TABLE OF CONTENTS

The Broadview Anthology of British Literature / edited by Joseph Black, Leonard Conolly, Kate Flint, Isobel Grundy, Don LePan, R.M. Liuzza, Jerome J. McGann, Anne Lake Prescott, Barry V. Qualls, Claire Waters
ISBN 978-1-55481-202-8 / 978-1-55481-290-5 / 978-1-55481-047-5 / 978-1-55481-311-7 / 978-1-55481-073-4 / 978-1-55111-614-3

The Broadview Introduction to Literature / edited by Lisa Chalykoff, Neta Gordon, Paul Lumsden
ISBN 978-1-55481-381-0

The Canterbury Tales / by Geoffrey Chaucer; edited by Robert Boenig, Andrew Taylor
ISBN 978-1-55481-106-9

Broadview Press is an independent, international publishing house, incorporated in 1985.

We welcome comments and suggestions regarding any aspect of our publications—please feel free to contact us at the addresses below or at broadview@broadviewpress.com.

North America
PO Box 1243, Peterborough, Ontario, Canada K9J 7H5
2215 Kenmore Ave., Buffalo, New York, USA 14207
Tel: (705) 743-8990; Fax: (705) 743-8353
email: customerservice@broadviewpress.com

UK, Europe, Central Asia, Middle East, Africa, India, and Southeast Asia
Eurospan Group, 3 Henrietta St., London WC2E 8LU, United Kingdom
Tel: 44 (0) 1767 604972; Fax: 44 (0) 1767 601640
email: eurospan@turpin-distribution.com

Australia and New Zealand
Footprint Books
c/o 1/6a Prosperity Parade, Warriewood, NSW 2012, Australia
Tel: (02) 9997 3973; Fax: (02) 9997 3185
email: info@footprint.com.au

www.broadviewpress.com

Broadview press acknowledges the financial support of the Government of Canada through the Canada Book Fund for our publishing activities.

Selected pages have been printed under Access Copyright license.

PRINTED IN CANADA

The Canterbury Tales

It is some indication of its popularity that *The Canterbury Tales* survives in so many manuscripts: fifty-five complete or nearly complete collections and a further twenty-eight manuscripts that contain one or more tales. Of these manuscripts, two of the earliest, the Hengwrt, now in the National Library in Wales, and the Ellesmere, now in the Huntington Library in San Marino, California, have provided the basis for most editions. The two manuscripts were copied by the same scribe, Adam Pynkhurst, in the first few years after Chaucer's death in 1400, or just possibly in the last year or two of Chaucer's life. The differences between the two manuscripts raise one of the great puzzles in Chaucerian scholarship: how close Chaucer came to finishing *The Canterbury Tales*. Ellesmere, generally agreed to be slightly later, presents the tales in an order that many modern readers have found to make strong artistic sense; Ellesmere also contains material—most notably the *Canon's Yeoman's Tale*, an account of a fraudulent alchemical workshop—that is missing from Hengwrt. On the other hand, many individual lines in Ellesmere contain small errors or are missing words. Why Pynkhurst, having managed to get an accurate (although incomplete) text from which to copy when he was writing the Hengwrt manuscript, should then have failed to do so when writing

Ellesmere remains unclear. This edition reproduces the text of the Ellesmere manuscript, preserving its spellings and modifying only its word division and punctuation. Where the text of the Ellesmere is clearly deficient or does not make sense, the editors have drawn on Hengwrt. In each case, these alterations are noted.

The Ellesmere manuscript includes a considerable number of marginal notes, or glosses. In the tales included in this anthology, these glosses are particularly numerous in *The Wife of Bath's Tale* and in *The Franklin's Tale*. Who first composed these glosses is still an open question, although there are strong grounds for believing that Chaucer himself composed quite a few of them. In these pages the texts of a number of the more interesting marginal glosses have been included in the notes at the bottom of the page.

The Ellesmere manuscript is large, its pages measuring roughly 15 by 11 inches, and elegantly decorated. It is the kind of luxury volume that might have been commissioned by an aristocrat, a prosperous London merchant, or a senior civil servant of the early fifteenth century. Various personal inscriptions in the manuscript indicate that it once belonged to John de Vere, who became the twelfth earl of Oxford in 1417, and whose guardians (possibly the book's first owners) were Thomas Beaufort, Duke of Exeter (one of the sons of John of Gaunt) and Henry IV's third son, John, Duke of Bedford, a great book collector.

The General Prologue

Chaucer's account of meeting a group of twenty-nine pilgrims at the Tabard Inn in Southwark, on the south bank of the Thames, has such an air of verisimilitude that it was once read as an account of an actual pilgrimage, with much attention devoted to determining just when it took place (1387 being the most favored date), how many days it took the pilgrims to get to Canterbury, and who the pilgrims were in real life. In fact, *The Canterbury Tales* draws on a tradition of medieval estates satire, poems that describe members of the three estates (those who pray, i.e., monks and nuns; those who fight, i.e., knights; and those who work, i.e., peasants) in terms of their characteristic vices. Many of Chaucer's most memorable and vivid characters, including his Friar and the Wife of Bath, are drawn from satirical figures found in such works as *Le Roman de la Rose* (*The Romance of the Rose*), in which a lover's quest for his lady (the rose) serves as an occasion for broad social commentary. Chaucer knew the work well, having translated it from French, and also knew the major example of English estates satire, William Langland's *Piers Plowman*, which Langland composed and then repeatedly reworked in the 1370s and 1380s.

Chaucer includes a Knight and a Plowman among his pilgrims, but for the most part they are drawn from the middle ranks of society, including prosperous members of the clergy, or first estate, such as the Friar, the Monk, and the Prioress, and those of the third estate who no longer fitted among the peasantry, such as the five prosperous Guildsmen, the Wife of Bath, the Merchant, the Physician, the Sergeant of Law, and the Manciple. Energetic and often clever, or at least sophisticated, the pilgrims are all professionally successful and—with a few exceptions—they thrive in the vibrant money economy of the later fourteenth century. To describe these people, Chaucer employs an affable and naively enthusiastic narrator, who mingles easily with them, admiring and even echoing their speeches, all apparently uncritically. As George Lyman Kittredge has observed, however, Chaucer was a professional tax collector and "a naïf collector of Customs would be a paradoxical monster." The poet and his narrator must not be confused.

The framing device of the pilgrimage allows Chaucer to explore the social tensions and moral debates of his day more freely than would otherwise be possible, transposing all conflict into an apparently innocent tale-telling competition. The question of who will tell the tale that offers the "best sentence and moost solaas" (line 798), i.e., the best moral meaning and the most enjoyment, is a standing invitation to probe beneath the surface and ask what the meaning of each tale really is. The pilgrimage frame also allows Chaucer to experiment with almost every major literary genre of his day and to assemble an encyclopedic compilation of ancient wisdom, history, and moral lessons. The learned aspect of this compilation is reinforced in the Ellesmere manuscript by the large number of marginal glosses, which identify the source for quotations and draw attention to particularly sententious passages.

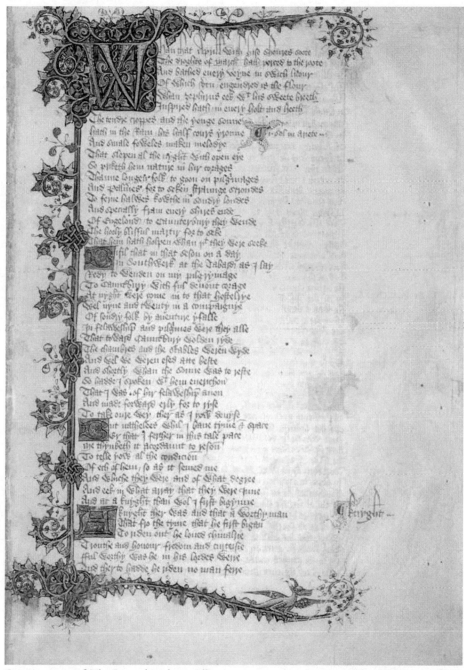

Opening page of *The General Prologue*, Ellesmere manuscript. (Reprinted by permission of the *Huntington Library, San Marino, California.* EL 26 C9 f. 1r.)

from *The Canterbury Tales*[1]

THE GENERAL PROLOGUE

Whan that Aprill with hise shoures° *showers*
   soote° *sweet*
The droghte° of March hath perced° *drought / pierced*
   to the roote
And bathed every veyne° in swich° licour° *vein / such / liquid*
Of which vertu° engendred is the flour,° *power / flower*
5   Whan Zephirus[2] eek° with his sweete breeth *also*
Inspired hath in every holt° and heeth° *wood / heath*
The tendre croppes and the yonge sonne
Hath in the Ram[3] his half cours yronne° *run*
And smale foweles° maken melodye *birds*
10   That slepen al the nyght with open eye,
So priketh° hem nature in hir corages,° *excites / their hearts*
Thanne longen folk to goon° on pilgrimages *go*
And palmeres° for to seken° straunge *pilgrims / seek*
   strondes° *shores*
To ferne halwes° kowthe° in sondry *far-off shrines / known*
   londes.
15   And specially, fram° every shires° ende *from / shire's*
Of Engelond to Caunterbury they wende,° *travel*
The hooly blisful martir[4] for to seke
That hem° hath holpen° whan that *them / helped*
   they were seeke.° *sick*
   Bifil° that in that seson° on a day *it happened / season*
20   In Southwerk[5] at the Tabard[6] as I lay
Redy to wenden° on my pilgrymage *travel*

To Caunterbury with ful devout corage,° *heart*
At nyght were come into that hostelrye° *inn*
Wel nyne° and twenty in a compaignye *nine*
25   Of sondry° folk by aventure yfalle[7] *various*
In felaweshipe, and pilgrimes were they alle
That toward Caunterbury wolden° ryde. *would*
The chambres° and the stables weren wyde,° *bedrooms / wide*
And wel we weren esed° atte beste. *made comfortable*
30   And shortly, whan the sonne was to reste,
So hadde I spoken with hem° everichon° *them / everyone*
That I was of hir° felaweshipe anon° *their / soon*
And made forward° erly° for to ryse *a pact / early*
To take oure wey ther as I yow devyse.° *as I will tell you*
35   But nathelees,° whil I have tyme and space, *nevertheless*
Er that I ferther° in this tale pace,° *further / go*
Me thynketh it° acordaunt° to resoun *it seems to me / according*
To telle yow al the condicioun° *i.e., character and estate*
Of ech of hem,° so as it semed me, *each of them*
40   And whiche they were and of what degree° *rank*
And eek° in what array° that they were inne, *also / clothing*
And at a knyght than wol I first bigynne.
   A Knyght ther was and that a worthy man,
That fro the tyme that he first bigan
45   To riden out, he loved chivalrie,
Trouthe and honour, fredom and curteisie.[8]
Ful worthy was he in his lordes werre° *war*
And therto hadde he riden, no man ferre,° *further*
As wel in Cristendom as in hethenesse° *pagan lands*
50   And evere honoured for his worthynesse.
At Alisaundre he was whan it was wonne.
Ful ofte tyme he hadde the bord bigonne[9]
Aboven alle nacions in Pruce.
In Lettow hadde he reysed° and in Ruce, *raided*
55   No Cristen man so ofte of his degree.
In Gernade at the seege eek° hadde he be *also*
Of Algezir, and riden in Belmarye.

---

[1] *The Canterbury Tales*   The present text of introductions to, and quotations for *The Canterbury Tales* have been prepared for *The Broadview Anthology of British Literature* by Robert Boenig and Andrew Taylor from their Broadview edition of the *Tales*.

[2] *Zephirus*   The name given to the personified west wind.

[3] *Ram*   The sign of the Zodiac for the early spring.

[4] *The hooly blisful martir*   St. Thomas Becket, Archbishop of Canterbury, was killed on 29 December 1170 during a dispute with his King, Henry II, by four knights who thought the king wished his death.

[5] *Southwerk*   Southwark is the region, now officially part of London but not so during Chaucer's time, on the southern bank of the Thames, directly across from the old city of London.

[6] *Tabard*   This is the name of Harry Bailly's inn. A "tabard" was a type of tunic often worn over chain-mail armor.

[7] *yfalle*   Encountered by chance.

[8] *Trouthe … curteisie*   Keeping one's word, preserving one's reputation or honor, generosity, and courtesy or courtly manners are central values in the code of chivalry.

[9] *hadde the bord bigonne*   Sat at the first table—an honor in victory banquets.

At Lyeys was he and at Satalye

Whan they were wonne and in the Grete See.

60 At many a noble armee° hadde he be.   *expedition*

At mortal batailles hadde he been fiftene

And foughten for oure feith° at Tramyssene   *faith*

In lystes° thries—and ay slayn his foo.   *jousting arenas*

This ilke° worthy knyght hadde been also   *same*

65 Somtyme with the lord of Palatye

Agayn another hethen° in Turkye,[1]   *heathen*

And everemoore he hadde a sovereyn° prys.°   *sovereign / reputation*

And though that he were worthy,° he was wys,°   *brave / prudent*

And of his port° as meeke as is a mayde.   *behavior*

70 He nevere yet no vileynye ne sayde

In al his lyf unto no maner wight.[2]

He was a verray,° parfit,° gentil° knyght.   *true / perfect / noble*

But for to tellen yow of his array,°   *appearance*

His hors° weren goode, but he was nat gay.°   *horses / finely dressed*

75 Of fustian° he wered a gypon°   *rough cloth / tunic*

Al bismotered° with his habergeon,°   *soiled / mail coat*

For he was late ycome° from his viage°   *arrived / voyage*

And wente for to doon° his pilgrymage.   *do*

With hym ther was his sone, a yong Squier,[3]

80 A lovyere° and a lusty° bacheler   *lover / vigorous*

With lokkes crulle° as they were leyd in presse.   *curled locks*

Of twenty yeer of age he was, I gesse.°   *guess*

Of his stature he was of evene lengthe°   *moderate height*

And wonderly delyvere° and of greet strengthe.   *quick*

85 And he hadde been somtyme in chyvachie°   *calvary expedition*

In Flaundres, in Artoys, and Pycardie[4]

And born hym weel as of so litel space°   *in so short a time*

In hope to stonden° in his lady grace.°   *stand / lady's favor*

Embrouded° was he as it were a meede,°   *embroidered / meadow*

90 Al ful of fresshe floures whyte and reede.°   *white and red*

Syngynge he was or floytynge° al the day.   *playing the flute*

He was as fressh as is the monthe of May.

Short was his gowne with sleves longe and wyde.

Wel koude he sitte on hors and faire ryde.

95 He koude songes make and wel endite,°   *compose verse*

Juste and eek daunce and weel putreye° and write.   *draw*

So hoote° he lovede, that by nyghtertale°   *hotly / nighttime*

He slepte namoore° than dooth a nyghtyngale.   *no more*

Curteis he was, lowely,° and servysable°   *humble / helpful*

100 And carf° biforn his fader at the table.   *carved (meat)*

A Yeman[5] hadde he and servantz namo°   *no more*

At that tyme for hym liste° ride so,   *desired*

And he was clad in cote° and hood of grene.   *coat*

A sheef of pecok arwes° bright and kene   *peacock arrows / sharp*

105 Under his belt he bar ful thriftily.°   *very carefully*

Wel koude he dresse his takel° yemanly.   *equipment*

His arwes drouped° noght with fetheres° lowe,   *drooped / feathers*

And in his hand he baar° a myghty bowe.   *bore*

A not heed° hadde he, with a broun   *close-cropped head*

visage.°   *face*

110 Of wodecraft wel koude° he al the usage.°   *knew / customs*

Upon his arm he baar° a gay bracer,°   *bore / leather arm guard*

And by his syde a swerd° and a bokeler°   *sword / small shield*

And on that oother syde a gay° daggere   *bright*

Harneised wel° and sharpe as point of spere;   *well-sheathed*

115 A cristophere° on his brest of silver   *St. Christopher medal*

sheene.°   *bright*

An horn he bar;° the bawdryk° was of grene.   *bore / shoulder-belt*

A forster° was he, soothly° as I gesse.°   *forester / truly / guess*

---

[1] *Alisaundre … Turkye* The locations of the Knight's battles are as follows: Alexandria in Egypt (1365), Prussia, Lithuania, Russia (the scenes of much fighting against hold-out pagans in the last decades of the fourteenth century), Grenada (in Spain) whose city Algezir was captured in 1344, Banu Merin (in North Africa), Ayash (Lyeys in Syria, captured in 1367), Antalya (Satalye, in modern Turkey, captured in 1361), Tlemcen (in modern Algeria), Balat (Palatye, in modern Turkey, involved in campaigning in both the 1340s and 1365), and Turkey. The places not identified with a specific date of battle saw protracted hostilities between Christians and non-Christians during the period in question. The "great sea" is the Mediterranean. It would, of course, have been impossible for a knight to have taken part in all these campaigns.

[2] *In … wight* He was never rude to anyone. Middle English often uses double or even triple negatives to intensify each other rather than to cancel each other out.

[3] *yong Squier* A squire would serve a knight, especially by helping to arm him, and would fight with him in battle. In some cases, as here, squires were young men training to be knights, but squires could also be older men, such as Chaucer.

[4] *In … Pycardie* These places in Flanders saw military action in 1383, as the English troops fought for Pope Urban VI against his rival, Anti-Pope Clement VII. The campaign, led by the war-loving Bishop of Norwich, was a great disaster for the English.

[5] *A Yeman* Yeoman, a small landholder or tenant farmer, often prosperous enough to serve as an infantryman or archer in a knight's retinue.

Ther was also a Nonne,° a Prioresse,[1]   *nun*
That of hir smylyng was ful° symple and coy.°   *very | modest*
120   Hire gretteste ooth was but "By Seint Loy!"[2]
And she was cleped° Madame Eglentyne.[3]   *called*
Ful weel she soong° the service dyvyne,[4]   *sung*
Entuned° in hir nose ful seemely.°   *intoned | seemly*
And Frenssh she spak ful faire and fetisly°   *elegantly*
125   After the scole° of Stratford atte Bowe:[5]   *school*
For Frenssh of Parys was to hire unknowe.°   *unknown*
At mete° wel ytaught° was she withalle.   *dinner | taught*
She leet° no morsel from hir lippes falle,   *let*
Ne wette hir fyngres in hir sauce depe.
130   Wel koude she carie a morsel and wel kepe,°   *take care*
That no drope ne fille upon hire brist.°   *breast*
In curteisie° was set ful muchel° hir list.° *courtesy | much | pleasure*
Hir over-lippe° wyped° she so clene,°   *upper lip | wiped | clean*
That in hir coppe° ther was no ferthyng°   *cup | coin-sized spot*
sene
135   Of grece° whan she dronken hadde hir draughte.° *grease | draft*
Ful semely after hir mete° she raughte.°   *food | reached*
And sikerly° she was of greet desport°   *surely | geniality*
And ful plesaunt and amyable° of port°   *amiable | bearing*
And peyned° hire to contrefete cheere°   *took pains | manners*
140   Of court and to been estalich° of manere   *stately*
And to ben holden° digne° of reverence.   *held | worthy*

But for to speken° of hire   *speak*
conscience,°   *tenderness of conscience*
She was so charitable and so pitous,°   *compassionate*
She wolde wepe° if that she saugh° a mous°   *weep | saw | mouse*
145   Kaught in a trappe if it were deed° or bledde.°   *dead | bleeding*
Of smale houndes hadde she that she fedde
With rosted flessh or milk and wastel breed.[6]
But soore wepte she if any of hem were deed°   *dead*
Or if men smoot it with a yerde° smerte.°   *yardstick | smartly*
150   And al was conscience and tendre herte.°   *tender heart*
Ful semyly hir wympul[7] pynched was;
Hir nose tretys,° hir eyen° greye as glas,   *shapely | eyes*
Hir mouth ful smal, and therto softe and reed.°   *red*
But sikerly, she hadde a fair forheed.
155   It was almoost a spanne brood,° I   *a hand's span across*
trowe,°   *believe*
For hardily° she was nat undergrowe.° *certainly | not undergrown*
Full fetys° was hir cloke, as I was war.°   *elegant | aware*
Of smal coral aboute hire arm she bar
A peire° of bedes, gauded° al with grene,[8]   *pair | divided*
160   And theron heng a brooch of gold ful sheene,°   *very shiny*
On which ther was first write° a crowned "A"   *written*
And after, "Amor vincit omnia."[9]
Another Nonne with hire hadde she
That was hir chapeleyne,° and Preestes° thre.   *chaplain | priests*
165   A Monk ther was, a fair for the maistrie,°   *i.e., better than all*
An outridere[10] that lovede venerie,°   *hunting*
A manly man, to been an abbot able.
Ful many a deyntee° hors hadde he in stable.   *fine*
And whan he rood, men myghte his brydel heere°   *hear*
170   Gynglen° in a whistlynge wynd als cleere°   *jingling | as clear*

---

[1]   *Prioresse* A prioress is either the second-in-command of an abbey, a large convent governed by an abbess, or is in charge of a priory, a smaller convent.

[2]   *Seint Loy* St. Eligius, a seventh-century Bishop of Noyon in France. He is patron saint of both goldsmiths and blacksmiths.

[3]   *Eglentyne* Eglantine, also known as sweet briar, is an early species of rose. It is known for its sweet, apple-like smell (which even the leaves emit if crushed) and five-petaled coral flowers, which appear once a year, in spring. Eglantine was not a common name in the Middle Ages.

[4]   *service dyvyne* Divine service; the phrase refers to the Office (or Canonical Hours)—the round of services dominated by psalm-singing that monks and nuns perform on a daily basis. The names of the individual services are Matins, Lauds, Prime, Terce, Sext, None, Vespers, and Compline.

[5]   *Stratford atte Bowe* Stratford-at-Bow is in Middlesex, just to the east of London. Chaucer's point, elaborated in the next line, is that the Prioress does not speak French properly but with a provincial accent. The Benedictine Priory of St. Leonard's was at Stratford-at-Bow and in Chaucer's day it had nine nuns, one of them named Argentine. The similarity of the names is suggestive, but Argentine was not the prioress there.

---

[6]   *wastel breed* White bread (which, in the Middle Ages, was a delicacy reserved for the nobility).

[7]   *wympul* Cloth folded cover the neck sides of the head, leaving only the face exposed. It was worn by both nuns and lay women.

[8]   *A ... grene* She carries a set of coral rosary beads, a chain of prayer-beads. These are divided at intervals by green beads. The green beads indicated the end of the "decade," one set of prayers, and the beginning of the next.

[9]   *Amor vincit omnia* Latin: Love conquers all.

[10]   *An outridere* An outrider was a monk whose job was to leave the cloister (which, as Chaucer makes clear below, was not the ideal thing for a monk to do) to take care of his monastery's business in the world at large. One of the common accusations made against monks was that they loved the secular world more than the cloister.

And eek as loude as dooth the chapel belle
Theras° this lord was kepere of the celle.[1]   *since*
The Reule° of Seint Maure or of Seint Beneit,[2]   *rule*
Bycause that it was old and somdel streit,°   *somewhat restrictive*
175 This ilke monk leet olde thynges pace°   *pass*
And heeld after the newe world the space.°   *course*
He yaf nat° of that text a pulled° hen   *gave not / plucked*
That seith that hunters beth nat hooly° men,   *not holy*
Ne that° a monk whan he is recchelees°   *nor when / negligent*
180 Is likned til° a fissh that is waterlees.   *likened to*
This is to seyn,° a monk out of his cloystre.°   *say / cloister*
But thilke° text heeld he nat worth an oystre.   *that same*
And I seyde his opinioun was good.
What° sholde he studie and make hymselven   *why*
      wood°   *crazy*
185 Upon a book in cloystre° alwey to poure°   *cloister / pore*
Or swynken° with his handes and laboure°   *work / labor*
As Austyn[3] bit?° How shal the world be served?   *commanded*
Lat Austyn have his owene swynk° to hym reserved!   *work*
Therfore he was a prikasour aright.°   *hard rider*
190 Grehoundes he hadde as swift as fowel° in flight.   *bird*
Of prikyng° and of huntyng for the hare   *riding*
Was al his lust.° For no cost wolde he spare.   *pleasure*
I seigh his sleves° ypurfiled° at the hond°   *sleeves / lined / hand*
With grys°—and that the fyneste° of a   *expensive gray fur / finest*
      lond.°   *the land*
195 And for to festne° his hood under his chyn°   *fasten / chin*
He hadde of gold ywroght° a ful° curious pyn:° *made / very / pin*
A love knotte in the gretter° ende ther was.   *bigger*
His heed was balled,[4] that shoon as any glas,
And eek his face as it hadde been enoynt.°   *anointed*

200 He was a lord ful fat and in good poynt,[5]
Hise eyen° stepe° and rollynge in his heed,   *eyes / bright*
That stemed as a forneys° of a leed,[6]   *furnace*
His bootes souple,° his hors in greet estaat.° *supple / in best shape*
Now certeinly he was a fair prelaat.°   *prelate*
205 He nas nat° pale as a forpyned goost.° *was not / distressed ghost*
A fat swan loved he best of any roost.°   *roast*
His palfrey[7] was as broun as is a berye.°   *berry*
    A Frere° ther was, a wantowne° and a   *friar / pleasure-seeking*
      merye,°   *merry*
A lymytour,[8] a ful solempne° man.   *imposing*
210 In alle the ordres foure[9] is noon° that kan°   *no one / knows*
So muchel° of daliaunce° and fair langage.   *much / flirtation*
He hadde maad° ful many a mariage   *made*
Of yonge wommen at his owene cost.
Unto his ordre he was a noble post!°   *pillar*
215 And wel biloved and famulier was he
With frankeleyns° ever al in his contree   *franklins (gentry)*
And with worthy wommen of the toun,
For he hadde power of confessioun,
As seyde hymself, moore than a curat,°   *curate (local priest)*
220 For of his ordre he was licenciat.°   *licensed*
Ful swetely° herde he confessioun,   *sweetly*
And plesaunt was his absolucioun.
He was an esy° man to yeve° penaunce,   *easy / give*
Theras° he wiste° to have a good   *where / thought*
      pitaunce.°   *donation*
225 For unto a povre° ordre for to yive°   *poor / give*
Is signe that a man is wel yshryve.°   *confessed*
For if he yaf,° he dorste° make avaunt,°   *gave / dared / assert*

---

[1] *celle* Priory or outlying house governed by the central monastery.

[2] *Seint Maure ... Seint Beneit* St. Benedict, a sixth-century Italian monk and abbot, compiled the famous Rule that goes by his name. It became normative for most of Western monasticism. St. Maurus, by legend one of his monks, was credited with bringing his Rule to France.

[3] *Austyn* "Austin" is the typical Middle English abbreviation for Augustine, the great Doctor of the Church and Bishop of Hippo in Northern Africa (354–430 CE). He was famous for his theological writings, particularly *The City of God* and *The Confessions*, the latter his spiritual autobiography. He is also credited with writing the Rule (followed by Augustinian canons and monks) to which this passage alludes.

[4] *His heed was balled* Monks shaved the crowns of their heads in a haircut known as a tonsure.

---

[5] *in good poynt* Idiomatic: in good condition.

[6] *of a leed* Under a cauldron.

[7] *palfrey* Everyday horse, as opposed to a destrier (war-horse) or a plowhorse.

[8] *lymytour* Friar licensed to preach, minister, and hear confessions in a specified, limited area.

[9] *In ... foure* There were four main orders of friars in the later Middle Ages—the Franciscans, the Dominicans, the Carmelites, and the Augustinians. Like monks, the friars took vows of poverty, chastity, and obedience, but they were supposed to go out in the world and preach to the laity, whereas monks were supposed to live apart from the world and devote themselves to prayer.

He wiste that a man was repentaunt.[1]
For many a man so hard is of his herte,
230 He may nat wepe° althogh hym soore   *weep*
        smerte.°   *sorely hurts*
Therfore instede of wepynge° and preyeres,°   *weeping / prayers*
Men moote yeve° silver to the povre freres!   *should give*
His typet[2] was ay farsed° ful of knyves   *stuffed*
And pynnes° for to yeven yonge   *pins*
        wyves.°   *give to young women*
235 And, certeinly, he hadde a murye note;°   *merry singing voice*
Wel koude he synge and pleyen on a rote.°   *play on a lyre*
Of yeddynges° he baar outrely° the   *songs / completely*
        pris.°   *prize*
His nekke° whit° was as the flour-de-lys.°   *neck / white / lily*
Therto he strong was as a champion.
240 He knew the tavernes wel° in al the toun   *well*
And everich hostiler and
        tappestere°   *each innkeeper and barmaid*
Bet° than a lazar° or a beggestere.°   *better / leper / female beggar*
For unto swich° a worthy man as he   *such*
Acorded nat as by his facultee[3]
245 To have with sike lazars aqueyntaunce.°   *sick lepers acquaintance*
It is nat honeste.° It may nat avaunce,°   *respectable / advance (one)*
For to deelen° with no swich poraille°   *deal / poor folk*
But al with riche° and selleres of vitaille.°   *rich / sellers of food*
And overal theras profit sholde arise,
250 Curteis he was and lowely° of servyse.   *humble*
Ther nas no° man nowher so vertuous;   *was not*
He was the beste beggere in his hous.°[4]   *convent*
For thogh a wydwe° hadde noght a sho,°   *widow / not a shoe*
So plesaunt was his "In principio,"[5]

255 Yet wolde he have a ferthyng° er he wente.   *farthing (coin)*
His purchas° was wel bettre than his rente,°   *income / expenses*
And rage° he koude as it were right a whelp.°   *cavort / dog*
In love-dayes ther koude he muchel° help,   *could he (offer) much*
For ther he was nat lyk a cloystrer°   *monk*
260 With a thredbare cope° as is a povre scoler,°   *cloak / poor student*
But he was lyk a maister or a pope.
Of double worstede° was his semycope°   *thick cloth / short-cloak*
That rounded as a belle out of the presse.°   *mold*
Somwhat he lipsed° for his wantownesse°   *lisped / affectation*
265 To make his Englissh sweete upon his tonge.
And in his harpyng, whan that he hadde songe,
Hise eyen° twynkled in his heed aryght°   *eyes / aright*
As doon° the sterres° in the frosty nyght.   *do / stars*
This worthy lymytour° was cleped Huberd.   *limiter*
270   A Marchant was ther with a forked berd;°   *beard*
In motlee° and hye° on horse he sat,   *multi-colored cloth / high*
Upon his heed a Flaundryssh° bevere° hat,   *Flemish / beaver*
His bootes clasped faire and fetisly.
Hise resons° he spak ful solempnely,   *opinions*
275 Sownynge° alwey th'encrees° of his   *concerning / increase*
        wynnyng.°   *profit*
He wolde° the see° were kept for anythyng   *wished / sea*
Bitwixe° Middelburgh and Orewelle.[6]   *between*
Wel koude he in eschaunge° sheeldes selle.[7]   *exchange*
This worthy man ful wel his wit bisette;°   *employed*
280 Ther wiste no wight that he was in dette,[8]
So estatly° was he of his governaunce,°   *dignified / management*
With his bargaynes and with his
        chevyssaunce.°   *money lending*
Forsothe,° he was a worthy man withalle.°   *truly / for all that*
But sooth to seyn, I noot how men hym calle.[9]

---

[1] *For ... repentaunt* For if a man gave money then he (the Friar) knew that man was repentant. The Friar is imposing a light penance in exchange for a donation to his order.

[2] *typet* Long ornamental piece of cloth worn either as a kind of scarf or as part of a hood or as sleeves. It provided a convenient place to put small objects.

[3] *For ... facultee* It was not appropriate according to his profession.

[4] The Hengwrt manuscript at this point includes the following two lines, usually numbered 252b and 252c: "And yaf a certeyn ferme for the graunt / Noon of his bretheren cam ther in his haunt" (And he paid a certain annual amount for the rights [to beg] / so that none of his brother friars came into his territory).

[5] *In principio* Latin: "In the beginning was the Word," the opening line of the Gospel of John.

---

[6] *Middelburgh and Orewelle* These two ports were in the Netherlands and in England respectively. There was much trade in the late Middle Ages between the two countries, particularly in textiles.

[7] *sheeldes selle* A shield, or *écu*, was a French coin. This kind of trade between national currencies was regarded with suspicion. It was often illegal and could be used as a way of surreptitiously charging interest on a loan (which the Church condemned as usury).

[8] *Ther ... dette* The syntax is ambiguous. Either "No one knew that he was in debt" (implying he was) or "No one knew him to be in debt" (implying he was not) or, since merchants were normally in debt, "No one knew how much he was in debt."

[9] *sooth ... calle* To tell the truth, I don't know what he was called.

285   A Clerk[1] ther was of Oxenford° also   *Oxford*

That unto logyk hadde longe ygo,° *who had [committed himself] to*

And leene° was his hors as is a rake.   *lean*

And he nas nat right° fat, I undertake,° *was not very / declare*

But looked holwe° and therto sobrely.° *hollow / soberly*

290   Ful thredbare was his overeste courtepy,° *overcoat*

For he hadde geten hym yet no benefice[2]

Ne was° so worldly for to have office.   *nor was (he)*

For hym was levere° have at his beddes   *would rather*

    heed°   *bed's head*

Twenty bookes clad° in blak or reed° *bound / red*

295   Of Aristotle and his philosophie

Than robes riche or fithele° or gay sautrie.° *fiddle / harp*

But al be that he was a philosophre,

Yet hadde he but litel gold in cofre.°[3] *little gold in a chest*

But al that he myghte of his freendes° hente,° *friends / obtain*

300   On bookes and on lernynge° he it spente   *learning*

And bisily° gan for the soules preye° *busily / prayed*

Of hem° that yaf° hym wherwith to   *them / gave*

    scoleye.°   *the means to study*

Of studie took he moost cure° and moost heede.   *care*

Noght o° word spak he moore than was neede,   *one*

305   And that was seyd in forme° and reverence   *formally*

And short and quyk and ful of hy sentence.° *meaning*

Sownynge in° moral vertu was his speche,   *resounding*

And gladly wolde he lerne and gladly teche.

A Sergeant of the Lawe[4] war° and wys° *shrewd / wise*

310   That often hadde been at the Parvys[5]

Ther was also, ful riche of excellence.

Discreet he was and of greet reverence—

He semed swich, his wordes weren so wise.

Justice° he was ful often in assise° *judge / court*

315   By patente and by pleyn commissioun,[6]

For his science° and for his heigh renoun.° *knowledge / renown*

Of fees and robes hadde he many oon;° *many a one*

So greet a purchasour[7] was nowher noon.° *nowhere at all*

Al was fee symple[8] to hym in effect.

320   His purchasyng myghte nat been infect.° *invalidated*

Nowher so bisy° a man as he ther nas,° *busy / was not*

And yet he semed bisier° than he was.   *seemed busier*

In termes° hadde he caas° and doomes   *files / cases*

    alle°   *judgments*

That from the tyme° of Kyng William[9] were   *time*

    yfalle.°   *given*

325   Therto he koude endite° and make a thyng.° *write / brief*

Ther koude no wight° pynchen° at his   *nobody / quibble*

    writyng.

And every statut koude he pleyn by rote.° *recite by heart*

He rood but hoomly° in a medlee° cote, *simply / multi-colored*

Girt with a ceint° of silk with barres° smale.   *belt / ornaments*

330   Of his arraye tell I no lenger tale.

---

[1] *Clerk* The term clerk can mean student or professor, priest or priest's assistant, or learned man or philosopher, depending on the context. University students were supposed to be preparing for the priesthood. Some became priests, which required a vow of celibacy, and could then win promotion in the ranks of the Church. Others only took minor orders (which meant they could marry), and either remained at university or, in many cases, became members of the growing royal, baronial, and civic administration. Chaucer's Clerk, who is studying advanced logic, is roughly the equivalent of a graduate student or junior professor.

[2] *benefice* Position as a priest or clergyman. In the Middle Ages there had developed a much-criticized custom of granting the income from some benefices to people who would apportion a small amount of the income to a poorer clergyman to do the work and then live off the rest. This practice made some bishops with multiple benefices very wealthy, and it became a means of supporting a well-connected scholar at one of the universities.

[3] *But ... cofre* Chaucer is punning on the word philosopher, which can also mean alchemist. The search for the Philosopher's Stone, thought to be the key to turning metal to gold, was a particular study of alchemists.

[4] *Sergeant of the Lawe* In late fourteenth-century England, a Sergeant of Law was not simply a lawyer; he was one of about twenty or so lawyers who functioned as legal advisors to the king and served as judges.

[5] *Parvys* Shortened form of "Paradise," a name given to the porch in front of large churches. Here the reference is to the porch of Saint Paul's Cathedral in London, where lawyers would meet with their clients, the lawyer's office being unknown to late-fourteenth-century England.

[6] *By ... commissioun* Letters patent were royal letters of appointment that were open, i.e., public, documents that anyone was allowed to read. The full commission gives the Sergeant the right to hear all legal cases in the Court of Assizes, circuit courts that would move from county to county.

[7] *purchasour* I.e., purchaser, someone who acquired feudal property by money rather than feudal service.

[8] *fee symple* Ownership without feudal obligations.

[9] *Kyng William* William the Conqueror, who ruled England from 1066 to 1087. His reign marked a turning point in English governance.

A Frankeleyn[1] was in his compaignye.
Whit° was his heed° as is a dayesye.°   *white / head / daisy*
Of his complexioun he was sangwyn;[2]
Wel loved he by the morwe a sope in wyn.[3]
335 To lyven° in delit° was evere his wone,°   *live / delight / custom*
For he was Epicurus[4] owene sone°   *son*
That heeld opinioun that pleyn delit°   *full delight*
Was verray° felicitee parfit.°   *true / perfect happiness*
An housholdere and that a greet was he;
340 Seint Julian[5] was he in his contree.
His breed,° his ale was always after oon;[6]   *bread*
A bettre envyned man° was nevere noon.   *man stocked with wine*
Withoute bake mete° was nevere his hous   *baked food*
Of fissh and flessh, and that so plentevous°   *plentiful*
345 It snewed° in his hous of mete and drynke,   *snowed*
Of alle deyntees° that men koude thynke.   *delicacies*
After the sondry° sesons° of the yeer   *various / seasons*
So chaunged he his mete° and his soper.°   *dinner / supper*
Ful° many a fat partrich° hadde he in   *very / partridge*
muwe°   *coop*
350 And many a breem° and many a luce° in   *bream / pike*
stuwe.°   *pond*
Wo° was his cook but if° his sauce were   *woe / unless*
Poynaunt° and sharpe° and redy al his   *pungent / spicy*
geere.°   *utensils*
His table dormant[7] in his halle alway

Stood redy covered al the longe day.
355 At sessiouns° ther was he lord and sire;   *court sessions*
Ful ofte tyme he was Knyght of the Shire.[8]
An anlaas° and a gipser° al of silk   *dagger / pouch*
Heeng° at his girdel whit° as morne°   *hung / white / morning*
milk.
A shirreve° hadde he been and countour.°   *sheriff / tax-collector*
360 Was nowher swich a worthy vavasour.°   *feudal land holder*
An Haberdasshere[9] and a Carpenter,
A Webbe,° a Dyere, and a Tapycer,°   *weaver / tapestry-maker*
And they were clothed alle in o° lyveree[10]   *one*
Of a solempne and a greet fraternitee.[11]
365 Ful fressh and newe hir geere° apiked° was.   *equipment / adorned*
Hir knyves were chaped° noght° with bras   *mounted / not / brass*
But al with silver, wroght ful clene° and weel   *made very elegantly*
Hire girdles° and hir pouches everydeel.°   *belts / every bit*
Wel semed° ech of hem a fair burgeys°   *seemed / citizen*
370 To sitten in a yeldehalle° on a deys.°   *guildhall / raised platform*
Everich° for the wisdom that he kan°   *everyone / knew*
Was shaply° for to been an alderman.[12]   *suitable*

---

[1] *Frankeleyn*   From the word franc or free, a wealthy independent landowner and a member of the minor gentry.

[2] *Of … sangwyn*   The Franklin's physiological makeup is dominated by blood, one of the four humors, which makes him red-faced and cheerful.

[3] *Wel … wyn*   He greatly loved in the morning bread soaked in wine. Such was the preferred breakfast for those wealthy enough to afford wine, which had to be imported from Gascony, the sole remaining territory England retained in what we now call France.

[4] *Epicurus*   The Greek philosopher Epicurus (341–270 BCE) maintained that the pursuit of pleasure was the natural state of humankind.

[5] *Seint Julian*   St. Julian, the patron saint of hospitality in the Middle Ages. Julian set up a way-station for travelers in penance for unwittingly killing his parents, who had unknowingly lodged in his house while journeying.

[6] *after oon*   Consistent, i.e., consistently good.

[7] *His table dormant*   Always standing. Most medieval tables on which meals were set were trestle tables, i.e., a long board placed on top of what we would call saw-horses. After the meal was over, the table would normally be taken down. Not so the Franklin's.

[8] *Knyght of the Shire*   Official designation for people chosen to represent their region in Parliament. Chaucer himself, while he was never knighted and only held the rank of squire, served as Knight of the Shire for Kent in 1386, the year before the fictitious pilgrimage to Canterbury takes place. The Franklin has also presided at the sessions of the Justices of the Peace (line 355) and served as Sheriff, the chief royal officer in a county who was responsible for collecting its taxes, and as the county auditor, who assisted the Sheriff.

[9] *Haberdasshere*   Seller of ribbons, buttons, hats, gloves, and small articles of clothing.

[10] *lyveree*   Uniform. Members of craft or religious guilds, as well as retainers of various lords, wore liveries. At this time the wearing of liveries encouraged factionalism and attendant violence, and there were some legal attempts to curb abuses.

[11] *fraternitee*   Trade guilds or religious guilds. The trade guilds regulated who was allowed to follow a given trade in a given town, and the religious guilds functioned as mutual aid societies, burying their dead and helping members who were sick or had fallen into poverty. These guildsmen, though identified by their trades, are members of a religious guild, since trade guilds admitted only members of a single trade.

[12] *alderman*   In late medieval England, as in some cities today, the board of aldermen governs under the mayor. The five guildsmen have prospered, rising from apprentices to masters. They are successful businessmen who run their own shop or shops, participate in civic government, and aspire, with their wives, to the status of the lesser gentry.

For catel° hadde they ynogh° and rente,°   *belongings / enough / rent*

And eek hir wyves° wolde it wel assente°   *wives / agree*

375 And elles° certeyn were they to blame.   *otherwise*

It is ful fair to been ycleped° "Madame"   *called*

And goon to vigilies[1] al bifore

And have a mantel roialliche ybore.°   *cloak royally carried*

A Cook° they hadde with hem° for the nones°   *cook / them / occasion*

380 To boille° the chiknes° with the marybones°   *boil / chickens / marrowbones*

And poudre-marchant tart and galyngale.[2]

Wel koude he knowe a draughte of Londoun ale.

He koude rooste and sethe° and boille° and frye,   *simmer / boil*

Maken mortreux° and wel bake a pye.   *stews*

385 But greet harm° was it as it thoughte me°   *pity / seemed to me*

That on his shyne° a mormal° hadde he.   *shin / ulcer*

For blankmanger[3] that made he with the beste.

A Shipman was ther wonynge° fer by weste.°   *living / far in the west*

For aught I woot,° he was of Dertemouthe.[4]   *all I know*

390 He rood° upon a rouncy° as he kouthe°   *rode / nag / could*

In a gowne of faldyng° to the knee.   *woolen cloth*

A daggere hangynge on a laas° hadde he   *lace*

About his nekke under his arm adoun.°   *downwards*

The hoote° somer hadde maad° his hewe° al broun,   *hot / made / color*

395 And certeinly he was a good felawe.

Ful many a draughte° of wyn° had he drawe°   *draft / wine / drawn*

Fro Burdeuxward whil that the chapman° sleepe.[5]   *merchant*

Of nyce° conscience took he no keepe.°   *scrupulous / notice*

If that he faught° and hadde the hyer hond,°   *if he fought / upper hand*

400 By water he sente hem hoom° to every lond.[6]   *home*

But of his craft° to rekene° wel his tydes,°   *ability / reckon / tides*

His stremes° and his daungers° hym bisides,°   *currents / dangers / all around him*

His herberwe° and his moone,° his lodemenage,°   *harborage / moon / piloting*

Ther nas noon swich° from Hull to Cartage.[7]   *was not such a one*

405 Hardy he was and wys to undertake;°   *wise in his endeavors*

With many a tempest hadde his berd° been shake.°   *beard / shaken*

He knew alle the havenes° as they were   *havens*

Fro Gootlond to the Cape of Fynystere[8]

And every cryke° in Britaigne° and in Spayne.°   *inlet / Brittany / Spain*

410 His barge ycleped was the Maudelayne.

With us ther was a Doctour of Physik.[9]

In al this world ne was ther noon hym lik°   *there was no one like him*

To speke of phisik° and of surgerye,   *medicine*

For he was grounded in astronomye.[10]

415 He kepte° his pacient a ful greet deel   *watched over*

In houres by his magyk natureel.[11]

Wel koude he fortunen the ascendent°   *calculate a planet's position*

Of hise ymages[12] for his pacient.

He knew the cause of everich° maladye,   *every*

---

[1] *vigilies* Church services held the night before an important holy day. The aldermen and their wives would lead the procession, with their cloaks carried by a servant.

[2] *And … galyngale* And tart ground spice and aromatic roots (such as ginger).

[3] *blankmanger* Stew of milk, rice, almonds, and chicken or fish.

[4] *Dertemouthe* I.e., Dartmouth, a port on the English Channel in the southwest of England, near Plymouth.

[5] *Ful … sleepe* Sailing home from Bordeaux with a cargo of wine, the Shipman would secretly steal some while the wine merchant (chapman) was asleep.

[6] *By … lond* I.e., he threw his defeated opponents overboard.

[7] *Hull to Cartage* Hull is a port in northern England; Cartage is either Carthage on the Mediterranean coast of North Africa or Cartagena in Spain.

[8] *Fro … Fynystere* Gotland is an island in the Baltic Sea off the coast of southern Sweden; Cape Finisterre is the point of land that juts out into the Atlantic Ocean in northwest Spain.

[9] *Doctour of Physik* Physician. The term "doctor" means "teacher," as everyone in the Middle Ages knew, so the type of doctor who taught medicine and sometimes practiced it needed to be distinguished from other types of doctors, who taught academic subjects in the universities.

[10] *For … astronomye* In the Middle Ages, physicians often based their schedules of treatment on astrological tables.

[11] *In … natureel* Hours are the times in the day when the various planetary influences were pronounced, when the Physician watched over (kepte) his patient. Natural magic is opposed to black magic, which involves contact with malicious spirits.

[12] *Of hise ymages* The practice of astrologically-based medicine involved the use of images of the planets as talismans.

420	Were it of hoot or coold or moyste or drye,[1]	
	And where they engendred and of what humour.	
	He was a verray, parfit praktisour:°	*practitioner*
	The cause yknowe° and of his harm the roote,°	*known / root*
	Anon he yaf° the sike man his boote.°	*gave / remedy*
425	Ful redy hadde he hise apothecaries°	*pharmacists*
	To sende hym drogges° and his letuaries,°	*drugs / syrups*
	For ech° of hem° made oother for to wynne.°*each / them / profit*	
	Hir° frendshipe nas nat newe° to	*their / recently*
	bigynne.°	*begun*
	Wel knew he the olde Esculapius	
430	And Deyscorides and eek Rufus,	
	Olde Ypocras, Haly, and Galyen,	
	Serapion, Razis, and Avycen,	
	Averrois, Damascien, and Constantyn,	
	Bernard and Gatesden and Gilbertyn.[2]	
435	Of his diete° mesurable° was he,	*diet / moderate*
	For it was of no superfluitee°	*excess*
	But of greet norissyng° and digestible.	*nourishment*
	His studie was but litel on the Bible.[3]	

---

[1] *He ... drye* Medieval medicine was also based on a theory, traceable back to Greek physicians such as the ones Chaucer mentions below, of the balance of the four bodily humors (blood, phlegm, black bile, and yellow bile) and their qualities of hot, cold, moist, and dry mentioned in this line.

[2] *Wel ... Gilbertyn* Aesculapius was a mythological demi-god, son to Apollo. Dioscorides, Rufus of Ephesus, Hippocrates (associated with the Hippocratic Oath physicians still swear), and Galen were famous Greek physicians. Galen (129–199) was particularly influential, since he set out the theory of four humors which was the basis of medieval medicine. "Haly" is probably the Persian physician Ali Ben el-Abbas (d. 994). Rhazes (d. c. 930) was an Arab astronomer and physician. Avicenna, or Ibn Sina (980–1037), and Averroes (1126–98) were Islamic philosophers and physicians. John of Damascus was a Syrian physician of the ninth century. Constantine the African came from Carthage, converted to Christianity, became a Benedictine monk, and taught at Salerno in Italy in the eleventh century. His work on aphrodisiacs earns him the title the "cursed monk" in *The Merchant's Tale*, line 1810. Islamic science was widely influential in the Middle Ages; it first brought Greek thought to the Latin West. The last three authorities are British. Bernard Gordon was a Scottish physician who taught at Montpellier in the fourteenth century. John Gaddesden (d. c. 1349) taught at Oxford and served as court doctor to Edward II. Gilbert was an English physician in the thirteenth century and the author of a major medical treatise.

[3] *His ... Bible* In the Middle Ages physicians were often thought to be religious skeptics, partly because of their knowledge of classical astronomy.

	In sangwyn° and in pers° he clad was al,	*red / blue*
440	Lyned with taffata and with sendal.[4]	
	And yet he was but esy of dispence.°	*moderate in spending*
	He kepte that he wan° in pestilence.°[5]	*what he earned / plague*
	For gold in phisik° is a cordial.°	*medicine / heart-medicine*
	Therfore he lovede gold in special.°	*especially*
445	A good Wif was ther of biside Bathe,[6]	
	But she was somdel deef,° and that was	*somewhat deaf*
	scathe.°	*a shame*
	Of clooth makyng she hadde swich an haunt,°	*skill*
	She passed hem of Ypres and of Gaunt.[7]	
	In al the parisshe° wif ne was ther noon	*parish*
450	That to the offrynge[8] bifore hire sholde goon.	*offering*
	And if ther dide, certeyn so wrooth° was she,	*angry*
	That she was out of alle charitee.	
	Hir coverchiefs° ful fyne were of ground°—	*kerchiefs / texture*
	I dorste swere° they weyeden° ten pound—*dared swear / weighed*	
455	That on a Sonday weren upon hir heed.	
	Hir hosen weren of fyn° scarlet reed,°	*fine / red*
	Ful streite yteyd° and shoes ful moyste°	*tightly laced / supple*
	and newe.	
	Boold° was hir face and fair and reed of hewe.°	*bold / color*
	She was a worthy womman al hir lyve.	
460	Housbondes at chirche dore° she hadde fyve,°[9]*church door / five*	
	Withouten° oother compaignye in youthe.	*apart from*
	But therof nedeth nat to speke as nowthe.°	*for now*

---

[4] *Lyned ... sendal* Taffeta and sendal are types of silk cloth; silk, imported from Asia, was a mark of status and wealth.

[5] *He ... pestilence* Possibly a reference to the Black Death, which killed at least a third of the population of England between 1348 and 1349, although there were later outbreaks of plague in 1362, 1369, and 1376.

[6] *Bathe* I.e., Bath, a town in southwest England near Bristol. It is famous for its hot springs (hence its name) and Roman ruins. The parish of St. Michael's, just north of Bath, was famous for its weavers.

[7] *Ypres ... Gaunt* Cities in Flanders (now north-western Belgium) known for cloth trading. There were also skilled weavers from these cities working in England.

[8] *offrynge* In eucharistic services, gifts are brought to the altar during the Offering, or Offertory.

[9] *Housbondes ... fyve* Marriage vows were exchanged on the church steps and were followed by a Mass inside the church.

And thries° hadde she been at Jerusalem.[1] *three times*
She hadde passed many a straunge strem.° *sea*
465 At Rome she hadde been and at Boloigne,
In Galice at Seint Jame and at Coloigne.
She koude muchel of wandrynge by the weye.[2]
Gat-tothed was she, soothly for to seye.[3]
Upon an amblere° esily° she sat, *saddle-horse / easily*
470 Ywympled[4] wel, and on hir heed° an hat *head*
As brood° as is a bokeler or a targe,° *broad / shield*
A foot mantel° aboute hir hipes large *outer skirt*
And on hir feet a paire of spores° sharpe. *spurs*
In felaweshipe wel koude she laughe and carpe.° *joke*
475 Of remedies of love she knew perchaunce,° *as it happened*
For she koude° of that art the olde daunce. *knew*

A good man was ther of religioun
And was a povre Persoun° of a toun, *poor parson*
But riche he was of hooly thoght° and werk.° *holy thought / work*
480 He was also a lerned man, a clerk,
That Cristes° gospel trewely wolde preche.° *Christ's / preach*
Hise parisshens° devoutly wolde he teche. *parishioners*
Benygne° he was and wonder diligent *benign*
And in adversitee ful pacient,
485 And swich° he was preved° ofte sithes.° *such / proven / many times*
Ful looth° were hym to cursen° for *reluctant / excommunicate*
   hise tithes,[5]
But rather wolde he yeven° out of doute° *give / without doubt*
Unto his povre parisshens aboute
Of his offryng and eek of his substaunce.
490 He koude in litel thyng have suffisaunce.[6]

---

[1] *And ... Jerusalem* Jerusalem was the greatest of all pilgrimages. From England, a trip there and back could take a couple of years. The other pilgrimages mentioned below are Rome, where the Apostles Peter and Paul were buried; Boulogne-sur-mer in France, famous for its miraculous image of the Blessed Virgin; Compostella in Galicia, where the relics of St. James were venerated; and Cologne, where the relics of the Three Kings (or Three Magi) were kept.

[2] *She ... weye* She knew much about wandering along the road.

[3] *Gat-tothed ... seye* According to medieval physiognomy, a gap between the teeth was a sign that a woman was bold, lecherous, faithless, and suspicious.

[4] *Ywympled* Wearing a wimple.

[5] *tithes* Periodic assessments made to determine one tenth of a person's goods, harvest, and animals, which would then be claimed by the Church. Parish priests could excommunicate parishioners who would not pay them.

[6] *He ... suffisaunce* He was able to have enough in little things.

Wyd° was his parisshe and houses fer asonder,° *wide / far apart*
But he ne lefte° nat for reyn° ne thonder *did not neglect / rain*
In siknesse nor in meschief° to visite *trouble*
The ferreste° in his parisshe muche and *farthest*
   lite,° *of greater or lesser (rank)*
495 Upon his feet and in his hand a staf.° *staff*
This noble ensample° to his sheepe he yaf, *example*
That firste he wroghte° and afterward that he taughte. *acted*
Out of the gospel he tho° wordes caughte,° *those / took*
And this figure° he added eek therto,° *figure of speech / to it*
500 "That if gold ruste, what shal iren° do?" *iron*
For if a preest be foul on whom we truste,
No wonder is a lewed man° to ruste, *layman*
And shame it is if a preest take keepe°— *heed*
A shiten° shepherde and a clene° *soiled with excrement / clean*
   sheepe.
505 Wel oghte° a preest ensample for to yeve *ought*
By his clennesse how that his sheepe sholde lyve.
He sette nat° his benefice to hyre *did not offer*
And leet° his sheepe encombred° in the myre° *left / stuck / mud*
And ran to Londoun unto Seint Poules[7]
510 To seken hym° a chauntrie° for soules *seek for himself / chantry*
Or with a bretherhed° to been withholde,°[8] *guild / hired*
But dwelleth at hoom and kepeth wel his
   folde° *sheepfold (i.e., flock)*
So that the wolf ne made° it nat *would not make*
   myscarie.° *come to grief*
He was a shepherde and noght° a mercenarie,° *not / mercenary*
515 And though he hooly were and vertuous,
He was nat to synful men despitous,° *scornful*
Ne of his speche daungerous° ne digne,° *proud / haughty*
But in his techyng discreet and benygne,° *kind*
To drawen folk to hevene by fairnesse,
520 By good ensample. This was his bisynesse.
But it were any persone obstinat,[9]
Whatso° he were of heigh or lough estat,° *whether / low class*

---

[7] *Seint Poules* St. Paul's Cathedral in London. The custom Chaucer refers to is related to the issue of benefices. A chantry is an endowed position, usually at large churches and cathedrals, in which a priest sings masses for the soul of the person who left money for the endowment. It involved very little work, unlike the Parson's toil described in his section of the General Prologue.

[8] *Or ... withholde* The brotherhood here is a guild. Guilds hired priests to serve as their chaplains.

[9] *But ... obstinat* But if anyone were obstinate.

Hym wolde he snybben° sharply for the nonys.°   *rebuke / occasion*

A bettre preest I trowe° that nowher noon ys.   *believe*

525 He waiteth after° no pompe and reverence,   *expected*

Ne maked° hym a spiced° conscience.   *affected / overly fastidious*

But Cristes loore° and hise apostles twelve   *teaching*

He taughte, but first he folwed it hymselve.

  With hym ther was a Plowman, was° his brother,   *(who) was*

530 That hadde ylad° of dong ful many a fother.°   *hauled / cartload*

A trewe swynkere° and a good was he,   *true worker*

Lyvynge in pees and parfit charitee.

God loved he best with al his hoole herte

At alle tymes, thogh he gamed or smerte,[1]

535 And thanne° his neighebore right° as hymselve.   *then / just*

He wolde thresshe° and therto dyke° and delve°   *thresh / dig / shovel*

For Cristes sake for every povre wight°   *poor person*

Withouten hire° if it lay in his myght.   *pay*

Hise tithes payde he ful faire and wel,

540 Bothe of his propre swynk° and his catel.°   *own work / possessions*

In a tabard° he rood upon a mere.°   *over-shirt / mare*

  Ther was also a Reve° and a Millere,   *reeve*

A Somnour°[2] and a Pardoner[3] also,   *summoner*

A Maunciple°[4] and myself. Ther were namo.°   *manciple / no more*

545   The Millere was a stout carl° for the nones.   *sturdy fellow*

Ful byg he was of brawn and eek of bones.

That proved wel,° for overal ther° he cam°   *was clear / everywhere / came*

At wrastlynge° he wolde have alwey the ram.[5]   *wrestling*

He was short-sholdred,° brood,° a thikke knarre.°   *stocky / broad / thick fellow*

550 Ther was no dore that he ne wolde heve of harre[6]

Or breke it at a rennyng° with his heed.   *by running at it*

His berd as any sowe° or fox was reed,   *sow*

And therto brood as though it were a spade.

Upon the cope° right of his nose he hade   *ridge*

555 A werte° and theron stood a toft of herys,°   *wart / tuft of hairs*

Reed as the brustles° of a sowes erys.°   *bristles / sow's ears*

Hise nosethirles° blake were and wyde.°   *nostrils / wide*

A swerd and a bokeler bar° he by his syde.   *bore*

His mouth as greet was as a greet forneys.°   *furnace*

560 He was a janglere° and a goliardeys,[7]   *joker*

And that was moost of synne° and harlotries.°   *sin / obscenities*

Wel koude he stelen° corn° and tollen thries,°   *steal / grain / take his toll (percentage) thrice*

And yet he hadde a thombe[8] of gold, pardee.°   *by God*

A whit cote° and a blew° hood wered° he.   *white coat / blue / wore*

565 A baggepipe wel koude he blowe and sowne,°   *sound*

And therwithal he broghte us out of towne.

  A gentil° Maunciple was ther of a temple   *gracious*

Of which achatours° myghte take exemple   *buyers*

For to be wise in byynge° of vitaille.°   *buying / food*

570 For wheither that he payde or took by taille,°   *credit*

Algate he wayted so in his achaat

That he was ay biforn and in good staat.[9]

Now is nat that of God a ful faire grace

That swich a lewed° mannes wit shal pace°   *unlearned / surpass*

575 The wisdom of an heepe° of lerned men?   *heap*

Of maistres hadde he mo° than thries ten°   *more / three times ten*

That weren° of lawe° expert and curious,°   *were / law / skilled*

Of whiche ther weren a duszeyne° in that hous   *dozen*

Worthy to been stywardes° of rente and lond   *stewards*

580 Of any lord that is in Engelond,

To maken hym lyve by his propre good°   *own means*

In honour dettelees°—but if he were wood—   *without debt*

---

[1] *At ... smerte* At all times, whether he rejoiced or suffered.

[2] *A Somnour* Deliverer of legal summonses to either secular or ecclesiastical courts, although more often the latter. The ecclesiastical courts were run by the Church and had jurisdiction over all clerics but also over any lay person charged with a moral offense such as adultery or fornication.

[3] *Pardoner* Seller of indulgences, which were writs authorized by the Church to raise money for charitable causes. Indulgences usually promised reduction of time in penance and, after death, in Purgatory.

[4] *Maunciple* Servant at one of the Inns of Court, the legal brotherhoods in London. The Inns of Court were also called temples.

[5] *ram* Typical prize for victors at trade fairs.

[6] *Ther ... harre* There was not a door that he would not heave off its hinges.

[7] *goliardeys* The reference is to Goliards, wandering scholars in the eleventh and twelfth centuries who were known for their rowdy life.

[8] *thombe* The reference is either to the proverb "An honest miller has a golden thumb," which implied that there was no such thing as an honest miller, or to the distinctive shape millers' thumbs acquired by continually feeling the grain while it was being ground, so that a "golden thumb" was a sign of a prosperous miller.

[9] *Algate ... staat* He was always so watchful in his purchasing (achaat) / That he always came out ahead (biforn) and did well.

Or lyve as scarsly° as hym list desire,°   *frugally / as he wanted*
And able for to helpen al a shire°   *an entire county*
585 In any caas° that myghte falle or happe,°   *situation / happen*
And yet this Manciple sette hir aller cappe.°   *cheated them all*
    The Reve was a sclendre,° colerik° man.[1]   *slender / angry*
His berd was shave° as ny° as ever he kan,   *shaven / closely*
His heer° was by his erys° ful round yshorn.°   *hair / ears / cut*
590 His tope was dokked° lyk a preest biforn.[2]   *clipped*
Ful longe were his legges and ful lene°—   *lean*
Ylyk° a staf° ther was no calf ysene.°   *like / staff / seen*
Wel koude he kepe a gerner° and a bynne;°   *granary / bin*
Ther was noon auditour koude of hym
    wynne.°   *get the better of*
595 Wel wiste° he by the droghte° and by the   *knew / drought*
    reyn°   *rain*
The yeldynge° of his seed and of his greyn.°   *yield / grain*
His lordes sheepe, his neet,° his dayerye,°   *cattle / dairy cows*
His swyn,° his hors, his stoor,° and his   *swine / livestock*
    pultrye°   *poultry*
Was hoolly° in this Reves governyng,   *wholly*
600 And by his covenant° yaf the rekenyng°   *contract / reckoning*
Syn° that his lord was twenty yeer of age.   *since*
Ther koude no man brynge hym in arrerage.°   *arrears*
Ther nas baillif ne hierde nor oother hyne,
That he ne knew his sleighte and his covyne.[3]
605 They were adrad° of hym as of the deeth.°[4]   *afraid / death*
His wonyng° was ful faire upon an heeth;°   *dwelling / heath*
With grene trees shadwed was his place.
He koude bettre than his lord purchace.°   *buy land*
Full riche he was, astored pryvely.°   *privately stocked*
610 His lord wel koude he plesen subtilly,°   *please subtly*
To yeve and lene° hym of his owene good°   *loan / goods*

And have a thank and yet a gowne and hood.[5]
In youthe he hadde lerned° a good myster:°   *learned / craft*
He was a wel good wrighte,° a carpenter.   *craftsman*
615 This Reve sat upon a ful good stot°   *farm horse*
That was al pomely° grey and highte° Scot.   *dappled / named*
A long surcote° of pers upon he hade,   *overcoat*
And by his syde he baar a rusty blade.
Of Northfolk° was this Reve of which I telle,   *Norfolk*
620 Biside a toun men clepen Baldeswelle.[6]
Tukked° he was as is a frere° aboute,[7]   *belted / friar*
And ever he rood the hyndreste° of oure route.°   *last / company*
    A Somonour was ther with us in that place
That hadde a fyr reed,° cherubynnes° face,[8]   *fire red / cherub-like*
625 For saucefleem° he was with eyen narwe.°   *blotchy / narrow eyes*
As hoot he was and lecherous as a sparwe,°[9]   *sparrow*
With scaled browes blake and piled berd.[10]
Of his visage° children were aferd.°   *face / afraid*
Ther nas quyksilver, lytarge, ne brymstoon,
630 Boras, cerice, ne oille of Tartre noon,[11]
Ne oynement° that wolde clense° and   *ointment / cleanse*
    byte°   *bite*
That hym myghte helpen of the whelkes° white   *blemishes*
Nor of the knobbes sittynge° on his chekes.°   *sitting / cheeks*
Wel loved he garleek, oynons, and eek lekes°   *leeks*
635 And for to drynken strong wyn reed as blood.
Thanne wolde he speke and crie° as he were wood.   *yell*

---

[5] *His lord ... hood* This reeve cheats his lord by storing away the lord's goods as his own and then using them to provide loans to the lord, receiving payment and thanks. Payment in the Middle Ages was most often in tangible goods, like the clothing mentioned here, rather than in money.

[6] *Baldeswelle* I.e., Bawdeswell, a town in the northern part of Norfolk, the northernmost county in East Anglia on the east coast of England.

[7] *Tukked ... aboute* Franciscan friars wore habits tied about the waist with ropes.

[8] *That ... face* Cherubim, the second highest order of angels, were bright red. See Ezekiel 1.13.

[9] *sparwe* Since sparrows travel in flocks, they had a reputation in the Middle Ages for being lecherous, similar to the more modern reputation of rabbits.

[10] *With ... berd* The Summoner's eyebrows have a disease called the scall, and his beard has been losing tufts of hair.

[11] *Ther ... noon* The unsuccessful remedies are mercury (sometimes known as quicksilver), lead monoxide (lytarge), sulfur (sometimes known as brimstone), borax, white lead (cerice), and cream of tartar.

---

[1] *The ... man* A reeve was someone, often originally a peasant, who served as a supervisor on a lord's estate. Among other things, reeves collected the portion of the harvest due to the lords and made sure peasants performed their customary labor for the lords. They were much resented. Chaucer's Reeve is dominated by choler, or yellow bile, which makes him suspicious and irritable.

[2] *His ... biforn* The top of his head was cut short in the front like a priest's haircut. This would have been an unfashionable cut for a layman, and suitable to a man who was poor, or miserly, or austere.

[3] *Ther nas ... covyne* There was not a bailiff (foreman), herdsman, or other worker whose tricks and deception he did not know.

[4] *adrad ... deeth* Death in general, or possibly the plague.

And whan that he wel dronken hadde the wyn,
Thanne wolde he speke no word but Latyn.
A fewe termes hadde he, two or thre,
640 That he had lerned out of som decree.°   *legal document*
No wonder is, he herde it al the day,
And eek ye knowen wel how that a jay°   *chattering bird*
Kan clepen "Watte"° as wel as kan the Pope.   *Walter*
But whoso koude in oother thyng him grope,°   *examine*
645 Thanne hadde he spent al his philosophie.
Ay° "Questio quid iuris!"[1] wold he crie.   *always*
He was a gentil harlot and a kynde;°   *noble and kindly scoundrel*
A bettre felawe° sholde men noght° fynde.   *fellow / not*
He wolde suffre for a quart of wyn
650 A good felawe to have his concubyn°   *mistress*
A twelf monthe° and excuse hym atte fulle.°   *a year / fully*
Ful prively° a fynch eek koude he pulle.[2]   *secretly / finch*
And if he foond° owher° a good felawe,   *found / anywhere*
He wolde techen° hym to have noon awe°   *teach / no respect*
655 In swich caas of the Ercedekenes curs—[3]
But if° a mannes° soule were in his purs.°   *unless / man's / purse*
For in his purs he sholde ypunysshed be:°   *be punished*
Purs is the Ercedekenes Helle, seyde he.
But wel I woot° he lyed° right in dede.°   *know / lied / indeed*
660 Of cursyng° oghte ech gilty man him drede;   *excommunication*
For curs wol slee° right as° assoillyng°   *kill / just as / absolution*
    savith.
And also war° him of a "Significavit"!"[4]   *beware*
In daunger° hadde he at his owene gise°   *power / pleasure*
The yonge girles[5] of the diocise°   *diocese*
665 And knew hir conseil° and was al hir reed.[6]   *their adviser*
A gerland° hadde he set upon his heed   *garland*

As greet as it were for an ale stake.[7]
A bokeleer hadde he, maad° hym of a cake.°   *made / loaf of bread*
    With hym ther was a gentil° Pardoner   *noble*
670 Of Rouncivale,[8] his freend and his compeer,°   *companion*
That streight° was comen fro the court of Rome.   *straight*
Ful loude he soong "Com Hider, Love, to Me;"[9]
This Somonour bar to hym a stif burdoun.[10]
Was nevere trompe° of half so greet a soun!   *trumpet*
675 This Pardoner hadde heer as yelow as wex,°   *wax*
But smothe it heeng as dooth a strike° of flex.°   *bunch / flax*
By ounces° henge hise lokkes that he hadde,   *strands*
And therwith he hise shuldres°   *shoulders*
    overspradde,°   *spread over*
But thynne° it lay by colpons° oon° and oon. *thin / strands / one*
680 But hood for jolitee° wered° he noon,   *fun / wore*
For it was trussed° up in his walet.°   *packed / bag*
Hym thoughte° he rood al of the newe   *it seemed to him*
    jet.°   *fashion*
Dischevelee° save° his cappe° he   *with his hair loose / except / cap*
    rood° al bare.   *rode*
Swiche glarynge° eyen hadde he as an hare.[11]   *bulging*
685 A vernycle[12] hadde he sowed° upon his cappe;   *sewn*
His walet° biforn° hym in his lappe,°   *wallet / before / lap*
Bretful° of pardoun, comen from Rome al hoot.   *brimful*

---

[1] *Questio quid iuris* Latin: Question: what point of the law? The expression was often used in the ecclesiastical courts.

[2] *Ful … pulle* Obscene expression that meant, literally, "to pluck a bird."

[3] *In … curs* In such a case of the excommunication (curse) of the archdeacon. An archdeacon was the ecclesiastical official in charge of the ecclesiastical court of a diocese.

[4] *Significavit* Latin: It signified. It is the first word in a writ authorizing the civil court to imprison someone who had been excommunicated.

[5] *yonge girles* In Middle English, girls can mean young people of both sexes, but here it may just mean young women.

[6] *was al hir reed* Was all their advice. Idiomatic: the Summoner was in their confidence.

---

[7] *ale stake* Ale-sign; a long pole hung with a garland that stuck out into the street and showed that ale was being sold on the premises.

[8] *Of Rouncivale* The Pardoner belongs to the Hospital of the Blessed Mary of Roncesvalles in London, a dependent house of the larger one at Roncesvalles, the mountain pass between Spain and France which many pilgrims used when they traveled to St. James of Compostela. Hospitals in the Middle Ages were not purely medical facilities; they also served as inns and poor houses.

[9] *Com Hider, Love, to Me* This song, "Come Here, Love, to Me," does not survive.

[10] *This … burdoun* The Summoner accompanied him with a strong bass. In medieval carols, each sung verse was separated by a burden, a kind of refrain. Carols originally had many subjects, not just the joys of Christmas.

[11] *hare* According to medieval lore, hares were hermaphroditic, becoming both male and female in order to reproduce. Bulging eyes were thought to be a sign of lust and folly.

[12] *vernycle* Badge depicting St. Veronica's veil, a relic at Rome. St. Veronica wiped Jesus' face with her veil as he carried the cross, and by miracle his image was imprinted upon it. Pilgrims collected such badges.

A voys° he hadde as smal° as hath a *voice / high-pitched*
   goot.° *goat*
No berd hadde he, ne never sholde° have: *would*
690 As smothe° it was as° it were late yshave.° *smooth / as if / shaven*
I trowe° he were a geldyng° or a mare.[1] *believe / gelding*
But of his craft fro° Berwyk into Ware[2] *from*
Ne was ther swich° another pardoner. *there was not such*
For in his male° he hadde a pilwe beer,° *bag / pillow-case*
695 Which that he seyde was oure Lady veyl;°[3] *Virgin Mary's veil*
He seyde he hadde a gobet° of the seyl° *piece / sail*
That Seint Peter hadde when that he wente
Upon the see til Jhesu Crist hym hente.°[4] *grabbed him*
He hadde a croys° of latoun° ful of stones, *cross / brass*
700 And in a glas° he hadde pigges bones. *glass*
But with thise relikes whan that he fond
A povre person dwellynge upon lond,
Upon a day he gat hym° moore moneye *got himself*
Than that the person gat in monthes tweye.
705 And thus with feyned° flaterye and japes° *pretended / jokes*
He made the person and the peple his apes.° *dupes*
But trewely, to tellen atte laste,
He was in chirche a noble ecclesiaste.° *churchman*
Wel koude he rede a lessoun° or a *lesson*
   storie,° *story (from the Bible)*
710 But alderbest° he song° an offertorie,[5] *best of all / sang*
For wel he wiste whan that song was songe
He moste preche° and wel affile° his *must preach / sharpen*
   tonge° *tongue*
To wynne° silver as he ful wel koude. *acquire*
Therfore he song the murierly° and loude. *more merrily*
715 Now have I toold yow shortly° in a clause *briefly*
Th'estaat,° th'array,° the nombre, *social position / appearance*
   and eek the cause
Why that assembled was this compaignye

In Southwerk at this gentil hostelry
That highte the Tabard, faste by the Belle.[6]
720 But now is tyme to yow° for to telle *you*
How that we baren° us that ilke nyght *behaved*
Whan we were in that hostelrie alyght,° *arrived*
And after wol I tell of oure viage
And al the remenaunt of oure pilgrimage.
725 But first I pray yow of youre curteisye
That ye n'arette it nat my vileynye,[7]
Thogh that I pleynly° speke in this mateere *plainly*
To telle yow hir wordes and hir cheere,° *comportment*
Ne thogh I speke hir wordes proprely.° *exactly*
730 For this ye knowen also wel as I:
Whoso° shal telle a tale after a man, *whoever*
He moot° reherce as ny° as ever he kan *should / closely*
Everich a word° if it be in his charge, *every word*
Al° speke he never so rudeliche° or *although / crudely*
   large,° *freely*
735 Or ellis° he moot° telle his tale untrewe, *else / must*
Or feyne thyng,° or fynde wordes newe. *falsify something*
He may nat spare althogh he were his brother;
He moot as wel seye o word as another.
Crist spak hymself ful brode° in Hooly *freely*
   Writ,° *holy scripture*
740 And wel ye woot no vileynye is it.
Eek Plato seith, whoso kan hym rede,
The wordes moote be cosyn° to the dede.°[8] *cousin / deed*
Also I prey yow to foryeve° it me *forgive*
Al° have I nat set folk in hir degree° *although / according to rank*
745 Heere in this tale as that they sholde stonde.
My wit° is short, ye may wel understonde. *intelligence*
   Greet chiere° made oure Hoost us everichon,° *cheer / everyone*

---

[1] *I ... mare* I believe he was either a gelding (a castrated horse) or a mare.

[2] *Berwyk into Ware* Berwick is in the extreme north of England near the border with Scotland; Ware is near London.

[3] *For ... veyl* Chaucer's point is that the Pardoner sells fraudulent relics (sacred objects associated with Jesus or the saints).

[4] *That ... hente* The reference is to Peter's unsuccessful attempt to imitate Christ by walking on the water. Christ had to rescue him. See Matthew 14.22–33.

[5] *offertorie* The Offertory was chanted when the congregation was bringing gifts to the altar.

[6] *Belle* Previous editors have capitalized this word, guessing that it was the name of another inn—there were several called the Bell in that area—or perhaps a house of prostitution. Perhaps the word should not be capitalized, as it may imply a notable bell in the neighborhood.

[7] *That ... vileynye* That you not attribute it to my lack of manners. Vileynye does not mean villainy in the modern sense. A villein was originally an inhabitant of a rural village; thus the word signifies the state of being rustic rather than civilized.

[8] *Eek ... dede* The reference is to Plato's *Timaeus*, the only one of his dialogues available in translation to the Latin West in the Middle Ages. The quotation is found in section 29. The passage is also discussed by Boethius in his *Consolation of Philosophy* (3, prose 12), a work that Chaucer had translated and drew upon frequently.

And to the soper sette he us anon.
He served us with vitaille at the beste;
750 Strong was the wyn, and wel to drynke us leste.° *it pleased us*
A semely° man oure Hoost was withalle *suitable*
For to been a marchal° in an halle.[1] *marshal*
A large man he was, with eyen stepe.° *bright*
A fairer burgeys° was ther noon in Chepe,[2] *citizen*
755 Boold of his speche and wys and wel ytaught,° *learned*
And of manhod hym lakked° right naught.° *lacked / nothing*
Eek therto° he was right a myrie man, *in addition*
And after soper pleyen° he bigan° *play / began*
And spak of myrthe amonges othere thynges
760 Whan that we hadde maad oure rekenynges[3]
And seyde thus, "Now lordynges, trewely,
Ye been° to me right welcome hertely.° *are / heartily*
For by my trouthe, if that I shal nat lye,
I saugh nat this yeer so myrie a compaignye
765 Atones° in this herberwe° as is now. *at once / inn*
Fayn° wolde I doon yow myrthe, wiste I° *gladly / if I knew*
how.
And of a myrthe I am right now bythoght° *in mind*
To doon yow ese,° and it shal coste *do you ease*
noght.° *nothing*
Ye goon to Caunterbury: God yow
speede!° *God bring you success!*
770 The blissful martir quite° yow youre meede!° *pay / reward*
And wel I woot as ye goon by the weye,
Ye shapen yow° to talen° and to pleye.° *intend / tell tales / play*
For trewely,° confort° ne myrthe is noon *truly / comfort*
To ride by the weye doumb as the stoon.[4]
775 And therfore wol I maken yow disport,° *entertainment*
As I seyde erst,° and doon yow som *first*
confort.° *bring you some comfort*
And if yow liketh° alle by oon assent° *pleases you / unanimously*
For to stonden at° my juggement° *abide by / judgment*
And for to werken° as I shal yow seye, *proceed*
780 Tomorwe, whan ye riden by the weye,
Now by my fader soule° that is deed,° *father's soul / dead*

But if ye be myrie, I wol yeve yow myn heed!
Hoold up youre hondes withouten moore speche."
Oure conseil° was nat° longe for to seche.° *counsel / not / seek*
785 Us thoughte° it was noght worth to make it wys,[5] *we thought*
And graunted hym withouten moore avys° *more debate*
And bad° hym seye his voirdit° as hym *asked / verdict*
leste.° *as he wanted*
"Lordynges," quod he, "now herkneth for the beste,
But taak it nought, I prey° yow, in desdeyn.° *beg / disdain*
790 This is the poynt, to speken short and pleyn,
That ech of yow to shorte° with oure weye *shorten*
In this viage shal telle tales tweye° *two*
To Caunterburyward,° I mene° it so, *towards Canterbury / mean*
And homward he shal tellen othere two
795 Of aventures that whilom° han bifalle.° *once / have happened*
And which of yow that bereth hym° best of *conducts himself*
alle,
That is to seyn, that telleth in this caas° *occasion*
Tales of best sentence° and moost solaas,° *meaning / enjoyment*
Shal have a soper at oure aller cost° *at all our cost*
800 Heere in this place, sittynge by this post,
Whan that we come agayn fro Caunterbury.
As for to make yow the moore mury,° *merry*
I wol myself goodly° with yow ryde, *gladly*
Right at myn owene cost, and be youre gyde.
805 And whoso wole my juggement withseye° *resist*
Shal paye al that we spenden by the weye.° *along the way*
And if ye vouchesauf° that it be so, *grant*
Tel me anon withouten wordes mo,
And I wol erly° shape me° therfore."° *early / get ready / for it*
810 This thyng was graunted and oure othes° swore° *oaths / sworn*
With ful glad herte, and preyden° hym also *asked*
That he wolde vouchesauf for to do so
And that he wolde been oure governour
And of oure tales juge° and reportour° *judge / referee*
815 And sette a soper at a certeyn pris° *price*
And we wol reuled been at his devys° *wish*
In heigh and lough.° And thus by oon° *all matters / one*
assent
We been acorded° to his juggement, *agreed*
And therupon the wyn was fet° anon.° *fetched / immediately*
820 We dronken and to reste wente echon° *each one*
Withouten any lenger taryynge.° *longer delaying*

---

[1] *For ... halle* A marshal is a steward or chief butler; a hall is a manor house or town house of a lord.

[2] *Chepe* Cheapside was the merchants' district in London.

[3] *Whan ... rekenynges* When we had paid our bills.

[4] *For ... stoon* For truly there is neither comfort nor mirth in riding along as silent as a stone.

[5] *to make it wys* Idiomatic: to make a big deal of it.

Amorwe,° whan that day gan° for to sprynge,°   *the next day / began / dawn*
Up roos° oure Hoost and was oure aller cok°   *rose / rooster for us all*
And gadrede° us togidre° all in a flok.°   *gathered / together / flock*
825 And forth we ridden,° a litel moore than paas,°   *rode / a horse's walking pace*
Unto the Wateryng of Seint Thomas.[1]
And there oure Hoost bigan his hors areste°   *rein in*
And seyde, "Lordynges, herkneth if yow leste!°   *please*
Ye woot youre foreward° and it yow recorde;°   *contract / recall*
830 If evensong° and morwesong° accorde,[2]   *evensong / matins*
Lat se° now who shal telle the firste tale.   *let us see*
As evere mote° I drynke wyn or ale,   *might*
Whoso be rebel to my juggement
Shal paye for al that by the wey is spent.
835 Now draweth cut er that we ferrer twynne;[3]
He which that hath the shorteste shal bigynne.
Sire Knyght," quod he, "my mayster and my lord,
Now draweth cut,° for that is myn accord.°   *a straw / decision*
Cometh neer," quod he, "my lady Prioresse,
840 And ye, sire Clerk, lat be youre shamefastnesse,°   *shyness*
Ne studieth noght.° Ley° hond° to every man."   *stop studying / lay / hand*

Anon to drawen every wight° bigan,   *person*
And shortly for to tellen as it was,
Were it by aventure or sort or cas,[4]
845 The sothe° is this: the cut° fil° to the knyght,   *truth / straw / fell*
Of which ful blithe° and glad was every wyght.   *very happy*
And telle he moste his tale as was reso un,°   *reasonable*
By foreward° and by composicioun,°   *agreement / arrangement*
As ye han herd. What nedeth wordes mo?
850 And whan this goode man saugh° that it was so,   *saw*
As he that wys was and obedient
To kepe his foreward by his free assent,
He seyde, "Syn° I shal bigynne the game,   *since*
What, welcome be the cut, a Goddes° name!   *in God's*
855 Now lat us ryde and herkneth what I seye."
And with that word we ryden forth oure weye.
And he bigan with right a myrie cheere°   *cheerful expression*
His tale anon, and seyde in this manere.[5]

---

[1] *Wateryng of Seint Thomas* The Watering of St. Thomas was the name given to a brook just outside London on the way to Canterbury.

[2] *If … accorde* I.e., if you still say in the morning what you said last evening.

[3] *Now … twynne* "Now draw a straw before we depart further."

[4] *Were … cas* Adventure, sort, and case mean roughly the same thing: chance.

[5] *His … manere* Hengwrt and some other manuscripts read "and seyde as ye may heere," not "and seyde in this manere," a suggestion that *The Canterbury Tales* were to be read aloud as well as silently.

The Miller's Prologue and Tale

When the Knight has finished his tale, much applauded by the "gentles," the Host turns to the pilgrim who, after the Prioress, ranks next in the social hierarchy: the Monk, a senior brother from a wealthy monastery. But the Miller, who has already placed himself at the head of the pilgrims to lead them out of town with his discordant bagpipes, has no respect for social hierarchy. He insists that he will "quyte" the Knight, that is, repay him or match him, and his tale does just that. With the insertion of *The Miller's Tale*, Chaucer breaks decisively from less dynamic frame narratives such as Boccaccio's *Decameron*, in which the stories are told by a homogeneous and harmonious group of aristocrats, and launches a social comedy in which the various tellers will contest each other's authority and values.

The Miller's Tale belongs to the medieval genre of the *fabliau,* a short tale of trickery often set among lower-class or bourgeois characters. These tales may have circulated orally, but they were also written down, and the written versions were enjoyed by aristocratic, not peasant, readers. Chaucer draws on two well-established *fabliau* plots. In the first, a young scholar cuckolds an old husband by making him believe that a second flood is coming; in the second, a young lover humiliates a rival by tricking him into a misdirected kiss. Chaucer may have drawn on a source that had already combined these two plots or may have combined them himself. Early critics, embarrassed by the tale's vulgarity, tended to regard it as a regrettable lapse and take Chaucer at his word when he apologizes in *The General Prologue* for his boorish lower-class characters, whom he designates as "churls" who insist on telling churlish stories. But Chaucer devoted all his powers of comic timing, sensual description, and social satire to expanding the basic story line into a comic masterpiece, in which the two plots come together when Nicholas calls for water.

The Miller tells his tale, a "legend or a life" (which would normally mean a saint's life) of the cuckolding of an old carpenter, in part to attack the Reeve, who is also a carpenter—and a professional rival, since reeves were expected to catch dishonest millers. The Miller's rivalry with the Knight, however, and his claim that he will "quyte" him, invite readers to observe how extensively his tale parallels that of the Knight. These parallels all serve to subvert the values of *The Knight's Tale*, calling into question its lengthy tribute to cosmic order, its chivalric dignity, and its depiction of refined love from afar. Whereas Palamon and Arcite are almost interchangeable, Nicholas, who is "hende" or handy in so many ways, is completely unlike the squeamish Absolon; and Alison, in complete contrast to the passive Emelye, is an energetic schemer, who participates gleefully in Absolon's humiliation.

Set in Oxford, *The Miller's Tale* gives a vivid sense of medieval student life and reveals the tensions between the more prosperous members of the peasantry and cunning clerics. Most unusually, the butt of the story, the old cuckolded husband, becomes a complex and often sympathetic character. John the carpenter is allowed to expand upon his philosophy of life, warning against prying into God's secrets, just as the Miller warns the Reeve not to pry into his wife's secrets. With the fast pace of burlesque or a modern situation comedy, *The Miller's Tale* is filled with vivid details of domestic life; it could not be more different from the Knight's, and its insistence that cleverness or proximity will triumph over high ideals is one of its many possible morals. The tale offers solace and *sentens,* but exactly what this *sentens* is remains the source of continual debate.

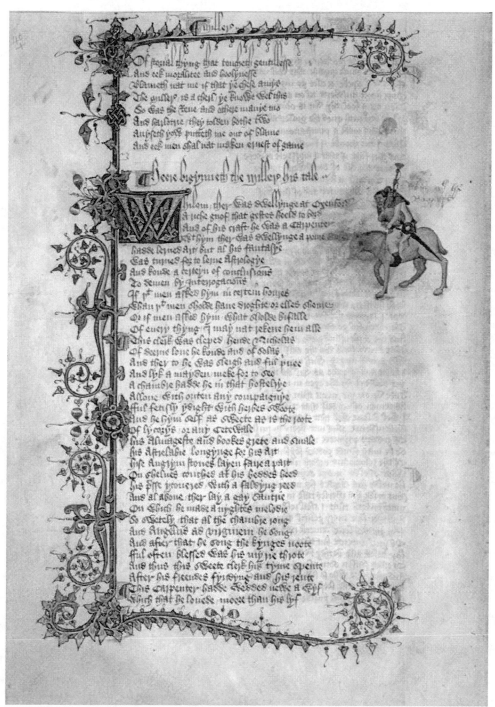

Opening page to *The Miller's Tale*, Ellesmere manuscript. (Reprinted by permission of *The Huntington Library, San Marino, California. EL 26 C9 f. 34v.*)

THE MILLER'S PROLOGUE

HERE FOLWEN THE WORDES BITWENE THE HOOST AND THE MILLERE

Whan that the Knyght hath thus his tale ytoold,° *told*
In al the route° ne was ther° yong *company / there was not*
    ne° oold *nor*
That he ne seyde° it was a noble storie *did not say*
And worthy for to drawen to memorie,° *learn by heart*
5 And namely° the gentils° *especially / gentlefolk*
    everich on.° *every one*
Oure Hoost lough° and swoor,° "So *laughed / swore*
    moot I gon,[1]
This gooth aright!° Unbokeled° is the *goes well / unbuckled*
    male.° *purse*
Lat se,° now, who shal telle another tale? *let's see*
For trewely, the game is wel bigonne.
10 Now telleth on, Sire Monk, if that ye konne,° *if you can*
Somwhat to quite with° the knyghtes tale." *match*
The Millere, that for dronken° was al pale *being drunk*
So that unnethe° upon his hors he sat, *scarcely*
He nolde° avalen° neither hood ne hat *would not / take off*
15 Ne abyde° no man for his curteisie,° *wait for / courtesy*
But in Pilates[2] voys° he gan° to crie *voice / began*
And swoor, "By armes and by blood and bones,[3]
I kan° a noble tale for the nones° *know / occasion*
With which I wol now quite° the Knyghtes tale!" *match*
20 Oure Hoost saugh° that he was dronke of ale *saw*
And seyde, "Abyd,° Robyn, my leeve° brother, *wait / dear*
Som bettre man shal telle us first another.
Abyde, and lat° us werken° thriftily."° *let / work / respectably*
    "By Goddes soule," quod° he, "that wol° nat I. *said / will*
25 For I wol speke or elles° go my wey."° *else / way*
Oure Hoost answerde, "Tel on a devele wey!° *in the devil's name*
Thou art a fool! Thy wit is overcome!"
    "Now herkneth,"° quod the Millere, *listen*
      "alle and some.° *one and all*

But first I make a protestacioun° *protest*
30 That I am dronke; I knowe it by my soun.° *sound*
And therfore if that I mysspeke or seye,° *say something wrong*
Wyte it° the ale of Southwerk, I preye.° *blame it on / pray*
For I wol tell a legende and a lyf[4]
Bothe of a carpenter and of his wyf,
35 How that a clerk° hath set the wrightes cappe."[5] *student*
    The Reve answerde and seyde, "Stynt thy
      clappe!° *shut your mouth*
Lat be thy lewed,° dronken° *ignorant / drunken*
    harlotrye!° *bawdiness*
It is a synne° and eek° a greet° folye° *sin / also / great / folly*
To apeyren° any man or hym° defame° *harm / him / slander*
40 And eek to bryngen wyves in swich° fame.° *such / dishonor*
Thou mayst ynogh° of othere thynges seyn."° *enough / speak*
    This dronke° Millere spak° ful° soone *drunken / spoke / very*
    agayn° *again*
And seyde, "Leve brother Osewold,
Who hath no wyf, he is no cokewold.[6]
45 But I sey nat therfore that thou art oon.° *one*
Ther been ful goode wyves many oon,° *a one*
And evere a thousand goode ayeyns° oon badde.° *against / bad*
That knowestow wel° thyself, but if° *you know well / unless*
    thou madde.° *are mad*
Why artow° angry with my tale now? *are you*
50 I have a wyf, Per Die,° as wel as thow, *by God*
Yet nolde° I for the oxen in my plogh° *would not / plow*
Take upon me moore than ynogh,° *enough*
As demen° of myself that I were oon.° *judge / one (i.e., a cuckold)*
I wol bileve° wel that I am noon.° *believe / none*
55 An housbonde shal nat been inquisityf° *inquisitive*
Of Goddes pryvetee° nor of his wyf. *secrets*
So he may fynde° Goddes foyson° there, *find / abundance*
Of the remenant nedeth nat enquere!"° *he need not inquire*
    What sholde I moore seyn, but this Millere,
60 He nolde° his wordes for no man *would not*
    forbere,° *forego*
But tolde his cherles° tale in his manere.° *boor's / manner*
M'athynketh° that I shal reherce° it heere, *I regret / repeat*

---

1 *So ... gon* I.e., as I hope to live.

2 *But in Pilates* I.e., Pontius Pilate, the Roman governor who condemned Jesus to be crucified. In medieval religious plays he was depicted as a loud, rampaging villain.

3 *By ... bones* Swearing during the Middle Ages and Renaissance often involved taking oaths on various parts of God's body—here God's arms, blood, and bones.

4 *legende and a lyf* Normally a "saint's life," or biography of a Christian saint.

5 *set the wrightes cappe* Made a fool of the carpenter.

6 *cokewold* I.e., cuckold: a husband whose wife has sex with another man.

And therfore every gentil° wight° I preye,°   *noble / person / pray*
For Goddes love demeth° nat° that I seye°   *judge / not / speak*
65   Of yvel entente,° but that I moot reherce°   *evil intent / repeat*
Hir° tales, all be they° bettre or werse,   *their / although they be*
Or elles° falsen° som of my mateere.°   *else / falsify / matter*
And therfore, whoso° list° it nat   *whoever / wishes*
yheere,°   *not to hear*
Turne over the leef,° and chese° another tale.   *page / choose*
70   For he shal fynde° ynowe,° grete° and   *find / enough / great*
smale,°   *small*
Of storial° thyng that toucheth gentillesse°   *historical / nobility*
And eek moralitee° and hoolynesse.°   *morality / holiness*
Blameth nat me if that ye chese amys.°   *choose wrongly*
The millere is a cherl.° Ye knowe wel this.   *boor*
75   So was the Reve, and othere manye mo,°   *more*
And harlotrie° they tolden bothe two.   *bawdiness*
Avyseth yow;° putteth me out of blame,   *be advised*
And eek men shal nat maken ernest° of game.°   *seriousness / joke*

THE MILLER'S TALE

HEERE BIGYNNETH THE MILLERE HIS TALE

Whilom° ther was dwellynge° at   *once / living*
Oxenford°   *Oxford*
80   A riche gnof° that gestes° heeld to bord,[1]   *fellow / guests*
And of his craft° he was a carpenter.   *profession*
With hym ther was dwellynge a povre° scoler°   *poor / student*
Hadde lerned° art, but al his fantasye°   *learned / interest*
Was turned for to lerne astrologye,
85   And koude a certeyn of conclusiouns[2]
To demen° by interrogaciouns°   *judge / questions*
If that men asked hym in certein houres[3]
Whan that men sholde have droghte° or elles   *drought*
shoures,°   *rain*
Or if men asked hym what sholde bifalle°   *happen*
90   Of every thyng—I may nat rekene° hem° all.   *count up / them*
This clerk was cleped° hende° Nicholas.   *named / handy*
Of deerne° love he koude° and of solas,°   *secret / knew / pleasure*

And therto he was sleigh° and ful privee°   *sly / very secretive*
And lyk° a mayden meke° for to see.   *like / meek*
95   A chambre° hadde he in that hostelrye,°   *room / lodging*
Allone° withouten any compaignye.   *alone*
Ful fetisly° ydight° with herbes[4]   *fashionably / decorated*
swoote,°   *sweet*
And he hymself as swete as is the roote°   *root*
Of lycorys° or any cetewale.[5]   *licorice*
100   His *Almageste*[6] and bookes grete and smale,
His astrelabie[7] longynge for° his art,   *pertaining to*
Hise augrym stones[8] layen° faire apart°   *lay / somewhat away*
On shelves couched° at his beddes heed,°   *arranged / bed's head*
His presse° ycovered° with a faldyng°   *cupboard / covered / cloth*
reed,°   *red*
105   And al above ther lay a gay sautrie[9]
On which he made a nyghtes° melodie°   *nightly / melody*
So swetely that al the chambre rong.°   *rang*
And *Angelus ad virginem*[10] he song,
And after that he song *The Kynges Noote*;[11]
110   Full often blessed was his myrie° throte!°   *merry / throat*
And thus this sweete clerk his tyme spente
After his freendes fyndyng[12] and his rente.°   *income*
This carpenter hadde wedded newe° a wyf   *newly married*
Which that he lovede moore than his lyf.

---

1   *heeld to bord*   Rented out rooms.

2   *koude a certeyn of conclusiouns*   Knew some (astrological) calculations.

3   *houres*   I.e., astrological hours—times when certain planets exerted a certain influence.

4   *ydight with herbes*   Spread with dried and sweet smelling herbs.

5   *cetewale*   The spice zedoary, similar to ginger.

6   *Almageste*   I.e., *Almagest*, the basic textbook for medieval astronomy. It was the work of Claudius Ptolemy (second century CE), who gives his name to the Ptolemaic system, in which the sun revolves around the earth. According to Ptolemy, the heavens comprised nine concentric crystal spheres that revolved and on which the planets and stars were affixed.

7   *astrelabie*   I.e., astrolabe, a scientific instrument used to measure angles of heavenly bodies. Chaucer wrote *The Treatise on the Astrolabe*, a prose work that is one of the first pieces of technical writing in the English language.

8   *augrym stones*   I.e., Augrim stones; they were marked with numbers and were used for making mathematical calculations.

9   *sautrie*   I.e., psaltery, a stringed musical instrument.

10   *Angelus ad virginem*   Latin: The Angel to the Virgin. The song, an antiphon used in liturgical service, depicts the conversation between the angel Gabriel and the Virgin Mary about the coming birth of Jesus.

11   *The Kynges Noote*   This song has not survived.

12   *After his freendes fyndyng*   According to what his friends gave him.

115 Of eighteteene yeer she was of age.
Jalous° he was and heeld hire narwe° in cage,[1]   *jealous / closely*
For she was yong and wylde and he was old,
And demed° hymself been° lik° a   *guessed / to be / likely*
    cokewold.°   *cuckold*
He knew nat Catoun,[2] for his wit° was   *intelligence*
    rude,°   *unformed*
120 That bad° man sholde wedde his   *who advised*
    simylitude.°   *equal*
Men sholde wedden after hire° estaat,°   *their / condition*
For youthe and elde° is often at debaat.°   *age / in dispute*
But sith° that he was fallen in the snare,°   *since / trap*
He moste endure as oother folk his care.°   *sorrow*
125   Fair was this yonge wyf and therwithal
As any wezele° hir body gent° and smal.   *weasel / delicate*
A ceynt° she werede° ybarred° al of silk,   *girdle / wore / striped*
A barmclooth° as whit° as morne° milk   *apron / white / morning*
Upon hir lendes,° ful of many a goore.°   *hips / pleat*
130 Whit° was hir smok° and   *white / undergarment*
    broyden° al bifoore°   *embroidered / in front*
And eek bihynde on hir coler° aboute   *collar*
Of col-blak° silk withinne and eek withoute.   *coal-black*
The tapes° of hir white voluper°   *ribbons / cap*
Were of the same suyte° of hir coler,   *pattern*
135 Hir filet° brood° of silk and set ful hye,°   *headband / broad / high*
And sikerly° she hadde a likerous° eye.   *certainly / flirtatious*
Ful smale ypulled° were hire browes° two,   *plucked / eyebrows*
And tho° were bent and blake° as any   *they / black*
    sloo.°   *sloeberry*
She was ful moore blisful° on to see   *much more pleasant*
140 Than is the newe perejonette tree,°   *pear tree*
And softer than the wolle° is of a wether.°   *wool / male sheep*
And by hir girdel° heeng a purs of   *belt*
    lether°   *hung a purse of leather*
Tasseled with grene° and perled° with   *green / decorated*
    latoun.°   *brass*
In al this world to seken° up and doun   *seek*
145 Ther nas° no man so wys° that koude   *was not / wise*
    thenche°   *imagine*

So gay a popelote° or swich a wenche.°   *doll / peasant girl*
Full brighter was the shynyng° of hir hewe°   *shining / complexion*
Than in the Tour° the noble° yforged°   *tower / gold coin / forged*
    newe![3]
But of hir song, it was as loude and yerne°   *eager*
150 As any swalwe° sittynge on a berne.°   *swallow / barn*
Therto she koude skippe° and make game°   *dance / play*
As any kyde° or calf folwynge his dame.°*kid (young goat) / mother*
Hir mouth was sweete as bragot° or the   *ale*
    meeth°   *mead (fermented honey)*
Or hoord° of apples leyd° in hey° or   *hoard / stored / hay*
    heeth.°   *heather*
155 Wynsynge° she was as is a joly° colt,   *skittish / pretty*
Long as a mast and uprighte° as a bolt.°   *straight / arrow*
A brooch° she baar° upon hir loue   *broach / wore*
    coler°   *low collar*
As brood° as is the boos[4] of a bokeler.°   *broad / shield*
Hir shoes were laced on hir legges hye.°   *high*
160 She was a prymerole,° a piggesnye°   *primrose / pig's eye (flower)*
For any lord to leggen° in his bedde   *lay*
Or yet for any good yeman° to wedde.   *yeoman*
    Now sire° and eft° sire, so bifel° the cas°   *sir / again / befell / event*
That on a day this hende° Nicholas   *handy*
165 Fil° with this yonge wyf to rage° and pleye   *fell / romp*
Whil that hir housbonde was at Oseneye,[5]
As clerkes been ful subtile° and ful queynte,°   *subtle / clever*
And prively° he caughte hire by the queynte[6]   *secretly / genitals*
And seyde, "Ywis,° but if° ich° have my wille,   *indeed / unless / I*
170 For deerne° love of thee, lemman,° I   *secret / sweetheart*
    spille,"°   *die*
And heeld hire harde by the haunche bones°   *thighs*
And seyde, "Lemman,° love me al at ones°   *sweetheart / immediately*
Or I wol dyen,° also° God me save!"   *die / as*

---

[1] *in cage* In a cage; i.e., he guarded her carefully.

[2] *Catoun* I.e., Cato. The *Distichs*, a widely circulating collection of proverbs and wise sayings in verse couplets, often used for teaching Latin in schools, were ascribed in the Middle Ages to the Roman writer Dionysius Cato.

[3] *Than ... newe* Gold coins were forged in the Tower of London.

[4] *boos* I.e., boss, the center bulge of a shield, occasionally used to injure an enemy.

[5] *Oseneye* I.e., Oseney, a small town just to the west of Oxford (now part of the modern city) where there was an abbey.

[6] *queynte* A rhyme on two homonyms (such as *blue / blew* or *guest / guessed*), near homonyms (such as *seke / seke*, i.e., *seek* and *sick* in the General Prologue, lines 18–19) or on two different meanings of the same word, as here with *queynte*, was known as "rime riche" and was much valued by the French court poets of Chaucer's day. The modern term "rich rhyme" has a slightly narrower meaning and is confined to rhymes on homonyms.

And she sproong° as a colt dooth° in the   sprang / does
trave,°   stall
175   And with hir heed she wryed° faste awey.   twisted
She seyde, "I wol nat kisse thee, by my fey!°   faith
Why, lat be, quod ich,°[1] lat be Nicholas,   I say
Or I wol crie 'Out, harrow, and allas!'[2]
Do wey° youre handes, for youre curteisye!"   let go
180   This Nicholas gan mercy for to crye
And spak so faire and profred° hire so faste   urged
That she hir love hym graunted atte last°   at last
And swoor hir ooth,° "By Seint Thomas of   oath
Kent,"°   St. Thomas à Becket
That she wol° been at his comandement   would
185   Whan that she may hir leyser° wel espie.°   leisure / see
"Myn housbonde is so ful of jalousie
That but° ye wayte° wel and been privee,°   unless / wait / secretive
I woot° right wel I nam° but deed," quod she.   know / am not
"Ye moste been ful deerne° as in this cas."°   secretive / business
190   "Nay, therof care thee noght,"° quod Nicholas,   have no care
"A clerk hadde lutherly biset his whyle[3]
But if° he koude a carpenter bigyle."°   unless / trick
And thus they been accorded° and ysworn°   agreed / sworn
To wayte a tyme° as I have told biforn.°   wait (for a time) / before
195   Whan Nicholas had doon° thus everideel°   done / every bit
And thakked° hire aboute the lendes° weel,°   patted / loins / well
He kiste hire sweete and taketh his sawtrie°   psaltery
And pleyeth° faste and maketh melodie.   plays
   Thanne fil it° thus that to the paryssh chirche   it happened
200   Cristes owene werkes° for to wirche,°   works / perform
This goode wyf wente on an haliday.[4]
Hir forheed° shoon° as bright as any day,   forehead / shone
So was it wasshen° whan she leet° hir werk.°   washed / left / work

Now was ther of that chirche° a parissh clerk[5]   church
205   The which that was ycleped° Absolon.[6]   called
Crul° was his heer, and as the gold it shoon,   curled
And strouted° as a fanne° large and   stretched out / fan
brode;°   broad
Ful streight and evene lay his joly shode.°   parting of his hair
His rode° was reed,° hise eyen greye as   complexion / red
goos,°   goose
210   With Poules wyndow[7] corven° on his shoos.°   carved / shoes
In hoses° rede° he wente fetisly.°   stockings / red / elegantly
Yclad° he was ful smal° and proprely   clothed / very tightly
Al in a kirtel° of a lyght waget.°   tunic / blue
Ful faire and thikke° been the poyntes° set,   thick / laces
215   And therupon he hadde a gay surplys°   surplice (liturgical garment)
As whit as is the blosme upon the rys.°   twig
A myrie° child° he was, so God me save.   merry / young man
Wel koude he laten blood° and clippe and shave[8]   let blood
And maken a chartre° of lond° or   contract / land
acquitaunce.°   quit-claim
220   In twenty manere koude he trippe and daunce
After the scole° of Oxenford tho,°   school / then
And with his legges casten to and fro
And pleyen songes on a smal
rubible.°   rebec (bowed stringed instrument)
Therto he song somtyme a loud quynyble,°   falsetto
225   And as wel koude he pleye on his
giterne.°   gittern (plucked stringed instrument)
In al the toun° nas° brewhous ne taverne   town / was not
That he ne visited° with his solas°   did not visit / comfort
Ther any gaylard tappestere° was.   merry bar-maid
But sooth to seyn, he was somdeel
squaymous°   somewhat squeamish

[1] *quod ich* Both Ellesmere and Hengwrt read "ich" here, yet modern editors emend to "she," under the assumption that Chaucer is here slipping in and out of direct discourse. The manuscript readings can be defended on the basis of her uttering these words: "Let me be, I said, let me be, Nicholas…!"

[2] *Out, harrow, and allas* Common cries of alarm to summon assistance.

[3] *lutherly biset his whyle* Wasted his time.

[4] *haliday* I.e., holy day; a saint's day or the day of a major religious celebration.

[5] *a parissh clerk* Absolon is an assistant to the parish priest. He is a member of the clergy and probably in minor orders and might, in due course, be ordained as a priest himself.

[6] *Absolon* The Biblical Absalom, son of King David, was famous for his beauty. Cf. 2 Samuel 14.25–26.

[7] *Poules wyndow* Fancy shoes were sometimes cut to produce a lattice pattern, which Chaucer compares to the stained glass rose window at St. Paul's Cathedral, London, which burned down in the disastrous fire in 1666.

[8] *clippe and shave* Medieval barbers not only worked on one's hair but also did minor surgery like letting blood. This procedure, which involved opening a vein and allowing blood to flow out, was considered important in keeping the body's four humors (one of which was blood) in balance, thus insuring good health.

230 Of fartyng, and of speche daungerous.°   *fastidious*
    This Absolon that jolif° was and gay   *jolly*
    Gooth° with a sencer° on the haliday,[1]   *goes / incense censer*
    Sensynge° the wyves° of the parisshe   *incensing / wives*
      faste.°   *diligently*
    And many a lovely look on hem° he caste,   *them*
235 And namely° on this carpenteris wyf.   *especially*
    To looke on hire hym thoughte a myrie lyf.
    She was so propre and sweete and likerous,
    I dar wel seyn if she hadde been a mous°   *mouse*
    And he a cat, he wolde hire° hente° anon.   *her / grab*
240 This parissh clerk, this joly Absolon,
    Hath in his herte swich a love longynge
    That of no wyf took he noon offrynge.°   *no offering*
    For curteisie, he seyde, he wolde noon.°   *wanted none*
      The moone, whan it was nyght, ful brighte shoon,
245 And Absolon his gyterne° hath ytake;°   *gittern / taken*
    For paramours° he thoghte for to wake.°   *love's sake / stay awake*
    And forth he gooth, jolif° and amorous,   *jolly*
    Til he cam to the carpenteres hous
    A litel after cokkes° hadde ycrowe°   *roosters / crowed*
250 And dressed° hym up by a   *approached*
      shot-wyndowe°   *hinged window*
    That was upon the carpenteris wal.°   *wall*
    He syngeth in his voys° gentil° and   *voice / refined*
      smal,°   *high-pitched*
    "Now deere lady, if thy wille be,
    I pray yow that ye wole thynke on me,"
255 Ful wel acordaunt° to his   *in accord*
      gyternynge.°   *playing of the gittern*
    This carpenter awook and herde synge
    And spak unto his wyf and seyde anon,
    "What, Alison, herestow nat° Absolon   *don't you hear*
    That chaunteth° thus under oure boures°   *who sings / bedroom's*
      wal?"
260 And she answerde hir housbonde therwithal,
    "Yis, God woot,° John! I heere it every deel."°   *God knows / every bit*
      This passeth forth. What wol ye bet than
      weel?°   *what more do you want?*
    Fro day to day this joly Absolon
    So woweth° hire that hym is wobigon.°   *woos / filled with woe*
265 He waketh al the nyght and al the day.

He kembeth° hise lokkes° brode and   *combs / hair*
      made hym gay.
He woweth hire by meenes° and brocage°   *go-betweens / agents*
And swoor he wolde been hir owene page.°   *young servant*
He syngeth brokkynge° as a nyghtyngale.   *twittering*
270 He sent hire pyment,° meeth,° and ale   *spiced wine / mead*
      spiced
And wafres° pipyng hoot° out of the   *wafer cakes / hot*
      gleede,°   *fire*
And for° she was of towne, he profreth meede.°   *because / money*
For som folk wol ben wonnen° for richesse,   *won*
And somme for strokes,° and somme for   *force*
      gentillesse.°   *nobility*
275 Somtyme to shewe his lightnesse° and maistrye°   *agility / ability*
He playeth Herodes[2] upon a scaffold° hye.°   *stage / high*
But what availleth hym as in this cas?
She loveth so this hende Nicholas
That Absolon may blowe the bukkes° horn.[3]   *buck's*
280 He ne hadde° for his labour but a scorn.   *did not have*
And thus she maketh Absolon hire ape,
And al his ernest° turneth til a jape.°   *seriousness / joke*
Ful sooth° is this proverbe, it is no lye,°   *true / lie*
Men seyn right thus: "Alwey the nye slye°   *near sly one*
285 Maketh the ferre° leeve° to be looth."°   *far / loved one / hated*
For though that Absolon be wood° or wrooth,°   *crazy / angry*
Bycause that he fer° was from hire sighte,   *far*
This nye Nicholas stood in his lighte.
      Now bere° thee wel, thou hende Nicholas,   *bear*
290 For Absolon may waille° and synge "Allas!"   *complain*
And so bifel it° on a Saterday   *it happened*
This carpenter was goon° til Osenay,°   *gone / to Oseney*
And hende Nicholas and Alisoun
Acorded° been to this conclusioun   *agreed*
295 That Nicholas shal shapen° hym a wyle°   *fabricate / scheme*
This sely,° jalous housbonde to bigyle,°   *simple / trick*
And if so be the game wente aright,
She sholde slepen° in his arm al nyght,   *sleep*
For this was his desir and hire° also.   *hers*
300 And right anon, withouten wordes mo,
This Nicholas no lenger wolde tarie,°   *delay*

---

[1] *Gooth … haliday* It was and is the custom in liturgical churches to burn incense in a censer, a metal container which hung from a chain and was swung about by a cleric called a thurifer.

[2] *Herodes* I.e., King Herod. Told of the birth of the Messiah, Herod ordered the slaughter of all male children born in Bethlehem, an event depicted in some religious plays.

[3] *blowe the bukkes horn* The expression "blow the buck's horn" more or less means "go whistle."

But dooth ful softe° unto his chambre carie° *quietly / carry*
Bothe mete° and drynke for a day or tweye° *food / two*
And to hire housbonde bad hire for to seye,° *asked her to say*
305 If that he axed° after Nicholas, *asked*
She sholde seye she nyste° where he was; *did not know*
Of al that day she saugh° hym nat° with eye. *saw / not*
She trowed° that he was in maladye,° *believed / sickness*
For° for° no cry hir mayde koude hym calle. *because / with*
310 He nolde° answere for thyng° that myghte *would not / anything*
      falle.° *happen*
    This passeth forth al thilke° Saterday, *that same*
That Nicholas stille° in his chambre lay *quietly*
And eet° and sleepe° or dide what hym *ate / slept*
      leste,° *what he wanted*
Til Sonday that the sonne gooth to reste.
315 This sely carpenter hath greet merveyle° *wondered greatly*
Of Nicholas or what thyng myghte hym eyle° *ail (trouble)*
And seyde, "I am adrad,° by Seint Thomas, *afraid*
It stondeth nat aright with Nicholas.
God shilde° that he deyde° sodeynly! *forbid / died*
320 This world is now ful tikel,° sikerly.° *uncertain / certainly*
I saugh today a cors° yborn° to chirche *body / carried*
That now on Monday last I saugh hym wirche!° *work*
    Go up," quod he unto his knave° *serving boy*
      anoon,° *immediately*
"Clepe° at his dore or knokke with a stoon. *call*
325 Looke how it is and tel me boldely."
    This knave gooth hym up ful sturdily
And at the chambre dore whil that he stood,
He cride and knokked as that he were wood,
"What how! What do ye, maister Nicholay?
330 How may ye slepen al the longe day?"
    But al for noght. He herde nat a word.
An hole he foond ful lowe upon a bord° *board*
Theras° the cat was wont° in for to *where / accustomed*
      crepe,° *creep*
And at that hole he looked in ful depe
335 Til at the laste he hadde of hym a sighte.
This Nicholas sat capyng evere uprighte° *gaping upwards*
As he had kiked° on the newe moone. *looked*
Adoun° he gooth and tolde his maister soone *down*
In what array° he saugh that ilke° man. *condition / same*
340   This carpenter to blessen[1] hym bigan° *began*

And seyde, "Help us, Seinte Frydeswyde![2]
A man woot litel what hym shal bityde!° *shall happen to him*
This man is falle° with his astromye° *fallen / astronomy*
In som woodnesse° or in som agonye.° *madness / fit*
345 I thoghte ay° wel how that it sholde be. *I always thought*
Men sholde nat knowe of Goddes pryvetee.° *secrets*
Yblessed° be alwey a lewed° man *blessed / uneducated*
That noght but oonly° his Bileve[3] kan.°*nothing other than / knows*
So ferde° another clerk with astromye:° *it happened / astronomy*
350 He walked in the feeldes° for to prye° *fields / pry (study foolishly)*
Upon the sterres,° what ther sholde bifalle, *stars*
Til he was in a marleput[4] yfalle.° *fallen*
He saugh nat that! But yet by Seint Thomas,
Me reweth° soore of hende Nicholas. *I have pity*
355 He shal be rated of° his studiyng *scolded for*
If that I may, by Jhesus hevene° kyng! *Heaven's*
Get me a staf° that I may underspore,° *staff / pry*
Whil that thou, Robyn, hevest of the dore.° *heave off the door*
He shal out of his studiyng, as I gesse."° *guess*
360 And to the chambre dore° he gan hym dresse.°*door / approached*
His knave° was a strong carl° for the *servant / fellow*
      nones,° *occasion*
And by the haspe° he haaf it of° *hinge / heaved it off*
      atones;° *at once*
Into° the floor the dore° fil° anon. *onto / door / fell*
This Nicholas sat ay° as stille as stoon° *ever / stone*
365 And evere caped° upward into the eir.° *gaped / air*
This carpenter wende° he were in despeir, *believed*
And hente° hym by the sholdres° myghtily *grabbed / shoulders*
And shook hym harde and cride spitously,° *loudly*
"What Nicholay! What, how! What! Looke adoun!
370 Awake and thenk° on Cristes Passioun! *think*
I crouche° thee from elves and fro *sign with the cross*
      wightes."° *evil creatures*
Therwith the nyght spel[5] seyde he anonrightes° *right away*

---

[1] *blessen* I.e., to bless oneself, to make the sign of the cross.

[2] *Seinte Frydeswyde* The Anglo-Saxon St. Frideswide, a young noblewoman who was persecuted for her desire to be a nun, is the patron saint of the town of Oxford. She was abbess of a monastery that was on the site of the present Christ Church, Oxford.

[3] *Bileve* Carpenter John's "Believe" is his Creed—the Apostle's Creed, which, along with the Lord's Prayer, was to be memorized by every Christian.

[4] *marleput* I.e., marl-pit, a ditch on a farm for keeping marl, a type of soil rich in clay and used for fertilizing fields.

[5] *nyght spel* Spell or charm said at night to ward off evil spirits.

On foure halves° of the hous aboute — *four corners*
And on the thresshfold° of the dore withoute. — *threshold*
375 "Jhesu Crist and Seint Benedight[1]
Blesse this hous from every wikked wight
For nyghtes nerye° the white Pater Noster:° — *save / Lord's Prayer*
Where wentestow, Seint Petres soster?"[2]
    And atte laste this hende Nicholas
380 Gan for to sike° soore and seyde, "Allas! — *sigh*
Shal al this world be lost eftsoones° now?" — *immediately*
    This carpenter answerde, "What seystow?° — *do you say*
What! Thynk on God as we doon, men that swynke."[3]
    This Nicholas answerde, "Fecche° me drynke, — *get*
385 And after wol I speke in pryvetee
Of certeyn thyng that toucheth me and thee.
I wol telle it noon oother° man certeyn." — *(to) no other*
    This carpenter goth doun and comth ageyn° — *comes again*
And broghte of myghty ale a large quart.
390 And whan that ech of hem had dronke his part,
This Nicholas his dore faste shette° — *shut*
And doun the carpenter by hym he sette.
    He seyde, "John, myn hoost, lief° and deere, — *beloved*
Thou shalt upon thy trouthe swere me here
395 That to no wight thou shalt this conseil° wreye,° — *counsel / betray*
For it is Cristes conseil that I seye!
And if thou telle man, thou art forlore,° — *lost*
For this vengeaunce thou shalt han therfore:° — *for it*
That if thou wreye° me, thou shalt be wood." — *betray*
400 "Nay, Crist forbede it for his hooly blood!"
Quod tho this sely man, "I nam no labbe.° — *am no blabber*
Ne, though I seye, I am nat lief to gabbe.° — *accustomed to gab*
Sey what thou wolt, I shal it nevere telle
To child ne wyf, by hym that harwed helle!"[4]

405 "Now John," quod Nicholas, "I wol nat lye.
I have yfounde° in myn astrologye — *found*
As I have looked in the moone bright
That now a Monday next° at quarter nyght[5] — *next Monday*
Shal falle a reyn,° and that so wilde and wood — *rain*
410 That half so greet° was nevere Noees° Flood. — *great / Noah's*
This world," he seyde, "in lasse° than an hour — *less*
Shal al be dreynt,° so hidous is the shour.° — *drowned / downpour*
Thus shal mankynde drenche° and lese hir lyf." — *drown*
    This carpenter answerde, "Allas, my wyf!
415 And shal she drenche? Allas, myn Alisoun!"
For sorwe° of this he fil° almoost adoun — *sorrow / fell*
And seyde, "Is ther no remedie in this cas?"
    "Why, yis, for Gode," quod hende Nicholas.
"If thou wolt werken° after loore° and — *act / teaching*
    reed.° — *advice*
420 Thou mayst nat werken after thyn owene
    heed,° — *head (intelligence)*
For thus seith Salomon,[6] that was ful trewe:
'Werk° al by conseil and thou shalt nat rewe!'° — *do / regret*
And if thou werken wolt by good conseil,
I undertake withouten mast and seyl° — *sail*
425 Yet shal I saven hire° and thee and me. — *save her*
Hastou nat herd how saved was Noe° — *Noah*
Whan that oure Lord hadde warned hym biforn° — *before*
That al the world with water sholde be lorn?"° — *lost*
    "Yis," quod this carpenter, "ful yoore ago."° — *very long ago*
430 "Hastou nat herd," quod Nicholas, "also,
The sorwe of Noe with his felaweshipe
Er that he myghte brynge his wyf to shipe?[7]
Hym hadde be levere,° I dar° wel — *he had rather / dare*
    undertake,° — *affirm*
At thilke tyme° than alle hise wetheres — *at that time*
    blake° — *black sheep*
435 That she hadde had a shipe hirself° allone. — *to herself*

[1] *Seint Benedight*   St. Benedict of Nursia was an early sixth-century abbot who wrote the famous Rule for monasteries.

[2] *For nyghtes ... soster*   These lines have never been satisfactorily explained and probably represent John's mangling of popular charms or invocations; *Where wentestow* Where did you go; *soster* Sister.

[3] *men that swynke*   Men who labor. John is making the old distinction between the three estates here. The first estate comprises those who pray (the profession for which Nicholas is studying), the second, those who fight (the nobility), and the third, those who work and thus provide the food for all three estates.

[4] *harwed helle*   The Harrowing of Hell (another subject of medieval religious drama) was the victorious entry Christ made into Hell between his death and resurrection to save the righteous souls held in limbo.

[5] *quarter nyght*   One-fourth of the way through the night.

[6] *Salomon*   Solomon, the ancient King of Israel, was known for his wisdom and was thought to be the author of several books of the Hebrew Bible. The reference here is to Ecclesiasticus 32.24. John makes a mistake here: Ecclesiasticus, part of the Greek Old Testament considered apocryphal by Protestants or deuterocanonical by Catholics, was written by Jesus ben Sirach, not Solomon, as Saint Augustine (among others) noted.

[7] *to shipe*   On board. The difficulty Noah has in getting his wife aboard the Ark is depicted in medieval drama.

And therfore woostou° what is best to doone? — *do you know*
This asketh° haste, and of an hastif — *requires*
   thyng° — *urgent business*
Men may nat preche or maken tariyng.° — *delay*
  "Anon, go gete us faste into this in° — *house*
440 A knedyng trogh° or ellis a kymelyn° — *kneading pot / tub*
For ech° of us—but looke that they be large— — *each*
In whiche we mowe swymme° as in a barge, — *may float*
And han therinne vitaille suffissant° — *enough food*
But for a day. Fy on° the remenant! — *disregard*
445 The water shal aslake° and goon away — *ebb*
Aboute pryme° upon the nexte day. — *prime (an early hour of prayer)*
But Robyn may nat wite° of this, thy knave,° — *know / servant*
Ne eek thy mayde Gille I may nat save.
Axe nat° why, for though thou aske me, — *ask not*
450 I wol nat tellen Goddes pryvetee.° — *secrets*
Suffiseth thee, but if thy wittes madde,
To han as greet a grace as Noe hadde.[1]
Thy wyf shal I wel saven, out of doute.° — *doubtless*
Go now thy wey, and speed thee heer aboute.
455   "But whan thou hast for hire and thee and me
Ygeten° us thise knedyng tubbes thre, — *gotten*
Thanne shaltow hange hem° in the roof ful hye, — *hang them*
That° no man of oure purveiaunce° spye. — *so that / preparations*
And whan thou thus hast doon as I have seyd
460 And hast oure vitaille faire in hem yleyd,° — *laid*
And eek an ax to smyte the corde° atwo° — *rope / in two*
Whan that the water comth, that we may go,
And breke an hole anheigh° up on the gable — *on high*
Unto the gardynward° over the stable, — *towards the garden*
465 That we may frely passen forth oure way
Whan that the grete shour is goon away.
Thanne shal I swymme as myrie,° I undertake,° — *merrily / expect*
As dooth the white doke° after hire drake.° — *duck / male duck*
Thanne wol I clepe,° 'How, Alison! How, John! — *call*
470 Be myrie, for the flood wol passe anon!'
And thou wolt seyn, 'Hayl,° maister Nicholay, — *hail*
Good morwe! I se thee wel, for it is day.'
And thanne shul° we be lordes al oure lyf — *shall*
Of al the world, as Noe and his wyf.
475   "But of o° thyng I warne thee ful right:° — *one / directly*
Be wel avysed on that ilke nyght° — *that same night*

That we ben entred° into shippes bord — *entered*
That noon of us ne speke nat a word,
Ne clepe,° ne crie, but been in his preyere, — *call*
480 For it is Goddes owene heeste° deere. — *commandment*
  "Thy wyf and thou moote hange fer° atwynne,° — *far / apart*
For that bitwixe yow shal be no synne,° — *sin*
Namoore in lookyng than ther shal in deede.
This ordinance° is seyd. Go, God thee speede! — *commandment*
485 Tomorwe at nyght, whan folk ben alle aslepe,
Into oure knedyng tubbes wol we crepe,
And sitten there abidyng Goddes grace.
Go now thy wey. I have no lenger space° — *no more time*
To make of this no lenger sermonyng.° — *speech*
490 Men seyn thus: 'Sende the wise and sey nothing.'
Thou art so wys, it nedeth thee nat to preche.° — *preach*
Go save oure lyf, and that I the biseche."° — *implore*
  This sely carpenter goth forth his wey.
Ful ofte he seith "Allas!" and "Weylawey!"
495 And to his wyf he tolde his pryvetee.° — *secret*
And she was war° and knew it bet° than he — *aware / better*
What al this queynte cast° was for to seye. — *unusual scheme*
But nathelees she ferde as° she wolde deye, — *acted as if*
And seyde, "Allas! Go forth thy wey anon.
500 Help us to scape° or we been lost echon!° — *escape / everyone*
I am thy trewe, verray° wedded wyf. — *faithful*
Go, deere spouse, and help to save oure lyf!"
  Lo, which a greet° thyng is affeccioun! — *what a great*
Men may dyen° of ymaginacioun,° — *die / imagination*
505 So depe° may impressioun be take.° — *deep / taken*
This sely carpenter bigynneth quake.° — *to shake*
Hym thynketh verraily° that he may see — *it truly appears to him*
Noees° Flood come walwynge° as the see — *Noah's / surging*
To drenchen° Alisoun, his hony deere. — *drown*
510 He wepeth, weyleth, maketh sory cheere.° — *a sorry face*
He siketh with ful many a sory swogh.° — *groan*
He gooth and geteth hym a knedyng trogh,
And after that a tubbe and a kymelyn,
And pryvely he sente hem to his in° — *house*
515 And heng hem in the roof in pryvetee.
His owene hand made laddres thre
To clymben by the ronges and the stalkes° — *shafts*
Into the tubbes hangynge in the balkes,° — *beams*
And hem vitailleth,° bothe trogh and tubbe, — *provides food for*
520 With breed and chese and good ale in a jubbe,° — *jug*
Suffisynge right ynogh as for a day.
But er that he hadde maad al this array° — *these preparations*

---

1 *Suffiseth ... hadde* It is enough for you (i.e., you should be grateful), unless you are insane, to have as much favor as Noah had (by being warned of the Flood).

He sente his knave and eek his wenche also

Upon his nede° to London for to go.   *need*

525 And on the Monday whan it drow to nyght,°   *approached night*

He shette° his dore withoute candel lyght   *shut*

And dresseth° alle thyng as it shal be.   *arranged*

And shortly, up they clomben alle thre.

They sitten stille, wel a furlong way.[1]

530   Now, "Pater Noster, clom!"° seyde Nicholay.   *be quiet*

And "Clom," quod John. And "Clom," seyde Alisoun.

This carpenter seyde his devocioun,°   *prayers*

And stille he sit and biddeth his preyere,°   *offers his prayers*

Awaitynge on the reyn, if he it heere.

535   The dede° sleepe, for wery° bisynesse,   *dead / weary*

Fil° on this carpenter, right as I gesse,°   *fell / guess*

About corfew° tyme[2] or litel moore.   *curfew*

For travaille° of his goost° he groneth soore   *labor / spirit*

And eft° he routeth,° for his heed°   *also / snores / head*

myslay.°   *lay wrong*

540 Doun of the laddre stalketh Nicholay,

And Alisoun ful softe adoun she spedde.°   *hastens*

Withouten wordes mo they goon to bedde

Theras° the carpenter is wont to lye.   *where*

Ther was the revel° and the melodye,   *fun*

545 And thus Alison and Nicholas

In bisynesse of myrthe and of solas

Til that the belle of laudes[3] gan to rynge

And freres° in the chauncel[4] gonne synge.°   *friars / began to sing*

This parissh clerk, this amorous Absolon

550 That is for love alwey so wobigon,°   *sorrowful*

Upon the Monday was at Oseneye

With a compaignye hym to disporte and

pleye,°   *play and have fun*

And axed upon cas° a cloistrer°   *asked by chance / monk*

Ful prively° after John the carpenter.   *very secretly*

555 And he drough hym apart° out of the chirche   *drew him aside*

And seyde, "I noot.° I saugh hym heere nat wirche   *don't know*

Syn° Saterday.[5] I trowe° that he be went°   *since / believe / is gone*

For tymber ther° oure abbot hath hym sent,   *timber where*

For he is wont° for tymber for to go   *accustomed*

560 And dwellen° at the grange° a day or two.[6]   *stay / farm-house*

Or elles he is at his hous, certeyn.

Where that he be, I kan nat soothly seyn."°   *truly say*

This Absolon ful joly was and light

And thoghte, "Now is tyme [to] wake° al nyght,   *to stay awake*

565 For sikirly,° I saugh hym nat stirynge°   *certainly / not stirring*

Aboute his dore syn day bigan to sprynge.°   *dawn*

"So moot I thryve,° I shall at cokkes crowe   *thrive*

Ful pryvely knokke at his wyndowe

That stant ful lowe upon his boures wal.°   *bedroom's wall*

570 To Alison now wol I tellen al

My love-longynge, for yet I shal nat mysse

That at the leeste wey° I shal hire kisse;   *very least*

Som maner° confort shal I have, parfay.°   *kind of / in faith*

My mouth hath icched° al this longe day: *itched*

575 That is a signe of kissyng atte leeste!

Al nyght me mette° eek I was at a feeste.°   *I dreamed / feast*

Therfore I wol goon slepe an houre or tweye

And al the nyght thanne° wol I wake and pleye."   *then*

Whan that the firste cok° hath crowe anon,   *rooster*

580 Up rist° this joly lovere Absolon   *rose*

And hym arraieth° gay at poynt devys.[7]   *dresses*

But first he cheweth greyn° of lycorys°   *a grain / licorice*

To smellen sweete er he hadde kembd his heer.

Under his tonge° a trewe-love[8] he beer,°   *tongue / carried*

585 For therby wende° he to ben gracious.°   *expected / attractive*

He rometh° to the carpenteres hous,   *roams*

And stille he stant° under the   *stands*

shot-wyndowe°—   *hinged window*

Unto his brist° it raughte,° it was so lowe—   *breast / reached*

And softe he knokketh with a semy soun.°   *quiet sound*

590 "What do ye, honycomb, sweete Alisoun,

My faire bryd,° my sweete cynamone?°   *bird / cinnamon*

Awaketh, lemman myn,° and speketh to me.   *my sweetheart*

Wel litel° thynken ye upon my wo,   *very little*

---

[1] *They … way* For the time it takes to walk a furlong (about an eighth of a mile).

[2] *corfew tyme* Curfew, from the French for "cover your fire," announced the time when all fires had to be covered and houses were shut up for the night.

[3] *laudes* I.e., Lauds, the monastic hour of prayer that occurs very early in the morning, before dawn.

[4] *chauncel* Chancel, the area of a church or chapel near the altar.

[5] *I … Saterday* I do not know. I have not seen him work here since Saterday.

[6] *And … two* Abbeys usually had outlying estates, such as this one where John the carpenter is working.

[7] *at poynt devys* I.e., at point devise: perfectly.

[8] *a trewe-love* Four-leaved clover.

That for youre love I swete° ther° I go. *sweat / where*

595 No wonder is thogh° that I swelte° *is it though / swelter*
 and swete;

I moorne° as dooth° a lamb after the tete.° *yearn / does / teat*

Ywis,° lemman,° I have swich love longynge *indeed / sweetheart*

That lik a turtel° trewe is my moornynge.° *turtle-dove / mourning*

I may nat ete namoore° than a mayde." *anymore*

600 "Go fro the wyndow, Jakke fool,"° she sayde. *Jack-fool*

"As help me God, it wol nat be 'com pa me.'° *come kiss me*

I love another, and elles° I were to blame, *else*

Wel bet° than thee, by Jhesu, Absolon. *better*

Go forth thy wey, or I wol caste a stoon,° *throw a stone*

605 And lat me slepe, a twenty devel wey!"[1]

 "Allas," quod Absolon, "and weylawey,

That trewe love was evere so yvel biset!° *ill bestowed*

Thanne kys me, syn° it may be no bet,° *since / better*

For Jhesus love and for the love of me."

610 "Wiltow thanne go thy wey?" quod she.

 "Ye, certes, lemman," quod this Absolon.

 "Thanne make thee redy," quod she. "I come anon."

And unto Nicholas she seyde stille,° *quietly*

"Now hust,° and thou shalt laughen al thy fille." *shush*

615 This Absolon doun sette hym on his knees

And seyde, "I am lord at alle degrees,° *in every way*

For after this I hope ther cometh moore.

Lemman, thy grace, and sweete bryd,° thyn oore!"° *bird / favor*

 The wyndow she undoth° and that in haste. *unlatched*

620 "Have do," quod she. "Com of and speed the faste,[2]

Lest that oure neighebores thee espie."° *see you*

 This Absolon gan wype his mouth ful drie.

Dirk° was the nyght as pich° or as the cole, *dark / pitch / coal*

And at the wyndow out she pitte° hir hole. *put*

625 And Absolon hym fil° no bet° ne wers,° *fell / better / worse*

But with his mouth he kiste° hir naked ers° *kissed / ass*

Ful savourly° er he was war° of this. *with relish / aware*

Abak° he stirte° and thoughte it was *backwards / jumped*
 amys,° *wrong*

For wel he wiste a womman hath no berd.° *beard*

630 He felte a thyng al rough and longe yherd° *long-haired*

And seyde, "Fy! Allas! What have I do?"° *done*

 "Tehee!" quod she, and clapte° the wyndow to, *slammed*

And Absolon gooth forth a sory° pas.° *sorry / step*

"A berd,° a berd!" quod hende Nicholas. *beard, trick*

635 "By Goddes corpus,° this goth° faire and weel!" *body / goes*

 This sely° Absolon herde every deel° *foolish / part*

And on his lippe° he gan for anger byte,° *lip / began to bite*

And to hymself he seyde, "I shall thee quyte!"° *repay*

 Who rubbeth now, who froteth° now his lippes *wipes*

640 With dust, with sond, with straw, with clooth, with
 chippes° *chips (of wood)*

But Absolon, that seith ful ofte, "Allas!

My soule bitake° I unto Sathanas° *commit / Satan*

But me were levere° than al this toun," quod he, *rather*

"Of this despit° awroken° for to be. *insult / avenged*

645 Allas," quod he, "Allas, I ne hadde
 ybleynt!"° *had not restrained (myself)*

His hoote love was coold and al yqueynt.° *quenched*

For fro that tyme that he hadde kist hir ers,

Of paramours° he sette nat a kers,[3] *love*

For he was heeled of his maladie.

650 Ful ofte paramours° he gan deffie,° *passionate love / defied*

And weepe as dooth a child that is ybete.° *beaten*

A softe paas° he wente over the strete° *quiet step / street*

Until° a smyth° men cleped daun° *unto / blacksmith / master*
 Gerveys,

That in his forge smythed plough° harneys. *plow*

655 He sharpeth shaar° and kultour° bisily. *plowshare / plow-blade*

This Absolon knokketh al esily° *quietly*

And seyde, "Undo,° Gerveys, and that anon." *open up*

 "What! Who artow?"° "I am heere Absolon." *are you*

"What! Absolon, for Cristes sweete tree,° *cross*

660 Why rise ye so rathe?° Ey,° benedicitee! *early / ah*

What eyleth° yow? Som gay gerl,° God it *ails / girl*
 woot,° *knows*

Hath broght yow thus upon the viritoot.[4]

By Seinte Note,[5] ye woot wel what I mene."

 This Absolon ne roghte nat a bene° *did not care a bean*

665 Of al his pley. No word agayn he yaf.° *gave*

He hadde moore tow° on his distaf[6] *flax*

Than Gerveys knew, and seyde, "Freend so deere,° *kind*

---

[1] *a twenty devel wey* For the sake of twenty devils.

[2] *Com … faste* "Hurry up," she said, "make haste and be quick."

[3] *sette nat a kers* Cared nothing. (A *kers* is a watercress.)

[4] *upon the viritoot* Up and about.

[5] *Seinte Note* I.e., St. Neot, a ninth-century monk from Glaston-
bury who became a hermit.

[6] *distaf* I.e., distaff, a tool used in making thread to be spun into
cloth.

That hoote° kultour° in the chymenee heere,   *hot / plow-blade*
As lene° it me. I have therwith to doone,°   *lend / do*
670 And I wol brynge it thee agayn ful soone."
     Gerveys answerde, "Certes, were it gold
Or in a poke° nobles° alle untold,°   *bag / gold coins / unnumbered*
Thou sholdest have,° as I am trewe smyth.   *have (it)*
Ey, Cristes foo,° what wol ye do therwith?"   *foe*
675 "Therof," quod Absolon, "be as be may.
I shal wel telle it thee tomorwe day,"
And caughte the kultour by the colde stele.°   *handle*
Ful softe out at the dore he gan to stele°   *began to steal*
And wente unto the carpenteris wal.
680 He cogheth° first and knokketh therwithal   *coughs*
Upon the wyndowe right° as he dide er.   *just*
     This Alison answerde, "Who is ther
That knokketh so? I warante it a theef."
     "Why, nay," quod he, "God woot, my sweete leef,°   *loved one*
685 I am thyn Absolon, my deerelyng.°   *darling*
Of gold," quod he, "I have thee broght a ryng.
My mooder yaf° it me, so God me save.   *gave*
Ful fyn° it is and therto wel ygrave.°   *fine / engraved*
This wol I yeve° thee if thou me kisse."   *give*
690 This Nicholas was risen for to pisse
And thoughte he wolde amenden° al the jape: *make better*
He sholde kisse his ers er that he scape.°   *escape*
And up the wyndowe dide he hastily,
And out his ers he putteth pryvely
695 Over the buttok to the haunche bon.°   *thigh*
And therwith spak this clerk, this Absolon:
"Spek, sweete bryd,° I noot nat°   *bird / do not know*
     where thou art."
     This Nicholas anon leet fle° a fart   *let fly*
As greet as it had been a thonder dent,°   *thunder-clap*
700 That with the strook he was almoost yblent.°   *blinded*
And he was redy with his iren hoot,°   *hot iron*
And Nicholas amydde the ers° he   *in the middle of the ass*
     smoot.°   *struck*
     Of gooth° the skyn° an   *off goes / skin*
     hande brede° about,   *a hand-breadth*
The hoote kultour brende° so his toute,°   *burned / rear*
705 And for the smert° he wende° for to dye.°   *pain / expected / die*
As he were wood for wo, he gan to crye,
"Help, water, water, help, for Goddes herte!"
     This carpenter out of his slomber sterte°   *jumped*
And herde oon crien,° "Water!" as he were wood,   *heard one cry*
710 And thoughte, "Allas, now comth Nowelis Flood!"

He sit hym up withouten wordes mo,
And with his ax he smoot the corde atwo,
And doun gooth al! He foond neither to selle,
Ne breed ne ale, til he cam to the celle[1]
715 Upon the floor, and there aswowne° he lay.   *in a faint*
     Up stirte hire Alison and Nicholay,
And criden, "Out!" and "Harrow!" in the strete.
The neighebores, bothe smale and grete,°   *big*
In ronnen° for to gauren on° this man   *ran in / gape at*
720 That yet aswowne he lay, bothe pale and wan,
For with the fal° he brosten hadde° his arm.   *fall / had broken*
But stonde he moste unto his owene harm.[2]
For whan he spak, he was anon bore doun°   *shouted down*
With° hende Nicholas and Alisoun.   *by*
725 They tolden every man that he was wood.
He was agast° so of Nowelis Flood   *afraid*
Thurgh fantasie° that of his vanytee°   *fantasy / folly*
He hadde yboght° hym knedyng tubbes thre   *bought*
And hadde hem hanged in the rove° above,   *roof*
730 And that he preyde° hem for Goddes love   *asked*
To sitten in the roof par compaignye.°   *for company*
     The folk gan laughen at his fantasye.
Into the roof they kiken° and they cape°   *stare / gape*
And turned al his harm unto a jape.°   *joke*
735 For what° so that this carpenter answerde,   *whatever*
It was for noght.° No man his reson° herde.   *nothing / explanation*
With othes° grete he was so sworn adoun°   *oaths / shouted down*
That he was holde° wood in al the toun,   *considered*
For every clerk° anonright heeld° with oother;   *scholar / agreed*
740 They seyde, "The man was wood, my leeve° brother."   *dear*
And every wight gan laughen of this stryf.°   *strife*
Thus swyved° was this carpenteris wyf   *made love to*
For al his kepyng° and his jalousye,   *guarding*
And Absolon hath kist hir nether° eye,   *lower*
745 And Nicholas is scalded in the towte.°   *rear*
This tale is doon, and God save al the rowte!°   *company*

HEERE ENDETH THE MILLERE HIS TALE

---

[1] *Ne ... celle* He did not find bread or ale to sell until he came to the bottom; i.e., he did not stop on his way down.

[2] *moste ... harm* This idiomatic expression has been interpreted differently. John the Carpenter must endure (or put up with, or take responsibility for) his own injury, or he must stand up for himself even though it turned out badly.

[handwritten: miller's mostly enjoyable]

3855 WHAN folk had laughen° at this nyce cas° — *laughed, silly matter*
Of Absolon and hende° Nicholas, — *handy*
Diverse° folk diversly° they seyde,° — *different, differently, said*
But for the moore part° they loughe and — *for the most part*
   pleyde.° — *played*
Ne° at this tale I saugh° no man hym greve,° — *nor, saw, become angry*

3860 But° it were oonly° Osewold the Reve. — *except, only*
Bycause he was of carpenteris craft,
A litel° ire° is in his herte° ylaft.° — *little, anger, heart, left*
He gan to grucche° and blamed it a lite.° — *complain, little*
"So theek,"° quod he, "ful wel koude° I — *As I thrive, very well could*
   yow quite° — *requite*

3865 With bleryng° of a proud milleres eye, — *blearing*
If that me liste speke of ribaudye.° — *If I wanted to speak of bawdiness*
But ik° am oold. Me list° no pley° for age. — *I, I desire, play*
Gras-tyme° is doon.° My fodder is now forage.[1] — *grass-time, done*
This white tope writeth° myne° olde yeris.° — *declare, my, years*

3870 Myn herte° is mowled° also as myne — *my heart, grown moldy*
   heris.° — *my hairs*
But if I fare as doth an open-ers.
That ilke° fruyt° is ever leng the wers,° — *same, fruit, gets ever worse*
Til it be roten° in mullok° or in stree.°[2] — *rotten, garbage, straw*
We olde men, I drede,° so fare we — *fear*

3875 Til we be roten,° kan° we nat° be rype.° — *rotten, can, not, ripe*
We hoppen° ay° whil that the world wol° — *dance, always, will*
   pype.° — *pipe (play music)*
For in oure wyl° ther stiketh° evere° a nayl,°[3] — *will, sticks, MS eve, nail*
To have an hoor heed° and a grene tayl° — *gray head, green tail*
As hath a leek.[4] For thogh oure myght be goon,° — *gone*

3880 Oure wyl desireth folie° evere° in oon. — *folly, always*
For whan we may nat doon,° than wol° we speke,° — *not do, will, speak*

[handwritten: carpenter offended]
[handwritten: Reeve old]
[handwritten: story of miller's manipulation]
[handwritten: sexual desires]

Yet in oure asshen° olde is fyr° yreke.° — *ashes, fire, raked over*
FOURE gleedes° han° we whiche I shal devyse:° — *embers, have, describe*
Avauntyng,° liyng,° anger, coveitise.° — *boasting, lying, coveting*

3885 Thise foure sparkles° longen° unto eelde.° — *sparks, belong, age*
Oure olde lemes° mowe° wel° been — *limbs, must, well*
   unweelde,° — *weak*
But wyl° ne shal nat faillen,° that is sooth.° — *will, shall not fail, truth*
And yet ik° have alwey a coltes° tooth[5] — *I, colt's*
As many a yeer° as it is passed henne° — *year, away*

3890 Syn° that my tappe° of lif° bigan to renne.° — *since, tap, life, run*
For sikerly,° whan I was bore,° anon° — *surely, born, immediately*
Deeth drough the tappe of lyf and leet it gon[6]
And ever sithe° hath so the tappe° yronne° — *since, tap, run*
Til that almoost al empty is the tonne.° — *tun (barrel)*

3895 The streem° of lyf° now droppeth° on the — *stream, life, drops*
   chymbe.° — *rim*
The sely° tonge may wel rynge° and chymbe°[7] — *silly, ring, chime*
Of wrecchednesse° that passed is ful — *wretchedness*
   yoore.° — *very long ago*
With olde folke, save dotage, is namoore."° — *no more*
WHAN that oure hoost hadde herd° this — *heard*
   sermonyng,° — *this sermonizing*

3900 He gan° to speke° as lordly as a kyng. — *began, speak*
He seide,° "What amounteth° al this wit? — *said, amounts*
What, shul we speke al day of hooly writ?° — *holy scriptures*
The devel° made a reve° for to preche° — *devil, reeve, preach*
And of a soutere,° shipman or a leche!°[8] — *cobbler, physician*

3905 Sey° forth thy tale, and tarie nat° the tyme.° — *say, tarry not, time*
Lo, Depeford, and it is half wey pryme![9]
Lo, Grenewych,[10] ther° many a shrewe° is inne!° — *where, scoundrel in*
It were al tyme° thy tale to bigynne!"° — *about time, begin*
"Now, sires," quod this Osewold the Reve,

3910 "I pray yow all that ye nat yow greve° — *you do not take offence*

---

1 My time in the pasture is over and now I am like a horse in the stable in winter who eats hay.

2 The medlar (a kind of plum) was known as an "open-ass" because it has a strong purgative effect. It only becomes edible when it is rotten.

3 I.e., we are always goaded by desire. A goad is a stick, often with a sharp metal point, used to drive animals.

4 "Green tail" is an expression, possibly proverbial, suggesting sexual activity. The image is also found in Boccaccio's *Decameron* in the introduction to the fourth day.

5 A proverbial expression for having the sexual desires of a young creature. Cf. Wife of Bath's prologue, line 602.

6 "Death drew the tap of life and let it run." The image is of a large barrel whose spigot has been turned open by Death, so that the beer or wine runs out.

7 The old man's babbling tongue is like the splashing of the beer or wine on the rim of the barrel.

8 I.e., the devil, who made a reve preach, also made a shipman or doctor (leach) from a cobbler. Hengwrt reads "Or of a soutere, a shipman, or a lech," which makes more sense and better meter.

9 Deptford is a town about three miles from Southwark on the road to Canterbury. Prime is an hour for prayer in the early morning.

10 Greenwich is about half a mile further on the road to Canterbury. Chaucer probably lived in Greenwich between about 1385 and 1398.

109

tells revenge story to Miller back (handwritten, left margin)

Proud Miller = Symkyn (handwritten, left margin)
-proud
-talented

wife: (handwritten, top right margin)
-well-dowry
-nunnery
-proud

Thogh° I answere and somdeel° sette his howve.[1] *though, somewhat*
For leveful is with force force of showve.[2]
THIS dronke° Millere hath ytoold° us heer° *drunken, told, here*
How that bigyled° was a carpenteer— *fooled*
3915 Paraventure° in scorn, for I am oon. *Perhaps*
And by youre leve,° I shal hym° quite° *leave, him, requite*
anoon.° *immediately*
Right in his cherles termes° wol I speke. *churl's terms*
I pray to God his nekke mote breke!° *neck might break*
He kan wel in myn eye seen a stalke,° *sliver*
3920 But in his owene he kan nat seen a balke."°[3] *beam*

THE REEVE'S TALE

HEERE BIGYNNETH THE REVES TALE

AT Trumpyngtoun, nat fer fro° Cantebrigge,[4] *far from*
Ther gooth° a brook and over that a brigge,° *runs, bridge*
Upon the which brook ther stant° a melle.° *stands, mill*
And this is verray° sooth° that I yow telle. *true, truth*
3925 A millere was ther dwellynge many a day.
As any pecok° he was proud and gay. *peacock*
Pipen° he koude and fisshe and nettes *play the bagpipe*
beete° *mend (fishing) nets*
And turne coppes[5] and wel wrastle° and *wrestle*
sheete.° *shoot (arrows)*
And by his belt° he baar° a long *on his belt, carried*
panade,° *short sword*
3930 And of a swerd° ful° trenchant° was the blade. *sword, very, sharp*
A joly poppere° baar° he in his pouche. *pretty dagger, carried*
Ther was no man for peril° dorste hym° touche. *dared, him*
A Sheffeld thwitel° baar° he in his hose.°[6] *knife, carried, stockings*
Round was his face and camuse° was his nose. *snub*
3935 As piled° as an ape was his skulle.° *bald, skull*

He was a market-betere° atte fulle.° *street fighter, utterly*
Ther dorste° no wight° hand upon hym legge,° *dared, person, lay*
That he ne swoor he sholde anon abegge.[7]
A theef he was of corn° and eek° of mele,° *grain, also, meal*
3940 And that a sly and usaunt° for to stele. *accustomed*
His name was hoote° deynous° Symkyn. *was called, arrogant*
A wyf he hadde ycomen° of noble kyn. *come, kindred*
The person° of the toun hir fader° was. *parson, her father*
With hire he yaf ful many a panne of bras,[8]
3945 For that Symkyn sholde° in his blood allye.° *should, ally*
She was yfostred° in a nonnerye,°[9] *brought up, convent of nuns*
For Symkyn wolde° no wyf, as he sayde, *wanted*
But if° she were wel ynorissed° and a *unless, well brought up*
mayde,° *virgin*
To saven° his estaat° of yomanrye.° *preserve, estate, yeomanry*
3950 And she was proud and peert° as is a pye.° *impudent, magpie*
A ful fair sighte was it upon hem° two *them*
On haly dayes° biforn hire wolde° he go *holy days, before her would*
With his typet° bounde aboute his heed,° *scarf, head*
And she cam° after in a gyte° of reed.° *came, gown, red*
3955 And Symkyn hadde hosen° of the same. *stockings*
Ther dorste° no wight° clepen hire° but *dared, person, call her*
"Dame."
Was noon° so hardy that wente by the weye,° *none, along the road*
That with hire dorste rage° or ones° pleye,° *romp, once, flirt*
But if° he wolde be slayn° of Symkyn *unless, wished to be killed by*
3960 With panade° or with knyf or boidekyn.° *sword, dagger*
For jalous° folk been perilous° everemo.° *jealous, dangerous, always*
Algate they wolde hire wyves wenden so.[10]
And eek,° for she was somdel° *also, since*
smoterlich,°[11] *somewhat soiled*
She was as digne° as water in a dich,° *haughty, ditch*
3965 As[12] ful of hoker° and of bismare.° *contempt, scorn*
Hir thoughte that a lady sholde hire spare,[13]

---

1 "Set his hood," is an expression that means "make him a fool."
2 There is a Latin gloss in the margin, "To repel force with force," referring to this well known legal principle.
3 These two lines paraphrase Matthew 7:3.
4 Trumpington is about three miles south of Cambridge, and there was a mill there in medieval times. There is a picture of the Reeve in the margin.
5 "Turn cups" probably refers to drinking an alcoholic drink in one gulp.
6 Sheffeld, in northern England, is still famous for its high-quality steel.
7 "That he did not swear that he should immediately pay for it."
8 The parson gave a large dowry (brass pans) because his daughter was illegitimate. Priests were not allowed to marry and were expected to be chaste.
9 Convents often served as schools for girls from well-off families.
10 "At any rate they want their wives to think so."
11 She is "soiled" because she is the illegitimate daughter of a priest.
12 Hengwrt reads "And." This reading is followed in most editions.
13 Probably, "She thought that a lady [like herself] should be reserved," or possibly, "She thought that a lady should treat her with respect" (although this would be an unusual use of "spare").

What for hire kynrede° and hir nortelrie,° — *her kindred, nurture*
That she hadde lerned° in the nonnerie.° — *learned, convent*
A DOGHTER hadde they bitwexe hem° two, — *between them*
3970 Of twenty yeer,° withouten any mo,° — *years old, more*
Savynge a child that was of half yeer° age. — *except, year*
In cradel° it lay and was a propre page.° — *cradle, handsome boy*
This wenche° thikke° and wel ygrowen° was, — *girl, thick, well-grown*
With kamuse° nose and eyen° greye as glas,° — *snub, eyes, glass*
3975 Buttokes brode° and brestes rounde and hye. — *buttocks broad*
But right° fair was hire heer,° I wol nat lye.° — *truly, her hair, not lie*
THIS person of the toun, for° she was feir,° — *because, fair*
In purpos was to maken hire his heir,° — *intended to make her his heir*
Bothe of his catel° and his mesuage.° — *belongings, household*
3980 And straunge° he made it of hir mariage.° — *difficult, her marriage*
His purpos was for to bistowe hire hye° — *bestow her high*
Into som° worthy blood of auncetrye,° — *some, ancestry [=nobility]*
For Hooly Chirches good moot been despended
On Hooly Chirches° blood that is descended.[1] — *Holy Church's*
3985 Therfore he wolde° his hooly° blood honoure,° — *wanted, holy, to honor*
Though that he Hooly Chirche sholde devoure.° — *should devour*
GREET sokene°[2] hath this millere, out of doute,° — *great monopoly, without doubt*
With whete° and malt of al the land aboute. — *wheat*
And nameliche° ther° was a greet° collegge° — *namely, there, great, college*
3990 Men clepen° the Soler Halle[3] at Cantebregge.° — *call, Cambridge*
Ther was hir° whete and eek° hir malt ygrounde.° — *their, also, ground up*
And on a day it happed° in a stounde,° — *happened, once*
Sik° lay the maunciple° on a maladye.°[4] — *sick, manciple, illness*
Men wenden° wisly that he sholde dye, — *expected*
3995 For which this millere stal° bothe mele° and corn° — *stole, meal (coarsely ground grain), grain*
An hundred tyme moore than biforn.
For therbiforn° he stal but curteisly,° — *before, courteously (discretely)*

But now he was a theef outrageously,° — *thief blatantly*
For which the wardeyn° chidde° and made fare.° — *warden, complained, made a fuss*
4000 But therof° sette the millere nat a tare[5] — *about this*
And craketh boost° and swoor° it was nat° so. — *cracks a boast, swore, not*
THANNE were ther yonge povre clerkes° two — *poor students*
That dwelten° in this halle of which I seye.° — *lived, spoke*
Testif° they were and lusty° for to pleye° — *headstrong, energetic, play*
4005 And oonly for hire° myrthe° and reverye.° — *just for their, mirth, wildness*
Upon the wardeyn bisily° they crye° — *eagerly, cry*
To yeve hem leve° but a litel stounde° — *give them leave, a little while*
To goon to mille and seen hir corn ygrounde.
And hardily they dorste leye hir nekke° — *dared wager their neck*
4010 The millere sholde not stele hem° half a pekke° — *[from] them, peck*
Or corn by sleighte° ne by force hem° reve.° — *trickery, them, rob*
And at the laste the wardeyn yaf hem leve.
John highte° that oon° and Aleyn heet that oother.° — *was called, one, other*
Of o toun were they born that highte Strother,[6]
4015 Fer° in the north, I kan nat telle° where. — *far, cannot tell*
THIS Aleyn maketh redy° al his gere,° — *ready, equipment*
And on an hors the sak° he caste anon.° — *sack, threw immediately*
Forth goth Aleyn the clerk and also John
With good swerd and bokeler° by hir syde.° — *shield, side*
4020 John knew the wey; hem neded no gyde.° — *they did not need a guide*
And at the mille the sak adoun° he layth.° — *down, lays*
Aleyn spak first: "Al hayl,° Symond, yfayth!° — *hello, in faith*
Hou fares thy faire doghter and thy wyf?"
"ALEYN, welcome," quod Symkyn, "by my lyf!
4025 And John also. How now! What do ye heer?"° — *here*
"SYMOND," quod John, "by God, nede has na peer![7]
Hym boes° serve hymselve that has na swayn,° — *he must, no servant*
Or elles° he is a fool, as clerkes° sayn." — *else, scholars, say*

---

1 "For the belongings of Holy Church must be spent on those who are descended from its blood" (i.e., the children of the clergy).
2 "Soken" was a term referring to a monopoly granted by a king or lord over a certain right or transaction.
3 Solar Hall is probably King's Hall, Cambridge, which had numerous solars or sun-rooms, upper rooms with large windows.
4 The manciple is responsible for the general upkeep of the college while the warden or master is a senior academic and the equivalent of a modern principal or president.
5 "Did not care at all." A "tare" is a weed, something of no value.
6 There is no town of this name in England, but there was a powerful Strother family in Northumbria.
7 "'Simon,' said John, 'by God, need has no peer (equal).'" Here Chaucer would normally write "hath." The students, from far in the north, speak a northern dialect of Middle English, often using *a* where Chaucer's southern English uses *o* (e.g., *ham* for *hom*) and ending the third-person indicative in *s* rather than in *th*.

Oure manciple—I hope° he wil be deed—   *expect*
4030 Swa werkes ay the wanges° in his heed,°   *so ache ever the teeth, head*
And forthy° is I come and eek° Alayn   *therefore, also*
To grynde oure corn and carie° it ham agayn.°   *carry, home again*
I pray yow spede° us heythen° that ye may."   *help, hence*
4035 What wol ye doon° whil° that it is in hande?"   *will you do, while*
"By God, right by the hopur¹ wil I stande,"
Quod John, "and se how that the corn gas° in.   *goes*
Yet saugh° I never by my fader kyn°   *saw, father's kin*
How that the hopur wagges til and fra."°   *hopper wags to and fro*
4040 Aleyn answerde, "John, wiltow swa?°   *will you so*
Thanne wil I be byneth,° by my croun,°   *beneath, crown (of head)*
And se how that the mele° falles doun°   *meal, falls down*
Into the trough. That sal° be my disport,°   *shall, amusement*
For, John, yfaith,° I may been° of youre sort.   *in faith, be*
4045 I is as ille° a millere as ar ye!"°   *ill, as are you*
This millere smyled of° hir nycetee°   *smiled about, foolishness*
And thoghte,° "Al° this nys doon° but for   *thought, all, is not done*
    a wyle.°   *trick*
They wene° that no man may hem° bigyle.°   *think, them, trick*
4050 But by my thrift, yet shal I blere hir eye°   *make their eye bleary*
For al° the sleighte° in hir° philosophye.   *all, trickery, their*
The moore° queynte crekes° that they make,   *more, clever tricks*
The moore wol I stele° whan I take.   *steal*
Instide of flour, yet wol I yeve° hem° bren.°   *give, them, bran*
'The gretteste clerkes been noght° wisest   *greatest scholars are not*
    men,'
4055 As whilom° to the wolf thus spak° the mare.²   *once, spoke*
Of al° hir° art counte I noght a tare."°   *all, their, care not at all*
Out at the dore° he gooth° ful pryvely°   *door, goes, very secretly*
Whan that he saugh his tyme° softely.°   *opportunity, quietly*
He looketh up and doun til he hath founde
4060 The clerkes hors° ther° as it stood   *students' horse, where*
    ybounde°   *tied*
Bihynde° the mille under a lefsel.°   *behind, arbor*
And to the hors he goth hym faire and wel.
He strepeth° of the brydel° right anon°   *strips, bridle, right away*
And whan the hors was laus° he gynneth° gon   *loose, went*

4065 Toward the fen° ther° wilde mares renne,°   *swamp, where, run*
And forth with "Wehee"° thurgh thikke and thurgh   *whinny*
    thenne.°   *thick and thin*
This millere gooth agayn. No word he seyde,
But dooth° his note° and with the clerkes   *does, business*
    pleyde°   *joked*
Til that hir corn was faire and weel ygrounde.
4070 And whan the mele° is sakked° and   *meal, put into sacks*
    ybounde,°   *bound*
This John goth° out and fynt° his hors away   *goes, finds*
And gan° to crie,° "Harrow and weylaway!"³   *began, cry*
Oure hors is lorn,° Alayn, for Goddes banes!°   *lost, bones*
Stepe on thy feet! Com° out, man, al atanes!°   *come, all at once*
4075 Allas, our wardeyn° has his palfrey° lorn!"°   *warden, horse, lost*
This Aleyn al forgat° bothe mele° and corn.°   *all forgot, meal, grain*
Al was out of his mynde° his housbondrie.°   *mind, stewardship*
"What! Whilk° way is he geen?"° he gan°   *which, has he gone, began*
    to crie.
The wyf cam° lepynge inward° with a ren.°   *came, running up, rein*
4080 She seyde, "Allas, youre hors goth° to the fen°   *goes, swamp*
With wilde mares as faste as he may go!
Unthank° come on his hand that boond   *a curse*
    hym° so   *bound him*
And he that bettre° sholde han knyt° the   *better, should have tied*
    reyne!"°   *rein*
"Allas!" quod Aleyn, "For Cristes peyne,°   *pain*
4085 Lay doun thy swerd,° and I wil myn alswa!°   *sword, also*
I is ful wight,° God waat,° as is a raa!°   *strong, knows, roe (deer)*
By God herte,° he sal nat scape° us   *God's heart, shall not escape*
    bathe!°   *both*
Why nadtow pit the capul in the lathe?⁴
Ilhayl,° by God, Alayn, thou is a fonne!"°   *bad luck, you are a fool*
4090 This sely clerkes° han° ful° faste yronne°⁵   *silly students, have, very, run*
Toward the fen, bothe Aleyn and eek John.
And whan the millere saugh that they were gon,
He half a busshel of hir° flour hath take°   *their, taken*
And bad° his wyf, "Go knede° it in   *commanded, knead*
    cake."°   *into a loaf of bread*
4095 He seyde, "I trowe° the clerkes were aferd,°   *believe, afraid*

---

1   The hopper is the mechanism that feeds the grain into the mill to be ground.
2   The story, which is found in Aesop's *Fables* and has several medieval versions, is that when the wolf offered to buy the mare's foal, she told him that the price was written on her hoof and that if he was a scholar he could come and read it. The wolf drew the moral after being kicked by the mare.
3   "Harrow and welaway" is the cry to raise help in an emergency.
4   "Why did you not put the horse in the barn?"
5   Ellesmere reads "yrenne." The emendation is from Hengwrt.

[handwritten marginal note, left:] Miller let lose students' horse so he can cheat freely

[handwritten marginal note, bottom right:] makes extra flour into cake

asks to be hosted in Miller house for night

Yet kan a millere make a clerkes berd[1]
For al his art. Now lat hem goon hir weye.°   *let them go their way*
Lo, wher they goon! Ye, lat the children pleye.
They gete hym nat so lightly, by my croun!"°   *crown*
4100 THISE sely clerkes rennen° up and doun   *run*
With "Keepe!° Keepe! Stand! Stand! Jossa!°   *Down here!, Whoa!*
    Warderere!°   *Watch out!*
Ga° whistle thou, and I shal kepe° hym here."°   *go, keep, him here*
But[2] shortly til that it was verray° nyght,   *true*
They koude nat thogh they do al hir myght°   *their might*
4105 Hir capul cacche.° He ran alwey so faste,   *their horse catch*
Til in a dych° they caughte hym atte laste.°   *ditch, at last*
WERY° and weet° as beest° is in the reyn°   *weary, wet, beast, rain*
Comth° sely° John and with hym comth Aleyn.   *comes, silly*
"Allas," quod John, "the day that I was born!
4110 Now are we dryve til hethyng and til scorn.°   *held up to mockery*
Oure corn° is stoln! Men° wil us fooles calle,   *grain, MS Me*
Bathe° the wardeyn° and oure felawes° alle,   *both, warden, fellows*
And namely the millere, weylaway!"°   *alas*
THUS pleyneth° John as he gooth by the   *laments*
    way°   *along the road*
4115 Toward the mille and Bayard in his hond.
The millere sittynge by the fyr he fond,°   *found*
For it was nyght and forther° myghte they noght.°   *further, not [go]*
But for the love of God they hym° bisoght°   *him, requested*
Of herberwe° and of ese° as for hir peny.°[4]   *lodging, food, penny*
4120 THE millere seyde° agayn, "If ther be eny,°   *replied, any*
Swich° as it is yet shal° ye have youre part.   *such, shall*
Myn hous is streit° but ye han lerned°   *my house is small, have learned*
    art.[5]
Ye konne° by argumentz make a place   *know how*
A myle° brood,° of twenty foot of space.   *mile, broad*
4125 Lat se° now if this place may suffise   *let's see*
Or make it rowm° with speche° as is youre   *roomy, speech*
    gise."°   *custom*

"Now, Symond," seyde John, "by Seint Cutberd,[6]
Ay° is thou myrie° and this is faire answerd.   *ever, merry*
I have herd seyd, 'Man sal taa° of twa   *shall take*
    thynges°   *two things*
4130 Slyk° as he fyndes or taa° slyk as he brynges.'°   *such, take, brings*
But specially, I pray thee, hoost deere,°   *dear host*
Get us som mete° and drynke° and make us   *food, drink*
    cheere,°   *welcome*
And we wil payen trewely atte fulle.°   *will pay truly the full amount*
With empty hand men may none haukes° tulle.°   *hawks, lure*
4135 Loo, heere° oure silver, redy° for to spende."   *here, ready*
THIS millere into toun his doghter sende
For ale and breed and rosted hem° a goos   *roasted them*
And boond° hire hors. It sholde nat goon   *tied up*
    loos.°   *not go loose*
And in his owene chambre° hem made a bed[7]   *own room*
4140 With sheetes and with chalons° faire yspred.°   *blankets, spread*
Noght from his owene bed ten foot or twelve
His doghter hadde a bed al by hirselve,
Right in the same chambre by and by.°   *nearby*
It myghte° be no bet° and cause   *might, better,*
    why:°   *[this is the] reason why*
4145 Ther was no roumer herberwe° in the place.   *larger room*
They soupen° and they speke hem to   *eat supper*
    solace°   *to comfort themselves*
And drynke evere strong ale atte beste.°   *of the best*
Aboute mydnyght wente they to reste.
WEL hath this millere vernysshed° his heed.°[8]   *varnished, head*
4150 Ful° pale he was for dronken° and nat reed.°   *very, drinking, not red*
He yexeth,° and he speketh thurgh the nose   *burps*
As he were on the quakke or on the pose.°   *hoarse or had a cold*
To bedde he goth and with hym goth his wyf.
As any jay she light was and jolyf,°   *jolly*
4155 So was hir joly whistle wel ywet.°[9]   *wet*
The cradel° at hir beddes feet° is set   *cradle, foot of her bed*

---

1   "Make a beard" is an expression for "make a fool of."
2   Ellesmere has a hole in the parchment after this word, one evidently present before the scribe worked on it since no word is missing from the text, as attested by Hengwrt.
3   Bayard was a typical name for a horse in the Middle Ages.
4   Since there were relatively few inns in the Middle Ages, residents of private homes often lodged travelers for money.
5   The sense of Symon's comment here is that the students have studied at the university, so they are practiced in logical argument, which can make something seem what it is not. A small house thus can seem big enough for two extra people.
6   The Anglo-Saxon Saint Cuthbert, who lived in the seventh century, was particularly venerated in the northern parts of England, which were home to Aleyn and John, as their accents reveal.
7   All family members in peasant households in the Middle Ages commonly slept in a home's main room.
8   "Varnished one's head" seems to have been an expression for getting drunk.
9   "Wetting one's whistle" is still today an expression for having a drink.

To rokken° and to yeve the child to sowke.° *rock, breast-feed*

And whan that dronken al was in the crowke,° *jug*

To bedde wente the doghter right anon.° *immediately*

4160 To bedde wente Aleyn and also John.

Ther nas namoore; hem neded no dwale.[1]

This millere hath so wisely bibbed° ale *sipped*

That as a hors° he fnorteth° in his sleepe. *horse, snores*

Ne of his tayl° bihynde° he took no keepe. *tail, behind*

4165 His wyf bar° hym a burdon[2] a ful° strong. *bore, very*

Men myghte° hir rowtyng° heere° two furlong.[3] *might, snoring, hear*

The wenche° rowteth eek° par *girl, also*
        compaignye.° *for company's sake*

ALEYN the clerk that herde this melodye,

He poked John and seyde, "Slepestow?° *Do you sleep?*

4170 Herdtow evere° slyk° a sang° er *Did you ever hear, such, song,*
        now?° *before*

Lo, whilk a cowplyng°[4] is ymel hem *what a compline*
        alle.° *among them all*

A wilde fyr° upon thair bodyes falle! *wildfire (painful skin disease)*

Wha herkned° evere slyk° a ferly° thyng? *who heard, such, marvelous*

Ye,° they sal° have the flour° of il° *yes, shall, flower (the best), ill*
        ending.

4175 This lange nyght ther tydes me na
        reste.° *long night there is no sleep for me*

But yet na fors,° al sal° be for the beste. *it does not matter, shall*

For John," seyde he, "als° evere moot° I thryve,° *as, might, thrive*

If that I may, yon° wenche wil° I swyve.° *yonder, will, have sex with*

Som esement° has lawe° yshapen° us, *some easement, law, shaped for*

4180 For, John, ther is a lawe that says thus:

That gif° a man in a point° be ygreved,° *if, matter, injured*

That in another he sal° be releved.° *shall, relieved*

Oure corn° is stoln.° Shortly is ne nay,° *grain, stolen, no denying [it]*

And we han° had an il° fit al this day. *have, ill*

4185 And syn° I sal° have neen amendement° *since, shall, no pay-back*

Agayn° my los,° I wil° have esement. *against, loss, will*

By God[es] sa[u]le,°[5] it sal° neen° other bee!"° *God's soul, shall, no, be*

THIS John answerde, "Alayn, avyse° thee! *be careful*

The millere is a perilous° man," he seyde, *dangerous*

4190 "And gif° that he out of his sleepe abreyde,° *if, awakes*

He myghte doon° us bathe° a vileynye."° *might do, both, harm*

ALEYN answerde, "I counte hym nat a flye."° *not [worth] a flea*

And up he rist,° and by the wenche he crepte.° *he gets up, crawled*

This wenche lay uprighte° and faste slepte, *on her back*

4195 Til he so ny° was, er° she myghte espie,° *near, before, see*

That it had been to° late for to crie.° *too, cry*

And shortly for to seyn,° they were aton.° *say, united*

Now pley,° Aleyn, for I wol speke of John. *play*

THIS John lith stille° a furlong wey or two,[6] *lies quietly*

4200 And to hymself he maketh° routhe° and wo.° *makes, pity, woe*

"Allas," quod° he, "this is a wikked jape!"° *said, wicked joke*

Now may I seyn that I is but an ape.

Yet has my felawe° somwhat° for his harm. *companion, something*

He has the milleris doghter in his arm.

4205 He auntred° hym and has his nedes *took a chance*
        sped,° *need's success*

And I lye° as a draf,[7] sek° in my bed. *lie, sick*

And whan this jape° is tald° another day, *joke, told*

I sal° been halde° a daf,° a cokenay.[8] *shall, be considered, weakling*

I wil arise° and auntre° it by my fayth!° *get up, risk, faith*

4210 'Unhardy is unseely.'[9] Thus men sayth."

And up he roos,° and softely° he wente *rose, quietly*

Unto the cradel and in his hand it hente° *grasped*

And baar° it softe unto the beddes feet. *carried*

SOONE after this the wyf hir rowtyng leet° *stopped snoring*

4215 And gan awake° and wente hire° out to pisse *awoke, herself*

And cam agayn° and gan hir cradel *came back*
        mysse° *missed her cradle*

And groped heer and ther. But she foond noon.

---

1   "They did not need for themselves any sleeping potion."

2   The burden of a medieval carol was its refrain, a line or phrase sung at the beginning and after each successive verse.

3   A furlong was a measure of distance 220 yards (or ⅛ mile). Originally, it was the length of the typical furrow made in the common fields by peasants when they ploughed.

4   The normal spelling in Middle English for compline, the sung prayers of monks and nuns in the late evening hours, would have been "complyn." Aleyn evidently mispronounces the word, mixing it up with "coupling," a word that could refer to the act of sex, unless the error is simply that of the scribe Adam Pinkhurst.

5   The emendation is from Hengwrt.

6   For the time it takes to walk a furlong (220 yards or ⅛ of a mile).

7   "Draf" is chaff, the waste material left over from grinding grain into flour, but "a draf" (a chaff) is an odd idiom. Hengwrt reads "draf sack" (a sack for chaff or refuse), which also makes better sense, since John is clearly not sick.

8   A "cockney" is a cock's egg. Folklore held that cocks did occasionally lay eggs but only tiny ones of no value.

9   The proverb John quotes roughly means, "The fearful one is the unhappy one."

"Allas," quod she, "I hadde almoost mysgoon.°   *made a mistake*
I hadde almoost goon° to the clerkes' bed!   *had almost gone, students'*
4220 Ey, benedicite,° thanne° hadde I foule   *Oh bless [me], then*
            ysped!"°   *done badly*
And forth she gooth til she the cradel fond.
She gropeth alwey forther° with hir hond   *further*
And foond° the bed and thoghte noght° but   *found, thought nothing*
            good,
Bycause that the cradel by it stood,
4225 And nyste wher° she was, for it was derk.°   *did not know where, dark*
But faire and wel° she creepe into° the   *well, creeps towards*
            clerk
And lith ful stille° and wolde han caught a   *lies very quietly*
            sleepe.°   *wanted to fall asleep*
Withinne° a while this John the clerk up leepe,°   *Within, jumped*
And on this goode wyf he leith on soore.°   *lays on vigorously*
4230 So myrie° a fit° hadde she nat ful   *merry, episode*
            yoore.°   *not for a long time*
He priketh harde° and soore as he were   *pierces vigorously*
            mad.°   *crazy*
This joly lyf° han° thise two clerkes lad°   *life, have, led*
Til that the thridde° cok bigan to synge.°   *third, cock began to crow*
ALEYN wax wery° in the dawenynge,°   *grew weary, dawn*
4235 For he had swonken° al° the longe nyght,   *labored, all*
And seyde,° "Fareweel,° Malyne, sweete   *said, farewell*
            wight,°   *person*
The day is come. I may no lenger byde.°   *no longer stay*
But everemo° wherso° I go or ryde,°   *ever more, wherever, ride*
I is thyn awen° clerk, swa° have I seel!"°   *your own, so, good luck*
4240 "Now, deere lemman,"° quod she, "go fare weel.°   *sweetheart, farewell*
But er° thow go, o thyng° I wol thee telle.   *before, one thing*
Whan that thou wendest homward by the
            melle,°   *you go homewards by the mill*
Right at the entree° of the dore° bihynde°   *entrance, door, behind*
Thou shalt a cake of half a busshel fynde
4245 That was ymaked° of thyn owene mele°   *made, meal*
Which that I heelpe my fader for to stele.°   *steal*
And, goode lemman,° God thee save and kepe!"°   *sweet heart, keep*
And with that word almoost she gan to wepe.°   *began to weep*
ALEYN up rist° and thoughte, "Er° that it   *rose up, Before,*
            dawe,°   *dawns*
4250 I wol go crepen in by my felawe,"

And fond the cradel with his hand anon."°   *immediately*
"By God," thoughte he, "Al wrang° I have   *wrong*
            mysgon!°   *gone wrong*
Myn heed° is toty° of my swynk° tonyght   *head, dizzy, work*
That maketh me that I go nat aright.°   *not right*
4255 I woot wel° by the cradel° I have   *know well, cradle*
            mysgo.°   *gone wrong*
Heere lith° the millere and his wyf also."   *here lies*
And forth he goth a twenty devel way[1]
Unto the bed theras° the millere lay.   *where*
He wende have cropen° by his felawe John.   *expected [to] have crept*
4260 And by the millere in he creepe° anon   *creeps in*
And caughte hym by the nekke. And softe° he   *quietly*
            spak.
He seyde, "Thou John, thou swynes heed!°   *pig's head*
            Awak,°   *awake*
For Cristes saule,° and heer° a noble game!   *soul, hear*
For by that lord that called is Seint Jame,°   *St. James*
4265 As I have thries° in this shorte nyght   *three times*
Swyved° the milleres doghter bolt   *had sex with*
            upright°   *lying on her back*
Whil thow hast° as a coward° been agast!"°   *while you have, afraid*
"YE° false harlot!"° quod the millere, "hast?°   *yes, villain, have [you]*
A, false traitour, false clerk," quod he,
4270 "Thow shalt be deed,° by Goddes dignitee!"°   *dead, dignity*
Who dorste° be so boold° to disparage°   *dares, bold, dishonor*
My doghter that is come of swich lynage!"°   *such lineage*
And by the throte bolle° he caughte Alayn,   *Adam's apple*
And he hente hym despitously
            agayn,°   *(Aleyn) grabbed him fiercely in return*
4275 And on the nose he smoot hym° with his fest.°   *hit him, fist*
Doun ran the blody streem° upon his brest,°   *bloody stream, breast*
And in the floor with nose and mouth tobroke°   *broken*
They walwe° as doon° two pigges° in a poke.°   *wallow, do, pigs, bag*
And up they goon° and doun agayn° anon   *go, down again*
4280 Til that the millere sporned at° a stoon.°   *stumbled on, stone*
And doun he fil bakward upon his wyf,
That wiste nothyng° of this nyce   *who knew nothing*
            stryf,°   *ludicrous strife*
For she was falle aslepe° a lite wight°   *had fallen asleep, a short time*
With John the clerk that waked hadde° al   *who had been awake*
            nyght.

_____

1   This cliché means "in the name of twenty devils."

39

Miller finds out

4285 And with the fal out of hir sleepe she breyde,° — *awoke*
"Help, hooly croys° of Bromholm,"¹ she seyde,° — *holy cross, said*
"In manus tuas, Lord, to thee I calle!²
Awak,° Symond, the feend° is on us falle!° — *awake, fiend, fallen*
Myn herte° is broken. Help! I nam but — *my heart*
    deed!° — *I am as good as dead*
4290 Ther lyth oon° upon my wombe° and on — *lies someone, stomach*
    myn heed.
Helpe, Symkyn, for the false clerkes fighte!"
THIS John stirte up° as soone as ever he myghte — *jumped up*
And graspeth by the walles° to and fro — *gropes along the walls*
To fynde a staf.° And she stirte up° also — *stick, got up*
4295 And knew the estres° bet° than dide° this John. — *interior, better, did*
And by the wal a staf she foond° anon — *found*
And saugh° a litel shymeryng° of a light, — *saw, little shimmering*
For at an hole in shoon the moone bright.
And by that light she saugh hem bothe two.
4300 But sikerly° she nyste° who was who, — *surely, did not know*
But as° she saugh a whit thyng° in hir eye. — *except that, white thing*
And whan she gan the white thyng espye,° — *saw the white thing*
She wende° the clerk hadde wered° a — *thought, had worn*
    volupeer,° — *nightcap*
And with the staf she drow ay neer and neer° — *drew ever nearer*

4305 And wende han hit° this Aleyn at the fulle° — *intended to hit, fully*
And smoot° the millere on the pyled skulle.° — *hit, bald skull*
And doun he gooth and cride,° "Harrow!³ I dye!"° — *cried, die*
Thise clerkes beete hym weel° and lete hym — *beat him well*
    lye° — *let him lie*
And greythen° hem and tooke° hir hors anon — *get dressed, took*
4310 And eek° hir mele,° and on hir wey° they gon. — *also, meal, their way*
And at the mille yet they tooke hir cake° — *their loaf*
Of half a busshel flour ful wel ybake.° — *very well baked*
THUS is the proude millere wel ybete° — *well beaten*
And hath ylost° the gryndynge° of the whete° — *lost, grinding, wheat*
4315 And payed° for the soper° everideel° — *paid, supper, every bit*
Of Aleyn and of John that bette hym weel.° — *beat him well*
His wyf is swyved° and his doghter als.° — *has had sex, as well*
Lo, swich° it is a millere to be fals!° — *such [is the result], false*
And therfore this proverbe is seyd° ful sooth:° — *said, in full truth*
4320 "Hym thar nat wene wel that yvele dooth."⁴
A gylour° shal hymself bigyled° be. — *trickster, tricked*
And God that sitteth heighe in Trinitee — *who sits high in Trinity*
Save al this compaignye° grete and smale!° — *company, great and small*
Thus have I quyt° the Millere in my tale. — *requited*

HEERE IS ENDED THE REVES TALE

John + Aleyn get cake & win

Miller punished

---

1   This was a famous shrine in Bromholm, in Norfolk, which claimed to have a piece of the true cross.
2   "Into your hands, Lord, to you I call." The Latin is a quotation from Luke 23:46, words that Jesus utters immediately before death on the cross.
3   "Harrow" is a word used to raise help in an emergency.
4   "He who does evil should not expect good."

The Wife of Bath's Prologue and Tale

With the opening words of her extremely long prologue, the Wife of Bath introduces one of her central themes, the conflict between the experience of life, which for the Wife means sexual experience foremost, and "auctoritee," the written commentary of learned men on religious, moral, and philosophical issues. These men, who included both the patristic writers (such as Saints Ambrose and Jerome) and classical philosophers, have little good to say about women, whom they repeatedly depict as deceitful, quarrelsome, and lecherous. Escape from this tradition, as the Wife herself indicates in her account of the debate between the man and the lion, is not easy. Just as all paintings of lions will always be painted by men, so in classical and medieval society almost all writing, especially writing that had official authority, was done by men. The Wife herself, in one of the tale's many layers of ventriloquism, places traditional criticisms of women in the mouths of her first three husbands, whom she accuses of abusing her with these repeated insults. The criticisms can also be found in her fifth husband's book, a compilation of misogynistic texts from Jerome and others, all counseling against marriage.

The great irony is that the Wife herself is drawn from this tradition. Her character is based in part on the Old Woman in *The Romance of the Rose*, a sexually experienced cynic who teaches young people the tricks of love, and both the Wife's history and the literary shape of her prologue and tale conform to many of the traditional misogynistic stereotypes found in her husband's book. The subtle layering of the text makes its final moral elusive. Readers continue to argue whether the Wife should be taken as a moral warning against unbridled carnality or admired for her independence, courage, and vitality. The glosses in the Ellesmere manuscript tend to support the first view, but the Wife herself has some telling comments to offer on men who write glosses.

The tale that the Wife finally tells is an Arthurian romance. It follows a well-established folk-tale plot in which a knight is given a year to answer a question or die and can only get the answer from an old and ugly woman who will not give it to him unless he promises either to marry her or, as in Chaucer's version, to give her whatever she wants, which later turns out to be marriage. In several versions, including *The Tale of Florent* in John Gower's *Confessio Amantis*, the question the knight must answer is what women most desire. Chaucer modifies the familiar story in a number of ways, so that the tale contributes to the argument the Wife has been making in her prologue. The knight in the Wife's version is not innocent—he is a rapist—and he objects to the marriage not just because the woman is old and ugly, but also because she is of low birth, an objection she counters in a long disquisition on the nature of true gentility. Even the knight's final choice, which in the other versions takes the form of "foul by day and fair by night" or the reverse, is subtly altered in keeping with the Wife's interests.

Detail, opening page of the Prologue to *The Wife of Bath's Tale*, Ellesmere manuscript; see color insert for full page. (Reprinted by permission of *The Huntington Library, San Marino, California.* EL 26 C9 f. 72r.)

THE WIFE OF BATH'S PROLOGUE

THE PROLOGUE OF THE WYVVES TALE OF BATHE

"Experience, though noon auctoritee
 Were in this world, were right ynogh to me[1]
To speke° of wo° that is in mariage. — *speak / woe*
For lordynges,° sith° I twelve yeer was of age, — *lords / since*
5 Ythonked° be God that is eterne on lyve,° — *thanked / eternally alive*
Housbondes at chirche dore° I have had fyve,° — *church door / five*
For I so ofte have ywedded° bee,°[2] — *wedded / been*
And alle were worthy men in hir° degree. — *their*
But me was toold certeyn° nat longe — *certainly*
  agoon° is, — *not long ago*
10 That sith that Crist ne wente° nevere but onis° — *did not go / once*
To weddyng in the Cane° of Galilee,[3] — *Cana*
By the same ensample° thoughte me° — *example / it seemed to me*
That I ne sholde° wedded be but ones.° — *should not / once*
Herkne eek° which a sharpe word — *listen also*
  for the nones° — *for the occasion*
15 Biside° a welle Jhesus, God and man, — *beside*
Spak° in repreeve° of the Samaritan;[4] — *spoke / rebuke*
'Thou hast yhad° fyve housbondes,' quod° he, — *have had / said*
'And that man the which that hath now thee° — *who now has you*
Is noght thyn housbonde.' Thus seyde he certeyn.
20 What that he mente therby,° — *meant by this*
  I kan nat seyn.° — *cannot say*
But that I axe,° why that the fifthe man — *ask*
Was noon housbonde to the Samaritan?
How manye myghte she have in mariage?
Yet herde I nevere tellen° in myn age — *never heard told*
25 Upon this nombre° diffinicioun.° — *number / definition*
Men may devyne° and glosen°[5] up and doun,° — *guess / gloss / down*
But wel I woot° expres° withoute lye,° — *well I know / clearly / lie*

God bad° us forto wexe° and multiplye.[6] — *commanded / to increase*
That gentil° text kan° I understonde! — *noble / can*
30 Eek wel I woot, he seyde myn housbonde
Sholde lete fader and mooder° — *should leave father and mother*
  and take me.[7]
But of no nombre° mencioun — *number*
  made he° — *did he make mention*
Of bigamye° or of octogamye.° — *bigamy / marriage to eight spouses*
Why sholde men speke° of it vileynye?° — *speak / as villainy*
35 "Lo heere° the wise kyng daun° Salamon: — *consider / master*
I trowe° he hadde wyves mo° than oon.°[8] — *believe / more / one*
As wolde God, it were leveful unto me[9]
To be refresshed° half so ofte° as he! — *refreshed / often*
Which yifte° of God hadde he for alle hise wyvys;° — *gift / wives*
40 No man hath swich° that in this world alyve° is. — *such / alive*
God woot,° this noble kyng, — *knows*
  as to my wit,° — *as far as I know*
The first nyght° had many a myrie° fit — *night / merry*
With ech° of hem,° so wel was hym° — *each / them / he was so lucky*
  on lyve.
Yblessed be God that I have wedded five![10]
45 Welcome the sixte, whanevere he shal.° — *whenever he shall arrive*
Forsothe,° I wol nat kepe me chaast in al° — *in truth / entirely chaste*
Whan myn housbonde is fro° the world ygon.° — *from / gone*
Som° Cristen° man shal wedde me — *some / Christian*
  anon,° — *immediately*
For thanne° th'apostle seith°[11] I am free — *then / the apostle says*

---

[1] *Experience ... me* Experience, even if there were no written authority in the world, would be quite enough for me. Authority, in this sense, refers to the writings of learned men, especially the patristic writers and ancient philosophers.

[2] *For ... bee* Many manuscripts have "If I so ofte myghte have ywedded be," i.e., if these multiple marriages were indeed lawful.

[3] *Cane of Galilee* See John 2.1–11.

[4] *Samaritan* See John 4.1–42.

[5] *glosen* Crucial points in the Bible, and other religious, philosophical, or legal texts were explained in glosses (comments written in the margins or between the lines).

---

[6] *God bad ... multiplye* See Genesis 6.1.

[7] *myn housbonde ... me* See Genesis 2.24.

[8] *I ... oon* According to the Bible, King Solomon had seven hundred wives and three hundred concubines. See 1 Kings 11.33.

[9] *As wolde ... me* If only God would permit that it should be lawful for me.

[10] *Yblessed ... five* Some manuscripts contain the following six-line passage:

"Of whiche I have pyked out the beste
Bothe of here nether purs and of here cheste.
Diverse scoles maken parfyt clerkes,
And diverse practyk in many sondry werkes,
Maken the workman parfit, sekirly;
Of five husbandes scoleiyng am I."

John Manly and Edith Rickert suggest that these lines are "a late Chaucerian insertion," i.e., part of a late rough draft of the poem.

[11] *th'apostle seith* I.e., St. Paul. See 1 Corinthians 7.25–38.

50 To wedde, a Goddes half, where it liketh me.[1]
He seith to be wedded is no synne:° — *sin*
'Bet° is to be wedded than to brynne.'°[2] — *better / burn*
What rekketh me,° thogh folk seye° — *what do I care / say*
vileynye° — *villainy*
Of shrewed° Lameth[3] and of bigamye?° — *cursed / bigamy*
55 I woot wel° Abraham[4] was an hooly° man — *know well / holy*
And Jacob eek, as ferforth as I kan,° — *as far as I know*
And ech of hem° hadde wyves mo than two — *them*
And many another man also.
Whanne° saugh° ye evere in manere° age — *when / saw / any*
60 That hye° God defended° mariage — *high / forbade*
By expres° word? I pray yow, telleth me. — *specific*
Or where comanded he virginitee?° — *virginity*
I woot as wel as ye,° it is no drede,[5] — *know as well as you*
Whan th'apostel° speketh of maydenhede°— *virginity*
65 He seyde that precept° therof° hadde he — *commandment / about*
noon.°[6] — *none*
Men may conseille° a womman to been oon,° — *counsel / single*
But conseillyng is nat comandement.
He putte it in oure owene juggement.° — *left it to our own judgment*
For hadde° God comanded maydenhede, — *had*
70 Thanne° hadde he dampned° weddyng — *then / condemned*
with the dede.° — *in the act*
And certein,° if ther were no seed ysowe° — *certainly / sown*
Virginitee, wherof thanne° sholde° it growe? — *how then / should*
Poul° ne dorste nat° — *St. Paul / dared not*
comanden atte leeste° — *command at least*
A thyng of which his maister° yaf° — *master / gave*
noon heeste.° — *no command*
75 The dart[7] is set up of virginitee:

Cacche whoso may. Who renneth best, lat see!°[8]
"But this word is nat taken of every
wight,° — *does not apply to everyone*
But theras God lust gyve it of his myght.[9]
I woot wel the apostel was a mayde.° — *virgin*
80 But nathelees,° thogh° that he wroot° — *nevertheless / though / wrote*
and sayde
He wolde° that every wight° were swich° — *wished / person / such*
as he,
Al nys but conseil° to virginitee. — *is not but advice*
And for to been° a wyf he yaf° me leve° — *be / gave / leave*
Of indulgence,° so it is no repreve° — *by permission / reproach*
85 To wedde me if my make° dye,° — *mate / should die*
Withouten excepcioun° of bigamye.° — *objection / bigamy*
Al° were it good no womman for to touche, — *although*
He mente° as in his bed or in his couche.° — *meant / couch*
For peril is bothe fyr and tow t'assemble.[10]
90 Ye knowe what this ensample° may resemble. — *example*
This is al and som,° that virginitee — *the whole matter*
Moore profiteth than weddyng in freletee;[11]
Freletee° clepe I° but if° that he and she — *weakness / I call it / unless*
Wolde lede° al hir lyf° in chastitee. — *would lead / their life*
95 "I graunte° it wel; I have noon envie,° — *grant / no envy*
Thogh maydenhede preferre bigamye.[12]
Hem liketh° to be clene,° body and — *they prefer / pure*
goost.° — *spirit*
Of myn estaat° I nyl nat° make no — *my condition / will not*
boost.° — *boast*
For wel ye knowe, a lord in his houshold,
100 He nath nat° every vessel al of gold. — *does not have*
Somme been of tree° and doon° hir° — *wood / do / their*
lord servyse.
God clepeth° folk to hym in sondry wyse.° — *calls / in different ways*
And everich hath° of God a propre — *everyone has*
yifte°— — *particular gift*
Som this, som that, as hym liketh shifte.° — *as he pleases to give*

---

[1] *To wedde … me* To wed, by God's permission, wherever I wish.

[2] *Bet … brynne* See 1 Corinthians 7.9.

[3] *Lameth* Lamech is the first to marry two wives. See Genesis 4.19.

[4] *Abraham* The patriarch Abraham, as recounted in the book of Genesis, was favored by God, yet he had more than one wife, as did his grandson Jacob.

[5] *it is no drede* Do not doubt it.

[6] *He … noon* Paul admits that he could find no justification for his view in the Old Testament. See 1 Corinthians 7.25.

[7] *dart* A spear was sometimes given as a prize for a race in England in the Middle Ages. Many editors prefer the reading "for virginity" (found in many other manuscripts), which makes virginity the competitor rather than the prize.

---

[8] *Cacche … see* Let whoever can catch it. Let us see who runs best.

[9] *But … myght* Except where God wishes, through his might, to impose this principle (of virginity).

[10] *fyr … t'assemble* To bring together fire and flax (flammable material of which wicks are made).

[11] *Moore … freletee* Remaining a virgin is better than marrying through weakness.

[12] *Thogh … bigamye* Though virginity be preferred to bigamy.

105   "Virginitee is greet perfeccioun
And continence° eek with devocioun.°   *chastity / religious devotion*
But Crist that of perfeccioun° is welle°   *perfection / well (source)*
Bad° nat every wight sholde go selle   *commanded*
Al that he hadde and gyve° it to the poore   *give*
110 And in swich wise folwe hym[1] and his foore.°   *steps*
He spak to hem that wolde lyve parfitly.°   *wished to live perfectly*
And, lordynges, by youre leve,° that am nat I!   *leave*
I wol bistowe° the flour° of myn age   *will bestow / flower*
In the actes and in fruyt° of mariage.   *fruit*
115   "Telle me also, to what conclusioun
Were membres ymaad° of generacioun?[2]   *made*
And for what profit° was a wight ywroght?°   *purpose / person made*
Trusteth° right wel, they were nat maad°   *believe me / not made*
    for noght.°   *nothing*
Glose whoso wole and seye bothe up and doun,[3]
120 That they were maad for purgacioun°   *releasing*
Of uryne° and oure bothe thynges   *urine*
    smale,°   *our two small things (sexual organs)*
And eek to knowe° a femele from a male,   *distinguish*
And for noon oother cause: sey° ye no?   *say*
The experience woot wel° it is   *experience (in general) knows well*
    noght so.
125 So that the clerkes° be nat with me wrothe,°   *theologians / angry*
I sey yis,° that they beth maked° for bothe!   *say yes / are made*
That is to seye, for office and for ese°   *pleasure*
Of engendrure,[4] ther we nat God
    displese.°   *where we do not displease God*
Why sholde men elles° in hir bookes sette°   *otherwise / set down*
130 That a man shal yelde to his wyf hire dette?[5]
Now, wherwith° sholde he make his   *with what*
    paiement°   *payment*
If he ne used° his sely° instrument?   *did not use / innocent*
Thanne were they maad upon a creature
To purge uryne° and for engendrure.°   *release urine / conception*

135   "But I seye noght° that every wight is holde°   *not / obligated*
That hath swich harneys,° as I of tolde,   *such equipment*
To goon° and usen hem° in engendrure.   *go / them*
They shul° nat take of chastitee no cure.°   *shall / attention*
Crist was a mayde° and shapen° as a man,   *virgin / formed*
140 And many a seint sith° the world bigan,   *since*
Yet lyved they evere in parfit° chastitee.   *perfect*
I nyl nat envye° no virginitee.   *will not envy*
Lat hem° be breed° of pured   *let them / bread*
    whete° seed,   *refined wheat*
And lat us wyves hoten° barly breed.   *be called*
145 And yet with barly breed, Mark telle kan,
Oure Lord refresshed° many a man.[6]   *gave food to*
In swich estaat° as God hath cleped us°   *condition / has called us*
I wol persevere.° I nam nat precius.°   *remain / fastidious*
In wyfhode I wol use myn instrument°   *sexual organ*
150 As frely° as my makere hath it sent.   *freely*
If I be daungerous,° God yeve° me sorwe.   *stand-offish / give*
Myn housbonde shal it have bothe eve and morwe
Whan that hym list com forth and paye his dette.[7]
An housbonde I wol have, I nyl nat lette,°   *will not stop*
155 Which shal° be bothe my dettour° and my   *who shall / debtor*
    thral°   *slave*
And have his tribulacioun° withal°   *tribulation / also*
Upon his flessh whil I am his wyf.
I have the power durynge° al my lyf   *during*
Upon his propre° body, and noght he.   *own*
160 Right thus the apostel[8] tolde it unto me
And bad° oure housbondes for to love us weel.°   *commanded / well*
Al this sentence me liketh every deel."[9]
    Up stirte° the Pardoner and that anon.°   *jumped / immediately*
"Now, Dame," quod he, "by God and by Seint John,
165 Ye been° a noble prechour° in this cas!°   *are / preacher / matter*
I was aboute to wedde a wyf, allas!
What sholde I bye it on my flessh so deere?[10]

---

[1] *swich wise* Such a manner; *folwe hym* Follow him.

[2] *membres ... of generacioun* Sexual organs.

[3] *Glose ... doun* Let whoever wishes to do so offer an interpretation and say both up and down.

[4] *Of engendrure* Of conception. The phrase "office and ease of engendrure" means for a purpose (that is, conceiving children) and for the pleasure of procreation.

[5] *yelde ... dette* Having sex. I.e., both partners owed each other a certain sexual fulfillment, lest sexual frustration drive one of them to adultery. The line is a quotation from 1 Corinthians 7.3.

[6] *And ... man* The reference here is to John 6.9 and the miracle of the loaves and fishes, not to a passage in the Gospel of Mark.

[7] *Whan ... dette* When he wishes to come forth and pay his debt.

[8] *the apostel* I.e., St. Paul, whose insights on marriage the Wife of Bath has been mentioning since she began to speak. In addition to the passage referred to above in note 5, Paul's other major pronouncement on marriage is in Ephesians 5.21–33.

[9] *Al ... deel* All this lesson (of Scripture) pleases me, every part (of it).

[10] *What ... deere* Why should I pay so dearly for it with my flesh.

Yet hadde I levere° wedde no wyf to yeere!"[1]   *rather | this year*

"Abyde,"° quod she, "my tale is nat bigonne!   *wait*

170 Nay, thou shalt drynken° of another tonne°   *drink | cask (of wine)*

Er that I go, shal savoure wors° than ale!   *that shall taste worse*

And whan that I have toold forth my tale

Of tribulacioun that is in mariage,

Of which I am expert in al myn age°—   *throughout my life*

175 This to seyn,° myself have been the whippe°—   *say | whip*

Than maystow chese wheither° thou   *choose whether*

wolt sippe°   *will sip*

Of that tonne that I shal abroche.°   *open*

Bewar of it er thou to ny° approche,°   *too near | approach*

For I shal telle ensamples° mo° than ten.   *examples | more*

180 Whoso that wol nat bewar by othere men,[1]

By hym shul othere men corrected be.

The same wordes writeth Protholomee.°   *Ptolemy*

Rede° it in his *Almageste* and take it there!"[2]   *read*

"Dame, I wolde praye° if youre wyl° it were,"   *ask | will*

185 Seyde this Pardoner, "as ye bigan

Telle forth youre tale. Spareth° for no man,   *spare*

And teche us yonge men of youre praktike!"°   *practice*

"Gladly, sires,° sith it may yow like.°   *sirs | it may please you*

But yet I praye to al this compaignye,

190 If that I speke after my fantasye,°   *fancy*

As taketh it nat agrief° that° I seye,   *take it not wrong | what*

For myn entente is but for to pleye.

"Now sire, now wol I telle forth my tale.

As evere moote° I drynken wyn or ale,   *might*

195 I shal seye sooth° of tho housbondes that I hadde,   *say the truth*

As thre of hem were goode and two were badde.

The thre men were goode and riche and olde.

Unnethe° myghte they the statut° holde   *scarcely | regulation*

In which that they were bounden° unto me.[3]   *bound*

200 Ye woot wel what I meene° of this, pardee.°   *mean | by God*

As help me God, I laughe whan I thynke

How pitously anyght° I made hem swynke!°   *at night | work*

And by my fey,° I tolde of it no stoor.°   *faith | set no store by it*

They had me yeven° hir° gold and hir   *given | their*

tresoor.°   *treasure*

205 Me neded nat do lenger diligence[4]

To wynne hir love or doon hem reverence.°   *honor them*

They loved me so wel, by God above,

That I ne tolde no deyntee of hir love.[5]

A wys° womman wol sette hire evere in   *wise*

oon°   *will always determine*

210 To gete hire° love theras° she hath   *get herself | where*

noon.°   *has none*

But sith I hadde hem° hoolly° in myn hond,   *them | wholly*

And sith they hadde me yeven° al hir lond,°   *given | all their land*

What sholde I taken heede° hem for to plese,°   *bother | please*

But if° it were for my profit and myn ese?°   *unless | pleasure*

215 I sette hem so a werk,° by my fey,°   *to work | faith*

That many a nyght they songen° 'Weilawey!'°   *sang | alas*

The bacon was nat fet° for hem, I trowe,°   *fetched | believe*

That som° men han° in Essex at Dunmowe.[6]   *some | have*

I governed hem so wel after my lawe,

220 That ech° of hem was ful blisful° and fawe°   *each | very happy | eager*

To brynge me gaye thynges° fro the fayre.°   *pretty things | fair*

They were ful glad whan I spak to hem faire,°   *nicely*

For, God it woot, I chidde hem spitously!°   *scolded them spitefully*

"Now herkneth hou° I baar me° proprely,   *how | bore myself*

225 Ye wise wyves that kan understonde.

Thus shul ye speke and beren hem on honde.[7]

For half so boldely kan ther no man

Swere° and lye° as kan a womman.   *swear | lie*

I sey nat this by° wyves that been wyse,   *about*

230 But if° it be whan they hem   *unless*

mysavyse.°   *give themselves bad advice*

A wys wyf, if that she kan hir good,°   *knows what is good for her*

Shal bere hym on hond the cow is wood[8]

And take witnesse of hir owene mayde°   *own maid*

---

[1] *Whoso ... men* The one who will not be warned (by examples offered) by others.

[2] *Rede ... there* The aphorism is not found in the *Almagest*, the great astrological treatise of Claudius Ptolemy (second century CE), but in the preface to one of the translations of his work.

[3] *In ... me* I.e., the three old husbands could barely fulfill their obligation to pay the marriage debt.

[4] *Me ... diligence* I did not need to make any more effort.

[5] *ne tolde ... love* Did not put any value on their love.

[6] *The bacon ... Dunmowe* In the village of Dunmow, it was the custom to award a side of bacon to a married couple if they did not quarrel for a year.

[7] *beren hem on honde* Either to deceive them or to accuse them falsely. The Wife does both to her husbands.

[8] *A wys ... wood* A wise woman can convince her husband that a tale-telling cowbird (a kind of jackdaw) who tells him she has been unfaithful is mad and use her own maid as a witness.

Of hir° assent, but herkneth°   her / listen to
   how I sayde:°   how I spoke
235 "'Sire olde kaynard,° is this thyn array?° dotard / your behavior
Why is my neighebores wyf so gay?°   well dressed
She is honoured over al ther she gooth.°   wherever she goes
I sitte at hoom. I have no thrifty clooth.°   appropriate clothing
What dostow° at my neighebores hous?   are you doing
240 Is she so fair? Artow° so amorous?   are you
What rowne° ye with oure mayde,° benedicite? whisper / maid
Sire olde lecchour,° lat thy japes° be!   sir old lecher / tricks
And if I have a gossib° or a freend,°   confidant / friend
Withouten gilt,° thou chidest° as a feend!° guilt / complain / fiend
245 If that I walke or pleye unto his hous,
Thou comest hoom as dronken as a mous[1]
And prechest° on thy bench, with yvel   preach
   preef!°   bad luck to you
  "'Thou seist° to me it is a greet   you say
   meschief°   great misfortune
To wedde a povre° womman for costage.°   poor / expense
250 And if she be riche and of heigh parage,°   lineage
Thanne seistow° it is a tormentrie°   you say / torment
To suffren° hire pride and hire malencolie.°   endure
And if she be fair, thou verray knave,[2]
Thou seyst that every holour° wol hire have: lecher
255 She may no while in chastitee abyde°   remain
That is assailled upon ech a syde.°   every side
  "'Thou seyst that som folk desiren us for richesse,
Somme for oure shape, somme for oure fairnesse
And som for she kan synge and daunce
260 And som for gentillesse° and som for   nobility
   daliaunce,°   flirtation
Som for hir handes and hir armes smale.°   slender
Thus goth al to the devel,° by thy tale!   devil
Thou seyst men may nat kepe° a castel wal,° not hold / wall
It may so longe assailled been overal!°   everywhere
265 "'And if that she be foul,° thou seist that she   ugly
Coveiteth every man that she may se.°   see
For as a spaynel° she wol on hym lepe,°   spaniel / leap
Til that she fynde som man hire to chepe.°   to buy her
Ne noon so grey goos gooth in the lake

270 As, seistow, wol been withoute make.[3]
And seyst it is an hard thyng for to welde,°   control
A thyng that no man wole his thankes helde.° willingly hold
  "'Thus seistow, lorel,° whan thow goost to bedde, fool
And that no wys man nedeth° for to wedde,   needs
275 Ne° no man that entendeth unto   nor
   hevene.°   intends to go to heaven
With wilde thonder dynt° and   thunder claps
   firy levene°   fiery lightening
Moote° thy welked nekke° be   may / withered neck
   tobroke!°   broken
  "'Thow seyst that droppyng° houses and eek smoke dripping
And chidyng° wyves maken men to flee   nagging
280 Out of hir owene houses. A, benedicitee,
What eyleth° swich an old man for to chide?   ails
  "'Thow seyst that we wyves wol oure vices hide
Til we be fast,° and thanne we wol hem shewe.° secure / show
Wel may that be a proverbe of a shrewe!°   villain
285 "'Thou seist that oxen, asses, hors,° and houndes, horses
They been assayd° at diverse stoundes;° tried / different times
Bacyns,° lavours° er that men hem bye,° basins / bowls / buy them
Spoones and stooles and al swich
   housbondrye,°   household equipment
And so been pottes,° clothes, and array.° pots / ornaments
290 But folk of wyves maken noon assay°   do not try them out
Til they be wedded. Olde dotard° shrewe!   foolish
Thanne seistow we wol oure vices shewe.
  "'Thou seist also that it displeseth me
But if° that thou wolt preyse° my beautee   unless / will praise
295 And but° thou poure° alwey upon my face   unless / gaze
And clepe° me "faire dame!" in every place,   call
And but thou make a feeste° on thilke° day feast / the same
That I was born, and make me fressh and gay,
And but thou do to my norice[4] honour
300 And to my chambrere° withinne my   chambermaid
   bour.°   bedroom
And to my fadres° folk° and his allyes: father's / relatives
Thus seistow, olde barel° ful of lyes!°   barrel / lies
  "'And yet of oure apprentice Janekyn,

---

[1] *dronken as a mous* It is not clear why mice are thought to be drunk, but the expression was common in medieval England.

[2] *thou verray knave* You true villain.

---

[3] *Ne noon ... make* Proverbial: There is no goose in the lake, no matter how grey, who does not have a mate.

[4] *norice* Nurse. Wealthy medieval people were attended to in their childhood by wet nurses, who often became, for a time, surrogate mothers.

For his crispe heer° shynynge° as gold so fyn,°   *curly hair / shining / fine*

305 And for he squiereth° me bothe up and doun,   *escorts*

Yet hastow° caught a fals suspecioun.   *you have*

I wol° hym noght,° though thou were deed tomorwe!   *want / not*

"'But tel me, why hydestow° with sorwe°   *do you hide / sorrow*

The keyes of my cheste° awey fro me?   *chest (safety box)*

310 It is my good° as wel as thyn, pardee!°   *possession / by God*

What, wenestow to make an ydiot of oure dame?[1]

Now by that lord that called is Seint Jame,°   *Saint James*

Thou shalt nat bothe, thogh° thou were wood,°   *though / crazy*

Be maister° of my body and of my good!°   *master / possessions*

315 That oon thou shalt forgo, maugree thyne eyen![2]

What nedeth thee of me to enquere° or spyen?°   *inquire / spy*

I trowe thou woldest loke me in thy chiste![3]

Thou sholdest seye, "Wyf, go wher thee liste.[4]

Taak youre disport!° I wol leve° no talys.°   *enjoyment / believe / tales*

320 I knowe yow for a trewe wyf, Dame Alys!"

We love no man that taketh kepe or charge°   *takes heed or cares*

Wher that we goon. We wol ben at oure large.°   *free*

"'Of alle men, blessed moot° he be,   *may*

The wise astrologien° Daun Protholome°   *astronomer / Master Ptolemy*

325 That seith this proverbe in his *Almageste*,

"Of alle men his wysdom is the hyeste°   *highest*

That rekketh nevere who hath the world in honde."[5]

By this proverbe thou shalt understonde:

Have thou ynogh, what thar thee recche or care[6]

330 How myrily° that othere folkes fare?°   *merrily / behave*

For certeyn, olde dotard,° by youre leve,°   *fool / leave*

Ye shul have queynte[7] right ynogh° at eve!°   *enough / at night*

He is to greet° a nygard° that wolde werne°   *too great / skinflint / refuse*

A man to lighte his candle at his lanterne.

335 He shal have never the lasse° light, pardee!   *less*

Have thou ynogh, thee thar nat pleyne thee.[8]

"'Thou seyst also that if we make us gay

With clothyng and with precious array,°   *expensive adornment*

That it is peril of° oure chastitee.   *a danger to*

340 And yet with sorwe thou most° enforce thee°   *must / support yourself*

And seye thise wordes in the apostles name:[9]

"In habit° maad° with chastitee and shame   *clothing / made*

Ye wommen shul apparaille yow,"° quod he   *dress yourselves*

"And noght° in tressed heer° and gay perree,°   *not / braided hair / jewels*

345 As perles,° ne with gold ne clothes riche."   *pearls*

After thy text° ne after thy rubriche°   *quotation / rubric*

I wol nat wirche° as muchel as a gnat![10]   *work*

"'Thou seydest this, that I was lyk° a cat.   *like*

For whoso wolde senge° a cattes skyn,   *singe*

350 Thanne wolde the cat wel dwellen in his in.°   *lodgings*

And if the cattes skyn be slyk° and gay,   *sleek*

She wol nat dwelle in house half a day,

But forth she wole° er any day be dawed°   *will go / dawned*

To shewe hir skyn and goon a caterwawed.[11]

355 This is to seye, if I be gay, sire shrewe,°   *sir villain*

I wol renne out my borel° for to shewe!   *cheap clothing*

"'Sire olde fool, what eyleth° thee to spyen?°   *ails / spy*

---

[1] *What ... dame*   What, do you expect to make an idiot of our lady? I.e., the Wife herself.

[2] *That ... eyen*   You must give up one of them, despite your eyes! (I.e., despite anything you can do.)

[3] *I trowe ... chiste*   I believe you would lock me in your chest. Medieval merchants used large locked chests to lock up their coins and their valuables.

[4] *Thou ... liste*   You should say, "Wife, go wherever you want."

[5] *That ... honde*   Who does not care who possesses the world.

[6] *Have ... care*   If you have enough, why do you need to bother yourself or care.

[7] *queynte*   Literally meaning elegant, clever, or pleasing thing, queynte is also a medieval euphemism for the female sexual organs.

[8] *Have ... thee*   If you have enough, you do not need to complain for yourself.

[9] *the apostles name*   St. Paul. The following quotation is from 1 Timothy 2.9.

[10] *After thy ... gnat*   I will not follow (work after) your quotation or your text in the smallest way, or, any more than a gnat would. In medieval service books and books of devotion, rubrics (whose name comes from the red ink in which they were written) were directions about how to use the texts to which they referred either in communal worship or private devotion.

[11] *caterwawed*   Caterwauling, the loud noise cats make while they are mating.

Thogh thou preye Argus[1] with hise hundred eyen

To be my wardecors,° as he kan° best.   *bodyguard / knows how*

360 In feith, he shal nat kepe me but me lest!°   *unless I want to be kept*

Yet koude I make his berd,° so moot I thee![2]   *fool him*

      "'Thou seydest eek that ther been thynges thre,°   *three things*

The whiche thynges troublen° al this erthe,   *trouble*

And that no wight may endure the ferthe.°   *fourth*

365 O leeve° sire shrewe! Jhesu° shorte° thy lyf!   *dear / Jesus / shorten*

Yet prechestow° and seyst an hateful wyf   *still you preach*

Yrekned is for° oon of thise   *is counted as*

      meschances.°   *misfortunes*

Been ther none othere resemblances

That ye may likne° youre parables to,   *liken*

370 But if a sely° wyf be oon of tho?°   *innocent / those*

      "'Thou liknest° wommenes love to helle,   *liken*

To bareyne° lond° ther° water may nat   *barren / land / where*

      dwelle.

Thou liknest it also to wilde fyr:

The moore° it brenneth,° the moore it hath   *more / burns*

      desir°   *desires*

375 To consumen° everythyng that brent wole be.   *consume*

Thou seyst, right as wormes° shendeth° a tree,   *grubs / harm*

Right so a wyf destroyeth hire housbond;

This knowe they that been to wyves bonde.'°   *bound*

      "Lordynges, right thus as ye have understonde

380 Baar I stifly myne olde housbondes on honde,

That thus they seyden in hir dronkenesse![3]

And al was fals, but that I took witnesse

On Janekyn and on my nece° also.   *niece*

O Lord, the pyne° I dide hem° and the wo,   *pain / to them*

385 Ful giltlees,° by Goddes sweete pyne!°   *guiltless / pain*

For as an hors I koude byte and whyne.°   *whinny*

I koude pleyne° thogh° I were in the   *complain / though*

      gilt,°   *guilty*

Or elles oftentyme hadde I been spilt.°   *destroyed*

Whoso comth° first to mille,° first   *whoever comes / mill*

      grynt.°   *grinds*

390 I pleyned first, so was oure werre° ystynt.°   *war / concluded*

They were ful glad to excuse hem° blyve°   *them / quickly*

Of thyng of which they nevere agilte hir lyve.[4]

Of wenches° wolde I beren hym on honde,°   *girls / accuse him*

Whan that for syk° unnethes° myghte he   *sickness / scarcely*

      stonde.

395 "Yet tikled° it his herte,° for that° he   *tickled / heart / because*

Wende° that I hadde of hym° so greet   *thought / for him*

      chiertee.°   *love*

I swoor° that al my walkynge° out by   *swore / walking*

      nyghte°   *night*

Was for t'espye° wenches that he dighte.°   *spy / had sex with*

Under that colour° hadde I many a myrthe,°   *pretense / mirth*

400 For al swich thyng was yeven° us in oure byrthe.°   *given / birth*

Deceite, wepyng, spynnyng° God hath yeve°   *spinning / given*

To wommen kyndely° whil that they may lyve.   *naturally*

And thus of o° thyng I avaunte° me: *one / boast*

Atte° ende, I hadde the bettre° in ech   *at the / better*

      degree°   *instance*

405 By sleighte,° or force, or by   *deceit*

      som maner thyng,°   *manner of thing*

As by continueel murmure° or   *continual murmur*

      grucchyng,°   *complaining*

Namely° abedde° hadden they   *especially / in bed*

      meschaunce;°   *misfortune*

Ther wolde I chide° and do hem no plesaunce.°   *nag / pleasure*

I wolde no lenger° in the bed abyde°   *longer / remain*

410 If that I felte his arm over my syde°   *side*

Til he had maad his raunsoun° unto me.   *paid his ransom*

Thanne wolde I suffre hym do his nycetee.°   *foolishness*

And therfore every man this tale I telle:

Wynne° whoso may, for al is for to selle.°   *win / for sale*

415 Wirh empty hand men may none° haukes° lure;   *no / hawks*

For wynnyng° wolde I al his lust endure   *profit*

And make me a feyned° appetit.   *pretended*

And yet in bacon[5] hadde I nevere delit.°   *delight*

That made me that evere I wolde hem chide,

420 For thogh the Pope hadde seten hem biside,°   *sat beside them*

I wolde nat spare hem at hir owene bord.°   *table*

For by my trouthe, I quitte hem,° word for word,   *requited them*

As° helpe me verray° God omnipotent!   *so / true*

Though I right now sholde make my testament,

425 I ne owe hem nat a word that it nys quit.°   *was not paid back*

---

[1] *Argus* Hundred-eyed creature of Greek mythology hired by Hera to guard her husband Zeus's mistress Io. He was killed by Hermes.

[2] *so moot I thee* I.e., indeed, or by my word.

[3] *Baar ... dronkenesse* I bore witness firmly to my old husbands that they said this when they were drunk.

[4] *Of ... lyve* Of a thing that they had never been guilty of in their lives.

[5] *bacon* Old meat preserved by salting; in other words, old men.

I broghte° it so aboute, by my wit,   *brought*

That they moste yeve it up° as for the beste   *had to give it up*

Or elles hadde we nevere been in reste.°   *at rest*

For thogh° he looked as a wood leoun,°   *although / crazy lion*

430   Yet sholde he faille of his conclusioun.°   *intent*

     "Thanne wolde I seye, 'Goodlief, taak keepe

How mekely looketh Wilkyn oure sheepe![1]

Com neer, my spouse. Lat me ba° thy cheke.   *kiss*

Ye sholde been al pacient and meke°   *meek*

435   And han° a sweete, spiced conscience,°   *have / delicate conscience*

Sith ye so preche° of Jobes pacience.°[2]   *preach / Job's patience*

Suffreth alwey,° syn ye so wel kan preche,   *endure always*

And but° ye do, certein we shal yow teche°   *unless / teach you*

That it is fair to have a wyf in pees.°   *peace*

440   Oon of us two moste bowen,° doutelees,°   *must bow / doubtless*

And sith a man is moore resonable

Than womman is, ye moste been suffrable.°   *you must be patient*

What eyleth yow,° to grucche° thus and   *ails you / complain*

    grone?°   *groan*

Is it for ye wolde have my queynte°   *female sexual organs*

    allone?°   *alone*

445   Wy,° taak it al! Lo, have it everydeel!°   *why / every bit*

Peter, I shrewe yow but ye love it weel![3]

For if I wolde selle my bele chose,[4]

I koude walke as fressh as is a rose.[5]

But I wol kepe it for youre owene tooth.°   *own taste (pleasure)*

450   Ye be to blame, by God, I sey yow sooth!'°   *tell you the truth*

     "Swiche manere wordes hadde we on honde.[6]

Now wol I speken of my fourthe housbonde.

     "My fourthe housbonde was a revelour°—   *party-goer*

This is to seyn, he hadde a paramour°—   *lover*

455   And I was yong and ful of ragerye,°   *high spirits*

Stibourne° and strong and joly° as a   *stubborn / pretty*

    pye.°   *magpie*

Wel koude I daunce to an harpe smale°   *small harp*

And synge,° ywis,° as any nyghtyngale   *sing / indeed*

Whan I had dronke a draughte of sweete wyn.°   *wine*

460   Metellius,[7] the foule cherl, the swyn,°   *swine*

That with a staf° birafte° his wyf hir lyf   *club / stole from*

For° she drank wyn, thogh I hadde been his wyf,   *because*

He sholde nat han daunted me fro drynke![8]

And after wyn, on Venus[9] moste° I thynke.   *must*

465   For also siker° as cold engendreth hayl,°   *as sure / causes hail*

A likerous° mouth moste han° a likerous   *lecherous / must have*

    tayl.°   *tail*

In wommen vinolent is no defence.[10]

This knowen lecchours° by experience.   *lechers*

     "But, Lord Crist, whan that

    it remembreth me°   *when I remember*

470   Upon my yowthe° and on my jolitee,°   *youth / gaiety*

It tikleth° me aboute myn herte roote.°   *tickles / heart's root*

Unto this day it dooth myn herte boote°   *does my heart good*

That I have had my world as in my tyme.°   *time*

But age, allas, that al wole envenyme,°   *will poison all*

475   Hath me biraft° my beautee and my   *stolen from me*

    pith.°   *strength*

Lat go! Farewel! The devel go therwith!°   *with it*

The flour is goon,° ther is namoore° to telle;   *gone / no more*

The bren° as I best kan now moste° I selle.   *bran / must*

But yet to be right myrie° wol I fonde.°   *merry / try*

480   Now wol I tellen of my fourthe housbonde.

     "I seye I hadde in herte° greet despit°   *heart / great anger*

That he of any oother° had delit.°   *any other (woman) / delight*

But he was quit,° by God and by Seint Joce![11]   *punished*

I made hym of the same wode° a croce.°   *wood / cross*

485   Nat of my body in no foul manere,°   *manner*

But certein I made folk swich cheere,°   *hospitality*

That in his owene grece° I made hym frye°   *own grease / fry*

For angre and for verray jalousie.°   *true jealousy*

---

[1] *Thanne ... sheepe* Then would I say, "Sweetheart, note well, how meekly Willie, our sheep (i.e., her husband) looks."

[2] *Jobes pacience* God allowed Satan to attempt to shake Job's faith through a series of terrible misfortunes. See the Biblical Book of Job.

[3] *Peter ... weel* By St. Peter!, I curse you unless you love it well, i.e., do you ever love it well.

[4] *bele chose* French: beautiful thing, i.e., sexual organs.

[5] *I ... rose* In other words, if I sold myself sexually, I could dress myself beautifully with the proceeds.

[6] *Swiche ... honde* We were occupied by this kind of conversation.

[7] *Metellius* See *Facta et dicta memorabilia* (*Memorable Facts and Deeds*), a collection of short stories for orators, written by Valerius Maximus (first century CE).

[8] *He ... drynke* He should not have prevented me from drink.

[9] *Venus* Goddess of love.

[10] *In ... defence* There is no defense in drunken women, i.e., they are defenseless.

[11] *Seint Joce* St. Judoc or St. Joyce was a seventh-century prince in Brittany who gave up his succession to the throne to become a priest. He was also famous for going on a pilgrimage to Rome.

By God, in erthe I was his purgatorie,°   *purgatory*
490   For which I hope his soule be in glorie.
For God it woot,° he sat ful ofte and song°   *knows it / sang*
Whan that his shoo°   *shoe*
      ful bitterly hym wrong.°   *hurt him very bitterly*
Ther was no wight save God and he that wiste°   *who knew*
In many wise° how soore° I hym twiste.°   *ways / sorely / tormented*
495   He deyde° whan I cam fro°   *died / came from (a pilgrimage to)*
      Jerusalem
And lith ygrave° under the roode beem,[1]   *lies buried*
Al° is his tombe° noght so curyus°   *although / tomb / elaborate*
As was the sepulcre of hym Daryus,°   *Darius*
Which that Appeles wroghte° subtilly.°[2]   *made / subtly*
500   It nys° but wast to burye hym preciously.°   *is not / expensively*
Lat hym° fare wel! God yeve° his soule reste.   *may he / give*
He is now in his grave and in his cheste.°   *coffin*
     "Now of my fifthe housbonde wol I telle.
God lete his soule nevere come in Helle!
505   And yet was he to me the mooste shrewe.
That feele I on my ribbes° al by rewe,°   *ribs / in a row*
And evere shal unto myn endyng day.
But in oure bed he was ful fressh and gay.
And therwithal so wel koude he me glose,°   *flatter*
510   Whan that he wolde han my bele chose,
That thogh he hadde me bet° on every bon,°   *beaten / bone*
He koude wynne agayn my love anon.
I trowe° I loved hym best for that he   *believe*
Was of his love daungerous° to me.   *standoffish*
515   We wommen han, if that I shal nat lye,
In this matere a queynte fantasye:°   *odd whim*
Wayte,° what° thyng we may nat lightly   *know (that) / whatever*
      have,
Therafter° wol we crie al day and crave!   *after it*
Forbede° us thyng,° and that desiren we;   *forbid / something*
520   Preesse on us faste, and thanne wol we fle.°   *flee*
With daunger oute we al oure chaffare;[3]

Greet prees° at market maketh   *crowd*
      deere ware,°   *expensive goods*
And to greet cheepe° is holde at   *too much merchandise*
      litel prys.°   *little price*
This knoweth every womman that is wys.
525   My fifthe housbonde, God his soule blesse,
Which that I took for love and no richesse,
He somtyme° was a clerk° of Oxenford°   *once / student / Oxford*
And hadde left scole° and wente at hom°   *school / home*
      to bord°   *rent a room*
With my gossib,° dwellynge in oure toun.   *confidant*
530   God have hir soule! Hir name was Alisoun.
She knew myn herte and eek my privetee°   *secrets*
Bet° than oure parisshe preest, as   *better*
      moot I thee!°   *may I thrive*
To hire biwreyed° I my conseil° al.   *revealed / counsel*
For hadde myn housbonde pissed on a wal°   *wall*
535   Or doon a thyng that sholde han cost his lyf,
To hire and to another worthy wyf
And to my nece,° which that I loved weel,   *niece*
I wolde han toold his conseil everydeel.°   *every bit*
And so I dide ful often, God it woot!°   *God knows it*
540   That made his face ful often reed and hoot°   *hot*
For verray° shame, and blamed hymself, for he   *true*
Had toold to me so greet a pryvetee.
     "And so bifel° that ones° in a Lente—[4]   *it happened / once*
So oftentymes I to my gossyb° wente,   *confidant*
545   For evere yet I loved to be gay
And for to walke in March, Averill, and May
Fro hous to hous to heere sondry talys°—   *various tales*
That Jankyn clerk and my gossyb Dame Alys
And I myself into the feeldes° wente.   *fields*
550   Myn housbonde was at Londoun al the Lente;
I hadde the bettre leyser° for to pleye   *better opportunity*
And for to se° and eek for to be seye°   *see / seen*
Of lusty folk. What wiste I wher my grace
Was shapen for to be or in what place?[5]
555   Therfore I made my visitaciouns°   *visits*

---

[1] *And ... beem* Her fourth husband was buried inside the local parish church under the cross-beam of the cross near the high altar, a place reserved for only the most influential members of a parish.

[2] *As was ... subtilly* The legendary tomb of Darius the Mede, fashioned by the Jewish sculptor Appeles, was famous for its beauty.

[3] *With ... chaffare* Either (where we are greeted) with scorn, we (put) out all our goods (i.e., are anxious to sell), or we (put) out all our goods with (a show of) scorn (i.e., as if we did not care if anyone buys them).

---

[4] *Lente* Period in the late winter and early spring when Christians prepare for Easter by fasting and doing penance.

[5] *What wiste ... place* How could I know where or in what place my good luck was destined to be? or possibly (to avoid the redundancy) how could I know whether I was destined to have good luck, or where?

To vigilies and to processiouns,[1]
To prechyng° eek and to thise pilgrimages,   *preaching*
To pleyes° of myracles and to mariages,   *plays*
And wered upon° my gaye scarlet gytes.°   *wore / robes*
560 Thise wormes, ne thise motthes,° ne thise mytes°   *moths / mites*
Upon my peril frete° hem never a deel,°   *eat / never a bit*
And wostow° why? For they were used weel.   *do you know*
    "Now wol I tellen forth what happed me.°   *happened to me*
I seye that in the feeldes walked we
565 Til trewely we hadde swich daliance,°   *flirtation*
This clerk and I, that of my purveiance°   *foresight*
I spak to hym and seyde° hym how that he,   *said to*
If I were wydwe,° sholde wedde me.   *widowed*
For certeinly I sey for no bobance,°   *pride*
570 Yet was I nevere withouten purveiance
Of mariage n'of° othere thynges eek.   *nor of*
I holde a mouses herte° nat worth a leek   *mouse's heart*
That hath but oon hole forto sterte° to,   *escape*
And if that faille,° thanne is al ydo.°[2]   *should fail / completely done for*
575   "I bar hym on honde° he hadde enchanted me;   *accused him*
My dame° taughte me that soutiltee.°   *mother / trick*
And eek I seyde I mette° of hym al nyght: *dreamed*
He wolde han slayn° me as I lay upright,°   *killed / on my back*
And al my bed was ful of verray blood.
580 But yet I hope that he shal do me good,
For blood bitokeneth° gold, as me was taught.[3]   *signifies*
And al was fals! I dremed of it right naught.°   *not at all*
But I folwed ay° my dammes
    loore,°   *followed ever / mother's teaching*
As wel of this as othere thynges° moore.°   *matters / more*
585   "But now sire, lat me se° what I shal seyn.   *see*
Aha! By God, I have my tale ageyn!°   *again*
    "Whan that my fourthe housbonde was on beere,°[4]   *bier*
I weepe algate° and made sory cheere,°   *continuously / face*

As wyves mooten,° for it is usage,°   *must / custom*
590 And with my coverchief° covered my visage.°   *kerchief / face*
But for that° I was purveyed of°   *because / provided with*
    a make,°   *mate*
I wepte but smal,° and that I undertake.°   *little / attest*
    "To chirche° was myn housbonde born   *church*
    amorwe,°   *in the morning*
With neighebores that for hym maden sorwe,°   *sorrow*
595 And Jankyn oure clerk was oon of tho.°   *one of those*
As help me God, whan that I saugh° hym go   *saw*
After the beere, me thoughte he hadde a paire
Of legges and of feet so clene° and faire,°   *neat / attractive*
That al myn herte I yaf° unto his hoold.°   *gave / possession*
600 He was, I trowe,° a twenty wynter oold,   *believe*
And I was fourty, if I shal seye sooth.°   *say the truth*
And yet I hadde alwey a coltes° tooth.   *colt's*
Gat-tothed I was, and that bicam me weel;[5]
I hadde the prente° of Seint Venus seel.[6]   *print*
605 As help me God, I was a lusty oon,
And faire and riche and yong and wel bigon.°   *established*
And trewely, as myne housbondes tolde me,
I hadde the beste 'quonyam'° myghte be.   *sexual organ*
For certes, I am al venerien[7]
610 In feelynge,° and myn herte is marcien.[8]   *feeling*
Venus me yaf° my lust, my likerousnesse,°   *gave / lecherousness*
And Mars yaf me my sturdy hardynesse.°   *courage*
Myn ascendent was Taur, and Mars therinne.[9]
Allas! Allas! That evere love was synne!°   *sin*
615 I folwed° ay° myn inclinacioun°   *followed / ever / inclination*
By vertu° of my constellacioun,°   *influence / constellation*
That made me I koude noght withdrawe°   *withhold*

---

[1] *To ... processiouns* To vigils and to processions. Vigils were church services held on the evening before the feast day of a saint. Ceremonial processions formed part of the service on the day itself.

[2] *I holde ... ydo* The mouse who has only one hole to which it can escape appears in various proverbs as well as in the *Romance of the Rose* (line 13554), whose character La Vieille, the old woman who knows all about love, is one of the models for the Wife of Bath. Not worth a leek means worth nothing at all.

[3] *blood ... taught* Blood could serve as a token or symbol of gold, which was often described as red.

[4] *beere* Bier, i.e., in his coffin.

---

[5] *Gat-tothed ... weel* I was gap-toothed, and that suited me well. Women with gaps between their teeth were said to have lustful and licentious natures.

[6] *I hadde ... seel* I had the imprint of Venus's seal; in other words, Venus has given the Wife of Bath a birthmark, another supposed indication of a lascivious nature.

[7] *venerien* In astrology, one who is influenced by the planet Venus—i.e., prone to love.

[8] *marcien* In astrology, one who is influenced by the planet Mars—i.e., war-like.

[9] *Myn ... therinne* At the moment when the Wife was born the constellation of stars known as Taurus (the Bull) was coming over the horizon (ascendant) along with the planet Mars. It was believed that if a woman is born with Venus and Mars ascending together she will be unchaste.

My chambre° of Venus from a good felawe.°   *organ / fellow*
Yet have I Martes° mark[1] upon my face—   *Mars's*
620 And also in another privee place.
For God so wys° be my savacioun,°   *wise / salvation*
I ne loved nevere° by no discrecioun   *never loved*
But evere folwed myn appetit,°   *appetite*
Al° were he short or long° or blak° or   *whether / tall / dark*
    whit.°   *fair*
625 I took no kepe,° so that he liked° me,   *did not care / pleased*
How poore he was ne eek of what degree.
    "What sholde I seye, but at the monthes ende,
This joly° clerk Jankyn that was so hende°   *pretty / handy*
Hath wedded me with greet solempnytee.°   *ceremony*
630 And to hym yaf° I al the lond and fee°   *gave / property*
That evere was me yeven° therbifoore.°   *given / before this*
But afterward repented me ful soore!°   *I regretted it sorely*
He nolde suffre nothyng of my list.[2]
By God, he smoot° me ones° on the lyst,°   *hit / once / ear*
635 For that° I rente° out of his book a leef,°   *because / tore / page*
That of the strook° myn ere° wax°   *blow / ear / grew*
    al deef.°   *completely deaf*
Stibourne° I was as is a leonesse°   *stubborn / lioness*
And of my tonge° a verray°   *tongue / true*
    jangleresse.°   *ceaseless talker*
And walke I wolde as I had doon biforn°   *before*
640 From hous to hous, although he had it sworn.°   *forbidden*
For which he often tymes wolde preche°   *preach*
And me of olde Romayn geestes[3] teche°   *teach*
How he Symplicius Gallus lefte his wyf
And hire forsook for terme° of al his lyf,   *the rest*
645 Noght but for open heveded,[4] he hir say,
Lookynge out at his dore° upon a day.   *door*
    "Another Romayn tolde he me by name,
That, for° his wyf was at a someres game°   *because / entertainment*
Withouten his wityng,° he forsook hire eke.   *knowledge*
650 And thanne wolde he upon his Bible seke°   *seek*
That ilke° proverbe of Ecclesiaste[5]   *same*

Where he comandeth and forbedeth faste°   *firmly*
Man shal nat suffre° his wyf go roule° aboute.   *allow / wander*
Thanne wolde he seye right thus, withouten doute:
655 "'Whoso that buyldeth his hous al of salwes[6]
And priketh° his blynde hors° over the   *spurs / blind horse*
    falwes°   *fields*
And suffreth his wyf to go seken halwes°   *shrines*
Is worthy to been° hanged on the galwes.'°[7]   *be / gallows*
But al for noght! I sette noght an hawe°   *hawthorn berry*
660 Of his proverbes n'of° his olde lawe,   *nor of*
Ne I wolde nat of hym° corrected be.   *by him*
I hate hym that my vices telleth me°   *tells me about*
And so doo mo,° God woot,° of us than I.   *do more / knows*
This made hym with me wood° al outrely:°   *crazy / entirely*
665 I nolde noght° forbere° hym in no cas.°   *would not / endure / case*
    "Now wol I seye° yow° sooth,° by   *tell / you / the truth*
    Seint Thomas,[8]
Why that I rente out of his book a leef,
For which he smoot me so that I was deef.
    "He hadde a book that gladly, nyght and day,
670 For his desport° he wolde rede° alway.   *fun / read*
He cleped° it *Valerie and Theofraste*,[9]   *called*
At which book he lough° alwey ful faste.°   *laughed / very much*
And eek ther was somtyme° a clerk° at Rome,   *once / theologian*
A cardinal that highte° Seint Jerome,   *was named*
675 That made a book, *Agayn° Jovinian*,[10]   *against*

---

[6] *Whoso ... salwes* Whoever builds his house of all willow branches.

[7] *Whoso ... galwes* Proverb.

[8] *Seint Thomas* There are three possible candidates for this St. Thomas: Thomas the apostle, mentioned in the Gospels; St. Thomas Aquinas, the thirteenth-century theologian (though his second name was more often used than not); and St. Thomas Becket, whose shrine the Canterbury pilgrims are journeying to visit. Thomas the apostle was often referred to as "Thomas of India." Becket is the likely reference.

[9] *Valerie and Theofraste* The Wife of Bath is actually referring to two separate works, often bound together into one volume in the Middle Ages—the *Dissuasio Valerii ad Rufinum* by the English scholar and courtier Walter Map (c. 1140–c. 1208) and the *Golden Book of Marriages* by Theophrastus, a supposed disciple of Aristotle. Both books were full of stories attacking women and discouraging men from marrying.

[10] *Seint Jerome* Late fourth and early fifth centuries, theologian who wrote many influential works, including a translation of the Bible into Latin; *Agayn Jovinian Against Jovinian*, which extolls virginity, is one of Chaucer's major sources for the "Wife of Bath's Prologue."

---

[1] *Martes mark* Red birthmark.

[2] *He ... list* He would not allow anything I desired.

[3] *Romayn geestes* Roman stories. Like the reference to Metellius above in line 460, the following are old misogynistic or anti-matrimonial stories dating back to ancient Rome.

[4] *Noght ... heveded* Just because he saw her bare-headed.

[5] *That ... Ecclesiaste* See Ecclesiasticus 25.34.

In which book eek ther was Tertulan,[1]
Crisippus,[2] Trotula,[3] and Helowys[4]
That was abbesse nat fer° fro Parys,   *not far*
And eek the *Parables of Salomon,*[5]
680 Ovides° *Art,*[6] and bookes many on.°   *Ovid's / many (other) books*
And alle thise were bounden in o° volume.   *one*
And every nyght and day was his custume
Whan he hadde leyser° and vacacioun°   *leisure / opportunity*
From oother worldly occupacioun
685 To reden on this *Book of Wikked Wyves.*[7]
He knew of hem mo legendes and lyves°   *biographies*
Than been° of goode wyves in the Bible.   *there are*
For, trusteth wel, it is an inpossible°   *impossibility*
That any clerk wol speke good of wyves
690 But if° it be of hooly seintes lyves,   *unless*
Ne of noon other womman never the mo.
Who peynted the leoun,[8] tel me who?
By God, if wommen hadde writen stories
As clerkes han° withinne hire° oratories,°   *have / their / chapels*
695 They wolde han writen of men moore wikkednesse
Than al the mark of Adam° may redresse.   *male sex (i.e., men)*
The children of Mercurie and Venus[9]

Been in hir wirkyng ful contrarius.[10]
Mercurie loveth wysdam° and science,°   *wisdom / knowledge*
700 And Venus loveth ryot° and dispence.°*parties / squandering money*
And for hire diverse disposicioun,°   *natures*
Ech falleth in otheres exaltacioun,°   *exaltation*
And thus, God woot, Mercurie is desolat
In Pisces, wher Venus is exaltat,°   *exalted*
705 And Venus falleth ther° Mercurie is reysed.   *where*
Therfore no womman of no clerk is preysed.
The clerk, whan he is oold and may noght° do   *cannot*
Of Venus werkes[11] worth his olde sho,°   *shoe*
Thanne sit he doun and writ in his dotage[12]
710 That wommen kan nat kepe hir mariage.
  "But now to purpos° why I tolde thee   *the reason*
That I was beten° for a book, pardee.°   *beaten / by God*
Upon a nyght Jankyn, that was oure sire,°   *master*
Redde on his book as he sat by the fire
715 Of Eva° first, that for hir wikkednesse   *Eve*
Was al mankynde broght to wrecchednesse,
For which Crist hymself was slayn,
That boghte° us with his herte blood agayn.   *who bought*
Lo, heere,° expres° of womman may ye fynde *here / specifically*
720 That womman was the los° of al mankynde.   *destruction*
  "Tho° redde he me how Sampson[13] loste hise   *then*
      heres:°   *hairs*
Slepynge, his lemman° kitte° it with hir   *lover / cut*
      sheres,°   *scissors*
Thurgh° which tresoun° loste he   *through / betrayal*
      bothe hise eyen.
  "Tho redde he me, if that I shal nat lyen,°   *lie*
725 Of Hercules and of his Dianyre,[14]
That caused hym to sette hymself afyre.°   *on fire*
Nothyng° forgat he the sorwe and wo   *not at all*

---

[1] *Tertulan* Early third-century theologian who wrote several treatises about the value of virginity.

[2] *Crisippus* Mentioned in Jerome's treatise, referred to in line 675, but none of his works survive.

[3] *Trotula* Female doctor who taught medicine at the University of Salerno in the eleventh century and wrote a treatise about gynecology.

[4] *Helowys* Tried to persuade her lover Abelard not to marry her, giving typical anti-matrimonial reasons. She eventually became the abbess of the Paraclete, a convent of nuns near Paris.

[5] *Parables of Salomon* Biblical Book of Proverbs.

[6] *Ovides Art* Ovid's *Art of Love* concludes with a long argument about why it is prudent to avoid love.

[7] *Book of Wikked Wyves* Title of the whole compendium volume mentioned above.

[8] *Who ... leoun* In medieval versions of the fable of Aesop, a man and a lion were having a dispute about who was the stronger. For proof, the man showed the lion a picture of a man killing a lion, and the lion then asked the man who painted the lion—implying the painting is biased. Then the lion ate the man.

[9] *The children ... Venus* I.e., scholars and lovers.

[10] *Been ... contrarius* In addition to influencing the body's humors (Cf. *General Prologue,* lines 413 ff.), the planets were thought to govern various parts of the body and various trades. Mercury was the planet of scholars and merchants, who, in their ways of doing things, are completely at odds with lovers.

[11] *Venus werkes* I.e., sex.

[12] *Thanne ... dotage* Then he sits down and writes in his old age.

[13] *Tho ... Sampson* See Judges 16.15–22.

[14] *Hercules ... Dianyre* Deianira was the wife of Hercules and inadvertently caused his death by giving him a shirt that she thought would keep him faithful. It was in fact poisoned and he had himself burned alive to escape the pain.

That Socrates hadde with hise wyves two,
How Xantippa[1] caste° pisse° upon his heed.°   *threw / urine / head*
730 This sely° man sat stille° as he were   *innocent / quietly*
            deed.°   *dead*
He wiped his heed. Namoore dorste° he seyn   *dared*
But, 'Er° that thonder stynte,° comth a   *before / stops*
            reyn.'°   *rain*
      "Of Phasipha, that was the queene of Crete,
For shrewednesse° hym thoughte the tale   *nastines*
            swete.°   *sweet*
735 Fy! Spek namoore! It is a grisly thyng,
Of hire horrible lust and hir likyng![2]
      "Of Clitermystra,[3] for hire lecherye,
That falsly made hire housbonde for to dye,°   *die*
He redde it with ful good devocioun.
740 "He tolde me eek for what occasioun
Amphiorax at Thebes loste his lyf:[4]
Myn housbonde hadde a legende° of his wyf,   *story*
Eriphilem, that for an ouche° of gold   *brooch*
Hath prively° unto the Grekes told   *secretly*
745 Wher that hir housbonde hidde hym in a place,
For which he hadde at Thebes sory° grace.   *sorry*
      "Of Lyvia tolde he me and of Lucye.[5]
They bothe made° hir° housbondes for to dye—   *caused / their*
That oon for love, that oother was for hate.
750 Lyvia hir housbonde upon an even° late   *evening*
Empoysoned° hath, for that she was his fo;°   *poisoned / foe*
Lucia likerous° loved hire housbonde so,   *lustfully*

That, for he sholde alwey upon hire thynke,
She yaf° hym swich a manere° love drynke°   *gave / type of / potion*
755 That he was deed° er it were by the morwe.°   *dead / morning*
And thus algates° housbondes han sorwe.°   *always / have sorrow*
      "Thanne tolde he me how that oon Latumyus[6]
Compleyned unto his felawe° Arrius   *friend*
That in his gardyn growed swich a tree
760 On which he seyde how that hise wyves thre
Hanged hemself° for herte° despitus.°   *themselves / heart / cruel*
'O leeve° brother,' quod this Arrius,   *dear*
'Yif° me a plante° of thilke° blissed tree,   *give / seedling / that*
And in my gardyn planted it shal bee.'
765   "Of latter date of wyves hath he red,
That somme han slayn hir housbondes in hir bed
And lete hir lecchour dighte hire al the nyght[7]
Whan that the corps lay in the floor upright,
And somme han dryve° nayles° in hir brayn[8]   *driven / nails*
770 Whil that they slepte, and thus they han hem slayn;
Somme han hem yeve poysoun in hire drynke.[9]
He spak moore harm than herte may bithynke.°   *imagine*
And therwithal° he knew of mo proverbes   *with all this*
Than in this world ther growen gras or herbes.
775 'Bet° is,' quod he, 'thyn habitacioun°   *better / dwelling place*
Be with a leoun or a foul dragoun
Than with a womman usynge° for to chyde.   *accustomed*
Bet is,' quod he, 'hye° in the roof abyde   *high*
Than with an angry wyf doun in the hous,
780 They been° so wikked and contrarious;   *are*
They haten that hir housbondes loveth ay.'[10]
He seyde, 'A womman cast° hir shame away   *throws*
Whan she cast of° hir smok.° And forthermo,   *off / undergarment*
A fair womman, but° she be chaast° also,   *unless / chaste*
785 Is lyk a gold ryng in a sowes° nose.'   *pig's*
Who wolde leeve or who wolde suppose°   *believe*
The wo that in myn herte was and pyne?°   *pain*
      "And whan I saugh he wolde nevere fyne°   *finish*
To reden on this cursed book al nyght,

---

[1] *Xantippa* I.e., Xanthippe (late fifth c. BCE) famously shrewish wife of the philosopher Socrates (469–399 BCE).

[2] *Phasipha ... likyng* In Greek mythology, Queen Pasiphae of Crete had sex with a bull and gave birth to the monster Minotaur; *likyng* Desire.

[3] *Clitermystra* I.e., Clytemnestra, who with her lover Aegisthus, murdered her husband Agamemnon when he returned from the Trojan war.

[4] *Amphiorax ... lyf* Amphiaraus hid so he would not have to fight in war, but his hiding place was betrayed by his wife Eriphyle, and he was killed in battle.

[5] *Of ... Lucye* Livia was either Augustus's wife, who poisoned several prominent Romans (including her own husband) for political gain, or Livilla, Livia's granddaughter, who poisoned her husband at the instigation of her lover Sejanus. Lucilla poisoned her husband, the Roman philosopher Lucretius (c. 99–c.55 BCE), author of *On the Nature of Things*, with a love-potion intended to increase his desire for her.

[6] *Thanne ... Latumyus* The incident related below is another misogynistic story from ancient Rome, for which Chaucer's source is probably Walter Map's *Dissuasio Valerii*.

[7] *And ... nyght* And let her lover have sex with her all night.

[8] *And ... brayn* See Judges 4.17–22.

[9] *Somme ... drynke* Some have given them poison in their drink.

[10] *They ... ay* They always hate what their husbands love.

790	Al sodeynly thre leves have I plyght°	plucked
	Out of his book, right as he radde. And eke	
	I with my fest° so took° hym on the cheke,	fist / hit
	That in oure fyr he fil° bakward adoun.	fell
	And he up stirte° as dooth a wood leoun,	jumps
795	And with his fest he smoot me on the heed,	
	That in° the floor I lay as I were deed.	on
	And whan he saugh how stille that I lay,	
	He was agast° and wolde han fled his way.°	afraid / away
	Til atte laste out of my swogh° I breyde.°	faint / awoke
800	'O hastow° slayn me, false theef?' I seyde.	have you
	'And for my land thus hastow mordred me!	
	Er° I be deed, yet wol I kisse thee.'	before
	"And neer he cam and kneled faire° adoun	pleasantly
	And seyde, 'Deere suster° Alisoun,	sister
805	As help me God, I shal thee nevere smyte!	
	That I have doon, it is thyself to wyte.°	blame
	Foryeve it me, and that I thee biseke!'°	beg
	And yet eftsoones° I hitte hym on the cheke	once more
	And seyde, 'Theef, thus muchel am I wreke.°	avenged
810	Now wol I dye. I may no lenger speke.'	
	But atte laste, with muchel care and wo,	
	We fille acorded° by usselven°	came to an agreement / ourselves
	two.	
	He yaf me al° the bridel° in myn hond	completely / bridle
	To han the governance of hous and lond,	
815	And of his tonge and his hond also,	
	And made hym brenne his book anon right tho.°	there
	And whan that I hadde geten° unto me	gotten
	By maistrie° al the soveraynetee,	mastery
	And that he seyde, 'Myn owene trewe wyf,	
820	Do as thee lust to terme of al thy lyf:[1]	
	Keepe thyn honour and keepe eek myn estaat.'—	
	After that day we hadden never debaat.°	disagreement
	God helpe me so, I was to hym as kynde	
	As any wyf from Denmark unto Ynde°	India
825	And also trewe, and so was he to me.	
	I prey to God that sit in magestee,	
	So blesse his soule for his mercy deere.	
	Now wol I seye° my tale, if ye wol heere."	tell

BIHOLDE THE WORDES BITWENE THE SOMONOUR
AND THE FRERE

	The Frere° lough° whan he hadde herd al this.	friar / laughed
830	"Now dame," quod he, "so have I joye or blis,	
	This is a long preamble of a tale!"	
	And whan the Somonour herde the Frere gale,°	speak up
	"Lo," quod the Somonour, "Goddes armes two![2]	
	A frere wol entremette hym evere mo![3]	
835	Lo, goode men, a flye and eek a frere	
	Wol falle in every dyssh and mateere![4]	
	What spekestow° of	what do you say
	preambulacioun?°	preambling
	What! Amble or trotte° or pees° or go sit doun!	trot / pace
	Thou lettest° oure disport° in this manere."	spoil / fun
840	"Ye, woltow so,° sire Somonour?"	will you say so
	quod the Frere.	
	"Now by my feith, I shal er that I go	
	Telle of a somonour swich a tale or two,	
	That alle the folk shal laughen in this place!"	
	"Now elles,° Frere, I bishrewe° thy face!"	otherwise / curse
845	Quod this Somonour, "and I bishrewe me	
	But if° I telle tales two or thre	unless
	Of freres er I come to Sidyngborne![5]	
	That I shal make thyn herte for to morne,°	mourn
	For wel I woot thy pacience is gon."	
850	Oure Hoost cride, "Pees,° and that anon!"	peace
	And seyde, "Lat the womman telle hire tale.	
	Ye fare° as folk that dronken were of ale!	behave
	Do, dame, telle forth youre tale, and that is best."	
	"Aldredy,° sire," quod she, "right as yow lest,°	ready / wish
855	If I have licence of this worthy Frere."	
	"Yis, dame," quod he, "tel forth, and I wol heere."	

HEERE ENDETH THE WYF OF BATHE HIR PROLOGE
AND BIGYNNETH HIR TALE

---

1. *Do ... lyf* Do as you wish as long as you live.

---

2. *Goddes armes two* God's two arms. This is an oath like those uniformly condemned by the Church.

3. *A ... mo* A friar will always put himself in the middle of things.

4. *Wol ... mateere* Will fall into every dish and matter.

5. *Sidyngborne* I.e., Sittingbourne, a small town about forty miles from London on the road to Canterbury.

THE WIFE OF BATH'S TALE

In th'olde dayes of Kyng Arthour,
Of which that Britons speken greet honour,[1]
Al was this land fulfild of° fairye.[2]   *filled up with*
860   The Elf Queene with hir joly compaignye
Daunced ful ofte in many a grene mede.°   *meadow*
This was the olde opinion, as I rede°—   *read*
I speke of manye hundred yeres ago.
But now kan no man se none elves mo,°   *no more elves*
865   For now the grete charitee and prayeres
Of lymytours[3] and othere hooly° freres   *holy*
That serchen every lond and every streem,
As thikke as motes° in the sonne beem,   *dust particles*
Blessynge halles, chambres, kichenes, boures,°   *bedrooms*
870   Citees, burghes,° castels, hye toures,°   *fortified towns / towers*
Thropes,° bernes,° shipnes,°   *villages / barns / stables*
       dayeryes°—   *dairies*
This maketh° that ther been° no fairyes.   *causes it / are*
For theras° wont° to walken was an elf,   *where / accustomed*
Ther walketh now the lymytour° hymself   *friar*
875   In undermeles° and in morwenynges,°   *early afternoons / mornings*
And seyth his matyns° and his hooly   *morning service*
       thynges°   *prayers*
As he gooth in his lymytacioun.°   *limited area*
Wommen may go saufly° up and doun: *safely*
In every bussh or under every tree
880   Ther is noon oother incubus[4] but he,
And he ne wol doon hem but dishonour.[5]
       And so bifel° that this Kyng Arthour   *it happened*
Hadde in hous a lusty bachelor°   *young knight*
That on a day cam ridynge fro ryver,°   *from a river*
885   And happed that, allone° as he was born,   *alone*
He saugh a mayde° walkynge hym biforn,° *maid / in front of him*
Of° which mayde anon, maugree° hir heed,° *from / despite / will*
By verray° force birafte° hire maydenhed,   *true / stole*
For which oppressioun was swich clamour°   *outcry*

---

[1] *Kyng Arthour ... honour* Legendary British king of roughly the fifth or sixth century CE, the subject of many medieval tales and romances.

[2] *fairye* Supernatural beings known as elves or fairies.

[3] *lymytours* Friars who were licensed to preach in a limited area in a parish or county.

[4] *incubus* Devilish spirit who would appear to women in dreams and thereby impregnate them.

[5] *ne ... dishonour* Will do them nothing but dishonor.

890   And swich pursute° unto the Kyng Arthour,   *appeal*
That dampned° was this knyght for to be   *condemned*
       deed°   *dead*
By cours of lawe, and sholde han lost his heed—
Paraventure° swich was the statut tho°—   *by chance / then*
But that the queene and othere ladyes mo
895   So longe preyden° the kyng of grace,°   *requested / mercy*
Til he his lyf hym graunted in the place
And yaf hym to the queene al at hir wille
To chese° wheither she wolde hym save or spille.° *choose / kill*
       The queene thanketh the kyng with al hir myght
900   And after this thus spak she to the knyght
Whan that she saugh hir tyme upon a day:
"Thou standest yet," quod she, "in swich array°   *condition*
That of thy lyf yet hastow° no suretee.°   *have you / certainty*
I grante thee lyf if thou kanst tellen me
905   What thyng is it that wommen moost desiren.
Bewar and keepe thy nekke boon° from iren!°   *bone / iron*
And if thou kanst nat tellen it anon,
Yet shal I yeve thee leve for to gon°   *go*
A twelf month and a day to seche° and leere°   *seek / learn*
910   An answere suffisant° in this mateere.   *sufficient*
And suretee° wol I han er that thou pace°—   *guarantee / leave*
Thy body for to yelden° in this place."   *return*
       Wo° was this knyght, and sorwefully he siketh,°   *sad / sighs*
But he may nat do al as hym liketh.°   *as he wishes*
915   And at the laste he chees° hym for to wende,° *chooses / go*
And come agayn right at the yeres° ende   *year's*
With swich answere as God wolde hym purveye,°   *provide*
And taketh his leve and wendeth forth his weye.
       He seketh every hous and every place
920   Whereas° he hopeth for to fynde grace   *where*
To lerne what thyng wommen loven moost,
But he ne koude arryven in no coost°   *region*
Wheras he myghte fynde in this mateere
Two creatures accordynge° in feere.°   *agreeing / together*
925   Somme seyde wommen loven best richesse;
Somme seyde honour, somme seyde jolynesse,°   *jollity*
Somme riche array.° Somme seyden lust   *clothing*
       abedde°   *in bed*
And oftetyme to be wydwe° and wedde.°   *widowed / married*
       Somme seyde that oure hertes been moost esed° *refreshed*
930   Whan that we been° yflatered and yplesed.   *are*
He gooth ful ny the sothe, I wol nat lye![6]

---

[6] *He ... lye* He gets very near the truth, I will not lie.

A man shal wynne us best with flaterye

And with attendance° and with bisynesse°   *attention / diligence*

Been we° ylymed[1] bothe moore and lesse.   *we are*

935   And somme seyn that we loven best

For to be free and so do right° as us lest°   *just / wish*

And that no man repreve us° of oure vice   *complain to us*

But seye that we be wise and nothyng° nyce.°   *not / foolish*

For trewely, ther is noon° of us alle,   *none*

940   If any wight° wol clawe° us on the galle,°   *person / claw / a sore*

That we nel kike,° for he seith us sooth.   *will not kick*

Assay° and he shal fynde it that so dooth.   *try*

For be we never so vicious° withinne,°   *wicked / within*

We wol been holden° wise and clene   *wish to be considered*

of synne.

945   And somme seyn that greet delit han we

For to been holden stable and eek secree,°   *discreet*

And in o° purpos stedefastly to dwelle,   *one*

And nat biwreye° thyng° that men us telle.   *betray / something*

But that tale is nat worth a rake-stele!°   *handle of a rake*

950   Pardee, we wommen konne nothyng hele.[2]

Witnesse on Myda.[3] Wol ye heere the tale?

Ovyde, amonges othere thynges smale,

Seyde Myda hadde under his longe heres°   *hairs*

Growynge upon his heed two asses eres,

955   The which vice he hydde as he best myghte

Ful subtilly° from every mannes sighte,   *carefully*

That save his wyf, ther wiste of it namo.°   *no one else*

He loved hire moost and triste° hire also.   *trusted*

He preyde° hire that to no creature   *asked*

960   She sholde tellen of his disfigure.°   *disfigurement*

She swoor hym nay: for al this world to wynne°   *gain*

She nolde° do that vileynye or synne   *would not*

To make hir housbonde han so foul a name.

She nolde nat telle it for hir owene shame.

965   But nathelees, hir thoughte that she dyde,°   *would die*

That° she so longe sholde a conseil° hyde.   *if / secret*

Hir thoughte it swal so soore aboute hir herte

That nedely som word hire moste asterte.[4]

And sith she dorste° telle it to no man,   *dared*

970   Doun to a mareys° faste by° she ran;   *marsh / close by*

Til she cam there hir herte was afyre.°   *on fire*

And as a bitore[5] bombleth° in the myre,°   *calls out / mud*

She leyde hir mouth unto the water doun.

"Biwreye me nat, thou water, with thy soun,"°   *sound*

975   Quod she. "To thee I telle it and namo:

Myn housbonde hath longe asses erys two!

Now is myn herte al hool.° Now is it oute!   *whole*

I myghte no lenger kepe it, out of doute."°   *without doubt*

Heere may ye se,° thogh we a tyme° abyde,   *see / for a time*

980   Yet out it moot!° We kan no conseil hyde.   *must (go)*

The remenant of the tale if ye wol heere,

Redeth Ovyde, and ther ye may it leere.°   *learn*

This knyght of which my tale is specially,

Whan that he saugh he myghte nat come therby,

985   This is to sey, what wommen love moost,

Withinne his brest ful sorweful was the goost.°   *spirit*

But hoom he gooth. He myghte nat sojourne.°   *delay*

The day was come that homward moste he tourne.

And in his wey it happed hym to ryde

990   In al this care under a forest syde

Wheras he saugh upon a daunce[6] go

Of ladyes foure and twenty and yet mo,

Toward the which daunce he drow ful yerne°   *drew very eagerly*

In hope that som wysdom sholde he lerne.

995   But certeinly, er he cam fully there,

Vanysshed was this daunce he nyste° where.   *knew not*

No creature saugh he that bar lyf,°   *bore life*

Save on the grene° he saugh sittynge a wyf°—   *meadow / woman*

A fouler° wight ther may no man devyse.°   *uglier / imagine*

1000   Agayn° the knyght this olde wyf gan ryse°   *towards / rose up*

And seyde, "Sire Knyght, heer forth ne lith° no   *lies*

wey.°   *road*

Tel me what that ye seken, by youre fey.°   *faith*

Paraventure it may the bettre be;

Thise olde folk kan° muchel° thyng," quod she.   *know / many*

---

[1]   *ylymed* Limed. Lime was used to catch birds.

[2]   *Pardee ... hele* By God, we women know nothing about how to keep a secret.

[3]   *Myda* I.e., Midas. See Ovid's *Metamorphoses*, Book 11 (although in Ovid's version it is the king's barber, not his wife, who whispers the secret).

[4]   *Hir thoughte ... asterte* It seemed to her that it became so sorely swollen around her heart. That by necessity some word had to burst out.

[5]   *bitore* I.e., bittern, a small heron.

[6]   *Wheras ... daunce* One way in which mortals were said to encounter elves was at night in the woods, where the elves performed a ritual dance.

1005   "My leeve° mooder,"° quod this knyght certeyn,   *dear / mother*

"I nam but° deed but if° that I kan seyn   *am as good as / unless*
What thyng it is that wommen moost desire.
Koude ye me wisse, I wolde wel quite youre hire."[1]

"Plight° me thy trouthe° heere in myn hand,"   *pledge / word*
quod she,

1010   "The nexte thyng that I require° thee,   *ask of*
Thou shalt it do if it lye in thy myght,
And I wol telle it yow° er it be nyght."   *to you*

"Have heer my trouthe," quod the knyght. "I grante."

"Thanne," quod she, "I dar° me wel avante°   *dare / boast*

1015   Thy lyf is sauf,° for I wol stonde therby.   *safe*
Upon my lyf, the queene wol seye as I.
Lat se° which is the proudeste of hem alle   *let's see*
That wereth on a coverchief° or a calle°   *kerchief / hairnet*
That dar seye nay of that I shal thee teche.°   *teach*

1020   Lat us go forth withouten lenger speche."
Tho° rowned° she a pistel° in his ere   *then / whispered / lesson*
And bad hym to be glad and have no fere.

Whan they be comen to the court, this knyght
Seyde he had holde° his day as he hadde hight°   *kept / promised*

1025   And redy was his answere, as he sayde.
Full many a noble wyf and many a mayde
And many a wydwe,° for that they been° wise,   *widow / are*
The queene hirself sittynge as justise,°   *sitting as a judge*
Assembled been° his answere for to heere,   *are*

1030   And afterward this knyght was bode°   *commanded*
appeere.°   *to appear*
To every wight comanded was silence
And that the knyght sholde telle in audience°   *in their hearing*
What thyng that worldly wommen loven best.
This knyght ne stood nat° stille as doth a best,°   *did not stand / beast*

1035   But to his questioun anon answerde
With manly voys,° that al the court it herde.   *voice*

"My lige° lady, generally," quod he,   *liege*
"Wommen desiren to have sovereynetee°   *to have sovereignty*
As wel over hir housbond as hir love
1040   And for to been in maistrie hym above.
This is youre mooste° desir, thogh ye me kille.   *greatest*
Dooth as yow list. I am at youre wille."

In al the court ne was ther° wyf ne mayde   *there was neither*
Ne wydwe that contraried that he sayde,

1045   But seyden he was worthy han° his lyf.   *to have*
And with that word up stirte° the olde wyf   *jumped*
Which that the knyght saugh sittynge in the grene.
"Mercy," quod she, "my sovereyn lady queene!
Er that youre court departe, do me right.
1050   I taughte this answere unto the knyght,
For which he plighte° me his trouthe° there,   *promised / word*
The firste thyng I wolde hym requere,
He wolde it do if it lay in his myght.
Bifore the court thanne preye° I thee, sire knyght,"   *ask*
1055   Quod she, "that thou me take unto thy wyf.
For wel thou woost° that I have kept thy lyf.   *know*
If I seye fals, sey nay, upon thy fey!"°   *faith*

This knyght answerde, "Allas and weylawey!°   *woe is me*
I woot° right wel that swich° was my   *know / such*
biheste.°   *promise*
1060   For Goddes love, as chees° a newe requeste!   *choose*
Taak° al my good,° and lat° my body go!"   *take / possessions / let*

"Nay thanne,"° quod she, "I shrewe,°   *then / curse*
us bothe two,
For thogh that I be foul, oold, and poore,
I nolde° for al the metal ne for oore°   *would not / ore*
1065   That under erthe° is grave° or lith° above   *earth / buried / lies*
But if thy wyf I were and eek thy love."

"My love!" quod he. "Nay, my dampnacioun!°   *damnation*
Allas, that any of my nacioun°   *family*
Sholde evere so foule disparaged° be!"   *badly shamed*
1070   But al for noght! Th'end is this: that he
Constreyned° was. He nedes moste hire wedde,   *compelled*
And taketh his olde wyf and gooth to bedde.

Now wolden som men seye paraventure°   *perhaps*
That for my necligence I do no cure°   *care*
1075   To tellen yow the joye and al th'array°   *the arrangements*
That at the feeste was that ilke° day   *same*
To which thyng shortly answere I shal.
I seye ther nas° no joye ne feeste at al.   *was no*
Ther nas° but hevynesse and muche sorwe.   *was nothing*
1080   For prively he wedded hire on a morwe,°   *morning*
And al day after hidde hym as an owle,
So wo was hym, his wyf looked so foule.

Greet was the wo the knyght hadde in his thoght
Whan he was with his wyf abedde ybroght.[2]

1085   He walweth,° and he turneth to and fro.   *writhes about*

---

[1] *Koude ... hire* If you could inform me, I would pay you back well.

[2] *Whan ... ybroght* It was a custom for wedding guests to escort the bride and groom to their bedroom.

His olde wyf lay smylynge° evere mo — *smiling*
And seyde, "O deere housbonde, benedicitee,° — *bless you*
Fareth° every knyght thus with his wyf as ye? — *behaves*
Is this the lawe of Kyng Arthures hous?
1090 Is every knyght of his so dangerous?° — *standoffish*
I am youre owene love and youre wyf;
I am she which that saved hath youre lyf.
And certes, yet ne dide° I yow nevere unright:° — *did not / injustice*
Why fare ye thus with me this firste nyght?
1095 Ye faren lyk a man had lost his wit.
What is my gilt?° For Goddes love, tel it, — *guilt*
And it shal been amended if I may."
    "Amended!" quod this knyght. "Allas, nay! Nay!
It wol nat been amended nevere mo.° — *forever more*
1100 Thou art so loothly° and so oold° also, — *ugly / old*
And therto comen of so lough° a kynde,° — *low / lineage*
That litel wonder is thogh° I walwe° and — *though / writhe*
    wynde.° — *twist about*
So wolde God myn herte wolde breste!"° — *burst*
"Is this," quod she, "the cause of youre unreste?"
1105 "Ye, certeinly," quod he, "no wonder is!"
"Now sire," quod she, "I koude amende al this
If that me liste° er it were dayes thre,° — *I wished / three days*
So wel ye myghte bere yow unto me.[1]
    But for° ye speken of swich gentillesse — *because*
1110 As is descended out of old richesse,
That therfore sholden ye be gentilmen,
Swich arrogance is nat worth an hen!
Looke who that is moost vertuous alway,
Pryvee and apert and moost entendeth ay
1115 To do the gentil dedes that he kan:[2]
Taak hym for the grettest gentilman.
Crist wole° we clayme° of hym oure — *desires that / claim*
    gentillesse,
Nat of oure eldres° for hire old richesse. — *ancestors*
For thogh they yeve us al hir heritage,
1120 For which we clayme to been of heigh parage,° — *lineage*
Yet may they nat biquethe° for nothyng — *bequeath*
To noon° of us hir vertuous lyvyng° — *none / living*
That made hem° gentilmen ycalled be, — *them*
And bad us folwen hem in swich degree.

1125 Wel kan the wise poete of Florence
That highte Dant° speken in this — *is named Dante*
    sentence.° — *matter*
Lo, in swich maner rym° is Dantes tale: — *such a kind of rhyme*
'Ful selde up riseth by his branches smale
Prowesse of man.[3] For God of his goodnesse
1130 Wole° that of hym we clayme oure gentillesse.' — *wishes*
For of oure eldres may we nothyng clayme
But temporel thyng° that man may hurte — *temporal things*
    and mayme.° — *maim*
Eek every wight woot this as wel as I.
If gentillesse were planted natureelly° — *implanted by nature*
1135 Unto a certeyn lynage doun the lyne,° — *line (of generations)*
Pryvee nor apert thanne wolde they nevere fyne
To doon of gentillesse the faire office.[4]
They myghte do no vileynye or vice.
    Taak fyr° and ber° it in the derkeste hous — *fire / carry*
1140 Bitwix this and the mount of Kaukasous° — *Caucasus*
And lat men shette the dores and go thenne:° — *go away*
Yet wole the fyr as faire lye° and brenne° — *blaze / burn*
As twenty thousand men myghte it biholde.
His° office natureel ay° wol it holde, — *its / ever*
1145 Up peril of my lyf, til that it dye.[5]
    Heere may ye se wel how that genterye
Is nat annexed° to possessioun, — *linked*
Sith folk ne doon hir operacioun° — *do not behave*
Alwey as dooth the fyr, lo, in his kynde.° — *according to its nature*
1150 For God it woot, men may wel often fynde
A lordes sone do shame and vileynye,
And he that wole han° pris of° his gentrye, — *will have / esteem for*
For he was born of a gentil hous
And hadde hise eldres noble and vertuous,
1155 And nel hymselven° do no gentil dedis° — *will not himself / deeds*
Ne folwen his gentil auncestre that deed° is, — *dead*
He nys nat° gentil, be he duc° or erl,° — *is not / duke / earl*
For vileyns synful dedes make a cherl.° — *churl*
For gentillesse nys but° renomee° — *is not / renown*
1160 Of thyne auncestres for hire heigh bountee,° — *their high goodness*

---

[1] *So … me* Provided that you might behave yourself well towards me.

[2] *Looke … kan* Look for whoever is always most virtuous in private and in public and always strives to do the most noble deeds.

[3] *Ful … man* The excellence of a man seldom extends to the further branches (of his family tree); i.e., the sons are seldom worthy of the father. Cf. Dante's *Convivio* 4 and *Purgatorio* 7.121.

[4] *Pryvee … office* Then they would never stop doing the fair office of gentle deeds either in private or in public.

[5] *His … dye* Upon my life, it will always perform its natural function (i.e., burn) until it dies.

512   GEOFFREY CHAUCER

Which is a strange° thyng to thy persone.   *separate*
Thy gentillesse cometh fro God allone.
Thanne comth oure verray gentillesse of grace;
It was nothyng biquethe us°   *bequeathed to us*
    with oure place.°   *social position*
1165   Thenketh how noble, as seith Valerius,
Was thilke° Tullius Hostillius,[1]   *that*
That out of poverte roos° to heigh noblesse.   *rose*
Reed Senek and redeth eek Boece:[2]
Ther shul ye seen expres° that no drede° is   *specifically / doubt*
1170 That he is gentil that dooth gentil dedis.
And therfore, leeve housbonde, I thus conclude,
Al° were it that myne auncestres weren   *although*
    rude,°   *of low birth*
Yet may the hye° God—and so hope I—   *high*
Grante me grace to lyven° vertuously.   *live*
1175 Thanne am I gentil whan that I bigynne°   *begin*
To lyven vertuously and weyve synne.°   *avoid sin*
    And theras° ye of poverte me repreeve,°   *since / reproach*
The hye God on whom that we bileeve
In wilful° poverte chees° to lyve his lyf.   *voluntary / chose*
1180 And certes, every man, mayden, or wyf
May understonde that Jesus Hevene kyng°   *King of Heaven*
Ne wolde nat chesen° vicious lyvyng.   *choose*
Glad° poverte is an honeste thyng, certeyn.   *joyful*
This wole Senec and othere clerkes° seyn.°   *writers / say*
1185 Whoso that halt hym payd of° his poverte,   *satisfied with*
I holde° hym riche, al° hadde he nat a sherte. *consider / although*
He that coveiteth° is a povere wight,   *covets*
For he wolde han that° is nat in his myght.   *what*
But he that noght hath ne coveiteth have°   *and does not covet*
1190 Is riche, although ye holde hym but a knave.
    Verray poverte, it syngeth properly.
Juvenal[3] seith of poverte myrily,°   *merrily*
'The povre man, whan he goth by the weye,°   *along the road*
Bifore the theves he may synge and pleye.'
1195 Poverte is hateful good and, as I gesse,
A ful greet bryngere° out of bisynesse.° *very great bringer / busyness*

A greet amendere° eek of sapience°   *improver / wisdom*
To hym that taketh it in pacience.°   *patience*
Poverte is this, although it seme alenge:°   *wretched*
1200 Possessioun that no wight wol chalenge.°   *claim*
Poverte ful ofte, whan a man is lowe,
Maketh° his God and eek hymself to knowe.   *causes*
Poverte a spectacle° is, as thynketh me,   *lens*
Thurgh° which he may hise verray° freendes see. *through / true*
1205 And therfore sire, syn that I noght yow greve,° *do not grieve you*
Of my poverte namoore° ye me repreve.   *no more*
Now sire, of elde° ye repreve me,   *old age*
And certes, sire, thogh noon auctoritee
Were in no book, ye gentils° of honour   *nobles*
1210 Seyn that men sholde an oold wight doon favour° *do honor*
And clepe° hym fader for youre gentillesse.   *call*
And auctours° shal I fynden, as I gesse.   *authorities*
Now ther° ye seye that I am foul and old: *where*
Than drede° you noght to been a cokewold.[4]   *fear*
1215 For filthe° and eelde,° also moot   *ugliness / old age*
    I thee,°   *might I thrive*
Been grete wardeyns upon° chastitee.   *guardians of*
But nathelees, syn I knowe youre delit,°   *delight*
I shal fulfille youre worldly appetit.
    Chese now," quod she, "oon of thise thynges tweye:° *two*
1220 To han me foul and old til that I deye
And be to yow a trewe, humble wyf
And nevere yow displese° in al my lyf,   *displease you*
Or elles° ye wol han me yong and fair   *else*
And take youre aventure of the repair
1225 That shal be to youre hous bycause of me,
Or in som oother place, may wel be.[5]
Now chese yourselven wheither that yow
    liketh."°   *whichever pleases you*
    This knyght avyseth° hym and sore   *considers*
    siketh,°   *sorely sighs*
But atte laste he seyde in this manere:
1230 "My lady and my love and wyf so deere,
I put me in youre wise governance.
Cheseth yourself which may be moost plesance°   *most pleasant*
And moost honour to yow and me also.
I do no fors° the wheither of the two,   *I do not care*

[1] *Valerius … Hostillius* Tullius Hostillius started life as a peasant and rose to become king. The story is told by the Roman writer Valerius Maximus.

[2] *Senek* I.e., Seneca, Stoic philosopher (c. 5 BCE–65 CE); *Boece* I.e., Boethius. See his *Consolation of Philosophy*, book 3, prose 6 and meter 3.

[3] *Juvenal* Roman poet and satirist (55–127 CE).

[4] *cokewold* I.e., cuckold, a man whose wife has been unfaithful to him.

[5] *And … be* And take your chances of the visiting (i.e., by lovers) at your house, or perhaps in some other places, in order to see me.

61

1235   For as yow liketh, it suffiseth me."

     "Thanne have I gete° of yow maistrie,"° quod *gotten / mastery*
     she,

     "Syn I may chese and governe as me lest?"°   *as I wish*

     "Ye certes, wyf," quod he, "I holde it best."

     "Kys me," quod she, "we be no lenger wrothe.°   *angry*

1240   For by my trouthe,° I wol be to yow bothe.   *truth*

     This is to seyn, ye, bothe° fair and good.   *indeed both*

     I prey to God that I moote sterven wood°   *die crazy*

     But° I to yow be also good and trewe   *unless*

     As evere was wyf, syn that the world was newe.

1245   And but° I be tomorn° as fair to seene   *unless / tomorrow*

     As any lady, emperice,° or queene   *empress*

     That is bitwixe the est and eke the west,

     Dooth° with my lyf and deth right° as yow lest.° *do / just / wish*

     Cast up the curtyn. Looke how that it is."

1250   And whan the knyght saugh verraily al this,

That she so fair was and so yong therto,

For joye he hente° hire in hise armes two.   *held*

His herte° bathed in a bath of blisse.   *heart*

A thousand tyme arewe° he gan hire kisse.   *in a row*

1255 And she obeyed hym in everythyng

That myghte doon hym plesance or likyng.°   *enjoyment*

     And thus they lyve unto hir lyves ende

In parfit° joye. And Jesu Crist us sende   *perfect*

Housbondes meeke, yonge, and fressh abedde°   *in bed*

1260 And grace to t'overbyde° hem that we wedde.   *control*

And eek I pray Jhesu shorte hir lyves°   *shorten their lives*

That nat wol be governed by hir wyves.

And olde and angry nygardes° of dispence,° *skinflints / spending*

God sende hem soone verray pestilence!

HEERE ENDETH THE WYVES TALE OF BATHE

The Pardoner's Prologue and Tale

The Pardoner calls himself "a full vicious man," yet, paradoxically, his tale is one of the few that has a completely straightforward moral: covetousness is the root of all evil. The tale is actually a popular sermon of the kind that the Pardoner has given so often that he knows it by rote. A story of three men who go in search of death, *The Pardoner's Tale* has at its core an *exemplum*, a short and gripping story with a clear moral message. To this exemplum a preacher might add, as the Pardoner does, dramatic denunciations of the Seven Deadly Sins, supported by Biblical quotations, and calls for repentance. Medieval popular preachers were often excellent storytellers, but the level of detail in *The Pardoner's Tale* goes beyond the needs of any sermon. Like the Miller, the Pardoner is a churl, and their two tales share an interest in the concrete and seamy aspects of daily life, down to such matters as how people rented rooms or poisoned rats. Although the time period is not specified the Pardoner's story captures the brutal joys of the tavern and the grim atmosphere of England in a time of plague, with the death cart making the rounds to retrieve the bodies, as it would have done during the Black Death of 1348–49. The enigmatic old man who cannot die but knows where death is to be found further enriches the basic *exemplum*.

The Pardoner's greatest modification of a popular sermon, however, is to offer a full commentary on his own art, describing his motivation (simple covetousness) and the various tricks, including blackmail, which he uses to persuade his listeners to buy his spurious relics and pardons. By holding out false promises of salvation, the Pardoner is endangering the souls of others and his own. His character has fascinated readers, perhaps because it is so enigmatic. There has been much discussion of what drives the Pardoner to such extensive self-revelation and why, having just explained his methods to the pilgrims, he is so rash as to make a final sales pitch for his relics. In one much-discussed line in *The General Prologue*, "I trowe [I believe] he were a gelding [a castrated stallion] or a mare," the narrator indicates that he does not precisely know what to make of the Pardoner, while defining him as other than "masculine." Based on this line and other features of his depiction, some have seen the Pardoner as a tormented outsider, anxious to win group approval, others as a figure of spiritual sterility, corrupted by his own covetousness and in turn corrupting those who listen to him.

Opening page of *The Pardoner's Tale*, Ellesmere manuscript (detail). (Reprinted by permission of *The Huntington Library, San Marino, California.* EL 26 C9 f. 138r.)

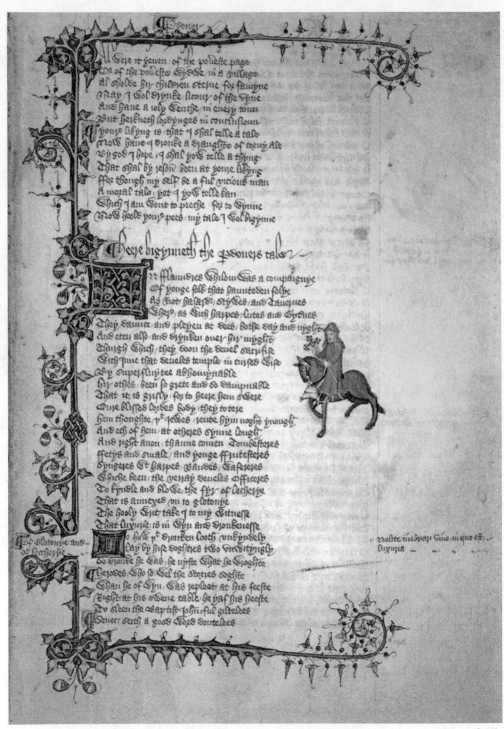

Opening page of *The Pardoner's Tale*, Ellesmere manuscript. (Reprinted by permission of *The Huntington Library, San Marino, California*. EL 26 C9 f. 138r.)

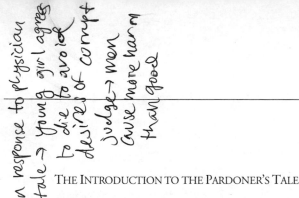

[handwritten margin note, top left]: in response to physician tale → young girl agrees to die to avoid desires of corrupt judge → men cause more harm than good

[handwritten margin note, top right]: Harry rlly wants a happy tale be hes sad about girl

THE INTRODUCTION TO THE PARDONER'S TALE

THE WORDES OF THE HOOST
TO THE PHISICIEN AND THE PARDONER

O ure Hoost gan to swere° as° he were *began to swear / as if*
  wood.° *crazy*
"Harrow!" quod he. "By nayles and by blood!"[1]
This was a fals° cherl° and a fals justice.° *false / churl / judge*
As shameful deeth° as herte° may devyse° *death / heart / imagine*
5 Come to thise° false juges° and hire *these / judges*
    advocatz!° *their lawyers*
Algate° this sely° mayde° is slayn,° *but / innocent / maid / killed*
    allas![2]
Allas, to deere° boughte she beautee! *too dearly*
Wherfore° I seye° al day as men may see, *therefore / say*
That yiftes° of Fortune and of nature *gifts*
10 Been° cause of deeth to many a creature. *are*
Of bothe yiftes that I speke of now
Men han ful ofte° moore for harm than *have very often*
    prow.° *profit*
But trewely,° myn owene maister° deere,° *truly / master / dear*
This is a pitous° tale for to here.° *pitiful / hear*
15 But nathelees,° passe over.° Is no *nevertheless / let it pass*
    fors.° *matter*
I pray to God so save thy gentil cors° *noble body*
And eek thyne urynals and thy jurdones,[3]
Thyn ypocras° and eek thy galiones° *hypocras / galians (medicines)*
And every boyste° ful of thy letuarie.° *box / medicine*
20 God blesse hem° and oure Lady, Seint Marie! *them*
So moot° I theen,° thou art a propre° man *might / thrive / fine*
And lyk° a prelat,° by Seint Ronyan![4] *like / prelate (high clergyman)*

Seyde I nat wel? I kan nat speke in terme.° *in the right jargon*
But wel I woot,° thou doost myn herte to *know*
  erme,° *make my heart grieve*
25 That I almoost have caught a cardynacle.[5]
By corpus bones,° but° I have triacle[6] *by God's bones / unless*
Or elles a draughte° of moyste° and *drink / moist*
    corny° ale, *malty (strong)*
Or but I heere anon° a myrie° tale, *immediately / merry*
Myn herte is lost for pitee of this mayde.
30 Thou beel amy,° thou Pardoner," he sayde, *good friend*
"Telle us som myrthe or japes° right anon." *jokes*
  "It shal be doon!" quod he, "by Seint Ronyon!
But first," quod he, "heere at this ale-stake[7]
I wol bothe drynke and eten° of a cake."° *eat / bread*
35   And right anon the gentils° gonne° to crye, *gentle folk / began*
"Nay, lat hym telle us of no ribaudye!° *ribald story*
Telle us som moral thyng that we may leere° *learn*
Som wit,° and thanne wol we gladly heere." *piece of wisdom*
  "I graunte, ywis,"° quod he. "But I moot *indeed*
    thynke° *must think*
40 Upon som honeste thyng° whil that I drynke." *respectable subject*

[handwritten: gets a little drunk]

[handwritten, right margin: tells Pardoner to tell happy tale]

[handwritten, right margin: nobles say to tell noble story]

THE PARDONER'S PROLOGUE

HEERE FOLWETH THE PROLOGE OF THE PARDONERS TALE

Radix malorum est Cupiditas. Ad Thimotheum 6.10[8]

"L ordynges,"° quod he, "in chirches° *lords / churches*
  whan I preche,° *preach*

---

[1] *Harrow … blood* *Harrow* Help; *Nails and blood* By Christ's nails and by Christ's blood, i.e., alas. Medieval swearing often referred to parts of Christ's body.

[2] *Harow … allas* The tale told previously, by the Physician, involved an innocent young girl who agrees to let her father kill her in order to save her from the lewd desires of a corrupt judge.

[3] *urynals* Vessels to hold urine; *jurdones* Jars. These were both part of the equipment medieval doctors used.

[4] *Seint Ronyan* There were several medieval saints called St. Ronan—a seventh-century Scottish hermit, a Breton bishop who died in Cornwall, a Scottish bishop who helped settle a dispute about the date of Easter, and an early bishop of Caesarea, whose arm was kept as a relic at Canterbury Cathedral. Most editors state that it was the Scottish hermit to whom the Host refers here, but the last

Saint Ronan, given his association with Canterbury, seems the most likely reference, for the pilgrims are traveling to the place where his relic was kept. There may also be a pun on runnions (male sexual organs).

[5] *cardynacle* The Host means heart attack, though he blunders for the proper word, which is cardiacle.

[6] *triacle* Medicine or cordial, usually made primarily from molasses.

[7] *ale-stake* Post set up outside a house when the people who lived there had brewed up some ale and were ready to sell it to those passing by.

[8] *Radix … 6.10* Latin: The root of evils is cupidity. From 1 Timothy 6.10. Cupidity is often translated as avarice, or love of money, but, like the word covetousness, it can also refer to any excessive or sinful love of earthly things.

[handwritten margin note: tells disguised speeches in church]

I peyne me to han° an hauteyn speche°   *take pains to have / dignified speech*
And rynge° it out as round° as gooth a belle,°   *ring / roundly / rings a bell*
For I kan° al by rote° that I telle.°   *know / by memory / say*
45 My theme[1] is alwey oon° and evere was: *always one*
Radix malorum est cupiditas.
    "First I pronounce° whennes° that I come,   *say / whence*
And thanne my bulles[2] shewe I alle and some.°   *one and all*
Oure lige lordes[3] seel° on my patente,°   *seal / license*
50 That shewe I first, my body to warente,°   *protect*
That no man be so boold,° ne preest ne clerk,[4]   *bold*
Me to destourbe° of Cristes hooly werk.   *disturb*
And after that thanne° telle I forth my tales.   *then*
Bulles of popes and of cardynales,°   *cardinals*
55 Of patriarkes° and bisshopes° I shewe,   *patriarchs / bishops*
And in Latyn° I speke a wordes fewe   *Latin*
To saffron with[5] my predicacioun°   *preaching*
And for to stire hem° to devocioun.   *stir them*
Thanne shewe I forth my longe cristal stones,°   *glass cases*
60 Ycrammed° ful of cloutes° and of bones.   *crammed / rags*
Relikes been they, as wenen they echoon.°   *as everyone believes*
Thanne have I in latoun° a sholder boon°   *brass / shoulder bone*
Which that was of an hooly Jewes sheepe.°   *holy Jew's sheep*
'Goode men,' I seye, 'taak of my wordes keepe.°   *heed*
65 If that this boon be wasshe° in any welle,   *washed*
If cow or calf or sheepe or oxe swelle°   *swell*
That any worm° hath ete° or worm ystonge,°   *snake / has eaten / stung*
Taak water of that welle and wassh his tonge,

And it is hool° anon. And forthermoor,   *healthy*
70 Of pokkes° and of scabbe° and every soor°   *pocks / scab / sore*
Shal every sheepe be hool that of this welle
Drynketh a draughte. Taak kepe° eek°   *take heed / also*
    what I telle!
If that the goode man that the beestes° oweth°   *beasts / owns*
Wol every wyke° er° that the cok° hym croweth°   *week / before / rooster / crows*
75 Fastynge° drynke of this welle a draughte,   *while fasting*
As thilke° hooly Jew oure eldres° taughte,   *that / ancestors*
Hise beestes and his stoor° shal multiplie.   *possessions*
    "And sire, also it heeleth° jalousie.   *heals*
For though a man be falle° in jalous rage,   *fallen*
80 Lat maken with this water his potage,°   *soup*
And nevere shal he moore his wyf mystriste,°   *mistrust*
Though he the soothe° of hir defaute° wiste,°   *truth / default / knew*
Al had she taken preestes two or thre.[6]
    "Heere is a miteyn° eek that ye may se.   *mitten*
85 He that his hand wol putte in this mitayn,
He shal have multipliyng of his grayn°   *grain*
Whan he hath sowen, be it whete° or otes,°   *wheat / oats*
So that he offre pens or elles grotes.[7]
    "Goode men and wommen, o° thyng warne I yow: *one*
90 If any wight° be in this chirche now   *person*
That hath doon° synne° horrible, that he   *committed / sin*
Dar nat for shame of it yshryven° be,   *confessed*
Or any womman, be she yong or old,
That hath ymaked° hir housbonde cokewold,[8]   *made*
95 Swich folk shal have no power ne no grace
To offren° to my relikes in this place.   *make an offering*
And whoso fyndeth hym out° of swich fame,°   *finds himself free / (ill-) repute*
They wol come up and offre on° Goddes name,   *in*
And I assoille hem° by the auctoritee°   *absolve them / authority*
100 Which that by bulle ygraunted was to me.
    "By this gaude° have I wonne° yeer° by yeer   *trick / gained / year*

---

[1] *theme* "Text." Medieval sermons were usually organized around a short passage from the Bible.

[2] *bulles* I.e., papal bulls (written documents which put official policy into effect). Pardoners had licenses from the Pope to raise money for charitable causes by selling indulgences (certificates that reduce the number of years the buyer must serve in Purgatory after death).

[3] *lige lordes* The liege lord in question might be the bishop or possibly even the king.

[4] *ne preest ne clerk* The term clerk can refer to students, scholars, or assistants to priests (as in *The Miller's Tale*), so neither priest nor clerk means not a member of the clergy. The parish clergy often regarded wandering preachers as interlopers.

[5] *To saffron with* To season with saffron, a very expensive yellow spice imported from the East.

[6] *Al ... thre* Even if she had taken two or three priests as lovers.

[7] *So ... grotes* Provided that he offers pennies or else groats (a coin worth fourpence).

[8] *cokewold* I.e., cuckold, a man whose wife has committed adultery.

An hundred mark sith I was pardoner.[1]
I stonde lyk a clerk° in my pulpet,   *cleric*
And whan the lewed peple[2] is doun yset,°   *settled down*
105 I preche so as ye han herd bifoore°   *have heard before*
And telle an hundred false japes° moore.   *tricks*
Thanne peyne I me° to strecche°   *I take pains / stretch*
    forth the nekke
And est° and west upon the peple° I bekke°   *east / people / nod*
As dooth a dowve° sittynge on a berne.°   *sitting / barn*
110 Myne handes and my tonge goon so yerne°   *eagerly*
That it is joye to se° my bisynesse.°   *see / busyness*
Of avarice and of swich cursednesse°   *cursedness*
Ys° al my prechyng, for to make hem free°   *is / generous*
To yeven hir pens°—and namely unto me.   *give their pence*
115 For myn entente° is nat but for to wynne°   *intent / profit*
And nothyng° for correccioun° of synne. *by no means / correction*
I rekke° nevere whan they been beryed,°   *care / buried*
Though that hir soules goon a blakeberyed![3]
For certes, many a predicacioun°   *sermon*
120 Comth ofte tyme of yvel entencioun—°   *evil intent*
Som for plesance° of folk and flaterye   *pleasure*
To been avaunced by ypocrisye°   *hypocrisy*
And som for veyneglorie° and som for hate.   *pride*
For whan I dar noon oother weyes° debate,   *in no other way*
125 Thanne wol I stynge° hym[4] with my tonge   *sting*
    smerte°   *sharp*
In prechyng, so that he shal nat asterte°   *escape*
To been defamed falsly if that he
Hath trespased° to my bretheren or to me.   *has done harm*
For though I telle noght° his propre° name,   *not / own*
130 Men shal wel knowe that it is the same
By signes and by othere circumstances.
Thus quyte° I folk that doon us displesances.° *pay back / offenses*
Thus spitte I out my venym under hewe°   *guise*
Of hoolynesse, to semen° hooly and trewe.   *seem*

135 "But shortly, myn entente I wol devyse:°   *describe*
I preche of nothyng but for coveityse.°   *covetousness*
Therfor my theme is yet and evere was
Radix malorum est cupiditas.
Thus kan I preche agayn° that same vice   *against*
140 Which that I use, and that is avarice.
But though myself be gilty in that synne,
Yet kan I maken oother folk to twynne°   *turn away*
From avarice and soore° to repente.   *sorely*
But that is nat my principal entente;°   *intent*
145 I preche nothyng but for coveitise.°   *covetousness*
Of this mateere it oghte ynogh suffise.° *should be sufficient*
    "Thanne telle I hem ensamples° many   *examples*
    oon°   *many a one*
Of olde stories longe tyme agoon,°   *ago*
For lewed peple° loven tales olde;   *laypeople*
150 Swiche thynges kan they wel reporte and holde.° *remember*
What? Trowe ye,° the whiles I may preche   *do you believe*
And wynne° gold and silver for I teche,° *gain / because I teach*
That I wol lyve in poverte wilfully?°   *willingly*
Nay, nay! I thoghte it nevere, trewely.
155 For I wol preche and begge in sondry landes;° *different countries*
I wol nat do no labour with myne handes
Ne make baskettes and lyve therby,
Bycause I wol nat beggen ydelly.°   *beg in vain*
I wol noon of the apostles countrefete![5]
160 I wol have moneie,° wolle,° chese, and   *money / wool*
    whete,°   *wheat*
Al° were it yeven° of the povereste page° *even if / given / poorest boy*
Or of the povereste wydwe° in a village,   *widow*
Al sholde hir children sterve° for famyne.   *die*
Nay, I wol drynke licour of the vyne
165 And have a joly wenche° in every toun.   *pretty girl*
But herkneth,° lordynges, in conclusioun: *listen*
Youre likyng° is that I shal telle a tale.   *pleasure*
Now have I dronke a draughte of corny ale,
By God, I hope I shal yow telle a thyng
170 That shal by resoun° been at youre liking.   *with reason*
For though myself be a ful° vicious man,   *very*
A moral tale yet I yow telle kan,
Which I am wont° to preche for to wynne.   *accustomed*
Now hoold youre pees!° My tale I wol bigynne.   *peace*

---

[1] *An ... pardoner* A hundred marks equaled over £66, making the Pardoner a wealthy man. In comparison, in 1367 Chaucer was granted an annual pension of 20 marks.

[2] *lewed peple* Uneducated, illiterate (in the medieval sense—i.e., unable to read Latin), or simple, but it can also refer to lay people in general. It does not have the modern meaning of sexual offensiveness.

[3] *a blakeberyed* Go picking blackberries (i.e., wandering).

[4] *hym* I.e., any opponent. Pardoners were much criticized by the parish clergy and by reformers.

[5] *noon ... countrefete* In the Gospels and the Book of Acts the apostles were enjoined to live in poverty so as to give surplus goods to the poor.

THE PARDONER'S TALE

HEERE BIGYNNETH THE PARDONERS TALE

175   In Flaundres° whilom° was a   *Flanders / once*
         compaignye°   *company*
    Of yonge folk that haunteden folye
    As riot, hasard, stywes, and tavernes,[1]
    Whereas° with harpes, lutes, and gyternes[2]   *where*
    They daunce and pleyen° at dees° bothe day and   *play / dice*
        nyght
180   And eten also and drynken over hir myght,°   *capacity*
    Thurgh which they doon the devel sacrifise° *sacrifice to the devil*
    Withinne that develes temple[3] in cursed wise°   *manner*
    By superfluytee° abhomynable.   *excess*
    Hir othes° been so grete and so dampnable°   *oaths / damnable*
185   That it is grisly° for to heere hem swere.   *horrible*
    Oure blissed° Lordes body they to-tere—°   *blessed / tear apart*
    Hem thoughte that Jewes rente hym noght ynough![4]
    And ech of hem at otheres synne° lough.°   *sin / laughed*
    And right anon thanne comen tombesteres°   *female acrobats*
190   Fetys° and smale° and yonge   *elegant / slender*
        frutesteres,°   *fruit-sellers*
    Syngeres with harpes, baudes,° wafereres,° *pimps / pastry-sellers*
    Whiche been° the verray devels officeres   *who are*
    To kyndle and blowe the fyr of lecherye
    That is annexed unto° glotonye.°   *allied with / gluttony*
195   The Hooly Writ° take I to my witnesse   *Bible*
    That luxurie° is in wyn° and dronkenesse.   *lust / wine*
      Lo how that dronken Looth[5] unkyndely°   *unnaturally*
    Lay by hise doghtres° two unwityngly!° *daughters / unknowingly*
    So dronke he was, he nyste° what he   *did not know*
        wroghte.°   *did*

200   Herodes,[6] whoso wel the stories soghte,[7]
    Whan he of wyn was replet° at his feeste,°   *most filled / feast*
    Right at his owene table he yaf° his heeste° *gave / command*
    To sleen° the Baptist John ful giltelees.[8]   *kill*
    Senec[9] seith a good word, doutelees.°   *doubtless*
205   He seith he kan no difference fynde
    Bitwix° a man that is out of his mynde   *between*
    And a man which that is dronkelewe,°   *often drunk*
    But that woodnesse,° fallen° in a   *madness / occurring*
        shrewe,°   *villain*
    Persevereth° lenger than dooth dronkenesse.   *lasts*
210   O glotonye, ful of cursednesse,
    O cause first of oure confusioun,
    O original of oure dampnacioun,[10]
    Til Crist hadde boght° us with his blood agayn! *redeemed*
    Lo how deere,° shortly for to seyn,°   *expensively / say*
215   Aboght° was thilke° cursed vileynye!   *purchased / that*
    Corrupt was al this world for glotonye.
      Adam oure fader and his wyf also
    Fro° Paradys to labour and to wo°   *from / woe*
    Were dryven° for that vice, it is no drede.°   *driven / doubt*
220   For whil that Adam fasted, as I rede,°   *read*
    He was in Paradys, and whan that he
    Eet° of the fruyt deffended° on the tree,   *ate / prohibited*
    Anon he was outcast to wo and peyne.
    O glotonye, on thee wel oghte us pleyne!°   *complain*
225   O, wiste a man how manye maladyes°   *diseases*
    Folwen of excesse and of glotonyes,
    He wolde been the moore mesurable°   *temperate*
    Of his diete, sittynge at his table.
    Allas, the shorte throte,° the tendre mouth   *throat*
230   Maketh that° est and west and north and south,   *causes*
    In erthe, in eir, in water man to swynke°   *labor*
    To gete a glotoun° deyntee° mete° *glutton / delicious / meat*
      and drynke.

---

[1] *Of yonge ... tavernes* Of young folk that gave themselves to foolish living, such as loud parties, gambling, brothels, and taverns.

[2] *gyternes* Like the harp and the lute, the medieval gittern was a plucked stringed instrument.

[3] *develes temple* I.e., a tavern.

[4] *Hem ... ynough* They thought that Jews did not tear him apart enough. The oaths figuratively tore God's body apart, according to the moralists. In the Middle Ages, Jews were usually blamed for Christ's crucifixion.

[5] *Looth* I.e., Lot. The story of how Lot, while drunk, made his daughters pregnant is recounted in Genesis 19.30–38.

---

[6] *Herodes* I.e., Herod, King of the Jewish people (74–3 BCE).

[7] *whoso ... soghte* As whoever consulted the stories carefully can confirm.

[8] *ful giltelees* Entirely guiltless. See Matthew 14.1–12.

[9] *Senec* I.e., Seneca, Roman playwright, orator, and philosopher (4 BCE–65 CE).

[10] *O cause ... dampnacioun* A reference to the role of gluttony in causing Adam and Eve to eat the forbidden fruit of the Tree of Knowledge in the Garden of Eden. See Genesis 2–3.

Of this matiere, O Paul,[1] wel kanstow trete:°   *can you write*
"Mete unto wombe° and wombe eek unto mete: *stomach*
235   Shal God destroyen bothe," as Paulus seith.[2]
Allas, a foul thyng is it, by my feith,
To seye this word, and fouler is the dede
Whan man so drynketh of the white and
    rede,°   *white and red wine*
That of his throte he maketh his pryvee,°   *latrine*
240   Thurgh thilke cursed superfluitee.°   *excess*
    The apostel[3] wepyng seith ful pitously,°   *pitifully*
"Ther walken manye of whiche yow toold
    have I.°   *I have told you*
I seye it now wepyng with pitous voys:°   *pitiful voice*
Ther been° enemys of Cristes croys°   *are / cross*
245   Of whiche the ende is deeth.° Wombe is hir god."[4]   *death*
O wombe, o bely, o stynkyng cod,°   *stinking bag (stomach)*
Fulfilled of donge° and of corrupcioun,   *filled with dung*
At either ende of thee foul is the soun!°   *sound*
How greet labour and cost is thee to fynde.°   *provide for*
250   Thise cookes, how they stampe° and streyne°   *pound / strain*
    and grynde
And turnen substaunce into accident[5]
To fulfillen al thy likerous° talent!°   *lecherous / inclination*
Out of the harde bones knokke they
The mary,° for they caste° noght awey   *marrow / throw*
255   That may go thurgh the golet° softe and swoote.°   *throat / sweet*
Of spicerie° of leef and bark and roote   *spices*
Shal been his sauce ymaked,° by delit°   *made / through delight*
To make° hym yet a newer appetit.   *give*
But certes, he that haunteth° swiche delices°   *follows / delights*
260   Is deed whil that he lyveth in tho° vices.[6]   *those*

---

[1] *Paul*   I.e., St. Paul.

[2] *Shal ... seith*   See 1 Corinthians 6.13.

[3] *apostel*   I.e., apostle, here St. Paul.

[4] *Ther walken ... god*   See Philippians 3.18–19.

[5] *And ... accident*   This distinction between the basic food and the flavors the cooks give to it draws on Aristotle's distinction between substance (essential inner reality) and its superficial qualities (accidents). This line could be read as an allusion to contemporary philosophical debates between Nominalists and Realists or to contemporary theological controversies concerning the process through which the bread and wine of the Eucharist are transformed into the body and blood of Christ.

[6] *he that ... vices*   Cf. 1 Timothy 5.6: "But she that lives in pleasure is dead while she lives."

A lecherous thyng is wyn, and dronkenesse
Is ful of stryvyng° and of wrecchednesse.   *quarreling*
O dronke man, disfigured is thy face!
Sour is thy breeth! Foul artow° to embrace!   *are you*
265   And thurgh thy dronke nose semeth the
    soun°   *the sound seems to come*
As though thou seydest ay° "Sampsoun, Sampsoun!"   *ever*
And yet, God woot,° Sampsoun drank nevere   *God knows*
    no wyn![7]
Thou fallest as it were a styked swyn.°   *stuck (i.e., speared) pig*
Thy tonge is lost and al thyn honeste cure.°   *care*
270   For dronkenesse is verray sepulture°   *tomb*
Of mannes wit and his discrecioun.
In whom that drynke hath dominacioun,
He kan no conseil° kepe, it is no drede.°   *counsel / doubt*
Now kepe yow fro the white and fro the rede
275   And namely fro the white wyn of Lepe[8]
That is to selle° in Fyssh Strete or in Chepe.[9]   *for sale*
This wyn of Spaigne° crepeth subtilly   *Spain*
In othere wynes growynge faste° by,[10]   *near*
Of which ther ryseth swich fumositee°   *such vapors*
280   That whan a man hath dronken draughtes thre°   *three*
And weneth° that he be at hoom° in Chepe,   *thinks / home*
He is in Spaigne, right at the toune of Lepe—
Nat at the Rochele ne at Burdeux toun—[11]
And thanne wol he seye, "Sampsoun, Sampsoun!"
285   But herkneth, lordes, o° word, I yow preye,   *one*
That alle the sovereyn actes, dar I seye,
Of victories in the Olde Testament
Thurgh verray° God that is omnipotent   *true*
Were doon in abstinence and in preyere.
290   Looketh the Bible, and ther ye may it leere.°   *learn*
    Looke, Attilla[12] the grete conquerour

---

[7] *And yet ... wyn*   As recounted in Judges 13, in which it is written that Samson's mother did not drink wine during her pregnancy.

[8] *Lepe*   Town in Spain.

[9] *Fyssh ... Chepe*   I.e., Fish Street and Cheapside, two market districts in London. Chaucer's father was a wine merchant on Fish Street.

[10] *This wyn ... by*   Expensive French wines, shipped through Bordeaux and La Rochelle, were often surreptitiously mixed with cheaper, but stronger, Spanish wines.

[11] *the Rochele ... Burdeux toun*   I.e., La Rochelle and Bordeaux.

[12] *Attilla*   I.e., Attila the Hun, a fifth-century nomadic chieftain who ravaged vast stretches of central Europe. According to medieval histories, such as those of Jordanes and Paul the Deacon, he died

Deyde° in his sleepe with shame and dishonour,   *died*
Bledynge° ay at his nose in dronkenesse.   *bleeding*
A capitayn° sholde lyve in sobrenesse.   *leader*
295   And over al this° avyseth yow° right wel   *above all / consider*
What was comaunded unto Lamwel.[1]
Nat Samuel[2] but Lamwel, seye I.
Redeth the Bible, and fynde it expresly°   *specifically*
Of wyn yevyng° to hem that han   *giving wine*
          justise.°   *have legal power*
300   Namoore of this, for it may wel suffise.
     And now I have spoken of glotonye,
Now wol I yow deffenden° hasardrye.°   *prohibit / gambling*
Hasard is verray mooder° of lesynges°   *mother / lying*
And of deceite and cursed forswerynges,°   *perjury*
305   Blasphemyng of Crist, manslaughtre, and
          wast° also   *wasteful spending*
Of catel° and of tyme. And forthermo,   *goods*
It is repreeve° and contrarie of° honour   *reproach / to*
For to ben holde° a commune hasardour.°   *be considered / gambler*
And ever the hyer° he is of estaat°   *higher / condition*
310   The moore is he holden° desolaat.°   *regarded as / vile*
If that a prynce° useth hasardrye,°   *prince / frequently gambles*
In alle governaunce and policye
He is as by commune opinioun
Yholde° the lasse° in reputacioun.   *held / less*
315   Stilboun,[3] that was a wys embassadour,
Was sent to Cornythe° in ful greet honour   *Corinth*
Fro Lacidomye° to maken hire alliaunce,   *Sparta*
And whan he cam, hym happed par chaunce[4]
That alle the gretteste that were of that lond
320   Pleyynge atte hasard he hem fond,
For which, as soone as it myghte be,
He stal hym° hoom agayn to his contree   *stole away*
And seyde, "Ther wol I nat lese° my name!   *lose*
Ne I wol nat take on me so greet defame°   *dishonor*
325   Yow for to allie° unto none hasardours.   *ally*
Sendeth otherewise° embassadours.   *other*

For by my trouthe, me were levere dye°   *rather die*
Than I yow sholde to hasardours allye.
For ye that been so glorious in honours
330   Shul nat allyen yow with hasardours,
As by my wyl,° ne as by my tretee."°   *will / treaty*
This wise philosophre thus seyde hee.
     Looke eek that to the kyng Demetrius,
The kyng of Parthes,° as the book seith° us,[5]   *Parthia / tells*
335   Sente him a paire of dees° of gold in scorn,   *dice*
For he hadde used hasard ther-biforn,°   *often gambled before this*
For which he heeld his glorie or his renoun
At no value or reputacioun.
Lordes may fynden oother maner pley°   *kinds of amusement*
340   Honeste ynough to dryve the day awey.
     Now wol I speke of othes° false and grete   *oaths*
A word or two, as olde bookes trete.
Greet sweryng° is a thyng abhominable,   *swearing*
And fals sweryng° is yet moore reprevable.°   *perjury / disgraceful*
345   The heighe God forbad sweryng at al,[6]
Witnesse on Mathew, but in special,°   *specially*
Of sweryng seith the hooly Jeremye,°   *Jeremiah*
"Thou shalt seye sooth thyne othes° and nat lye   *truly your oaths*
And swere in doom° and eek in rightwisnesse."[7]   *judgment*
350   But ydel sweryng is a cursednesse.
Bihoold and se that in the firste table°   *tablet (of Moses)*
Of heighe Goddes heestes° honorable   *commandments*
Hou that the seconde heeste of hym° is this   *them*
"Take nat my name in ydel or amys."[8]
355   Lo, rather° he forbedeth swich   *earlier (in the commandments)*
          sweryng
Than homycide or any cursed thyng.
I seye that as by ordre thus it stondeth.°   *stands*

from drink on the night that he took a new bride.

[1]   *Lamwel*   I.e., Lemuel, King of Massa, whose mother warns him not to drink wine. See Proverbs 31.4–5.

[2]   *Samuel*   I.e., the prophet Samuel. See 1 Samuel.

[3]   *Stilboun*   I.e., Chilon, an ambassador who is mentioned in John of Salisbury's *Polycraticus*, 1.5.

[4]   *And … chaunce*   And when he came, it happened to him by chance.

[5]   *The kyng … us*   King Demetrius of Parthia has not been securely identified, but John of Salisbury tells his story in the *Policraticus* immediately after that of Chilon.

[6]   *The heighe … al*   See Matthew 5.34.

[7]   *Thou … rightwisnesse*   See Jeremiah 4.2; *rightwisnesse* Righteousness.

[8]   *Take … amys*   See Deuteronomy 5.7–21. In the Middle Ages the first two commandments were normally grouped as one, making what is now considered the third commandment the second, as it is here. The tenth commandment was then broken into two to make up the difference; *amys* In vain.

This knowen that hise heestes understondeth,[1]

How that the seconde heeste° of God is   *second commandment*
that.

360 And forther over,° I wol thee telle al plat°   *furthermore | plainly*

That vengeance shal nat parten° from his hous   *depart*

That of his othes° is to° outrageous.   *oaths | too*

"By Goddes precious herte!" and "By his nayles"°   *nails*

And "By the blood of Crist that is in Hayles,[2]

365 Sevene is my chaunce and thyn is cynk° and treye!"°[3]   *five | three*

By Goddes armes, if thou falsly pleye,

This daggere shal thurghout thyn herte go!"°   *pierce*

This fruyt° cometh of the bicched bones two—[4]   *fruit*

Forsweryng,° ire,° falsnesse, homycide.   *perjury | anger*

370 Now for the love of Crist that for us dyde,

Lete° youre othes, bothe grete and smale.   *leave*

But sires, now wol I telle forth my tale.

    Thise riotours° thre of whiche I telle   *party-goers*

Longe erst er° prime° rong° of any belle   *before | early morning | rang*

375 Were set hem in a taverne to drynke.

And as they sat, they herde a belle clynke°   *ring*

Biforn° a cors° was° caried   *before | corpse | that was being*
to his grave.

That oon of hem gan callen to his knave,°   *servant*

"Go bet,"° quod he, "and axe° redily°   *quickly | ask | eagerly*

380 What cors is this that passeth heer forby,

And looke that thou reporte his name weel."

    "Sire," quod this boy, "it nedeth never a deel.°   *it is not necessary*

It was me toold er ye cam heer two houres.[5]

He was, pardee,° an old felawe° of youres,   *by God | friend*

385 And sodeynly he was yslayn tonyght.

For dronke as he sat on his bench upright

Ther cam a privee theef° men clepeth° Deeth,   *secret thief | call*

That in this contree al the peple sleeth,

And with his spere he smoot° his herte atwo°   *cut | in two*

390 And wente his wey withouten wordes mo.

He hath a thousand slayn this pestilence.°[6]   *during this epidemic*

And maister, er ye come in his presence,

Me thynketh that it were necessarie

For to bewar of swich an adversarie.

395 Beth° redy for to meete hym everemoore.°   *be | always*

Thus taughte me my dame.° I sey namoore."   *mother*

"By seinte Marie," seyde this taverner,°   *tavern keeper*

"The child seith sooth, for he hath slayn this yeer

Henne° over a mile withinne a greet° village   *from here | large*

400 Bothe man and womman, child and hyne°   *hired hand*
and page.

I trowe° his habitacioun° be there.   *believe | dwelling*

To been avysed° greet wysdom it were,   *warned*

Er° that he dide° a man a dishonour."°   *lest | cause | harm*

    "Ye, Goddes armes," quod this riotour,

405 "Is it swich peril with hym for to meete?

I shal hym seke by wey° and eek by strete,°   *road | street*

I make avow° to Goddes digne° bones.   *a vow | worthy*

Herkneth, felawes, we thre been al ones.°   *are three together*

Lat ech of us holde up his hand til oother,°   *to the other*

410 And ech of us bicomen° otheres brother,   *become*

And we wol sleen this false traytour, Deeth!

He shal be slayn, which that so manye sleeth,

By Goddes dignitee er it be nyght!"

    Togidres° han thise thre hir trouthes plight°   *together | promised*

415 To lyve and dyen ech of hem for oother

As though he were his owene yborn° brother.   *born*

And up they stirte° al dronken in this rage.   *jumped*

And forth they goon towardes that village

Of which the taverner hadde spoke biforn.

420 And many a grisly° ooth thanne han they sworn,   *horrible*

And Cristes blessed body they torente.°   *tear apart (with their oaths)*

Deeth shal be deed, if that they may hym hente!°   *catch him*

    Whan they han goon[7] nat fully half a mile

---

[1] *This ... understondeth* Those who understand his commandments know this.

[2] *Hayles* I.e., Hales Abbey in Gloucestershire, a monastery that claimed to have some of Christ's blood as a relic.

[3] *Sevene ... treye* The modern game of craps is a version of medieval hazard, in which the player rolling the dice must call out the numbers he hopes to get.

[4] *bicched bones two* Two cursed bones; i.e., the dice, which were made of bone in the Middle Ages.

[5] *It ... houres* It was told to me two hours ago, before you came here.

[6] *Ther cam ... pestilence* The reference here is doubtless to plague, the Black Death that spread from Italy across Europe, hit England in 1348, and in the space of a year killed at least a third of the population. There were further outbreaks in 1361–62, 1369, and 1375–76.

[7] *han goon* Have gone. Chaucer frequently alternates between the simple past (the rioters jumped up, the old man met with them) and the present or the perfect forms (the rioters have gone rather than had gone or went, which we would expect in modern English).

Right° as they wolde han troden over a stile,[1]   *just*

425 An oold man and a povre° with hem   *poor*
       mette.°   *encountered them*
   This olde man ful mekely° hem grette°   *meekly / greeted*
   And seyde thus: "Now, lordes, God yow see!"°   *watch over*
      The proudeste of thise riotours three
   Answerde agayn, "What, carl,° with sory   *peasant*
       grace!°   *bad luck to you*
430 Why artow al forwrapped,° save thy face?   *wrapped up*
   Why lyvestow° so longe in so greet age?"   *live you*
      This olde man gan looke in his visage°   *face*
   And seyde thus: "For° I ne kan nat fynde   *because*
   A man, though that I walked into Ynde,°   *India*
435 Neither in citee nor in no village,
   That wolde chaunge his youthe for myn age.
   And therfore moot I han° myn age stille,   *I must have*
   As longe tyme as it is Goddes wille.
   Ne deeth, allas, ne wol nat han my lyf.
440 Thus walke I lyk a restelees° kaityf,°   *restless / wretch*
   And on the ground which is my moodres° gate   *mother's*
   I knokke with my staf° bothe erly and late   *walking stick*
   And seye, 'Leeve° Mooder, leet me in!   *dear*
   Lo how I vanysshe°—flessh and blood and skyn!   *waste away*
445 Allas, whan shul my bones been at reste?
   Mooder, with yow wolde I chaunge my cheste°   *money box*
   That in my chambre° longe tyme hath be,°   *room / been*
   Ye, for an heyre clowt° to wrappe me.'[2]   *hair-shirt*
   But yet to me she wol nat do that grace,°   *favor*
450 For which ful pale and welked° is my face.   *withered*
      "But sires, to° yow it is no curteisye   *in*
   To speken to an old man vileynye,°   *insults*
   But° he trespasse° in word or elles in dede.   *unless / offend*
   In Hooly Writ ye may yourself wel rede
455 'Agayns° an oold man hoor° upon   *in the presence of / gray*
       his heed
   Ye sholde arise.'[3] Wherfore° I yeve° yow   *therefore / give*
       reed:°   *advice*
   Ne dooth unto an oold man noon harm now,

Namoore than that ye wolde° men did to yow[4]   *desire*
In age—if that ye so longe abyde.°   *live long enough*
460 And God be with yow, where° ye go° or ryde.   *wherever / walk*
   I moot go thider as° I have to go."   *thither where*
      "Nay, olde cherl, by God thou shalt nat so!"
   Seyde this oother hasardour° anon.   *gambler*
   "Thou partest nat° so lightly, by Seint John!   *do not get away*
465 Thou spak right now of thilke traytour Deeth,
   That in this contree° alle oure freendes sleeth.   *country*
   Have heer my trouthe:° as thou art his espye,°   *on my word / spy*
   Telle where he is, or thou shalt it abye,°   *pay for it*
   By God and by the hooly sacrement!°   *holy sacrament (the Eucharist)*
470 For soothly, thou art oon of his assent°   *plot*
   To sleen us yonge folk, thou false theef!"
      "Now sires," quod he, "if that ye be so leef,°   *desirous*
   To fynde Deeth, turne up this croked wey.°   *crooked way*
   For in that grove I lafte hym, by my fey,°   *faith*
475 Under a tree, and there he wole abyde.°   *wait*
   Noght for youre boost he wole him nothyng hyde.[5]
   Se ye that ook?° Right there ye shal hym fynde.   *oak*
   God save yow that boghte agayn° mankynde[6]   *redeemed*
   And yow amende!"° Thus seyde this olde man.   *make you better*
480 And everich° of thise riotours ran   *each*
   Til he cam to that tree, and ther they founde
   Of floryns° fyne of gold ycoyned° rounde   *florins (coins) / coined*
   Wel ny° an eighte busshels, as hem   *very nearly*
       thoughte.°   *it seemed to them*
   No lenger thanne° after Deeth they soughte,   *then*
485 But ech of hem so glad was of that sighte,
   For that the floryns been so faire and brighte,
   That doun° they sette hem° by this precious   *down / themselves*
       hoord.°   *hoard*
   The worste of hem, he spak the firste word.
      "Bretheren," quod he, "taak kepe° what I seye.   *pay attention to*
490 My wit is greet, though that I bourde° and pleye.   *joke*
   This tresor hath Fortune unto us yeven°   *given*
   In myrthe and joliftee° oure lyf to lyven.   *jollity*
   And lightly° as it comth, so wol we spende.   *easily*
   Ey, Goddes precious dignitee! Who wende°   *expected*

---

[1] *stile* Steps to get over a wall or fence.

[2] *Mooder ... me* People in the Middle Ages sometimes wore shirts made of hair, which irritated the body, expecting the pain to gain them spiritual benefit. Here the old man wishes to be buried in such a shirt, exchanging it for the chest that holds his money.

[3] *Agayns ... arise* See Leviticus 19.3.

[4] *Namoore ... yow* Cf. the Golden Rule from Matthew 7:12: "So whatever you wish that men would do to you, do so to them."

[5] *Noght ... hyde* He will not hide himself in any way because of your boasting.

[6] *God ... mankynde* May God, who redeemed mankind (by sending his Son Jesus Christ to die on the Cross), save you.

495 Today that we sholde han so fair a grace?
But myghte this gold be caried fro this place
Hoom to myn hous, or elles unto yours—
For wel ye woot that al this gold is oures—
Thanne were we in heigh felicitee.°   *great happiness*
500 But trewely, by daye it may nat bee.°   *not be*
Men wolde seyn that we were theves stronge°   *downright thieves*
And for oure owene tresor doon us honge.°   *cause us to be hanged*
This tresor moste ycaried be by nyghte
As wisely and as slyly as it myghte.
505 Wherfore I rede° that cut° among us alle   *advise / lots*
Be drawe° and lat se wher the cut wol falle,   *drawn*
And he that hath the cut with herte blithe°   *happy*
Shal renne to towne, and that ful swithe,°   *quickly*
And brynge us breed and wyn ful prively.°   *secretly*
510 And two of us shul kepen subtilly°   *cleverly*
This tresor wel. And if he wol nat tarie,°   *delay*
Whan it is nyght we wol this tresor carie
By oon assent° whereas us thynketh best."   *in agreement*
That oon of hem the cut° broghte in his fest°   *lots / fist*
515 And bad hem drawe and looke where it wol falle.
And it fil on the yongeste of hem alle,
And forth toward the toun he wente anon.
And also soone as that he was gon,
That oon spak thus unto that oother:
520 "Thow knowest wel thou art my sworn brother;
Thy profit° wol I telle thee anon.   *your advantage*
Thou woost wel that oure felawe is agon,
And heere is gold, and that ful greet plentee,°   *a great deal of it*
That shal departed° been among us thre.   *divided*
525 But nathelees, if I kan shape it so,
That it departed were among us two,
Hadde I nat doon a freendes torn° to thee?"   *friend's turn*
    That oother answerde, "I noot hou° that   *do not know how*
        may be.
He woot how that the gold is with us tweye.°   *two*
530 What shal we doon? What shal we to hym seye?"
    "Shal it be conseil?"° seyde the firste shrewe.°   *our plan / villain*
"And I shal tellen in a wordes fewe
What we shal doon and bryngen it wel aboute."
    "I graunte," quod that oother, "out of doute,°   *without doubt*
535 That by my trouthe I shal thee nat biwreye."°   *betray*
    "Now," quod the firste, "thou woost wel we be tweye,
And two of us shul strenger be than oon.

Looke whan that he is set, that right anoon
Arys° as though thou woldest with hym pleye,   *arise*
540 And I shal ryve° hym thurgh the sydes tweye°   *stab / two sides*
Whil that thou strogelest° with hym as in game,°   *struggle / jest*
And with thy daggere, looke thou do the same.
And thanne shal al this gold departed be,
My deere freend, bitwixen me and thee.
545 Thanne may we bothe oure lustes° all fulfille   *pleasures*
And pleye at dees° right at oure owene wille."   *dice*
And thus acorded been° thise shrewes tweye   *are agreed*
To sleen° the thridde, as ye han herd me seye.   *kill*
    This yongeste, which that wente unto the toun,
550 Ful ofte in herte he rolleth up and doun
The beautee of thise floryns newe and brighte.
"O Lord," quod he, "if so were that I myghte
Have al this tresor to myself allone,
Ther is no man that lyveth under the trone°   *throne*
555 Of God that sholde lyve so murye° as I!"   *merry*
And atte laste the feend° oure enemy   *devil*
Putte in his thought that he sholde poyson beye°   *buy*
With which he myghte sleen° hise felawes tweye,   *kill*
For why the feend foond hym in swich lyvynge
560 That he hadde leve hym to sorwe brynge.[1]
For this was outrely° his fulle entente,   *utterly*
To sleen hem bothe and nevere to repent.
And forth he gooth—no lenger wolde he tarie—
Into the toun unto a pothecarie°   *apothecary*
565 And preyde hym that he hym wolde selle
Som poysoun that he myghte hise rattes° quelle.°   *rats / kill*
And eek ther was a polcat in his hawe,
That, as he seyde, hise capouns hadde yslawe.[2]
And fayn° he wolde wreke hym,° if he   *gladly / avenge himself*
        myghte,
570 On vermyn that destroyed° hym by nyghte.   *harmed*
    The pothecarie answerde, "And thou shalt have
A thyng that, also° God my soule save,   *as*
In al this world ther is no creature
That eten or dronken hath of this confiture°   *concoction*

---

[1] *For why ... brynge* Because the devil found him living in such a way (i.e., so sinfully) that he had permission (from God) to bring him to sorrow (i.e., damnation).

[2] *And eek ... yslawe* And also there was a polcat (a type of weasel) in his yard that, as he said, had killed his poultry.

575	Noght° but the montance° of a corn° of whete, *nothing / size / grain*
	That he ne shal his lif anon° forlete.° *immediately / lose*
	Ye, sterve° he shal, and that in lasse while° *die / less time*
	Than thou wolt goon a paas° nat but a mile, *at a walking pace*
	The poysoun is so strong and violent."
580	This cursed man hath in his hond yhent° *taken*
	This poysoun in a box, and sith° he ran *afterwards*
	Into the nexte strete° unto a man *street*
	And borwed hym° large botels thre. *borrowed from him*
	And in the two his poyson poured he.
585	The thridde he kepte clene for his owene drynke.
	For al the nyght he shoope° hym for to swynke° *intended / labor*
	In cariynge of the gold out of that place.
	And whan this riotour with sory grace° *wretched misfortune*
	Hadde filled with wyn hise grete botels thre,
590	To hise felawes agayn repaireth he.
	What nedeth it to sermone° of it moore? *talk*
	For right so° as they hadde cast° his deeth bifoore, *just as / determined*
	Right so they han hym slayn, and that anon.
	And whan that this was doon, thus spak that oon:° *the first*
595	"Now lat us sitte and drynke and make us merie,
	And afterward we wol his body berie."° *bury*
	And with that word it happed hym par cas° *by chance*
	To take the botel ther the poysoun was,
	And drank and yaf his felawe drynke also,
600	For which anon they storven° bothe two. *died*
	But certes, I suppose that Avycen[1]
	Wroot° nevere in no *Canoun* ne in no fen° *wrote / chapter*
	Mo wonder° signes° of empoisonyng° *more terrible / symptoms* / *poisoning*
	Than hadde thise wrecches two er hir endyng.° *before their death*
605	Thus ended been thise homycides° two *murderers*
	And eek the false empoysonere° also. *poisoner*
	O cursed synne of alle cursednesse,
	O traytours° homycide, o wikkednesse, *traitorous*
	O glotonye, luxurie,° and hasardrye, *lust*

610	Thou blasphemour of Crist with vileynye
	And othes grete° of usage° and of pride! *great oaths / habit*
	Allas, mankynde, how may it bitide° *happen*
	That to thy creatour, which that the wroghte° *who made you*
	And with his precious herte blood thee boghte,° *redeemed*
615	Thou art so fals and so unkynde,° allas? *unnatural*
	Now goode men, God foryeve yow youre trespas
	And ware° yow fro the synne of avarice! *guard*
	Myn hooly pardoun may yow all warice,° *save*
	So° that ye offre nobles or sterlynges[2] *provided*
620	Or elles silver broches, spoones, rynges.
	Boweth youre heed under this hooly bulle.° *license*
	Com up, ye wyves, offreth of youre wolle;° *wool*
	Youre names I entre heer in my rolle° anon. *list*
	Into the blisse of Hevene shul ye gon.
625	I yow assoille° by myn heigh power, *pardon*
	As ye were born. And lo, sires, thus I preche.
	And Jesu Crist that is oure soules leche° *soul's physician*
	So graunte yow his pardoun to receyve.
	For that is best; I wol yow nat deceyve.
630	"But sires, o° word forgat I in my tale. *one*
	I have relikes and pardoun in my male° *pouch*
	As faire as any man in Engelond,
	Whiche were me yeven° by the Popes hond.° *given / hand*
	If any of yow wole of devocioun° *in devotion*
635	Offren and han myn absolucioun,
	Com forth anon, and kneleth heere adoun,
	And mekely° receyveth my pardoun. *meekly*
	Or elles taketh pardoun as ye wende,° *go*
	Al newe and fressh at every miles ende,
640	So that ye offren alwey newe° and newe *anew*
	Nobles or pens,° whiche that be goode and trewe.[3] *pence*
	It is an honour to everich° that is heer *everyone*
	That ye mowe° have a suffisant° pardoneer *may / capable*
	T'assoille yow in contree° as ye ryde *the country*
645	For aventures° whiche that may bityde.° *accidents / befall*
	Paraventure° ther may fallen oon or two *perhaps*
	Doun of his hors and breke his nekke atwo.° *in two*

---

[1] *Avycen* I.e., Avicenna or Ibn Sina (980–1037 CE), a Persian philosopher who wrote, among other things, a treatise about medicine entitled *Liber Canonis Medicinae* (*The Book of the Canon of Medicine*). The word *Canon* in the next line refers to this book. It was divided into chapters called "fens," from the Arabic word for a part of a science.

---

[2] *nobles or sterlynges* Gold and silver coins respectively.

[3] *Nobles ... trewe* Forgery and also the clipping of coins (i.e., shaving off some of the silver or gold from the edges) were major concerns in Chaucer's day.

Looke which a seuretee° is it to yow alle   *guarantee*
That I am in youre felaweshipe yfalle,°   *fallen into your company*
650 That may assoille yow bothe moore and
        lasse°   *greater and lesser (of rank)*
Whan that the soule shal fro the body passe.
I rede° that oure Hoost heere shal bigynne,°   *advise / begin*
For he is moost envoluped in synne.
Com forth, sire Hoost, and offre first anon,
655 And thou shalt kisse my relikes everychon.
Ye, for a grote unbokele anon thy purs."[1]

    "Nay, nay," quod he, "thanne have I Cristes curs!°   *curse*
Lat be,"° quod he. "It shal nat be so, thee'ch!   *leave it be*
Thou woldest make me kisse thyn olde breech°   *pants*
660 And swere it were a relyk of a seint—
Though it were with thy fundement° depeint!°   *anus / stained*
But by the croys which that Seint Eleyne[2] fond,
I wolde I hadde thy coillons° in myn hond   *testicles*
Instide of relikes or of seintuarie!°   *reliquaries*
665 Lat kutte hem of!° I wol with thee hem   *let them be cut off*
        carie.°   *carry*

They shul be shryned° in an   *enshrined*
        hogges toord!"°   *hog's turd*
    This Pardoner answerde nat a word.
So wrooth° he was, no word ne wolde he seye.   *angry*
    "Now," quod oure Hoost, "I wol no lenger pleye°   *joke*
670 With thee ne with noon oother angry man!"
But right anon the worthy knyght bigan°   *began*
Whan that he saugh that al the peple lough,°   *laughed*
"Namoore of this! For it is right ynough!°   *quite enough*
Sire Pardoner, be glad and myrie of cheere.°   *merry of face*
675 And ye, sire Hoost, that been to me so deere,
I prey yow that ye kisse the Pardoner.
And Pardoner, I prey thee, drawe thee neer,
And as we diden,° lat us laughe and pleye!"   *did*
Anon they kiste and ryden forth hir weye.°   *their way*

HEERE IS ENDED THE PARDONERS TALE

---

[1] *Ye ... purs*   Yes, unbuckle your purse immediately for a groat (fourpenny coin).

[2] *Seint Eleyne*   I.e., St. Helena, the mother of the fourth-century Roman emperor Constantine. Legend had it that she went to the Holy Land and found there the cross on which Christ was crucified.

The Nun's Priest's Prologue and Tale

In the full *Canterbury Tales* this tale is preceded by *The Monk's Tale*, in which the Monk recites a long list of tragedies, which for him are simply stories of those who have fallen suddenly from great rank. This wearies the Knight, who interrupts him. When the Monk refuses to tell stories of hunting instead, the Host calls peremptorily upon the Nun's Priest. The Nun's Priest, who is not even described in the *General Prologue*, is at first almost a nonentity. By the end of his tale, however, he will have won whole-hearted admiration, at least from the rather undiscerning Host, whose response (also included here) is contained in a passage that does not appear in the Ellesmere Manuscript.

The tale offered by the Nun's Priest is a beast fable of the kind told by Aesop. It revolves around animals who are all too human in their follies, and it teaches a clear moral lesson: beware of flatterers. The Nun's Priest expands on this simple structure, beginning with a rich rhetorical evocation of the rooster Chauntecleer's crowing, which he contrasts to the austere life of the poor widow who owns him. The tale then moves into an elaborate debate on dream lore, in which the hen Pertelote speaks for the materialist for whom dreams are the result of indigestion, and Chauntecleer for those who see them as veiled prophecies. This debate alone takes up nearly half the lines in the tale. Throughout, the tale fluctuates between a world in which Chauntecleer and Pertelote are aristocratic lovers and a world in which they are just barnyard fowl. Much of the comedy lies in the elaborate rhetorical language, which is both celebrated and mocked. The Nun's Priest is clearly a master of this art, and it is typical of the tale's comic approach to the eloquence it proudly displays that he should invoke Geoffrey of Vinsauf and his basic textbook on rhetoric. This is a work that, while it is several steps up on Pertelote's only written authority, an elementary grammar drawn from the moral writings of Cato, is scarcely sophisticated. For all its comedy, the tale contains one of Chaucer's grimmest and most pointed historical references, to the rebels in 1381 who hunted down and murdered Flemish weavers.

The Nun's Priest ends by suggesting that the tale exists only for its moral, the fruit, and that we should discard the story, the chaff. All that is written, he tells us, is written for our doctrine, a line Chaucer repeats in his *Retraction*. But the Nun's Priest also tells us that his story is as true as that of Lancelot de Lake (line 445), that he speaks only in game (line 495), and that when he criticizes women his words are those of Chauntecleer (line 498). Filled with references to books and sayings, such as Chauntecleer's comment that "Mulier est hominis confusio" (Latin: Woman is man's confusion, line 397), that are misrepresented or otherwise untrustworthy, the tale does not allow such an easy distinction between literary art and moral content.

Opening page of *The Nun's Priest's Tale*, Ellesmere manuscript (detail).
(Reprinted by permission of *The Huntington Library, San Marino, California.* EL 26 C9 f. 179r.)

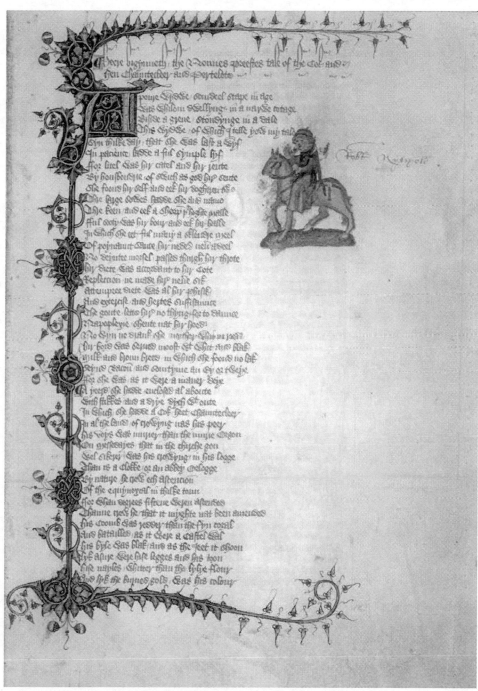

Opening page of *The Nun's Priest's Tale*, Ellesmere manuscript. (Reprinted by permission of *The Huntington Library, San Marino, California. EL 26 C9 f. 179r.*)

THE NUN'S PRIEST'S PROLOGUE

HEERE STYNTETH THE KNYGHT THE MONK OF HIS TALE[1]

THE PROLOGE OF THE NONNES PREESTES TALE

"Hoo,"° quod° the Knyght, "good sire,   whoa / said
  namoore° of this!   no more
That ye han seyd is right ynough, ywis,[2]
And muchel moore,° for litel   much more
  hevynesse°   a little heaviness
Is right ynough° to muche folk,° I gesse.   enough / many people
5 I seye° for me it is a greet disese,°   say / great discomfort
Whereas° men han been in greet welthe° and   where / wealth
  ese,°   ease
To heeren° of hire° sodeyn fal,° allas!   hear / their / sudden fall
And the contrarie° is joye and greet solas,°   contrary / comfort
As whan a man hath been in povre° estaat,°   poor / condition
10 And clymbeth° up, and wexeth° fortunate,   climbs / grows
And there abideth° in prosperitee.   remains
Swich° thyng is gladsom,° as it   such a / pleasant
  thynketh° me,   seems to
And of swich thyng were goodly for to telle."
  "Ye,"° quod oure Hoost, "by Seint Poules belle,[3]   yes
15 Ye seye right sooth.° This Monk, he clappeth   truth
  lowed.°   chatters loudly
He spak how Fortune covered with a clowde°   cloud
I noot° nevere what, and also of a tragedie   know not
Right now ye harde,° and, pardee,° no   heard / by God
  remedie°   remedy
It is for to biwaille° ne° compleyne°   bewail / nor / lament
20 That that° is doon,° and als° it is a   which / done / also
  peyne,°   pain
As ye han seyd, to heere of hevynesse.°   sadness
  "Sire Monk, namoore of this, so God yow blesse!
Youre tale anoyeth al this compaignye.
Swich talkyng is nat worth a boterflye!°   butterfly
25 For therinne is ther no desport° ne game.   sport

Wherfore,° sire Monk, daun° Piers by   therefore / sir
  youre name,
I pray yow hertely° telle us somwhat elles.° heartily / something else
For sikerly, nere° clynkyng° of youre   were it not for / clinking
  belles
That on youre bridel° hange on every syde,   bridle
30 By Hevene Kyng° that° for us alle   the King of Heaven / who
  dyde,°   died
I sholde er° this han° fallen doun for sleepe,   before / have
Althogh the slough° had never been so deepe.   mud
Thanne hadde youre tale al be° toold in veyn.°   been / vain
For certeinly, as that thise clerkes seyn,°   these scholars say
35 Whereas° a man may have noon° audience,   where / no
Noght helpeth it° to tellen his sentence.° it is of no use / meaning
And wel I woot, the substance is in me
If anythyng shal wel reported be.[4]
Sire, sey° somwhat of huntyng, I yow preye."   tell us
40 "Nay," quod this Monk, "I have no lust° to   desire
  pleye.°   play
Now lat° another telle as I have toold."   let
  Thanne spak oure Hoost with rude speche°   rough speech
  and boold°   bold
And seyde unto the Nonnes Preest°   Nun's Priest
  anon,°   immediately
"Com neer, thou Preest. Com hyder,° thou sire John![5]   here
45 Telle us swich thyng as may oure hertes glade.°   gladden
Be blithe,° though thou ryde upon a jade.°   happy / bad horse
What thogh° thyn hors be bothe foul and lene?°   though / lean
If he wol serve thee, rekke nat a bene!°   do not care a bean
Looke that thyn herte be murie° everemo."   merry
50 "Yis sire," quod he, "yis, Hoost, so moot I go.°   as I may go
But° I be myrie, ywis,° I wol be blamed."   unless / indeed
And right anon his tale he hath attamed,°   has begun
And thus he seyde unto us everichon,°   everyone
This sweete preest, this goodly man, sire John.

EXPLICIT[6]

---

[1] *Heere ... Tale* Here the Knight stops the Monk from telling his tale. The Monk's tragic tale recounted the fall of numerous people from greatness to wretchedness and misery.

[2] *That ... ywis* What you have said is quite enough, indeed.

[3] *Seint Poules belle* I.e., the bell of St. Paul's Cathedral in London.

[4] *the substance ... be* Either I have the stuff (substance) in me (i.e., the power) to understand if a story is well told, or possibly, if a story is well told, I know when I have grasped the substance of it.

[5] *thou sire John* The Host addresses the Nun's Priest with the familiar *thou*, not the polite *you* that he uses for the Knight, the Monk, or most of the other gentle folk.

[6] *Explicit* Latin: Here it ends.

THE NUN'S PRIEST'S TALE

HEERE BIGYNNETH THE NONNES PREESTES TALE OF THE COK AND HEN, CHAUNTECLEER AND PERTELOTE

55 A povre° wydwe° somdeel° stape° in age   *poor / widow / somewhat / advanced*
Was whilom° dwellyng° in a narwe° cottage   *once / living / small*
Biside° a grene[1] stondynge° in a dale.   *beside / standing*
This wydwe of which I telle yow my tale,
Syn° thilke° day that she was last a wyf   *since / that*
60 In pacience ladde° a ful° symple lyf,   *led / very*
For litel° was hir catel° and hir rente.°   *little / possessions / income*
By housbondrie° of swich° as God hire° sente   *frugal use / such / her*
She foond° hirself and eek° hir doghtren° two.   *provided for / also / daughters*
Thre° large sowes hadde she and namo,°   *three / no more*
65 Thre keen,° and eek a sheepe that highte° Malle.   *cows / was called*
Ful sooty was hir bour° and eek hir halle°   *bedroom / hall*
In which she eet° ful many a sklendre meel.°   *ate / meager meal*
Of poynaunt° sauce hir neded never a deel;°   *spicy / portion*
No deyntee° morsel passed thurgh hir throte.°   *dainty / throat*
70 Hir diete was accordant to hir cote.°   *in accord with her cottage*
Repleccioun° ne made hire nevere sik.°   *gluttony / sick*
Attempree° diete was al hir phisik,°   *temperate / medical remedy*
And excercise and hertes suffisaunce.°   *heart's content*
The goute lette hire nothyng for to daunce,[2]
75 N'apoplexie° shente° nat hir heed.°   *nor stroke / harmed / head*
No wyn ne drank she, neither whit ne reed.
Hir bord° was served moost with whit and blak—   *table*
Milk and broun breed, in which she foond no lak,[3]
Seynd bacoun° and somtyme an ey° or tweye.°   *smoked bacon / egg / two*
80 For she was, as it were, a maner° deye.°   *kind of / dairy farmer*

A yeerd° she hadde enclosed al aboute   *yard*
With stikkes° and a drye dych[4] withoute,   *sticks*
In which she hadde a cok° heet° Chauntecleer.[5]   *rooster / named*
In al the land of crowyng° nas° his peer.   *crowing / there was not*
85 His voys° was murier° than the murie orgon°   *voice / merrier / organ*
On messedayes that in the chirche gon.[6]
Wel sikerer° was his crowing in his logge°   *reliable / lodging*
Than is a clokke or an abbey orlogge.°   *monastery clock*
By nature he crew° ech ascencioun°   *crowed / each ascension*
90 Of the equynoxial[7] in thilke° toun.   *that*
For whan degrees fiftene weren ascended,
Thanne crew he that it myghte nat been amended.°   *could not be improved*
His coomb° was redder than the fyn° coral   *coxcomb / fine*
And batailled° as it were a castel wal.[8]   *crenellated*
95 His byle° was blak, and as the jeet° it shoon.°   *bill / jet (gemstone) / shone*
Lyk asure° were his legges and his toon,°   *azure / toes*
Hise nayles° whitter than the lylye flour,°   *nails / lily flower*
And lyk the burned° gold was his colour.   *polished*
This gentil° cok hadde in his governaunce°   *noble / control*
100 Sevene hennes for to doon° al his plesaunce,°   *do / pleasure*
Whiche were hise sustres° and his paramours°   *his sisters / lovers*
And wonder lyk° to hym as of colours,   *marvelously similar*
Of whiche the faireste hewed° on hir throte°   *colored / her throat*
Was cleped° faire damoysele° Pertelote.   *called / damsel*
105 Curteys° she was, discreet, and debonaire°   *courteous / gracious*
And compaignable,° and bar° hirself so faire°   *friendly / behaved / well*
Syn thilke day that she was seven nyght oold,°   *nights old*

---

[4] *drye dych* Contrasts with the moat of a castle.

[5] *Chauntecleer* From the French, "clear singer." Chauntecleer is the name of the rooster in *The Romance of Renard*, which tells the adventures of a wily fox and contains one of the best known medieval versions of the story told by the Nun's Priest.

[6] *On ... gon* That go (i.e., are played—the organ, an instrument of many pipes, was spoken of as plural) in Church on feast days.

[7] *By nature ... equynoxial* The sense of this passage is that Chauntecleer crows when each hourly point of the celestial equator rises past the horizon.

[8] *And ... wal* The crenelation on a castle's walls is the alternation of high, squared masonry with blank spaces. This would provide cover for the archers defending the castle against the arrows of the attackers.

---

[1] *grene* I.e., green, a common area in a village used for pasturage or other agricultural pursuits that did not demand the plowing of the green into a field.

[2] *The goute ... daunce* The gout (a disease affecting the feet and brought on by over-eating or drinking) by no means hindered her from dancing.

[3] *in ... lak* Either defect or lack, so either: In which she found no fault, or of which she had no shortage.

That trewely, she hath the herte in hoold°   *holds the heart*
Of Chauntecleer, loken° in every lith.°   *locked / limb*
110 He loved hire so, that wel was hym therwith.
And swich a joye was it to here hem° synge,   *them*
Whan that the brighte sonne bigan to sprynge,°   *rise*
In sweete accord,° "My Lief Is Faren in Londe."[1]   *harmony*
For thilke tyme,° as I have understonde,   *at that time*
115 Beestes and briddes° koude speke and synge.   *birds*
    And so bifel° that in the dawenynge,°   *it happened / at dawn*
As Chauntecleer among hise wyves alle
Sat on his perche° that was in the halle,   *perch*
And next hym sat this faire Pertelote,
120 This Chauntecleer gan gronen° in his throte   *began to groan*
As man that in his dreem is drecched soore.°   *sorely disturbed*
And whan that Pertelote thus herde hym roore,°   *roar*
She was agast° and seyde, "O herte deere,   *afraid*
What eyleth° yow to grone in this manere?   *ails*
125 Ye been° a verray° slepere. Fy!° For shame!"   *are / good / fie*
    And he answerde and seyde thus: "Madame,
I pray yow that ye take it nat agrief.°   *amiss*
By God, me thoughte I was in swich meschief°   *such trouble*
Right now, that yet myn herte is soore afright.
130 Now God," quod he, "my swevene recche aright,[2]
And kepe my body out of foul prisoun!
Me mette° how that I romed up and doun   *I dreamed*
Withinne oure yeerd, wheereas° I saugh a beest   *where*
Was lyk an hound, and wolde han maad areest°   *grabbed hold*
135 Upon my body and han had me deed!°   *have had me dead*
His colour was bitwixe yelow and reed,°   *red*
And tipped was his tayl° and bothe hise eeris°   *tail / his ears*
With blak, unlyk° the remenant of hise heeris;°   *unlike / hairs*
His snowte° smal with glowynge eyen tweye.°   *nose / two*
140 Yet° of his look for feere° almoost I deye.   *still / fear*
This caused me my gronyng, doutelees."°   *doubtless*
    "Avoy!"° quod she. "Fy on yow, hertelees!°   *shame / coward*
Allas," quod she, "for by that God above,
Now han ye lost myn herte and al my love.
145 I kan nat love a coward, by my faith!
For certes,° whatso° any womman seith,   *certain / whatever*
We alle desiren, if it myghte bee,

To han housbondes hardy,° wise, and free,°   *brave / generous*
And secree° and no nygard° ne no fool,   *discreet / cheapskate*
150 Ne hym that is agast° of every tool,°   *afraid / weapon*
Ne noon avauntour,° by that God above.   *nor any braggart*
How dorste° ye seyn, for shame, unto youre love   *dare*
That anythyng myghte make yow aferd?°   *afraid*
Have ye no mannes herte,° and han a berd?°   *man's heart / beard*
155 Allas, and konne ye been agast of swevenys?°   *be afraid of dreams*
Nothyng, God woot,° but vanitee° in   *knows / foolishness*
    swevene is!
Swevenes engendren of° replecciouns°   *are caused by / overeating*
And ofte of fume° and of complecciouns[3]   *stomach-gas*
Whan humours been° to habundant° in a   *are / too abundant*
    wight.°   *person*
160 Certes, this dreem which ye han met° tonyght   *have dreamed*
Cometh of greet superfluytee°   *excess*
Of youre rede colera, pardee,[4]
Which causeth folk to dreden° in hir dremes   *fear*
Of arwes° and of fyr° with rede lemes,°   *arrows / fire / red flames*
165 Of grete beestes that they wol hem byte,°   *will bite them*
Of contek° and of whelpes° grete and lyte,°   *conflict / dogs / small*
Right° as the humour of malencolie[5]   *just*
Causeth ful many a man in sleepe to crie
For feere of blake beres° or boles° blake   *black bears / bulls*
170 Or elles blake develes wole hem take.
Of othere humours koude I telle also
That werken° many a man in sleepe ful wo,°   *cause / much woe*
But I wol passe° as lightly as I kan.   *pass over*
    "Lo Catoun,[6] which that was so wys° a man,   *wise*
175 Seyde he nat thus: 'Ne do no fors of dremes'?[7]

---

[1] *My ... Londe* My dear one has traveled into (a foreign) land. This is the title of a popular song, one version of which, from c. 1500, has survived in a manuscript at Trinity College, Cambridge.

[2] *Now ... aright* "Now God," he said, "interpret my dream correctly."

---

[3] *complecciouns* I.e., complexions, or temperaments. Medieval medical theory maintained that what we now call personality was a function of the balance in the body of the four bodily fluids known as humors. If these fluids were unbalanced, disease would result.

[4] *Of ... pardee* Of your red choler, by God. Choler was one of the four bodily humors. The red choler was formed of yellow bile, which is hot and dry.

[5] *malencolie* I.e., melancholy, another of the four humors. It was formed of a black bile, which was cold and dry.

[6] *Catoun* I.e., Dionysius Cato, a Roman politician who was believed in the Middle Ages to be the author of a widely-circulating collection of proverbs which was often used to teach basic Latin grammar.

[7] *Seyde ... dremes* Said he not this: "Do not pay attention to dreams"?

Now sire," quod she, "whan ye flee° fro the bemes,° — *fly down / beams*

For Goddes love, as taak som laxatyf!° — *take some laxative*

Up° peril of my soule and of my lyf, — *upon*

I conseille° yow the beste—I wol nat lye°— — *counsel / lie*

180 That bothe of colere° and of malencolye — *choler*

Ye purge yow,° and for ye shal nat tarie,° — *yourself / so you do not delay*

Though in this toun is noon apothecarie,° — *no pharmacist*

I shal myself to herbes° techen yow, — *about herbs*

That shul been for youre heele° and for youre prow,° — *health / profit*

185 And in oure yeerd° tho° herbes shal I fynde, — *yard / those*

The whiche han of hire propretee° by kynde° — *their property / nature*

To purge yow bynethe and eek above.

Foryet nat this, for Goddes owene love!

Ye been ful coleryk of compleccioun.

190 Ware the sonne in his ascencioun

Ne fynde yow nat repleet of humours hoote.[1]

And if it do, I dar wel leye° a grote[2] — *bet*

That ye shul° have a fevere terciane[3] — *shall*

Or an agu° that may be youre bane.° — *ague (fever) / cause of death*

195 A day or two ye shul have digestyves° — *stomach medicines*

Of wormes, er ye take youre laxatyves[4]

Of lawriol,° centaure,° and fumetere,° — *laurel / centaury / fumaria*

Or elles of ellebor,° that groweth there; — *hellebore*

Of katapuce° or of gaitrys beryis,° — *euphorbia / rhamus berries*

200 Of herbe yve,° growyng in oure yeerd ther mery is.° — *herb-ivy / where it is merry*

Pekke hem up right as they growe, and ete hem yn.° — *eat them up*

Be myrie,° housbonde, for youre fader kyn!° — *merry / father's kin*

Dredeth no dreem. I kan sey yow namoore."

"Madame," quod he, "*graunt mercy*[5] of youre loore!° — *advice*

205 But nathelees, as touchyng° daun Catoun,° — *pertaining to / Master Cato*

That hath of° wysdom swich a greet renoun,° — *for / fame*

Though that he bad° no dremes for to drede, — *commanded*

By God, men may in olde bookes rede

Of many a man moore of auctorite

210 Than evere Caton was, so moot I thee,° — *so might I thrive*

That al° the revers° seyn of this sentence, — *completely / opposite*

That han wel founden° by experience — *have found out well*

That dremes been significaciouns° — *are signs*

As wel of joye as of tribulaciouns° — *troubles*

215 That folk enduren in this lif present.

Ther nedeth make of this noon argument.

The verray preeve° sheweth it in dede.° — *true proof / deed*

"Oon of the gretteste auctour[6] that men rede

Seith thus: that whilom° two felawes wente — *once*

220 On pilgrimage in a ful good entente,

And happed so° they coomen in a toun, — *it so happened*

Wheras ther was swich congregacioun° — *a gathering*

Of peple, and eek so streit of herbergage,° — *such a shortage of lodging*

That they ne founde as muche as o° cotage — *one*

225 In which they bothe myghte logged bee,

Wherfore they mosten of necessitee

As for that nyght departen compaignye.° — *part company*

And ech of hem gooth to his hostelrye° — *lodging place*

And took his loggyng as it wolde falle.° — *would happen*

230 That oon of hem was logged in a stalle° — *stall*

Fer° in a yeerd, with oxen of the plough. — *far*

That oother man was logged wel ynough,

As was his aventure° or his fortune, — *chance*

That us governeth alle as in commune.° — *in common*

235 "And so bifel that, longe er it were day,

This man mette in his bed, theras° he lay, — *where*

How that his felawe gan upon hym calle° — *to call*

And seyde, 'Allas, for in an oxes stalle

This nyght I shal be mordred ther I lye!

240 Now helpe me, deere brother, or I dye.

In alle haste com to me,' he sayde.

---

[1] *Ware ... hoote* Beware that the sun when it is climbing does not find you when you are (already) full of hot humors. The movements of the planets were thought to affect a patient's balance of humors.

[2] *grote* Coin equal to four pence.

[3] *fevere terciane* I.e., tertian fever. Medieval people classified the types of fevers they would contract by how frequently they recurred. This one would return every third day—meaning every other day, in which the first day is counted, as is the non-fever day and the recurring-fever day. The disease is possibly malaria.

[4] *laxatyves* The laxatives listed by the hen are all types of bitter herbs.

---

[5] *graunt mercy* From the French "grand merci" or "much thanks." Chauntecleer, as an aristocrat, employs French phrases.

[6] *Oon ... auctour* The Roman orator and writer (auctour) Cicero (106–43 BCE) tells the story in *On Divination*, and it is also found in the *Memorable Deeds and Sayings of Valerius Maximus* (written c. 30–31 CE).

This man out of his sleepe for feere abrayde,° *woke up*
But whan that he was wakened of his sleepe,
He turned hym° and took of it no keepe.° *turned over / notice*
245 Hym thoughte his dreem nas but a vanitee.° *folly*
Thus twies in his slepyng dremed hee,
And atte thridde tyme yet his felawe
Cam as hym thoughte and seide, 'I am now slawe.° *slain*
Bihoold my bloody woundes depe and wyde.
250 Arys° up erly in the morwe tyde,° *arise / morning-time*
And at the west gate of the toun,' quod he,
'A carte ful of donge° ther shaltow° se° *dung / shall you / see*
In which my body is hid ful prively.° *secretly*
Do thilke carte arresten boldely.[1]
255 My gold caused my mordre, sooth to sayn,'° *true to say*
And tolde hym every point how he was slayn
With a ful pitous face, pale of hewe.° *color*
And truste wel, his dreem he foond ful trewe.
For on the morwe, as soone as it was day,
260 To his felawes in° he took the way, *friend's inn*
And whan that he cam to this oxes stalle,
After his felawe he bigan to calle.
"The hostiler° answerde hym anon *innkeeper*
And seyde, 'Sire, youre felawe is agon.° *gone*
265 As soone as day he wente out of the toun.'
"This man gan fallen in suspecioun,° *to be suspicious*
Remembrynge on hise dremes that he mette.° *dreamed*
And forth he gooth—no lenger wolde he lette°— *delay*
Unto the west gate of the toun and fond° *found*
270 A dong-carte, as it were to donge lond° *to manure a field*
That was arrayed in that same wise° *way*
As ye han herd the dede man devyse.° *describe*
And with an hardy herte he gan to crye,
'Vengeance and justice of this felonye!
275 My felawe mordred is this same nyght,
And in this carte heere he lith,° gapyng *lies*
upright.° *facing upright*
I crye out on the ministres,'° quod he, *magistrates*
'That sholden kepe° and reulen° this citee! *care for / rule*
Harrow!° Allas! Heere lith my felawe slayn!' *help*
280 What sholde I moore unto this tale sayn?
The peple out sterte° and caste the cart to grounde, *jumped up*
And in the myddel of the dong they founde
The dede man that mordred was al newe.° *recently*

"O blisful° God that art so just and trewe, *blessed*
285 Lo how that thou biwreyest° mordre alway! *reveal*
Mordre wol out.° That se we day by day. *will be found out*
Mordre is so wlatsom° and abhomynable° *repulsive / abominable*
To God, that is so just and resonable,
That he ne wol nat suffre it heled° be, *concealed*
290 Though it abyde a yeer or two or thre.
Mordre wol out! This my conclusioun.
And right anon, ministres of that toun
Han hent° the cartere, and so soore° hym *arrested / sorely*
pyned,° *tortured*
And eek the hostiler so soore engyned,° *tortured on a rack*
295 That they biknewe° hire wikkednesse anon *confessed*
And were anhanged° by the nekke bon.° *hanged / neck-bone*
"Heere may men seen that dremes been to
drede.° *are to be feared*
And certes, in the same book I rede,
Right in the nexte chapitre after this—
300 I gabbe° nat, so have I joye or blis— *babble*
Two men that wolde han° passed over see° *would have / the sea*
For certeyn cause into a fer contree,° *distant country*
If that the wynd° ne hadde been contrarie, *wind*
That made hem in a citee for to tarie° *delay*
305 That stood ful myrie° upon an haven-syde.° *merrily / harbor-side*
But on a day agayn the eventyde,° *towards evening*
The wynd gan chaunge and blew right as hem
leste.° *they wanted*
Jolif° and glad, they wente unto hir reste *jolly*
And casten° hem ful erly for to saille. *decided*
310 But herkneth: to that o man fil a greet mervaille.[2]
That oon of hem, in slepyng as he lay,
Hym mette° a wonder dreem agayn the *dreamed*
day.° *toward daybreak*
Hym thoughte a man stood by his beddes syde
And hym comanded that he sholde abyde° *wait*
315 And seyde hym thus: 'If thou tomorwe wende,° *go*
Thow shalt be dreynt.° My tale is at an ende.' *drowned*
He wook and tolde his felawe what he mette
And preyde hym his viage° to lette;° *voyage / delay*
As for that day he preyde hym to byde.° *wait*
320 His felawe, that lay by his beddes syde,
Gan for to laughe, and scorned hym ful faste.° *very much*
'No dreem,' quod he, 'may so myn herte agaste° *frighten*

---

[1] *Do ... boldely* Cause that cart to be seized boldly.

[2] *But ... mervaille* But listen! To one man there happened a great marvel.

That I wol lette for to do my thynges.°   *business*

I sette nat a straw by thy dremynges!°   *dreams*

325 For swevenes been but vanytees° and japes.°   *nonsense / tricks*

Men dreme al day of owles or of apes,

And of many a maze° therwithal.°   *delusion / with it all*

Men dreme of thyng that nevere was ne shal.°   *nor shall be*

But sith I see that thou wolt heere abyde,

330 And thus forslewthen° wilfully thy tyde,°   *waste / time*

God woot, it reweth me!° And have good day!'   *I regret it*

And thus he took his leve° and wente his way.   *leave*

But er that he hadde half his cours yseyled,°   *sailed*

Noot I nat° why, ne what myschaunce°   *I know not / went wrong*

     it eyled,

335 But casuelly° the shippes botme° rente,°   *by chance / bottom / split*

And shipe and man under the water wente

In sighte of othere shippes it bisyde°   *beside it*

That with hem seyled at the same tyde.°   *tide*

And therfore, faire Pertelote, so deere,

340 By swiche ensamples olde yet maistow leere°   *may you learn*

That no man sholde been to recchelees°   *too careless*

Of dremes. For I seye thee douteles

That many a dreem ful soore is for to drede!

"Lo in the *Lyf of Seint Kenelm*[1] I rede,

345 That was Kenulphus sone,° the noble kyng   *Cenwulf's son*

Of Mercenrike,° how Kenelm mette° a thyng   *Mercia / dreamed*

A lite er° he was mordred on a day.   *little before*

His mordre in his avysioun° he say.°   *vision / saw*

His norice° hym expowned° every deel°   *nurse / explained / part*

350 His swevene, and bad hym for to kepe hym

     weel°   *protect himself*

For traisoun.° But he nas but° sevene   *from treason / was only*

     yeer oold,

And therfore litel tale hath he toold°   *paid little attention*

Of any dreem, so hooly° is his herte.   *holy*

By God, I hadde levere than my sherte

355 That ye hadde rad his Legende as have I,[2]

Dame Pertelote! I sey yow trewely,

Macrobeus, that writ the avisioun

In Affrike of the worthy Cipioun,[3]

Affermeth° dremes and seith that they   *affirms (the validity of)*

     been

360 Warnynge of thynges that men after seen.°   *see afterwards*

And forthermoore, I pray yow, looketh wel

In the Olde Testament of Daniel,

If he heeld° dremes any vanitee.°   *considered / folly*

Reed eek of Joseph,[4] and ther shul ye see

365 Wher dremes be somtyme—I sey nat alle°—   *not always*

Warnynge of thynges that shul after falle.°   *happen*

Looke of Egipte° the kyng daun Pharao,°   *Egypt / Lord Pharoah*

His bakere and his butiller° also,   *butler*

Wher° they ne felte noon° effect   *whether / did not feel any*

     in dremes.

370 Whoso wol seken actes of sondry remes°   *various realms*

May rede of dremes many a wonder thyng.

Lo Cresus,[5] which that was of Lyde kyng,

Mette he nat° that he sat upon a tree,   *did he not dream*

Which signified he sholde anhanged° bee?   *hanged*

375 Lo heere Adromacha,° Ectores° wyf,   *Andromache / Hector's*

That day that Ector sholde lese his lyf

She dremed on the same nyght biforn

How that the lyf of Ector sholde be lorn°   *lost*

If thilke day he wente into bataille.

380 She warned hym, but it myghte nat availle.°   *could not help*

He wente for to fighte natheles,°   *nevertheless*

---

[1] *Lyf ... Kenelm* This is a saint's life, or hagiography, of Kenelm (Cenhelm), a seven-year-old Anglo-Saxon king of Mercia who was murdered at the command of his aunt.

[2] *I hadde ... I* I would rather that you had read this saint's life than that I had my shirt, or, as we might say, I'd give my shirt to have you read it.

[3] *In ... Cipioun* The Roman writer Macrobius (c. 400 CE) wrote a commentary on the part of Cicero's *Republic* called "The Dream of Scipio." This book tells how Scipio Africanus Minor, a Roman consul, dreamed of meeting his famous ancestor, Scipio Africanus Major (so-called because he defeated Hannibal, the great general of Carthage, in North Africa) and urged him to pursue virtue for the sake of reward in a future life. Chauntecleer misinterprets his name, assuming the dream happened in Africa.

[4] *Daniel ... Joseph* Both Daniel and Joseph were famous for their ability to interpret dreams. Daniel interpreted the dream of King Nebuchadnezzar to predict that the king would be banished for seven years (see Daniel 4). Joseph interpreted his own dream to predict that he would be lord over his brothers, interpreted the dreams of Pharaoh's butler and his baker to predict that the former would be restored to office but the latter hanged, and interpreted Pharaoh's dream to predict that Egypt would have seven years of good harvest followed by seven years of famine (see Genesis 37.5–11; 40.1–23; 41.1–32).

[5] *Cresus* The Monk had mentioned the dream of Croesus, the fabulously rich king of Lydia who was conquered by King Cyrus of Persia, in the previous tale.

But he was slayn anon of Achilles.[1]
But thilke is al to° longe for to telle,   *too*
And eek it is ny° day. I may nat dwelle.°   *near / not delay*
385 Shortly I seye, as for conclusioun,
That I shal han of this avisioun
Adversitee. And I seye forthermoor
That I ne telle of laxatyves no stoor!°   *set no store in laxatives*
For they been venymes,° I woot° it weel.   *venomous / know*
390 I hem diffye,° I love hem never a deel!°   *reject them / not at all*
    "Now lat us speke of myrthe° and   *mirth*
        stynte° al this.   *be silent about*
Madame Pertelote, so have I blis,°   *happiness*
Of o° thyng God hath sent me large grace,°   *one / great favor*
For whan I se the beautee of youre face—
395 Ye been so scarlet reed° aboute youre eyen—   *red*
It maketh al my drede for to dyen.
For also siker° as *In principio*,[2]   *as certain*
Mulier est hominis confusio.[3]
Madame, the sentence° of this Latyn is,   *meaning*
400 'Womman is mannes joye and al his blis.'
For whan I feele anyght° youre softe side—   *at night*
Albeit that I may nat on yow ryde,°   *ride*
For that oure perche is maad° so narwe,° allas!   *made / narrow*
I am so ful of joye and of solas
405 That I diffye° bothe swevene and dreem!"[4]   *defy*
And with that word he fly° doun fro the beem,°   *flew / beam*
For it was day, and eek hise hennes alle,°   *did also all his hens*
And with a "chuk" he gan hem for to calle,
For he hadde founde a corn lay° in the yerd.   *kernel that lay*
410 Real° he was. He was namoore aferd,   *regal*
And fethered Pertelote twenty tyme

And trad as ofte er it was pryme.[5]
He looketh as it were° a grym leoun,°   *as if he were / fierce lion*
And on hise toos° he rometh° up and doun.   *his toes / roams*
415 Hym deigned nat to sette his foot to grounde.
He chukketh° whan he hath a corn yfounde,   *clucks*
And to hym rennen thanne° hise wyves alle.   *run then*
Thus roial° as a prince is in an halle   *regal*
Leve° I this Chauntecleer in his pasture,   *leave*
420 And after wol I telle his aventure.
    Whan that the monthe in which the world bigan,
That highte March, whan God first maked man,[6]
Was compleet, and passed were also,
Syn March bigan, thritty dayes and two,[7]
425 Bifel° that Chauntecleer in al his pryde,   *it happened*
Hise sevene wyves walkynge by his syde,
Caste up hise eyen to the brighte sonne,
That in the signe of Taurus hadde yronne
Twenty degrees and oon° and somwhat   *twenty-one degrees*
    moore,
430 And knew by kynde° and by noon oother   *nature*
    loore°   *teaching*
That it was pryme,° and crew with blisful   *early morning*
    stevene.°   *voice*
"The sonne," he seyde, "is clomben upon hevene
Fourty degrees and oon and moore, ywis.
Madame Pertelote, my worldes blis,
435 Herkneth thise blisful briddes,° how they synge,   *birds*
And se the fresshe floures, how they sprynge.°   *bloom*
Ful is myn herte of revel° and solas."   *amusement*
But sodeynly hym fil° a sorweful cas,°   *befell / event*
For evere the latter ende of joye is wo.
440 God woot that worldly joye is soone ago!°   *gone*
And if a rethor° koude faire endite,°   *rhetorician / write well*

---

[1] *Lo heere … Achilles*   The narrative of the Trojan war recounted by Dares Phrygius (one of the standard versions of the story in the Middle Ages) includes the story of the dream of Hector's wife. Homer's *Iliad*, which was not well known in western Europe at the time, does not include the episode.

[2] *In principio*   Latin: in the beginning; i.e., as certain as the Bible. These words begin both the book of Genesis and the Gospel of John.

[3] *Mulier … confusio*   Latin: woman is the confusion of man.

[4] *That … dreem*   Chauntecleer appears to distinguish between two kinds of dreams here, but it is not clear what the difference is. Medieval dream theory distinguished between prophetic dreams and those that had no special significance, but the terms swevene and dreme (and also mete) cover both.

[5] *And fethered … pryme*   He covered Pertelote with his feathers twenty times and copulated with her as often before it was the hour of prime (early morning).

[6] *That … man*   According to various medieval authorities, including Saint Basil and the English monastic writer Bede, God created the world at the spring equinox.

[7] *Was compleet … two*   The phrasing is ambiguous but the events seem to take place on May 3, when all of March and a further thirty-two days had passed. This date is in keeping with the position of the sun in the sky and the other astrological information. May 3 was considered an unlucky day and is also the day on which Palamon escapes from prison in *The Knight's Tale* (lines 604–05).

He in a cronycle saufly° myghte it write   *safely*
As for a sovereyn notabilitee.°   *very notable thing*
Now every wys man, lat hym herkne me.°   *listen to me*
445 This storie is also trewe, I undertake,°   *swear*
As is *The Book of Launcelot de Lake*,[1]
That wommen holde in ful greet reverence.
Now wol I come agayn to my sentence.°   *purpose*
  A colfox[2] ful of sly iniquitee,°   *malice*
450 That in the grove hadde woned° yeeres three,   *lived*
By heigh ymaginacioun forncast,[3]
The same nyght thurghout° the hegges°   *through / hedge*
  brast°   *burst*
Into the yerd ther° Chauntecleer the faire   *where*
Was wont, and eek hise wyves, to repaire,°   *retire*
455 And in a bed of wortes° stille° he lay   *herbs / quietly*
Til it was passed undren° of the day,   *dawn*
Waitynge his tyme° on Chauntecleer to falle,   *opportunity*
As gladly doon thise homycides alle°   *all these murderers*
That in await liggen° to mordre men.   *lie in wait*
460 O false mordrour, lurkynge in thy den!
O newe Scariot,° newe Genylon!°   *(Judas) Iscariot / Ganelon*
False dissymulour,° o Greek Synon,   *liar*
That broghtest Troye al outrely° to sorwe![4]   *utterly*
O Chauntecleer, acursed be that morwe
465 That thou into that yerd flaugh° fro the bemes!   *flew*
Thou were ful wel ywarned by thy dremes
That thilke day was perilous to thee,
But what that God forwoot° moot nedes   *foreknows*
  bee,°   *necessarily be*

After° the opinioun of certein clerkis.°   *according to / scholars*
470 Witnesse on hym that any parfit clerk is,[5]
That in scole° is greet altercacioun°   *the universities / debate*
In this mateere, and greet disputisoun,
And hath been of an hundred thousand men.[6]
But I ne kan nat bulte it to the bren[7]
475 As kan the hooly doctour Augustyn,°   *holy scholar Augustine*
Or Boece, or the Bisshope Bradwardyn—[8]
Wheither that Goddes worthy forwityng°   *foreknowledge*
Streyneth° me nedely° to doon a thyng—   *constrains / necessarily*
"Nedely" clepe° I symple necessitee—   *call*
480 Or elles, if free choys be graunted me
To do that same thyng or do it noght,
Though God forwoot it er that it was wroght,°   *done*
Or if his wityng° streyneth° never a   *knowing / constrains*
  deel°   *not at all*
But by necessitee condicioneel.[9]

---

[1] *The Book ... Lake* This is the title of any one of a number of Arthurian romances that recount the adventures of Sir Lancelot, including his love affair with Guinevere, wife of King Arthur.

[2] *colfox* Fox with black feet, ears, and tail.

[3] *By ... forncast* Foreseen by exalted imagination. What this means is disputed. Many editors take it to refer to the mind or conception (ymaginacioun) of God, which foresees all events. Others take "ymaginacioun" as a reference, expressed in deliberately and ridiculously grandiose language, to Chauntecleer's dream, or as a reference to the plotting of the fox. In each case, the word "forncast" introduces the theme of predestination discussed in lines 468–85.

[4] *O newe ... sorwe* In the Gospel, Judas Iscariot betrayed Christ by identifying him to the Roman soldiers who came to arrest him; in *The Song of Roland*, Ganelon betrayed Roland with a plot that led to his death in the pass at Roncesvalles; and in *The Iliad*, Sinon betrayed Troy by suggesting the Greeks conceal themselves in a wooden horse to gain access to the city.

[5] *Witnesse ... is* As any fully qualified scholar can testify.

[6] *But what ... men* The question of how God's foreknowledge could be reconciled with human free will was always important in medieval theology, but the debate flared up in Chaucer's day. The radical theologian John Wycliffe (d. 1394), best known for initiating the translation of the Bible into English, argued that God's omniscience gave him absolute knowledge of who would be saved or damned. This meant for Wycliffe that there was no justification for the institutions of the earthly church or for penitential practices such as confession or pilgrimage.

[7] *But ... bren* But I cannot separate (the kernels) from the bran. That is, the Nun's Priest cannot sort out the issues in the debate about God's foreknowledge.

[8] *As kan ... Bradwardyn* The great patristic writer St. Augustine (d. 430 CE), the late Roman scholar Boethius (d. 524 CE), and Thomas Bradwardine, chancellor of Oxford and very briefly Archbishop of Canterbury (who died of the Black Death in 1349), all wrote about the concept of predestination. Although stressing God's omniscience, all three were thoroughly orthodox in their insistence that humans have free will.

[9] *necessitee condicioneel* Boethius distinguishes between simple necessity and conditional necessity in his *Consolation of Philosophy* 5, prose 6, and then draws on God's status outside time to resolve the theological dilemma. To use Boethius's example, that a man must die is a matter of simple necessity. But if you know someone is walking, while he must then necessarily be walking, the necessity is only conditional; i.e., it depends on the condition of the man having decided to take a walk. From your perspective, he could have chosen not to do so. The issue here is whether God, in knowing in advance all future events and choices, necessarily removes free choice (for how can God be wrong?). The solution, proposed   [continued ...]

485 I wol nat han to do of° swich mateere.   *have to do with*
My tale is of a cok, as ye may heere,
That took his conseil of his wyf with sorwe
To walken in the yerd upon that morwe
That he hadde met that dreem that I of tolde.
490 Wommennes conseils been ful ofte colde.°   *bad*
Wommannes conseil broghte us first to wo
And made Adam out of Paradys to go,
Theras° he was ful myrie° and wel at ese.   *where / merry*
But for I noot° to whom it myght displese,   *since I do not know*
495 If I conseil of wommen wolde blame,
Passe over, for I seye it in my game.°   *in jest*
Rede auctours° where they trete of swich mateere,   *authors*
And what they seyn of wommen ye may heere.
Thise been the cokkes wordes and nat myne!
500 I kan noon harm of no womman divyne!°   *imagine*
    Faire in the soond° to bathe hire myrily   *sand*
Lith° Pertelote, and alle hire sustres by°   *lies / nearby*
Agayn the sonne.° And Chauntecleer so free   *in the sunshine*
Soong murier° than the mermayde in the   *sang more merrily*
    see—
505 For Phisiologus[1] seith sikerly°   *surely*
How that they syngen wel and myrily—
And so bifel that as he caste his eye
Among the wortes° on a boterflye,   *herbs*
He was war° of this fox that lay ful lowe.   *aware*
510 Nothyng ne liste hym thanne for to crowe,[2]
But cride anon, "Cok! Cok!" and up he sterte
As man that was affrayed in his herte.
For natureelly a beest desireth flee
Fro his contrarie° if he may it see,   *enemy*
515 Though he never erst hadde seyn it with his eye.
    This Chauntecleer, whan he gan hym espye,°   *spotted him*
He wolde han fled, but that the fox anon

Seyde, "Gentil sire, allas, wher wol ye gon?
Be ye affrayed of me, that am youre freend?
520 Now certes, I were worse than a feend°   *fiend*
If I to yow wolde° harm or vileynye!°   *intended*
I am nat come youre conseil for t'espye.°   *to spy on your council*
But trewely, the cause of my comynge
Was oonly for to herkne° how that ye synge.   *listen*
525 For trewely, ye have as myrie° a stevene°   *merry / voice*
As any aungel that is in Hevene.
Therwith ye han in musyk moore feelynge
Than hadde Boece[3] or any that kan synge.
My lord, youre fader, God his soule blesse,
530 And eek youre mooder of hire gentillesse
Han in myn hous ybeen to my greet ese.
And certes, sire, ful fayn° wolde I yow plese.   *very gladly*
But for men speke of syngyng, I wol yow seye—
So moote I brouke wel myne eyen tweye—[4]
535 Save yow,° herde I nevere man yet synge   *apart from yourself*
As dide youre fader in the morwenynge.
Certes, it was of herte° al that he song!   *from the heart*
And for to make his voys the moore strong,
He wolde so peyne hym° that with bothe hise eyen   *take pains*
540 He moste wynke°—so loude he wolde cryen—   *had to wink*
And stonden on his tip-toon° therwithal,°   *tip-toes / in doing so*
And strecche forth his nekke long and smal.°   *slender*
And eek he was of swich discrecioun°   *discernment*
That ther nas no man in no regioun
545 That hym in song or wisedom myghte passe.°   *surpass*
I have wel rad° in *Daun Burnel the Asse*,[5]   *read*
Among hise vers,° how that ther was a cok,   *verses*
For that° a preestes sone yaf° hym a knok   *because / gave*
Upon his leg whil he was yong and nyce,°   *silly*
550 He made hym for to lese his benefice.

---

by Boethius, is this idea of conditional necessity: to know about an event is not necessarily to cause it. As he says, "God sees those future events which happen of free will as present events; so that these things when considered with reference to God's sight of them do happen necessarily as a result of the condition of divine knowledge; but when considered in themselves they do not lose the absolute freedom of their nature."

[1] *Phisiologus* The supposed author of a bestiary, a book explaining the allegorical significances of various animals. According to this work, mermaids use their sweet singing to lure sailors to their deaths.

[2] *Nothyng ... crowe* He did by no means want then to crow.

---

[3] *Boece* Boethius not only wrote *The Consolation of Philosophy*, which Chaucer translated, but also wrote the basic university textbook on music used in the Middle Ages.

[4] *So ... tweye* So may I enjoy the use of my eyes, a common expression meaning little more than "indeed," but it is ill suited to express musical appreciation.

[5] *Daun ... Asse* Title of a twelfth-century Latin satire by Nigel Wireker about a foolish donkey, Master Brunellus, who becomes a wandering scholar. The episode described below concerns a young man who was about to be ordained and to receive a benefice. The cock, whom he had injured in his youth, took its revenge by not crowing, causing the man to oversleep and miss his opportunity for a benefice.

But certeyn, ther nys no° comparisoun   *is no*
Bitwixe the wisedom and discrecioun
Of youre fader and of his subtiltee.°   *cleverness*
Now syngeth, sire, for seinte charitee!°   *holy charity*
555   Lat se, konne ye youre fader countrefete?"°   *imitate*
    This Chauntecleer hise wynges gan to bete°   *beat*
As man that koude his traysoun° nat espie,°   *betrayal / perceive*
So was he ravysshed with his flaterie.
Allas, ye lordes, many a fals flatour°   *false flatterer*
560   Is in youre courtes,° and many a losengeour°   *courts / flatterer*
That plesen yow wel moore, by my feith,
Than he that soothfastnesse° unto yow seith.   *truth*
Redeth Ecclesiaste[1] of° flaterye.   *on*
Beth war,° ye lordes, of hir trecherye!   *beware*
565   This Chauntecleer stood hye upon his toos,
Strecchynge his nekke, and heeld his eyen cloos°   *closed*
And gan to crowe loude for the nones.°   *occasion*
And Daun Russell the fox stirte up atones°   *jumped up at once*
And by the gargat° hente° Chauntecleer   *throat / grabbed*
570   And on his bak toward the wode hym beer,
For yet° ne was ther no man that hym sewed.°   *as yet / pursued*
    O Destinee, that mayst nat been eschewed!°   *avoided*
Allas, that Chauntecleer fleigh fro the bemes!
Allas, his wyf ne roghte nat° of dremes!   *paid no attention*
575   And on a Friday fil al this meschaunce!
    O Venus, that art goddesse of plesaunce,[2]
Syn that thy servant was this Chauntecleer,
And in thy servyce dide al his poweer°   *all he could*
Moore for delit than world to
    multiplye,°   *to increase the world (procreate)*
580   Why woldestow suffre° hym on thy day to   *would you allow*
    dye?[3]

O Gaufred,[4] deere maister soverayn,°   *sovereign teacher*
That whan thy worthy kyng Richard was slayn
With shot,° compleynedest° his deeth so soore,   *arrow / lamented*
Why ne hadde I now thy sentence° and thy   *meaning*
    loore°   *learning*
585   The Friday for to chide as diden ye?
For on a Friday soothly° slayn was he.   *truly*
Thanne wolde I shewe yow how that I koude pleyne
For Chauntecleres drede and for his peyne!
Certes swich cry ne lamentacioun
590   Was nevere of ladyes maad° whan Ylioun°   *made / Ilion (Troy)*
Was wonne,° and Pirrus° with his streite   *conquered / Pyrrhus*
    swerd,°   *drawn sword*
Whan he hadde hent° Kyng Priam by the berd°   *seized / beard*
And slayn hym, as seith us *Eneydos*,°   *Aeneid*
As maden alle the hennes in the clos°   *yard*
595   Whan they had seyn of Chauntecleer the sighte.
But sodeynly Dame Pertelote shrighte°   *shrieked*
Ful louder than dide Hasdrubales wyf
Whan that hir housbonde hadde lost his lyf
And that the Romayns hadde brend° Cartage.[5]   *burned*
600   She was so ful of torment and of rage
That wilfully into the fyr she sterte
And brende hirselven with a stedefast herte.
    O woful hennes, right so criden ye
As, whan that Nero[6] brende the citee
605   Of Rome, cryden senatours wyves,
For that hir housbondes losten alle hir lyves.
Withouten gilt this Nero hath hem slayn.
Now turne I wole to my tale agayn.
    This sely° wydwe and eek hir doghtres two   *innocent*
610   Herden thise hennes crie and maken wo,
And out at dores stirten they anon
And syen the fox toward the grove gon

---

[1] *Ecclesiaste* Ecclesiasticus 12.16 warns against deceptive enemies but does not specifically mention flattery. The reference might be a mistake for Ecclesiastes or for Proverbs, other books of the Bible that were, like Ecclesiasticus, attributed to King Solomon.

[2] *O ... plesaunce* In classical mythology, Venus is the goddess of love.

[3] *Why ... dye* According to medieval astrology, each of the planets had special influence on a given day of the week. Venus, who gives her name to Friday (*Veneris dies*) in Romance languages, controlled that day.

[4] *Gaufred* I.e., Geoffrey of Vinsauf, whose treatise *Poetria Nova*, a basic manual on how to write rhetorically elaborate poetry, is alluded to by Chaucer in the following lines. King Richard is Richard I, the Lion-hearted, who in 1199 was wounded on a Friday while besieging a castle and later died of his wound.

[5] *Hasdrubales ... Cartage* I.e., Hasdrubal (245–207 BCE), Carthaginian general, who died in battle at the Metaurus River in central Italy when he met the army of Caius Claudius Nero. Carthage was destroyed by Scipio Africanus in 146 BCE.

[6] *Nero* Nero (r. 54–68 CE), Emperor of Rome, who had his city burned while he stood by, according to Suetonius, playing the bagpipes. In the previous tale the Monk narrates his tragedy.

And bar upon his bak the cok away,
And cryden, "Out! Harrow!" and "Weylaway!"° *alas*
615 Ha! Ha! The fox!" And after hym they ran,
And eek with staves° many another man; *clubs*
Ran Colle oure dogge, and Talbot and Gerland,[1]
And Malkyn with a dystaf° in hir hand. *spinning staff*
Ran cow and calf and the verray hogges,
620 So fered° for berkyng of the dogges *afraid*
And shoutyng of the men and wommen eek.
They ronne so hem thoughte hir herte breek;[2]
They yolleden° as feendes° doon in Helle. *yelled / fiends*
The dokes° cryden as men wolde hem quelle,° *ducks / kill them*
625 The gees° for feere flowen° over the trees, *geese / flew*
Out of the hyve° cam the swarm of bees. *hive*
So hydous° was the noyse,° a, *hideous / noise*
benedicitee,° *ah, bless us*
Certes he Jakke Straw and his meynee° *gang*
Ne made nevere shoutes half so shrille,
630 Whan that they wolden any Flemyng kille,[3]
As thilke day was maad upon the fox.
Of bras they broghten bemes and of box,
Of horn, of boon, in whiche they blewe and powped,[4]
And therwithal° they skriked° and they *with this / shrieked*
howped.° *whooped*
635 It semed as that Hevene sholde falle.
    Now, goode men, I prey yow, herkneth alle.
Lo how Fortune turneth sodeynly
The hope and pryde of hir enemy.
This cok that lay upon the foxes bak,
640 In al his drede unto the fox he spak
And seyde, "Sire, if that I were as ye,
Yet wolde I seyn, as wys° God helpe me, *wise*
'Turneth agayn, ye proude cherles° alle! *churls*
A verray pestilence upon yow falle!° *fall upon you*
645 Now I am come unto the wodes syde.° *border*

Maugree youre heed,° the cok shal heere *despite your efforts*
abyde.
I wol hym ete,° in feith, and that anon!'" *eat*
    The fox answerde, "In feith, it shal be don!"
And as he spak that word al sodeynly,
650 This cok brak° from his mouth delyverly° *broke / quickly*
And heighe upon a tree he fleigh anon.
And whan the fox saugh that he was gon,
    "Allas!" quod he. "O Chauntecleer, allas!
I have to yow," quod he, "ydoon trespas,° *done wrong*
655 In as muche as I maked yow aferd
Whan I yow hente° and broghte into this yerd.[5] *seized*
But sire, I dide it of no wikke° entente. *wicked*
Com doun, and I shal telle yow what I mente.
I shal seye sooth° to yow, God help me so!" *tell the truth*
660   "Nay, thanne," quod he, "I shrewe° us bothe two! *curse*
And first I shrewe myself, bothe blood and bones,
If thou bigyle° me any ofter° than ones!° *trick / more often / once*
Thou shalt namoore thurgh thy flaterye
Do me to synge and wynke with myn eye!
665 For he that wynketh whan he sholde see
Al wilfully,° God lat hym nevere thee!"° *voluntarily / thrive*
    "Nay," quod the fox, "but God yeve° hym *give*
meschaunce° *misfortune*
That is so undiscreet° of governaunce° *indiscreet / behavior*
That jangleth° whan he sholde holde his pees!"° *chatters / peace*
670   Lo, swich it is for to be recchelees° *reckless*
And necligent° and truste on flaterye! *negligent*
    But ye that holden° this tale a folye° *consider / folly*
As of a fox or of a cok and hen,
Taketh the moralite,° goode men. *moral*
675 For Seint Paul seith that al that writen is,
To oure doctrine° it is ywrite, ywis.[6] *for our teaching*
Taketh the fruyt,° and lat the chaf be *fruit*
stille.° *let the chaff alone*

---

[1] *Colle … Talbot and Gerland* Names for dogs.
[2] *They … breek* They ran so (fast) that they thought their hearts would burst.
[3] *Certes … kille* Jack Straw was the name of one of the leaders of the Uprising of 1381; about thirty or forty Flemish merchants and weavers were murdered in London during this period of violence and rioting.
[4] *Of bras … powped* They brought trumpets (bemes) made of brass and boxwood and of horn and of bone, on which they blew and puffed.

[5] *into this yerd* This seems an obvious slip that should instead read "out of this yerd," as this line does in some manuscripts. Derek Pearsall, however, in the Variorum edition, defends "into" by suggesting that the fox is still trying to deceive Chauntecleer and so refers to the place they have come to as "this yerd" as if it were the kind of safe enclosure the rooster were used to.
[6] *For Seint … ywis* Cf. Romans 15.4. Chaucer cites the same line in his "Retraction" and it is also paraphrased at the beginning of the medieval translation and allegorical interpretation of Ovid's *Metamorphoses*, the *Ovide Moralisé*.

Now, goode God, if that it be thy wille,
As seith my lord,[1] so make us alle goode men,
680   And brynge us to his heighe blisse. Amen!

HEERE IS ENDED THE NONNES PREESTES TALE

THE NUN'S PRIEST'S EPILOGUE[2]

"Sire Nonnes Preest," oure Hoost seide anoon,
"Iblissed° be thy breche° and every   *blessed / buttocks*
      stoon!°   *testicles*
This was a murie tale of Chauntecleer.
But by my trouthe, if thou were seculer°   *a lay man*

685   Thow woldest be a tredefoul[3] aright.
For if thou have corage° as thou hast myght,°   *spirit / power*
The were nede° of hennes, as I   *you would have need of*
      wene,°   *think*
Ya, moo° than sevene tymes seventeen!   *more*
Se which braunes° hath this gentil° preest,   *what muscle / fine*
690   So gret a nekke and swich a large breest.°   *chest*
He loketh as a sperhauke° with hise eyen.   *sparrowhawk*
Him nedeth nat his colour° for to dyghen°   *complexion / dye*
With brasile ne with greyn of Portingale.[4]
Now sire, faire falle yow° for your tale."   *may good befall you*
695   And after that he with ful murie chere
Seide unto another as ye shuln here.
—c. 1476

---

[1]   *my lord*   The Nun's Priest might be referring to the Archbishop of Canterbury, Christ, or, since he is attached to the nunnery at Stratford-at-Bow near London, his immediate ecclesiastical superior, the Bishop of London.

[2]   *The … Epilogue*   This epilogue is found in nine manuscripts but not in either Ellesmere or Hengwrt. It seems most likely that the epilogue is part of an earlier draft that Chaucer later abandoned, incorporating some of the lines into the Host's words to the Monk.

[3]   *tredefoul*   Copulator with chickens, a rooster.

[4]   *brasile … Portingale*   Imported red dyes.

SIR THOMAS WYATT

c. 1503 – 1542

During Thomas Wyatt's brief, 39-year lifespan, English men and women served two kings; three lord chancellors were executed; England waged war in four other lands (Scotland, Wales, Ireland, and France); and Henry VIII married five of his six wives, most of whom met sorry ends. Wyatt lived his entire adult life in service to the court, amidst the political intrigue and turmoil that accompanied the reign of King Henry VIII, and was twice imprisoned in the Tower of London. A few of his poems portray an idyllic life in the countryside away from the machinations of the king and his courtiers, yet they can carry a subtext about the ambient political disorder or the court's political dramas. One of his most famous poems, "Whoso list to hunt," based on a sonnet written by Petrarch (1304–74), is thought to express longing for Anne Boleyn, Henry's future second wife. Wyatt wrote in many poetic forms, but he is best known for the artistry of his satires and songs and, along with Henry Howard, Earl of Surrey (1517–47), for introducing the Italian sonnet to England.

Son of Anne Skinner and Sir Henry Wyatt, Thomas Wyatt was born in 1503 into wealth and status at Allington Castle in Kent, England. His later career as a statesman followed that of his father, as did his political trials and tribulations. Henry Wyatt had been imprisoned and tortured for over two years by the court of King Richard III for his loyalty to the Tudors. When Henry Tudor became King Henry VII, the elder Wyatt was made a Privy Councillor, and he was later knighted by Henry VIII.

Although it is not certain, it appears that Thomas Wyatt entered St. John's College, Cambridge at age twelve, and that he may have graduated by the age of sixteen. He was a man of many accomplishments, adept at music and poetry as well as politics, and he soon became a valued member of King Henry's court. After serving in various minor positions, Wyatt began his diplomatic career in 1526 with missions to France, Rome, and Venice, where, we may surmise, he acquired his knowledge of Italian sonnets. (At about this time Wyatt became estranged from his wife, Elizabeth Brooke, daughter of Lord Cobham, whom he had married at a young age.) He was knighted in 1536 but soon afterward had his first falling out with King Henry and was imprisoned in the Tower of London. Wyatt might have been under suspicion of having had an affair with Anne Boleyn when she was still unmarried; Henry VIII had divorced Catherine of Aragon for Boleyn and thereby provoked England's break with the Roman Catholic Church. Although Anne and five (almost certainly wrongly accused) lovers were all executed, Wyatt was released after a month.

Most of Wyatt's work to this point had been love poems, often containing themes of disappointment or unrequited love but rarely dark in tone. By contrast, poems written after his imprisonments can express bitterness.

Wyatt eventually regained both the king's favor and his diplomatic status. Unfortunately, though, he lost a great ally upon the fall and execution of the statesman Thomas Cromwell, in 1540, and in 1541 he was imprisoned again, this time on trumped-up charges of treason. Once again he was spared and was briefly in favor with the king. Wyatt succumbed to fever the next year, however, and died in Dorset in 1542.

[handwritten margin note: had affair w/ Anne Boleyn, possibly reciprocated → Anne married off to King → Wyatt writes poems]

Few of Wyatt's poems were printed in his lifetime, but many appeared in Richard Tottel's 1557 volume *Songes and Sonettes* (later to become known as *Tottel's Miscellany*); a third of the volume is made up of Wyatt's work. Some years later, the Elizabethan critic George Puttenham summarized Sir Thomas Wyatt's importance to the English literary tradition in terms that remain broadly accepted today: "[Wyatt and Surrey] travailed into Italie, and there tasted the sweet and stately measures and stile of the Italian Poesie as novices newly crept out of the schooles of Dante, Arioste and Petrarch. They greatly pollished our rude & homely maner of vulgar Poesie, from that it had been before, and for that cause may justly be said the first reformers of our English meetre and stile."

(Please note that additional poems by Sir Thomas Wyatt appear in the Elizabethan Sonnet and Lyric section elsewhere in the volume.)

Sonnets[1]

10[2]

The long love that in my thought doth harbour
And in mine heart doth keep his residence
Into my face presseth with bold pretence
And therein campeth, spreading his banner.
She that me learneth° to love and suffer   teaches
And will° that my trust and lust's negligence   wishes
Be reined by reason, shame,° and reverence,   modesty
With his hardiness° taketh displeasure.   daring
Wherewithal unto the heart's forest he fleeth,
Leaving his enterprise with pain and cry,
And there him hideth and not appeareth.
What may I do when my master feareth,
But in the field with him to live and die?
For good is the life ending faithfully.
—1557

29[3]

The pillar perished is whereto I leant,
The strongest stay of mine unquiet mind;
The like of it no man again can find—
From east to west still seeking though he went—

To mine unhap,° for hap° away hath rent   misfortune / chance
Of all my joy the very bark and rind,
And I, alas, by chance am thus assigned
Dearly to mourn till death do it relent.°   abate
But since that thus it is by destiny,
What can I more but have a woeful heart,
My pen in plaint,° my voice in woeful cry,   complaint, lament
My mind in woe, my body full of smart,°   pain
And I myself, myself always to hate
Till dreadful death do cease my doleful state?
—1557

31

Farewell, Love, and all thy laws forever.
Thy baited hooks shall tangle me no more.
Senec[4] and Plato call me from thy lore
To perfect wealth my wit for to endeavour.[5]
In blind error when I did persevere,
Thy sharp repulse, that pricketh ay so sore,
Hath taught me to set in trifles no store
And 'scape forth, since liberty is lever.°   dearer
Therefore, farewell. Go trouble younger hearts
And in me claim no more authority.
With idle youth go use thy property,
And thereon spend thy many brittle darts.
For hitherto, though I have lost all my time,
Me lusteth° no longer rotten boughs to climb.   desire
—1557

---

[1] *Sonnets* For additional sonnets by Sir Thomas Wyatt, please refer to the Elizabethan Sonnet and Lyric section in this anthology.

[2] *10* This poem is an adaptation of sonnet 140 from Petrarch's *Rime sparse* (*Scattered Rhymes*), also translated by Wyatt's friend Henry Howard, Earl of Surrey.

[3] *29* An imitation of Petrarch's *Rime* 269. There has been some speculation that Wyatt here laments the execution of Thomas Cromwell, Wyatt's former patron.

[4] *Senec* Seneca, a Roman essayist and philosopher (c. 4 BCE—65 CE).

[5] *wealth* Well-being; *wit* Intellect; *endeavour* Exert.

⌘⌘⌘

The Continental Background

FRANCESCO PETRARCH (1304–1374)

The influence of Petrarch's sonnet sequence, about his unfulfilled love for Laura, was immense, and provided European love poets with a way to shape the erotic experience in terms of frustration, self-scrutiny, self-division, praise, and longing and to express this through elaborate metaphor, paradox, and an intense focus on detail. Whether the object of imitation, revision, or satire, Petrarch's approach to love long remained the discourse against which and through which poets defined themselves when writing on love.

from *Rime Sparse*

134

Pace non trovo et non ò da far guerra,
e temo et spero, et ardo et son un ghiaccio,
et volo sopra 'l cielo et giacco in terra,
et nulla stringo et tutto 'l mondo abbraccio.
5   Tal m'à in pregion, che non m'apre né serra,
né per suo mi riten né sciolglie il laccio,
et non m'ancide Amore et non mi sferra,
né mi vuol vivo, né mi trae d'impaccio.
Veggio senza occhi, et non ò lingua et grido,
10   et bramo di perir, et cheggio aita,
et ò in odio me stesso et amo altrui.
Pascomi di dolor, piangendo rido,
egualmente mi spiace morte et vita.
In questo stato son, Donna, per vui.
—WRITTEN MID-14TH CENTURY

134

I find no peace and all my war is done,
I fear and hope, I burn and freeze like ice;
I fly above the wind yet can I not arise;
And naught I have and all the world I season°   *seize upon*
5   That[1] looseth nor locketh holdeth me in prison
And holdeth me not, yet can I 'scape no wise,
Nor letteth me live nor die at my device.°   *own choice*
And yet of death it giveth none occasion.
Without eyen° I see and without tongue I   *eyes*
plain;°   *complain*
10   I desire to perish, and yet I ask health;
I love another, and thus I hate myself;
I feed me in sorrow and laugh in all my pain;
Likewise displeaseth me both death and life:
And my delight[2] is causer of this strife.
—C. 1520S (TRANS. SIR THOMAS WYATT)

---

[1] *That*   Which (i.e., Love).

[2] *my delight*   His paradoxical pleasure in loving but also the lady—Laura, in Petrarch's poem.

140

Amor, che nel penser mio vive et regna
e 'l suo seggio maggior nel mio cor tene,
talor armato ne la fronte vene;
ivi si loca et ivi pon sua insegna.
5 Quella ch' amare et sofferir ne 'nsegna
e vol che 'l gran desio, l'accesa spene
ragion, vergogna, et reverenza affrene,
di nostro ardir fra se stessa si sdegna.
Onde Amor paventoso fugge al core,
10 Lasciando ogni sua impresa, et piange et trema;
ivi s'asonde et non appar più fore.
Che poss' io far, temendo il mio signore,
    se non star seco infin a l'ora estrema?
    ché bel fin fa chi ben amando more.
—WRITTEN MID-14TH CENTURY

140

Love, that doth reign and live within my thought
And built his seat° within my captive breast,   *dwelling*
Clad in the arms wherein with me he fought
Oft in my face he doth his banner rest.
5 But she that taught me love and suffer pain,
My doubtful hope and eke° my hot desire   *also*
With shamefast° look to shadow° and
    refrain,°   *modest / conceal; hold back*
Her smiling grace converteth straight to ire.
And coward Love then to the heart apace
10 Taketh his flight, where he doth lurk and plain;°   *complain*
His purpose lost, and dare not show his face.
For my lord's guilt thus faultless bide I pain,
    Yet from my lord[1] shall not my foot remove:
    Sweet is the death that taketh end by love.
—C. 1530S (TRANS. HENRY HOWARD, EARL OF SURREY)

189

Passa la nave mia colma d'oblio
per aspro mare a mezza notte il verno
enfra Scilla et Caribdi, et al governo
siede 'l signore anzi 'l nimico mio;
5 à ciascun remo un penser pronto et rio
che la tempesta e 'l fin par ch' abbi a scherno;
la vela rompe un vento umido eterno
di sospir, di speranze et di desio;
pioggia di lagrimar, nebbia di sdegni
10 bagna et rallenta la già stanche sarte
che son d'error con ignoranzia attorto.
Celansi i duo mei dolci usati segni,
    morta fra l'onde è la ragion et l'arte
    tal ch' i' 'ncomincio a desperar del porto.
—WRITTEN MID-14TH CENTURY

189

My galley charged with forgetfulness
Through sharp seas in winter nights doth pass
'Tween rock and rock;[2] and eke° mine enemy, alas,   *also*
That is my lord,[3] steereth with cruelness;
5 And every oar a thought in readiness,
As though that death were light° in such a case.   *easy*
An endless wind doth tear the sail apace
Of forcèd sighs and trusty fearfulness.
A rain of tears, a cloud of dark disdain,
10 Hath done the wearied cords°   *ship's rigging*
    great hinderance,
    Wreathèd with error and eke with ignorance
The stars be hid that led me to this pain;
    Drownèd is reason that should me consort,°   *accompany*
    And I remain despairing of the port.
—C. 1520S (TRANS. SIR THOMAS WYATT)

---

1 *lord* I.e., Love—the speaker's feudal lord.

2 *'Tween rock and rock* Petrarch specifies Scylla and Charybdis, the dangerous monsters who lived on a rock and in the whirlpool on either side of a narrow channel through which Ulysses must sail in Homer's *Odyssey*.

3 *lord* I.e., Cupid, Love.

190

Una candida cerva sopra l'erba
  verde m'apparve con duo corna d'oro,
  fra due riviere all'ombra d'un alloro,
  levando 'l sole a la stagione acerba.
5 Era sua vista sì dolce superba
  ch' i' lasciai per seguirla ogni lavoro,
come l'avaro che 'n cercar tesoro
con diletto l'affanno disacerba.
"Nessun mi tocchi," al bel collo d'intorno
10 scritto avea di diamanti et di topazi.
  "Libera farmi al mio Cesare parve."
Et era 'l sol già vòlto al mezzo giorno,
gli occhi miei stanchi di mirar, non sazi,
quand' io caddi ne l'acqua et ella sparve.
—WRITTEN MID-14TH CENTURY

190

Whoso list° to hunt, I know where is a
  hind,°
But as for me, alas, I may° no more:
The vain travail° hath wearied me so sore
I am of them that farthest come behind.
5 Yet may I by no means my wearied mind
  Draw from the deer: but, as she fleeth afore,
Fainting I follow. I leave off therefore,
Since in a net I seek to hold the wind.
Who list to hunt, I put him out of doubt,
10 As well as I may spend his time in vain.
  And, graven with diamonds in letters plain,
There is written her fair neck round about:
"Noli me tangere,[1] for Caesar's I am,
And wild for to hold, although I seem tame."
—C. 1520S (ADAPTED BY SIR THOMAS WYATT)

° wishes
° female deer
° can
° effort

---

[1] *Noli me tangere* "Do not touch me," words said by Christ after the Resurrection. Early commentators on Petrarch often read this as signifying that Laura considered herself bound by the laws of chaste marriage as decreed by Augustus Caesar. Wyatt's readers who identified the deer with Anne Boleyn (whom Wyatt knew and perhaps loved), would have read the lines as suggesting that the "hind" belongs to Henry VIII.

EDMUND SPENSER
1552? – 1599

Edmund Spenser has consistently been accorded a special place in the history of English literature. In the seventeenth century John Milton, as much impressed by *The Faerie Queene*'s subtle treatment of the moral virtues as by its aesthetic charm, called him "our sage and serious Spenser, whom I dare to name a better teacher than Scotus or Aquinas." In the nineteenth, Wordsworth wrote of "Sweet Spenser, moving through his clouded heaven / With the moon's beauty and the moon's soft pace." And in the twentieth and twenty-first centuries poets and critics have continued to hold Spenser and *The Fairie Queene* in extraordinarily high regard.

Spenser's career as a servant of the Crown was less glorious. He was not the moping failure some have thought him (he had steady work in Ireland helping the English govern its often rebellious and resentful population), but in England he was never the courtier that he seems to have wanted to be. His bid for more direct royal patronage was the first part of *The Faerie Queene* (1590). This is an allegorical epic poem with debts to Virgil, elements of Arthurian and Italian epic or romance, traces of medieval pilgrimage allegory, Chaucerian moments, and passages indebted to a range of other genres from the fabliau to the pastoral. The central if often absent figure is Prince Arthur, the future British king, who is seeking the always absent heroine, Gloriana, queen of Fairyland and an allegorical "mirror," Spenser told his friend Sir Walter Ralegh in a letter published at the end of the volume, of Queen Elizabeth in her public role as ruler. Modern scholars may perceive veiled criticisms of Elizabeth in the poetry, but the queen either did not notice or thought it wise to read the epic as purely complimentary, so she gave the author a generous yearly pension of fifty pounds.

Little is known with any certainty of Spenser's early life, although his writings provide some information. He was born, probably in London, to parents of modest means, and it was as an "impoverished" student that he entered the Merchant Taylors' School, headed by the scholar Richard Mulcaster, remembered today for his impassioned defense of the English language. There Spenser studied Latin, Greek, and possibly Hebrew; he also learned French and Italian. From there he went to Pembroke Hall (now Pembroke College) at Cambridge University, where he was registered as a "sizar," a poor student who was required to work for his keep, earning his bachelor's degree in 1573 and his M.A. in 1576. While at Pembroke, Spenser made friends with Gabriel Harvey, soon to be a prominent Cambridge don, who introduced him to useful patrons and whose correspondence with the young poet demonstrates a shared interest in poetic theory, genres, and metrics.

In 1579 Spenser produced his first significant, if pseudonymous, publication, *The Shepheardes Calender*, a set of illustrated pastoral poems for each month of the year and written, says a prefatory poem, by one "Immerito." The work, dedicated to Philip Sidney, comes with a preface and annotations by the still unidentified "E.K." In this innovative work, which saw a number of editions, Spenser exploits a genre that hearkened back to Theocritus and Virgil in the third and first centuries BCE but that had since added the potential for religious and political commentary because of the Christian associations of "pastor" and "flock." The book's presentation is fashionably Continental and the metrical variation innovative, yet the language is deliberately old-fashioned, reminiscent of

Chaucer and with a name for the protagonist—Colin Clout—taken from the work of an earlier poet, John Skelton.

In that same year, 1579, Spenser was in the service, as secretary, of the Earl of Leicester, an important royal advisor and at one point suitor to Queen Elizabeth. There he would have met Sidney, Leicester's nephew, and Edward Dyer, both poets and both eventually knighted, whose friendship, or at least notice, would have seemed valuable. Sidney may have helped Spenser later gain an appointment as secretary to Lord Grey, the Lord Deputy of Ireland. It is not quite clear how Spenser regarded Grey's brutality against the Spanish troops who supported the Irish rebels, but his later tract, *A Vewe of the Present State of Ireland* (printed 1633—see the anthology's online component, *Literature in Ireland, Gaelic Scotland, and Wales* for excerpts), whatever the ambiguities of its dialogue form and a few residual doubts about its authorship, displays little regard for the Irish and even less for the insurgents. After Grey was recalled to England, Spenser remained in Ireland and continued to work as a civil servant, gaining considerable acreage and a small castle.

In 1589 Spenser traveled with Sir Walter Ralegh to England, where in 1590 he published the first three books of *The Faerie Queene*, on which he had been working for about a decade. Politically as well as poetically motivated, this Protestant, but hardly "Puritan," epic creates a romance world filled with monsters, giants, knights, and enchanters, allegorical personifications who enact a subtle, complex, and often elusive interplay between the Aristotelian or Christian virtues and their enemies, both those active out in the world and those operating within the leading figures' own souls. According to his letter to Ralegh, Spenser hoped to write twelve books, but only six were completed (the second set being published in the 1596 edition): the "legends" of holiness, temperance, chastity, friendship, justice, and courtesy, as well as a fragment on "Mutabilitie." Spenser won his pension, but Elizabeth's patronage seems to have gone no further, perhaps because his satirical "Mother Hubberds Tale," included in his *Complaints* (1591), angered the authorities.

In between the first and second installments of *The Faerie Queene* Spenser published his *Complaints*, a collection of poems; *Colin Clouts Come Home Againe* (1595), a sometimes satirical anti-court pastoral; *Astrophel*, an elegy for Philip Sidney (1596); and *Amoretti and Epithalamion* (1595), sonnets that commemorate Spenser's courtship of Elizabeth Boyle, followed by a magnificently stately marriage hymn celebrating their wedding. The sonnets, which depart from the Petrarchan tradition of adulterous or futile desire, are structured by allusions to the liturgical year; the twenty-four stanzas of the "Epithalamion" allude to the day (June 11, then the summer solstice), and its 365 long lines recall the year.

In 1597 Spenser became Sheriff of Cork, but later that year Irish rebels ransacked and burned his castle. He returned to London carrying dispatches for the Privy Council, but his time there was to be short. He died early in 1599 and is buried in Westminster Abbey, next to Chaucer. A memorial erected in 1620 reads, in part, "Heare lyes … the body of Edmond Spencer, the prince of poets in his tyme; whose divine spirit needs noe other witnesse then the works which he left behinde him."

⌘ ⌘ ⌘

The Faerie Queene

In a letter to his friend Sir Walter Ralegh, Spenser writes that his unfinished *Faerie Queene* aimed to "fashion" a gentleman or noble person who would combine the virtues represented by twelve knightly heroes. In his epic poem, each of the books features one of these knights, who represents a virtue and who struggles to fight the specific vices that threaten his quest. The hero of Book 1's "Legend of Holinesse," is Saint George (the Redcrosse Knight), patron saint of England and, with God's help, slayer of a satanic dragon that has been threatening a royal family and its kingdom, Eden. In the legend as it came down to Spenser, George rescues the royal maiden and the kingdom by defeating the dragon but

from *Amoretti*[1]

1

Happy ye leaves° when as those lilly hands,   *pages*
  which hold my life in their dead doing[2] might,
  shall handle you and hold in loves soft bands,°   *bonds*
  lyke captives trembling at the victors sight.
5 And happy lines, on which with starry light,
  those lamping° eyes will deigne   *blazing*
    sometimes to look
  and reade the sorrowes of my dying spright,°   *spirit*
  written with teares in harts close bleeding book.
  And happy rymes bath'd in the sacred brooke,
10   of Helicon[3] whence she derivèd is,
  when ye behold that Angels blessèd looke,
  my soules long lackèd foode, my heavens blis.
Leaves, lines, and rymes, seeke her to please alone,
  whom if ye please, I care for other none.

3

The soverayne beauty which I doo admyre,
  witnesse the world how worthy to be prayzed:
  the light wherof hath kindled heavenly fyre,
  in my fraile spirit by her from basenesse raysed.
5 That being now with her huge brightnesse dazed,
  base thing I can no more endure to view:
  but looking still on her I stand amazed,
  at wondrous sight of so celestiall hew.°   *form*
So when my toung would speak her praises dew,°   *due*
10   it stoppèd is with thoughts astonishment:
  and when my pen would write her titles true,
  it ravisht is with fancies wonderment:
Yet in my hart I then both speake and write,
  The wonder that my wit cannot endite.

6

Be nought dismayd that her unmovèd mind
  doth still persist in her rebellious pride:
  such love not lyke to lusts of baser kynd,

  the harder wonne, the firmer will abide.
5 The duresull° Oake, whose sap is not yet dride,   *durable*
  is long ere it conceive the kindling fyre:
  but when it once doth burne, it doth divide,
  great heat, and makes his flames to heaven aspire.
So hard it is to kindle new desire,
10   in gentle brest that shall endure for ever:
  deepe is the wound, that dints° the parts entire   *strikes*
  with chast affects, that naught but death can sever.
Then thinke not long in taking litle paine,
  to knit the knot, that ever shall remaine.

15

Ye tradefull° Merchants, that with   *engaged in trading*
    weary toyle,°   *toil*
  do seeke most pretious things to make your gain;
  and both the Indias[4] of their treasures spoile,
  what needeth you to seeke so farre in vaine?
5 For loe° my love doth in her selfe containe   *behold*
  all this worlds riches that may farre be found,
  if Saphyres, loe her eies be Saphyres plaine,
  if Rubies, loe hir lips be Rubies sound:°   *pure*
If Pearles, hir teeth be pearles both pure and round;
10   if Yvorie, her forhead yvory weene;°   *seems*
  if Gold, her locks are finest gold on ground;
  if silver, her faire hands are silver sheene.°   *beautiful*
But that which fairest is, but few behold,
  her mind adornd with vertues manifold.

22

This holy season[5] fit to fast and pray,
  Men to devotion ought to be inclynd:
  therefore, I lykewise on so holy day,[6]
  for my sweet Saynt some service fit will find.
5 Her temple fayre is built within my mind,
  in which her glorious ymage placèd is,
  on which my thoughts doo day and night attend
  lyke sacred priests that never thinke amisse.
There I to her as th'author of my blisse,
10   will builde an altar to appease her yre:
  and on the same my hart will sacrifise,
  burning in flames of pure and chast desyre:

---

[1] *Amoretti* Italian: Little loves. This sonnet sequence is generally read as a description of Spenser's courtship of and marriage to Elizabeth Boyle (whom he had married in the previous year, 1594).

[2] *dead doing* Death-dealing.

[3] *Helicon* One of the mountains sacred to the Nine Muses, the goddesses of the arts and sciences. The sacred spring which flows from Helicon is the Hippocrene.

---

[4] *both the Indias* I.e., the East and West Indies.

[5] *This holy season* Lent.

[6] *holy day* Ash Wednesday.

The which vouchsafe O goddesse to accept,
   amongst thy deerest relicks to be kept.

26

Sweet is the Rose, but growes upon a brere;°   *thorny bush*
   Sweet is the Junipere, but sharpe his bough;
   sweet is the Eglantine,° but pricketh nere;   *sweet-briar*
   sweet is the firbloome,[1] but his braunches rough.
5 Sweet is the Cypresse, but his rynd° is tough,   *bark*
   sweet is the nut, but bitter is his pill;°   *shell*
   sweet is the broome-flowre,[2] but yet sowre enough;
   and sweet is Moly,[3] but his root is ill.
So every sweet with soure is tempred still,
10   that maketh it be coveted the more:
   for easie things that may be got at will,
   most sorts of men doe set but little store.
Why then should I accoumpt° of little paine,   *think much*
   that endlesse pleasure shall unto me gaine.

34[4]

Lyke as a ship that through the Ocean wyde,
   by conduct of some star doth make her way,
   whenas a storme hath dimd her trusty guyde,
   out of her course doth wander far astray.
5 So I whose star, that wont with her bright ray,
   me to direct, with cloudes is overcast,
   doe wander now in darknesse and dismay,
   through hidden perils round about me plast.°   *placed*
Yet hope I well, that when this storme is past
10   my Helice the lodestar[5] of my lyfe
   will shine again, and looke on me at last,
   with lovely light to cleare my cloudy grief,
Till then I wander carefull° comfortlesse,   *full of cares*
   in secret sorow and sad pensivenesse.

37

What guyle is this, that those her golden tresses,
   She doth attyre under a net of gold:

---

[1] *firbloome* Fruit of the fir tree.

[2] *broome-flowre* Large yellow flower of the broom shrub, a common English plant.

[3] *Moly* Mythical herb with a white flower and black root, taken by Odysseus to ward off the spells of the witch Circe.

[4] *34* Modifies Petrarch's *Rima* 189, or one of the many adaptations.

[5] *Helice* The constellation Ursa Major; *lodestar* North Star, Polaris, in the constellation of Ursa Minor.

and with sly° skill so cunningly them dresses,   *dexterous*
   that which is gold or heare,° may scarse be told?   *hair*
5 Is it that mens frayle eyes, which gaze too bold,
   she may entangle in that golden snare:
   and being caught may craftily enfold,
   theyr weaker harts, which are not wel aware?
Take heed therefore, myne eyes, how ye doe stare
10   henceforth too rashly on that guilefull net,
   in which if ever ye entrappèd are,
   out of her bands° ye by no meanes shall get.   *bonds*
Fondnesse° it were for any being free,   *foolishness*
   to covet fetters, though they golden bee.

54

Of this worlds Theatre in which we stay,
   My love lyke the Spectator ydly sits
   beholding me that all the pageants° play,   *parts*
   disguysing diversly my troubled wits.
5 Sometimes I joy when glad occasion fits,
   and mask in myrth lyke to a Comedy:
   soone after when my joy to sorrow flits,
   I waile and make my woes a Tragedy.
Yet she beholding me with constant eye,
10   delights not in my merth nor rues° my smart:°   *pities / pain*
   but when I laugh she mocks, and when I cry
   she laughes, and hardens evermore her hart.
What then can move her? if nor merth nor mone,°   *moan*
   she is no woman, but a sencelesse stone.

64

Comming to kisse her lyps, (such grace I found)
   Me seemd I smelt a gardin of sweet flowres:
   that dainty odours from them threw around
   for damzels fit to decke their lovers bowres.
5 Her lips did smell lyke unto Gillyflowers,°   *carnations*
   her ruddy cheekes lyke unto Roses red:
   her snowy browes lyke budded Bellamoures,[6]
   her lovely eyes lyke Pincks[7] but newly spred,
Her goodly bosome lyke a Strawberry bed,
10   her neck lyke to a bounch of Cullambynes:°   *columbines*
   her brest lyke lillyes, ere theyr leaves be shed,
   her nipples lyke yong blossomd Jessemynes,°   *jasmines*

---

[6] *Bellamoures* Unidentified.

[7] *Pincks* Dianthus plants, the flowers of which can be red, white, pink, or variegated.

Such fragrant flowres doe give most odorous smell,
  but her sweet odour did them all excell.

67[1]

Lyke as a huntsman after weary chace,
  Seeing the game from him escapt away,
  sits downe to rest him in some shady place,
  with panting hounds beguilèd of their pray:
5 So after long pursuit and vaine° assay,°   *fruitless / attempt*
  when I all weary had the chace forsooke,
  the gentle deare returnd the selfe-same way,
  thinking to quench her thirst at the next brooke.
There she beholding me with mylder looke,
10   sought not to fly, but fearelesse still did bide:
  till I in hand her yet halfe trembling tooke,
  and with her owne goodwill hir fyrmely tyde.
Strange thing me seemd to see a beast so wyld,
  so goodly wonne with her owne will beguyld.° *deceived*

68

Most glorious Lord of lyfe that on this day,[2]
  Didst make thy triumph, over death and sin:
  and having harrowd hell didst bring away[3]
  captivity thence captive us to win:
5 This joyous day, deare Lord, with joy begin,
  and grant that we for whom thou diddest dye
  being with thy deare blood clene washt from sin,
  may live for ever in felicity.
And that thy love we weighing worthily,
10   may likewise love thee for the same againe:
  and for thy sake that all lyke deare[4] didst buy,
  with love may one another entertayne.
So let us love, deare love, lyke as we ought,
  love is the lesson which the Lord us taught.

69

The famous warriors of the anticke world,[5]
  Used Trophees to erect in stately wize:° *ways*
  in which they would the records have enrold,
  of theyr great deeds and valarous emprize.
5 What trophee then shall I most fit devize,
  in which I may record the memory
  of my loves conquest, peerelesse beauties prise,
  adorn'd with honour, love, and chastity.
Even this verse vowd to eternity,
10   shall be thereof immortall moniment:
  and tell her prayse to all posterity,
  that may admire such worlds rare wonderment.
The happy purchase of my glorious spoile,
  gotten at last with labour and long toyle.

70

Fresh spring the herald of loves mighty king,
  In whose cote armour richly are displayd
  all sorts of flowers the which on earth do spring
  in goodly colours gloriously arrayd.
5 Goe to my love, where she is carelesse layd,
  yet in her winters bowre not well awake:
  tell her the joyous time wil not be staid° *halted*
  unlesse she doe him by the forelock take.[6]
Bid her therefore her selfe soone ready make,
10   to wayt on love amongst his lovely crew:
  where every one that misseth then her make,° *mate*
  shall be by him amearst° with penance dew.° *immersed / due*
Make hast therefore sweet love, whilest it is
    prime,° *spring*
  for none can call againe the passèd time.

74

Most happy letters fram'd by skilfull trade,° *application*
  with which that happy name[7] was first desynd:
  the which three times thrise happy hath me made,
  with guifts of body, fortune and of mind.
5 The first my being to me gave by kind,° *nature*
  from mothers womb deriv'd by dew° descent, *due*
  the second is my sovereigne Queene most kind,
  that honour and large richesse to me lent.

---

[1] *67* An adaptation of the Italian poet Petrarch's *Rima* 190 (also adapted by Thomas Wyatt, Torquato Tasso, and Marguerite de Navarre). Spenser significantly changes Petrarch's original ending, turning Petrarch's lament into a happy celebration of the realization of his desires.

[2] *this day* Easter.

[3] *having ... away* Before his Resurrection, Christ descended into Hell to rescue the good Israelites who had died before his birth—an event referred to as the Harrowing of Hell.

[4] *lyke deare* At the same cost. I.e., Christ redeemed all people at the same cost.

[5] *anticke world* I.e., antique world, classical Greece and Rome.

[6] *by ... take* Seize the time or take the opportunity.

[7] *that happy name* Elizabeth, the name shared by Spenser's mother, Queen, and wife.

The third my love, my lives last ornament,
10   by whom my spirit out of dust was raysed:°   *raised*
     to speake her prayse and glory excellent,
     of all alive most worthy to be praysed.
Ye three Elizabeths for ever live,
     that three such graces[1] did unto me give.

75

One day I wrote her name upon the strand,°   *shore*
     but came the waves and washèd it away:
     agayne I wrote it with a second hand,
     but came the tyde, and made my paynes his pray.° *prey*
5   Vayne man, sayd she, that doest in vaine assay,°   *attempt*
     a mortall thing so to immortalize.
     for I my selve shall lyke to this decay,
     and eek° my name bee wypèd out lykewize.   *also*
Not so, (quod° I) let baser things devize°   *said / plan*
10   to dy in dust, but you shall live by fame:
     my verse your vertues rare shall eternize,
     and in the hevens wryte your glorious name.
Where whenas death shall all the world subdew,
     our love shall live, and later life renew.

80

After so long a race as I have run
     Through Faery land, which those six books[2] compile,
     give leave to rest me being halfe fordonne,°   *overcome*
     and gather to my selfe new breath awhile.
5   Then as a steed refreshèd after toyle,
     out of my prison I will breake anew:
     and stoutly will that second worke assoyle,°   *discharge*
     with strong endevour and attention dew.°   *due*
Till then give leave to me in pleasant mew,°   *seclusion*
10   to sport my muse and sing my loves sweet praise:
     the contemplation of whose heavenly hew,°   *form*
     my spirit to an higher pitch will rayse.
But let her prayses yet be low and meane,°   *common*
     fit for the handmayd of the Faery Queene.

82

Joy of my life, full oft for loving you
     I blesse my lot, that was so lucky placed:
     but then the more your owne mishap I rew,°   *pity*
     that are so much by so meane° love   *common*
     embased.°   *lowered*
5   For had the equall hevens so much you graced
     in this as in the rest, ye mote invent
     som hevenly wit, whose verse could have
     enchased°   *engraved*
     your glorious name in golden moniment.
But since ye deignd so goodly to relent
10   to me your thrall,° in whom is little worth,   *bondage*
     that little that I am, shall all be spent,
     in setting your immortall prayses forth.
Whose lofty argument° uplifting me,   *theme*
     shall lift you up unto an high degree.

89

Lyke as the Culver° on the barèd bough,   *dove*
     Sits mourning for the absence of her mate:
     and in her songs sends many a wishfull vow,
     for his returne that seemes to linger late.
5   So I alone now left disconsolate,
     mourne to my selfe the absence of my love:
     and wandring here and there all desolate,
     seek with my playnts° to match that   *laments*
     mournful dove
Ne joy of ought° that under heaven doth   *anything*
     hove,°   *dwell*
10   can comfort me, but her owne joyous sight:
     whose sweet aspect both God and man can move,
     in her unspotted° pleasauns° to delight.   *pure / pleasure*
Dark is my day, whyles her fayre light I mis,
     and dead my life that wants such lively° blis.   *vital*
—1594

---

[1] *three such graces*   I.e., Three Graces, sister goddesses of beauty, mirth, and bounty.

[2] *those six books*   The six completed books of *The Faerie Queene*.

WILLIAM SHAKESPEARE
<u>1564 – 1616</u>

The plays of Shakespeare are foundational works of Western culture; in the English-speaking world they have influenced subsequent literary culture more broadly and more deeply than any other group of texts except the books of the Bible. The language and imagery of the plays; their ways of telling stories; their innovative dramatic qualities; the characters that populate them (and the ways in which these characters are created); the issues and ideas the plays explore (and the ways in which they explore them)—all these have powerfully shaped English literature and culture over the past four centuries. And this shaping influence has continually touched popular culture as well as more "elevated" literary and academic worlds. From the eighteenth century on Shakespeare's plays have held the stage with far greater frequency than those of any other playwright, and in the twentieth century many have been made into popular films (some of the best of which are films in Japanese and in Russian). Even outside the English-speaking world the plays of Shakespeare receive unparalleled exposure; in the Netherlands, for example, his plays have been performed in the late twentieth and early twenty-first centuries more than twice as often as those of any other playwright. In 2000 he headed the list both on the BBC "person of the millennium" poll and on the *World Almanac*'s poll listing the 10 "most influential people of the second millennium." The fact that a playwright, a member of the popular entertainment industry, has continued to enjoy this kind of cultural status—ranked above the likes of Newton, Churchill, Galileo, and Einstein—is worth pausing over. Why are these plays still performed, read, watched, filmed, studied, and appropriated four centuries after they were written? What is the source of his ongoing cultural currency?

There are many ways to answer this question. One is surely that the plays tell great stories. Fundamental, psychologically sophisticated stories, about love, death, growing up, families, communities, guilt, revenge, jealousy, order and disorder, self-knowledge and identity. Another, just as surely, is that they tell them with extraordinary verbal facility in almost all respects: Shakespeare is generally regarded as unsurpassed in his choice of individual words and his inventiveness in conjuring up striking images; in his structuring of the rhythm of poetic lines; in balancing sentences rhetorically; in shaping long speeches; and in crafting sparkling dialogue. A third is that the characters within the stories are uniquely engaging and memorable. In large part this can be attributed to Shakespeare's ingenuity: within the English literary tradition he more or less invented the psychologically realistic literary character; within the European literary tradition he more or less also invented the strong, independent female character. The bare bones of his characters are typically provided by other sources, but the flesh and blood is of Shakespeare's making. Fourth, and perhaps most important of all, Shakespeare's plays tell their stories in ways that are open-ended emotionally and intellectually: no matter how neatly the threads of story may be knitted together at the end, the threads of idea and of emotion in Shakespeare's plays are never tied off. It is this openness of the plays, their availability for reinterpretation, that enables them to be endlessly re-staged, rewritten, re-interpreted—and to yield fresh ideas and fresh feelings time and time again.

Given the centrality of Shakespeare to Western culture, the wish of many readers to know far more than we do about his life is understandable. In fact we do know a fair amount about the facts of his life—given late sixteenth- and early seventeenth-century norms, perhaps more than we might expect to know of someone of his class and background. But we know a good deal less of Shakespeare than we do of some other leading writers of his era—Ben Jonson, for example, or John Donne. And, perhaps most frustrating of all, we know almost nothing of an intimate or personal nature about Shakespeare.

Shakespeare (whose surname also appears on various documents as Shakespear, Shakspere, Shaxpere, and Shagspere) was baptized in Stratford-upon-Avon on 26 April 1564. Reasonable conjecture, given the customs of the time, suggests that he was born two-to-four days earlier; the date that has been most frequently advanced is 23 April (the same day of the year on which he died in 1616, and also the day on which St. George, England's patron saint, is traditionally honored). His father, John, was a glove-maker and also a local politician: first an alderman and then bailiff, a position equivalent to mayor. Some scholars have argued that he had remained a Catholic in newly-Protestant England, and that Shakespeare thus grew up in a clandestinely Catholic home; though the evidence for this is suggestive, it is not conclusive. (If Shakespeare had grown up Catholic, that background might lead readers to see some of his history plays in a different perspective, and might lend even greater poignancy to images such as that of the "bare ruined choirs" of Sonnet 73, with its suggestion of the destruction of the monasteries destroyed by Henry VIII following the break with Rome.)

Stratford-upon-Avon had a good grammar school, which is generally presumed to have provided William's early education, though no records exist to confirm this. Not surprisingly, he did not go on to university, which at the time would have been unusual for a person from the middle class. (Even Ben Jonson, one of the finest classicists of the period, did not attend university.) Shakespeare's first exposure to theater was probably through the troupes of traveling players that regularly toured the country at that time.

On 28 November 1562, when Shakespeare was eighteen, he was married to Anne Hathaway, who was eight years his senior. Six months later, in May of 1583, Anne gave birth to their first daughter, Susanna; given the timing, it seems reasonable to speculate that an unexpected pregnancy may have prompted a sudden marriage. In February 1585, twins, named Hamnet (Shakespeare's only son, who was to die at the age of eleven) and Judith, were born. Some time later, probably within the next three years, Shakespeare moved to London, leaving his young family behind. There has been considerable speculation as to his reasons for leaving Stratford-upon Avon, but no solid evidence has been found to support any of the numerous theories. Certainly London was then (as now) a magnet for ambitious young men, and in the late 1580s it was effectively the only English city conducive to the pursuit of a career as a writer or in the theater.

It is not known exactly when Shakespeare joined the professional theater in London, but by 1592 several of his plays had reached the stage–the three parts of *Henry VI*, probably *The Comedy of Errors* and *Titus Andronicus*, possibly others. The earliest extant mention of him in print occurs in 1592: a sarcastic jibe by an embittered older playwright, Robert Greene. Greene calls Shakespeare "an upstart crow beautified with our feathers," probably referring to Shakespeare's work on the series of *Henry VI* plays, which may well have involved the revision of material by other writers who had originally worked on the play. In any case, from 1594 on, Will Shakespeare is listed as a member of the company called The Lord Chamberlain's Men (later called The King's Men, when James I became their patron).

Professional theater in London did not become firmly established until 1576, when the first permanent playhouses opened. By the late 1580s four theaters were in operation—an unprecedented level of activity, and one that in all probability helped to nurture greater sophistication on the part of audiences. Certainly it was a hothouse that nurtured an extraordinary growth of theatrical agility on the part of Elizabethan playwrights. Shakespeare, as both playwright and actor in The Lord Chamberlain's Men, was afforded opportunities of forging, testing and reworking his written work in the heat of rehearsals and performances—opportunities that were not open to other playwrights.[1] And in Christopher Marlowe he had a rival playwright of a most extraordinary sort. It seems safe to conjecture that the two learned a good deal about play construction from each other. In the late 1580s and early 1590s they both adopt virtually simultaneously the practice of having their characters express their intentions in advance of the unfolding action, thereby encouraging the formation of audience expectations; they also begin to make it a practice to interpose some other action between the exit and the re-entry of any character, thereby further fostering the creation of a sense of temporal and spatial illusion of a sort quite new to the English stage.

In his early years in London Shakespeare also established himself as a non-dramatic poet—and sought aristocratic patronage in doing so. In the late sixteenth century the writing of poetry was accorded considerable respect, the writing of plays a good deal less. It was conventional for those not of aristocratic birth themselves to seek a patron for their writing—as Shakespeare evidently did with the Earl of Southampton, a young noble to whom he dedicated two substantial poems of mythological narrative, Venus and Adonis (1593) and The Rape of Lucrece (1594). (It is a measure of the enormity of Shakespeare's achievement that these poems, which would be regarded as major works of almost any other writer of the period, are an afterthought in most considerations of Shakespeare's work.) Before the end of the century Shakespeare was also circulating his sonnets, as we know from the praise of Francis Meres, who wrote in 1598 that the "sweet, witty soul" of the classical poet of love, Ovid, "lives in mellifluous and honey-tongued Shakespeare, witness his Venus and Adonis, his Lucrece, his sugared sonnets among his private friends, etc." Such circulation among "private friends" was common practice at the time, and was not necessarily followed by publication. When Shakespeare's sonnets were finally published, in 1609, the dedication was from the printer rather than the author, suggesting that Shakespeare may not have authorized their publication.

There are thirty-eight extant plays by Shakespeare (if Two Noble Kinsmen is included in the total). Unlike most other playwrights of the age, he wrote in every major dramatic genre. His history plays (most of them written in the 1590s) include Richard III, Henry IV, Part 1 and Part 2, and Henry V. He wrote comedies throughout his playwriting years; the succession of comedies that date from the years 1595–1601, including Much Ado About Nothing, As You Like It and Twelfth Night, may represent his most successful work in this genre, though some have argued that The Merchant of Venice (c. 1596) and the "dark comedies" which date from between 1601 and 1604 (including All's Well That Ends Well and Measure for Measure) resonate even more deeply. The period of the "dark comedies" substantially overlaps with the period in which Shakespeare wrote a succession of great tragedies. Hamlet may have been written as early as 1598–99, but Othello, King Lear, and Macbeth were written in succession between 1601 and 1606. Several of his last plays are romance-comedies—notably Cymbeline, The Winter's Tale and The Tempest (all of which date from the period 1608–11).

Shakespeare was a shareholder in The Lord Chamberlain's Men, and it was in that capacity rather than as a playwright or actor that he made a good deal of money. There was at the time no equivalent

[1] From the nineteenth century onwards (though, perhaps tellingly, never before that), the suggestion has occasionally been put forward that Shakespeare never wrote the plays attributed to him, and that someone else–perhaps Francis Bacon, perhaps Edward de Vere, 17th Earl of Oxford–was actually the author. These conspiracy theories have sometimes gained popular currency, but scholars have never found any reason whatsoever to credit any of them. One of the many reasons such theories lack credibility follows from our sure knowledge that Shakespeare was an actor in many of the plays that bear his name as author. If Shakespeare had not written the plays himself it would surely have been impossibly difficult to conceal that fact from all the members of the rest of the company, in rehearsal as well as in performance, over the course of many, many years.

to modern laws of copyright, or to modern conventions of payment to the authors of published works. Nineteen of Shakespeare's plays were printed individually during Shakespeare's lifetime, but it is clear that many of these publications did not secure his co-operation. It has often been hypothesized that some of the printers of the most obviously defective texts (referred to by scholars as "bad quartos") are pirated editions dictated from memory to publishers by actors; there is some evidence to support this theory, though even if correct it leaves many textual issues unresolved.

The first publication of Shakespeare's collected works did not occur until 1623, several years after his death, when two of his fellow actors, John Heminges and Henry Condell, arranged to have printed the First Folio, a carefully prepared volume (by the standards of the time) that included thirty-six of Shakespeare's plays. Eighteen of these were appearing for the first time, and four others for the first time in a reliable edition. (*Two Noble Kinsmen*, which was written in collaboration with a younger playwright, John Fletcher, and *Pericles*, of which it appears Shakespeare was not the sole author, were both excluded, although the editors did include *Henry VIII*, which is now generally believed to have been another work in which Fletcher had a hand.)

A vital characteristic of Shakespeare's plays is their extraordinary richness of language. After several centuries of forging a new tongue out of its polyglot sources, the English language in the sixteenth century had entered a period of steady growth in its range, as vocabulary expanded to meet the needs of an increasingly complex society. Yet its structure over this same time (no doubt in connection with the spread of print culture) was becoming increasingly stable. When we compare the enormous difference between the language of Chaucer, who was writing in the late fourteenth century, and that of Shakespeare, writing in the late sixteenth century, it is remarkable to see how greatly the language changed over those two centuries—considerably more than it has changed in the four centuries from Shakespeare's time to our own. English was still effectively a new language in his time, with immense and largely unexplored possibilities for conveying subtleties of meaning. More than any other, Shakespeare embarked on that exploration; his reading was clearly very wide,[1] as was his working vocabulary. But he expanded the language as well as absorbing it; a surprising number of the words Shakespeare used are first recorded as having been used in his work.

The popular image of Shakespeare's last few years is that first expressed by Nicholas Rowe in 1709:

> The latter part of his life was spent, as all men of good sense wish theirs may be, in ease, retirement, and the conversation of his friends. He had the good fortune to gather together an estate equal to his occasion, and, in that, to his wish; and is said to have spent some years before his death at his native Stratford.

We know for a fact that around 1610 Shakespeare moved from London to Stratford, where his family had continued to live throughout the years he had spent in London, and the move has often been referred to as a "retirement." Shakespeare did not immediately give up playwriting, however: *The Tempest* (1611), *Henry VIII* (c. 1612) and *Two Noble Kinsmen* (c. 1613) all date from after his move to Stratford. By the time he left London Shakespeare was indeed a relatively wealthy man, with

---

[1] In his early years in London Shakespeare may well have acquired much of his reading material from Richard Field, a man from Stratford-upon-Avon of about Shakespeare's age who was in the book trade. Field printed Shakespeare's early poems, *Venus and Adonis* and *The Rape of Lucrece*, and it is certainly possible that the two men had some understanding by which Shakespeare borrowed some of the books he read, which otherwise might have been prohibitively expensive. (Among the works printed by Field was a multi-volume Thomas North translation of Plutarch's *Lives*, of which Shakespeare made extensive use.) Shakespeare also lodged for a time in London with a French Huguenot family named Montjoy, whose home may have been the source for some of the French books that his plays demonstrate a familiarity with. And he may also have had the use of the libraries of one or more of his aristocratic patrons.

substantial investments both in real estate and in the tithes of the town (an arrangement that would be comparable to buying government bonds today).

After 1613 we have no record of any further writing; he died on 23 April 1616, aged 52. In his will, Shakespeare left his extensive property to the sons of his daughter, Susanna (described in her epitaph as "witty above her sex"). To his wife, he left his "second-best bed"—a bequest which many have found both puzzling and provocative. He was buried as a respectable citizen in the chancel of the parish church, where his gravestone is marked not with a name, but a simple poem:

> Good friend, for Jesus' sake forbear
> To dig the dust enclosed here.
> Blest be the man that spares these stones,
> And curst be he that moves my bones.

Shakespeare's work appears to have been extremely well regarded in his lifetime; soon after his death a consensus developed that his work—his plays in particular—constitute the highest achievement in English literature. In some generations he has been praised most highly for the depth of his characterization, in others for the dense brilliance of his imagery, in others for the extraordinary intellectual suggestiveness of the ideas that his characters express (and occasionally embody). But in every generation since the mid-seventeenth century a consensus has remained that Shakespeare stands without peer among English authors.

In most generations the study of Shakespeare has also helped to shape the development of literary criticism and theory. From John Dryden and Samuel Johnson to Samuel Taylor Coleridge to Northrop Frye, works central to the development of literary theory and criticism have had Shakespeare as their subject. And in the past 50 years Shakespeare has been a vital test case in the development of feminist literary theory, of post-colonial theory, and of political, cultural, and new historicist criticism: just as with each generation people of the theater develop new ways of playing Shakespeare that yield fresh insight, so too do scholars develop new ways of reading texts through reading Shakespeare.

[Note to instructors: *King Lear* and *Twelfth Night* are among over 400 available editions from Broadview, any one of which may be packaged together with this anthology volume at no extra cost to the student.]

Venus and Adonis

London's theaters were among the first public gathering places to close in times of plague. During the 1592–93 outbreak, Shakespeare turned his focus to narrative poetry—*The Rape of Lucrece* as well as *Venus and Adonis*—and successfully sought the patronage of Henry Wriothesley, the nineteen-year-old Earl of Southampton. Dedicated to Wriothesley, *Venus and Adonis* was the first poem that Shakespeare filed with the Stationers' Register, and the first known work of his to appear in printed form.

Venus and Adonis belongs to a sub-genre of poetry often referred to as *epyllia* (singular: *epyllion*)—narrative poems based on classical mythology that deal with the subject of love. The source material for this poem appears in Ovid's *Metamorphoses* (the relevant excerpts are included below, under the heading "In Context"). Like another well-known epyllion of the English Renaissance, Christopher Marlowe's *Hero and Leander*, *Venus and Adonis* diverges in interesting ways from its classical source. Shakespeare presents a version that is far longer than the story as it appears in Ovid; that delves in far greater detail into the psyches of its two characters; that posits a distinction between love and lust that is nowhere to be found in the classical source; and that is written in a tone that is quite distinct from

The Sonnets

Begun in the 1590s, intermittently revised, and with some of its contents already circulating, Shakespeare's *Sonnets* was printed in 1609 under obscure circumstances. Did Shakespeare authorize publication by the printer Thomas Thorpe? Did he organize the sonnets himself? Is there a pattern to them? The 154 sonnets, concluding with two light poems on Cupid, are followed by a long "Lover's Complaint" in a female voice. How does this poem fit the volume, and do we know with any certainty that Shakespeare is the author of it as well?

The volume's structure parallels that of sonnet collections in the 1590s, such as Samuel Daniel's *Delia* and Spenser's *Epithalamion and Amoretti*. Is Shakespeare merely following this example or subtly commenting on it? Who is the "W.H." whom the printer Thorpe calls "the only begetter" of the sonnets? No one knows. Nor, despite sometimes wild speculation, do we know the identity of the beautiful but faithless young man to whom many of the sonnets are addressed (or if there is only one young man), or that of the "dark lady" whom the lover treats with erotic admiration and moral contempt, or that of the rival poet to whom some sonnets allude. Is the lady always the same woman? Sonnet 145 seems to pun on "Hathaway," maiden name of Shakespeare's wife, Anne. Who is the presumed speaker of these sonnets? Several sonnets pun on the "Will"—a useful name, for it could also denote a faculty of the soul, sexual desire, and even the genitals.

For many years the sonnets received little attention or respect. The second edition of Shakespeare's poems, a shabby volume published by John Benson (1640), feminizes some pronouns, runs some sonnets together, and plagiarizes some commentary; it did the sonnets' reputation no good, and it was not until relatively recently that their splendor and power was fully acknowledged.

One source of older generations' unease with the sonnets was the passion with which the speaker addresses a younger man. It is conventional to think that the first 126 sonnets are to or about this youth and most of the remainder to or about a "dark lady," but many of the sonnets leave the gender of the addressee unspecified. Some of those undeniably involving the young man are clearly expressive of strong homoerotic desire, but the extent to which such desire is acted upon is much less clear. Sonnet 20 seems to say that a sexual relation between the speaker and his friend is impossible, but for some recent critics the poem's puns hint at the opposite. However we read them, such ardent expressions of love and longing for a fellow man are unusual, although not unparalleled, in the literature either of Renaissance England or the Continent.

Also unusual is the lover's sexually reciprocated but problematic love for a compliant if unfaithful woman. This is another respect in which Shakespeare makes a show of revising the Petrarchan tradition familiar to him from Renaissance poetry, in which the love of the male wooer was typically not reciprocated by his female beloved. Much as Shakespeare was clearly indebted to the Petrarchan tradition, he departed from it in a variety of ways.

In form, Petrarch and most other Italian poets had made it a practice to divide their sonnets formally into an octave followed by a sestet. Henry Howard, Earl of Surrey, had been instrumental in the development of an "English" sonnet pattern of three quatrains followed by a couplet. Shakespeare varies the structure of his sonnets in a number of ways, but generally employs rhyme schemes deriving from the "English" pattern (most commonly: *abab cdcd efef gg*).

Whether or not we read *Sonnets* as a sequence, certain recurrent motifs are worth noticing: desire and "will" in every sense, the ruinous passage of time together with the physical and poetic means of surmounting its ravages, the cyclical and poignant beauty of the natural world, and the paradoxes involved in loving the unworthy. Just as notable is the language, which offers an astonishing array of puns, syntactic or lexical ambiguities, and metaphors that evolve through associative connections with a logic just below the surface sense of the verse. Note, for example, how Sonnet 60 moves from ocean waves, to crooked eclipses that must involve the moon (which affects the ocean), to the (curved) plow that makes agricultural furrows, that parallels the wrinkles of bent age, and to Time's curved scythe. Shakespeare can also be funny, though—as witness Sonnet 135's bawdy insinuations, or the resigned (bitter? amused?) puns in Sonnet 138 on lying to and lying with a lover.

⌘ ⌘ ⌘

Sonnets

1

From fairest creatures we desire increase,°   *progeny*
   That thereby beauty's rose might never die,
But as the riper should by time[1] decease
His tender° heir might bear his memory: *young*
5 But thou, contracted[2] to thine own bright eyes,
Feed'st thy light's flame with self-substantial fuel,[3]
Making a famine where abundance lies,[4]
Thyself thy foe, to thy sweet self too cruel.
Thou that art now the world's fresh° ornament,   *unspoiled*
10 And only herald to the gaudy[5] spring,
Within thine own bud buriest thy content,[6]
And, tender churl, mak'st waste in niggarding.[7]
    Pity the world, or else this glutton[8] be,
    To eat the world's due, by the grave and thee.[9]

2

When forty[10] winters shall besiege thy brow,
   And dig deep trenches in thy beauty's field,
Thy youth's proud livery,° so gazed on now,   *uniform*
Will be a tattered weed° of small worth held: *garment*
5 Then being asked, where all thy beauty lies,
Where all the treasure of thy lusty° days,   *vigorous*
To say, within thine own deep-sunken eyes,
Were an all-eating shame and thriftless[11] praise.
How much more praise deserved thy beauty's use[12]
10 If thou couldst answer, "This fair child of mine
Shall sum my count, and make my old excuse,"[13]
Proving his beauty by succession° thine: *legal inheritance*
    This were to be new made when thou art old,
    And see thy blood warm when thou feel'st it cold.

12

When I do count the clock[14] that tells the time,
   And see the brave° day sunk in hideous   *splendid*
   night;
When I behold the violet past prime,
And sable curls all silvered o'er with white:
5 When lofty trees I see barren of leaves,
Which erst from heat did canopy the herd,[15]
And summer's green all girded° up in sheaves   *bundled*
Borne on the bier with white and bristly beard:[16]

---

[1] *But* But rather that; *riper* Older; *by time* Because of the passage of time.

[2] *contracted* Betrothed; also confined.

[3] *Feed'st ... fuel* Like a candle, you consume your own substance with self-love; cf. the story of Narcissus in Ovid, *Metamorphoses* 3.464 ("I am burned by love of myself / I produce and am consumed by flames").

[4] *Making ... lies* Cf. *Metamorphoses* 3.466 ("my very abundance makes me poor").

[5] *only* Chief; *gaudy* Brightly colored, but not in the modern pejorative sense.

[6] *content* Contentment; also, essence.

[7] *churl* Here, miser; *mak'st ... niggarding* Cf. *Romeo and Juliet* 1.1.223; *niggarding* Behaving in a miserly fashion.

[8] *this glutton* This kind of glutton.

[9] *To ... thee* What should belong to the world will be consumed first by yourself, then by death.

---

[10] *forty* Number signifying many and, in Shakespeare's time, corresponding to late middle age.

[11] *thriftless* Wasteful or unprofitable.

[12] *deserved ... use* Would thy beauty's use deserve; *use* Proper employment, also engagement for profit, as in money on loan.

[13] *sum my count* Display the total of my assets; *make ... excuse* Justify or make reparation for my old age.

[14] *count the clock* Count the sounds of the clock.

[15] *erst* Formerly; *canopy the herd* Provide shade for livestock.

[16] *bier* Barrow or litter for carrying crops, but more often associated with the bearing of a corpse to the grave; *white ... beard* As on wheat or barley after harvest.

Then of thy beauty do I question make,
10   That thou among the wastes of time must go,
Since sweets and beauties do themselves forsake,[1]
And die as fast as they see others grow,
    And nothing 'gainst time's scythe can make defence
    Save breed° to brave° him, when he   *reproduce / defy*
    takes thee hence.

15

When I consider° everything that grows *consider that*
  Holds in perfection but a little moment;
That this huge stage presenteth naught but shows[2]
Whereon the stars in secret influence[3] comment;
5 When I perceive that men as plants increase,
Cheered and checked even by the self-same sky,
Vaunt° in their youthful sap, at height decrease, *exult*
And wear their brave state out of memory:[4]
Then the conceit of this inconstant stay[5]
10 Sets you, most rich in youth, before my sight,
Where wasteful[6] time debateth with decay
To change your day of youth to sullied[7] night:
    And all in war with time for love of you
    As he takes from you, I engraft[8] you new.

16

But wherefore° do not you a mightier way *why*
  Make war upon this bloody tyrant, time,
And fortify yourself in your decay
With means more blessed than my barren rhyme?
5 Now stand you on the top of happy hours,

---

[1] *sweets* Pleasures, or people or things affording pleasure; *themselves forsake* Lose their essence through time.

[2] *this huge stage* The world as stage was a common notion in the Renaissance; cf. Shakespeare's *As You Like It* 2.7.139–40: "All the world's a stage / And all the men and women merely players"; *shows* Theatrical displays.

[3] *secret influence* The supposed life effects of the stars on human life and temperament.

[4] *wear … memory* Decay until their glory fades from memory.

[5] *conceit* Thought; conception; *inconstant stay* Constant state ("stay") of inconstancy, or change, as in the aging process.

[6] *wasteful* In the sense of wasting or destructive.

[7] *sullied* Tarnished; made gloomy or dull.

[8] *engraft* Insert a scion, or shoot, from one tree into the bark of another, from which it gains sustenance.

And many maiden gardens, yet unset,° *unplanted*
With virtuous wish would bear your living flowers,
Much liker[9] than your painted counterfeit:
So should the lines of life that life repair,[10]
10 Which this, time's pencil or my pupil pen,
Neither in inward worth nor outward fair,° *beauty*
Can make you live yourself in eyes of men:
    To give away yourself[11] keeps yourself still,° *always*
    And you must live drawn by your own sweet skill.

18

Shall I compare thee to a summer's day?
  Thou art more lovely and more temperate:
Rough winds do shake the darling buds of May,
And summer's lease hath all too short a date:
5 Sometime too hot the eye of heaven shines,
And often is his gold complexion dimmed;
And every fair° from fair sometime declines, *beauty*
By chance, or nature's changing course, untrimmed:
But thy eternal summer shall not fade,
10 Nor lose possession of that fair thou ow'st,° *own*
Nor shall death brag thou wander'st in his shade
When in eternal lines to time thou grow'st:
    So long as men can breathe or eyes can see,
    So long lives this, and this gives life to thee.

19

Devouring time, blunt thou the lion's paws,
  And make the earth devour her own sweet brood;
Pluck the keen teeth from the fierce tiger's jaws,
And burn the long-lived Phoenix in her blood;[12]
5 Make glad and sorry seasons as thou fleet'st,
And do whate'er thou wilt, swift-footed time,
To the wide world and all her fading sweets:° *pleasures*
But I forbid thee one most heinous crime,
O carve not with thy hours my love's fair brow,
10 Nor draw no lines there with thine antique[13] pen;

---

[9] *liker* More like you.

[10] *lines of life* Bloodlines of your descendants, or the outlines of you reflected in them; *repair* Restore.

[11] *give away yourself* Marry.

[12] *Phoenix* Mythical bird that after living five or six centuries burns itself in a nest of spices and then rises from the ashes renewed to begin another cycle; *in her blood* Alive.

[13] *antique* Ancient.

Him in thy course untainted[1] do allow
For beauty's pattern to succeeding men.
    Yet do thy worst, old Time, despite thy wrong,
    My love shall in my verse ever live young.

20

A woman's face with nature's own hand painted
Hast thou, the master mistress of my passion;
A woman's gentle heart, but not acquainted
With shifting change, as is false women's fashion;
5 An eye more bright than theirs, less false in rolling,[2]
Gilding the object whereupon it gazeth;
A man in hue,° all hues in his controlling,   *appearance*
Which steals men's eyes and women's souls amazeth;
And for a woman wert thou first created,
10 Till nature as she wrought thee fell a-doting,
And by addition[3] me of thee defeated,
By adding one thing to my purpose nothing:
    But since she pricked[4] thee out for women's pleasure,
    Mine be thy love, and thy love's use[5] their treasure.

23

As an unperfect actor[6] on the stage,
Who with his fear is put besides[7] his part;
Or some fierce thing, replete with too much rage,
Whose strength's abundance weakens his own heart;
5 So I, for fear of trust,[8] forget to say
The perfect ceremony[9] of love's right,°   *due*
And in mine own love's strength seem to decay,
O'ercharged with burden of mine own love's might:
O let my books be then the eloquence
10 And dumb presagers[10] of my speaking breast,

---

[1] *untainted* Unmarked, unhurt.

[2] *rolling* Glancing at lovers.

[3] *by addition* I.e., of male genitals.

[4] *pricked* Selected; "prick" was also slang for penis.

[5] *love's use* Sexual pleasure and probably the suggestion of reproduction and increase, with a pun on "usury."

[6] *unperfect actor* Actor who does not remember his lines accurately.

[7] *is put besides* Loses track of, forgets.

[8] *for … trust* Afraid to trust myself, or perhaps afraid of not being trusted.

[9] *perfect ceremony* Precise words demanded by the situation.

[10] *dumb presagers* Silent signals.

Who plead for love, and look for recompense,
More than that tongue that more hath more expressed:
    O learn to read what silent love hath writ!
    To hear with eyes belongs to love's fine wit.[11]

29

When in disgrace with fortune and men's eyes
I all alone beweep my outcast state,
And trouble deaf heav'n with my bootless° cries,   *unavailing*
And look upon myself, and curse my fate,
5 Wishing me like to one more rich in hope,
Featured like him,[12] like him with friends possessed,
Desiring this man's art° and that man's scope,   *skill*
With what I most enjoy contented least;
Yet in these thoughts myself almost despising,
10 Haply° I think on thee, and then my state,   *by chance*
Like to the lark at break of day arising,
From sullen° earth sings hymns at   *dark, gloomy*
    heaven's gate;
    For thy sweet love remembered such wealth brings
    That then I scorn to change my state with kings.

30

When to the sessions° of sweet silent   *judicial sittings*
thought
I summon up remembrance of things past,[13]
I sigh the lack of many a thing I sought,
And with old woes new wail my dear time's waste;
5 Then can I drown an eye (unused to flow)
For precious friends hid in death's dateless night,
And weep afresh love's long since cancelled woe,
And moan th'expense° of many a vanished sight.   *loss*
Then can I grieve at grievances foregone,°   *past*
10 And heavily from woe to woe tell° o'er   *count*
The sad account of fore-bemoanéd moan,
Which I new pay, as if not paid before;
    But if the while I think on thee, dear friend,
    All losses are restored, and sorrows end.

---

[11] *belongs … wit* Is characteristic of love's subtle intelligence.

[12] *Featured like him* With physical attractions like his.

[13] *summon* Call to court; *remembrance … past* Cf. Geneva Bible (1560), *Wisdom* 11.10: "For their grief was double with mourning, and the remembrance of things past."

33

Full many a glorious morning have I seen
Flatter the mountain tops with sovereign eye,
Kissing with golden face the meadows green,
Gilding pale streams with heavenly alchemy;
5 Anon° permit the basest clouds to ride   *soon*
With ugly rack[1] on his celestial face,
And from the forlorn world his visage hide,
Stealing unseen to west with this disgrace:
Even so my sun one early morn did shine
10 With all triumphant splendour on my brow;
But out alack,[2] he was but one hour mine,
The region cloud[3] hath masked him from me now.
　　Yet him for this, my love no whit[4] disdaineth:
　　Suns of the world may stain,[5] when heaven's sun
　　　　staineth.

35

No more be grieved at that which thou hast done;
Roses have thorns, and silver fountains mud;
Clouds and eclipses stain both moon and sun,
And loathsome canker° lives in sweetest bud.   *caterpillar*
5 All men make faults, and even I, in this,
Authorizing thy trespass with compare,°   *comparisons*
Myself corrupting, salving thy amiss,[6]
Excusing these sins more than these sins are:[7]
For to thy sensual fault I bring in sense;[8]
10 Thy adverse party is thy advocate,[9]
And 'gainst myself a lawful plea commence:
Such civil war is in my love and hate
　　That I an accessary needs must be
　　To that sweet thief which sourly robs from me.

36

Let me confess that we two must be twain,°   *separate*
Although our undivided loves are one;
So shall those blots° that do with me remain,   *disgraces*
Without thy help, by me be borne alone.
5 In our two loves there is but one respect,[10]
Though in our lives a separable spite;[11]
Which, though it alter not love's sole effect,[12]
Yet doth it steal sweet hours from love's delight.
I may not evermore acknowledge[13] thee,
10 Lest my bewailed guilt should do thee shame,
Nor thou with public kindness honour me,
Unless thou take[14] that honour from thy name:
　　But do not so;[15] I love thee in such sort,
　　As thou being mine, mine is thy good report.

55

Not marble, nor the gilded monuments
Of princes, shall outlive this powerful rhyme;
But you shall shine more bright in these contents[16]
Than unswept stone, besmeared with sluttish time.[17]
5 When wasteful war shall statues overturn
And broils° root out the work of masonry,   *violent quarrels*
Nor Mars[18] his sword, nor war's quick° fire,   *vigorous*
　　shall burn
The living record of your memory:
'Gainst death, and all oblivious[19] enmity,
10 Shall you pace forth; your praise shall still find room
Even in the eyes of all posterity
That wear this world out to the ending doom.[20]

[1] *rack* Mass of clouds driven by the wind in the upper air.

[2] *out alack* An expression of sharp regret.

[3] *region cloud* Clouds of the upper air.

[4] *no whit* Not the least bit.

[5] *stain* Lose luster or brightness.

[6] *salving thy amiss* Excusing or explaining away your wrong.

[7] *Excusing … are* My making excuses for your sins is worse than the actual sins themselves.

[8] *bring in sense* Add spurious reasoning.

[9] *adverse party* Legal opponent; *advocate* Legal defender.

[10] *one respect* A single, and hence mutual, regard.

[11] *a separable spite* An injury or misfortune capable of separating us.

[12] *love's sole effect* Our unity in love.

[13] *acknowledge* Greet or recognize in public.

[14] *Unless thou take* Without taking.

[15] *do not so* Do not display such public kindness toward me.

[16] *these contents* The contents of these poems.

[17] *Than … time* Than in dust-covered stone dirtied by the passage of time, which is dirty and grimy ("sluttish") in its effects.

[18] *Mars* Roman god of war.

[19] *oblivious* Bringing about oblivion.

[20] *ending doom* Last Judgment at the end of the world.

So till the judgement that yourself arise,[1]
You live in this, and dwell in lovers' eyes.

60

Like as the waves make towards the pebbled shore,
   So do our minutes hasten to their end,
Each changing place with that which goes before,
In sequent toil all forwards do contend.
5 Nativity, once in the main° of light,   *broad expanse*
Crawls to maturity; wherewith being crowned
Crooked eclipses 'gainst his glory fight,
And time, that gave, doth now his gift confound.°   *ruin*
Time doth transfix° the flourish set on youth,   *pierce*
10 And delves the parallels[2] in beauty's brow;
Feeds on the rarities of nature's truth,
And nothing stands[3] but for his scythe to mow.
      And yet to times in hope my verse shall stand,
      Praising thy worth, despite his cruel hand.

64

When I have seen by time's fell hand defaced
   The rich proud cost[4] of outworn buried age;[5]
When sometime lofty towers I see down razed,
And brass eternal slave to mortal rage;[6]
5 When I have seen the hungry ocean gain
Advantage on the kingdom of the shore,
And the firm soil win of the wat'ry main,°   *ocean*
Increasing store° with loss, and loss with store;   *gain*
When I have seen such interchange of state,
10 Or state itself confounded,° to decay,   *ruined*
Ruin hath taught me thus to ruminate:
That time will come and take my love away.
      This thought is as a death, which cannot choose
      But weep[7] to have that which it fears to lose.

65

Since brass, nor stone, nor earth, nor boundless sea,
   But sad mortality o'er-sways° their power,   *overcomes*
How with this rage[8] shall beauty hold a plea,[9]
Whose action is no stronger than a flower?
5 O how shall summer's honey breath hold out
Against the wrackful° siege of batt'ring days   *destructive*
When rocks impregnable are not so stout,
Nor gates of steel so strong, but time decays?
O fearful meditation! Where, alack,
10 Shall time's best jewel from time's chest lie hid?
Or what strong hand can hold his swift foot back,
Or who his spoil° o'er beauty can forbid?   *plunder*
      O none, unless this miracle have might:
      That in black ink my love may still shine bright.

71

No longer mourn for me when I am dead
   Than you shall hear[10] the surly sullen bell[11]
Give warning to the world that I am fled
From this vile world, with vilest worms to dwell:
5 Nay, if you read this line, remember not
The hand that writ it, for I love you so
That I in your sweet thoughts would be forgot,
If thinking on me then should make you woe.[12]
O if (I say) you look upon this verse,
10 When I, perhaps, compounded am with clay,
Do not so much as my poor name rehearse,°   *utter*
But let your love even° with my life decay;   *along*
      Lest the wise world should look into your moan,[13]
      And mock you with me[14] after I am gone.

73

That time of year thou mayst in me behold,
   When yellow leaves, or none, or few do hang
Upon those boughs which shake against the cold,

---

[1] *That ... arise* When you yourself are resurrected.

[2] *delves the parallels* Digs the trenches, i.e., forms the wrinkled lines; cf. Sonnet 2.2: "... dig deep trenches in thy beauty's field."

[3] *stands* Grows to full height, as a plant ready for harvest.

[4] *rich ... cost* Prideful and extravagant splendor.

[5] *outworn ... age* Antiquity worn out and obscured by time.

[6] *brass ... rage* Brass, known for its durability, but also subject ultimately to the fatally destructive effects of time.

[7] *cannot ... weep* Can only weep.

[8] *with this rage* Against this destructive action.

[9] *hold a plea* Present a legal case.

[10] *you shall hear* The span of time during which you hear.

[11] *surly ... bell* Passing-bell, rung solemnly from the church to announce a death, customarily one chime for each year of the deceased's lifespan.

[12] *make you woe* Cause you grief.

[13] *look ... moan* Question the cause of your grief.

[14] *with me* Along with me, and perhaps in the same manner.

Bare ruined choirs[1] where late the sweet birds sang;
5   In me thou seest the twilight of such day
As after sunset fadeth in the west,
Which by and by black night doth take away,
Death's second self[2] that seals up all in rest;
In me thou seest the glowing of such fire
10 That on the ashes of his youth doth lie,
As the deathbed, whereon it must expire,
Consumed with that which it was nourished by;
    This thou perceiv'st, which makes thy love more
        strong,
    To love that well, which thou must leave°   lose
        ere long.

74

But be contented when that fell° arrest   cruel
Without all bail shall carry me away.[3]
My life hath in this line[4] some interest,
Which for memorial still[5] with thee shall stay.
5   When thou reviewest this, thou dost review
The very part was consecrate to thee.
The earth can have but earth, which is his due;
My spirit is thine, the better part of me.
So then thou hast but° lost the dregs of life,   only
10 The prey of worms, my body being dead,
The coward conquest of a wretch's knife,
Too base of thee to be remembered.
    The worth of that is that which it contains,[6]
    And that is this, and this with thee remains.

80

O how I faint° when I of you do write,   lose heart
    Knowing a better spirit[7] doth use your name,
And in the praise thereof spends all his might,
To make me tongue-tied speaking of your fame.

---

[1] *choirs* Parts of churches designated for singers.

[2] *Death's second self* Sleep.

[3] *But be ... away* Some modern editors punctuate these lines with a semi-colon after "contented" and a comma after "away."

[4] *in this line* I.e., in this verse.

[5] *for memorial still* As a remembrance always.

[6] *The worth of that ... contains* The value of the body is that it contains the spirit.

[7] *a better spirit* A rival poet of superior gifts, referred to in Sonnet 79.

---

5   But since your worth, wide as the ocean is,
The humble as the proudest sail doth bear,°   carry along
My saucy bark,[8] inferior far to his,
On your broad main° doth wilfully appear.   ocean
Your shallowest help will hold me up afloat,
10 Whilst he upon your soundless° deep doth   immeasurable
        ride;
Or, being wracked, I am a worthless boat,
He of tall building, and of goodly pride.
    Then if he thrive, and I be cast away,
    The worst was this: my love was my decay.

87

Farewell—thou art too dear[9] for my possessing,
    And like enough thou know'st thy estimate.°   value
The charter of thy worth gives thee releasing;[10]
My bonds in thee are all determinate.°   expired
5   For how do I hold thee but by thy granting,
And for that riches where is my deserving?[11]
The cause of this fair gift in me is wanting,
And so my patent° back again is swerving.   title to property
Thyself thou gav'st, thy own worth then not knowing,
10 Or me to whom thou gav'st it else mistaking;
So thy great gift, upon misprision° growing,   error
Comes home again, on better judgement making.
    Thus have I had thee as a dream doth flatter:
    In sleep a king, but waking no such matter.

93

So shall I live supposing thou art true
    Like a deceived husband; so love's face
May still seem love to me, though altered new—
Thy looks with me, thy heart in other place.
5   For there can live no hatred in thine eye,
Therefore in that I cannot know thy change.[12]
In many's looks the false heart's history
Is writ in moods and frowns and wrinkles strange;

---

[8] *bark* Small boat.

[9] *too dear* Both "too expensive" and "too much loved."

[10] *The charter ... releasing* The document stating your value releases you (from any associated debts).

[11] *for that riches ... deserving?* How do I deserve the rich reward (of being granted your affection)?

[12] *in that ... change* From your eye I cannot know that your heart has changed.

But heav'n in thy creation did decree
10 That in thy face sweet love should ever dwell;
Whate'er thy thoughts or thy heart's workings be,
Thy looks should nothing thence but sweetness tell.
    How like Eve's apple doth thy beauty grow
    If thy sweet virtue answer not thy show![1]

94

They that have power to hurt and will do none,
    That do not do the thing they most do show,[2]
Who, moving others, are themselves as stone,
Unmovèd, cold, and to temptation slow—[3]
5 They rightly do inherit heaven's graces,
And husband° nature's riches from   *conserve*
    expense;°   *spending*
They are the lords and owners of their faces,
Others but stewards° of their excellence.   *managers*
The summer's flower is to the summer sweet
10 Though to itself it only live and die,
But if that flower with base infection meet
The basest weed outbraves his dignity;[4]
    For sweetest things turn sourest by their deeds:
    Lilies that fester smell far worse than weeds.

97

How like a winter hath my absence been
    From thee, the pleasure of the fleeting year!
What freezings have I felt, what dark days seen,
What old December's bareness everywhere!
5 And yet this time removed[5] was summer's time,
The teeming autumn big with[6] rich increase
Bearing the wanton burden of the prime,[7]

Like widowed wombs after their lords' decease:
Yet this abundant issue° seemed to me   *offspring*
10 But hope of orphans, and unfathered fruit;
For summer and his pleasures wait on thee,[8]
And thou away, the very birds are mute;
    Or if they sing, 'tis with so dull a cheer
    That leaves look pale, dreading the winter's near.

98

From you have I been absent in the spring,
    When proud pied° April, dressed   *particolored*
        in all his trim,°   *adornment*
Hath put a spirit of youth in everything,
That° heavy Saturn[9] laughed, and leaped   *such that*
    with him.
5 Yet nor the lays° of birds, nor the sweet smell   *songs*
Of different flowers in odour and in hue,
Could make me any summer's story tell,
Or from their proud lap[10] pluck them where they grew;
Nor did I wonder at the lily's white,
10 Nor praise the deep vermilion in the rose;
They were but° sweet, but figures of delight,   *merely*
Drawn after you, you pattern of all those.
    Yet seemed it winter still, and, you away,
    As with your shadow I with these did play.

105

Let not my love be called idolatry,
    Nor my beloved as an idol show,[11]
Since all alike my songs and praises be
To one, of one, still such, and ever so.
5 Kind is my love today, tomorrow kind,[12]
Still constant in a wondrous excellence.
Therefore my verse, to constancy confined,
One thing expressing, leaves out difference.
"Fair, kind, and true" is all my argument,
10 "Fair, kind, and true" varying to other words,

---

[1] *How like ... thy show* How much your beauty grows to resemble the attractiveness of the apple to Eve (i.e., that it will lead to the downfall of the one attracted to it) if your virtue does not match your appearance.

[2] *the thing they most do show* It is not entirely clear what this thing is, but it probably relates to romantic or sexual activity; "though they inspire love, they do not reciprocate," is one possible paraphrase.

[3] *to temptation slow* Slow to respond to temptation.

[4] *But if that flower ... dignity* The most common weed will outshine a lovely flower that has been infected by disease.

[5] *time removed* Time of my absence.

[6] *big with* Great with, about to give birth to.

[7] *burden* Contents of a womb; *prime* Spring.

---

[8] *wait on thee* Hold themselves in abeyance until you are present.

[9] *Saturn* Planetary God associated astrologically with the melancholy humor.

[10] *their proud lap* The rich earth that nurtures them.

[11] *as an idol show* Seem to be (perhaps also with a pun on "idle"—"be called an insignificant creature of appearances").

[12] *Kind ... kind* Both "of one sort today, and the same tomorrow," and "kind" in the sense of "having a gentle and sympathetic nature."

And in this change is my invention spent,[1]
Three themes in one, which wondrous scope affords.
Fair, kind, and true have often lived alone,
Which three till now never kept seat in one.

106

When in the chronicle of wasted time[2]
I see descriptions of the fairest wights,[3]
And beauty making beautiful old rhyme,
In praise of ladies dead, and lovely knights;
5 Then in the blazon[4] of sweet beauties best,
Of hand, of foot, of lip, of eye, of brow,
I see their antique pen would have expressed
Even such a beauty as you master° now: *possess*
So all their praises are but prophecies
10 Of this our time, all you prefiguring;
And for° they looked but with divining eyes   *since*
They had not skill enough your worth to sing;
   For we which now behold these present days
   Have eyes to wonder, but lack tongues to praise.

109

O never say that I was false of heart,
Though absence seemed my flame to qualify;
As easy might I from myself depart
As from my soul which in thy breast doth lie:
5 That is my home of love; if I have ranged,
Like him that travels I return again,
Just to the time,[5] not with the time exchanged,[6]
So that myself bring water for my stain;[7]
Never believe, though in my nature reigned
10 All frailties that besiege all kinds of blood,
That it could so preposterously be stained,°   *corrupted*
To leave for nothing all thy sum of good:

---

[1] *varying … spent* My inventiveness is used up in finding other words (to express the same thought).

[2] *wasted time* Time gone by, with "chronicles" suggesting previous eras, or "olden times."

[3] *fairest wights* Most beautiful people, again with an archaic flavor by Shakespeare's time.

[4] *blazon* Description catalogue of a beloved's body.

[5] *Just … time* Exactly on time.

[6] *not … exchanged* Not changed during the time spent away.

[7] *So … stain* So that my return, unchanged, might erase the fault of my absence; *water* Possibly, tears of repentence.

For nothing this wide universe I call,
Save thou, my rose; in it thou art my all.

110

Alas, 'tis true, I have gone here and there,
And made myself a motley to the view,[8]
Gored[9] mine own thoughts, sold cheap what is most
   dear,
Made old offences of affections new.[10]
5 Most true it is that I have looked on truth°   *constancy*
Askance and strangely;° but by all above,   *coldly*
These blenches[11] gave my heart another youth,[12]
And worse essays[13] proved thee my best of love.
Now all is done, save what shall have no end;
10 Mine appetite I never more will grind°   *whet*
On newer proof,° to try° an older friend,   *experience / test*
A god in love, to whom I am confined:°   *devoted*
   Then give me welcome, next my heaven the best,
   Even to thy pure and most most loving breast.

116

Let me not to the marriage of true minds
Admit impediments;[14] love is not love
Which alters when it alteration finds,
Or bends with the remover[15] to remove.
5 O no, it is an ever-fixed mark,
That looks on tempests and is never shaken;
It is the star to every wand'ring bark,°   *boat*

---

[8] *motley* Fool (from the motley, or particolored clothing traditionally worn by jesters); *to the view* In appearance, in the eyes of society.

[9] *Gored* Altered, as a garment is altered by inserting a gore, or wedge-shaped piece of cloth, and perhaps even mutilated, like a person gored by a horned animal.

[10] *Made … new* Committed infidelity by pursuing new relationships.

[11] *blenches* Flinchings or deviations (from constancy).

[12] *gave … youth* Rejuvenated my affections for you.

[13] *worse essays* Experiments with inferior loves.

[14] *impediments* Cf. the marriage service in the Book of Common Prayer (c. 1552): "If any of you know cause, or just impediment, why these two persons should not be joined together in holy Matrimony, ye are to declare it."

[15] *remover* One who changes, e.g., ceases to love.

Whose worth's unknown, although his height be taken.[1]
Love's not Time's fool, though rosy lips and cheeks
10 Within his bending sickle's compass° come;   *sweep*
Love alters not with his brief hours and weeks,
But bears it out even to the edge of doom.
     If this be error and upon me proved,
     I never writ, nor no man ever loved.

117

Accuse me thus: that I have scanted[2] all
  Wherein I should your great deserts repay,
Forgot upon your dearest love to call,
Whereto all bonds do tie me day by day;
5 That I have frequent been with unknown minds,
And given to time your own dear-purchased right;[3]
That I have hoisted sail to all the winds
Which should transport me farthest from your sight.
Book° both my wilfulness and errors down,   *record*
10 And on just proof surmise accumulate;[4]
Bring me within the level° of your frown,   *aim*
But shoot not at me in your wakened hate:
     Since my appeal says[5] I did strive to prove°   *test*
     The constancy and virtue of your love.

127

In the old age[6] black was not counted fair,°   *beautiful*
  Or if it were, it bore not beauty's name;
But now is black beauty's successive° heir,   *legitimate*
And beauty slandered with a bastard shame:[7]
5 For since each hand hath put on nature's power,[8]
Fairing the foul with art's false borrowed face,

Sweet beauty hath no name, no holy bower,[9]
But is profaned, if not lives in disgrace.
Therefore my mistress' eyes are raven black,
10 Her eyes so suited,° and they mourners seem   *attired*
At such who, not born fair, no beauty lack,[10]
Sland'ring creation with a false esteem;[11]
     Yet so they mourn, becoming of[12] their woe,
     That every tongue says beauty should look so.

128

How oft when thou, my music, music play'st
  Upon that blessed wood[13] whose motion sounds
With thy sweet fingers, when thou gently sway'st°   *direct*
The wiry concord[14] that mine ear confounds,°   *dazzles*
5 Do I envy those jacks° that nimble leap,   *keys*
To kiss the tender inward° of thy hand,   *palm*
Whilst my poor lips, which should that harvest reap,
At the wood's boldness by thee blushing stand?
To be so tickled they would change their state
10 And situation with those dancing chips,[15]
O'er whom thy fingers walk with gentle gait,
Making dead wood more blessed than living lips.
     Since saucy jacks[16] so happy are in this,
     Give them thy fingers, me thy lips to kiss.

129

Th'expense of spirit in a waste° of shame   *desolation*
  Is lust in action; and till action, lust
Is perjured, murd'rous, bloody, full of blame,
Savage, extreme, rude, cruel, not to trust;°   *be trusted*
5 Enjoyed no sooner but despised straight;
Past reason hunted, and no sooner had,

---

[1] *Whose ... taken* Referring to the "star" of the previous line, most likely the North Star, whose altitude can be reckoned for navigation purposes using a sextant, but whose essence remains unknown.

[2] *scanted* Provided grudgingly or insufficently for.

[3] *given ... right* Spent elsewhere the time you had a right to expect I should spend with you.

[4] *on ... accumulate* On the basis of my proven misdeeds, add others on suspicion.

[5] *my appeal says* My defense is that.

[6] *the old age* Earlier times.

[7] *beauty ... shame* The former (fair) conception of beauty has been discredited as illegitimate and false.

[8] *each ... power* Everyone has assumed the power to mimic natural beauty (through cosmetics).

[9] *name* Legitimate title; *holy bower* Sacred dwelling-place.

[10] *who ... lack* (1) Who, lacking natural beauty, have acquired it artificially; (2) Who, not being of fair coloration, are in accord with current ideals of beauty.

[11] *Sland'ring ... esteem* Devaluing natural beauty with false praise accorded to the artificial.

[12] *becoming of* Suiting well.

[13] *blessed wood* Probably a virginal, a small, legless harpsichord on which the strings were plucked rather than struck.

[14] *wiry concord* Harmony produced by the plucking of the strings.

[15] *dancing chips* The keys.

[16] *saucy jacks* Common slang for impertinent fellows, but here referring also to the aforementioned keys.

Past reason hated as a swallowed bait,
On purpose laid to make the taker mad;
Mad in pursuit, and in possession so,
10 Had, having, and in quest to have, extreme;
A bliss in proof,° and proved, a very woe;   *experience*
Before, a joy proposed; behind, a dream.
    All this the world well knows, yet none knows well
    To shun the heaven that leads men to this hell.

130

My mistress' eyes are nothing like the sun;
  Coral is far more red than her lips' red;
If snow be white, why then her breasts are dun;
If hairs be wires, black wires grow on her head;
5 I have seen roses damasked,° red and white,   *parti-colored*
But no such roses see I in her cheeks;
And in some perfumes is there more delight
Than in the breath that from my mistress reeks.
I love to hear her speak, yet well I know
10 That music hath a far more pleasing sound;
I grant I never saw a goddess go;°   *walk*
My mistress when she walks treads on the ground.
    And yet, by heaven, I think my love as rare
    As any she[1] belied with false compare.

135

Whoever hath her wish,[2] thou hast thy Will,[3]
  And Will to boot, and Will in
    overplus;°   *superabundance*
More than enough am I, that vex thee still,
To thy sweet will making addition thus.
5 Wilt thou, whose will is large and spacious,
Not once vouchsafe to hide my will in thine?
Shall will in others seem right gracious,
And in my will no fair acceptance shine?
The sea, all water, yet receives rain still,
10 And in abundance addeth to his store;
So thou, being rich in Will, add to thy Will
One will of mine, to make thy large Will more:

Let no unkind,° no fair beseechers kill;   *unkindness*
Think all but one,[4] and me in that one Will.

136

If thy soul check[5] thee that I come so near,
  Swear to thy blind soul[6] that I was thy Will,
And will, thy soul knows, is admitted there;
Thus far for love my love-suit sweet fulfil.
5 Will will fulfil the treasure of thy love,
Ay, fill it full with wills, and my will one;
In things of great receipt° with ease we prove   *capacity*
Among a number one is reckoned none.
Then in the number let me pass untold,
10 Though in thy store's account I one must be.
For nothing hold° me, so it please thee hold   *regard*
That nothing, me, a something sweet to thee.
    Make but my name thy love, and love that still;° *always*
    And then thou lov'st me, for my name is Will.

138

When my love swears that she is made of truth,
  I do believe her, though I know she lies,
That she might think me some untutored youth
Unlearnèd in the world's false subtleties.
5 Thus vainly thinking that she thinks me young,
Although she knows my days are past the best,
Simply I credit her false-speaking tongue;
On both sides thus is simple truth suppressed.
But wherefore says she not she is unjust?°   *unfaithful*
10 And wherefore say not I that I am old?
O love's best habit is in seeming trust,
And age in love[7] loves not t'° have years told: *to*
    Therefore I lie with her, and she with me,
    And in our faults by lies we flattered be.

143

Lo, as a careful housewife[8] runs to catch
  One of her feathered creatures broke away,

---

[1] *any she* Any woman.

[2] *Whoever … wish* No matter what other women may wish for or attain.

[3] *Will* In Shakespeare's time, the word could also refer to sexual desire and even to the genitals.

[4] *Think … one* Think of all your suitors as one.

[5] *check* Restrain or rebuke.

[6] *blind soul* Blind by nature, being enclosed within the body, or blinded by passion.

[7] *age in love* An older person in love, or in matters of love.

[8] *careful* Attentive, but also perhaps "full of cares," or anxious; *housewife* Pronounced "hussif" in Shakespeare's time.

Sets down her babe, and makes all swift dispatch°   *haste*
In pursuit of the thing she would have stay;
5 Whilst her neglected child holds her in chase,[1]
Cries to catch her whose busy care is bent°   *determined*
To follow that which flies before her face,
Not prizing° her poor infant's discontent: *considering*
So run'st thou after that which flies from thee,
10 Whilst I, thy babe, chase thee afar behind.
But if thou catch thy hope,[2] turn back to me,
And play the mother's part, kiss me, be kind:
    So will I pray that thou mayst have thy Will,
    If thou turn back and my loud crying still.°   *soothe*

144

Two loves I have, of comfort and despair,
  Which, like two spirits, do suggest° me   *tempt*
    still:°   *always*
The better angel is a man right fair,
The worser spirit a woman coloured ill.[3]
5 To win me soon to hell[4] my female evil
Tempteth my better angel from my side,
And would corrupt my saint to be a devil,
Wooing his purity with her foul pride;
And whether that[5] my angel be turned fiend
10 Suspect I may, yet not directly° tell;   *exactly*
But being both from me both to each friend,[6]
I guess one angel in another's hell.
    Yet this shall I ne'er know, but live in doubt,
    Till my bad angel fire my good one out.[7]

146

Poor soul, the centre of my sinful earth,
  ...[8] these rebel powers that thee array;[9]
Why dost thou pine[10] within and suffer dearth,
Painting thy outward walls so costly gay?
5 Why so large cost, having so short a lease,
Dost thou upon thy fading mansion spend?
Shall worms, inheritors of this excess,
Eat up thy charge?[11] Is this thy body's end?
Then soul, live thou upon thy servant's loss,
10 And let that[12] pine to aggravate thy store;[13]
Buy terms[14] divine in selling hours of dross;°   *scum*
Within be fed, without° be rich no more: *externally*
    So shalt thou feed on death, that feeds on men,
    And death once dead, there's no more dying then.

147

My love is as a fever, longing still°   *continually*
  For that which longer nurseth the disease,
Feeding on that which doth preserve the ill,
Th'uncertain° sickly appetite to please: *fitful*
20 My reason, the physician to my love,
Angry that his prescriptions are not kept,
Hath left me, and I, desperate, now approve°   *accept that*
Desire is death, which physic did except.[15]
Past cure I am, now reason is past care,
25 And frantic mad with ever more unrest;
My thoughts and my discourse as madmen's are,

---

[1] *holds ... chase* Chases after her.

[2] *thy hope* The object of your hope.

[3] *coloured ill* Of a dark or ugly complexion or temperament.

[4] *hell* For the equation of hell with sexual intercourse, cf. Sonnet 129.14: "... the heaven that leads men to this hell."

[5] *whether that* Whether or not.

[6] *being ... friend* Both spirits being apart from me and together (and friendly) with each other.

[7] *fire ... out* Expel or reject my good angel; to "fire out" meant to drive someone or something away from a place by setting a fire, as, e.g., in fox hunting; *fire* Possibly "fever," with perhaps a glancing reference to venereal disease.

[8] *...* The earliest printed version repeats the words "my sinful earth," an apparent misprint; Shakespeare's words are not known. Possible substitutions include "Rebuke," "Foiled by," or "Fooled by."

[9] *these rebel ... thee array* I.e., the body that clothes you (which rebels against your soul).

[10] *pine* Dwindle from longing.

[11] *thy charge* Your expense; also, a possession for which you are responsible.

[12] *that* I.e., the body.

[13] *aggravate thy store* Increase your riches.

[14] *terms* Periods of time; also agreements.

[15] *Desire ... except* The sexual desire objected to by my physician is deadly.

At random¹ from the truth vainly expressed:²
  For I have sworn thee fair, and thought thee bright,
  Who art as black as hell, as dark as night.

153

Cupid laid by his brand,³ and fell asleep;
  A maid of Dian's⁴ this advantage° found,   *opportunity*
And his love-kindling fire did quickly steep°   *plunge*
In a cold valley-fountain⁵ of that ground,
5 Which borrowed from this holy fire of love
A dateless° lively heat still° to endure,   *endless / always*
And grew° a seething bath, which yet men prove   *grew into*
Against strange maladies a sovereign° cure: *potent*
But at my mistress' eye love's brand new fired,⁶
10 The boy for trial needs would⁷ touch my breast;
I, sick withal, the help of bath desired,
And thither hied,⁸ a sad distempered guest,

But found no cure; the bath for my help lies
  Where Cupid got new fire: my mistress' eye.

154

The little love-god° lying once asleep,   *Cupid*
  Laid by his side his heart-inflaming brand,⁹
Whilst many nymphs, that vowed chaste life to keep,¹⁰
Came tripping by; but in her maiden hand
5 The fairest votary¹¹ took up that fire
Which many legions of true hearts had warmed;
And so the general of hot desire¹²
Was, sleeping, by a virgin hand disarmed.
This brand she quenched in a cool well by,°   *nearby*
10 Which from love's fire took heat perpetual,
Growing° a bath and healthful remedy   *growing into*
For men diseased; but I, my mistress' thrall,
  Came there for cure, and this by that I prove:
  Love's fire heats water, water cools not love.

—1609

---

¹ *At random* Wandering.

² *vainly expressed* Expressing myself foolishly or fecklessly.

³ *Cupid … brand* Cupid, Roman god of love, often pictured as a small boy carrying a torch (brand) used to kindle erotic love in the hearts of mortals; *laid by* Set aside.

⁴ *maid of Dian's* Diana, Roman goddess of the moon and the hunt, known for her chastity, was attended by young virgin nymphs (maids).

⁵ *cold valley-fountain* One of the cool springs associated with the dwelling-place of Diana.

⁶ *new fired* Reignited.

⁷ *for trial* To test the flame; *needs would* Wanted to.

⁸ *thither hied* Hastened there.

⁹ *heart-inflaming brand* Torch used by Cupid to kindle erotic love in the hearts of mortals.

¹⁰ *nymphs … keep* Attendants of the chaste goddess Diana, who themselves took a vow of chastity.

¹¹ *fairest votary* Most beautiful of those vowed to chastity.

¹² *general … desire* Cupid, pictured as the commander of erotic passion.

On this and the following page appear facsimile reproductions of two pages from the 1609 quarto edition of Shakespeare's sonnets. The facsimile pages include some sonnets that may be compared with annotated texts in modernized spelling appearing elsewhere in these pages, and others that are provided here only in this facsimile form, without mediation.

SHAKE-SPEARES

70
THat thou are blam'd shall not be thy defect,
For slanders marke was euer yet the faire,
The ornament of beauty is suspect,
A Crow that flies in heauens sweetest ayre.
So thou be good, slander doth but approue,
Their worth the greater beeing woo'd of time,
For Canker vice the sweetest buds doth loue,
And thou present'st a pure vnstayined prime.
Thou hast past by the ambush of young daies,
Either not assayld, or victor beeing charg'd,
Yet this thy praise cannot be soe thy praise,
To tye vp enuy, euermore inlarged,
        If some suspect of ill maskt not thy show,
        Then thou alone kingdomes of hearts shouldst owe.

71
NOe Longer mourne for me when I am dead,
Then you shall heare the surly sullen bell
Giue warning to the world that I am fled
From this vile world with vildest wormes to dwell:
Nay if you read this line, remember not,
The hand that writ it, for I loue you so,
That I in your sweet thoughts would be forgot,
If thinking on me then should make you woe.
O if (I say) you looke vpon this verse,
When I (perhaps) compounded am with clay,
Do not so much as my poore name reherse;
But let your loue euen with my life decay.
        Least the wise world should looke into your mone,
        And mocke you with me after I am gon.

72
O Least the world should taske you to recite,
What merit liu'd in me that you should loue
After my death (deare loue) for get me quite,
For you in me can nothing worthy proue.
Vnlesse you would deuise some vertuous lye,

To

SONNETS.

To doe more for me then mine owne defert,
And hang more praife vpon deceafed I,
Then nigard truth would willingly impart.
O leaft your true loue may feeme falce in this,
That you for loue fpeake well of me vntrue,
My name be buried where my body is,
And liue no more to fhame nor me, nor you.
  For I am fhamd by that which I bring forth,
  And fo fhould you, to loue things nothing worth.

73

THat time of yeeare thou maift in me behold,
  When yellow leaues, or none, or few doe hange
Vpon thofe boughes which fhake againft the could,
Bare rn'wd quiers, where late the fweet birds fang.
In me thou feeft the twi-light of fuch day,
As after Sun-fet fadeth in the Weft,
Which by and by blacke night doth take away,
Deaths fecond felfe that feals vp all in reft.
In me thou feeft the glowing of fuch fire,
That on the afhes of his youth doth lye,
As the death bed, whereon it muft expire,
Confum'd with that which it was nurrifht by.
  This thou perceu'ft, which makes thy loue more ftrong,
  To loue that well, which thou muft leaue ere long.

74

BVt be contented when that fell areft,
  With out all bayle fhall carry me away,
My life hath in this line fome intereft,
Which for memoriall ftill with thee fhall ftay.
When thou reueweft this, thou doeft reuew,
The very part was confecrate to thee,
The earth can haue but earth, which is his due,
My fpirit is thine the better part of me,
So then thou haft but loft the dregs of life,
The pray of wormes, my body being dead,
The coward conqueft of a wretches knife,

To

CHRISTOPHER MARLOWE
1564 – 1593

Christopher Marlowe's small body of work—seven plays, as well as a number of poems written during six productive years—profoundly influenced the course of English Renaissance drama. His plays set precedents for English history plays, tragedy, and heroic drama, while his newly supple and powerful blank verse (unrhymed iambic pentameter) impressed Ben Jonson as Marlowe's "mighty line." Had his writing career not been cut so short by a lethal tavern brawl he might have rivaled Shakespeare as the finest dramatist of his age.

Marlowe was born in Canterbury on 26 February 1564, in the same year as Shakespeare. His father was a shoemaker and a bondsman but also an actor; his mother was the daughter of a clergyman—and both theater and theology would help shape him. Despite his father's fairly humble occupation, Marlowe was well educated, first at King's School, in Canterbury, and then at Cambridge University's Corpus Christi College. His education at Cambridge, which was paid for by a foundation set up by Matthew Parker, Archbishop of Canterbury, included history, philosophy, and the theology of the Protestant Reformation, one version of which, despite a large and sometimes surreptitiously active Catholic minority, was now the orthodoxy of the officially established Church of England. In 1584 he earned his B.A.

During the latter part of his time at Cambridge, Marlowe frequently disappeared for extended periods. It is likely, some historians believe, that Marlowe had been recruited as a spy by Queen Elizabeth's Privy Council, which had longstanding fears of subversive Catholic activity at home and abroad. He spent time in the French city of Rheims, a refuge for many English Catholic expatriates, and perhaps helped uncover a Catholic plot to assassinate Elizabeth. This theory is strengthened by the actions of the Council upon Marlowe's return to England. Marlowe applied for his M.A., a degree normally granted automatically upon application once a certain amount of time had elapsed since the granting of a B.A., but the university refused him on multiple grounds. Not only had Marlowe failed to pursue ordination after his theological studies (as was expected of theology students); he had also spent considerable time among Catholics in France, and was therefore suspected of Catholic sympathies. Marlowe asked the Privy Council to intercede on his behalf and it obliged by sending a letter to the Cambridge authorities indicating that Marlowe "had done Her Majesty good service, & deserved to be rewarded for his faithful dealing." Moreover, says the letter severely, "it was not Her Majesty's pleasure that anyone employed, as [Marlowe] had been, in matters touching the benefit of his country, should be defamed by those that are ignorant in th' affairs he went about." Marlowe was granted his M.A. in 1587.

In the same year, Marlowe left Cambridge and moved to London to pursue his career as a playwright. His London years were marked by violence. In 1589 he spent two weeks in Newgate Prison, charged with the murder of one William Bradley, although he was acquitted and released, and in 1592 court records indicate that he was implicated in a street fight in which another man was killed. Through these same years, however, Marlowe's career soared. He had the luxury of being hired by the Lord Admiral's Company, which meant that the finest of London's actors would perform his plays. His first major plays, including *Tamburlaine the Great*—a grandiloquently written and violence-filled play—were produced in 1587 and were wildly popular. Over the next six years Marlowe completed at least five more plays: *The Jew of Malta* (c. 1589), *Edward II* (c. 1592), *The Massacre of Paris* (printed c. 1593), *Dido, Queen of Carthage* (printed in 1594), and *The Tragical History of Doctor Faustus* (?1593). In recent decades *Edward II* has drawn critical notice for its ambivalent portrayal of homoerotic love in conflict with political and marital duty, while the darkly comic *Jew of Malta*, whose Christians are quite as wicked as the Jewish protagonist, is significant in understanding early modern English views of the Jew as "other." *Faustus*, however, remains the most widely read and performed of Marlowe's plays. Based on an old Czech and German legend, the play presents a scholar who sells his soul to the devil in exchange for knowledge and power. As always, this proves a bad bargain: Faustus fritters away his power on pointless magic tricks and must, eventually, disappear in anguish into Hell. Marlowe's sympathies are hard to identify: the play may be read as orthodox (the anti-Catholic humor would not displease audiences or ecclesiastical authorities in England) but it may also raise difficult questions about free will and an implacable God.

Marlowe is also known for his poetry, including translations from Lucan's *Pharsalia* and Ovid's *Amores*. His most famous English poems are the unfinished "Hero and Leander," a tragic love story lightened by witty rhymes, outrageous metaphors, and a view of erotic love at once skeptical and sympathetic, and "The Passionate Shepherd to His Love," a poem based in part on Virgil's homo-erotic Second Eclogue (Marlowe's version was soon treated as entirely heterosexual but recent criticism has noted its ambiguity in this regard). Unfortunately, piecing together Marlowe's *oeuvre* is a complicated matter. We have, for example, two quite different versions of *Doctor Faustus* (1604 and 1616).

Marlowe's death on 30 May 1593 has been the subject of much controversy. According to the coroner's report, Marlowe and a number of his acquaintances were dining at Eleanor Bull's House, a tavern just outside London. A heated argument arose between Marlowe and a fellow diner, Ingram Frizer, over the bill. The report states that Marlowe attacked Frizer with a knife and injured him on the back of the head. Frizer wrested the knife from Marlowe's grasp and sank its blade two inches into Marlowe's skull, just above the right eye. Marlowe died instantly. Was there a conspiracy behind this? Marlowe had maintained connections from his spying days and at the time of his death was in the presence of men with connections to his former employer, Sir Francis Walsingham, who as Secretary of State was responsible for the government's intelligence operations. Marlowe had recently been arrested on charges of atheism (an imprecisely defined offence which could be laid against anyone expressing unorthodox theological opinions) and was due to go on trial in a few days. Some scholars have speculated that members of the government feared that Marlowe would identify other "atheists" in high positions or perhaps reveal espionage secrets should he appear in a court of law, and so had him assassinated.

Marlowe was buried in an unmarked grave on the grounds of St. Nicholas's Church, Deptford, on 1 June 1593. Not until July 2002, more than 400 years after he died, was he memorialized in the prestigious Poet's Corner of Westminster Abbey.

[Note to instructors: *Dr. Faustus the B Text* as well as several other Marlowe plays are among over 400 available editions from Broadview, any one of which may be packaged together with this anthology volume at no extra cost to the student.]

Hero and Leander

Christopher Marlowe's *Hero and Leander* is an epyllion, or little epic. Marlowe evokes the epic tradition in his very first lines, where he mentions the Hellespont, the narrow strait that divides Europe from Asia, Greece from Troy. But Marlowe soon reveals that his is not a story of imperialist

The Passionate Shepherd to His Love

Come live with me and be my love,
And we will all the pleasures prove°   *experience*
That valleys, groves, hills, and fields,
Woods, or steepy mountain yields.

5   And we will sit upon the rocks,
Seeing the shepherds feed their flocks,
By shallow rivers to whose falls
Melodious birds sing madrigals.[5]

And I will make thee beds of roses
10   And a thousand fragrant posies,
A cap of flowers, and a kirtle°   *skirt*
Embroidered all with leaves of myrtle;

A gown made of the finest wool
Which from our pretty lambs we pull;
15   Fair linèd slippers for the cold,
With buckles of the purest gold;

A belt of straw and ivy buds,
With coral clasps and amber studs:
And if these pleasures may thee move,
20   Come live with me, and be my love.

The shepherd swains° shall dance and sing   *rustic lovers*
For thy delight each May morning:
If these delights thy mind may move,
Then live with me and be my love.
—1599

---

[5] *madrigals* Part-songs for several voices, often with pastoral or amatory associations.

The Tragical History of Doctor Faustus

The Tragical History of Doctor Faustus is a work that employs belief from both the medieval and modern worlds. At its core is a story, of which there are various medieval versions, of a man selling his soul to the devil. Yet the play is plotted in a way that differs strikingly from the conventions of most medieval drama with, for example, a progression of scenes structured to suggest the passage of time in the real world. (Whereas in most medieval plays characters may exit at the end of one scene and reappear immediately at the beginning of the next in a different place or at a different time, Marlowe and Shakespeare broke new ground in the early 1590s, always providing for some passage of time in such circumstances.) The play posits sinister magical worlds that may seem far-fetched to the modern mind; in the late sixteenth century the lines that now divide what we term "science" from "superstition" had barely begun to be drawn and—again like Shakespeare—Marlowe mixes the comic and the tragic in ways that may jar on some modern sensibilities. Yet its treatment of the connections between the worlds of religion, magic, and science; of the connections between knowledge and power; and of the bitter fruits of excessive ambition resonate deeply with modern readers and modern audiences. So too does the material of the story itself, which has been recast by many authors in the intervening centuries—most notably by Goethe in the eighteenth century (*Faust*, 1790) and by Thomas Mann in the twentieth century (*Dr. Faustus*, 1947).

Not surprisingly, a somewhat uneasy relationship exists between *Dr. Faustus* and traditional Christian doctrine, Protestant or Catholic. However much the ambition of Faustus leads to damning sin, we are made to sense something attractive in his soaring visions. And in numerous other respects, too, the play puts forward religious notions from outside the mainstream (that hell may also be a state of mind, for example, and that there may be legitimate ties between the practices of magic and those of Christianity). Yet the play remains a memorable and provocative literary exploration of Christian doctrine. Do we have free will? What are the limits of God's forgiveness?

Marlowe's *Dr. Faustus* exists in two substantially different versions. There has been a great deal of scholarly discussion of the differences between the two, and debate over which is closest to what Marlowe himself wrote.

Marlowe probably completed the play in 1592 or early 1593 (he died on 30 May of that year). We know that between September of 1594 and October of 1597 the play was performed 25 times at the Rose Theatre by the Admiral's Men, with Edward Alleyn playing Faustus. The same company added the play to their repertory again when they opened the Fortune Theatre as their new house in late 1602. (Payment of £4 was made at this time on behalf of the Admiral's Men to two individuals "for there adicyones in doctor fostes.")

The first printed text that has come down to us is that of 1604 (commonly known as the "A" text). A much longer version was published in 1616; it included numerous new scenes (the majority of them comic) and a variety of other revisions throughout. Some of these revisions were evidently forced by the 1606 "Act to restrain Abuses of Players," which forbad actors "in any Stage play … jestingly or prophanely" from speaking or using "the holy Name of God or of Christ Jesus, or of the Holy Ghoste or of the Trinitie, which are not to be spoken but with feare and reverence." Thus Faustus's characterization of God as "unpleasant, harsh, contemptible, and vile" 1.1.110 is cut from the 1616 (or "B") text; similarly, his vision of Christ's blood and the frowns of an angry God (5.2.70–77) are radically altered. The reasons for and the source of the various other differences between the A and B texts remain in dispute among scholars. Michael Keefer, whose edition of the play appears in these pages, has argued persuasively not only that the "A" text is "shorter, harsher, more focused, and more disturbing" than the 1616 "B" text but also that it is much closer to the play as it was performed in the 1590s. The edition here has been adapted from Keefer's edition, which is based on the 1604 "A" text. For the text of all the 1616 revisions, together with a full scholarly discussion of the differences between the two versions, readers are invited to consult Keefer's full edition of the play, which appears as part of the Broadview Editions series.

The Tragical History of Doctor Faustus
("A" Text)

DRAMATIS PERSONAE

John Faustus, *doctor of theology*
Wagner, *a student, and Faustus's servant; also speaks the part of Chorus*
Good Angel
Evil Angel
Valdes and Cornelius, *magicians*
Three Scholars, *colleagues of Faustus at Wittenberg University*
Mephastophilis, *a devil*
Clown (Robin)
Rafe, *another clown*
Lucifer
Belzebub
The Seven Deadly Sins
Pope
Cardinal of Lorraine
Friar
Vintner
Charles V, Emperor of Germany
Knight
Alexander the Great and his Paramour, *spirits*
Horse-courser
Duke of Vanholt and his Duchess
Helen of Troy, a spirit
Old Man
Devils, Friars, Attendants

PROLOGUE

(*Enter Chorus.*)

CHORUS. Not marching now in fields of Thracimene
  Where Mars did mate[1] the Carthaginians,
  Nor sporting in the dalliance of love
  In courts of kings where state is overturn'd,
5 Nor in the pomp of proud audacious deeds
  Intends our muse to vaunt° his heavenly verse. *display proudly*
  Only this, gentlemen: we must perform
  The form of Faustus' fortunes, good or bad.
  To patient judgments we appeal our plaud,[2]
10 And speak for Faustus in his infancy:
  Now is he born, his parents base of stock,
  In Germany, within a town call'd Rhodes;[3]
  Of riper years to Wittenberg[4] he went,
  Whereas his kinsmen chiefly brought him up.
15 So soon he profits in divinity,
  The fruitful plot of scholarism grac'd,
  That shortly he was grac'd[5] with doctor's name,
  Excelling all whose sweet delight disputes[6]

---

[1] *Mars did mate* Mars "allied himself with" or "rivaled." Hannibal's Carthaginian army inflicted a crushing defeat upon the Romans at the battle of Lake Trasummenus in 217 BCE.

[2] *appeal our plaud* Appeal for our applause.

[3] *Rhodes* Roda (now Stadtroda), near Weimar.

[4] *Wittenberg* The University of Wittenberg was famous under Martin Luther as a Protestant center of learning.

[5] *grac'd* At Cambridge it was and still is by the "grace" or decree of the university Senate that degrees are conferred; Marlowe's name appears in the Grace Book in 1584 and 1587 for the B.A. and M.A. degrees respectively.

[6] *whose ... disputes* It is possible to construe "disputes" as a verb; more probably the expression is elliptical and means "whose sweet delight consists in disputes."

In heavenly matters of theology,
20   Till swoll'n with cunning[1] of a self-conceit,
His waxen wings[2] did mount above his reach
And melting heavens conspir'd his overthrow.
For falling to a devilish exercise,
And glutted now with learning's golden gifts,
25   He surfeits upon cursed necromancy;
Nothing so sweet as magic is to him,
Which he prefers before his chiefest bliss:
And this the man that in his study sits.

(*Exit.*)

ACT 1, SCENE 1[3]

(*Faustus in his study.*)

FAUSTUS.   Settle thy studies, Faustus, and begin
To sound the depth of that thou wilt profess.[4]
Having commenc'd,[5] be a divine in show,
Yet level at the end of every art,[6]
5   And live and die in Aristotle's works:
Sweet *Analytics*,[7] 'tis thou hast ravish'd me—
Bene disserere est finis logices.[8]
Is to dispute well logic's chiefest end?
Affords this art no greater miracle?
10   Then read no more, thou hast attain'd the end.
A greater subject fitteth Faustus' wit:°   *understanding*

Bid *on kai me on*[9] farewell; Galen[10] come,
Seeing *ubi desinit philosophus, ibi incipit medicus*.[11]
Be a physician Faustus, heap up gold,
15   And be eterniz'd for some wondrous cure!
Summum bonum medicinae sanitas.[12]
The end of physic° is our bodies' health.   *medicine*
Why Faustus, hast thou not attain'd that end?
Is not thy common talk sound aphorisms?[13]
20   Are not thy bills hung up as monuments,
Whereby whole cities have escap'd the plague,
And thousand desperate maladies been eas'd?
Yet art thou still but Faustus, and a man.
Couldst thou make men to live eternally,
25   Or being dead, raise them to life again,
Then this profession were to be esteem'd.
Physic farewell; where is Justinian?
Si una eademque res legatur duobus,
alter rem, alter valorem rei,[14] *etc.*
30   A petty case of paltry legacies!
Exhereditare filium non potest pater, nisi—[15]
Such is the subject of the *Institute*[16]
And universal body of the law.
This study fits a mercenary drudge
35   Who aims at nothing but external trash—

---

[1] *cunning* Knowledge, erudition, cleverness; sometimes with negative connotations.

[2] *waxen wings* Allusion to the story of Icarus (cf. Ovid, *Metamorphoses* 8.183–235): escaping with his father Daedalus from Minos's island kingdom of Crete, Icarus ignored his father's warning about the wings he had made for them and flew too close to the sun.

[3] *ACT 1, SCENE 1* Neither the 1604 nor the 1616 texts of the play contains any act or scene divisions; all such divisions in modern editions of the play are therefore editorial.

[4] *profess* Affirm faith in or allegiance to.

[5] *commenc'd* Taken a degree.

[6] *level ... art* Take aim at the final purpose or limit of every discipline.

[7] *Analytics* Name of two treatises on logic by Aristotle, whose works still dominated the university curriculum.

[8] *Bene ... logices* Latin: To argue well is the end or purpose of logic (a definition derived not from Aristotle but from Cicero).

---

[9] *on kai me on* Transliteration of Greek words meaning "being and not being," the subject of an ancient Greek philosophical treatise.

[10] *Galen* Claudius Galenus (c. 130–200 CE), most famous of ancient writers on medicine.

[11] *ubi ... medicus* Latin: where the philosopher leaves off, there the physician begins. Freely translated from Aristotle, *Sense and Sensibilia* 436a.

[12] *Summum ... sanitas* Latin: The supreme good of medicine is health. Translated from Aristotle, *Nicomachean Ethics* 1094a.

[13] *sound aphorisms* Reliable medical precepts.

[14] *Si ... rei* Latin: If one and the same thing is bequeathed to two persons, one of them shall have the thing, the other the value of the thing. Derived in part from 2.20 of the *Institutes*, a compilation of Roman law carried out at the command of the emperor Justinian in the sixth century.

[15] *Exhereditare ... nisi*— Latin: A father cannot disinherit his son except—. An incomplete formulation of a rule from Justinian's *Institutes* 2.12.

[16] *Institute* "Institute" here means "founding principle," and may refer also to Justinian's *Institutes*.

Too servile[1] and illiberal for me.
When all is done, divinity is best:
Jerome's Bible,[2] Faustus, view it well.
Stipendium peccati mors est.[3] Ha! *Stipendium, etc.*
40 The reward of sin is death? That's hard.
Si peccasse negamus, fallimur,
et nulla est in nobis veritas.[4]
If we say that we have no sin
We deceive ourselves, and there's no truth in us.
45 Why then belike we must sin,
And so consequently die.
Ay, we must die, an everlasting death.
What doctrine call you this? *Che sarà, sarà,*
What will be, shall be? Divinity, adieu!
50 These metaphysics[5] of magicians
And necromantic books are heavenly!
Lines,[6] circles,[7] seals, letters and characters:[8]
Ay, these are those that Faustus most desires,
O, what a world of profit and delight,
55 Of power, of honor, of omnipotence,

Is promis'd to the studious artisan![9]
All things that move between the quiet poles[10]
Shall be at my command. Emperors and kings
Are but obey'd in their several provinces,
60 Nor can they raise the wind, or rend the clouds;[11]
But his dominion that exceeds° in this   excels
Stretcheth as far as doth the mind of man!
A sound magician is a mighty god:
Here tire, my brains, to get° a deity!   beget

(Enter Wagner.)

65 Wagner, commend me to my dearest friends,
The German Valdes and Cornelius;
Request them earnestly to visit me.
WAGNER. I will, sir.

(Exit.)

FAUSTUS. Their conference will be a greater help to me
70 Than all my labors, plod I ne'er so fast.

(Enter the Good Angel and the Evil Angel.)

GOOD ANGEL. O Faustus, lay that damned book aside,
And gaze not on it, lest it tempt thy soul
And heap God's heavy wrath upon thy head!
Read, read the Scriptures; that is blasphemy.
75 EVIL ANGEL. Go forward, Faustus, in that famous art
Wherein all nature's treasury is contain'd:
Be thou on earth as Jove[12] is in the sky,
Lord and commander of these elements![13]

(Exeunt Angels.)

---

[1] *Too servile* To contrast the liberal arts with "servile" or "mechanical" studies and practices is an Elizabethan commonplace.

[2] *Jerome's Bible* Vulgate, prepared mainly by St. Jerome in the fourth century, was the Latin text of the Bible used by the Roman Catholic church.

[3] *Stipendium ... est* This is the first of several quotations from the Latin Vulgate Bible. This quotation is the first half of Romans 6.23, a verse which in the Geneva Bible (1560) is translated as follows: "For the wages of sin is death: but the gift of God is eternal life through Jesus Christ our Lord."

[4] *Si peccasse ... veritas* 1 John 1.8. Faustus has again quoted only the first half of an antithetical statement: he notices the condemnation of sinners by the law of God, but not the conditional promise of divine mercy which immediately follows in 1 John 1.9. In the Geneva Bible, 1 John 1.8–9 is rendered as follows: "If we say that we have no sin, we deceive our selves, and truth is not in us. If we acknowledge our sins, he is faithful and just, to forgive us our sins, and to cleanse us from all unrighteousness."

[5] *metaphysics* Science of the supernatural.

[6] *Lines* Reference to the occult art of geomancy, or divination by means of astrologically determined patterns of points and lines.

[7] *circles* Magic circles protected the practitioner of ceremonial magic from evil spirits.

[8] *seals, letters and characters* Talismanic symbols of the planets and of the angels, spiritual intelligences, and daemons that were believed to govern them.

---

[9] *artisan* Practitioner of an art.

[10] *quiet poles* This could refer either to the poles of the outermost celestial sphere or, more probably, to those of the earth.

[11] *raise ... clouds* Blasphemous echo of Jeremiah 10.13 (which speaks of God's power over clouds, lightning and wind).

[12] *Jove* The substitution of the supreme god of the pagan Roman pantheon for the Christian God is common in Renaissance texts and in Elizabethan poetry.

[13] *these elements* Earth, water, air and fire, here used as a metonymy for the world contained by the sphere of the moon which these elements were thought to constitute.

FAUSTUS.   How am I glutted with conceit[1] of this!
80   Shall I make spirits fetch me what I please,
Resolve me of all ambiguities,
Perform what desperate enterprise I will?
I'll have them fly to India for gold,
Ransack the ocean for orient pearl
85   And search all corners of the new found world
For pleasant fruits and princely delicates;
I'll have them read me strange philosophy
And tell the secrets of all foreign kings;
I'll have them wall all Germany with brass
90   And make swift Rhine[2] circle fair Wittenberg;
I'll have them fill the public schools with silk
Wherewith the students shall be bravely[3] clad;
I'll levy soldiers with the coin they bring,
And chase the Prince of Parma[4] from our land
95   And reign sole king of all our provinces;
Yea, stranger engines for the brunt° of war   *assault, onset*
Than was the fiery keel at Antwerp's bridge[5]
I'll make my servile spirits to invent.
Come, German Valdes and Cornelius,
100   And make me blest with your sage conference!

(Enter Valdes and Cornelius.)

Valdes, sweet Valdes, and Cornelius,
Know that your words have won me at the last
To practise magic and concealed arts:
Yet not your words only, but mine own fantasy,

105   That will receive no object, for my head
But ruminates on necromantic skill.[6]
Philosophy is odious and obscure;
Both law and physic are for petty wits;
Divinity is basest of the three,
110   Unpleasant, harsh, contemptible and vile;
'Tis magic, magic, that hath ravish'd me.
Then, gentle friends, aid me in this attempt,
And I, that have with concise syllogisms[7]
Gravell'd° the pastors of the German church   *confounded*
115   And made the flowering pride of Wittenberg
Swarm to my problems as the infernal spirits
On sweet Musaeus[8] when he came to hell,
Will be as cunning as Agrippa was,
Whose shadows[9] made all Europe honor him.
120   VALDES.   Faustus, these books, thy wit, and our experience
Shall make all nations canonize us.
As Indian Moors[10] obey their Spanish lords,
So shall the subjects[11] of every element
Be always serviceable to us three:
125   Like lions shall they guard us when we please,
Like Almain rutters[12] with their horsemen's staves,°   *lances*
Or Lapland giants trotting by our sides;
Sometimes like women, or unwedded maids,
Shadowing° more beauty in their airy brows   *harboring*
130   Than has the white breasts of the queen of love.[13]
From Venice shall they drag huge Argosies,[14]

---

[1] *conceit* Thought, notion.

[2] *Rhine* River in Germany.

[3] *bravely* Splendidly. University regulations forbade students to wear fine clothing: their scholars' gowns were to be made of woolen cloth in somber colors, and silk-lined hoods could only be worn by the holders of doctoral degrees.

[4] *Prince of Parma* Alessandro Farnese, Duke of Parma, a grandson of the emperor Charles V and the foremost general of his time. Parma served as Spanish governor of the Netherlands from 1578 until his death in 1592; he was hated by Protestants as a tyrant. He commanded the force that the Spanish Armada was to have transported across the Channel in 1588 for the invasion of England.

[5] *fiery ... bridge* On 4 April 1585 the Netherlanders sent two fireships loaded with explosives against the pontoon bridge over the river Scheldt which formed part of Parma's siegeworks around Antwerp; one of them reached its target and destroyed part of the bridge, killing many Spanish soldiers. Parma had the bridge rebuilt, and Antwerp subsequently surrendered.

[6] *Yet ... skill* Faustus is saying that his imagination is so preoccupied with thoughts of magic that he can think of no other subjects.

[7] *syllogisms* Particular form of argument from logic.

[8] *Musaeus* Legendary pre-Homeric Greek poet, a pupil of Orpheus. In Virgil's *Aeneid*, Musaeus is represented as standing in the midst of a crowd of spirits in the underworld, head and shoulders above the rest.

[9] *Agrippa ... shadows* Henricus Cornelius Agrippa of Nettesheim (1486–1535), said to be "the greatest conjurer in Christendom." Agrippa distinguished between two kinds of necromancy: *necyomantia*, the reviving of corpses by means of a blood sacrifice, and *scyomantia*, in which only the shadow of a dead person is invoked.

[10] *Indian Moors* Native peoples of the Americas.

[11] *subjects* Spirits. "Subjects" carries the additional implication of subjection to a sovereign will (here, that of the magician).

[12] *Almain rutters* German soldiers.

[13] *queen of love* Venus, Roman goddess of love.

[14] *Argosies* Richly laden merchant ships.

And from America the golden fleece[1]
That yearly stuffs old Philip's treasury,[2]
If learned Faustus will be resolute.
135 FAUSTUS. Valdes, as resolute am I in this
As thou to live, therefore object it not.
CORNELIUS. The miracles that magic will perform
Will make thee vow to study nothing else.
He that is grounded in[3] astrology,
140 Enrich'd with tongues,[4] well seen in minerals,[5]
Hath all the principles magic doth require.
Then doubt not, Faustus, but to be renown'd
And more frequented° for this mystery   sought out
Than heretofore the Delphian oracle.[6]
145 The spirits tell me they can dry the sea
And fetch the treasure of all foreign wrecks,
Ay, all the wealth that our forefathers hid
Within the massy° entrails of the earth.   heavy, massive
Then tell me Faustus, what shall we three want?
150 FAUSTUS. Nothing, Cornelius. O, this cheers my soul!
Come, show me some demonstrations magical,
That I may conjure in some lusty grove
And have these joys in full possession.
VALDES. Then haste thee to some solitary grove,
155 And bear wise Bacon's and Albanus' works,[7]
The Hebrew Psalter, and New Testament;
And whatsoever else is requisite
We will inform thee ere our conference cease.
CORNELIUS. Valdes, first let him know the words of art,
160 And then, all other ceremonies learn'd,
Faustus may try his cunning by himself.
VALDES. First I'll instruct thee in the rudiments,
And then wilt thou be perfecter than I.

---

[1] *golden fleece* In Greek mythology, Jason and his crew sailed in the Argo on a quest for the Golden Fleece.

[2] *golden … treasury* Annual fleet that shipped gold and silver from the Americas to Spain.

[3] *grounded in* Firmly established in.

[4] *Enrich'd with tongues* Improved by knowledge of (ancient) languages.

[5] *well … minerals* Well versed in the properties of minerals.

[6] *Delphian oracle* Oracle of Apollo at Delphi, the most famous and authoritative of ancient Greek oracles.

[7] *wise Bacon's and Albanus' works* Roger Bacon (c. 1214–94), an English Franciscan philosopher, was reputed also to have been a magician "Albanus" is an error for Pietro d'Abano or Petrus de Aponus (c. 1250–1316), a physician who was posthumously convicted of sorcery and burned in effigy by the Inquisition.

FAUSTUS. Then come and dine with me, and after meat
165 We'll canvas every quiddity[8] thereof.
For ere I sleep I'll try what I can do;
This night I'll conjure though I die therefore.

(*Exeunt.*)

ACT 1, SCENE 2

(*Enter two scholars.*)

FIRST SCHOLAR. I wonder what's become of Faustus, that
was wont to make our schools ring with *sic probo*.[9]
SECOND SCHOLAR. That shall we presently° know, for   *at once*
see: here comes his boy.

(*Enter Wagner.*)

5 FIRST SCHOLAR. How now sirrah,[10] where's thy master?
WAGNER. God in heaven knows.
SECOND SCHOLAR. Why, dost not thou know?
WAGNER. Yes, I know, but that follows not.
FIRST SCHOLAR. Go to sirrah, leave your jesting, and tell
10 us where he is.
WAGNER. That follows not necessary by force of argu-
ment, which you, being licentiate,[11] should stand
upon;[12] therefore acknowledge your error and be atten-
tive.
15 SECOND SCHOLAR. Why, didst thou not say thou
knew'st?
WAGNER. Have you any witness on't?
FIRST SCHOLAR. Yes, sirrah, I heard you.
WAGNER. Ask my fellow if I be a thief!
20 SECOND SCHOLAR. Well, you will not tell us.

---

[8] *canvas every quiddity* Discuss every essential particular.

[9] *sic probo* Latin: thus I prove; the cry of triumph with which Faustus would have clinched his victories in disputation.

[10] *sirrah* Term of address that expresses the speaker's contempt, the addressee's social inferiority, or both.

[11] *licentiate* Licensed by an academic degree to proceed to further studies.

[12] *stand upon* Insist on.

WAGNER.   Yes sir, I will tell you; yet if you were not dunces[1] you would never ask me such a question, for is not he *corpus naturale*, and is not that *mobile*?[2] Then wherefore should you ask me such a question? But that
25   I am by nature phlegmatic, slow to wrath and prone to lechery (to love I would say), it were not for you to come within forty foot of the place of execution[3]—although I do not doubt but to see you both hanged the next sessions. Thus having triumphed over you, I will
30   set my countenance like a precisian,[4] and begin to speak thus: Truly, my dear brethren, my master is within at dinner with Valdes and Cornelius, as this wine if it could speak would inform your worships; and so the Lord bless you, preserve you, and keep you,[5] my dear
35   brethren, my dear brethren.

(*Exit.*)

FIRST SCHOLAR.   Nay then, I fear he is fallen into that damned art, for which they two are infamous through the world.
SECOND SCHOLAR.   Were he a stranger, and not allied to
40   me, yet should I grieve for him. But come, let us go and inform the Rector, and see if he by his grave counsel can reclaim him.
FIRST SCHOLAR.   O, but I fear me nothing can reclaim him.
45   SECOND SCHOLAR.   Yet let us try what we can do.

(*Exeunt.*)

---

[1]   *dunces*   Renaissance humanists opposed both the hair-splitting complexity of scholastic logic. As a result, the name of Johannes Duns Scotus (c. 1265–1308), one of the most subtle medieval logicians, came to connote sophistical quibbling and, by extension, stupidity.

[2]   *corpus naturale ... mobile*   Latin: a body that is natural or subject to change—an adaptation of Aristotle's statement of the subject-matter of physics.

[3]   *place of execution*   Scene of action; in this case, the dining-room.

[4]   *precisian*   Puritan, one who is precise and scrupulous about religious observances. Having parodied the logic of scholastic disputation, Wagner proceeds to parody the discourse of excessive piety.

[5]   *the Lord ... keep you*   Numbers 6.24. In quoting these words as an exit line, Wagner is mocking the language with which religious services were (and are) commonly brought to a close.

ACT 1, SCENE 3

(*Enter Faustus to conjure.*)

FAUSTUS.   Now that the gloomy shadow of the earth,
Longing to view Orion's drizzling look,[6]
Leaps from th'antarctic world[7] unto the sky
And dims the welkin° with her pitchy breath,   *sky*
5   Faustus, begin thine incantations,
And try if devils will obey thy hest,°   *command*
Seeing thou hast pray'd and sacrific'd to them.
Within this circle is Jehovah's name,
Forward and backward anagrammatiz'd,[8]
10   The breviated° names of holy saints,   *abbreviated*
Figures of every adjunct to[9] the heavens,
And characters of signs and erring stars[10]
By which the spirits are enforc'd to rise;
Then fear not, Faustus, but be resolute,
15   And try the uttermost magic can perform.
Sint mihi dei Acherontis propitii! Valeat numen triplex
Iehovae! Ignei, aerii, aquatici spiritus salvete! Orientis princeps
Belzebub, inferni ardentis monarcha, et Demogorgon, propitia-
mus vos ut appareat et surgat Mephastophilis. Quid tu moraris?
20   *Per Iehovam, Gehennam et consecratam aquam quam nunc*
spargo, signumque crucis quod nunc facio, et per vota nostra,
ipse nunc surgat nobis dicatus Mephastophilis.[11]

---

[6]   *Orion's drizzling look*   Constellation of Orion associated in classical poetry with winter storms.

[7]   *th'antarctic world*   If one believes the sun to revolve around the earth, and lives in the northern hemisphere, then the sun will be conceived of as shining on the southern hemisphere when it is night in the northern, and re-emerging from "th'antarctic world" at dawn.

[8]   *anagrammatiz'd*   Cabalist mystics believed that hidden meanings were present in every possible recombination of letters in the Hebrew scriptures, and practitioners of Cabalistic magic saw the names of God in particular as containing occult secrets of divine power and knowledge.

[9]   *adjunct to*   Heavenly body attached to.

[10]   *characters ... stars*   Diagrams representing the constellations of the zodiac (one Latin term for which was *signa*) and the planets.

[11]   *Sint ... Mephastophilis*   Latin: May the gods of Acheron be propitious to me. Away with the threefold divinity of Jehovah! Hail, spirits of fire, air, and water! Belzebub, Prince of the East, monarch of burning hell, and Demogorgon, we invoke your favor that Mephastophilis may appear and ascend. Why do you delay? By Jehovah, Gehenna, and the holy water which I now sprinkle, by the sign of the cross which I now make, and by our vows, may Mephastophilis himself now rise to serve us!;   [continued ...]

(*Enter a devil.*)

I charge thee to return and change thy shape.
Thou art too ugly to attend on me;
25 Go, and return an old Franciscan friar:
That holy shape becomes a devil best.

(*Exit devil.*)

I see there's virtue[1] in my heavenly words,
Who would not be proficient in this art?
How pliant is this Mephastophilis,
30 Full of obedience and humility:
Such is the force of magic and my spells!
Now, Faustus, thou art conjurer laureate[2]
That canst command great Mephastophilis!
Quin redis, Mephastophilis, fratris imagine![3]

(*Enter Mephastophilis.*)

35 MEPHASTOPHILIS.   Now, Faustus, what wouldst thou
        have me do?
FAUSTUS.   I charge thee wait upon me whilst I live
To do whatever Faustus shall command,
Be it to make the moon drop from her sphere
Or the ocean to overwhelm the world.
40 MEPHASTOPHILIS.   I am a servant to great Lucifer,[4]
And may not follow thee without his leave;
No more than he commands must we perform.
FAUSTUS.   Did not he charge thee to appear to me?
MEPHASTOPHILIS.   No, I came hither of my own accord.
45 FAUSTUS.   Did not my conjuring speeches raise thee?
        Speak.

MEPHASTOPHILIS.   That was the cause, but yet *per accidens*,[5]
For when we hear one rack° the name of God,   torture
Abjure the Scriptures and his saviour Christ,
We fly, in hope to get his glorious[6] soul;
50 Nor will we come unless he use such means
Whereby he is in danger to be damn'd.
Therefore the shortest cut for conjuring
Is stoutly[7] to abjure the Trinity,[8]
And pray devoutly to the prince of hell.
55 FAUSTUS.   So Faustus hath already done,
And holds this principle:
There is no chief but only Belzebub,
To whom Faustus doth dedicate himself.
This word "damnation" terrifies not him,
60 For he confounds hell in Elysium:[9]
His ghost be with the old philosophers!
But leaving these vain trifles of men's souls,
Tell me, what is that Lucifer thy lord?
MEPHASTOPHILIS.   Arch-regent and commander of all spirits.
65 FAUSTUS.   Was not that Lucifer an angel once?
MEPHASTOPHILIS.   Yes Faustus, and most dearly lov'd
        of God.
FAUSTUS.   How comes it then that he is prince of devils?
MEPHASTOPHILIS.   O, by aspiring pride and insolence,
For which God threw him from the face of heaven.
70 FAUSTUS.   And what are you that live with Lucifer?
MEPHASTOPHILIS.   Unhappy spirits that fell with Lucifer,
Conspir'd against our God with Lucifer,
And are for ever damn'd with Lucifer.
FAUSTUS.   Where are you damn'd?
75 MEPHASTOPHILIS.   In hell.
FAUSTUS.   How comes it then that thou art out of hell?
MEPHASTOPHILIS.   Why this is hell, nor am I out of it:
Think'st thou that I who saw the face of God
And tasted the eternal joys of heaven

Mephastophilis Compound of three Greek words indicating negation (*me*), light (*phos*), and loving (*philis*); in its original form, the name thus means "not-light-loving"—perhaps parodying the Latin "Lucifer," or "light-bearer."

[1] *virtue* Power.

[2] *laureate* Crowned with laurel; of proved distinction.

[3] *Quin ... imagine* Latin: Why do you not return, Mephastophilis, in the shape of a friar!

[4] *Lucifer* The name appears in Isaiah 14.12.

[5] *per accidens* Scholastics distinguished between an efficient cause, i.e., an agent which itself produced an effect, and a cause *per accidens*, which was related to the final effect only in having provided an occasion for the intervention of some external agent.

[6] *glorious* Splendid; possibly also boastful.

[7] *stoutly* Courageously, resolutely.

[8] *Trinity* In orthodox Christian belief, the three persons (God the Father, Son, and Holy Spirit) of the Godhead.

[9] *confounds ... Elysium* Identifies Hell with Elysium; confuses the two; undoes Hell through belief in Elysium (in ancient Greece, the place in the afterworld reserved for heroes).

80   Am not tormented with ten thousand hells
        In being depriv'd of everlasting bliss?
        O Faustus, leave these frivolous demands,
        Which strike a terror to my fainting soul.
        FAUSTUS.   What, is great Mephastophilis so passionate
85   For being deprived of the joys of heaven?
        Learn thou of Faustus manly fortitude
        And scorn those joys thou never shalt possess.
        Go, bear these tidings to great Lucifer:
        Seeing Faustus hath incurr'd eternal death
90   By desperate thoughts against Jove's deity,
        Say he surrenders up to him his soul,
        So[1] he will spare him four and twenty years,
        Letting him live in all voluptuousness,
        Having thee ever to attend on me
95   To give me whatsoever I shall ask,
        To tell me whatsoever I demand,
        To slay mine enemies and aid my friends,
        And always be obedient to my will.
        Go, and return to mighty Lucifer,
100   And meet me in my study at midnight,
        And then resolve me of thy master's mind.
        MEPHASTOPHILIS.   I will, Faustus.

        (*Exit.*)

        FAUSTUS.   Had I as many souls as there be stars
        I'd give them all for Mephastophilis!
105   By him I'll be a great emperor of the world,
        And make a bridge thorough[2] the moving air
        To pass the ocean with a band of men;
        I'll join the hills that bind the Afric shore,
        And make that country continent to[3] Spain,
110   And both contributory to my crown;
        The emperor shall not live but by my leave,
        Nor any potentate of Germany.
        Now that I have obtain'd what I desire,
        I'll live in speculation of this art
115   Till Mephastophilis return again.

        (*Exit.*)

---

[1]   *So*   On condition that.

[2]   *thorough*   I.e., through.

[3]   *continent to*   Continuous with.

ACT 1, SCENE 4

(*Enter Wagner and the Clown.*)[4]

WAGNER.   Sirrah boy, come hither.
CLOWN.   How, "boy"? Swowns[5] boy, I hope you have
    seen many boys with such pickadevaunts[6] as I have.
    "Boy," quotha?
5   WAGNER.   Tell me sirrah, hast thou any comings in?[7]
CLOWN.   Ay, and goings out[8] too, you may see else.
WAGNER.   Alas, poor slave: see how poverty jesteth in his
    nakedness. The villain is bare, and out of service,[9] and so
    hungry that I know he would give his soul to the devil
10 for a shoulder of mutton, though it were blood raw.
CLOWN.   How, my soul to the devil for a shoulder of
    mutton though 'twere blood raw? Not so, good friend:
    b'urlady[10] I had need have it well roasted, and good
    sauce to it, if I pay so dear.
15 WAGNER.   Well, wilt thou serve me, and I'll make thee
    go like *Qui mihi discipulus?*[11]
CLOWN.   How, in verse?
WAGNER.   No sirrah, in beaten silk[12] and stavesacre.[13]
CLOWN.   How, how, knave's acre? Ay, I thought that
20 was all the land his father left him. Do ye hear, I would
    be sorry to rob you of your living.
WAGNER.   Sirrah, I say in stavesacre!
CLOWN.   Oho, oho, stavesacre! Why then belike,[14] if I

---

[4]   *Clown*   Boorish rustic, a fool. This character is presumably to be
identified with the Robin of 2.2 and 3.2.

[5]   *Swowns*   Contraction of "God's wounds" (a mild oath).

[6]   *pickadevaunts*   Short beards trimmed to a point; apparently from
the French *piqué devant,* "peaked in front," possibly with an obscene
double entendre.

[7]   *comings in*   Earnings.

[8]   *goings out*   Expenses; a punning reference to the fact that the
Clown is bursting out of his tattered clothes.

[9]   *out of service*   Unemployed.

[10]   *b'urlady*   Contraction of "by Our Lady."

[11]   *Qui mihi discipulus*   Latin: You who are my pupil. The opening
words of a didactic poem which appeared in the standard elementary
Latin textbook used in Elizabethan schools.

[12]   *beaten silk*   Embroidered silk; with a punning suggestion that
Wagner will thrash his servant.

[13]   *stavesacre*   Preparation against lice made from the seeds of a plant
related to the delphinium.

[14]   *belike*   In all likelihood.

were your man I should be full of vermin.

25 WAGNER. So thou shalt, whether thou beest with me or no. But sirrah, leave your jesting, and bind yourself presently unto me for seven years,[1] or I'll turn all the lice about thee into familiars,[2] and they shall tear thee to pieces.

30 CLOWN. Do you hear, sir? You may save that labor: they are too familiar with me already, swowns they are as bold with my flesh as if they had paid for my meat and drink.

WAGNER. Well, do you hear, sirrah? Hold, take these 35 guilders.

CLOWN. Gridirons, what be they?

WAGNER. Why, French crowns.

CLOWN. Mass, but for the name of French crowns, a man were as good have as many English counters.[3] And 40 what should I do with these?

WAGNER. Why now, sirrah, thou art at an hour's warning whensoever or wheresoever the devil shall fetch thee.

CLOWN. No, no; here, take your gridirons again.

45 WAGNER. Truly, I'll none of them.

CLOWN. Truly, but you shall.

WAGNER. Bear witness I gave them him!

CLOWN. Bear witness I give them you again!

WAGNER. Well, I will cause two devils presently to fetch 50 thee away. Baliol,[4] and Belcher!

CLOWN. Let your Balio and Belcher come here, and I'll knock them, they were never so knocked since they were devils! Say I should kill one of them, what would folks

say? "Do ye see yonder tall[5] fellow in the round slop,[6] he 55 has killed the devil": so I should be called "kill-devil" all the parish over.

(*Enter two devils, and the clown runs up and down crying.*)

WAGNER. Balio and Belcher, spirits away!

(*Exeunt.*)

CLOWN. What, are they gone? A vengeance on them, they have vile long nails. There was a he-devil and a she-60 devil. I'll tell you how you shall know them: all he-devils has horns,[7] and all she-devils has clefts[8] and cloven feet.

WAGNER. Well sirrah, follow me.

CLOWN. But do you hear: If I should serve you, would you teach me to raise up Banios and Belcheos?

65 WAGNER. I will teach thee to turn thyself to anything: to a dog, or a cat, or a mouse, or a rat, or any thing.

CLOWN. How? A Christian fellow to a dog or a cat, a mouse or a rat? No, no, sir. If you turn me into anything, let it be in the likeness of little pretty frisking flea, 70 that I may be here and there and everywhere: O, I'll tickle the pretty wenches' plackets,[9] I'll be amongst them i'faith!

WAGNER. Well sirrah, come.

CLOWN. But do you hear, Wagner?

75 WAGNER. How? Baliol and Belcher!

CLOWN. O Lord! I pray sir, let Banio and Belcher go sleep.

WAGNER. Villain, call me Master Wagner, and see that you walk attentively, and let your right eye be always 80 diametrally fixed upon my left heel, that thou mayest *quasi vestigiis nostris insitere.*[10]

(*Exit.*)

---

[1] *seven years* Standard period of time for an apprenticeship or a contract of indentured labor.

[2] *familiars* Attendant spirits of witches and sorcerers, who took the form of animals.

[3] *guilders ... English counters* Wagner professes to give the Clown Dutch guilders. Observing, it would seem, that the coins have holes punched in them, the Clown mis-hears the word as "gridirons"—whereupon Wagner re-identifies the coins as French crowns. A proclamation of 1587 authorized members of the public to strike holes in French crowns, which in the late 1580s and early 1590s were notoriously debased, and often counterfeit. From the sixteenth until the early nineteenth century, English merchants issued privately minted counters or tokens which circulated without having any officially accepted value; "counter" often denoted a debased or counterfeit coin; *Mass* An oath: "by the Mass."

[4] *Baliol* Deformation of "Belial," a name which occurs in the Bible (e.g., 2 Corinthians 6.15).

---

[5] *tall* Valiant, handsome.

[6] *round slop* Baggy breeches.

[7] *horns* Standard demonic equipment, perhaps with an overtone of cuckoldry.

[8] *clefts* Vulvas.

[9] *plackets* Pockets in women's skirts; metaphorically, a woman's genitals.

[10] *quasi vestigiis nostris insitere* Latin: as if walking in our footsteps.

CLOWN.   God forgive me, he speaks Dutch fustian.[1]
Well, I'll follow him, I'll serve him, that's flat.

(*Exit.*)

ACT 2, SCENE 1

(*Enter Faustus in his study.*)

FAUSTUS.   Now Faustus, must thou needs be damn'd,
And canst thou not be saved.
What boots° it then to think of God or heaven?   *avails*
Away with such vain fancies, and despair,
5   Despair in God, and trust in Belzebub.
Now go not backward: no Faustus, be resolute.
Why waverest thou? O, something soundeth in mine ears:
"Abjure this magic, turn to God again."
Ay, and Faustus will turn to God again.
10   To God? He loves thee not;
The god thou serv'st is thine own appetite,
Wherein is fix'd the love of Belzebub:
To him I'll build an altar and a church,
And offer lukewarm blood of new-born babes!

(*Enter Good Angel, and Evil.*)

15   GOOD ANGEL.   Sweet Faustus, leave that execrable art.
FAUSTUS.   Contrition, prayer, repentance: what of these?
GOOD ANGEL.   O, they are means to bring thee unto
heaven.
EVIL ANGEL.   Rather illusions, fruits of lunacy,
That makes men foolish that do trust them most.
20   GOOD ANGEL.   Sweet Faustus, think of heaven and
heavenly things.
EVIL ANGEL.   No Faustus, think of honor and of
wealth.

(*Exeunt Angels.*)

FAUSTUS.   Of wealth?

Why, the signory° of Emden[2] shall be mine!   *lordship, rule*
When Mephastophilis shall stand by me
25   What God can hurt me?[3] Faustus, thou art safe;
Cast° no more doubts. Come, Mephastophilis,   *emit, ponder*
And bring glad tidings[4] from great Lucifer!
Is't not midnight? Come Mephastophilis,
Veni, veni, Mephastophilis![5]

(*Enter Mephastophilis.*)

30   Now tell me, what says Lucifer thy lord?
MEPHASTOPHILIS.   That I shall wait on Faustus whilst
he lives,
So he will buy my service with his soul.
FAUSTUS.   Already Faustus hath hazarded that for thee.
MEPHASTOPHILIS.   But now thou must bequeath it
solemnly,
35   And write a deed of gift with thine own blood,
For that security craves great Lucifer.
If thou deny it I will back to hell.
FAUSTUS.   Stay Mephastophilis, and tell me,
What good will my soul do thy lord?
40   MEPHASTOPHILIS.   Enlarge his kingdom.
FAUSTUS.   Is that the reason why he tempts us thus?
MEPHASTOPHILIS.   *Solamen miseris socios habuisse
doloris.*[6]
FAUSTUS.   Why, have you any pain that tortures others?
MEPHASTOPHILIS.   As great as have the human souls of
men.
45   But tell me, Faustus, shall I have thy soul?
And I will be thy slave and wait on thee,
And give thee more than thou hast wit to ask.
FAUSTUS.   Ay Mephastophilis, I give it thee.
MEPHASTOPHILIS.   Then stab this arm courageously,
50   And bind thy soul, that at some certain day
Great Lucifer may claim it as his own:

---

[1]   *fustian*   Bombast, nonsense. Fustian was a coarse cloth made of cotton and flax; the word was metaphorically applied to inflated or inappropriately lofty language.

[2]   *Emden*   Prosperous port in northwest Germany which conducted an extensive trade with England.

[3]   *When … me?*   Blasphemous distortion of Romans 8.31: "If God be on our side, who can be against us?"

[4]   *glad tidings*   Cf. Luke 2.10: "I bring you glad tidings of great joy."

[5]   *Veni, veni, Mephastophilis!*   Latin: Come, O come, Mephastophilis!—a blasphemous echo of the twelfth-century Advent hymn *Veni, veni, Emmanuel* (Come, O Come Redeemer).

[6]   *Solamen … doloris*   Latin: It is a comfort to the wretched to have had companions in misfortune.

And then be thou as great as Lucifer!
FAUSTUS.   Lo Mephastophilis, for love of thee
  I cut mine arm, and with my proper° blood   *own*
55 Assure my soul to be great Lucifer's,
  Chief lord and regent of perpetual night.
  View here the blood that trickles from mine arm,
  And let it be propitious for my wish.
MEPHASTOPHILIS.   But Faustus, thou must
60 Write it in manner of a deed[1] of gift.
FAUSTUS.   Ay, so I will. But Mephastophilis,
  My blood congeals, and I can write no more.
MEPHASTOPHILIS.   I'll fetch thee fire to dissolve it
  straight.

(Exit.)

FAUSTUS.What might the staying of my blood portend?
65 Is it unwilling I should write this bill?°   *contract*
  Why streams it not, that I may write afresh?
  "Faustus gives to thee his soul"; ah, there it stay'd.
  Why should'st thou not? Is not thy soul thine own?
  Then write again: "Faustus gives to thee his soul."

(Enter Mephastophilis with a chafer[2] of coals.)

70 MEPHASTOPHILIS.   Here's fire: come Faustus, set it on.
FAUSTUS.   So: now the blood begins to clear again;
  Now will I make an end immediately.
MEPHASTOPHILIS.   *(Aside.)* O, what will not I do to
  obtain his soul!
FAUSTUS.   *Consummatum est:*[3] this bill is ended,
75 And Faustus hath bequeath'd his soul to Lucifer.
  But what is this inscription on mine arm?
  Homo fuge![4] Whither should I fly?
  If unto God he'll throw thee down to hell.
  My senses are deceiv'd: here's nothing writ.
80 O yes, I see it plain! Even here is writ

---

[1] *deed* Legally binding document.

[2] *chafer* Saucepan or chafing-dish.

[3] *Consummatum est* Latin: It is finished. According to the Gospel of John, these were the last words of Jesus on the cross (John 19.30).

[4] *Homo fuge* Latin: Man, flee! The words occur in the Vulgate text of 1 Timothy 6.11, but this line as a whole alludes more distinctly to Psalm 139.7–8: "Whither shall I go from thy spirit? or whither shall I flee from thy presence? If I ascend into heaven, thou art there: if I lie down in hell, thou art there."

Homo fuge; yet shall not Faustus fly.
MEPHASTOPHILIS.   I'll fetch him somewhat to delight
  his mind.

(Exit. Enter with devils, giving crowns and rich apparel to Faustus, and dance, and then [the devils] depart.)

FAUSTUS.   Speak Mephastophilis: what means this show?
MEPHASTOPHILIS.   Nothing, Faustus, but to delight
  thy mind,
85 And let thee see what magic can perform.
FAUSTUS.   But may I raise such spirits when I please?
MEPHASTOPHILIS.   Ay Faustus, and do greater things
  than these.
FAUSTUS.   Then there's enough for a thousand souls!
  Here Mephastophilis, receive this scroll,
90 A deed of gift, of body and of soul:
  But yet conditionally, that thou perform
  All articles prescrib'd between us both.
MEPHASTOPHILIS.   Faustus, I swear by hell and Lucifer
  To effect all promises between us made.
95 FAUSTUS.   Then hear me read them.
  On these conditions following:
  First, that Faustus may be a spirit in form and substance;
  Secondly, that Mephastophilis shall be his servant, and at
    his command;
  Thirdly, that Mephastophilis shall do for him, and bring
    him whatsoever;
100 *Fourthly, that he shall be in his chamber or house*
    invisible;
  Lastly, that he shall appear to the said John Faustus at all
    times, in what form or shape soever he please;
  I, John Faustus of Wittenberg, Doctor, by these presents[5]
  do give both body and soul to Lucifer, Prince of the East,
  and his minister Mephastophilis, and furthermore grant
105 *unto him that four and twenty years being expired, and*
  these articles above written being inviolate, full power to
  fetch or carry the said John Faustus, body and soul, flesh,
  blood, or goods, into their habitation wheresoever.
                             By me, John Faustus.

MEPHASTOPHILIS.   Speak Faustus, do you deliver this as
  your deed?
110 FAUSTUS.   Ay, take it, and the devil give thee good on't.

---

[5] *these presents* Legal articles being presented.

MEPHASTOPHILIS.   So. Now, Faustus, ask me what
   thou wilt.
FAUSTUS.   First will I question with thee about hell.
   Tell me, where is the place that men call hell?
MEPHASTOPHILIS.   Under the heavens.
115 FAUSTUS.   Ay, so are all things else; but whereabouts?
MEPHASTOPHILIS.   Within the bowels of these elements,
   Where we are tortur'd and remain forever.
   Hell hath no limits, nor is circumscrib'd
   In one self° place, but where we are is hell,   *single, particular*
120 And where hell is there must we ever be;
   And to be short, when all the world dissolves
   And every creature shall be purify'd,
   All places shall be hell that is not heaven.
FAUSTUS.   Come, I think hell's a fable.
125 MEPHASTOPHILIS.   Ay, think so still, till experience
   change thy mind.
FAUSTUS.   Why, think'st thou then that Faustus shall
   be damn'd?
MEPHASTOPHILIS.   Ay, of necessity, for here's the scroll
   Wherein thou hast given thy soul to Lucifer.
FAUSTUS.   Ay, and body too, but what of that?
130 Think'st thou that Faustus is so fond° to imagine   *foolish*
   That after this life there is any pain?
   Tush, these are trifles and mere old wives' tales.
MEPHASTOPHILIS.   But I am an instance to prove the
   contrary,
   For I tell thee I am damn'd, and now in hell.
135 FAUSTUS.   Nay, and this be hell, I'll willingly be damn'd!
   What, sleeping, eating, walking and disputing?
   But leaving this, let me have a wife, the fairest maid in
   Germany, for I am wanton and lascivious, and cannot
   live without a wife.
140 MEPHASTOPHILIS.   How, a wife? I prithee Faustus, talk
   not of a wife.
FAUSTUS.   Nay, sweet Mephastophilis, fetch me one,
   for I will have one.
MEPHASTOPHILIS.   Well, thou wilt have one. Sit there
145 till I come; I'll fetch thee a wife in the devil's name.

(Enter a devil dressed like a woman, with fireworks.)[1]

MEPHASTOPHILIS.   Tell, Faustus: how dost thou like
   thy wife?
FAUSTUS.   A plague on her for a hot whore!

(Exit devil.)

MEPHASTOPHILIS.   Tut, Faustus, marriage is but a
   ceremonial toy.°   *trifle*
   If thou lov'st me, think no more of it.
150 I'll cull thee out the fairest courtesans
   And bring them every morning to thy bed.
   She whom thine eye shall like, thy heart shall have,
   Be she as chaste as was Penelope,[2]
   As wise as Saba,[3] or as beautiful
155 As was bright Lucifer before his fall.
   Hold, take this book: peruse it thoroughly.
   The iterating of these lines brings gold;
   The framing of this circle on the ground
   Brings whirlwinds, tempests, thunder and lightning.
160 Pronounce this thrice devoutly to thyself,
   And men in armor shall appear to thee,
   Ready to execute what thou desir'st.
FAUSTUS.   Thanks, Mephastophilis; yet fain would I have
   a book wherein I might behold all spells and incanta-
165 tions, that I might raise up spirits when I please.
MEPHASTOPHILIS.   Here they are in this book.

(There turn to them.)

FAUSTUS.   Now would I have a book where I might see
   all characters[4] and planets of the heavens, that I might
   know their motions and dispositions.
170 MEPHASTOPHILIS.   Here they are too.

(Turn to them.)

FAUSTUS.   Nay, let me have one book more, and then I
   have done, wherein I might see all plants, herbs, and
   trees that grow upon the earth.
MEPHASTOPHILIS.   Here they be.

---

[1] *fireworks* In the comic sequences of sixteenth-century pageants and plays, fireworks were often attached to the costumes of devils and clowns in ways designed to make fun of sexual and excretory functions.

[2] *Penelope* Faithful wife of Odysseus, hero of the Trojan War and Homer's *Odyssey*.

[3] *Saba* Queen of Sheba, who in 1 Kings 10.1–13 comes to Jerusalem to test King Solomon's knowledge of God.

[4] *characters* Talismanic symbols of the planets and of the spiritual powers that govern them.

175 FAUSTUS. O, thou art deceived.
MEPHASTOPHILIS. Tut, I warrant thee.[1]

(*Turn to them. Exeunt.*)

ACT 2, SCENE 2[2]

(*Enter Robin the ostler with a book in his hand.*)

ROBIN. O, this is admirable! Here I ha' stolen one of Doctor Faustus' conjuring books, and i'faith I mean to search some circles[3] for my own use: now will I make all the maidens in our parish dance at my pleasure stark
5 naked before me, and so by that means I shall see more than I ever felt, or saw yet.

(*Enter Rafe, calling Robin.*)

RAFE. Robin, prithee come away! There's a gentleman tarries to have his horse, and he would have his things rubbed and made clean: he keeps such a chafing with
10 my mistress about it, and she has sent me to look thee out; prithee come away!
ROBIN. Keep out, keep out, or else you are blown up, you are dismembered. Rafe! Keep out, for I am about a roaring[4] piece of work.
15 RAFE. Come, what dost thou with that same book? Thou canst not read.
ROBIN. Yes, my master and mistress shall find that I can read: he for his forehead,[5] she for her private study.[6] She's born to bear with[7] me, or else my art fails.
20 RAFE. Why Robin, what book is that?
ROBIN. What book? Why, the most intolerable book for conjuring that e'er was invented by any brimstone devil!

RAFE. Canst thou conjure with it?
ROBIN. I can do all these things easily with it: first, I can
25 make thee drunk with hippocras[8] at any tavern in Europe for nothing; that's one of my conjuring works.
RAFE. Our master parson says that's nothing.
ROBIN. True, Rafe. And more, Rafe, if thou hast any mind to Nan Spit our kitchen maid, then turn her and
30 wind her[9] to thine own use, as often as thou wilt, and at midnight.
RAFE. O brave Robin, shall I have Nan Spit, and to mine own use? On that condition I'll feed thy devil with horse-bread[10] as long as he lives, of free cost.
35 ROBIN. No more, sweet Rafe: let's go and make clean our boots which lie foul upon our hands; and then to our conjuring, in the devil's name!

(*Exeunt.*)

ACT 2, SCENE 3

(*Enter Faustus in his study, and Mephastophilis.*)

FAUSTUS. When I behold the heavens then I repent
And curse thee, wicked Mephastophilis,
Because thou hast depriv'd me of those joys.
MEPHASTOPHILIS. Why Faustus,
5 Think'st thou heaven is such a glorious thing?
I tell thee 'tis not half so fair as thou
Or any man that breathes on earth.
FAUSTUS. How prov'st thou that?
MEPHASTOPHILIS.   'Twas made for man,
10 Therefore is man more excellent.
FAUSTUS. If it were made for man, 'twas made for me:
I will renounce this magic and repent.

---

[1] *I warrant thee* I assure you.

[2] *ACT 2, SCENE 2* In both the 1604 and the 1616 texts of the play this scene, together with the scene numbered Act 3, Scene 2 in the present edition, appear in succession.

[3] *circles* Magic circles, and also women's vaginas.

[4] *roaring* Noisy, riotous.

[5] *forehead* Deceived husbands or cuckolds were said to wear horns on their foreheads.

[6] *private study* With a quibble on private parts.

[7] *to bear with* To put up with; also (another bawdy quibble) to lie under, to bear the weight of his body.

[8] *hippocras* Wine flavored with spices.

[9] *Nan Spit ... wind her* One of the humblest occupations in the kitchen of a large household or inn was that of the turnspit, whose job was to stand by the open fireplace and crank the horizontally mounted spit on which roasting meat was impaled. Robin tempts Rafe with the thought of sexually impaling and "turning" this kitchen maid—of treating her, in effect, as she treats a roast of meat.

[10] *horse-bread* Bread made of beans, bran, etc. for horses—but apparently sometimes eaten also by the very poor. Rafe seems to be aware of the popular superstition according to which familiar spirits took the form of animals, and were fed like pets by the witches to whom they attached themselves.

(*Enter Good Angel and Evil Angel.*)

GOOD ANGEL.   Faustus, repent yet, God will pity thee.
EVIL ANGEL.   Thou art a spirit, God cannot pity thee.
15 FAUSTUS.   Who buzzeth° in mine ears I am a spirit?   *whispers*
Be I a devil, yet God may pity me.
Ay, God will pity me if I repent.
EVIL ANGEL.   Ay, but Faustus never shall repent.

(*Exeunt Angels.*)

FAUSTUS.   My heart's so harden'd I cannot repent.
20 Scarce can I name salvation, faith, or heaven,
But fearful echoes thunders in mine ears,
"Faustus, thou art damn'd!" Then swords and knives,
Poison, guns, halters,[1] and envenom'd steel
Are laid before me to dispatch myself,
25 And long ere this I should have done the deed
Had not sweet pleasure conquer'd deep despair.
Have I not made blind Homer sing to me
Of Alexander's love and Oenone's death?[2]
And hath not he that built the walls of Thebes
30 With ravishing sound of his melodious harp[3]
Made music with my Mephastophilis?
Why should I die, then, or basely despair?
I am resolv'd: Faustus shall ne'er repent.
Come Mephastophilis, let us dispute again,
35 And reason of divine astrology.[4]
Speak, are there many spheres above the moon?
Are celestial bodies but one globe,

As is the substance of this centric earth?[5]
MEPHASTOPHILIS.   As are the elements, such are the
heavens,
40 Even from the moon unto the empyreal orb,
Mutually folded on each other's spheres,
And jointly move upon one axle-tree
Whose termine is term'd the world's wide pole.
Nor are the names of Saturn, Mars, or Jupiter
45 Feign'd, but are erring stars.
FAUSTUS.   But tell me, have they all one motion, both
situ et tempore?[6]
MEPHASTOPHILIS.   All jointly move from east to west in
four and twenty hours upon the poles of the world, but
50 differ in their motions upon the poles of the zodiac.
FAUSTUS.   These slender questions Wagner can decide:
Hath Mephastophilis no greater skill?
Who knows not the double notion of the planets?[7]
The first is finish'd in a natural day,
55 The second thus: Saturn in thirty years,
Jupiter in twelve, Mars in four, the Sun, Venus, and
Mercury in a year, the Moon in twenty-eight days.[8]

---

[1] *halters* Hangman's nooses.

[2] *Alexander's ... death* These are matters which Homer left unsung; Faustus would have been the first to hear them from his lips. Paris (also named Alexandros), a son of King Priam and Queen Hecuba of Troy, was cast out by his parents (for it was prophesied that he should cause the destruction of Troy) and brought up among the shepherds of Mount Ida, where he won the love of Oenone. Asked by Hera, Athena, and Aphrodite to award a golden apple to the most beautiful goddess, he succumbed to Aphrodite's bribe of the love of the fairest woman alive, abandoned Oenone and abducted Helen from Sparta, thus provoking the Trojan War. Later, having been wounded by a poisoned arrow, he could have been healed only by Oenone; after jealously refusing to cure him, she was overwhelmed with remorse and threw herself onto his funeral pyre.

[3] *he ... harp* Amphion and his brother built the walls of Thebes; the music of Amphion's lyre magically moved huge stones into place.

[4] *astrology* Not clearly distinguished from astronomy until the seventeenth century.

[5] *the substance of this centric earth* The elements (earth, water, air, and fire) that make up "the substance of this centric earth" were thought to be concentrically disposed; so also, in the old geocentric cosmology, were the spheres that governed the motions of those wandering or "erring" stars, the planets. Mephastophilis says there are nine spheres: those of the planets, including the moon and the sun; the firmament, to which the fixed stars are attached; and the empyrean, the outermost and motionless sphere of the universe. (He apparently conflates the *primum mobile*, thought of by some astronomers as a distinct sphere that imparts motion to the heavens, with the firmament.) All of this is utterly commonplace. The systems developed by ancient astronomers were enormously more complex: Eudoxus (fourth century BCE) required twenty-seven, and Ptolemy (second century CE) more than eighty variously revolving spheres, including epicyclic and eccentric ones, to explain the motions of the planets.

[6] *situ et tempore* Latin: in position and time; i.e., in the direction of their revolutions around the earth and in the time these take.

[7] *poles ... planets* The apparent diurnal motion of the planetary spheres "upon one axle-tree" (the northern "termine" of which nearly coincides with the star Polaris) is of course due, in post-Copernican terms, to the earth's rotation upon its axis. The second component of the planets' apparent "double motion" is an effect of the differences between the earth's period of revolution around the sun and theirs.

[8] *first ... days* The periods of planetary revolution given by Faustus correspond for the most part to the then-accepted figures: Saturn 28 years, Jupiter 12 years, Mars 2 years, Venus, Mercury, and, of course, the sun 1 year, and the moon 1 month. The actual—as opposed to apparent—periods for the inner planets are of course much less: $7\frac{1}{2}$ and 3 months respectively.

Tush, these are freshmen's suppositions! But tell me, hath every sphere a dominion or *intelligentia?*[1]

60 MEPHASTOPHILIS.   Ay.

FAUSTUS.   How many planets or spheres are there?

MEPHASTOPHILIS.   Nine: the seven planets, the firmament, and the empyreal heaven.

FAUSTUS.   But is there not *coelum igneum, et crystallinum?*[2]

65 MEPHASTOPHILIS.   No, Faustus, they be but fables.

FAUSTUS.   Resolve me then in this one question: Why are not conjunctions, oppositions, aspects,[3] eclipses all at one time, but in some years we have more, in some less?

70 MEPHASTOPHILIS.   *Per inaequalem motum respectu totius.*[4]

FAUSTUS.   Well, I am answered. Now tell me who made the world.

MEPHASTOPHILIS.   I will not.

FAUSTUS.   Sweet Mephastophilis, tell me.

MEPHASTOPHILIS.   Move° me not, Faustus.   *anger*

75 FAUSTUS.   Villain, have I not bound thee to tell me any thing?

MEPHASTOPHILIS.   Ay, that is not against our kingdom. This is. Thou are damn'd, think thou of hell.

FAUSTUS.   Think, Faustus, upon God that made the world!

MEPHASTOPHILIS.   Remember this.

(Exit.)

80 FAUSTUS.   Ay, go accursed spirit to ugly hell:
'Tis thou hast damn'd distressed Faustus' soul.
Is't not too late?

(Enter Good Angel and Evil Angel.)

EVIL ANGEL.   Too late.

GOOD ANGEL.   Never too late, if Faustus can repent.

85 EVIL ANGEL.   If thou repent, devils shall tear thee in pieces.

GOOD ANGEL.   Repent, and they shall never raze° thy skin.   *graze*

(Exeunt Angels.)

FAUSTUS.   Ah Christ, my Saviour,
Seek to save distressed Faustus' soul!

(Enter Lucifer, Belzebub, and Mephastophilis.)

LUCIFER.   Christ cannot save thy soul, for he is just;

90 There's none but I have interest in[5] the same.

FAUSTUS.   O, what art thou that look'st so terribly?

LUCIFER.   I am Lucifer, and this is my companion prince in hell.

FAUSTUS.   O Faustus, they are come to fetch away thy soul!

LUCIFER.   We come to tell thee thou dost injure us.

95 Thou talk'st of Christ, contrary to thy promise.

BELZEBUB.   Thou should'st not think of God.

LUCIFER.   Think of the devil.

BELZEBUB.   And of his dam° too.   *woman*

FAUSTUS.   Nor will I henceforth:[6] pardon me in this,

100 And Faustus vows never to look to heaven,
Never to name God or to pray to him,
To burn his Scriptures, slay his ministers,
And make my spirits pull his churches down.

LUCIFER.   So shalt thou show thyself an obedient servant,

105 and we will highly gratify thee for it.

BELZEBUB.   Faustus, we are come from hell to show thee some pastime. Sit down, and thou shalt behold the Seven Deadly Sins appear to thee in their own proper shapes and likeness.

110 FAUSTUS.   That sight will be as pleasing unto me as Paradise was to Adam, the first day of his creation.

LUCIFER.   Talk not of Paradise, or creation, but mark the show.
Go, Mephastophilis, fetch them in.

(Enter the Seven Deadly Sins.)

---

1 *dominion or intelligentia*   It was widely believed that the planets were moved or guided by angels or intelligences.

2 *coelum igneum, et crystallinum*   Latin: a fiery, and a crystalline heaven.

3 *conjunctions ... aspects*   Astrological terms referring respectively to the apparent proximity of two planets, to their positioning on opposite sides of the sky, and to any other angular relation between their positions.

4 *Per inaequalem motum respectu totius*   Latin: Through an unequal motion with respect to the whole.

5 *interest in*   Legal claim upon.

6 *Nor ... henceforth*   I.e., think of God.

BELZEBUB.   Now Faustus, question them of their names
and dispositions.

FAUSTUS.   That shall I soon: what art thou, the first?

PRIDE.   I am Pride. I disdain to have any parents. I am
like Ovid's flea,[1] I can creep into every corner of a
wench: sometimes like a periwig I sit upon her brow;
next like a necklace I hang about her neck; then like a
fan of feathers I kiss her lips; and then, turning myself
to a wrought smock, do what I list. But fie, what a smell
is here? I'll not speak a word more, unless the ground be
perfumed and covered with a cloth of arras.[2]

FAUSTUS.   Thou art a proud knave indeed. What art
thou, the second?

COVETOUSNESS.   I am Covetousness, begotten of an old
churl in an old leathern bag; and might I have my wish,
I would desire that this house and all the people in it
were turned to gold, that I might lock you up in my
good chest. O, my sweet gold!

FAUSTUS.   What art thou, the third?

WRATH.   I am Wrath. I had neither father nor mother;
I leapt out of a lion's mouth when I was scarce half an
hour old, and ever since I have run up and down the
world with this case[3] of rapiers, wounding myself when
I had nobody to fight withal. I was born in hell, and
look to it: for some of you shall be my father.

FAUSTUS.   What art thou, the fourth?

ENVY.   I am Envy, begotten of a chimney-sweeper and
an oyster wife.[4] I cannot read, and therefore wish all
books were burned; I am lean with seeing others eat. O,
that there would come a famine through all the world,
that all might die, and I live alone: then thou should'st
see how fat I would be. But must thou sit and I stand?
Come down, with a vengeance![5]

FAUSTUS.   Away, envious rascal! What art thou, the fifth?

GLUTTONY.   Who I, sir? I am Gluttony. My parents are
all dead, and the devil a penny they have left me, but a
bare pension, and that buys me thirty meals a day and
ten bevers:[6] a small trifle to suffice nature. O, I come of
a royal parentage: my grandfather was a gammon of
bacon,[7] my grand-mother a hogshead[8] of claret[9] wine.
My god-fathers were these: Peter Pickleherring[10] and
Martin Martlemas-beef.[11] O, but my godmother she was
a jolly gentlewoman, and well-beloved in every good
town and city: her name was Mistress Margery March-
beer.[12] Now, Faustus, thou hast heard all my progeny,
wilt thou bid me to supper?

FAUSTUS.   No, I'll see thee hanged: thou wilt eat up all
my victuals.

GLUTTONY.   Then the devil choke thee.

FAUSTUS.   Choke thyself, glutton! What art thou, the
sixth?

SLOTH.   I am Sloth. I was begotten on a sunny bank,
where I have lain ever since, and you have done me
great injury to bring me from thence. Let me be carried
thither again by Gluttony and Lechery. I'll not speak
another word for a king's ransom.

FAUSTUS.   What are you, mistress minx,[13] the seventh
and last?

LECHERY.   Who I, sir? I am one that loves an inch of raw
mutton[14] better than an ell[15] of fried stock-fish,[16] and
the first letter of my name begins with Lechery.

LUCIFER.   Away, to hell, to hell.

---

[1]   *Ovid's flea*   The poem being referenced, *Elegia de pulice*, was
written in imitation of Ovid, and wrongly ascribed to him. In it is a
line addressed to the flea: "You go wherever you wish; nothing,
savage, is hidden from you."

[2]   *cloth of arras*   Tapestry fabric of the kind woven at Arras in
Flanders; to use it as a floor covering would be grossly ostentatious.

[3]   *case*   Pair.

[4]   *begotten ... wife*   I.e., filthy and foul-smelling woman.

[5]   *with a vengeance*   With a curse on you.

[6]   *bevers*   Drinks; also light meals or snacks.

[7]   *gammon of bacon*   Bottom piece of a flitch of bacon.

[8]   *hogshead*   Wine-barrel of a standard size, holding (in modern
terms) 225 liters or 63 American gallons—the equivalent of 25 cases
of a dozen bottles of wine.

[9]   *claret*   Light red wine from the Bordeaux region.

[10]   *Pickleherring*   Clown figure associated with carnival festivities and
popular farces.

[11]   *Martlemas-beef*   Martinmas, or St. Martin's Day (November 11),
was the traditional time to slaughter cattle that could not be fed over
the winter, and to commence the production of salt beef; it was
therefore also a time for feasting on "green" or unsalted beef.

[12]   *March-beer*   Strong beer brewed in March.

[13]   *minx*   Hussy, wanton woman.

[14]   *raw mutton*   Metaphor for prostitutes; the expression here takes
on a phallic meaning.

[15]   *ell*   Measure of length (equal in England to some forty-five
inches), commonly contrasted to an inch.

[16]   *stock-fish*   Unsalted dried fish, sometimes abusively associated
with the flaccid male organ.

(*Exeunt the Sins.*)

Now Faustus, how dost thou like this?
FAUSTUS.   O, this feeds my soul.
LUCIFER.   Tut, Faustus, in hell is all manner of delight.
FAUSTUS.   O, might I see hell, and return again, how
180   happy were I then!
LUCIFER.   Thou shalt. I will send for thee at midnight. In
mean time, take this book, peruse it thoroughly, and
thou shalt turn thyself into what shape thou wilt.
FAUSTUS.   Great thanks, mighty Lucifer:
185   This will I keep as chary° as my life.   *carefully*
LUCIFER.   Farewell, Faustus, and think on the devil.
FAUSTUS.   Farewell, great Lucifer. Come, Mephastophilis.

(*Exeunt all.*)

ACT 3, CHORUS.

(*Enter the Chorus [Wagner].*)

WAGNER.   Learned Faustus,
To know the secrets of astronomy
Graven in the book of Jove's high firmament,
Did mount him up to scale Olympus' top,[1]
5   Where sitting in a chariot burning bright,[2]
Drawn by the strength of yoked dragons' necks,
He views the clouds, the planets and the stars,
The tropics, zones, and quarters[3] of the sky,
From the bright circle of the horned moon
10   Even to the height of *primum mobile,*[4]
And whirling round with this circumference
Within the concave compass of the pole,
From east to west his dragons swiftly glide,

---

[1] *to scale Olympus' top*   I.e., to ascend to the dwelling-place of the
gods, on the top of Mount Olympus.

[2] *chariot … bright*   Parodic echo of the vision of the divine chariot-
throne in Ezekiel 1.13–28.

[3] *tropics … quarters*   Tropics of Cancer and Capricorn, the arctic
and antarctic circles and the equator divided the celestial sphere into
five belts or zones; traditional astronomy also quartered the celestial
sphere with two other circles that passed through its north and south
poles: the solstitial colure, which intersects the two tropics at the
solstitial points (those at which the ecliptic meets the tropics); and
the equinoctial colure, which intersects the equator at the equinoc-
tial points (those at which the ecliptic crosses the equator).

[4] *From … mobile*   From the lowest to the highest of the spheres.

And in eight days did bring him home again.
15   Not long he stay'd within his quiet house
To rest his bones after his weary toil,
But new exploits do hale him out again,
And mounted then upon a dragon's back
That with his wings did part the subtle° air,   *rarified*
20   He now is gone to prove cosmography,[5]
That measures coasts and kingdoms of the earth.
And as I guess, will first arrive at Rome
To see the Pope, and manner of his court,
And take some part of holy Peter's[6] feast,
25   The which this day is highly solemniz'd.

(*Exit.*)

ACT 3, SCENE 1

(*Enter Faustus and Mephastophilis.*)

FAUSTUS.   Having now, my good Mephastophilis,
Pass'd with delight the stately town of Trier,[7]
Environ'd round with airy mountain tops,
With walls of flint, and deep entrenched lakes,
5   Not to be won by any conquering prince;
From Paris next, coasting the realm of France,
We saw the river Main fall into Rhine,
Whose banks are set with groves of fruitful vines;
Then up to Naples, rich Campania,[8]
10   Whose buildings, fair and gorgeous to the eye
(The streets are straightforth and pav'd with finest brick),
Quarters the town in four equivalents.
There saw we learned Maro's[9] golden tomb,

---

[5] *to prove cosmography*   To put geography to the test. Cosmography
was sometimes thought of as a science that maps the universe as a
whole, thus incorporating geography and astronomy.

[6] *holy Peter*   St. Peter.

[7] *Trier*   City on the Moselle River, capital of an electoral state of
the Holy Roman Empire, which under the rule of Elector-Arch-
bishop Johann von Schönenburg was subjected during the 1580s and
1590s to a violent wave of witch-hunts.

[8] *Campania*   In ancient usage, the plain surrounding the city of
Capua; since medieval times, Naples has been the principal city of
this region. (In modern Italy the name Campania is applied to a
much larger area.)

[9] *Maro*   Virgil, or Publius Vergilius Maro, died at Naples in 19
BCE. In part because his fourth Eclogue was interpreted as a
prophecy of the coming of Christ, he acquired a reputation during
the medieval period as a necromancer. His supposed (continued)

The way[1] he cut, an English mile in length,
15 Thorough a rock of stone in one night's space.
From thence to Venice, Padua, and the rest,
In midst of which a sumptuous temple stands,
That threats the stars[2] with her aspiring top.
Thus hitherto hath Faustus spent his time.
20 But tell me now, what resting place is this?
Hast thou, as erst° I did command,   first
Conducted me within the walls of Rome?

MEPHASTOPHILIS.   Faustus, I have, and because we will
    not be unprovided,
I have taken up his Holiness' privy chamber[3] for our use.
25 FAUSTUS.   I hope his Holiness will bid us welcome.
MEPHASTOPHILIS.   Tut, 'tis no matter, man, we'll be
    bold with his good cheer.
And now my Faustus, that thou may'st perceive
What Rome containeth to delight thee with,
Know that this city stands upon seven hills
30 That underprop the groundwork of the same;
Just through the midst runs flowing Tiber's stream,
With winding banks that cut it in two parts,
Over the which four stately bridges lean,
That make safe passage to each part of Rome.
35 Upon the bridge call'd Ponte Angelo
Erected is a castle passing strong,[4]
Within those walls such stores of ordnance are,
And double cannons,[5] fram'd of carved brass,
As match the days within one complete year—
40 Besides the gates and high pyramides[6]
Which Julius Caesar brought from Africa.
FAUSTUS.   Now, by the kingdoms of infernal rule,

Of Styx, Acheron, and the fiery lake
Of ever-burning Phlegethon,[7] I swear
45 That I do long to see the monuments
And situation of bright splendent Rome.
Come therefore, let's away.
MEPHASTOPHILIS.   Nay Faustus, stay: I know you'd
    fain see the Pope,
And take some part of° holy Peter's feast,   in
50 Where thou shalt see a troop of bald-pate friars
Whose *summum bonum*[8] is in belly-cheer.
FAUSTUS.   Well, I am content to compass°   contrive
    then some sport,
And by their folly make us merriment.
Then charm me, that I may be invisible,
55 To do what I please
Unseen of any whilst I stay in Rome.

(*Mephastophilis charms him.*)[9]

MEPHASTOPHILIS.   So, Faustus: now
Do what thou wilt, thou shalt not be discern'd.

(*Sound a sennet.*[10] *Enter the Pope and the Cardinal of
Lorraine*[11] *to the banquet, with Friars attending.*)

POPE.   My lord of Lorraine, will't please you draw near?
60 FAUSTUS.   Fall to, and the devil choke you and you
    spare.[12]

---

tomb stands on the promontory of Posilipo on the Bay of Naples, at
the Naples end of a tunnel, nearly half a mile in length, which cuts
through the promontory—and which, as Petrarch wrote, "the insipid
masses conclude was made by Virgil with magical incantations."

[1] *way*   Road. The tunnel is in fact some seven yards wide.

[2] *sumptuous ... stars*   Saint Mark's in Venice. The "aspiring top"
would have to be that of the campanile, which stands at some
distance from the church.

[3] *privy chamber*   Bedchamber.

[4] *castle ... strong*   Papal fortress of Castel San Angelo.

[5] *double cannons*   Cannons of very large caliber.

[6] *pyramides*   Obelisk, in this case the one brought to Rome from
Egypt by the emperor Caligula (not Julius Caesar), and moved to its
present site in the Piazza San Pietro in 1586. The word is singular, not
plural.

---

[7] *Styx, Acheron ... Phlegethon*   Three of the four rivers of Hades, the
Greek underworld.

[8] *summum bonum*   Latin: highest good.

[9] *Mephastophilis charms him*   According to Henslowe's *Diary* the
Admiral's Men owned a "robe for to go invisible," a prop which may
have been used here.

[10] *sennet*   Flourish on the trumpet to announce a ceremonial
entrance.

[11] *Cardinal of Lorraine*   This position was held during the sixteenth
century by several members of the powerful Guise family: Jean de
Guise (1498–1550); Charles de Guise (1524–74), who helped
foment the wars of religion that convulsed France for decades after
1562 and acquired a reputation for dissimulation and cruelty; and
Louis de Guise (1555–88), who along with his brother, Henri, third
Duc de Guise (1550–88), was assassinated by King Henri III. As
leaders of the pro-Spanish and ultra-Catholic Ligue, and thus major
figures in the Spanish-led campaign against Protestantism, Louis and
Henri de Guise were feared and detested in England.

[12] *and you spare*   If you eat sparingly.

POPE.   How now, who's that which spake? Friars, look about!

FRIAR.   Here's nobody, if it like[1] your Holiness.

POPE.   My lord, here is a dainty dish was sent me from the Bishop of Milan.

65 FAUSTUS.   I thank you, sir.

(*Snatch it.*)

POPE.   How now, who's that which snatched the meat from me? Will no man look? My lord, this dish was sent me from the Cardinal of Florence.

FAUSTUS.   You say true, I'll ha' it.

(*Snatch it.*)

70 POPE.   What, again! My lord, I'll drink to your grace.

FAUSTUS.   I'll pledge your grace.

(*Snatch it.*)

LORRAINE.   My lord, it may be some ghost newly crept out of purgatory come to beg a pardon of your Holiness.

POPE.   It may be so. Friars, prepare a dirge[2] to lay the

75 fury of this ghost. Once again, my lord, fall to. (*The Pope crosses himself.*[3])

FAUSTUS.   What, are you crossing your self? Well, use that trick no more, I would advise you.

(*Cross again.*)

FAUSTUS.   Well, there's the second time. Aware the

80 third, I give you fair warning.

(*Cross again, and Faustus hits him a box of the ear, and they all run away.*)

Come on, Mephastophilis, what shall we do?

MEPHASTOPHILIS.   Nay, I know not; we shall be cursed with bell, book and candle.[4]

FAUSTUS.   How? Bell, book and candle, candle, book and bell,

85 Forward and backward, to curse Faustus to hell.

Anon you shall hear a hog grunt, a calf bleat, and an ass bray,

Because it is Saint Peter's holy day!

(*Enter all the Friars to sing the dirge.*)

FRIAR.   Come brethren, let's about our business with good devotion.

(*They sing this:*)

Cursed be he that stole away his Holiness' meat from the table.

90   *Maledicat dominus!*[5]

Cursed be he that struck his Holiness a blow on the face.

   Maledicat dominus!

Cursed be he that took Friar Sandelo a blow on the pate.

   Maledicat dominus!

95 *Cursed be he that disturbeth our holy dirge.*

   Maledicat dominus!

Cursed be he that took away his Holiness' wine.

Maledicat dominus! Et omnes sancti![6] *Amen.*

(*Faustus and Mephastophilis beat the Friars and fling fireworks among them, and so exeunt.*)

ACT 3, SCENE 2

(*Enter Robin and Rafe with a silver goblet.*)

ROBIN.   Come Rafe, did I not tell thee we were for ever made by this Doctor Faustus' book? *Ecce signum,*[7] here's

---

[1] *like* Please.

[2] *dirge* Originally "dirige," the first word of the Latin antiphon at matins in the Office of the Dead ("Dirige, Domine, Deus meus, in conspectu tuo viam meum": "Direct, O Lord, my God, my way in thy sight").

[3] *crosses himself* Makes the sign of the cross, the preliminary to Roman Catholic prayer.

[4] *bell, book and candle* At the end of the ritual of excommunication, which is performed to debar a member of the Church from the sacraments, the bell is tolled, the book closed, and the candle extinguished. That ritual is confused here with the office of exorcism, performed to banish evil spirits.

[5] *Maledicat dominus* Latin: May the Lord curse him.

[6] *Et omnes sancti!* Latin: And (may) all the saints (curse him).

[7] *Ecce signum* Latin: Behold the sign.

a simple purchase for horse-keepers! Our horses shall eat no hay as long as this lasts.

(*Enter the Vintner.*)

5 RAFE. But Robin, here comes the Vintner.
ROBIN. Hush, I'll gull[1] him supernaturally. Drawer,[2] I hope all is paid. God be with you; come Rafe.
VINTNER. Soft,[3] sir; a word with you. I must yet have a goblet paid from you ere you go.
10 ROBIN. I a goblet? Rafe, I a goblet? I scorn you, and you are but a etc.[4] I a goblet? Search me!
VINTNER. I mean so, sir, with your favor.

(*Searches Robin.*)

ROBIN. How say you now?
VINTNER. I must say somewhat to your fellow. You, sir.
15 RAFE. Me, sir? Me, sir! Search your fill! Now, sir, you may be ashamed to burden honest men with a matter of truth.
VINTNER. Well, t'one of you hath this goblet about you.
ROBIN. You lie, drawer, 'tis afore me. Sirrah you, I'll
20 teach ye to impeach[5] honest men: stand by, I'll scour you for a goblet. Stand aside, you had best, I charge you in the name of Belzebub! Look to the goblet, Rafe.[6]
VINTNER. What mean you, sirrah?
ROBIN. I'll tell you what I mean.

(*He reads.*)

25 *Sanctabulorum periphrasticon*—Nay, I'll tickle you, Vintner! Look to the goblet, Rafe. *Polypragmos Belseborams framanto pacostiphos tostu Mephastophilis, etc.*[7]

(*Enter Mephastophilis; sets squibs[8] at their backs; they run about.*)

VINTNER. *O nomine Domine!* What mean'st thou, Robin? Thou hast no goblet!
30 RAFE. *Peccatum peccatorum!* Here's thy goblet, good Vintner!
ROBIN. *Misericordia pro nobis!*[9] What shall I do? Good devil, forgive me now, and I'll never rob thy library more!
35 MEPHASTOPHILIS. Monarch of hell, under whose black survey
Great potentates do kneel with awful fear,
Upon whose altars thousand souls do lie,
How am I vexed with these villains' charms!
From Constantinople am I hither come
40 Only for pleasure of these damned slaves.
ROBIN. How, from Constantinople? You have had a great journey, will you take sixpence in your purse to pay for your supper, and be gone?
MEPHASTOPHILIS. Well villains, for your presumption,
45 I transform thee into an ape, and thee into a dog, and so be gone!

(*Exit.*)

ROBIN. How, into an ape? That's brave, I'll have fine sport with the boys; I'll get nuts and apples enow.[10]
RAFE. And I must be a dog.
50 ROBIN. I'faith, thy head will never be out of the pottage pot.

(*Exeunt.*)

---

[1] *gull* Trick.

[2] *Drawer* An insult: Robin pretends to mistake the Vintner (or innkeeper) for his employee, the tapster or drawer who serves the customers.

[3] *Soft* Softly, slowly; here carrying an imperative force, as in "not so fast!"

[4] *etc.* Substitute for a scatological or obscene expression.

[5] *impeach* Accuse.

[6] *Look … Rafe* Robin and Rafe are apparently passing the goblet back and forth between them.

[7] *Sanctabulorum … Mephastophilis, etc.* Robin's incantation is gibberish, though some of it comes close to deviating into sense. The Greek *periphrastikos* means "circumlocutory." In Greek *polypragmosyne* means "curiosity" or "meddlesomeness," and a *polypragmon* is a "busybody." The first four words of the invocation might then be translated as "Busy-body Belseborams … of beating-around-the-bush holy-molydoms!"

[8] *squibs* Fireworks.

[9] *O … nobis* Garbled scraps of liturgical Latin.

[10] *enow* Enough.

ACT 4, CHORUS

(*Enter Chorus.*)

CHORUS.   When Faustus had with pleasure ta'en the view
 Of rarest things and royal courts of kings,
 He stay'd his course, and so returned home,
 Where such as bear his absence but with grief,
5 I mean his friends and nearest companions,
 Did gratulate his safety with kind words,
 And in their conference of what befell
 Touching his journey through the world and air
 They put forth questions of astrology,
10 Which Faustus answer'd with such learned skill
 As[1] they admir'd and wonder'd at his wit.
 Now is his fame spread forth in every land;
 Amongst the rest of Emperor is one,
 Carolus the Fifth,[2] at whose palace now
15 Faustus is feasted 'mongst his noblemen.
 What there he did in trial of his art
 I leave untold, your eyes shall see perform'd.

(*Exit.*)

ACT 4, SCENE 1

(*Enter Emperor, Faustus, and a Knight, with attendants.*)

EMPEROR.   Master Doctor Faustus, I have heard strange
report of thy knowledge in the black art, how that none
in my empire, nor in the whole world, can compare
with thee for the rare[3] effects of magic: they say thou
5 hast a familiar spirit, by whom thou canst accomplish
what thou list.[4] This therefore is my request: that thou
let me see some proof of thy skill, that mine eyes may be
witnesses to confirm what mine ears have heard re-
ported; and here I swear to thee, by the honor of mine
10 imperial crown, that whatever thou doest, thou shalt be

no ways prejudiced or endamaged.[5]

KNIGHT.   (*Aside.*) I'faith, he looks much like a conjurer.

FAUSTUS.   My gracious sovereign, though I must confess
myself far inferior to the report men have published,
15 and nothing answerable[6] to the honor of your imperial
Majesty, yet for that[7] love and duty binds me thereunto,
I am content to do whatsoever your Majesty shall
command me.

EMPEROR.   Then Doctor Faustus, mark what I shall say.
20 As I was sometime solitary set
 Within my closet,[8] sundry thoughts arose
 About the honor of mine ancestors:
 How they had won by prowess such exploits,
 Got riches, subdu'd so many kingdoms,
25 As we that do succeed,[9] or they that shall
 Hereafter possess our throne shall,
 I fear me, never attain to that degree
 Of high renown and great authority;
 Amongst which kings is Alexander the Great,
30 Chief spectacle of the world's pre-eminence,[10]
 The bright shining of whose glorious acts
 Lightens the world with his reflecting beams,
 As when I hear but motion° made of him   *mention*
 It grieves my soul I never saw the man.
35 If therefore thou, by cunning of thine art,
 Canst raise this man from hollow vaults below
 Where lies entomb'd this famous conqueror,
 And bring with him his beauteous paramour,[11]
 Both in their right shapes, gesture, and attire
40 They us'd to wear during their time of life,
 Thou shalt both satisfy my just desire
 And give me cause to praise thee whilst I live.

FAUSTUS.   My gracious lord, I am ready to accomplish
your request, so far forth as by art and power of my
45 spirit I am able to perform.

KNIGHT.   (*Aside.*) I'faith that's just nothing at all.

FAUSTUS.   But if it like your Grace, it is not in my ability
to present before your eyes the true substantial bodies of

---

[1] *As* That.

[2] *Carolus the Fifth* Charles V (1500–58), King of Spain and Holy Roman Emperor from 1518 and 1519 respectively until his abdication in 1555. The historical Doctor Faustus never made an appearance at the imperial court. Contemporary *magi*, however, had connections with the courts of both the emperor Maximilian (Charles V's grandfather and immediate predecessor) and Charles V.

[3] *rare* Remarkable, extraordinary.

[4] *what thou list* Whatever you wish.

---

[5] *endamaged* Harmed.

[6] *nothing answerable* Quite unequal.

[7] *for that* Because.

[8] *closet* Study, inner chamber.

[9] *succeed* Follow in dynastic succession.

[10] *pre-eminence* Pre-eminent people.

[11] *paramour* Mistress, consort (i.e., Roxane of Oxyartes).

those two deceased princes, which long since are con-
50 sumed to dust.

KNIGHT.   (*Aside.*) Ay, marry[1] Master Doctor, now there's
a sign of grace in you when you will confess the truth.

FAUSTUS.   But such spirits as can lively resemble Alexan-
der and his paramour shall appear before your Grace, in
55 that manner that they best lived in, in their most
flourishing estate, which I doubt not shall sufficiently
content your imperial Majesty.

EMPEROR. Go to,[2] Master Doctor, let me see them
presently.[3]

60 KNIGHT. Do you hear, Master Doctor? You bring
Alexander and his paramour before the Emperor?

FAUSTUS. How then, sir?

KNIGHT. I'faith, that's as true as Diana turned me to a
stag.

65 FAUSTUS. No sir, but when Actaeon[4] died, he left the
horns for you. Mephastophilis, be gone.

(*Exit Mephastophilis.*)

KNIGHT.   Nay, and[5] you go to conjuring, I'll be gone.

(*Exit Knight.*)

FAUSTUS. I'll meet with[6] you anon for interrupting me
so. Here they are, my gracious lord.

(*Enter Mephastophilis with Alexander and his paramour.*)

70 EMPEROR. Master Doctor, I heard this lady while she
lived had a wart or mole in her neck. How shall I know
whether it be so or no?

FAUSTUS. Your highness may boldly go and see.

(*Emperor does so; then spirits exeunt.*)

---

[1] *marry* Here, expression used to give emphasis to a statement.

[2] *Go to* Normally an expression of incredulity, it appears here to
express mild demurral, or perhaps encouragement, with the same
range of meanings as "Come, come."

[3] *presently* At once.

[4] *Diana ... Actaeon* Actaeon, a hunter, witnessed the goddess
Diana and her nymphs bathing; the goddess transformed him into
a stag and he was torn to pieces by his own dogs.

[5] *and* If.

[6] *meet with* Get even with.

EMPEROR. Sure these are no spirits, but the true sub-
75 stantial bodies of these two deceased princes.[7]

FAUSTUS. Will't please your highness now to send for
the knight that was so pleasant with me here of late?

EMPEROR. One of you call him forth.

(*Enter the Knight with a pair of horns on his head.*)

How now, sir knight? Why, I had thought thou had'st
80 been a bachelor, but now I see thou hast a wife, that not
only gives thee horns but makes thee wear them. Feel on
thy head!

KNIGHT.   Thou damned wretch and execrable dog,
Bred in the concave of some monstrous rock,
85 How dar'st thou thus abuse a gentleman?
Villain, I say, undo what thou hast done!

FAUSTUS. O not so fast, sir; there's no haste but good.[8]
Are you remembered how you crossed me in my confer-
ence with the Emperor? I think I have met with you for
90 it.

EMPEROR. Good Master Doctor, at my entreaty release
him. He hath done penance sufficient.

FAUSTUS. My gracious lord, not so much for the injury[9]
he offered me here in your presence, as to delight you
95 with some mirth, hath Faustus worthily requited this
injurious knight; which being all I desire, I am content
to release him of his horns. And sir knight, hereafter
speak well of scholars. Mephastophilis, transform him
straight.[10] Now, my good lord, having done my duty, I
100 humbly take my leave.

EMPEROR. Farewell, Master Doctor; yet ere you go,
expect from me a bounteous reward.

(*Exeunt Emperor, Knight, and attendants.*)

ACT 4, SCENE 2

FAUSTUS. Now Mephastophilis, the restless course
That time doth run with calm and silent foot,
Shortening my days and thread of vital life,

---

[7] *princes* Used in this period to refer, not to a male ruler, but any
ruler.

[8] *there's ... good* Common proverb: "No haste but good (speed)."

[9] *injury* Insult.

[10] *straight* At once.

Calls for the payment of my latest years.

5   Therefore, sweet Mephastophilis,

Let us make haste to Wittenberg.

MEPHASTOPHILIS.   What, will you go on horseback, or on foot?

FAUSTUS.   Nay, till I am past this fair and pleasant green I'll walk on foot.

(*Enter a Horse-courser.*)[1]

10 HORSE-COURSER.   I have been all this day seeking one Master Fustian; mass,[2] see where he is. God save you, Master Doctor.

FAUSTUS.   What, horse-courser, you are well met.

HORSE-COURSER.   Do you hear, sir? I have brought you

15 forty dollars for your horse.

FAUSTUS.   I cannot sell him. If thou lik'st him for fifty, take him.

HORSE-COURSER.   Alas sir, I have no more. I pray you, speak for me.

20 MEPHASTOPHILIS.   I pray you, let him have him. He is an honest fellow, and he has a great charge,[3] neither wife nor child.

FAUSTUS.   Well, come, give me your money. My boy will deliver him to you. But I must tell you one thing before

25 you have him: ride him not into the water at any hand.[4]

HORSE-COURSER.   Why sir, will he not drink of all waters?

FAUSTUS.   O yes, he will drink of all waters, but ride him not into the water. Ride him over hedge or ditch, or

30 where thou wilt, but not into the water.

HORSE-COURSER.   Well, sir, now am I a made man for ever! I'll not leave[5] my horse for forty. If he had but the quality of hey ding ding, hey ding ding, I'd make a brave living on him: he has a buttock so slick as an eel.[6]

35 Well, God-bye[7] sir, your boy will deliver him me. But hark ye sir, if my horse be sick or ill at ease, if I bring his water[8] to you, you'll tell me what it is?

FAUSTUS.   Away, you villain! What, dost thou think I am a horse-doctor?

(*Exit Horse-courser.*)

40 What art thou, Faustus, but a man condemn'd to die? Thy fatal time[9] doth draw to final end; Despair doth drive distrust into my thoughts. Confound these passions with a quiet sleep: Tush, Christ did call the thief upon the cross.[10]

45 Then rest thee, Faustus, quiet in conceit.

(*Sleeps in his chair. Enter Horse-courser all wet, crying.*)

HORSE-COURSER.   Alas, alas, Doctor Fustian, quotha? Mass, Doctor Lopus[11] was never such a doctor: has given me a purgation,[12] has purged me of forty dollars, I shall never see them more. But yet like an ass as I was, I

50 would not be ruled by him, for he bade me I should ride him into no water. Now I, thinking my horse had some rare quality that he would not have had me know of, I like a venturous youth rid him into the deep pond at the town's end. I was no sooner in the middle of the pond,

55 but my horse vanished away, and I sat upon a bottle[13] of hay, never so near drowning in my life! But I'll seek out my doctor, and have my forty dollars again, or I'll make

---

[1] *Horse-courser* Horse dealer.

[2] *Fustian* Clownish deformation of "Faustus"; bombast, nonsense; *mass* Contraction of "By the Mass."

[3] *charge* Burden (of family responsibilities).

[4] *at any hand* Under any circumstances.

[5] *leave* Sell.

[6] *hey ding ding ... eel* "Hey ding-a-ding" is a common refrain in popular songs. The phrase has sexual overtones, and "buttock so slick as an eel" implies sexual potency; thus, the "brave living" that the horse-courser anticipates will presumably come from stud fees.

[7] *God-bye* Contraction of "God be with you."

[8] *water* Urine.

[9] *fatal time* Time allotted by fate.

[10] *the thief ... cross* See Luke 23.43.

[11] *Doctor Lopus* Doctor Roderigo Lopez, a Portuguese *marrano*, or Christianized Jew, and personal physician to Queen Elizabeth. Lopez incurred the enmity of the Earl of Essex, who in January 1594 accused him of high treason; he was tried (and convicted) on 28 February on charges that included attempting to poison the queen, and was executed on 7 June—more than a year after Marlowe's death. Although Lopez was well-known even before his appointment as the queen's physician in 1586 (he had previously been household physician to the Earl of Leicester), the past-tense allusion to him suggests that in its present form this scene must have been written after Marlowe's death.

[12] *purgation* Emetic.

[13] *bottle* From the French "botte," meaning bundle.

it dearest[1] horse. O, yonder is his snipper-snapper.[2] Do you hear? you, hey-pass,[3] where's your master?

60 MEPHASTOPHILIS.   Why sir, what would you? You cannot speak with him.

HORSE-COURSER.   But I will speak with him.

MEPHASTOPHILIS.   Why, he's fast asleep; come some other time.

65 HORSE-COURSER.   I'll speak with him now, or I'll break his glass windows[4] about his ears.

MEPHASTOPHILIS.   I tell thee, he hath not slept this eight nights.

HORSE-COURSER.   And he have not slept this eight

70 weeks I'll speak with him.

MEPHASTOPHILIS.   See where he is, fast asleep.

HORSE-COURSER.   Ay, this is he. God save ye Master Doctor! Master Doctor, Master Doctor Fustian, forty dollars, forty dollars for a bottle of hay!

75 MEPHASTOPHILIS.   Why, thou seest he hears thee not.

HORSE-COURSER.   So ho, ho! So ho, ho![5] (*Hallow in his ear.*) No, will you not wake? I'll make you wake ere I go!

(*Pull him by the leg, and pull it away.*)

Alas, I am undone! What shall I do?

80 FAUSTUS.   O my leg, my leg! Help, Mephastophilis! Call the officers, my leg, my leg!

MEPHASTOPHILIS.   Come villain, to the constable.

HORSE-COURSER.   O Lord, sir: let me go, and I'll give you forty dollars more.

85 MEPHASTOPHILIS.   Where be they?

HORSE-COURSER.   I have none about me; come to my ostry,[6] and I'll give them you.

MEPHASTOPHILIS.   Be gone, quickly.

(*Horse-courser runs away.*)

FAUSTUS.   What, is he gone? Farewell he, Faustus has his

90 leg again, and the horse-courser, I take it, a bottle of hay

---

[1] *dearest* Most expensive. If the horse-courser can't have his money back, he'll take revenge.

[2] *snipper-snapper* Conceited young fellow, smart-aleck.

[3] *hey-pass* Expression used by fairground conjurors or jugglers.

[4] *glass windows* Spectacles.

[5] *So ho, ho* Huntsman's cry.

[6] *ostry* Hostelry, inn.

for his labor. Well, this trick shall cost him forty dollars more.

(*Enter Wagner.*)

How now, Wagner, what's the news with thee?

WAGNER.   Sir, the Duke of Vanholt doth earnestly

95 entreat your company.

FAUSTUS.   The Duke of Vanholt! An honorable gentleman, to whom I must be no niggard[7] of my cunning. Come Mephastophilis, let's away to him.

(*Exeunt.*)

ACT 4, SCENE 3

(*Enter to them the Duke, and the Duchess; the Duke speaks.*)

DUKE.   Believe me, Master Doctor, this merriment hath much pleased me.

FAUSTUS.   My gracious lord, I am glad it contents you so well. But it may be, madam, you take no delight in this.

5 I have heard that great-bellied[8] women do long for some dainties or other: what is it, madam? Tell me, and you shall have it.

DUCHESS.   Thanks, good Master Doctor, and for I see your courteous intent to pleasure me, I will not hide

10 from you the thing my heart desires; and were it now summer, as it is January, and the dead time of winter, I would desire no better meat[9] than a dish of ripe grapes.

FAUSTUS.   Alas, madam, that's nothing. Mephastophilis, be gone.

(*Exit Mephastophilis.*)

15 Were it a greater thing than this, so it would content you, you should have it.

(*Enter Mephastophilis with the grapes.*)

Here they be, madam, will't please you to taste on them?

DUKE. Believe me, Master Doctor, this makes me

20 wonder above the rest, that being in the dead time of

---

[7] *niggard* Parsimonious person, one who shares only grudgingly.

[8] *great-bellied* Pregnant.

[9] *meat* Food.

winter, and in the month of January, how you should come by these grapes.

FAUSTUS. If it like your Grace, the year is divided into two circles over the whole world, that when it is here
25   winter with us, in the contrary circle it is summer with them, as in India, Saba, and farther countries in the east;[1] and by means of a swift spirit that I have, I had them brought hither, as ye see. How do you like them, madam, be they good?

30   DUCHESS. Believe me, Master Doctor, they be the best grapes that e'er I tasted in my life before.

FAUSTUS. I am glad they content you so, madam.

DUKE. Come, madam, let us in, where you must well reward this learned man for the kindness he hath
35   showed to you.

DUCHESS. And so I will, my lord, and whilst I live rest beholden for this courtesy.

FAUSTUS. I humbly thank your Grace.

DUKE. Come Master Doctor, follow us, and receive your
40   reward.

(*Exeunt.*)

ACT 5, SCENE 1

(*Enter Wagner alone.*)

WAGNER. I think my master means to die shortly,
For he hath given to me all his goods;
And yet methinkes[2] if that death were near
He would not banquet and carouse and swill
5   Amongst the students, as even now he doth,
Who are at supper with such belly-cheer
As Wagner ne'er beheld in all his life.
See where they come: belike the feast is ended.

(*Exit. Enter Faustus with two or three scholars.*)

FIRST SCHOLAR. Master Doctor Faustus, since our
10   conference about fair ladies, which was the beautiful'st in all the world, we have determined with[3] our selves

that Helen of Greece was the admirablest lady that ever lived. Therefore, Master Doctor, if you will do us so much favor as to let us see that peerless dame of Greece,
15   whom all the world admires for majesty, we should think ourselves much beholding unto you.

FAUSTUS. Gentlemen,
For that[4] I know your friendship is unfeign'd
(And Faustus' custom is not to deny
20   The just requests of those that wish him well),
You shall behold that peerless dame of Greece
No otherways for pomp and majesty
Than when Sir Paris cross'd the seas with her
And brought the spoils to rich Dardania.[5]
25   Be silent then, for danger is in words.

(*Music sounds, and Helen passeth over the stage.*)

SECOND SCHOLAR. Too simple is my wit to tell her praise,
Whom all the world admires for majesty.

THIRD SCHOLAR. No marvel though the angry Greeks pursued[6]
With ten years' war the rape° of such a queen,   abduction
30   Whose heavenly beauty passeth all compare.

FIRST SCHOLAR. Since we have seen the pride of nature's works,
And only paragon of excellence,

(*Enter an old man.*)

Let us depart, and for this glorious deed
Happy and blest be Faustus evermore.
35   FAUSTUS. Gentlemen, farewell, the same I wish to you.

(*Exeunt scholars.*)

OLD MAN. Ah, Doctor Faustus, that I might prevail
To guide thy steps unto the way of life,
By which sweet path thy may'st attain the goal
That shall conduct thee to celestial rest.
40   Break heart, drop blood, and mingle it with tears,
Tears falling from repentant heaviness

---

[1] *two circles ... east* The two "circles" should of course be the northern and southern hemispheres. Saba is the land of the Queen of Sheba, now Yemen.

[2] *methinkes* Modernized spelling would upset the rhythm of this line.

[3] *determined with* Settled among.

[4] *For that* Because.

[5] *Dardania* Troy, referred to here by the name of the founder of the Trojan dynasty, Dardanus.

[6] *pursued* Sought to avenge.

Of thy most vile and loathsome filthiness,
The stench whereof corrupts the inward soul
With such flagitious[1] crimes of heinous sins
45 As no commiseration may expel
But mercy, Faustus, of thy Saviour sweet,
Whose blood alone must wash away thy guilt.[2]
FAUSTUS.   Where art thou, Faustus?[3] wretch, what hast
     thou done?
Damn'd art thou, Faustus, damn'd, despair and die!
50 Hell claims his right, and with a roaring voice
Says, "Faustus, come, thine hour is almost come!"

(Enter Mephastophilis, who gives him a dagger.)

And Faustus now will come to do thee right.
OLD MAN.   Ah stay, good Faustus, stay thy desperate steps:
I see an angel hovers o'er thy head,
55 And with a vial full of precious grace[4]
Offers to pour the same into thy soul:
Then call for mercy and avoid despair.
FAUSTUS.   Ah my sweet friend, I feel thy words
To comfort my distressed soul.
60 Leave me awhile to ponder on my sins.
OLD MAN.   I go, sweet Faustus, but with heavy cheer,
Fearing the ruin of thy hopeless soul.

     (Exit.)

FAUSTUS.   Accursed Faustus, where is mercy now?
I do repent, and yet I do despair:
65 Hell strives with grace for conquest in my breast;
What shall I do to shun the snares of death?
MEPHASTOPHILIS.   Thou traitor, Faustus, I arrest thy soul
For disobedience to my sovereign lord.
Revolt,[5] or I'll in piece-meal tear thy flesh!

---

[1] *flagitious* Extremely wicked, infamous.

[2] *no … guilt* Cf. Revelation 1.5: "Jesus Christ … loved us, and washed us from our sins in his own blood." *The Prayer-Book of Queen Elizabeth* (1559) specifies that if a person in "extremity of sickness … do truly repent him of his sins, and steadfastly believe that Jesus Christ … shed his blood for his redemption" (135), this is the equivalent of taking communion.

[3] *Where … Faustus?* Cf. Genesis 3.9: "The Lord God called to the man, and said unto him, Where art thou?"

[4] *vial … grace* The old man here individualizes an image from Revelation 5.8, in which elders worshiping before the throne of God carry "golden vials full of odors, which are the prayers of saints."

[5] *Revolt* Reverse your course of action.

70 FAUSTUS.   I do repent I e'er offended him.
Sweet Mephastophilis, entreat thy lord
To pardon my unjust presumption,
And with my blood again I will confirm
My former vow I made to Lucifer.
75 MEPHASTOPHILIS.   Do it then quickly, with unfeigned
     heart,
Lest greater danger do attend thy drift.[6]
FAUSTUS.   Torment, sweet friend, that base and
     crooked age
That durst dissuade me from thy Lucifer,
With greatest torments that our hell affords.
80 MEPHASTOPHILIS.   His faith is great, I cannot touch his
     soul.
But what I may afflict his body with
I will attempt, which is but little worth.
FAUSTUS.   One thing, good servant, let me crave of thee
To glut the longing of my heart's desire:
85 That I might have unto° my paramour   *as*
That heavenly Helen which I saw of late,
Whose sweet embracings may extinguish clean
These thoughts that do dissuade me from my vow,
And keep mine oath I made to Lucifer.
90 MEPHASTOPHILIS.   Faustus, this, or what else thou
     shalt desire
Shall be perform'd in the twinkling of an eye.

(Enter Helen.)

FAUSTUS.   Was this the face that launch'd a thousand ships
And burnt the topless° towers of Ilium?°   *soaring / Troy*
Sweet Helen, make me immortal with a kiss;
95 Her lips suck forth my soul, see where it flies!
Come Helen, come, give me my soul again;
Here will I dwell, for heaven be in these lips,
And all is dross that is not Helena.

(Enter old man.)

I will be Paris, and for love of thee
100 Instead of Troy shall Wittenberg be sack'd,
And I will combat with weak Menelaus[7]

---

[6] *drift* Conscious or unconscious tendency or aim.

[7] *weak Menelaus* Book 3 of Homer's *Iliad* recounts the duel between Alexandros or Paris and Menelaus. Paris challenged all the best of the Achaeans to single combat, but recoiled in fear from Menelaus. Having agreed that Helen and her possessions should go to the victor, Paris was defeated, but saved from   [continued …]

And wear thy colours on my plumed crest;
Yea, I will wound Achilles in the heel
And then return to Helen for a kiss.
105 O, thou art fairer than the evening air
Clad in the beauty of a thousand stars;
Brighter art thou than flaming Jupiter
When he appear'd to hapless Semele,[1]
More lovely than the monarch of the sky
110 In wanton Arethusa's[2] azur'd arms,
And none but thou shalt be my paramour.

(*Exeunt.*)

OLD MAN. Accursed Faustus, miserable man,
That from thy soul exclud'st the grace of heaven
And fliest the throne of his tribunal seat!

(*Enter the devils.*)

115 Satan begins to sift me[3] with his pride;
As in this furnace God shall try my faith,
My faith, vile hell, shall triumph over thee!
Ambitious fiends, see how the heaven smiles
At your repulse, and laughs your state to scorn:
120 Hence, hell, for hence I fly unto my God.

(*Exeunt.*)

ACT 5, SCENE 2

(*Enter Faustus with the scholars.*)

FAUSTUS. Ah, gentlemen!
FIRST SCHOLAR. What ails Faustus?
FAUSTUS. Ah, my sweet chamber-fellow, had I lived
with thee, then had I lived still, but now I die eternally.
5 Look, comes he not, comes he not?

---

death by Aphrodite, who carried him in a mist into his own
bedchamber. There, although shamed in Helen's eyes as in everyone
else's, he promptly took her to bed.

[1] *hapless Semele* One of Jupiter's human mistresses, she was
persuaded by Juno to ask him to come to her in the same form in
which he embraced Juno in heaven, and was consumed by fire.

[2] *Arethusa* Nymph who, bathing in the river Alpheus, aroused the
river-god's lust; fleeing from him, she was transformed into a
fountain. No classical myth links her with Jupiter or the sun-god.

[3] *sift me* Cf. Christ's words to Peter at the last supper: "Simon,
Simon, behold, Satan hath desired to have you, and he may sift you
as wheat" (Luke 22.31).

SECOND SCHOLAR. What means Faustus?
THIRD SCHOLAR. Belike he is grown into some sickness,
by being over-solitary.
FIRST SCHOLAR. If it be so, we'll have physicians to cure
10 him. 'Tis but a surfeit,[4] never fear, man.
FAUSTUS. A surfeit of deadly sin, that hath damned both
body and soul.
SECOND SCHOLAR. Yet Faustus, look up to heaven;
remember, God's mercies are infinite.
15 FAUSTUS. But Faustus' offence can ne'er be pardoned:
the serpent that tempted Eve may be saved, but not
Faustus. Ah gentlemen, hear me with patience, and
tremble not at my speeches. Though my heart pants and
quivers to remember that I have been a student here
20 these thirty years, O would I had never seen Wittenberg,
never read book: and what wonders I have done, all
Germany can witness, yea all the world, for which
Faustus hath lost both Germany and the world, yea
heaven itself, heaven the seat of God, the throne of the
25 blessed, the kingdom of joy, and must remain in hell for
ever—hell, ah, hell, for ever! Sweet friends, what shall
become of Faustus, being in hell for ever?
THIRD SCHOLAR. Yet Faustus, call on God.
FAUSTUS. On God, whom Faustus hath abjured? on
30 God, whom Faustus hath blasphemed? Ah my God, I
would weep, but the devil draws in my tears. Gush forth
blood instead of tears, yea life and soul! Oh, he stays my
tongue; I would lift up my hands, but see, they hold
them, they hold them!
35 ALL. Who, Faustus?
FAUSTUS. Lucifer and Mephastophilis. Ah, gentlemen,
I gave them my soul for my cunning.[5]
ALL. God forbid!
FAUSTUS. God forbade it indeed, but Faustus hath done
40 it: for the vain pleasure of four and twenty years hath
Faustus lost eternal joy and felicity. I writ them a bill
with mine own blood, the date is expired, the time will
come, and he will fetch me!
FIRST SCHOLAR. Why did not Faustus tell of this before,
45 that divines might have prayed for thee?
FAUSTUS. Oft have I thought to have done so, but the
devil threatened to tear me in pieces if I named God, to
fetch both body and soul if I once gave ear to divinity,

---

[4] *surfeit* Excessive indulgence in food or drink, and the resulting
disorder of the system.

[5] *cunning* Knowledge.

and now 'tis too late: gentlemen, away, lest you perish
50   with me.

SECOND SCHOLAR.   O what may we do to save Faustus?

FAUSTUS.   Talk not of me, but save yourselves, and
depart.

THIRD SCHOLAR.   God will strengthen me, I will stay
55   with Faustus.

FIRST SCHOLAR.   Tempt not God, sweet friend, but let
us into the next room, and there pray for him.

FAUSTUS.   Ah, pray for me, pray for me; and what noise
soever[1] ye hear, come not unto me, for nothing can
60   rescue me.

SECOND SCHOLAR.   Pray thou, and we will pray that
God may have mercy upon thee.

FAUSTUS.   Gentlemen, farewell. If I live till morning, I'll
visit you; if not, Faustus is gone to hell.

65   ALL.   Faustus, farewell.

(*Exeunt scholars. The clock strikes eleven.*)

FAUSTUS.   Ah Faustus,
Now hast thou but one bare hour to live,
And then thou must be damn'd perpetually.
Stand still, you ever-moving spheres of heaven.
70   That time may cease, and midnight never come!
Fair nature's eye, rise, rise again, and make
Perpetual day, or let this hour be but a year,
A month, a week, a natural day,
That Faustus may repent, and save his soul.
75   *O lente lente currite noctis equi!*[2]
The stars move still, time runs, the clock will strike,
The devil will come, and Faustus must be damn'd.
O, I'll leap up to my God: who pulls me down?
See, see where Christ's blood streams in the firmament:
80   One drop would save my soul, half a drop! Ah, my Christ,
Ah rend not my heart for the naming of my Christ,[3]
Yet I will call on him, oh spare me Lucifer!
Where is it now? 'tis gone,
And see where God stretcheth out his arm
85   And bends his ireful brows!

Mountains and hills, come, come, and fall on me
And hide me from the heavy wrath of God.[4]
No, no?
Then will I headlong run into the earth.
90   Earth, gape! O no, it will not harbor me.
You stars that reign'd at my nativity,
Whose influence hath allotted death and hell,
Now draw up Faustus like a foggy mist
Into the entrails of yon laboring cloud,
95   That when you vomit forth into the air
My limbs may issue from your smoky mouths,
So that my soul may but ascend to heaven.

(*The watch° strikes.*)   clock

Ah, half the hour is past: 'twill all be past anon.
Oh God, if thou wilt not have mercy on my soul,
100   Yet for Christ's sake, whose blood hath ransom'd me,
Impose some end to my incessant pain:
Let Faustus live in a hell a thousand years,
A hundred thousand, and at last be sav'd.
O, no end is limited to damned souls.[5]
105   Why wert thou not a creature wanting soul?
Or why is this immortal that thou hast?
Ah, Pythagoras' metempsychosis,[6] were that true
This soul should fly from me, and I be chang'd
Unto some brutish beast.
110   All beasts are happy, for when they die
Their souls are soon dissolv'd in elements,
But mine must live still to be plagu'd in hell.
Curst be the parents that engender'd me;
No Faustus, curse thyself, curse Lucifer
115   That hath depriv'd thee of the joys of heaven!

(*The clock strikes twelve.*)

O it strikes, it strikes, now body, turn to air
Or Lucifer will bear thee quick° to hell!   alive

(*Thunder and lightning.*)

O soul, be changed into little water drops
And fall into the ocean, ne'er be found;
120   My God, my God, look not so fierce on me!

---

[1]   *soever*   I.e., whatsoever.

[2]   *O lente … equi*   Latin: O gallop slowly, slowly, you horses of the
night! Ovid, *Amores* 1.8.40.

[3]   *rend … Christ*   Cf. Joel 2.12–13, where, faced by a terrifying
prospect of destruction that makes the earth quake and the heavens
tremble, and that darkens the sun, moon and stars, the Israelites are
exhorted to "rend their hearts in repentance."

[4]   *Mountains … God*   Cf. Luke 23.30, Revelation 6.16, Hosea 10.8.

[5]   *no end … souls*   I.e., damnation is endless.

[6]   *metempsychosis*   Doctrine of the transmigration of souls.

(*Enter devils.*)

Adders and serpents, let me breathe awhile!
Ugly hell gape not, come not Lucifer,
I'll burn my books, ah Mephastophilis!

(*Exeunt with him.*)

EPILOGUE

(*Enter Chorus.*)

CHORUS.   Cut is the branch that might have grown full
straight,

And burned is Apollo's laurel bough
That sometime grew within this learned man:
Faustus is gone, regard his hellish fall,
Whose fiendful fortune may exhort the wise
Only to wonder[1] at unlawful things,
Whose deepness doth entice such forward wits
To practice more than heavenly power permits.

(*Exit.*)

Terminat hora diem, terminat Author opus.[2]
—?1594 (FIRST PRINTED 1604)

———————————

[1]   *Only to wonder*   To be content with wondering.
[2]   *Terminat ... opus*   Latin: The hour ends the day; the author ends his work.

Sir Walter Ralegh
1554 – 1618

Sir Walter Ralegh was one of the leading courtiers, adventurers, and literary figures of the Elizabethan era. Intermittently regarded as a hero and a traitor in his lifetime, Ralegh profited richly and suffered considerably from his proximity to Elizabeth I—but fared considerably worse after James I replaced Elizabeth on the throne. Known for his gallantry, for his fighting ability, for his effort at colonization in Virginia, and for bringing the practice of smoking tobacco into European culture, Ralegh was also the author of literary work that ranged from love poetry to exploration narratives to an unfinished history of the world.

Born into the lesser gentry at Hayes Barton, Devon, Ralegh went to France in 1569 to fight for the Huguenots in the French religious civil wars. By 1572, he was studying at Oriel College, Oxford, only to leave over a year later without a degree. Ralegh finished his education in the Inns of Court, including Lyon's Inn and the Middle Temple, and it was during these years that his first poem was probably printed. It is often difficult to date or even attribute Ralegh's poems accurately, for like many courtiers, Ralegh generally circulated his verses in manuscript.

Ralegh's poetry is characterized by an intensely personal treatment of such conventional themes as love, loss, beauty, and time. The majority of his poems are short lyrics—many of them occasional, written in response to particular events.

After embarking with his stepbrother, Humphrey Gilbert, on an unsuccessful colonizing expedition to North America in 1578, Ralegh spent a year and a half fighting in Ireland. He returned to England in 1581 and caught the Queen's attention, eventually emerging as her new favorite and reaping substantial rewards, including a monopoly over wine licences in 1583 and a knighthood in 1585. A grant of 42,000 Irish acres on which to establish English colonists, made in 1587, brought Ralegh back to Ireland several times, and he was responsible for bringing an acquaintance, Edmund Spenser, back to England and introducing him to the Queen in 1589.

Ralegh's rapid rise to prominence at Elizabeth I's court was abruptly halted in 1592 after the discovery of his secret marriage to Elizabeth Throckmorton, one of the Queen's attendants. The Queen had him imprisoned in the Tower of London for several months—the occasion for his long poem, *The Ocean to Cynthia*, Ralegh's lament over Elizabeth's displeasure. This, Ralegh's most ambitious and sprawling poem, is a work that exists only in fragments, the longest of them over five hundred lines long. Five years elapsed before Ralegh was again in the Queen's good graces, a period during which he traveled to Guiana (1595), published a report on his adventures entitled *The Discovery of the Large, Rich, and Beautiful Empire of Guiana* (1596), developed his Irish plantations, and participated in the attack on Cadiz (1596). Always critical of Spain's colonial and naval power, Ralegh never lost interest in North America, sponsoring reconnaissance and colonizing expeditions in the late 1580s to the areas now known as Virginia and the Carolinas.

Following James I's accession in 1603, Ralegh returned to the Tower of London for nearly thirteen years after a dubious treason conviction for allegedly supporting Arabella Stuart's claim to the throne. Rarely idle, Ralegh kept abreast of the political and intellectual climate during his imprisonment by entertaining numerous visitors (including James's son, Prince Henry), conducting scientific experiments, compounding drugs, and writing. His most notable work from this period is *The Historie of the World* (1614), a three-volume overview of world events from creation to the second century BCE. Ralegh was released in 1617 to make a second journey to Guiana in search of the gold mine that he claimed to have found on his first voyage. Returning empty-handed in 1618, he was imprisoned under his former sentence for disobeying James's orders to avoid any acts of violence against the Spanish, and then beheaded. Despite a reputation for unorthodoxy and even atheism, Ralegh made a pious if showy end and replied, when asked if he should not face east (toward Jerusalem), "What matter how the head lie, so the heart be right?"

[Please note that an exchange of poems between Sir Walter Ralegh and Elizabeth I appears with other writings by Elizabeth earlier in this volume.]

⌘⌘⌘

But could youth last and love still breed,
Had joys no date nor age no need,[4]
Then these delights my mind might move
To live with thee and be thy love.
—1600

The Nymph's Reply to the Shepherd[2]

If all the world and love were young,
And truth in every shepherd's tongue,
These pretty pleasures might me move
To live with thee and be thy love.

5   Time drives the flocks from field to fold
When rivers rage and rocks grow cold,
And Philomel[3] becometh dumb;
The rest complains of cares to come.

The flowers do fade, and wanton° fields   *unrestrained, unruly*
10   To wayward winter reckoning yields;
A honey tongue, a heart of gall,°   *bitterness, rancor*
Is fancy's spring, but sorrow's fall.

Thy gowns, thy shoes, thy beds of roses,
Thy cap, thy kirtle,° and thy posies   *tunic or skirt*
15   Soon break, soon wither, soon forgotten—
In folly ripe, in reason rotten.

Thy belt of straw and ivy buds,
Thy coral clasps and amber studs,
All these in me no means can move
20   To come to thee and be thy love.

---

[2] *The Nymph's ... Shepherd*   Response to Christopher Marlowe's "The Passionate Shepherd to His Love."

[3] *Philomel*   I.e., the nightingale doesn't sing. In classical mythology, Philomela, the daughter of the King of Athens, was transformed into a nightingale after being pursued and raped by her brother-in-law, Tereus, King of Thrace.

JOHN DONNE
1572 – 1631

John Donne was an innovator: his work represented something new in poetry, and his contemporaries knew it. Donne set out to startle his readers with his disdain for convention, writing poems that challenged expectations about what was appropriate in poetic subject, form, tone, language, and imagery. He was not afraid of being difficult, or ambiguous, or contradictory from one poem to another: like the speaker of his "Holy Sonnet 19," in Donne "contraries meet in one." Some critics and readers try to smooth out these "contraries" by separating Donne's works into the secular verse written by "Jack Donne" (Donne's own phrase), the witty young man-about-London whose love poems combine erotic energy with high-minded argument; and the religious verse written later in life by Dr. John Donne, Dean of St. Paul's Cathedral, the learned Anglican minister famous for his electrifying sermons. But this neat division is complicated by the fact that many of his poems are impossible to date. Donne wrote primarily for manuscript circulation: only a handful of his poems were printed before he died. Some religious poetry may therefore have been written earlier than once thought, and some love lyrics later. In any case, Donne frequently blurs any differences between the sacred and the secular, erotic love and divine love: he can present erotic love as a form of religious experience, and religious devotion as an erotic experience. Donne's voice, moreover, ranges across a multitude of roles and postures, from misogynist cynicism and self-mocking sophistry to tender idealism and devout if still painfully self-conscious religious passion.

With his colloquial language, rough meter, sometimes swaggeringly masculine persona, and elaborately worked out philosophical (or wittily pseudo-philosophical) conceits, Donne's poetry breaks with the late Elizabethan poets: even when expressing difficult or ambiguous thoughts, they tended to prefer lines of smooth and highly decorated elegance. Donne's new manner caught the imagination of many poets, and his work was immensely influential for much of the seventeenth century. Times and tastes change, however, and what had been thought wit in 1600 by 1700 had come to seem mere fancy, unrestrained by judgment. In 1693, for example, John Dryden argued that Donne "affects the metaphysics ... where nature only should reign," claiming that his love poetry "perplexes [women's minds] ... with nice speculations of philosophy, when he should engage their hearts." In the eighteenth century, Samuel Johnson labeled Donne and his followers "Metaphysical Poets" who "ransacked" nature to create startling and strained conceits. (Because of the objections of scholars who point out that the term is misleading, the long-popular term "metaphysical" is currently losing ground.) Thanks to further shifts in sensibility, and thanks also to the praise of T.S. Eliot, who found in Donne's difficulty and intellectual dazzle a model for modernist poetic practice, Donne's work moved again in the twentieth century to the center of the English poetic canon.

Born in London in 1572, Donne was the son of a prosperous ironmonger. The family was Catholic at a time when the government viewed all Catholics with suspicion and prosecuted those it thought seditious. Donne's mother, Elizabeth, was related to Thomas More and was beheaded as a traitor for refusing to support Henry VIII's rejection of the Pope's authority. Two of her uncles lived in exile; another, a Jesuit, was incarcerated; and in 1593 Donne's brother Henry died of a fever while imprisoned for harboring a priest. Thus, Donne well understood religious persecution, which is why some have speculated that his conversion to the Church of England, however sincere, must have felt at times like a betrayal. First educated by Jesuits, at age eleven Donne entered Oxford, and then studied at Cambridge. He took no degree, perhaps because graduation required accepting the Church of England's thirty-nine "articles of religion." In 1592 he began legal studies at Lincoln's Inn, and over the next few years wrote many of the love lyrics that were known at first to a few friends and then, especially in the next century, found a large readership. A set of five satires mocking English life, laws, and mores (including those of courtiers) also dates from these years; they helped intensify a fashion in the late 1590s for biting verse satire. The most powerful, "Satire III," explores with surprising candor, if no conclusion, the risks and dilemmas of choosing a version of Christianity to follow.

After taking part in the 1596 and 1597 anti-Spanish expeditions to Cadiz and the Azores, in 1598 Donne was appointed secretary to Sir Thomas Egerton, Lord Keeper of the Great Seal. By now his future seemed assured—he had distanced himself from the Roman Catholic Church and had served in Parliament. In 1601, however, he nearly wrecked his prospects by a secret marriage to Egerton's 17-year-old-niece, Ann More. When the marriage was discovered, Donne wrote to her father, Sir George More, begging that Ann not "feel the terror of your sudden anger," but Sir George disinherited his daughter and had Donne dismissed from his position and briefly imprisoned. Years of poverty and unemployment lay before the couple and their family (Ann eventually had twelve children, seven of whom survived). Donne found some support, however, from various friends and patrons, among them Sir Robert Drury, for whom he wrote two long "Anniversary" poems (1611–12) lamenting the death of Sir Robert's daughter, Elizabeth.

During this difficult period Donne finally renounced his Roman Catholicism and within a few years published two anti-Catholic tracts: *Pseudo-Martyr* (1610), which argues that Catholics should take the Oath of Allegiance to the crown, and the satirical *Ignatius His Conclave* (1611), which describes a meeting of Jesuits in Hell. King James was pleased but insisted that Donne be ordained before receiving an appointment. Donne complied and was shortly thereafter made a royal chaplain and a Reader in Divinity at Lincoln's Inn. He soon suffered a personal loss, however, when his wife died during childbirth at age 33, a sorrow to which Donne probably alludes in his seventeenth "Holy Sonnet," when he mentions that "she whom I loved hath paid her last debt." Most of his "Holy Sonnets," however (including "Death Be not Proud"), seem to have been written before his ordination and reflect earlier hopes and anguish. In 1621 Donne was appointed Dean of St. Paul's, and attracted large audiences for his intellectually challenging and emotionally stirring sermons, many of which were published, both during and after his life.

During a grave illness in the mid-1620s, Donne wrote his popular *Devotions upon Emergent Occasions* (1624), a series of prose meditations that include his famous assertion of human interconnectedness ("No man is an island"). Donne survived, but he never lost his fascination with death. He delivered his last sermon, "Death's Duel," early in 1631 before Charles I. His audience, it was later said, sensed that he was in effect preaching his own funeral sermon; he died that March. Donne is buried at St. Paul's Cathedral; his monument is modeled on a portrait of himself taken while he was still alive and dressed for the occasion in his shroud. His collected *Poems* were printed in 1633 and was reprinted several times before his reputation faded with the coming of the Restoration and a new generation's taste for neoclassical poetry.

⌘⌘⌘

from *Songs and Sonnets*[1]

The Good-Morrow

I wonder by my troth, what thou, and I
Did, till we loved? were we not weaned till then?
But sucked on country pleasures, childishly?
Or snorted we in the seven sleepers' den?[2]
5   'Twas so; but° this, all pleasures fancies be   *except for*
If ever any beauty I did see,
Which I desired, and got, 'twas but a dream of thee.

And now good-morrow to our waking souls,
Which watch not one another out of fear;
10 For love, all love of other sights controls,
And makes one little room, an every where.
Let sea-discoverers to new worlds have gone,
Let maps[3] to others, worlds on worlds have shown,
Let us possess one world,[4] each hath one, and is one.

15 My face in thine eye, thine in mine appears,
And true plain hearts do in the faces rest,
Where can we find two better hemispheres,
Without sharp North, without declining West?
What ever dies, was not mixed equally;[5]
20 If our two loves be one, or, thou and I
Love so alike that none do slacken, none can die.
                                    —1633[6]

---

[1] *Sonnets*   Donne uses the term as a general one for love poems or love songs, rather than referring specifically to the 14-line sonnet; his secular love poetry includes no traditional 14-line sonnets.

[2] *seven sleepers' den*   In early Christian legend, seven youths walled up in a cave during a persecution who slept for nearly 200 years.

[3] *maps*   Probably astronomical maps.

[4] *one world*   Many manuscript versions have "our world."

[5] *What ever ... equally*   Classical medical theory held that disease was the result of improper balance among the body's elements.

[6] *1633*   Much uncertainty and inconsistency surrounds the dates of composition and publication for Donne's work. We do not follow our usual format here of organizing the author's works chronologically by publication date; the texts are sorted instead by traditional categories.

Song ("Go, and catch a falling star")

Go, and catch a falling star,
   Get with child a mandrake root,[7]
Tell me, where all past years are,
   Or who cleft the Devil's foot,
5 Teach me to hear mermaids singing,
Or to keep off envy's stinging,
         And find
         What wind
Serves to advance an honest mind.

10 If thou be'st born to strange sights,
      Things invisible to see,
Ride ten thousand days and nights,
      Till age snow white hairs on thee,
Thou, when thou return'st, wilt tell me
15 All strange wonders that befell thee,
         And swear,
         No where
Lives a woman true, and fair.

If thou find'st one, let me know,
20   Such a pilgrimage were sweet;
Yet do not, I would not go,
      Though at next door we might meet;
Though she were true, when you met her,
And last, till you write your letter,
25   Yet she
         Will be
False, ere I come, to two, or three.
                        —1633

Woman's Constancy

Now thou hast loved me one whole day,
   To-morrow when thou leavest, what wilt thou say?
Wilt thou then antedate some new-made vow?
         Or, say that now
5 We are not just those persons, which we were?
Or, that oaths made in reverential fear
Of Love, and his wrath, any may forswear?
Or, as true deaths, true marriages untie,

---

[7] *mandrake root*   Plant whose forked root resembles a human body.

10 So lovers' contracts, images of those,
Bind but till sleep, death's image, them unloose?
            Or, your own end to justify,
For having purposed change, and falsehood, you
Can have no way but falsehood to be true?
Vain lunatic,[1] against these 'scapes I could
15   Dispute, and conquer, if I would;
            Which I abstain to do,
For by to-morrow, I may think so too.
—1633

The Sun Rising

Busy old fool, unruly Sun,
      Why dost thou thus,
Through windows, and through curtains call on us?
Must to thy motions lovers' seasons run?
5   Saucy pedantic wretch, go chide
            Late schoolboys and sour prentices,
      Go tell court-huntsmen that the King will ride,
      Call country ants to harvest offices;
Love, all alike, no season knows, nor clime,
10 Nor hours, days, months, which are the rags of time.

            Thy beams, so reverend, and strong
            Why shouldst thou think?
I could eclipse and cloud them with a wink,
But that I would not lose her sight so long:
15   If her eyes have not blinded thine,
            Look, and tomorrow late, tell me,
      Whether both the Indias of spice and mine[2]
      Be where thou leftst them, or lie here with me.
Ask for those kings whom thou saw'st yesterday,
20 And thou shalt hear, All here in one bed lay.

            She's all states, and all princes, I,
            Nothing else is.
Princes do but play us; compared to this,
All honor's mimic, all wealth alchemy.[3]

___

[1] *lunatic* Under the control of the moon, thus inconstant, subject to change.

[2] *Indias of spice and mine* The East Indies (source of spice and perfume) and West Indies (source of gold and precious metals).

[3] *alchemy* Here, flashy rubbish.

25   Thou sun art half as happy as we,
      In that the world's contracted thus:
      Thine age asks ease, and since thy duties be
      To warm the world, that's done in warming us.
Shine here to us, and thou art everywhere;
30 This bed thy center is, these walls, thy sphere.
—1633

The Canonization

For God's sake hold your tongue, and let me love,
      Or chide my palsy, or my gout,
My five gray hairs, or ruined fortune flout,
      With wealth your state, your mind with arts improve,
5   Take you a course, get you a place,[4]
            Observe his honour, or his grace,[5]
And the King's real, or his stamped face
            Contemplate;[6] what you will, approve,[7]
            So you will let me love.

10 Alas, alas, who's injured by my love?
      What merchant's ships have my sighs drowned?
Who says my tears have overflowed his ground?
      When did my colds a forward spring remove?
            When did the heats which my veins fill
15   Add one more to the plaguy bill?[8]
Soldiers find wars, and lawyers find out still
      Litigious men, which quarrels move,
      Though she and I do love.

Call us what you will, we are made such by love;
20   Call her one, me another fly,[9]

___

[4] *course … place* Take a course of action; get yourself a position.

[5] *his honour … his grace* Cultivate contacts with political or religious dignitaries.

[6] *stamped face / Contemplate* Look at the king's face stamped on coins: in effect, "go think about money."

[7] *what you will, approve* Do whatever you want.

[8] *plaguy bill* Weekly list of those who had died of the plague.

[9] *me another fly* Call her a fly (butterfly or moth), and call me one too.

We're tapers too, and at our own cost die,[1]
   And we in us find the eagle and the dove.[2]
      The phoenix riddle[3] hath more wit
      By us; we two being one, are it.
25 So, to one neutral thing both sexes fit,
   We die and rise the same, and prove
      Mysterious by this love.

We can die by it, if not live by love,
   And if unfit for tombs and hearse
30 Our legend be, it will be fit for verse;
   And if no piece of chronicle° we prove,   *history*
      We'll build in sonnets° pretty rooms;[4]   *love poems*
      As well a well wrought urn becomes
The greatest ashes, as half-acre tombs,
35   And by these hymns, all shall approve
      Us canonized for love.

And thus invoke us: You whom reverend love
   Made one another's hermitage;
You, to whom love was peace, that now is rage;
40   Who did the whole world's soul contract,[5]
         and drove
      Into the glasses of your eyes
      (So made such mirrors, and such spies,
That they did all to you epitomize)
      Countries, towns, courts: beg from above
45   A pattern of your love.
   —1633

---

1 *We're tapers ... die* "To die" was slang for reaching orgasm, and each sexual act was popularly believed to shorten one's life by one day. The two lovers are compared to moths attracted to a candle, and to the self-consuming candle (taper) itself: moths, candle, and lovers all pay for doing what they do by their very nature.

2 *eagle and the dove* Symbols of (masculine) strength and (feminine) gentleness, now united in the lovers.

3 *phoenix riddle* Only one mythical phoenix ever lived at a time; the bird mysteriously renewed itself by rising from the ashes of its own funeral pyre. The "riddle" of its unisex existence makes better sense (has "more wit") when compared with the two lovers: like the phoenix, they combine "both sexes" to make "one neutral thing" which dies, then rises the same (with the traditional play on the sexual resonances of dying and rising).

4 *rooms* In Italian, "stanza" means "room."

5 *contract* Manuscript versions have "extract."

Song ("Sweetest love, I do not go")

Sweetest love, I do not go
For weariness of thee,
Nor in hope the world can show
   A fitter love for me;
5   But since that I
Must die at last, 'tis best
To use my self in jest
   Thus by feigned deaths[6] to die.

Yesternight the sun went hence,
10   And yet is here today,
He hath no desire nor sense,
   Nor half so short a way:
      Then fear not me,
But believe that I shall make
15 Speedier journeys, since I take
   More wings and spurs than he.

O how feeble is man's power,
   That if good fortune fall,
Cannot add another hour,
20   Nor a lost hour recall!
      But come bad chance,
And we join to it our strength,
And we teach it art and length,
   Itself o'er us to advance.

25 When thou sigh'st, thou sigh'st not wind,
   But sigh'st my soul away,
When thou weep'st, unkindly kind,
   My life's blood doth decay.
      It cannot be
30 That thou lov'st me, as thou say'st,
If in thine my life thou waste,
   Thou art the best of me.

Let not thy divining heart
   Forethink me any ill,
35 Destiny may take thy part,
   And may thy fears fulfil;
      But think that we

---

6 *feigned deaths* Separations from the beloved.

Are but turned aside to sleep;
They who one another keep
40   Alive, ne'er parted be.
—1633

Air and Angels

Twice or thrice had I loved thee,
    Before I knew thy face or name;
So in a voice, so in a shapeless flame,[1]
Angels affect us oft, and worshipped be;
5   Still when, to where thou wert, I came,
Some lovely glorious nothing I did see.
      But since my soul, whose child love is,
Takes limbs of flesh, and else could nothing do,
      More subtle than the parent is
10 Love must not be, but take a body too;
      And therefore what thou wert, and who,
          I bid Love ask, and now
That it assume thy body, I allow,
And fix itself in thy lip, eye, and brow.

15 Whilst thus to ballast love, I thought,
And so more steadily to have gone,
With wares which would sink admiration,
I saw I had love's pinnace[2] overfraught;
      Ev'ry thy hair for love to work upon
20 Is much too much, some fitter must be sought;
      For, nor in nothing, nor in things
Extreme, and scatt'ring bright, can love inhere;
      Then as an angel, face and wings
Of air, not pure as it, yet pure doth wear,
25   So thy love may be my love's sphere;
          Just such disparity
As is 'twixt air and angels' purity,
'Twixt women's love, and men's will ever be.
—1633

---

[1] *shapeless flame*   Unsteady, or suddenly flaring, flame.

[2] *pinnace*   Small, light ship, unsuited for carrying the figurative cargo of the beloved's many beauties.

Break of Day[3]

'Tis true, 'tis day; what though it be?
    O wilt thou therefore rise from me?
Why should we rise because 'tis light?
Did we lie down because 'twas night?
5 Love, which in spite of darkness brought us hither,
Should in despite of light keep us together.

Light hath no tongue, but is all eye;
If it could speak as well as spy,
This were the worst that it could say,
10 That being well, I fain would stay,
And that I loved my heart and honor so,
That I would not from him, that had them, go.

Must business thee from hence remove?
Oh that's the worst disease of love,
15 The poor, the foul, the false, love can
Admit, but not the busied man.
He which hath business, and makes love, doth do
Such wrong, as when a married man doth woo.
—1612, 1633

The Anniversary

All kings, and all their favourites,
    All glory of honours, beauties, wits,
The sun itself, which makes times, as they pass,
Is elder by a year, now, than it was
5 When thou and I first one another saw:
All other things to their destruction draw,
    Only our love hath no decay;
This, no tomorrow hath, nor yesterday,
Running it never runs from us away,
10 But truly keeps his first, last, everlasting day.

    Two graves must hide thine and my corse,°   corpse
    If one might, death were no divorce:
Alas, as well as other princes, we
(Who prince enough in one another be)

---

[3] *Break of Day*   First printed, with a musical setting, in William Corkine's *Second Book of Airs* (1612). The speaker is a woman.

15 Must leave at last in death, these eyes, and ears,
Oft fed with true oaths, and with sweet salt tears;
    But souls where nothing dwells but love
(All other thoughts being inmates) then shall prove
This, or a love increased there above,
20 When bodies to their graves, souls from their
    graves remove.

    And then we shall be throughly° blest,   *thoroughly*
    But we no more than all the rest,
Here upon earth, we're kings, and none but we
Can be such kings, nor of such subjects be;
25 Who is so safe as we? where none can do
Treason to us, except one of us two.
    True and false fears let us refrain,
Let us love nobly, and live, and add again
Years and years unto years, till we attain
30 To write threescore: this is the second of our reign.
    —1633

Twicknam Garden[1]

Blasted with sighs, and surrounded with tears,
Hither I come to seek the spring,
    And at mine eyes, and at mine ears,
Receive such balms, as else cure everything;
5   But O, self traitor, I do bring
The spider[2] love, which transubstantiates all,
    And can convert manna to gall,
And that this place may throughly be thought
    True Paradise, I have the serpent[3] brought.

10 'Twere wholesomer for me, that winter did
    Benight the glory of this place,
    And that a grave frost did forbid
These trees to laugh and mock me to my face;

---

[1] *Twicknam Garden* Twickenham Park (pronounced, and often in the period spelled, Twicknam) was the home of Lucy, Countess of Bedford (1581–1627), a friend and patron of Donne and other writers, including Ben Jonson, Samuel Daniel, and Michael Drayton.

[2] *spider* Spiders were believed to transform everything they ate into poison.

[3] *serpent* Emblem of envy, and of temptation.

    But that I may not this disgrace
15 Endure, nor leave this garden, Love, let me
    Some senseless piece of this place be;
Make me a mandrake, so I may groan here,[4]
    Or a stone fountain weeping out my year.

Hither with crystal vials, lovers come,
20 And take my tears, which are love's wine,
    And try° your mistress' tears at home,   *test*
For all are false, that taste not just like mine;
    Alas, hearts do not in eyes shine,
Nor can you more judge woman's thoughts by tears,
25 Than by her shadow, what she wears.
O perverse sex, where none is true but she,
    Who's therefore true, because her truth kills me.
—1633

A Valediction: of Weeping

Let me pour forth
    My tears before thy face, whil'st I stay here,
For thy face coins them, and thy stamp they bear,
And by this mintage they are something worth,
5   For thus they be
        Pregnant of thee;
Fruits of much grief they are, emblems of more,
When a tear falls, that thou falls which it bore,
So thou and I are nothing then, when on a diverse shore.

10   On a round ball[5]
A workman that hath copies by, can lay
An Europe, Afric, and an Asia,[6]
And quickly make that, which was nothing, All,
        So doth each tear,
15   Which thee doth wear,
A globe, yea world by that impression grow,
Till thy tears mixed with mine do overflow

---

[4] *mandrake ... groan here* Plant whose forked root was thought to resemble the human body, and reputed to shriek or groan; the printed edition has "grow," but many manuscripts have "groan," which better parallels the weeping fountain in the next line.

[5] *round ball* Blank globe, on which printed maps could be placed to make a world.

[6] *Asia* Pronounced in the period as a three-syllable word.

This world, by waters sent from thee, my heaven
   dissolved so.

     O more than Moon,
20 Draw not up seas to drown me in thy sphere,
Weep me not dead, in thine arms, but forbear
To teach the sea what it may do too soon;
     Let not the wind
     Example find,
25 To do me more harm than it purposeth;
Since thou and I sigh one another's breath,
Who e'r sighs most is cruellest, and hastes the
   other's death.[1]
   —1633

The Flea

Mark but this flea, and mark in this,
How little that which thou deny'st me is;
It sucked me first,[2] and now sucks thee,
And in this flea our two bloods mingled be;[3]
5 Thou know'st that[4] this cannot be said
A sin, nor shame, nor loss of maidenhead,
   Yet this enjoys before it woo,
   And pampered swells with one blood made of two,
   And this, alas, is more than we would do.

10 Oh stay, three lives in one flea spare,
Where we almost, nay more than married are:
This flea is you and I, and this
Our marriage bed, and marriage temple is;
Though parents grudge, and you, we're met
15 And cloistered in these living walls of jet.°   *black stone*
   Though use° make you apt to kill me,   *habit*
   Let not to that, self murder added be,
   And sacrilege, three sins in killing three.

---

1 *Who e'r sighs ... death* According to folklore, sighing shortened life (each sigh was said to cost one drop of blood).

2 *It sucked me first* "Me it sucked first" in many manuscripts.

3 *mingled be* The speaker's subsequent argument hinges on the traditional belief that blood mixed during sexual intercourse.

4 *Thou know'st that* "Confess it" in many manuscripts.

Cruel and sudden, hast thou since
20 Purpled thy nail in blood of innocence?
Wherein could this flea guilty be,
Except in that drop which it sucked from thee?
Yet thou triumph'st, and say'st that thou
Find'st not thy self, nor me the weaker now;
25   'Tis true, then learn how false, fears be;
   Just so much honor, when thou yield'st to me,
   Will waste, as this flea's death took life from thee.
—1633

A Nocturnal upon St. Lucy's Day,
Being the Shortest Day[5]

'Tis the year's midnight, and it is the day's,
Lucy's, who scarce seven hours herself unmasks;
The sun is spent, and now his flasks°   *the stars*
Send forth light squibs, no constant rays;
5   The world's whole sap is sunk:
The general balm[6] the hydroptic° earth hath drunk,   *thirsty*
Whither, as to the bed's-feet, life is shrunk,
Dead and interred; yet all these seem to laugh,
Compared with me, who am their epitaph.

10 Study me then, you who shall lovers be
At the next world, that is, at the next spring:
   For I am every dead thing,
   In whom Love wrought new alchemy.
     For his art did express°   *extract*
15 A quintessence even from nothingness,
From dull privations, and lean emptiness;
He ruined me, and I am re-begot
Of absence, darkness, death; things which are not.

All others, from all things, draw all that's good,
20 Life, soul, form, spirit, whence they being have;
   I, by love's limbeck,[7] am the grave
   Of all that's nothing. Oft a flood
     Have we two wept, and so

---

5 *St Lucy's Day, Being the Shortest Day* 13 December, the shortest day of the year in the old Julian calendar.

6 *general balm* The innate, vital sap believed to preserve all things.

7 *limbeck* Retort, or still (apparatus for distillation).

Drowned the whole world, us two; oft did we grow
25   To be two chaoses, when we did show
Care to aught else; and often absences
Withdrew our souls, and made us carcasses.

But I am by her death (which word wrongs her)
Of the first nothing the elixir grown;
30   Were I a man, that I were one
        I needs must know; I should prefer,
            If I were any beast,
Some ends, some means; yea plants, yea stones detest,
And love; all, all some properties invest;
35   If I an ordinary nothing were,
As shadow, a light and body must be here.

But I am none; nor will my sun renew.
You lovers, for whose sake the lesser sun
        At this time to the Goat[1] is run
40   To fetch new lust, and give it you,
            Enjoy your summer all;
Since she enjoys her long night's festival,
Let me prepare towards her, and let me call
This hour her vigil, and her eve, since this
45   Both the year's, and the day's deep midnight is.
—1633

The Bait

Come live with me, and be my love,
    And we will some new pleasures prove
Of golden sands, and crystal brooks,
With silken lines, and silver hooks.

5   There will the river whispering run
Warmed by thy eyes, more than the sun.
And there the enamoured fish will stay,
Begging themselves they may betray.

When thou wilt swim in that live bath,
10   Each fish, which every channel hath,
Will amorously to thee swim,
Gladder to catch thee, than thou him.

1 *Goat* The constellation Capricorn, into whose sign the sun enters
at the winter solstice; goats were associated with lust.

If thou, to be so seen, be'st loth,
By sun or moon, thou dark'nest both,
15   And if myself have leave to see,
I need not their light, having thee.

Let others freeze with angling reeds,
And cut their legs with shells and weeds,
Or treacherously poor fish beset,
20   With strangling snare, or windowy net.

Let coarse bold hands, from slimy nest
The bedded fish in banks out-wrest,
Or curious traitors, sleave-silk[2] flies,
Bewitch poor fishes' wand'ring eyes.

25   For thee, thou need'st no such deceit,
For thou thyself art thine own bait;
That fish, that is not catched thereby,
Alas, is wiser far than I.
—1633

The Apparition

When by thy scorn, O murd'ress, I am dead,
        And that thou thinkst thee free
From all solicitation from me,
Then shall my ghost come to thy bed,
5   And thee, feigned vestal,[3] in worse arms shall see;
Then thy sick taper will begin to wink,
And he, whose thou art then, being tired before,
Will, if thou stir, or pinch to wake him, think
        Thou call'st for more,
10   And in false sleep will from thee shrink,
And then, poor aspen° wretch, neglected thou   *trembling*
Bathed in a cold quicksilver sweat[4] wilt lie,
        A verier ghost than I;

2 *sleave-silk* Silk in the form of fine filaments.

3 *feigned vestal* Pretended virgin. The original has "fained," the
common variant spelling in the period; many editions retain "fained"
(eager, glad).

4 *quicksilver sweat* Shiny coating of sweat; from quicksilvering, the
application of a thin coat of an alloy using mercury (quicksilver).
That mercury was also used to relieve the symptoms of syphilis adds
to Donne's insult.

What I will say, I will not tell thee now,
15 Lest that preserve thee; and since my love is spent,
    I'd rather thou shouldst painfully repent,
    Than by my threatnings rest still innocent.
    —1633

A Valediction: Forbidding Mourning

As virtuous men pass mildly away,
    And whisper to their souls to go,
Whilst some of their sad friends do say,
    The breath goes now, and some say, no:

5 So let us melt, and make no noise,
    No tear-floods, nor sigh-tempests move,
'Twere profanation of our joys,
    To tell the laity our love.

Moving of the earth° brings harms and fears,   *earthquakes*
10   Men reckon what it did and meant,
But trepidation of the spheres,[1]
    Though greater far, is innocent.

Dull sublunary[2] lovers' love
    (Whose soul is sense) cannot admit
15 Absence, because it doth remove
    Those things which elemented it.

But we by a love, so much refined
    That our selves know not what it is,
Inter-assured of the mind,
20   Care less, eyes, lips, and hands to miss.

Our two souls therefore, which are one,
    Though I must go, endure not yet
A breach, but an expansion,
    Like gold to airy thinness beat.

If they be two, they are two so
25   As stiff twin compasses[3] are two:
Thy soul, the fixed foot, makes no show
    To move, but doth, if the other do.

And though it in the center sit,
30   Yet when the other far doth roam,
It leans, and hearkens after it,
    And grows erect, as that comes home.

Such wilt thou be to me, who must
    Like the other foot, obliquely run;
35 Thy firmness makes my circle just,
    And makes me end, where I begun.
    —1633

The Ecstasy

Where, like a pillow on a bed,
    A pregnant bank swelled up, to rest
The violet's reclining head,
    Sat we two, one another's best.
5 Our hands were firmly cemented
    With a fast balm, which thence did spring;
Our eye-beams twisted, and did thread
    Our eyes upon one double string.
So to engraft our hands, as yet
10   Was all our means to make us one,
And pictures in our eyes to get°   *beget*
    Was all our propagation.
As 'twixt two equal armies, Fate
    Suspends uncertain victory,
15 Our souls (which to advance their state,
    Were gone out) hung 'twixt her and me.
And whilst our souls negotiate there,
    We like sepulchral statues lay;
All day, the same our postures were,
20   And we said nothing, all the day.
If any, so by love refined,
    That he soul's language understood,
And by good love were grown all mind,
    Within convenient distance stood,

---

[1] *trepidation of the spheres*   The precession of the equinox, thought to be caused by movements in the celestial spheres.

[2] *sublunary*   Beneath the moon, hence corruptible and subject to change (because subject to the consequences of the Fall from Paradise).

[3] *twin compasses*   Single drawing compass (with twin "feet").

25 He (though he knew not which soul spake,
      Because both meant, both spake the same)
   Might thence a new concoction take,[1]
      And part far purer than he came.
   This ecstasy doth unperplex
30   (We said) and tell us what we love;
   We see by this, it was not sex;
      We see, we saw not what did move:
   But as all several souls contain
      Mixture of things, they know not what,
35 Love, these mixed souls doth mix again,
      And makes both one, each this, and that.
   A single violet transplant,
      The strength, the colour, and the size
   (All which before was poor and scant)
40   Redoubles still, and multiplies.
   When love with one another so
      Interinanimates two souls,
   That abler soul, which thence doth flow,
      Defects of loneliness controls.
45 We then, who are this new soul, know
      Of what we are composed, and made,
   For the atomies of which we grow
      Are souls, whom no change can invade.
   But O alas, so long, so far
50   Our bodies why do we forbear?
   They're ours, though they're not we, we are
      The intelligences, they the sphere.
   We owe them thanks, because they thus
      Did us, to us, at first convey,
55 Yielded their forces, sense, to us,
      Nor are dross to us, but allay.°   alloy
   On man heaven's influence works not so,
      But that it first imprints the air;
   So soul into the soul may flow,
60   Though it to body first repair.
   As our blood labours to beget
      Spirits, as like souls as it can,
   Because such fingers need to knit
      That subtle knot, which makes us man:
65 So must pure lovers' souls descend
      To affections, and to faculties,
   Which sense may reach and apprehend,
      Else a great prince in prison lies.

To our bodies turn we then, that so
70   Weak men on love revealed may look;
   Love's mysteries in souls do grow,
      But yet the body is his book.
   And if some lover, such as we,
      Have heard this dialogue of one,
75 Let him still mark us, he shall see
      Small change when we're to bodies gone.
   —1633

The Relic

When my grave is broke up again
   Some second guest to entertain
   (For graves have learned that woman-head[2]
   To be to more than one a bed)
5   And he that digs it, spies
A bracelet of bright° hair about the bone,   fair
      Will he not let us alone,
And think that there a loving couple lies,
Who thought that this device might be some way
10 To make their souls, at the last busy day,
Meet at this grave, and make a little stay?

      If this fall in a time, or land,
         Where mis-devotion doth command,[3]
         Then he that digs us up will bring
15   Us to the Bishop, and the King,
            To make us relics; then
Thou shalt be a Mary Magdalen, and I
      A something else thereby;
All women shall adore us, and some men;
20 And since at such times miracles are sought,
I would have that age by this paper taught
What miracles we harmless lovers wrought.

      First, we loved well and faithfully,
         Yet knew not what we loved, nor why,
25   Difference of sex no more we knew,
         Than our guardian angels do;
            Coming and going, we

---

[1] *new concoction take*   Be even further refined.

[2] *woman-head*   Womanishness (a play on "maidenhead").

[3] *If this fall ... command*   That is, in a time or place where people prayed to saints and venerated relics: in effect, were Roman Catholic.

Perchance might kiss, but not between those meals;
    Our hands ne'er touched the seals,
30 Which nature, injured by late law,[1] sets free:
These miracles we did; but now, alas,
All measure, and all language, I should pass,
Should I tell what a miracle she was.
—1633

from *Elegies*

Elegy 1. Jealousy[2]

Fond° woman, which wouldst have thy   *foolish*
  husband die,
And yet complain'st of his great jealousy.
If swollen with poison, he lay in his last bed,
His body with a sere-bark° covered,   *dry crust*
5 Drawing his breath as thick and short as can
The nimblest crocheting[3] musician,
Ready with loathsome vomiting to spew
His soul out of one hell into a new,
Made deaf with his poor kindred's howling cries,
10 Begging with few feigned tears great legacies,
Thou wouldst not weep, but jolly and frolic be,
As a slave which to-morrow should be free.
Yet weep'st thou when thou seest him hungerly
Swallow his own death, heart's-bane jealousy.
15 Oh give him many thanks, he's courteous,
That in suspecting kindly warneth us.
We must not, as we used, flout openly
In scoffing riddles his deformity;
Nor at his board, together being sat,
20 With words, nor touch, scarce looks, adulterate.
Nor when he, swol'n and pampered with great fare,
Sits down and snorts, caged in his basket chair,
Must we usurp his own bed any more,
Nor kiss and play in his house, as before.
25 Now I see many dangers; for that is
His realm, his castle, and his diocese.

But if, as envious men which would revile
Their prince, or coin his gold, themselves exile
Into another country, and do it there,
30 We play in another house, what should we fear?
There we will scorn his household policies,
His silly plots and pensionary spies,°   *servants*
As the inhabitants of Thames' right side[4]
Do London's mayor, or Germans, the Pope's pride.[5]
—1633

Elegy 8. The Comparison[6]

As the sweet sweat of roses in a still,
  As that which from chafed musk cat's pores
     doth trill,°   *flow*
As the almighty balm° of the early East,   *morning dew*
Such are the sweat drops of my mistress' breast,
5 And on her neck her skin such lustre sets,
They seem no sweat drops, but pearl carcanets.°   *necklaces*
Rank sweaty froth thy mistress' brow defiles,
Like spermatic issue of ripe menstruous boils,
Or like that scum, which, by need's lawless law
10 Enforced, Sanserra's starved men did draw
From parboiled shoes, and boots, and all the rest
Which were with any sovereign fatness blest,[7]
And like vile lying stones in saffroned tin,[8]
Or warts, or weals, they hang upon her skin.
15 Round as the world's her head, on every side,
Like to that fatal ball which fell on Ide,[9]

---

1 *late law* Human law, which came after the original "law" of nature.

2 *Elegy 1. Jealousy* Numbered "Elegy 4" in some modern editions.

3 *crotcheting* Crotchets are grace notes; in effect, "quick-fingered."

---

4 *Thames' right side* Southwark, where the theaters were, was outside the jurisdiction of London authorities.

5 *Pope's pride* Germany was the birthplace of the Reformation, which challenged the authority of the Pope.

6 *Elegy 8. The Comparison* Numbered "Elegy 2" in some modern editions.

7 *From parboiled shoes ... fatnes blest* The King's Catholic army laid siege to the Protestants of Sancerre, France, for nine months in 1573; the town's inhabitants were reduced to eating anything made out of leather.

8 *lying stones in saffroned tin* Artificial jewels set in false gold (gilded tin).

9 *fatal ball which fell on Ide* The golden apple inscribed "To the fairest" that Eris, goddess of discord, brought to a wedding in revenge for not being invited. Hera, Athena, and Aphrodite competed for the prize, and Paris, a herdsman [continued ...]

Or that whereof God had such jealousy,
As, for the ravishing thereof we die.[1]
Thy head[2] is like a rough-hewn statue of jet,°   *black stone*
20 Where marks for eyes, nose, mouth, are yet scarce set;
Like the first Chaos, or flat seeming face
Of Cynthia,° where the earth's shadows her   *the moon*
    embrace.
Like Proserpine's white beauty-keeping chest,[3]
Or Jove's best fortune's urn,[4] is her fair breast.
25 Thine's like worm eaten trunks, clothed in seal's skin,
Or grave, that's dirt without, and stink within.
And like that slender stalk, at whose end stands
The woodbine quivering, are her arms and hands,
Like rough-barked elmboughs, or the russet skin
30 Of men late scourged for madness, or for sin,
Like sun-parched quarters on the city gate,[5]
Such is thy tanned skin's lamentable state.
And like a bunch of ragged carrots stand
The short swoll'n fingers of thy gouty hand.
35 Then like the chemic's masculine equal° fire,   *evenly heating*
Which in the limbeck's[6] warm womb doth inspire
Into the earth's worthless dirt a soul of gold,
Such cherishing heat her best loved part doth hold.
Thine's like the dread mouth of a fired gun,
40 Or like hot liquid metals newly run
Into clay moulds, or like to that Aetna[7]
Where round about the grass is burnt away.

---

on Mount Ida (near Troy), had to choose the winner. His choice of Aphrodite led to the Trojan war. The elegy invites the reader to compare that beauty competition with the one it offers.

[1] *ravishing ... we die* The forbidden fruit of the Tree of the Knowledge of Good and Evil in Eden.

[2] *Thy head* That is, the head of thy mistress, as opposed to "her head" (the speaker's mistress) of line 15. The poem proceeds to contrast the qualities of the speaker's "her" with those of "thy" or "thine" mistress.

[3] *beauty-keeping chest* In classical story, Psyche was required to travel to the underworld and ask Prosperina (Persephone) to place in a box a gift of beauty for Venus.

[4] *Jove's best fortune's urn* From Homer, *Iliad*: Zeus (Jove) kept two urns in his palace, one filled with good gifts, the other with evil ones.

[5] *Like sun-parched ... city gate* The dessicated body parts of "quartered" criminals, impaled as warning to would-be offenders on city gates.

[6] *limbeck* Alchemical still or retort.

[7] *Aetna* Volcano in Sicily.

Are not your kisses then as filthy, and more,
As a worm sucking an envenomed sore?
45 Doth not thy fearful hand in feeling quake,
As one which gath'ring flowers, still fears a snake?
Is not your last act harsh, and violent,
As when a plough a stony ground doth rent?
So kiss good turtles,° so devoutly nice   *turtledoves*
50 Are priests in handling reverent sacrifice,
And such in searching wounds the surgeon is
As we, when we embrace, or touch, or kiss.
Leave her, and I will leave comparing thus,
She, and comparisons are odious.
—1633

Elegy 19. To His Mistress Going to Bed[8]

Come Madam, come, all rest my powers defy,
  Until I labour, I in labour lie.
The foe oft-times, having the foe in sight,
Is tired with standing though they never fight.
5 Off with that girdle, like heaven's zone glistering,
But a far fairer world encompassing.
Unpin that spangled breastplate,[9] which you wear
That the eyes of busy fools may be stopped there.
Unlace your self: for that harmonious chime[10]
10 Tells me from you that now 'tis your bed time.
Off with that happy busk,° which I envy,   *corset*
That still can be, and still can stand so nigh.
Your gown's going off, such beauteous state reveals,
As when from flowr'y meads the hill's shadow steals.
15 Off with that wiry coronet and show
The hairy diadem which on you doth grow.
Now off with those shoes, and then softly tread
In this love's hallowed temple, this soft bed.
In such white robes, Heaven's angels used to be

---

[8] *Elegy 19. To His Mistress Going to Bed* Censoring authorities refused to let the publisher include this elegy in early collections of Donne's poems; it was first printed in an anthology, *The Harmony of the Muses* (1654), and did not appear in an edition of Donne's poems until 1669. It is numbered "Elegy 8" in some modern editions.

[9] *spangled breastplate* The stomacher; it covered the chest and was often richly ornamented.

[10] *chime* The lady wears a chiming watch.

20   Received by men: thou, angel, bringst with thee
A heaven like Mahomet's Paradise,[1] and though
Ill spirits walk in white, we easily know
By this these angels from an evil sprite:
Those set our hairs, but these our flesh upright.

25   Licence my roving hands, and let them go,
Behind, before, above, between, below.[2]
Oh my America, my newfound land,
My kingdom, safeliest when with one man manned,
My mine of precious stones: my empery,°   empire

30   How blest am I in this discovering thee!
To enter in these bonds, is to be free;
Then where my hand is set, my seal shall be.

        Full nakedness, all joys are due to thee;
As souls unbodied, bodies unclothed must be

35   To taste whole joys. Gems which you women use
Are like Atlanta's balls,[3] cast in men's views,
That when a fool's eye lighteth on a gem,
His earthly soul may covet theirs, not them.
Like pictures, or like books' gay coverings, made

40   For lay-men,[4] are all women thus arrayed;
Themselves are mystic books, which only we
(Whom their imputed grace[5] will dignify)
Must see revealed. Then since I may know,
As liberally as to a midwife show

45   Thyself: cast all, yea, this white linen hence,

There is no penance, much less innocence.[6]
    To teach thee, I am naked first; why then
What needst thou have more covering than a man.
—1654

---

[1] *Mahomet's Paradise*   Heaven of erotic bliss. The sensual aspects of the Islamic version of Paradise are described in the Koran sura 55, 54–56, sura 56, 12–40, and sura 76, 12–22.

[2] *Behind, before … below*   The order of the words in this line varies in the manuscripts and printed editions.

[3] *Atlanta's balls*   In classical legend, Atalanta said she would only marry a man who could defeat her in footrace. Her suitor Hippomenes won the challenge by dropping three golden balls as he ran; Atalanta stopped to pick them up. The speaker here reverses the story's gender dynamic.

[4] *lay-men*   Referring to the traditional use of images to instruct non-clerics ("lay-men") who could not read the Bible itself; and to the ornate bindings commissioned by wealthy owners to cover books they probably would never read. The speaker proceeds to argue that women are like these kinds of pictures or books: externally beautiful, but only a favored few may "read" what lies inside.

[5] *imputed grace*   Theological term associated with Protestantism: the justifying grace ascribed to a person through Christ's righteousness.

[6] *this white … innocence*   The color white is associated with both penitence and innocence. In some manuscripts and in the 1654 and 1669 printed editions, this line reads "There is no penance due to innocence," a more theologically conventional reading. Some manuscripts read "Here is no penance, much less innocence."

Oh I shall soon despair, when I do see
That Thou lov'st mankind well, yet wilt not choose me,
And Satan hates me, yet is loth to lose me.
—1633

5[3]

I am a little world made cunningly
　Of elements, and an angelic sprite,
But black sin hath betrayed to endless night
My world's both parts, and (oh) both parts must die.
5　You which beyond that heaven which was most high
Have found new spheres, and of new lands can write,
Pour new seas in mine eyes, that so I might
Drown my world with my weeping earnestly,
Or wash it, if it must be drowned no more:
10　But oh it must be burnt; alas the fire
Of lust and envy have burnt it heretofore,
And made it fouler; let their flames retire,
And burn me O Lord, with a fiery zeal
Of Thee and Thy house, which doth in eating heal.
—1635

6[4]

This is my play's last scene, here heavens appoint
　My pilgrimage's last mile; and my race
Idly, yet quickly run, hath this last pace,
My span's last inch, my minute's last point,
5　And gluttonous death will instantly unjoint
My body and soul, and I shall sleep a space,
But my ever-waking part shall see that face
Whose fear already shakes my every joint:
Then, as my soul, to heaven her first seat, takes flight,
10　And earth-born body in the earth shall dwell,
So, fall my sins, that all may have their right,
To where they're bred, and would press me, to hell.
Impute me righteous,[5] thus purged of evil,
For thus I leave the world, the flesh, and devil.
—1633

from *Holy Sonnets*

2[2]

As due by many titles I resign
　Myself to thee, O God, first I was made
By thee, and for Thee, and when I was decayed
Thy blood bought that, the which before was Thine;
5　I am Thy son, made with Thyself to shine,
Thy servant, whose pains Thou hast still repaid,
Thy sheep, Thine image, and, till I betrayed
Myself, a temple of Thy Spirit divine;
Why doth the devil then usurp on me?
10　Why doth he steal, nay ravish, that's Thy right?
Except Thou rise and for Thine own work fight,

---

[2]　*2*　Numbered as Sonnet 1 in some modern editions.

---

[3]　*5*　Numbered as Sonnet 2 (of those added in 1635) in some modern editions.

[4]　*6*　Numbered as Sonnet 3 in some modern editions.

[5]　*Impute me righteous*　Key idea of Protestant theology: justifying grace is imputed to a person through Christ's righteousness.

AEMILIA LANYER
1569 – 1645

Aemilia Lanyer published her one book of poetry at a time when it was unusual for an English woman to publish her writing, especially under her full name. It was even more unusual for a middle-class woman to approach publication as a means of making money; to choose herself female patrons; and to make carefully planned use of poems addressed to them in order to raise the status of her work. Lanyer did all of these things.

Because Lanyer was not born into the nobility, many of the details of her personal life are sketchy, cobbled together from court and church records, information gleaned from her poems, and the professional journals of Simon Forman, an astrologer whom she consulted in 1597. She was born to Baptista Bassano and Margaret Johnson, a couple in a common-law marriage, in January 1569. Her father was an Italian musician in the courts of Edward VI and Elizabeth I, so although Aemilia Bassano was not of noble birth, she had access to aristocratic circles and was probably educated along with the young ladies of the court, likely in classical literature and rhetoric.

At age 18, Aemilia Bassano became the mistress of Henry Carey, Lord Hunsdon, who was then serving as Lord Chamberlain to Queen Elizabeth. The affair continued for five years, until she became pregnant. To avoid embarrassment, Carey married her off to another court musician, Alfonso Lanyer, on 18 October 1592, and provided her with an annual stipend of £40. Lanyer bore a son in early 1593, and named him Henry. Lanyer's marriage to Alfonso was not happy: according to Simon Forman's journals, "her husband hath dealt hardly with her and spent and consumed her goods and she is now ... in debt." The couple had one child together in December 1598, named Odillya, who died at the age of ten months.

Despite her domestic situation, Lanyer maintained her connection with aristocratic families, particularly with a circle of intellectual court women, to whom she later dedicated many poems. Some time before 1609, she stayed with Margaret Clifford, Countess of Cumberland, and her daughter Anne at the estate where they were then living, Cookham Dean. The visit influenced Lanyer profoundly, as she relates in "The Description of Cooke-ham," the first "country house" poem published in English. While at Cookham Dean, she says, she experienced a spiritual awakening, inspired by the piety of the countess.

In 1611, at age 42, she published her volume of verse, *Salve Deus Rex Judæorum* (*Hail, God, King of the Jews*). Although the book focuses on virtue and religion, topics considered appropriate for a woman, it is nevertheless a radical (although not unprecedented) work for its time. Among its topics is the traditional and misogynistic maltreatment of women. The title poem, a lively narrative of the passion of Christ, interrupts its story once to argue that Eve, and, by extension, womankind, have been unjustly made to bear the chief responsibility for eating the fruit of the forbidden tree: that sin pales in comparison to the sin of the men who deliberately sentenced Christ to death. She commends the intervention of Pilate's wife and contrasts the behavior of Christ's male disciples, who forsook or denied him, with that of the women who stayed with him to the end.

After her husband died in 1613, Lanyer founded a school for the children of nobility and other wealthy families as a means of supporting herself. The only details concerning the remainder of her life come from court records, which indicate that she had considerable legal troubles, first concerning her school, then regarding the estate of her son, Henry, who died in October 1633. Lanyer died at age 76, and was buried 3 April 1645, at St. James Church, Clerkenwell.

⌘ ⌘ ⌘

To the Virtuous Reader[1]

Often have I heard that it is the property[2] of some women not only to emulate the virtues and perfections of the rest, but also by all their powers of ill-speaking to eclipse the brightness of their deserved fame; now contrary to this custom, which men I hope unjustly lay to their charge, I have written this small volume or little book, for the general use of all virtuous ladies and gentlewomen of this kingdom; and in commendation of some particular persons of our own sex, such as for the most part are so well known to myself and others, that I dare undertake fame dares not to call any better. And this have I done to make known to the world that all women deserve not to be blamed, though some forgetting they are women themselves, and in danger to be condemned by the words of their own mouths, fall into so great an error, as to speak unadvisedly against the rest of their sex; which if it be true, I am persuaded they can show their own imperfection in nothing more; and therefore could wish (for their own ease, modesties and credit) they would refer such points of folly to be practised by evil-disposed men, who forgetting they were born of women, nourished of women, and that if it were not by the means of women, they would be quite extinguished out of the world, and a final end of them all, do like vipers deface the wombs wherein they were bred,[3] only to give way and utterance to their want of discretion and goodness. Such as these, were they that dishonoured Christ, his apostles and prophets, putting them to shameful deaths. Therefore we are not to regard any imputations, that they undeservedly lay upon us, no otherwise than to make use of them to our own benefits, as spurs to virtue, making us fly all occasions that may colour their unjust speeches to pass current.[4] Especially considering that they have tempted even the patience of God himself, who gave power to wise and virtuous women to bring down their pride and arrogance. As was cruel Cesarius by the discreet counsel of noble Deborah,[5] judge and prophetess of Israel, and resolution of Jael,[6] wife of Heber the Kenite; wicked Haman, by the divine prayers and prudent proceedings of beautiful Hester;[7] blasphemous Holofernes, by the invincible courage, rare wisdom, and confident carriage of Judith;[8] and the unjust judges, by the innocence of chaste Susanna;[9] with infinite others, which for brevity's sake I will omit. As also in respect it pleased our Lord and Saviour Jesus Christ, without the assistance of man, being free from original and all other sins, from the time of his conception till the hour of his death, to be begotten of a woman, born of a woman, nourished of a woman, obedient to a woman; and that he healed women, pardoned women, comforted women, yea, even when he was in his greatest agony and bloody sweat, going to be crucified, and also in the last hour of his death, took care to dispose of a woman; after his resurrection, appeared first to a woman, sent a woman to declare his most glorious resurrection to the rest of his disciples. Many other examples I could allege of diverse faithful and virtuous women, who have in all ages not only been confessors, but also endured most cruel martyrdom for their faith in Jesus Christ. All which is sufficient to enforce all good Christians and honourable-minded men to speak reverently of our sex, and especially of all virtuous and good women. To the modest censures of both which I refer these my imperfect endeavours, knowing that according to their own excellent dispositions they will rather cherish, nourish, and increase the least spark of virtue where they find it, by their favourable and best interpretations, than quench it by wrong constructions. To whom I wish with all increase of virtue, and desire their best opinions.
—1611

---

[1] *To the Virtuous Reader*   Printed as a preface to Lanyer's book *Salve Deus Rex Judæorum*, selections from which are included below.

[2] *property*   Habit.

[3] *vipers ... bred*   It was thought that at birth the viper's young bit through the sides of the mother in order to be born, killing her.

[4] *pass current*   Seem legitimate.

[5] *Deborah*   Ruler of Israel who defeated the army of Sisera (Cesarius), a Canaanite general (see Judges 4).

[6] *Jael*   Woman who killed Sisera by driving a tent peg through his head (see Judges 4).

[7] *Hester*   Jewish queen (also called Esther) who saved the Jews from a genocidal plot concocted by Haman by appealing to Xerxes, King of Persia (see Esther 3–7).

[8] *Judith*   Woman who killed the Babylonian general Holofernes by cutting off his head (see Judith 8–12).

[9] *Susanna*   Woman who resisted the advances of two judges, who then unjustly charged her with adultery (see Daniel and Susanna 13).

from *Salve Deus Rex Judæorum*[1]

"Invocation"

Sith° *Cynthia*[2] is ascended to that rest   *since*
Of endless joy and true eternity,
That glorious place that cannot be expressed
By any wight° clad in mortality,   *creature*
5 In her almighty love so highly blest,
And crowned with everlasting sovereignty;
    Where saints and angels do attend her throne,
    And she gives glory unto God alone.

To thee, great Countess,[3] now I will apply
10 My pen, to write thy never dying fame;
That when to heaven thy blessed soul shall fly,
These lines on earth record thy reverend name:
And to this task I mean my muse to tie,
Though wanting skill I shall but purchase blame:
15   Pardon (dear Lady) want of woman's wit
    To pen thy praise, when few can equal it.

*   *   *

"Eve's Apology in Defense of Women"

745 Now Pontius Pilate[4] is to judge the cause
Of faultless Jesus, who before him stands,
Who neither hath offended prince, nor laws,
Although he now be brought in woeful bands.
O noble governor, make thou yet a pause,
750 Do not in innocent blood inbrue° thy hands;[5]   *defile*
    But hear the words of thy most worthy wife,
    Who sends to thee, to beg her Savior's life.[6]

Let barb'rous cruelty far depart from thee,
And in true justice take affliction's part;
755 Open thine eyes, that thou the truth may'st see.
Do not the thing that goes against thy heart,
Condemn not him that must thy Savior be;
But view his holy life, his good desert.°   *merit*
    Let not us women glory in men's fall.[7]
760   Who had power given to overrule us all.

Till now your indiscretion sets us free.
And makes our former fault much less appear;
Our mother Eve, who tasted of the tree,[8]
Giving to Adam what she held most dear,
765 Was simply good, and had no power to see;
The after-coming harm did not appear:
    The subtle serpent that our sex betrayed
    Before our fall so sure a plot had laid.

That undiscerning ignorance perceived
770 No guile or craft that was by him intended;
For had she known of what we were bereaved,[9]
To his request she had not condescended.
But she, poor soul, by cunning was deceived;
No hurt therein her harmless heart intended:
775   For she alleged° God's word, which he[10] denies,   *affirmed*
    That they should die, but even as gods be wise.

But surely Adam cannot be excused;
Her fault though great, yet he was most to blame;
What weakness offered, strength might have refused,
780 Being lord of all, the greater was his shame.
Although the serpent's craft had her abused,
God's holy word ought all his actions frame,°   *shape*
    For he was lord and king of all the earth,
    Before poor Eve had either life or breath,

[1] *Salve Deus Rex Judæorum* The complete text of Lanyer's book is available on the website component of this anthology.

[2] *Cynthia* Goddess of the moon, often identified with Queen Elizabeth I, who died in 1603.

[3] *Countess* Margaret Clifford, Countess of Cumberland (1560–1616), Lanyer's patroness.

[4] *Pontius Pilate* Roman governor of Judea, who presided over the trial of Jesus (see Matthew 27.11–26).

[5] *Do ... hands* Reference to Matthew 27.24, in which Pilate washes his hands to demonstrate that he does not consider himself responsible for what happens to Jesus.

[6] *hear ... life* Pilate received a message from his wife, urging him not to convict Jesus (see Matthew 27.19).

[7] *men's fall* Fall into a sin, by crucifying Christ, greater than Eve's "original" sin.

[8] *Eve ... tree* According to Genesis 3.6, Eve ate the fruit of the tree of the knowledge of good and evil. She shared the fruit with Adam, and as a consequence the two were banished from the Garden of Eden.

[9] *bereaved* Robbed (of eternal life).

[10] *he* I.e., the serpent (see Genesis 3.4–5).

785 Who being framed° by God's eternal hand   *formed*
The perfectest man that ever breathed on earth;
And from God's mouth received that strait° command, *strict*
The breach whereof he knew was present death;
Yea, having power to rule both sea and land,
790 Yet with one apple won to lose that breath[1]
        Which God had breathed in his beauteous face,
        Bringing us all in danger and disgrace.

And then to lay the fault on Patience' back,
That we (poor women) must endure it all.
795 We know right well he did discretion lack,
Being not persuaded thereunto at all.
If Eve did err, it was for knowledge sake;
The fruit being fair persuaded him to fall:
        No subtle serpent's falsehood did betray him;
800   If he would eat it, who had power to stay° him?   *stop*

Not Eve, whose fault was only too much love,
Which made her give this present to her dear,
That what she tasted he likewise might prove,°   *experience*
Whereby his knowledge might become more clear;
805 He never sought her weakness to reprove
With those sharp words which he of God did hear;
        Yet men will boast of knowledge, which he took
        From Eve's fair hand, as from a learned book.

If any evil did in her remain,
810 Being made of him,[2] he was the ground of all.
If one of many worlds[3] could lay a stain
Upon our sex, and work so great a fall
To wretched man by Satan's[4] subtle train,
What will so foul a fault amongst you all?
815   Her weakness did the serpent's words obey,
        But you in malice God's dear Son betray,

Whom, if unjustly you condemn to die,
Her sin was small to what you do commit;
All mortal sins that do for vengeance cry
820 Are not to be compared unto it.
If many worlds would altogether try
By all their sins the wrath of God to get,
        This sin of yours surmounts them all as far
        As doth the sun another little star.[5]

825 Then let us have our liberty again,
And challenge° to yourselves no sovereignty.   *attribute*
You came not in the world without our pain,
Make that a bar against your cruelty;
Your fault being greater, why should you disdain
830 Our being your equals, free from tyranny?
        If one weak woman simply did offend,
        This sin of yours hath no excuse nor end,

To which, poor souls, we never gave consent.
Witness, thy wife, O Pilate, speaks for all,
835 Who did but dream, and yet a message sent
That thou shouldest have nothing to do at all
With that just man[6] which, if thy heart relent,
Why wilt thou be a reprobate[7] with Saul[8]
        To seek the death of him that is so good,
840   For thy soul's health to shed his dearest blood?
—1611

The Description of Cooke-ham[9]

Farewell (sweet Cooke-ham) where I first obtained
Grace from that grace where perfect grace remained;
And where the muses gave their full consent,
I should have power the virtuous to content;

---

[1] *breath* God breathed life into Adam (see Genesis 2.7).

[2] *made … him* According to Genesis 2.21–22, Eve was made from one of Adam's ribs.

[3] *many worlds* As the first man, Adam was the father of all humans. Human beings were sometimes likened to individual worlds in the literature of the time.

[4] *Satan's* Belonging to the serpent, traditionally identified with Satan.

[5] *sun … star* As the sun outshines the other stars in the sky, so the sin of killing Jesus is greater in magnitude. In earlier understandings of astronomy, the sun was thought to be much larger than the stars.

[6] *just man* I.e., Jesus.

[7] *a reprobate* Damned.

[8] *Saul* King of Israel, who tried to kill David (see 1 Samuel 19.9–24).

[9] *Cooke-ham* Cookham Dean, a country house in Berkshire, UK, leased by the brother of Lanyer's patroness, Margaret Clifford, Countess of Cumberland.

5   Where princely palace willed me to indite°   *write*
       The sacred story of the soul's delight.[1]
       Farewell (sweet place) where virtue then did rest,
       And all delights did harbour in her breast;
       Never shall my sad eyes again behold
10   Those pleasures which my thoughts did then unfold;
       Yet you (great lady) mistress of that place,[2]
       From whose desires did spring this work of grace,
       Vouchsafe° to think upon these pleasures past   *are prepared*
       As fleeting, worldly joys that could not last,
15   Or as dim shadows of celestial pleasures,
       Which are desired above all earthly treasures.
       Oh how (methought) against you thither came
       Each part did seem some new delight to frame!
       The house received all ornaments to grace it,
20   And would endure no foulness to deface it.
       The walks put on their summer liveries,°   *uniforms*
       And all things else did hold like similes:
       The trees with leaves, with fruits, with flowers clad,
       Embraced each other, seeming to be glad,
25   Turning themselves to beauteous canopies
       To shade the bright sun from your brighter eyes;
       The crystal streams with silver spangles graced,
       While by the glorious sun they were embraced;
       The little birds in chirping notes did sing,
30   To entertain both you and that sweet spring;
       And Philomela[3] with her sundry lays,
       Both you and that delightful place did praise.
       Oh, how methought each plant, each flower, each tree
       Set forth their beauties then to welcome thee;
35   The very hills right humbly did descend,
       When you to tread upon them did intend.
       And as you set your feet, they still did rise,
       Glad that they could receive so rich a prize.
       The gentle winds did take delight to be
40   Among those woods that were so graced by thee
       And in sad murmur uttered pleasing sound,
       That pleasure in that place might more abound;
       The swelling banks delivered all their pride,

       When such a phoenix once they had espied.
45   Each arbour, bank, each seat, each stately tree
       Thought themselves honoured in supporting thee.
       The pretty birds would oft come to attend thee,
       Yet fly away for fear they should offend thee;
       The little creatures in the burrow by
50   Would come abroad to sport them in your eye;[4]
       Yet fearful of the bow in your fair hand
       Would run away when you did make a stand.
       Now let me come unto that stately tree,
       Wherein such goodly prospects you did see;
55   That oak that did in height his fellows pass,
       As much as lofty trees, low-growing grass;
       Much like a comely cedar, straight and tall,
       Whose beauteous stature far exceeded all;
       How often did you visit this fair tree,
60   Which seeming joyful in receiving thee,
       Would like a palm tree spread his arms abroad,
       Desirous that you there should make abode;
       Whose fair green leaves much like a comely veil
       Defended Phoebus[5] when he would assail;
65   Whose pleasing boughs did lend a cool fresh air,
       Joying his happiness when you were there;
       Where being seated, you might plainly see
       Hills, vales and woods, as if on bended knee
       They had appeared, your honour to salute,
70   Or to prefer° some strange unlooked-for suit;°   *proffer / request*
       All interlaced with brooks and crystal springs,
       A prospect fit to please the eyes of kings;
       And thirteen shires appear all in your sight,
       Europe could not afford much more delight.
75   What was there then but gave you all content,
       While you the time in meditation spent,
       Of their creator's power, which there you saw
       In all his creatures held a perfect law,
       And in their beauties did you plain descry°   *discern*
80   His beauty, wisdom, grace, love, majesty.
       In these sweet woods how often did you walk
       With Christ and his apostles there to talk;
       Placing his holy writ° in some fair tree,   *scripture*
       To meditate what you therein did see;

---

[1] *sacred ... delight Salve Deus Rex Judeaeorum*, to which this poem
is appended.

[2] *you ... place* Margaret Clifford, Countess of Cumberland (1560-
1616).

[3] *Philomela* Nightingale. In Greek mythology, Philomela was a
woman who was changed into a nightingale.

---

[4] *sport ... eye* Entertain you.

[5] *Phoebus* Sun. "Phoebus" is an epithet for Apollo, Greek and
Roman god of the sun.

85 With Moses you did mount his holy hill,[1]
To know his pleasure and perform his will.
With lovely David you did often sing,
His holy hymns to heaven's eternal king.[2]
And in sweet music did your soul delight,
90 To sound his praises, morning, noon and night.
With blessed Joseph you did often feed
Your pined brethren when they stood in need.[3]
And that sweet lady sprung from Clifford's race,
Of noble Bedford's blood, fair stem of grace,
95 To honourable Dorset now espoused,[4]
In whose fair breast true virtue then was housed;
Oh, what delight did my weak spirits find
In those pure parts of her well-framed mind;
And yet it grieves me that I cannot be
100 Near unto her, whose virtues did agree
With those fair ornaments of outward beauty,
Which did enforce from all both love and duty.
Unconstant fortune, thou art most to blame,
Who casts us down into so low a frame,°   state
105 Where our great friends we cannot daily see,
So great a difference is there in degree.°   social status
Many are placed in those orbs of state,
Parters° in honour, so ordained by fate,   dividers
Nearer in show, yet farther off in love,
110 In which the lowest always are above.
But whither am I carried in conceit?°   thought
My wit too weak to conster° of the great.   understand
Why not? although we are but born of earth,
We may behold the heavens, despising death;
115 And loving heaven that is so far above,
May in the end vouchsafe° us entire love.   grant
Therefore sweet memory, do thou retain
Those pleasures past, which will not turn again;

Remember beauteous Dorset's[5] summer sports,[6]
120 So far from being touched by ill reports;
Wherein myself did always bear a part,
While reverend love presented my true heart;
Those recreations let me bear in mind,
Which her sweet youth and noble thoughts did find;
125 Whereof deprived, I evermore must grieve,
Hating blind fortune, careless to relieve.
And you, sweet Cooke-ham, whom these ladies leave,
I now must tell the grief you did conceive
At their departure; when they went away,
130 How everything retained a sad dismay;
Nay long before, when once an inkling came,
Methought each thing did unto sorrow frame;
The trees that were so glorious in our view,
Forsook both flowers and fruit, when once they knew
135 Of your depart, their very leaves did wither,
Changing their colours as they grew together.
But when they saw this had no power to stay you,
They often wept, though speechless, could not pray you;
Letting their tears in your fair bosoms fall,
140 As if they said: "Why will ye leave us all?"
This being vain, they cast their leaves away,
Hoping that pity would have made you stay;
Their frozen tops, like age's hoary hairs,
Shows their disasters, languishing in fears;
145 A swarthy rivelled rine[7] all overspread
Their dying bodies, half-alive, half-dead.
But your occasions called you so away,
That nothing there had power to make you stay;
Yet did I see a noble, grateful mind,
150 Requiting each according to their kind;
Forgetting not to turn and take your leave
Of these sad creatures, powerless to receive
Your favour, when with grief you did depart,
Placing their former pleasures in your heart;
155 Giving great charge to noble memory,
There to preserve their love continually;
But specially the love of that fair tree,
That first and last you did vouchsafe to see;
In which it pleased you oft to take the air,
160 With noble Dorset, then a virgin fair;

---

[1] *Moses ... hill* In Exodus 24.9 Moses climbs Mount Sinai in order to see God.

[2] *With ... king* David was then supposed to be the author of most or all of Psalms, songs written in praise of God.

[3] *With ... need* Reference to Genesis 42.25, in which Joseph, as governor of Egypt, provides his deceitful brothers with food in order to save them from starvation.

[4] *sweet lady ... espoused* Margaret Clifford's daughter, Lady Anne Clifford (1589–1675), married Richard Sackville, Earl of Dorset (1589–1624). Lady Anne's maternal grandfather was Francis Russell, Earl of Bedford (1527–85). A selection from her diary is in this anthology.

---

[5] *Dorset* Lady Anne Clifford.

[6] *summer sports* E.g., country dances and outdoor games.

[7] *rivelled rine* Wrinkled bark.

Where many a learned book was read and scanned;
To this fair tree, taking me by the hand,
You did repeat the pleasures which had passed,
Seeming to grieve they could no longer last.
165 And with a chaste, yet loving kiss took leave,
Of which sweet kiss I did it soon bereave;°   *rob*
Scorning a senseless creature should possess
So rare a favour, so great happiness.
No other kiss it could receive from me,
170 For fear to give back what it took of thee;
So I, ungrateful creature, did deceive it,
Of that which you vouchsafed in love to leave it.
And though it oft had giv'n me much content,
Yet this great wrong I never could repent;
175 But of the happiest made it most forlorn,
To show that nothing's free from fortune's scorn,
While all the rest with this most beauteous tree,
Made their sad consort sorrow's harmony.
The flowers that on the banks and walks did grow,
180 Crept in the ground, the grass did weep for woe.
The winds and waters seemed to chide together,
Because you went away, they knew not whither.
And those sweet brooks that ran so fair and clear,
With grief and trouble wrinkled did appear.
185 Those pretty birds that wonted° were to sing,   *accustomed*
Now neither sing, nor chirp, nor use their wing;
But with their tender feet on some bare spray,°   *branch*
Warble forth sorrow, and their own dismay.
Fair Philomela leaves her mournful ditty,
190 Drowned in dead sleep, yet can procure no pity;
Each arbour, bank, each seat, each stately tree
Looks bare and desolate now, for want of thee;
Turning green tresses° into frosty grey,   *hair*
While in cold grief they wither all away.
195 The sun grew weak, his beams no comfort gave,
While all green things did make the earth their grave;
Each briar, each bramble, when you went away,
Caught fast your clothes, thinking to make you stay;
Delightful Echo,[1] wonted to reply
200 To our last words, did now for sorrow die;
The house cast off each garment that might grace it,
Putting on dust and cobwebs to deface it.
All desolation then there did appear,
When you were going whom they held so dear.
205 This last farewell to Cooke-ham here I give;
When I am dead thy name in this may live,
Wherein I have performed her noble hest,°   *command*
Whose virtues lodge in my unworthy breast,
And ever shall, so long as life remains,
210 Tying my heart to her by those rich chains.
—1611

To the Doubtful Reader[2]

Gentle reader, if thou desire to be resolved,[3] why I give this title, *Salve Deus Rex Judæorum,*[4] know for certain, that it was delivered unto me in sleep many years before I had any intent to write in this manner, and was quite out of my memory, until I had written the Passion of Christ, when immediately it came into my remembrance, what I had dreamed long before; and thinking it a significant token, that I was appointed to perform this work, I gave the very same words I received in sleep as the fittest title I could devise for this book.
—1611

---

[1] *Echo* Nymph in Greek mythology who was prevented by a curse from saying anything other than what others said.

[2] *To the Doubtful Reader* Printed at the conclusion of *Salve Deus Rex Judæorum; Doubtful* Curious.

[3] *be resolved* Understand.

[4] *Salve … Judæorum* Latin: Hail, God, King of the Jews.

LADY MARY WROTH
1587 – 1651

Lady Mary Wroth wrote the first work of prose fiction and the first amatory sonnet sequence published by a woman in English. Her court romance, *The Countess of Montgomery's Urania* (1621) exploits multiple Renaissance genres—sonnet, ballad, madrigal, pastoral narrative and song, among others—with penetrating observation, worldly skepticism, and emotional subtlety. Wroth's work was admired by a number of poets of her day—Ben Jonson, who dedicated his play *The Alchemist* (1610) to her, proclaimed that her verse had made him "a better lover, and much better poet"—and although her reputation faded during the ensuing centuries, today Mary Wroth is recognized as a significant Jacobean writer and pioneer.

Born Mary Sidney in 1587, Wroth was a member of an illustrious political and literary family that included her uncle, Sir Philip Sidney, her aunt, Mary Sidney Herbert, Countess of Pembroke (herself a poet and patron of poets), and her father, Sir Robert Sidney, a statesman and minor poet. Educated by tutors, Mary was already an accomplished scholar, musician, and dancer by the time of her arranged marriage in 1604 to a wealthy landowner, Sir Robert Wroth. The union was not a happy one, but it did propel Lady Mary further into the life of the Jacobean court, where she performed in Ben Jonson's *Masque of Blackness* in 1605 and *Masque of Beauty* in 1608, and, in her family's tradition, bestowed friendship and patronage on poets such as Jonson and George Chapman.

On her husband's death in 1614, Wroth was left with an infant son (who died in 1616) and crushing debts. She was also free to pursue more openly a long-time illicit affair with her cousin, William Herbert, with whom she eventually had two illegitimate children. This affair, and financial constraints, may have limited Wroth's access to court and spurred her to write more seriously. She polished her sonnets, already circulating in manuscript as early as 1605, and in 1621 appended them to a 558-page prose romance, *Urania*, dedicated to the Countess of Montgomery. Because of its fictionalized allusions to actual court personages and events, the book offended those who saw themselves depicted too transparently. One such person, Sir William Denny, complained to the King and circulated a scathing poem criticizing Wroth as a "hermaphrodite" and "monster," an "oyster" gaping open to every tide. Denny's attack sparked a wittily vigorous reply in which Wroth mimicked the exact form of Denny's verse, rewriting his lines one by one. But in the end the attacks on her found their mark; she withdrew the edition of *Urania* and published no more work during her lifetime. (A second part of *Urania*, a few other poems, and a pastoral drama, *Love's Victory*, remained unpublished until our own time.)

Scandalous elements aside, *Urania* is a groundbreaking work because it uses genres traditionally written by men—episodic pastoral narrative of the sort we find in Sir Philip Sidney's *Arcadia*, and the digressive adventures of the Alexandrian romance—in untraditional ways to examine the social situation of women in actual court society. Wroth's prose is plainer than Sidney's and her outlook even more skeptical of romantic ideals. ("Credit no thing" is a typical warning.) Centering on the friendship of the shepherdess Urania (modeled on the Countess of Montgomery) with the princess Pamphilia (modeled on Wroth herself) and Pamphilia's frustrated love for the faithless Amphilanthus (whose name means "lover of two"), the story branches into multiple episodes and characters, interspersed with over fifty poems and songs in various genres. While celebrating the power of female desire, Wroth does not shrink from depicting the casual brutality of relations between the sexes: women seduced and abandoned, the indignity of forced marriages, the tortures of jealousy and deception.

In *Pamphilia to Amphilanthus*, the sequence of 83 sonnets and 20 songs that follows *Urania*, Wroth, no doubt influenced by her famous uncle's *Astrophil and Stella*, again applies herself to a genre traditionally (although by now by no means exclusively) reserved for males. She again deftly employs a somewhat outdated convention—the Petrarchan sonnet—in ways that highlight love's tensions and contradictions. Pamphilia addresses not her beloved, as does the authorial voice in many Petrarchan sonnets, but herself ("I with my spirit talk and cry"), as well as Cupid, Time, Fortune, and other personifications of her trials. As Paula Payne observes, "Astrophil is writing to win his love, but Pamphilia is writing to discover her self." If so, she may in this regard be more genuinely and interestingly Petrarchan than some of Petrarch's later and lesser followers. The climax of *Pamphilia to Amphilanthus* is a technical *tour de force*, a "corona" of fourteen sonnets in which the last line of the first becomes the first line of the next. The line that begins and ends it ("In this strange labyrinth how shall I turn?") is emblematic of Wroth's skill in combining the elegant detachment of the Petrarchan form with a heightened emotional urgency: love, it turns out, is not the "thread" that she had expected to lead her from the labyrinth, for the "corona" leaves her there.

Mary Wroth lived her final decades in obscurity, struggling with debt, and died in 1651. In the youthful portrait of her which survives, she is pictured holding, not the gloves or fan customary in female portraits of the time, but an archlute—symbol of the poet.

⌘ ⌘ ⌘

from *Pamphilia to Amphilanthus*

1

When night's black mantle could most darkness prove,°   *display*
And sleep death's Image did my senses hire°   *engage*
From knowledge of my self, then thoughts did move
Swifter than those most swiftness need require:
5 In sleep, a Chariot drawn by winged desire
I saw: where sat bright Venus Queen of love,
And at her feet her son,[1] still adding fire
To burning hearts which she did hold above,
But one heart flaming more than all the rest
10 The goddess held, and put it to my breast,
Dear son, now shoot said she: thus must we win;
He her obeyed, and martyred my poor heart,
I, waking hoped as dreams it would depart
Yet since: O me: a lover I have been.

6

My pain, still smothered in my grieved breast,
Seeks for some ease, yet cannot passage find
To be discharged of this unwelcome guest;
When most I strive, more fast his burdens bind,
5 Like to a ship, on Goodwins[2] cast by wind
The more she strives, more deep in sand is pressed
Till she be lost; so am I, in this kind°   *manner*
Sunk, and devoured, and swallowed by unrest,
Lost, shipwrecked, spoiled, debarred of smallest hope
10 Nothing of pleasure left; save° thoughts have scope,   *unless*
Which wander may: Go then, my thoughts, and cry
Hope's perished; Love tempest-beaten; Joy lost;
Killing despair hath all these blessings crossed
Yet faith still cries, Love will not falsify.

---

1 *her son* Cupid, customarily pictured as a winged infant carrying a bow and a quiver of arrows for piercing hearts, and torches to set them ablaze.

2 *Goodwins* The Goodwins, or Goodwin Sands, a dangerous shoal off the coast of Kent proverbially associated with shipwrecks in Wroth's time.

7

Love leave° to urge, thou know'st thou hast   cease
    the hand;°   upper hand
'Tis cowardice, to strive where none resist:
Pray thee leave off, I yield unto thy band;°   bond
Do not thus, still, in thine own power persist,
5 Behold I yield: let forces be dismissed;
I am thy subject, conquered, bound to stand,
Never thy foe, but did thy claim assist
Seeking thy due of those who did withstand;
But now, it seems, thou would'st I should thee love;
10 I do confess, 'twas thy will made me choose;
And thy fair shows[1] made me a lover prove
When I my freedom did, for pain, refuse.
Yet this Sir God,[2] your boyship I despise;
Your charms I obey, but love not want of eyes.[3]

13

Dear, famish not what you your self gave food;
    Destroy not what your glory is to save;
Kill not that soul to which you spirit gave;
In pity, not disdain your triumph stood;
5 An easy thing it is to shed the blood
Of one, who at your will, yields to the grave;
But more you may true worth[4] by mercy crave
When you preserve, not spoil, but nourish good;
Your sight is all the food I do desire;
10 Then sacrifice me not in hidden fire,
Or stop the breath which did your praises move:
Think but how easy 'tis a sight to give;
Nay ev'n desert; since by it I do live,
I but chameleon-like[5] would live, and love.

14

Am I thus conquered? have I lost the powers
    That to withstand, which joys° to ruin me?   delights
Must I be still while it my strength devours
And captive leads me prisoner, bound, unfree?

---

[1] *shows* Displays (of power).

[2] *Sir God* Mocking address to Cupid.

[3] *want of eyes* Blindness, a proverbial attribute of love, and of Cupid.

[4] *worth* Pun on "Wroth," which was pronounced "worth."

[5] *chameleon-like* The chameleon could survive for long periods without food, and was thus reputed to live on air.

5 Love first shall leave men's fancies to them free,
Desire shall quench love's flames, spring hate°   shall hate
    sweet showers,
Love shall loose all his darts, have sight, and see
His shame, and wishings hinder happy hours;
Why should we not love's purblind° charms   almost blind
    resist?
10 Must we be servile, doing what he list?°   wishes
No, seek some host to harbour thee: I fly°   flee from
Thy babish° tricks, and freedom do profess;   babyish
But O my hurt, makes my lost heart confess
I love, and must: So farewell liberty.

15

Truly poor Night thou welcome art to me:
    I love thee better in this sad attire
Than that which raiseth some men's fancies higher
Like painted outsides which foul inward be;
5 I love thy grave, and saddest looks to see,
Which seems° my soul, and dying heart entire,   resembles
Like to the ashes of some happy fire
That flamed in joy, but quenched in misery:
I love thy count'nance, and thy sober pace
10 Which evenly goes, and as of loving grace
To us, and me among the rest oppressed
Gives quiet, peace to my poor self alone,
And freely grants day leave when thou art gone
To give clear light to see all ill° redressed.   misery

22

Like to the Indians, scorched with the sun,
    The sun which they do as their God adore
So am I used by love, for ever more
I worship him, less favors have I won,
5 Better are they who thus to blackness run,
And so can only whiteness' want deplore
Than I who pale, and white am with grief's store,° abundance
Nor can have hope, but to see hopes undone;
Besides, their sacrifice received's in sight
10 Of their chose saint: mine hid as worthless rite;
Grant me to see where I my offerings give,
Then let me wear the mark of Cupid's might

In heart as they in skin of Phoebus' light[1]
Not ceasing offerings to love while I Live.

23

When every one to pleasing pastime hies°　*hastens*
　Some hunt, some hawk, some play, while some
　　delight
In sweet discourse, and music shows joy's might
Yet I my thoughts do far above these prize.
5　The joy which I take, is that free from eyes[2]
I sit, and wonder at this daylike night
So to dispose themselves, as void° of right;　*bereft*
And leave true pleasure for poor vanities;
When others hunt, my thoughts I have in chase;
10　If hawk,[3] my mind at wished end doth fly,
Discourse,[4] I with my spirit talk, and cry
While others, music choose as greatest grace.
O God, say I, can these fond° pleasures move?　*foolish*
Or music be but in sweet thoughts of love?

35

False hope which feeds but to destroy, and spill
　What it first breeds;[5] unnatural to the birth
Of thine own womb; conceiving but to kill,
And plenty gives to make the greater dearth,
5　So Tyrants do who falsely ruling earth
Outwardly grace them, and with profit's fill
Advance those who appointed are to death
To make their greater fall to please their will.
Thus shadow they their wicked vile intent
10　Colouring evil with a show of good
While in fair shows° their malice so is spent;　*spectacles*
Hope kills the heart, and tyrants shed the blood.
For hope deluding brings us to the pride°　*peak*
Of our desires the farther down to slide.

---

[1] *as ... light* As Indians, "scorched with the sun," show "in their skins" the mark of Phoebus, the sun-god.

[2] *eyes* The eyes, or gaze, of others.

[3] *If hawk* If they (others) hawk.

[4] *Discourse* When others discourse.

[5] *spill ... breeds* As in a miscarriage.

SONG [LOVE, A CHILD, IS EVER CRYING]

Love, a child, is ever crying,
　Please him, and he straight is flying;
　Give him, he the more is craving,
　Never satisfied with having.

5　His desire have no measure,
　Endless folly is his treasure;
　What he promiseth he breaketh;
　Trust not one word that he speaketh.

He vows nothing but false matter,
10　And to cozen° you he'll flatter;　*deceive*
　Let him gain the hand, he'll leave you,
　And still glory to deceive you.

He will triumph in your wailing,
　And yet cause be of your failing:
15　These his virtues are, and slighter
　Are his gifts, his favours lighter.

Feathers are as firm in staying,
　Wolves no fiercer in their preying.
　As a child then leave him crying,
20　Nor seek him, so giv'n to flying.

A CROWN OF SONNETS DEDICATED TO LOVE

77

In this strange labyrinth how shall I turn?
　Ways° are on all sides while the way I miss:　*paths*
　If to the right hand, there in love I burn;
　Let me go forward, therein danger is;
5　If to the left, suspicion hinders bliss;
　Let me turn back, shame cries I ought return,
　Nor faint, though crosses° with my fortunes kiss;　*troubles*
　Stand still is harder, although sure to mourn.[6]
Thus let me take the right, or left-hand way,
10　Go forward, or stand still, or back retire:
　I must these doubts endure without allay°　*relief*
　Or help, but travail[7] find for my best hire.

---

[6] *although sure to mourn* Although sure to make me mourn.

[7] *travail* Hard work, but also with a pun on "travel."

Yet that which most my troubled sense doth move,
Is to leave all, and take the thread of Love.[1]

78

15 Is to leave all, and take the thread of love,
     Which line straight leads unto the soul's content,
     Where choice delights with pleasure's wings do move,
     And idle fancy never room had lent.
     When chaste thoughts guide us, then our minds are bent
20   To take that good which ills from us remove:
       Light of true love brings fruit which none repent;
       But constant lovers seek and wish to prove.
     Love is the shining star of blessing's light,
       The fervent fire of zeal, the root of peace,
25   The lasting lamp, fed with the oil of right,
       Image of faith, and womb for joy's increase.
     Love is true virtue, and his end's delight,
     His flames are joys, his bands true lovers' might.

79

     His flames are joys, his bands true lovers' might,
30   No stain is there, but pure, as purest white,
       Where no cloud can appear to dim his light,
       Nor spot defile, but shame will soon requite.
     Here are affections, tried by love's just might
       As gold by fire, and black discerned by white;
35   Error by truth, and darkness known by light,
       Where faith is valued, for love to requite.
     Please him, and serve him, glory in his might
       And firm he'll be, as innocency white,
       Clear as th'air, warm as sun's beams, as day light
40   Just as truth, constant as fate, joyed to requite.
     Then love obey, strive to observe his might
     And be in his brave court a glorious light.

80

     And be in his brave court a glorious light
       Shine in the eyes of faith, and constancy
45   Maintain the fires of love, still burning bright,
       Not slightly sparkling, but light flaming be.
     Never to slack till earth no stars can see,

Till sun, and moon do leave to us dark night,
  And second chaos once again do free
50 Us, and the world from all divisions spite,
Till then affections which his followers are,
  Govern our hearts, and prove his power's gain,
  To taste this pleasing sting, seek with all care
  For happy smarting is it with small pain.
55 Such as although it pierce your tender heart,
  And burn, yet burning you will love the smart.

81

And burn, yet burning you will love the smart,
  When you shall feel the weight of true desire,
  So pleasing, as you would not wish your part
60 Of burden should be missing from that fire.
But faithful and unfeigned heat aspire
  Which sin abolisheth, and doth impart
  Salves to all fear, with virtues which inspire
  Souls with divine love; which shows his chaste art.
65 And guide he is to joyings, open eyes
  He hath to happiness, and best can learn
  Us means how to deserve, this he descries,°   *perceives*
  Who blind, yet doth our hiddenest thoughts discern.
Thus we may gain since living in blest love,
70 He may our prophet,[2] and our tutor prove.

82

He may our prophet, and our tutor prove,
  In whom alone we do this power find,
  To join two hearts as in one frame to move
  Two bodies, but one soul to rule the mind
75 Eyes which must care to one dear object bind,
  Ears to each other's speech as if above
  All else, they sweet, and learned were; this kind
  Content of lovers witnesseth true love.
It doth enrich the wits, and make you see
80 That in your self which you knew not before,
  Forcing you to admire such gifts should be
  Hid from your knowledge, yet in you the store.
Millions of these adorn the throne of Love,
How blest be they then, who his favours
     prove?°   *experience*

---

[1] *thread of Love* Referring to the myth of Ariadne, who gave her beloved Theseus a spool of thread to unwind behind him as he traveled through the labyrinth of the Minotaur; by following the thread he could find his way back out.

[2] *prophet* This appears as "profit" in an earlier version of the poem.

83

85 How blest be they, then, who his favours prove,
   A life whereof the birth is just desire?
     Breeding sweet flame, which hearts invite to move,
     In these loved eyes which kindle Cupid's fire,
  And nurse his longings with his thoughts entire,
90   Fixed on the heat of wishes formed by love,
     Yet whereas fire destroys, this doth aspire,[1]
     Increase, and foster all delights above.
  Love will a painter make you, such, as you
     Shall able be to draw your only dear,
95   More lively, perfect, lasting, and more true
     Than rarest workman, and to you more near.
  These be the least, then all must needs confess,
  He that shuns love, doth love himself the less.

84

He that shuns love, doth love himself the less,
100   And cursed he whose spirit not admires
     The worth of love, where endless blessedness
     Reigns, and commands, maintained by heavenly fires.
  Made of virtue, joined by truth, blown by desires,
     Strengthened by worth, renewed by carefulness,
105   Flaming in never changing thoughts: briars
     Of jealousy shall here miss welcomeness.
  Nor coldly pass in the pursuits of love
     Like one long frozen in a sea of ice:
     And yet but chastely let your passions move,
110   No thought from virtuous love your minds entice.
  Never to other ends your fancies place,
  But where they may return with honour's grace.

85

But where they may return with honour's grace,
   Where Venus' follies can no harbour win,
115   But chased are, as worthless of the face,
     Or style of love, who hath lascivious been.
  Our hearts are subject to her son, where sin
     Never did dwell, or rest one minute's space;
     What faults he hath in her did still begin,
120   And from her breast he sucked his fleeting pace.
  If lust be counted love 'tis falsely named
     By wickedness, a fairer gloss to set

Upon that vice, which else makes men ashamed
     In the own phrase to warrant, but beget
125 This child for love,[2] who ought like monster born,
Be from the court of Love, and Reason torn.

86

Be from the court of Love, and Reason torn,
   For Love in Reason now doth put his trust,
   Desert° and liking are together born   *worthiness*
130   Children of Love and Reason, parents just.
  Reason adviser is, Love ruler must
     Be of the state, which crown he long hath worn;
     Yet so, as neither will in least mistrust
     The government where no fear is of scorn.
135 Then reverence both their mights thus made of one,
     But wantonness, and all those errors shun,
     Which wrongers be, impostures, and alone
     Maintainers of all follies ill begun.
  Fruit of a sour,[3] and unwholesome ground
140 Unprofitably pleasing, and unsound.

87

Unprofitably pleasing, and unsound.
   When heaven gave liberty to frail dull earth,
   To bring forth plenty that in ills abound,[4]
   Which ripest, yet do bring a certain dearth.
145 A timeless, and unseasonable birth,
     Planted in ill, in worse time springing found,
     Which hemlock[5] like might feed a sick wit's mirth
     Where unruled vapours[6] swim in endless round.
  Then joy we not in what we ought to shun,
150   Where shady pleasures show, but true born fires
     Are quite quenched out, or by poor ashes won,
     Awhile to keep those cool, and wan desires.
  O no, let Love his glory have, and might
  Be giv'n to him, who triumphs in his right.

---

[2] *which else … love* Which otherwise makes men ashamed in the same phrase to affirm that lust is the child of love.

[3] *sour* Acidic and dank.

[4] *When heaven … abound* See Genesis 1.11–12.

[5] *hemlock* Herb that was commonly used as a sedative, poisonous in higher doses.

[6] *vapours* Exhalations of air from the stomach that, according to medical wisdom of the time, caused mental illnesses such as depression and nervousness.

---

[1] *aspire* Ascend or rise. This appears as "respire" (i.e., "restore hope") in an earlier version of the poem.

88

155   Be giv'n to him who triumphs in his right;
    Nor fading be, but like those blossoms fair,
    Which fall for good, and lose their colours bright,
    Yet die not, but with fruit their loss repair:
  So may Love make you pale with loving care,
160   When sweet enjoying shall restore that light,
    More clear in beauty, then we can compare,
    If not to Venus in her chosen might.[1]
  And who so give themselves in this dear kind,
    These happinesses shall attend them still,
165   To be supplied with joys enriched in mind,
    With treasures of content, and pleasures fill.
  Thus love to be divine, doth here appear,
  Free from all fogs, but shining fair and clear.

89

  Free from all fogs, but shining fair, and clear,
170   Wise in all good, and innocent in ill,
    Where holy friendship is esteemed dear,
    With truth in love, and justice in our will.
  In love these titles only have their fill
    Of happy life-maintainer, and the mere
175   Defence of right, the punisher of skill,
    And fraud, from whence directions doth appear.
  To thee then, lord commander of all hearts,
    Ruler of our affections, kind, and just,
    Great king of love, my soul from feigned smarts,
180   Or thought of change, I offer to your trust,
  This crown,[2] my self, and all that I have more,
  Except my heart, which you bestowed before.

90

  Except my heart, which you bestowed before,
    And for a sign of conquest gave away
185   As worthless to be kept in your choice store;
    Yet one more spotless with you doth not stay.
  The tribute which my heart doth truly pay,
    Is faith untouched, pure thoughts discharge the score
    Of debts for me, where constancy bears sway,
190   And rules as lord, unharmed by envy's sore.
  Yet other mischiefs fail not to attend,
    As enemies to you, my foes must be,

  Cursed jealousy doth all her forces bend
    To my undoing, thus my harms I see.
195   So though in love I fervently do burn,
  In this strange labyrinth how shall I turn?
—1621

Railing Rhymes Returned upon the Author by Mistress Mary Wroth

Hermaphrodite[3] in sense in Art a monster
  As by your railing rhymes the world may
    conster°   *construe*
Your spiteful words against a harmless book
Shows that an ass much like the sire doth look
5 Men truly noble fear no touch of blood
Nor question make of others much more good
Can such comparisons seem the want° of wit *lack*
When oysters have inflamed your blood with it
But it appears your guiltiness gaped wide
10 And filled with Dirty doubt your brain's swollen tide
Both friend and foe in deed you use alike
And your mad wit in sherry equal strike
These slanderous flying flames raised from the pot[4]
You know are false and raging makes you hot
15 How easily now do you receive your own
Turned on your self from whence the squib was thrown
When these few lines not thousands writ at least
Mainly thus prove your self the drunken beast
This is far less to you than you have done
20 A Thread but of your own all words worse spun
By which you lively see in your own glass[5]
How hard it is for you to lie and pass
Thus you have made yourself a lying wonder
Fools and their pastimes should not part asunder.
—1983 (WRITTEN C. 1621)

---

1 *might* This appears as "night" in an earlier version of the poem.

2 *This crown* I.e., this crown of sonnets.

3 *Hermaphrodite* Possessing both male and female sexual organs; often used pejoratively to describe a mannish woman or an effeminate man.

4 *pot* Drinking vessel (for liquor).

5 *glass* Mirror, but here perhaps also drinking-glass.

IN CONTEXT

The Occasion of "Railing Rhymes"

Wroth's "Railing Rhymes" was written in response to the following attack by Lord Denny.

Edward Denny, Baron of Waltham, To Pamphilia from the Father-in-Law of Seralius (c. 1621)[1]

Hermaphrodite in show, in deed a monster
As by thy words and works all men may conster°   *construe*
Thy wrathful spite conceived an Idle° book   *worthless*
Brought forth a fool which like the dam doth look
5 Wherein thou strikes at some man's noble blood
Of kin to thine[2] if thine be counted good
Whose vain comparison for want° of wit   *lack*
Takes up the oystershell to play with it
Yet common oysters such as thine gape wide
10 And take in pearls or worse at every tide
Both friend and foe to thee are even alike
Thy wit runs mad not caring who it strike
These slanderous flying f[l]ames rise from the pot
For potted wits inflamed are raging hot
15 How easy wer't to pay thee with thine own
Returning that which thou thyself hast thrown
And write a thousand lies of thee at least
And by thy lines describe a drunken beast
This were no more to thee than thou hast done
20 A Thread but of thine own which thou hast spun
By which thou plainly seest in thine own glass
How easy 'tis to bring a lie to pass
Thus hast thou made thyself a lying wonder
Fools and their Babbles seldom part asunder
25 Work o th' Works leave idle books alone
For wise and worthier women have writ none.
—1983 (WRITTEN C. 1621)

---

[1] *Seralius* A character in Wroth's court pastoral *The Countess of Montgomery's Urania* (1621), whose satirical resemblance to Denny's son-in-law was transparent enough to suggest embarrassing parallels to a recent Denny family scandal. Denny wrote angry letters to Wroth demanding withdrawal of her book and circulated this poem questioning her honesty and the appropriateness of a woman pursuing the vocation of writing.

[2] *Of kin to thine* As good, or noble, as yours.

KATHERINE PHILIPS
1632 – 1664

Katherine Philips, known also by her *nom de plume* "Orinda" whom some called "the Matchless Orinda," was the first Englishwoman to enjoy widespread public acclaim as a poet during her lifetime. Despite prejudice against seeing women's secular works in print, her male peers recognized Philips as a poet of the first rank. As early as 1651, Henry Vaughan paid tribute to her "new miracles in Poetrie," and in 1663 Abraham Cowley proclaimed her verse "then Man more strong, and more then Woman sweet." In the guise of her literary persona Orinda, Philips dramatized, within her self-devised Society of Friendship, the ideals—and the realities and tribulations—of Platonic love with wit, elegance, and clarity. Thus the Society—whether fully or partly imaginary—helped establish a literary standard for her generation and Orinda herself a model for the female writers who followed her. Toward the end of her fairly short life Philips also broke new ground as a playwright and

translator: although other women had written or translated dramas, her translation of Corneille's neoclassical *Pompey* was the first rhymed version of a French tragedy in English and the first English play written by a woman to be performed on the professional stage.

Orinda was born Katherine Fowler in London on 1 January 1632, into a prosperous middle-class family with strong Puritan leanings. Friendships made at the boarding school she attended from 1640 to about 1645 probably influenced Philips's eventual shift to the Royalist cause. Certainly at school she began to write verse within a coterie of friends and to cultivate a taste for the French romances and Cavalier plays from which she would later choose many of the pet names she gave members of her Society of Friendship.

In 1648, Philips, then 16, married James Philips and moved with him to Cardigan in Wales, which was to remain her family home for the rest of her life. Since her husband was a prominent Parliamentarian, however, she accompanied him occasionally on trips to London, where she befriended a circle of Cavalier writers gathered around the composer Henry Lawes and devoted to the memory of William Cartwright, who had died in 1643. It was her prefatory poem to the 1651 edition of Cartwright's works, in fact, that marked Philips's first appearance in print, and she contributed her "To the much honoured Henry Lawes" and "Mutuall Affection between Orinda and Lucasia" (later retitled as "Friendship's Mysterys") to Lawes's *Second Book of Ayres* in 1655. By this time, her poems were being read in manuscript as public chronicles of a literary and social clique.

The Society of Friendship had its origins in the cult of Neoplatonic love imported from the continent in the 1630s by Charles I's French wife, Henrietta Maria. Adherents indulged in elaborate rhetoric about the mingling of souls, and often adopted pseudonyms drawn from French pastoral romances or Cavalier dramas. With her literary gifts, however, and her intuitive sense of the value of deep friendships in a time of war and social schism, Philips enriched this convention as a cultural ideal of harmony and personal friendships to set against the faithless, war-torn public world. At the same time many of her poems (which she herself evidently valued highly) address public, political events.

During the 1650s the Society of Friendship probably numbered at least 20 people of both sexes, but Philips's literary energies were concentrated on her two closest female friends, Mary Aubrey ("Rosania")—until the latter's marriage in 1652 caused an estrangement—and then, in the succeeding decade, Anne Owen Lewis ("Lucasia"). The degree to which these friendships and the poetry that sprang from them include an erotic component is a subject of debate among scholars; what is agreed is that these poems have always attracted the keenest critical attention from readers of Philips's works. Initially strongly influenced by John Donne, Philips eventually matched the best of the Cavalier lyricists in freshness of wit, elegant invention, and pleasing rhythm.

Hoping to bolster her husband's political fortunes after the Restoration in 1660, Philips wrote many Royalist occasional pieces and became a friend of Sir Charles Cotterell, Master of Ceremonies to the King. She dubbed him "Poliarchus" and carried on a lively correspondence with him that was published after her death. While visiting the newly married Anne Owen in Ireland in 1662, Philips translated Corneille's *Mort de Pompée* from French alexandrines into fine English heroic couplets. The play was an instant success in Dublin and London in 1663, introducing Philips to wider celebrity as a playwright. (She left a second Corneille translation, *Horace*, unfinished, however.)

A supposedly illicit edition of Philips's poems appeared early in 1664. Germaine Greer and others have suggested that Philips engineered the publication of this edition in such a way that she could disown it. In any event, the publisher, Richard Marriott, withdrew the edition before Philips (who rushed to London to deal with the situation) had time to compel him to do so. It was during this same visit to London that Philips contracted smallpox; she died in June of that year, seemingly at the height of her powers. An authorized volume of her collected verse, published by Henry Herringman in 1667, exerted enormous influence on female poets of the succeeding generations, such as Anne Killigrew and Anne Finch, the Countess of Winchilsea. Praised for her modesty and Christian virtue as well as for her poetry, Philips, in her brief career as playwright, helped to pave the way for the acceptance of the somewhat less modest and less virtuous Aphra Behn. Finally, as Orinda, she asserted a female claim to what had been so often thought an exclusively male sphere: ideal friendship. As she claims in "A Friend":

> … for men t'exclude
> Women from friendship's capacity,
> Is a design injurious and rude,
> Only maintain'd by partial tyranny.
> Love is allow'd to us, and Innocence,
> And noblest friendships do proceed from thence.

⌘⌘⌘

A Married State

A married state affords but little ease
The best of husbands are so hard to please.
This in wives' careful° faces you may spell°   *careworn / discern*
Though they dissemble° their misfortunes well.   *conceal*
5 A virgin state is crowned with much content;°   *contentment*
It's always happy as it's innocent.

No blustering husbands to create your fears;
No pangs of childbirth to extort your tears;
No children's cries for to offend your ears;
10 Few worldly crosses° to distract your prayers: *difficulties*
Thus are you freed from all the cares that do
Attend on matrimony and a husband too.
Therefore Madam, be advised by me
Turn, turn apostate to° loves levity.   *reject, forsake*

15   Suppress wild nature if she dare rebel.
      There's no such thing as leading apes in hell.[1]
      —c. 1648

Upon the Double Murder of King Charles
In Answer to a Libelous Rhyme made by V. P.[2]

I think not on the state, nor am concerned
    Which way soever that great helm is turned,
But as that son whose father's danger nigh
Did force his native dumbness, and untie
5   His fettered organs:[3] so here is a cause
That will excuse the breach of nature's laws.
Silence were now a sin: nay passion now
Wise men themselves for merit would allow.
What noble eye could see, (and careless pass)
10   The dying lion kicked by every ass?[4]
Hath Charles so broke God's laws, he must not have
A quiet crown, nor yet a quiet grave?
Tombs have been sanctuaries; thieves lie here
Secure from all their penalty and fear.
15   Great Charles his double misery was this,
Unfaithful friends, ignoble enemies;
Had any heathen been this prince's foe,
He would have wept to see him injured so.
His title was his crime, they'd reason good
20   To quarrel at the right they had withstood.
He broke God's laws, and therefore he must die,
And what shall then become of thee and I?

Slander must follow treason; but yet stay,°   *stop*
Take not our reason with our king away.
25   Though you have seized upon all our defense,
Yet do not sequester° our common sense.   *confiscate*
But I admire not at this new supply:
No bounds will hold those who at scepters fly.
Christ will be King, but I ne'er understood,
30   His subjects built his kingdom up with blood
(Except their own) or that he would dispense
With his commands, though for his own defense.
Oh! to what height of horror are they come
Who dare pull down a crown, tear up a tomb![5]
      —1667

On the Third of September, 1651[6]

As when the glorious magazine of light[7]
    Approaches to his canopy of night,
He with new splendor clothes his dying rays,
And double brightness to his beams conveys;
5   As if to brave° and check his ending fate,   *defy*
Puts on his highest looks in 's lowest state;
Dressed in such terror as to make us all
Be anti-Persians,[8] and adore his fall;
Then quits the world, depriving it of day,
10   While every herb and plant does droop away:
So when our gasping English royalty
Perceived her period° now was drawing nigh,   *end*
She summons her whole strength to give one blow,
To raise her self, or pull down others too.
15   Big with revenge and hope, she now spake more
Of terror than in many months before;
And musters her attendants, or to save
Her from, or wait upon° her to the grave: *escort*
Yet but enjoyed the miserable fate
20   Of setting majesty, to die in state.
Unhappy Kings! who cannot keep a throne,

---

[1] *leading apes in hell* The proverbial fate of spinsters after death.

[2] *V.P.* Vavasor Powell (1617–70), an itinerant Nonconformist preacher and one of the Fifth Monarchists, who believed in the imminent Second Coming and the illegitimacy of earthly kings. The verses alluded to by Philips have not survived.

[3] *that son ... fettered organs* Referring to the ancient Greek tale in which Croesus, King of Lydia, was saved from summary execution during the sack of Sardis by his mute son, who, speaking for the first time, identified his father as King and thus a man to be taken alive (Herodotus 1.85).

[4] *dying lion kicked by every ass* The dying Lion in Aesop's fable "The Sick Lion," who is assaulted in his helplessness by the various beasts, his subjects. On being finally kicked in the face by the Ass, the Lion proclaims, "This is a double death." Aesop's moral reads, "Only cowards insult dying majesty." The Scottish lion was also the dominant figure on the Stuart coat of arms.

[5] *tear up a tomb* Deface the honor and memory of the dead king.

[6] *Third of September, 1651* The date of the Battle of Worcester, in which Oliver Cromwell decisively defeated Charles II and the Royalist cause, bringing the English Civil War to an end.

[7] *magazine of light* The sun, pictured as a storehouse of light.

[8] *anti-Persians* Anti-sun, referring to the ancient Persian worship of Mithra, later identified with the sun.

Nor be so fortunate to fall alone!
Their weight sinks others: Pompey could not fly,
But half the world must bear him company;[1]
25   Thus captive Sampson could not life conclude,
Unless attended with a multitude.[2]
Who'd trust to greatness now, whose food is air,[3]
Whose ruin sudden, and whose end despair?
Who would presume upon his glorious birth,
30   Or quarrel for a spacious share of earth,
That sees such diadems become thus cheap,
And heroes tumble in the common heap.
O! give me virtue then, which sums up° all,   *encompasses*
And firmly stands when crowns and scepters fall.
—1667

To My Excellent Lucasia, on Our Friendship

17th. July 1651[4]

I did not live until this time
Crowned my felicity,
When I could say without a crime,
    I am not thine, but thee.
5   This carcass° breathed, and walked, and slept,   *body*
    So that the world believed
There was a soul the motions kept;
    But they were all deceived.
For as a watch by art° is wound   *mechanical skill*
10   To motion, such was mine:
But never had Orinda found

A soul till she found thine;
Which now inspires, cures and supplies,
    And guides my darkened breast:
15   For thou art all that I can prize,
    My joy, my life, my rest.
Nor bridegroom's nor crowned conqueror's mirth
    To mine compared can be:
They have but pieces of this earth,
20   I've all the world in thee.
Then let our flame still light and shine,
    (And no bold° fear control)   *strong*
As innocent as our design,°   *intent*
    Immortal as our soul.
—1667

Friendship's Mystery, To My Dearest Lucasia

Come, my *Lucasia*, since we see
    That Miracles Mens faith do move,
By wonder and by prodigy[5]
    To the dull angry world let's prove
5   There's a Religion in our Love.

For though we were design'd t' agree,
    That Fate no liberty destroyes,
But our Election is as free
    As Angels, who with greedy choice
10   Are yet determin'd to their joyes.

Our hearts are doubled by the loss,
    Here Mixture is Addition grown;
We both diffuse, and both ingross:
    And we whose minds are so much one,
15   Never, yet ever are alone.

We court our own Captivity
    Than Thrones more great and innocent:
'Twere banishment to be set free,
    Since we wear fetters whose intent
20   Not Bondage is, but Ornament.

original spelling

---

[1]   *Pompey...company*   The Roman general Pompey fled to Egypt after being defeated by Julius Caesar at Pharsalus (48 BCE), where 15,000 of his men were killed. Pompey's defeat and subsequent assassination in Egypt brought an end to the Civil War of the Triumvirate.

[2]   *captive Sampson ... multitude*   Captured and blinded by the Philistines, the biblical hero Samson brought down the pillars of the temple at Gaza, killing thousands of his enemies along with himself. See Book of Judges 16.

[3]   *whose food is air*   Who is changeable and inconstant as the chameleon, which had the ability to endure long periods without food, and was thus reputed to live on air.

[4]   *Lucasia ... 1651*   Philips met her close friend Anne Owen (Lucasia) in 1651.

[5]   *prodigy*   Miracle or extraordinary event.

Divided joyes are tedious found,
    And griefs united easier grow:
We are our selves but by rebound,
    And all our Titles shuffled so,
25 Both Princes, and both Subjects too.

Our Hearts are mutual Victims laid,
    While they (such power in Friendship lies)
Are Altars, Priests, and Off'rings made:
    And each Heart which thus kindly dies,
30 Grows deathless by the Sacrifice.
    —1667

On the Death of My First and Dearest Child, Hector Philips[1]

1

Twice forty months of wedlock I did stay,[2]
  Then had my vows crowned with a lovely boy,
And yet in forty days he dropt away,
  O swift vicissitude of human joy.

2

5 I did but see him and he disappeared,
  I did but pluck the rosebud and it fell,
A sorrow unforeseen and scarcely feared,
  For ill can mortals their afflictions spell.

3

And now (sweet babe) what can my trembling heart
10 Suggest to right my doleful fate or thee,
Tears are my Muse and sorrow all my Art,
  So piercing groans must be thy eulogy.

4

Thus whilst no eye is witness of my moan,
  I grieve thy loss (ah boy too dear to live)

15 And let the unconcerned world alone,
  Who neither will, nor can refreshment give.

5

An off'ring too for thy sad tomb I have,
  Too just a tribute to thy early hearse,
Receive these gasping numbers to thy grave,
20 The last of thy unhappy mother's verse.
  —1667 (WRITTEN 1655)

Friendship in Emblem,[3] or the Seal, To My Dearest Lucasia

The hearts thus intermixed speak
  A love that no bold shock can break;
For joined and growing, both in one,
  Neither can be disturbed alone.

5 That means a mutual knowledge too;
  For what is't either heart can do,
Which by its panting sentinel°   *guard*
  It does not to the other tell?

That friendship hearts so much refines,
10 It nothing but itself designs:
The hearts are free from lower ends,
  For each point to the other tends.

They flame, 'tis true, and several ways,
  But still those flames do so much raise,
15 That while to either they incline
  They yet are noble and divine.

From smoke or hurt those flames are free,
  From grossness° or mortality: *vulgarity*
The hearts (like Moses' bush[4] presumed)
20 Warmed and enlightened, not consumed.

---

[1] *Hector Philips* According to a manuscript copy of this poem, Philips's son Hector was born 23 April 1655 and died about ten days later, on 2 May. She would have one other child, a daughter named Katherine, the following year.

[2] *Twice forty ... stay* Philips was married in August 1648, almost seven years before Hector was born.

---

[3] *Emblem* Drawing expressing an allegory, or representing a quality. Often these were accompanied by a motto and some lines of verse; this poem describes the symbolic elements in an emblem of friendship.

[4] *Moses' bush* The Angel of the Lord appears to Moses in a burning bush, which, miraculously, is not consumed by the fire (see Exodus 3.2–5).

The compasses that stand above
Express this great immortal Love;
For friends, like them, can prove this true,
They are, and yet they are not, two.

25 And in their posture is expressed
Friendship's exalted interest:
Each follows where the other leans,
And what each does, the other means.

And as when one foot does stand fast,
30 And t'other circles seeks to cast,
The steady part does regulate
And make the wanderer's motion straight.

So friends are only two in this,
T'reclaim each other when they miss:
35 For whose'er will grossly fall,
Can never be a friend at all.

And as that useful instrument
For even lines was ever meant;
So friendship from good angels springs,
40 To teach the world heroic things.

As these are found out in design
To rule and measure ev'ry line;
So friendship governs actions best,
Prescribing law to all the rest.

45 And as in nature nothing's set
So just as lines and numbers met;
So compasses for these b'ing made,
Do friendship's harmony persuade.

And like to them, so friends may own
50 Extension, not division:
Their points, like bodies, separate;
But head, like souls, knows no such fate.

And as each part so well is knit,
That their embraces ever fit:
55 So friends are such by destiny,
And no third can the place supply.

There needs no motto to the seal:
But that we may the mine reveal
To the dull eye, it was thought fit
60 That friendship only should be writ.

But as there is degrees of bliss,
So there's no friendship meant by this,
But such as will transmit to fame
Lucasia's and Orinda's name.
—1664 (WRITTEN C. 1653)

JONATHAN SWIFT
1667 – 1745

In *The Life of the Rev. Dr. Jonathan Swift* (1784), Thomas Sheridan called him "a man whose original genius and uncommon talents have raised him, in the general estimation, above all the writers of the age"—a list that included Defoe, Dryden, and Pope. If Swift's talents did indeed raise him above most writers of his time, he was entirely at one with his age in his penchant for satire, so notably illustrated in his most famous work, *Gulliver's Travels*. His aim in *Gulliver's Travels*, as he put it in a letter to Alexander Pope, was "to vex the world, not to divert it." Yet he understood that even the most pointed satire would often miss its mark. He once commented that satire "is a sort of glass, wherein beholders do generally discover everybody's face but their own." He held the glass up to hypocrites and bombasts of many forms, but he particularly loathed religious and political tyranny. *A Tale of a Tub* and "A Modest Proposal" are enduring protests against such oppression.

Swift was born in Ireland to Abigail Errick Swift; his English father died before he was born. At the age of one, Swift was kidnapped and taken to England by his nursemaid; he was not re-united with his mother until after he had reached the age of three. He studied at Kilkenny School and then moved on to Trinity College at the University of Dublin when he was fourteen. When he completed his education, he made what he thought would be a permanent move to England. There he took employment as secretary to retired politician, Sir William Temple, through whom Swift made several lifelong friends.

During the 1690s Swift composed urban pastoral poetry, odes, and two early satires. *The Battle of the Books* was written in defense of Temple and against the "moderns" who were, in Swift's view, unwisely neglecting "ancient" modes of learning. In *A Tale of a Tub*, Swift mocked the religious and intellectual foolishness of the sort that prompts absurd flights of fancy. The narrative focuses on the adventures of three brothers of different religious persuasions, representing Roman Catholicism, Anglicanism, and Calvinism, but chapters of narrative alternate with inventively irrelevant digressions, including the famous "Digression in Praise of Digressions."

Swift seemed destined to keep returning, for one reason or another, to Ireland. He studied for the Anglican priesthood in Dublin from 1694 to 1696 before returning to Temple's service, but after his employer's death in 1699 he traveled to Ireland as secretary and chaplain to Earl Berkeley and was then appointed Vicar of Laracor in the Dublin area. He returned to England in 1707 as an emissary of the Irish clergy, seeking a reduction in tax on their incomes. Queen Anne had little sympathy, however; the pious but literal-minded queen had misread *A Tale of a Tub* as an attack on established religion rather than a defense of it. Swift's poem "The Windsor Prophecy" did not help matters, as the attack on the Duchess of Somerset, a Whiggish favorite of the Queen, further consolidated her opposition both to his causes and to him personally. Lacking promotion in England, Swift had little choice but to return to Ireland, where he was installed as Dean of St. Patrick's Cathedral in 1713. He was never to achieve his goal of holding high religious office in London.

In the early 1700s Swift began to distinguish himself by his political pamphleteering and his comical literary hoaxes, some of them published in Richard Steele's periodical *The Tatler* (which also published some of his best-known poems). In 1708, for example, he composed "An Argument Against Abolishing Christianity in England." Whatever his relation to authority in general, Swift was all his life a defender of the established religion, and his argument was really aimed against the Whig attempt to abolish certain forms of discrimination against Roman Catholics and Dissenters by repealing the Test Act, which imposed certain civil disabilities on those who refused Church of England sacraments. Swift's strategy was to conflate arguments against the Test Act with arguments against the Church itself, while opening a disturbing split in his argument between real or primitive Christianity (which is irrelevant, he says, because nobody practices it) and nominal Christianity.

While in Temple's service, Swift had tutored Temple's eight-year-old ward, Esther Johnson (or "Stella," as he would come to call her), and when she came of age he convinced her and a companion to live near him in Dublin. While separated from her when he was in England, he wrote her a series of letters that was published much later as *Journal to Stella* (written 1710–13). In the *Journal* Swift adopted a private, often obscure language—a "nursery talk" full of neologisms, irregular spellings, and novel grammatical usages. Swift's and Johnson's relationship endured to the end of her life in 1728 and was marked by an annual birthday poem; the survivors are some of his most charming poems. The dynamics of his emotional life remain obscure: he conducted a simultaneous relationship with "Vanessa" (Esther Vanhomrigh), who was a more rebellious character than Johnson and who followed him, without invitation, to Ireland from England. This relationship too produced a remarkable poem, *Cadenus and Vanessa*, in which Swift relates the story of their friendship from his own point of view, leaving its ending open.

Swift counted among his friends many of the leading lights of London's literary scene, including Joseph Addison (until politics divided the two), Alexander Pope, and John Gay, and counted his "banishment" to Ireland as "the greatest unhappiness" of his life. Although he made a number of return visits to England, after 1727 his home was "wretched Dublin, in miserable Ireland." Swift also suffered from undiagnosed Ménières disease, a debilitating inner-ear disease causing dizziness, headaches, depression, and deafness.

A preoccupation with death and decay lends a sharply pessimistic tone to Swift's later satires. Rereading these works several years later, Samuel Johnson despaired at ever discovering "by what depravity of intellect [Swift] took delight in revolting ideas from which almost every other mind shrinks with disgust." Swift was often accused of misanthropy, but in a letter to Alexander Pope he endeavored to counter the charge, insisting that while he had "ever hated all nations, professions, and communities," he did indeed love "individuals." Swift has often also been accused of misogyny on account of such poems as "The Lady's Dressing Room," in which a man is abruptly cured of his passion when he discovers his beloved's bedroom to be disgustingly squalid.

If Swift was embittered by Ireland, the nation, which remained entirely subject to English rule, was to benefit greatly by its association with him. Swift wrote numerous pamphlets and tracts in opposition to British policy, among them *A Modest Proposal* (1729), a brilliantly macabre send-up of English hard-heartedness toward the Irish and of the number-crunching approach to public policy, which puts economic utility first. In his *Proposal*, Swift recommends that the Irish could solve their problems of famine and overpopulation by raising their children for export as a food source for the English.

Swift often proudly anticipated public opposition to his views. Foreseeing the hostile reaction to his founding of St. Patrick's Hospital, Ireland's first mental asylum, he wrote *Verses on the Death of Dr. Swift* (1739), which predicts and responds to hostilities and objections. His legacy, he hoped, would be based not on fashionable and worldly expectations, but on his commitment to identifying and rooting out abuses. Translated from the Latin, the epitaph on his tomb in St. Patrick's Cathedral reads: "*Here is laid the body of Jonathan Swift, Doctor of Divinity, Dean of this Cathedral Church, where fierce indignation can no longer rend the heart. Go, traveller, and imitate if you can this earnest and dedicated champion of liberty. He died on the 19th day of October 1745 AD. Aged 78 years.*"

⌘⌘⌘

A Modest Proposal

For Preventing the Children of Poor People in Ireland from Being a Burden to Their Parents or the Country, and for Making Them Beneficial to the Public

It is a melancholy object to those who walk through this great town,[1] or travel in the country, when they see the streets, the roads, and cabin doors crowded with beggars of the female sex, followed by three, four, or six children, all in rags and importuning every passenger[2] for an alms. These mothers, instead of being able to work for their honest livelihood, are forced to employ all their time in strolling[3] to beg sustenance for their helpless infants, who, as they grow up, either turn thieves for want of work, or leave their dear native country to fight for the Pretender in Spain, or sell themselves to the Barbados.[4]

I think it is agreed by all parties that this prodigious number of children in the arms, or on the backs, or at the heels of their mothers, and frequently of their fathers, is, in the present deplorable state of the kingdom, a very great additional grievance; and therefore, whoever could find out a fair, cheap, and easy method of making these children sound and useful members of the commonwealth would deserve so well of the public as to have his statue set up for a preserver of the nation.

But my intention is very far from being confined to provide only for the children of professed beggars; it is

---

[1] *this great town* I.e., Dublin.

[2] *passenger* Passerby.

[3] *strolling* Wandering, roving.

[4] *the Pretender* James Francis Edward Stuart, son of James II who was deposed from the throne in the Glorious Revolution due to his overt Catholicism. Catholic Ireland was loyal to Stuart, and the Irish were often recruited by France and Spain to fight against England; *Barbados* Because of the extreme poverty in Ireland, many Irish people emigrated to the West Indies, selling their labor to sugar plantations in advance to pay for the voyage.

of a much greater extent, and shall take in the whole number of infants at a certain age who are born of parents in effect as little able to support them as those who demand our charity in the streets.

As to my own part, having turned my thoughts for many years upon this important subject and maturely weighed the several schemes of other projectors,[1] I have always found them grossly mistaken in their computation. 'Tis true, a child just dropped from its dam may be supported by her milk for a solar year with little other nourishment, at most not above the value of two shillings, which the mother may certainly get, or the value in scraps, by her lawful occupation of begging; and it is exactly at one year old that I propose to provide for them in such a manner as, instead of being a charge upon their parents or the parish, or wanting food and raiment for the rest of their lives, they shall on the contrary contribute to the feeding, and partly to the clothing, of many thousands.

There is likewise another great advantage in my scheme, that it will prevent those abortions, and that horrid practice of women murdering their bastard children, alas, too frequent among us, sacrificing the poor innocent babes, I doubt,[2] more to avoid the expense than the shame, which would move tears and pity in the most savage and inhuman breast.

The number of souls in this kingdom being usually reckoned one million and a half, of these I calculate there may be about two hundred thousand couple whose wives are breeders, from which number I subtract thirty thousand couples who are able to maintain children, although I apprehend there cannot be as many under the present distresses of the kingdom; but this being granted, there will remain one hundred and seventy thousand breeders.

I again subtract fifty thousand for those women who miscarry, or whose children die by accident or disease within the year. There only remain one hundred and twenty thousand children of poor parents annually born. The question therefore is how this number shall be reared and provided for, which, as I have already said, under the present situation of affairs is utterly impossible by all the methods hitherto proposed. For we can neither employ them in handicraft or agriculture; we

neither build houses (I mean in the country) nor cultivate land.[3] They can very seldom pick up a livelihood by stealing till they arrive at six years old, except where they are of towardly parts,[4] although I confess they learn the rudiments much earlier, during which time they can however be properly looked upon only as probationers, as I have been informed by a principal gentleman in the county of Cavan, who protested to me that he never knew above one or two instances under the age of six, even in a part of the kingdom so renowned for the quickest proficiency in that art.

I am assured by our merchants that a boy or a girl before twelve years old is no saleable commodity; and even when they come to this age, they will not yield above three pounds, or three pounds and half a crown at most, on the Exchange,[5] which cannot turn to account[6] either to the parents or the kingdom, the charge of nutriment and rags having been at least four times that value.

I shall now therefore humbly propose my own thoughts, which I hope will not be liable to the least objection.

I have been assured by a very knowing American[7] of my acquaintance in London that a young healthy child well nursed is at a year old a most delicious, nourishing, and wholesome food, whether stewed, roasted, baked, or boiled; and I make no doubt that it will equally serve in a fricassee or a ragout.[8]

I do therefore humbly offer it to public consideration that of the hundred and twenty thousand children already computed, twenty thousand may be reserved for breed, whereof only one fourth part to be males, which is more than we allow to sheep, black cattle, or swine, and my reason is that these children are seldom the fruits of marriage, a circumstance not much regarded by our savages; therefore, one male will be sufficient to serve four females. That the remaining hundred thou-

---

[3] *neither build ... land*   The British placed numerous restrictions on the Irish agricultural industry, retaining the majority of land for the grazing of sheep. The vast estates of British absentee landlords further contributed to Ireland's poverty.

[4] *towardly parts*   Promising; exceptionally able.

[5] *on the Exchange*   At the market.

[6] *turn to account*   Result in profit.

[7] *American*   I.e., Native American.

[8] *fricassee or a ragout*   Stews.

[1] *projectors*   Those who design or propose experiments or projects.

[2] *doubt*   Think.

sand may at a year old be offered in sale to the persons of quality and fortune through the kingdom, always advising the mother to let them suck plentifully of the last month, so as to render them plump and fat for a good table. A child will make two dishes at an entertainment for friends, and when the family dines alone, the fore or hind quarter will make a reasonable dish, and seasoned with a little pepper or salt will be very good boiled on the fourth day, especially in winter.

I have reckoned upon a medium that a child just born will weigh twelve pounds, and in a solar year if tolerably nursed increase to twenty-eight pounds.

I grant this food will be somewhat dear,[1] and therefore very proper for landlords, who, as they have already devoured most of the parents, seem to have the best title to the children.

Infants' flesh will be in season throughout the year, but more plentiful in March, and a little before and after. For we are told by a grave author,[2] an eminent French physician, that, fish being a prolific diet,[3] there are more children born in Roman Catholic countries about nine months after Lent than at any other season; therefore, reckoning a year after Lent, the markets will be more glutted than usual because the number of popish infants is at least three to one in this kingdom, and therefore it will have one other collateral advantage by lessening the number of papists among us.

I have already computed the charge of nursing a beggar's child (in which list I reckon all cottagers,[4] labourers, and four fifths of the farmers) to be about two shillings per annum, rags included, and I believe no gentleman would repine to give ten shillings for the carcass of a good fat child, which, as I have said, will make four dishes of excellent nutritive meat when he hath only some particular friend or his own family to dine with him. Thus the Esquire[5] will learn to be a good landlord and grow popular among his tenants; the mother will have eight shillings net profit and be fit for work till she produces another child.

Those who are more thrifty (as I must confess the times require) may flay the carcass, the skin of which, artificially[6] dressed, will make admirable gloves for ladies and summer boots for fine gentlemen.

As to our city of Dublin, shambles[7] may be appointed for this purpose in the most convenient parts of it, and butchers we may be assured will not be wanting, although I rather recommend buying the children alive and dressing them hot from the knife, as we do roasting pigs.

A very worthy person, a true lover of his country, and whose virtues I highly esteem, was lately pleased, in discoursing on this matter, to offer a refinement upon my scheme. He said that, many gentlemen of this kingdom having of late destroyed their deer, he conceived that the want of venison might be well supplied by the bodies of young lads and maidens, not exceeding fourteen years of age nor under twelve, so great a number of both sexes in every county being now ready to starve for want of work and service; and these to be disposed of by their parents if alive, or otherwise by their nearest relations. But with due deference to so excellent a friend and so deserving a patriot, I cannot be altogether in his sentiments; for as to the males, my American acquaintance assured me from frequent experience that their flesh was generally tough and lean, like that of our schoolboys, by continual exercise, and their taste disagreeable, and to fatten them would not answer the charge. Then as to the females, it would, I think with humble submission, be a loss to the public because they soon would become breeders themselves. And besides, it is not improbable that some scrupulous people might be apt to censure such a practice (although indeed very unjustly) as a little bordering upon cruelty, which, I confess, hath always been with me the strongest objection against any project, however well intended.

But in order to justify my friend, he confessed that this expedient was put into his head by the famous Psalmanazar,[8] a native of the island of Formosa, who came from thence to London above twenty years ago,

1 *dear* Expensive.

2 *grave author* Sixteenth-century satirist François Rabelais. See his *Gargantua and Pantagruel*.

3 *prolific diet* Causing increased fertility.

4 *cottagers* Country dwellers.

5 *Esquire* Commoner; person without any other title.

6 *artificially* Artfully, skillfully.

7 *shambles* Slaughterhouses.

8 *Psalmanazar* George Psalmanazar (1679?–1763), a French adventurer who pretended to be a Formosan and published an account of Formosan customs, *Historical and Geographical Description of Formosa* (1704), which was later exposed as fraudulent. The story Swift recounts here is found in the second edition of Psalmanazar's work.

and in conversation told my friend that in his country, when any young person happened to be put to death the executioner sold the carcass to persons of quality as a prime dainty, and that in his time the body of a plump girl of fifteen, who was crucified for an attempt to poison the emperor, was sold to his Imperial Majesty's Prime Minister of State and other great Mandarins of the court, in joints from the gibbet,[1] at four hundred crowns. Neither indeed can I deny that if the same use were made of several plump young girls in this town who, without one single groat[2] to their fortunes, cannot stir abroad without a chair,[3] and appear at the playhouse and assemblies in foreign fineries which they never will pay for, the kingdom would not be the worse.

Some persons of a desponding spirit are in great concern about that vast number of poor people who are aged, diseased, or maimed, and I have been desired to employ my thoughts what course may be taken to ease the nation of so grievous an encumbrance. But I am not in the least pain upon that matter because it is very well known that they are every day dying and rotting by cold and famine, and filth and vermin, as fast as can be reasonably expected. And as to the younger labourers, they are now in almost as hopeful a condition. They cannot get work, and consequently pine away for want of nourishment to a degree that if at any time they are accidentally hired to common labour, they have not strength to perform it; and thus the country and themselves are happily delivered from the evils to come.

I have too long digressed, and therefore shall return to my subject. I think the advantages by the proposal which I have made are obvious and many, as well as of the highest importance.

For first, as I have already observed, it would greatly lessen the number of papists, with whom we are yearly overrun, being the principal breeders of the nation as well as our most dangerous enemies, and who stay at home on purpose with a design to deliver the kingdom to the Pretender, hoping to take their advantage by the absence of so many good Protestants, who have chosen rather to leave their country than stay at home and pay tithes against their conscience to an Episcopal curate.

Secondly, the poorer tenants will have something valuable of their own, which by law may be made liable to distress[4] and help to pay their landlord's rent, their corn and cattle being already seized, and money a thing unknown.

Thirdly, whereas the maintenance of an hundred thousand children from two years old and upwards cannot be computed at less than ten shillings apiece per annum, the nation's stock will be thereby increased fifty thousand pounds per annum, besides the profit of a new dish introduced to the tables of all gentlemen of fortune in the kingdom who have any refinement in taste, and the money will circulate among ourselves, the goods being entirely of our own growth and manufacture.

Fourthly, the constant breeders, besides the gain of eight shillings sterling per annum by the sale of their children, will be rid of the charge of maintaining them after the first year.

Fifthly, this food would likewise bring great customs to taverns, where the vintners will certainly be so prudent as to procure the best receipts[5] for dressing it to perfection, and consequently have their houses frequented by all the fine gentlemen who justly value themselves upon their knowledge in good eating. And a skilful cook who understands how to oblige his guests will contrive to make it as expensive as they please.

Sixthly, this would be a great inducement to marriage, which all wise nations have either encouraged by rewards or enforced by laws and penalties. It would increase the care and tenderness of mothers toward their children, when they were sure of a settlement for life to the poor babes, provided in some sort by the public, to their annual profit instead of expense. We should soon see an honest emulation[6] among the married women, which of them could bring the fattest child to market. Men would become as fond of their wives during the time of their pregnancy as they are now of their mares in foal, their cows in calf, or sows when they are ready to farrow, nor offer to beat or kick them (as it is too frequent a practice) for fear of a miscarriage.

---

[1] *gibbet* Gallows.

[2] *groat* Silver coin equal in value to four pence. It was removed from circulation in 1662, and thereafter "a groat" was used metaphorically to signify any very small sum.

[3] *chair* Sedan chair, which seated one person and was carried on poles by two men.

[4] *distress* Seizure of property for the payment of debt.

[5] *receipts* Recipes.

[6] *emulation* Rivalry.

Many other advantages might be enumerated: for instance, the addition of some thousand carcasses in our exportation of barreled beef; the propagation of swine's flesh and improvement in the art of making good bacon, so much wanted among us by the great destruction of pigs, too frequent at our tables, which are no way comparable in taste or magnificence to a well-grown, fat yearling child, which, roasted whole, will make a considerable figure at a Lord Mayor's feast or any other public entertainment. But this and many others I omit, being studious of brevity.

Supposing that one thousand families in this city would be constant customers for infants' flesh, besides others who might have it at merry-meetings, particularly weddings and christenings, I compute that Dublin would take off annually about twenty thousand carcasses, and the rest of the kingdom (where probably they will be sold somewhat cheaper) the remaining eighty thousand.

I can think of no one objection that will possibly be raised against this proposal, unless it should be urged that the number of people will be thereby much lessened in the kingdom. This I freely own, and it was indeed one principal design in offering it to the world. I desire the reader will observe that I calculate my remedy for this one individual kingdom of Ireland, and for no other that ever was, is, or, I think, ever can be upon earth. Therefore let no man talk to me of other expedients:[1] of taxing our absentees at five shillings a pound; of using neither clothes nor household furniture, except what is of our own growth and manufacture; of utterly rejecting the materials and instruments that promote foreign luxury; of curing the expensiveness of pride, vanity, idleness, and gaming[2] in our women; of introducing a vein of parsimony, prudence, and temperance; of learning to love our country, wherein we differ even from Laplanders and the inhabitants of Topinamboo;[3] of quitting our animosities and factions, nor act any longer like the Jews, who were murdering one another at the very moment their city was taken;[4] of being a little cautious not to sell our country and consciences for nothing; of teaching landlords to have at least one degree of mercy toward their tenants; lastly, of putting a spirit of honesty, industry, and skill into our shopkeepers, who, if a resolution could now be taken to buy only our native goods, would immediately unite to cheat and exact upon us in the price, the measure, and the goodness, nor could ever yet be brought to make one fair proposal of just dealing, though often in earnest invited to it.

Therefore I repeat, let no man talk to me of these and the like expedients till he hath at least some glimpse of hope that there will ever be some hearty and sincere attempt to put them in practice.

But as to myself, having been wearied out for many years with offering vain, idle, visionary thoughts, and at length utterly despairing of success, I fortunately fell upon this proposal, which, as it is wholly new, so it hath something solid and real, of no expense and little trouble, full in our own power, and whereby we can incur no danger in disobliging England. For this kind of commodity will not bear exportation, the flesh being of too tender a consistence to admit a long continuance in salt, although perhaps I could name a country[5] which would be glad to eat up our whole nation without it.

After all, I am not so violently bent upon my own opinion as to reject any offer, proposed by wise men, which shall be found equally innocent, cheap, easy, and effectual. But before something of that kind shall be advanced in contradiction to my scheme, and offering a better, I desire the author or authors will be pleased maturely to consider two points.

First, as things now stand, how they will be able to find food and raiment for one hundred thousand useless mouths and backs.

And secondly, there being a round million of creatures in human figure throughout this kingdom whose whole subsistence, put into a common stock, would leave them in debt two million of pounds sterling, adding those who are beggars by profession to the

---

[1] *other expedients* All of which Swift had already proposed in earnest attempts to remedy Ireland's poverty. See, for example, his *Proposal for the Universal Use of Irish Manufactures*. In early editions the following proposals were italicized to show the suspension of Swift's ironic tone.

[2] *gaming* Gambling.

[3] *Topinamboo* District in Brazil.

[4] *Jews ... was taken* According to the history of Flavius Joseph, Roman Emperor Titus's invasion and capture of Jerusalem in 70 BCE was aided by the fact that factional fighting had divided the city.

[5] *a country* I.e., England.

bulk of farmers, cottagers, and labourers with their wives and children, who are beggars in effect.

I desire those politicians who dislike my overture, and may perhaps be so bold to attempt an answer, that they will first ask the parents of these mortals whether they would not at this day think it a great happiness to have been sold for food at a year old in the manner I prescribe, and thereby have avoided such a perpetual scene of misfortunes as they have since gone through by the oppression of landlords, the impossibility of paying rent without money or trade, the want of common sustenance, with neither house nor clothes to cover them from the inclemencies of the weather, and the most inevitable prospect of entailing[1] the like or greater miseries upon their breed forever.

I profess in the sincerity of my heart that I have not the least personal interest in endeavoring to promote this necessary work, having no other motive than the public good of my country by advancing our trade, providing for infants, relieving the poor, and giving some pleasure to the rich. I have no children by which I can propose to get a single penny, the youngest being nine years old, and my wife past childbearing.

—1729

WILLIAM BLAKE
1757 – 1827

"I labor upwards into futurity," etched William Blake onto the back of one of the copper plates which constituted the "tablets" of his visionary art. A poet and artist whose work was sorely undervalued during his own lifetime, Blake recognized that his was a genius before its time. The mysterious and powerful poetry that he crafted to convey his vision would eventually be recognized as having revolutionary significance; for the past century or more Blake has been recognized as a great poet of the Romantic era.

Blake was born one November evening in 1757 above his parents' hosiery shop in the Soho district of London. James and Catherine Blake, religious Dissenters whose non-compromising beliefs were those of a growing number of tradespeople, allowed their son to pursue a program of self study that saved him from being schooled under the institutional authorities he instinctively abhorred. Although his parents were generally indulgent, there are hints that Blake balked even under their natural expressions of authority. He received a thrashing for declaring he had seen the face of God, and was accused of lying when he reported passing a tree bespangled with angels. Since his family could not afford the expense of artistic training, he was apprenticed at fourteen to a highly respected engraver, with whom he lived for seven years while learning the trade which would thereafter earn him his living.

During the period of his apprenticeship, Blake began writing the poems that were eventually collected in *Poetical Sketches* (1783)—the only volume of his verse originally printed by letter-press rather than by the "illuminated" methods he later originated. Of his parents and three siblings, Blake retained lasting affection only for his younger brother, Robert. Blake claimed to communicate daily with the spirit of Robert after his early death from tuberculosis. Indeed, the unique style of relief etching or "Illuminated Printing" which Blake later devised was imparted, he claimed, by Robert in a visitation. Etching words backwards into copper plates so that they would reverse to normal upon printing, Blake in 1788 produced his first illuminated texts with "All Religions Are One" and "There is No Natural Religion." It was a defining moment for him, one in which words and images converged into an indivisible and prophetic expression. He soon applied his new method of printing to a larger project, the poetic and pictorial depiction of a young soul descending into the realm of matter, recounted in *The Book of Thel*.

Blake's words and designs "interanimate each other," in the words of one critic; a master of color, he, at times, achieved unearthly effects in his hand-tinted books, of which no two copies were exactly the same. Rather than reflecting the tones of the natural world, Blake's color—and indeed the vividness of his verse—aim towards the supernatural. Similarly, what separates his poetry from that of contemporaries, such as Wordsworth and Coleridge is his lack of interest in "painting Nature." For Blake, the true aim of art was to tune the senses and the imaginative faculties to the higher pitch of a spiritual reality, not to the natural world. For this reason, Blake detested what he called the "muddy" colors, nuanced shade work, and secular sensibilities of an artist such as Rembrandt, while revering the determined outlines, bright colors and unequivocal contrasts of light and dark achieved by High Renaissance painters such as Michelangelo and Raphael.

The bold, declarative and (to some modern eyes) exaggerated style which Blake admired in painting is paralleled in many of his literary preferences. His work has close associations with the declamatory traditions of prophecy, of the aphorism, of the political pamphlet, and of the proverb. *The Marriage of Heaven and Hell* (1790) contains some of his most chiseled epigrams: "The cut worm forgives the plow" and "The tigers of wrath are wiser than the horses of instruction." The Bible was a tremendous imaginative reserve upon which he drew all of his life. He admired Dante, Milton, Spenser, and Shakespeare, supplied commissioned designs for editions of Milton's *L'Allegro*, *Il Penseroso*, *Paradise Lost*, and *Paradise Regained*, and left behind an unfinished series of watercolors illustrating Dante's work. He was also influenced by the architecture and sepulchral art of Westminster Abbey and by the literary gothic of Edward Young's *Night Thoughts* and Robert Blair's *The Grave*, versions of which he illustrated. If he was in many respects an outsider to his own culture, Blake was fully a man of the times in his love of the popular "forgeries" of James Macpherson (author of the "Ossian" poems) and Thomas Chatterton, as well as in his enjoyment of works of Gothic fiction such as Ann Radcliffe's *The Mysteries of Udolpho* (1794).

On at least two occasions Blake struck out to earn a reputation as an artist in his own right. The first occasion came at the end of his apprenticeship, when he submitted a portfolio to the Royal Academy of Arts (under the presidency of Sir Joshua Reynolds—and was accepted into the Academy. Yet he failed to emerge out of obscurity, and was forced to set up an engraver's shop. For twenty years Blake would resign himself to the grueling schedule of a copy engraver, recognized only by a few of his friends as a formidably original artist, and almost wholly overlooked as a poet. In 1809, energized by a gallery showing of works by Dürer, Michelangelo, Giulio Romano, and others, Blake renewed his association with the Royal Academy to launch a solo exhibition of his own work. With the exception of a caustic review or two, the public remained unmoved by—possibly unready for—the idiosyncratic light Blake cast upon subjects such as "The Body of Abel found by Adam and Eve."

Blake found his soul mate in Catherine Boucher, the illiterate daughter of a market gardener. He taught her to read and trained her in the preparation of copper plates, the hand coloring of prints, and the stitching of pages into bound copies. Catherine was evidently a submissive, devoted wife, and some have denigrated Blake's traditional and even misogynist approach to marriage, citing his pronouncement that "the female ... lives from the light of the male." At the same time, however, Blake approved of the arguments for sexual equality made by Mary Wollstonecraft in *A Vindication of the Rights of Woman* (1793). Blake radically proposed that carnal pleasure was a portal to the divine. In *Visions of the Daughters of Albion* (1793), Blake abjures sexual domination and celebrates "the moment of desire!" in a manner highly unconventional at the time. Visitors to the Blake home reported coming across the couple reading naked in a garden house in their back yard, enjoying the innocence of their private Eden and rejecting the narratives of shame and the Fall.

The rewriting of the Biblical drama of the Creation and Fall that underlies nearly all of Blake's work was influenced by radical Dissenters who celebrated nudity as a symbol of unfallen humanity. Blake was also influenced by the mystical systems of Emmanuel Swedenborg and Jacob Boehme, and tapped into veins of esoteric knowledge related to the cabbalistic teachings of the Freemasons, the Rosicrucians, and Paracelsus. He also had associations with decidedly non-mystical political movements that were bravely calling for democratic reforms at a time when the English monarchy was intent on quashing sympathizers with American War of Independence and the French Revolution.

Blake never fully participated in an organized movement of any kind, be it religious or political. His was "a voice crying in the wilderness," an unsystematizable voice urging men and women to realize their "human form divine." Unwilling to conform to any system not of his own creation, Blake's language grew increasingly esoteric and opaque in later major prophecies such as *The Four Zoas*, *Milton* (1804) and *Jerusalem* (1804–20).

One vision that Blake explores over and over again is that of an earthly Eden triumphing over forces of repression. This is the common theme of *The French Revolution* (1791), *America: A Prophecy*

(1793), *Europe: A Prophecy* (1794), and *The Book of Urizen* (1794). When Blake summons Albion, figure of the human form divine in *Jerusalem*, to "Awake!" he is calling for a spiritual revolution in which humanity awakens to the knowledge that the republic of heaven is immanent.

Blake imagined the spiritual dimensions of the geography of London in particularly vivid detail. That the material double of his holy city was corrupt lends a sharp edge to Blake's vision. As one Blake biographer writes, "it was a time when mobs and rioters often controlled large areas of the city; there were riots by sailors, silk-weavers, coal-heavers, hatters, glass-grinders ....and bloody demonstrations over the price of bread." The biting simplicity of "The Chimney Sweeper" and "The Little Black Boy" in Blake's *Songs of Innocence and of Experience* (1789–94) are testimony to his acute sensitivity to the realities of poverty and exploitation that accompanied the "dark satanic mills" of the industrial revolution.

In this London, Blake admitted to living in fear that his artistic vision and eccentric tendency to converse with angels and ghosts would land him in trouble with the authorities—a fear horribly realized in 1803. The Blakes had been generously invited by William Hayley, an eminent poet and wealthy patron of the arts, to live in a country cottage at Felpham. One day a drunken private in the Royal Dragoons, John Scofield, fell into a heated argument with Blake at his garden gate. Blake physically evicted the abusive soldier from the premises. Scofield subsequently accused Blake of making seditious remarks against the Crown, an offense punishable by death. Hayley generously paid for his friend's bail and his defense, and Blake was eventually acquitted, to the thunderous approval of the court. However, the incident stamped itself upon his sensitive mind; he raised it to mythological proportions in the convoluted poetic symbology of *Jerusalem*, where the Law is figured as the nauseous region of "Bowlahoola," while Scofield and his cohorts appear as "ministers of evil."

As the culture around him placed increasing faith in the physical laws of natural science, Blake's insistence on the incorruptible coordinates of imaginative truth cast him as an increasing oddity. Many of Blake's contemporaries considered him insane. London was shifting to a secular orientation under the rise of industrial culture. Against the grain of the times, Blake continued producing labor-intensive printings of illuminated books, none of which proved to be a commercial success. Only twenty-eight copies of *Songs of Innocence and of Experience* are known to exist, sixteen of *The Book of Thel*, nine of *The Marriage of Heaven and Hell*, and five of *Jerusalem*.

In his last years, just as he had reconciled himself to poverty and obscurity, Blake attracted the first following he had ever enjoyed, a small group of painters called "the Ancients." Charles Lamb and a few other writers of the period also expressed admiration, but the glimmerings of a full-fledged "Blake industry" did not appear until years after his death, when his art and poetry were discovered by Dante Gabriel Rossetti and the Pre-Raphaelites. Rossetti and, later, William Butler Yeats edited volumes of Blake's poems, and appreciation grew of his powerful poetic as well as painterly achievements. By the middle of the twentieth century, academics around the world were devoting themselves to the scholarly study of Blake's work, which was also exerting a profound influence on the literary and popular culture of the time. Blake was an inspiration to the generation of Beat poets clustered around Allen Ginsberg and to many in the 'sixties counterculture who took up his call to open the "doors of perception" (words straight from *The Marriage of Heaven and Hell*), trying everything from the hallucinogenic drugs proposed by Aldous Huxley, to communal living and free love, to approximate his visionary universe. The future had finally caught up with William Blake.

⌘ ⌘ ⌘

from *Songs of Innocence and of Experience*
Showing the Two Contrary States of the
Human Soul

Title page, *Songs of Innocence and of Experience*.

from *Songs of Innocence*

Introduction

Piping down the valleys wild
Piping songs of pleasant glee
On a cloud I saw a child.
And he laughing said to me.

5   'Pipe a song about a Lamb:'
So I piped with merry chear.[1]

---

[1]   *chear*   The usual practice of this anthology regarding moderniza-
tion of spelling and punctuation has not been followed in the case
of Blake; his idiosyncrasies have been retained.

'Piper pipe that song again'
So I piped, he wept to hear.

'Drop thy pipe thy happy pipe
10   Sing thy songs of happy chear.'
So I sung the same again,
While he wept with joy to hear

'Piper sit thee down and write
In a book that all may read—'
15   So he vanish'd from my sight
And I pluck'd a hollow reed

And I made a rural pen,
And I stain'd the water clear,
And I wrote my happy songs
20   Every child may joy to hear
—1789

The Ecchoing Green

The Sun does arise,
    And make happy the skies.
The merry bells ring
To welcome the Spring.
5   The sky-lark and thrush,
The birds of the bush,
Sing louder around,
To the bells chearful sound.
While our sports shall be seen
10   On the Ecchoing Green.
Old John with white hair
Does laugh away care,
Sitting under the oak,
Among the old folk.
15   They laugh at our play,
And soon they all say.
'Such such were the joys.
When we all girls & boys,
In our youth-time were seen.
20   On the Ecchoing Green.'

Till the little ones weary
No more can be merry
The sun does descend,
And our sports have an end:
25 Round the laps of their mothers.
Many sisters and brothers,
Like birds in their nest,
Are ready for rest:
And sport no more seen,
30 On the darkening Green.
—1789

The Lamb

Little Lamb who made thee
Dost thou know who made thee
Gave thee life & bid thee feed.
By the stream & o'er the mead;
5 Gave thee clothing of delight,
Softest clothing wooly bright;
Gave thee such a tender voice,
Making all the vales rejoice;
   Little Lamb who made thee
10   Dost thou know who made thee

   Little Lamb I'll tell thee,
   Little Lamb I'll tell thee:
He is called by thy name,
For he calls himself a Lamb:

15 He is meek & he is mild,[1]
He became a little child:
I a child & thou a lamb,
We are called by his name.
   Little Lamb God bless thee
20   Little Lamb God bless thee.
—1789

[1] *He ... mild* Cf. Charles Wesley, "Gentle Jesus, meek and mild."

"The Little Black Boy."

The Little Black Boy

My mother bore me in the southern wild,
And I am black, but O! my soul is white.
White as an angel is the English child:
But I am black as if bereav'd of light.

5 My mother taught me underneath a tree
And sitting down before the heat of day.
She took me on her lap and kissed me.
And pointing to the east began to say.

'Look on the rising sun! there God does live
10 And gives his light. and gives his heat away.
And flowers and trees and beasts and men receive
Comfort in morning joy in the noon day.

'And we are put on earth a little space.
That we may learn to bear the beams of love.
15 And these black bodies and this sun-burnt face
Is but a cloud, and like a shady grove.

'For when our souls have learn'd the heat to bear
The cloud will vanish we shall hear his voice.
Saying: "come out from the grove my love & care,
20   And round my golden tent like lambs rejoice."'

Thus did my mother say and kissed me.
And thus I say to little English boy.
When I from black and he from white cloud free,
And round the tent of God like lambs we joy:

25   Ill shade him from the heat till he can bear.
To lean in joy upon our fathers knee
And then Ill stand and stroke his silver hair.
And be like him and he will then love me.
—1789

The Chimney Sweeper [1]

When my mother died I was very young,
   And my father sold me while yet my tongue,
Could scarcely cry 'weep weep weep weep.' [2]
So your chimneys I sweep & in soot I sleep. [3]

5   Theres little Tom Dacre who cried when his head
That curl'd like a lambs back, was shav'd. so I said.
'Hush Tom never mind it, for when your head's bare.
You know that the soot cannot spoil your white hair.'

And so he was quiet, & that very night.
10   As Tom was a sleeping he had such a sight,
That thousands of sweepers Dick, Joe Ned & Jack
Were all of them lock'd up in coffins of black,

And by came an Angel who had a bright key,
And he open'd the coffins & set them all free.
15   Then down a green plain leaping laughing they run

And wash in a river and shine in the Sun. [4]

Then naked & white, all their bags left behind.
They rise upon clouds, and sport in the wind.
And the Angel told Tom if he'd be a good boy.
20   He'd have God for his father & never want joy.

And so Tom awoke and we rose in the dark
And got with our bags & our brushes to work.
Tho' the morning was cold, Tom was happy & warm.
So if all do their duty, they need not fear harm.
—1789

The Divine Image

To Mercy Pity Peace and Love,
   All pray in their distress:
And to these virtues of delight
Return their thankfulness.

5   For Mercy Pity Peace and Love.
Is God our father dear:
And Mercy Pity Peace and Love.
Is Man his child and care.

For Mercy has a human heart
10   Pity a human face:
And Love, the human form divine.
And Peace, the human dress.

Then every man of every clime,
That prays in his distress,
15   Prays to the human form divine
Love Mercy Pity Peace.

And all must love the human form,
In heathen, turk or jew. [5]

---

[1]   *The Chimney Sweeper*   Children were often forced to climb up chimneys to clean them—a filthy, dangerous, and unhealthy job. A law ameliorating their working conditions was passed in 1788, but it was rarely enforced.

[2]   *weep ... weep*   The child is attempting to say "sweep," the chimney-sweeper's street cry. The act of 1788 should have prevented the apprenticing of children younger than eight.

[3]   *in soot I sleep*   The sweeps used their bags of soot as blankets.

[4]   *And wash ... Sun*   The act of 1788 called for weekly washings for sweeps.

[5]   *heathen ... jew*   Cf. Isaac Watts, "Praise for the Gospel": "Lord, I ascribe it to thy Grace / And not to Chance, as others do, / That I was born of *Christian* Race, / And not a *Heathen*, or a *Jew*." Whereas Watt's emphasis had been on the theological underpinnings for a hierarchy of birth that took for granted the inferiority of other races and religions, Blake's emphasis is on loving even those whom his society despises.

Where Mercy, Love & Pity dwell,
20 There God is dwelling too.
—1789

Holy Thursday [1]

'Twas on a Holy Thursday their innocent faces clean
The children walking two & two in red & blue
    & green[2]
Grey headed beadles[3] walkd before with wands as
    white as snow
Till into the high dome of Pauls they like Thames
    waters flow

5 O what a multitude they seemd these flowers of
    London town
Seated in companies they sit with radiance all their own
The hum of multitudes was there but multitudes of
    lambs
Thousands of little boys & girls raising their innocent
    hands

Now like a mighty wind they raise to heaven the voice
    of song
10 Or like harmonious thunderings the seats of heaven
    among
Beneath them sit the aged men wise guardians of the poor
Then cherish pity, lest you drive an angel from your
    door[4]
—1789

Infant Joy

"I have no name,
    I am but two days old."
What shall I call thee?
"I happy am
5 Joy is my name."
Sweet joy befall thee!

Pretty joy!
Sweet joy but two days old,
Sweet joy I call thee;
10 Thou dost smile.
I sing the while
Sweet joy befall thee.
—1789

Nurse's Song

When the voices of children are heard on the
    green
And laughing is heard on the hill,
My heart is at rest within my breast
And every thing else is still

5 'Then come home my children, the sun is gone down
And the dews of night arise
Come come leave off play. and let us away
Till the morning appears in the skies.'

'No no let us play, for it is yet day
10 And we cannot go to sleep
Besides in the sky, the little birds fly
And the hills are all coverd with sheep'

'Well well go & play till the light fades away
And then go home to bed'
15 The little ones leaped & shouted & laugh'd
And all the hills ecchoed.
—1789

---

[1] *Holy Thursday* Each year since 1782, the 6,000 children in London's charity schools had been brought to St. Paul's Cathedral for an annual service of thanks-giving. Though "Holy Thursday" is the name given to Ascension Day, these services always occurred on a Thursday, usually in May, but never on Ascension Day.

[2] *in ... green* The school uniforms.

[3] *beadles* Officials.

[4] *cherish ... door* Cf. Hebrews 13.2, "Be not forgetful to entertain strangers; for thereby some have entertained angels unawares."

Title page, *Songs of Experience*.

from *Songs of Experience*

Introduction

H ear the voice of the Bard!
 Who Present, Past, & Future sees
Whose ears have heard,
The Holy Word,

5   That walk'd among the ancient trees.[1]
Calling[2] the lapsed Soul
And weeping in the evening dew:
That[3] might controll
The starry pole;
10 And fallen fallen light renew!

---

[1]   *Holy Word ... trees*   Cf. Genesis 3.8: "And they heard the voice of the Lord God walking in the garden in the cool of the day: and Adam and his wife hid themselves from the presence of the Lord God amongst the trees of the garden."

[2]   *Calling*   The subject here is ambiguous, and could either be the bard or the Holy Word.

[3]   *That*   Most likely the referent here is the lapsèd soul, but it may also be the Holy Word.

Frontispiece, *Songs of Experience*.

O Earth, O Earth return!
Arise from out the dewy grass;
Night is worn,
And the morn
15 Rises from the slumberous mass.

'Turn away no more:
Why wilt thou turn away
The starry floor[1]
The watry shore
20 Is giv'n thee till the break of day.'
—1794

The Clod & the Pebble

Love seeketh not Itself to please.
Nor for itself hath any care;
But for another gives its ease.
And builds a Heaven in Hells despair.'

5 So sang a little Clod of Clay.
Trodden with the cattles feet:
But a Pebble of the brook.
Warbled out these metres meet.

'Love seeketh only Self to please,
10 To bind another to Its delight;
Joys in anothers loss of ease,
And builds a Hell in Heavens despite.'[2]
—1794

Holy Thursday

Is this a holy thing to see.
In a rich and fruitful land,
Babes reducd to misery.
Fed with cold and usurous hand?[3]

5 Is that trembling cry a song?
Can it be a song of joy?
And so many children poor?
It is a land of poverty!

And their sun does never shine.
10 And their fields are bleak & bare.
And their ways are fill'd with thorns
It is eternal winter there.

For where-e'er the sun does shine.
And where-e'er the rain does fall:
15 Babe can never hunger there,
Nor poverty the mind appall.
—1794

The Chimney Sweeper

A little black thing among the snow:
Crying 'weep, weep,' in notes of woe!
'Where are thy father & mother? say?'
'They are both gone up to the church to pray.

5 'Because I was happy upon the heath.
And smil'd among the winters snow:
They clothed me in the clothes of death.
And taught me to sing the notes of woe.

'And because I am happy & dance & sing.
10 They think they have done me no injury:
And are gone to praise God & his Priest & King
Who make up a heaven of our misery.'
—1794

The Sick Rose

O Rose thou art sick.
The invisible worm.
That flies in the night
In the howling storm:

5 Has found out thy bed
Of crimson joy:

---

1 *starry floor* The sky, the floor of heaven.

2 *builds ... despite* In Milton's *Paradise Lost* (1.254–55), Satan declares, "The mind is its own place, and in itself / Can make a Heaven of Hell, a Hell of Heaven."

3 *usurous hand* I.e., the hand of someone engaged in lending money at interest.

And his dark secret love
Does thy life destroy.
—1794

The Fly

Little Fly
Thy summers play.
My thoughtless hand
Has brush'd away.

5   Am not I
A fly like thee?[1]
Or art not thou
A man like me?

For I dance
10 And drink & sing:
Till some blind hand
Shall brush my wing.

If thought is life
And strength & breath:
15 And the want
Of thought is death;[2]

Then am I
A happy fly,
If I live,
20 Or if I die.
—1794

The Tyger

Tyger Tyger, burning bright,
In the forests of the night;
What immortal hand or eye.
Could frame thy fearful symmetry?

5   In what distant deeps or skies.
Burnt the fire of thine eyes?

On what wings dare he aspire?[3]
What the hand. dare seize the fire?[4]

And what shoulder, & what art,
10 Could twist the sinews of thy heart?
And when thy heart began to beat,
What dread hand? & what dread feet?

What the hammer? what the chain,
In what furnace was thy brain?
15 What the anvil? what dread grasp.
Dare its deadly terrors clasp!

When the stars threw down the spears[5]
And water'd heaven with their tears:

---

[1] *Am ... thee* Cf. Shakespeare, *King Lear* 4.1.36–37: "As flies to wanton boys, are we to the gods, / They kill us for their sport."

[2] *If thought...death* Cf. René Descartes's statement "Cogito, ergo sum" ("I think, therefore I am").

[3] *what ... aspire* In Greek mythology, Icarus fashioned wings of wax and feathers; these melted when he attempted to fly too close to the sun.

[4] *What ... fire* Prometheus stole fire from heaven to give to humans.

[5] *threw down the spears* Either in surrender or as an act of rebellion —it is uncertain which.

Did he smile his work to see?
20 Did he who made the Lamb make thee?[1]

Tyger Tyger burning bright,
In the forests of the night:
What immortal hand or eye.
Dare frame thy fearful symmetry?
—1794

Ah! Sun-Flower

Ah Sun-flower! weary of time,
   Who countest the steps of the Sun:
Seeking after that sweet golden clime
Where the travellers journey is done.

5 Where the Youth pined away with desire,
And the pale Virgin shrouded in snow:
Arise from their graves and aspire.
Where my Sun-flower wishes to go.
—1794

The Garden of Love

I went to the Garden of Love.
   And saw what I never had seen:
A Chapel was built in the midst,
Where I used to play on the green.[2]

5 And the gates of this Chapel were shut,
And 'Thou shalt not'[3] writ over the door;
So I turn'd to the Garden of Love,
That so many sweet flowers bore.

And I saw it was filled with graves,
10 And tomb-stones where flowers should be:
And Priests in black gowns. were walking their
      rounds,

And binding with briars.[4] my joys & desires.
—1794

London

I wander thro' each charter'd[5] street,
   Near where the charter'd Thames does flow,
And mark in every face I meet
Marks of weakness, marks of woe.

5 In every cry of every Man,
In every Infants cry of fear.
In every voice; in every ban.
The mind-forg'd manacles I hear

How the Chimney-sweepers cry
10 Every blackning Church appalls.
And the hapless Soldiers sigh
Runs in blood down Palace walls

But most thro' midnight streets I hear
How the youthful Harlots curse[6]
15 Blasts the new born Infants tear[7]
And blights with plagues the Marriage hearse.
—1794

The Human Abstract

Pity would be no more.
   If we did not make somebody Poor:
And Mercy no more could be.
If all were as happy as we;

5 And mutual fear brings peace;
Till the selfish loves increase.

---

[1] *Did he … thee*   Tigers are not mentioned in the Bible.

[2] *A Chapel … green*   Possibly a reference to the erection of a chapel on South Lambeth Green in 1793.

[3] *Thou shalt not*   The phrase that introduces most of the Ten Commandments (Exodus 20.3–17).

[4] *binding with briars*   Prior to the nineteenth century, binding graves with briars was a common practice.

[5] *charter'd*   Privileged, licensed. While charters grant freedoms, they often do so for a select minority (such as merchants) and thereby simultaneously oppress the majority.

[6] *Harlots curse*   Referring both to the oaths she utters and the venereal diseases she spreads.

[7] *Blasts … tear*   A reference to the blindness caused in infants if they contract certain venereal diseases (such as gonorrhea) from the mother.

Then Cruelty knits a snare,
And spreads his baits with care.

He sits down with holy fears,
10 And waters the ground with tears;
Then Humility takes its root
Underneath his foot.

Soon spreads the dismal shade
Of Mystery over his head;
15 And the Catterpiller and Fly.
Feed on the Mystery.

And it bears the fruit of Deceit.
Ruddy and sweet to eat;
And the Raven his nest has made
20 In its thickest shade.

The Gods of the earth and sea.
Sought thro' Nature to find this Tree
But their search was all in vain:
There grows one in the Human Brain
—1794

5 And I waterd it in fears,
Night & morning with my tears:
And I sunned it with smiles,
And with soft deceitful wiles.

And it grew both day and night.
10 Till it bore an apple bright.
And my foe beheld it shine,
And he knew that it was mine.

And into my garden stole.
When the night had veild the pole;
15 In the morning glad I see.
My foe outstretchd beneath the tree.
—1794

Infant Sorrow

My mother groand! my father wept.
Into the dangerous world I leapt:
Helpless, naked. piping loud;
    Like a fiend hid in a cloud.

5 Struggling in my fathers hands:
Striving against my swadling bands:
Bound and weary I thought best
To sulk upon my mothers breast.
—1794

A Poison Tree[1]

I was angry with my friend;
I told my wrath, my wrath did end.
I was angry with my foe:
I told it not, my wrath did grow.

[1] *the Poison Tree* Another version of this poem is entitled "Christian Forbearance."

WILLIAM WORDSWORTH
1770 – 1850

Since about 1815, William Wordsworth has been acknowledged as a central figure in the English Romantic Movement. *Lyrical Ballads*, produced in conjunction with Samuel Taylor Coleridge though largely Wordsworth's project, marks a decisive break with the formalism and neo-classicism of eighteenth-century literature. It became the touchstone of a new literary sensibility that gave its faith to the benevolence of feeling, and of the vehicle it associated most with feeling: a poetry of sincerity. And it established the idea of Nature as the measure by which to judge whether a poem's expression of feeling was genuine or not.

Wordworth's poems respond powerfully to the major developments of his day—including the French Revolution, war, and industrialization. That response, however, was marked by many tensions and contradictions. It is the play of those contradictions that give such weight and continued authority to Wordsworth's work.

Wordsworth was born in the Lake District of England, in West Cumberland, and spent his boyhood absorbing the natural beauty around him. The death of his mother when he was eight, and of his father only five years later, unsettled the lives of William and his four siblings. Their situation was worsened by the fact that the only substantial legacy their father left was a sum owed to him by his employer, Lord Lonsdale, who withheld the money until his death in 1802. Along with his three brothers, William was sent to school at Hawkshead. His sister Dorothy—later his muse, confidante, and secretary—found herself shifting among various relatives.

At Hawkshead Wordsworth and his brothers boarded at the home of Ann Tyson, who became a surrogate mother to Wordsworth, encouraging his love of nature and tolerating his habit of roaming the countryside. Wordsworth paid close attention to and frequently conversed with the town's working people. His observations would inform the representation of many of the humble rural characters who appear in his poetry. Leaving the Lake District for the first time in 1787, he entered St. John's College, Cambridge. During this period he made two walking tours with his friend Robert Jones, first through France and the Alps during a crucial period of the French Revolution, and later through Wales (excursions described in Books Six and Fourteen respectively of the 1850 *Prelude*).

These adventures quickened Wordsworth's belief in the healing powers of nature and of his own responsive imagination, and they also awakened radical sentiments. While traveling in France in 1791–1792 he was swept up in the heady excitement that followed the French Revolution (1789). Young Wordsworth also fell in love with Annette Vallon, whose politics (Royalist) and religion (Catholic) he did not share, and they produced a daughter, Caroline, out of wedlock. Too poor to remain in France, which was now at war with England, Wordsworth returned to his country a divided man, his disillusionment growing as France fell into a Reign of Terror.

Financial concerns fed Wordsworth's doubts about his political convictions and his choice of vocation. In 1795, however, Wordsworth received a legacy of £900 from a friend, Raisley Calvert, whom he had nursed through his final illness. With this sum, and a rent-free cottage in Alfoxden provided by other friends, Wordsworth was able to set up housekeeping with his sister Dorothy, with his friend Coleridge not far away at Nether Stowey. (Describing his relationship with Coleridge in an 1832 letter to a friend, Wordsworth declared, "He and my beloved sister are the two beings to whom my intellect is most indebted.") Long walks and talks with Coleridge resulted in an extraordinary literary collaboration, *Lyrical Ballads, with a few other poems* (1798), a slender, anonymously-published volume that opens with Coleridge's literary ballad "The Rime of the Ancient Mariner" and closes with Wordsworth's blank-verse meditation, "Lines, Composed a Few Miles Above Tintern Abbey." The volume sought to combat what the authors saw as the increasingly marginal position of the poet in society, and the overly artificial language on which poetry relied.

As Coleridge and Wordsworth had expected, critics attacked the tone and subject matter of the volume. In the *Preface to the Second Edition* (1800)—perhaps the most famous poetic manifesto in the language—Wordsworth explained and defended the decision he made "to choose incidents and situations from common life, and to relate or describe them, throughout, as far as was possible, in a selection of language really used by men." In poems such as "Michael" and "The Brothers" (added to the 1800 edition of *Lyrical Ballads*), Wordsworth shows the strength and dignity with which the Lake District's inhabitants endure hardship, living in harmony with the natural world, removed from the taint of urban superficiality. Wordsworth was thus in an important sense what he is often taken to be, a "poet of nature." But his main object was not to depict directly "the beautiful and permanent forms of nature" but rather to explore how "the passions of men are incorporated with" such forms, and to depict the "ennobling interchange" between the natural world and the mental world. It is the mind, ultimately, that was Wordsworth's "haunt, and the main region of my song."

After a brief, inhospitable stay in Germany in 1798–99, during which Wordsworth wrote the "Lucy" poems (the identity of "Lucy" is unknown) and Coleridge assimilated German philosophy, Wordsworth and his sister returned to England and took up residence at Dove Cottage in Grasmere. Here Dorothy kept journals that have since become famous in their own right, and Wordsworth composed some of his finest lyrics, including "Resolution and Independence," "The Solitary Reaper" (a memorial of his walking tour through Scotland), and *Ode: Intimations of Immortality from Recollections of Early Childhood*, all of which were later published in his *Poems, in Two Volumes* (1807).

In 1802, Wordsworth married a childhood friend, Mary Hutchinson, and began a period of relative tranquility and poetic fruitfulness, although these years were not without grief and disappointment. By 1812, two of his five children were dead, his brother John had been lost at sea, his friendship with Coleridge (whose health was deteriorating as his opium addiction deepened) had become strained, and *Poems, in Two Volumes* had suffered damaging reviews.

Then in 1814 Wordsworth published *The Excursion*, a long blank-verse meditation that was a forecast and first installment of his planned epic, *The Recluse*. The book was poorly reviewed, even ridiculed. Nevertheless, Wordworth by this time had gained a growing audience of devoted admirers, and his reputation from this low point began to establish itself firmly.

Like *The Excursion*, *The Prelude*, which Wordsworth had begun in 1799, was intended as a subsidiary piece that would be incorporated into *The Recluse*. He completed a two-book version of *The Prelude* in 1799 and a much expanded thirteen-book poem in 1805. He then continued to revise the poem for the rest of his life. This epic in blank verse—which Coleridge, upon hearing it, declared a "prophetic Lay"—describes the growth of the poet's mind from earliest memories to adulthood. By the end of his journey in the poem, Wordsworth reaffirms both providential design and the revolutionary potential of the imagination. *The Prelude* is a great, long lesson showing "how the mind of Man becomes / A thousand times more beautiful than the earth / On which he dwells."

In 1813, the Wordsworth household left Dove Cottage for the more expansive environs of Rydal Mount. There the poet, his beloved sister, and his wife lived out their days. The move was made possible by Wordsworth's improved financial situation, the result of a literary patronage granted by

Lord Lonsdale and a position as Stamp Distributor for Westmorland. In the eyes of the younger generation (including Percy Shelley, Lord Byron, and Robert Browning), the patronage and the government position seemed to transform the once radical poet into a hypocritical and complacent hireling. As they saw it, Wordsworth had abandoned his early commitment to be the voice of the disenfranchised and the poor. Increasingly skeptical of external revolutions and political agitation, Wordsworth saw himself not as having abandoned his ideals but rather as having internalized—or spiritualized—his commitment to truth and liberty.

During his middle and old age Wordsworth wrote numerous sonnets, including *Ecclesiastical Sketches* (1822), inspired by his brother Christopher, a clergyman and scholar. Having begun as a poetic and political revolutionary, he ended his life an iconic figure of the early Victorian era. Queen Victoria crowned him her Poet Laureate in 1843, and admirers flocked to the Lake District to seek him out in his home. The influence of his poetic style remained strong until well into the twentieth century, and Victorian writers of prose and poetry alike—including Tennyson, Charles Dickens, George Eliot, and Elizabeth Gaskell—acknowledged their debt to the life he had breathed into ways of thinking about nature, poetic feeling, and the human imagination.

⌘⌘⌘

⌘⌘⌘

from *Lyrical Ballads, 1798*

ADVERTISEMENT

It is the honourable characteristic of Poetry that its materials are to be found in every subject which can interest the human mind. The evidence of this fact is to be sought, not in the writings of Critics, but in those of Poets themselves.

The majority of the following poems are to be considered as experiments. They were written chiefly with a view to ascertain how far the language of conversation in the middle and lower classes of society is adapted to the purposes of poetic pleasure. Readers accustomed to the gaudiness and inane phraseology of many modern writers, if they persist in reading this book to its conclusion, will perhaps frequently have to struggle with feelings of strangeness and awkwardness: they will look round for poetry, and will be induced to enquire by what species of courtesy these attempts can be permitted to assume that title. It is desirable that such readers, for their own sakes, should not suffer the solitary word Poetry, a word of very disputed meaning, to stand in the way of their gratification; but that, while they are perusing this book, they should ask themselves if it contains a natural delineation of human passions, human characters, and human incidents; and if the answer be favourable to the author's wishes, that they should consent to be pleased in spite of that most dreadful enemy to our pleasures, our own pre-established codes of decision.

Readers of superior judgment may disapprove of the style in which many of these pieces are executed. It must be expected that many lines and phrases will not exactly suit their taste. It will perhaps appear to them that, wishing to avoid the prevalent fault of the day, the author has sometimes descended too low, and that many of his expressions are too familiar, and not of sufficient dignity. It is apprehended that the more conversant the reader is with our elder writers, and with those in modern times who have been the most successful in painting manners and passions, the fewer complaints of this kind will he have to make.

An accurate taste in poetry, and in all the other arts, Sir Joshua Reynolds[1] has observed, is an acquired talent, which can only be produced by severe thought, and a long continued intercourse with the best models of composition. This is mentioned not with so ridiculous a purpose as to prevent the most inexperienced reader from judging for himself; but merely to temper the

---

[1] *Sir Joshua Reynolds* Renowned portrait and history painter, and first President of the Royal Academy (1723–92).

rashness of decision, and to suggest that if poetry be a subject on which much time has not been bestowed, the judgment may be erroneous, and that in many cases it necessarily will be so.

The tale of Goody Blake and Harry Gill is founded on a well-authenticated fact which happened in Warwickshire. Of the other poems in the collection, it may be proper to say that they are either absolute inventions of the author, or facts which took place within his personal observation or that of his friends. The poem of the Thorn, as the reader will soon discover, is not supposed to be spoken in the author's own person: the character of the loquacious narrator will sufficiently show itself in the course of the story. The Rime of the Ancyent Marinere was professedly written in imitation of the style, as well as of the spirit of the elder poets; but with a few exceptions, the Author believes that the language adopted in it has been equally intelligible for these three last centuries. The lines entitled Expostulation and Reply, and those which follow, arose out of conversation with a friend who was somewhat unreasonably attached to modern books of moral philosophy.

We Are Seven

A simple child, dear brother Jim,
That lightly draws its breath,
And feels its life in every limb,
What should it know of death?

5   I met a little cottage girl,
She was eight years old, she said;
Her hair was thick with many a curl
That cluster'd round her head.

She had a rustic, woodland air,
10   And she was wildly clad;
Her eyes were fair, and very fair
—Her beauty made me glad.

"Sisters and brothers, little maid,
How many may you be?"

15   "How many? seven in all," she said,
And wondering looked at me.

"And where are they, I pray you tell?"
She answered, "Seven are we,
And two of us at Conway[1] dwell,
20   And two are gone to sea.

"Two of us in the church-yard lie,
My sister and my brother,
And in the church-yard cottage, I
Dwell near them with my mother."

25   "You say that two at Conway dwell,
And two are gone to sea,
Yet you are seven; I pray you tell
Sweet Maid, how this may be?"

Then did the little Maid reply,
30   "Seven boys and girls are we;
Two of us in the church-yard lie,
Beneath the church-yard tree."

"You run about, my little maid,
Your limbs they are alive;
35   If two are in the church-yard laid,
Then ye are only five."

"Their graves are green, they may be seen,"
The little Maid replied,
"Twelve steps or more from my mother's door,
40   And they are side by side.

"My stockings there I often knit,
My 'kerchief there I hem;
And there upon the ground I sit—
I sit and sing to them.

45   "And often after sunset, Sir,
When it is light and fair,
I take my little porringer,[2]
And eat my supper there.

---

[1] *Conway* Seaport of southern Wales.

[2] *porringer* Small metal or earthenware basin from which broth or porridge is eaten.

"The first that died was little Jane;
50 In bed she moaning lay,
Till God released her of her pain,
And then she went away.

"So in the church-yard she was laid,
And all the summer dry,
55 Together round her grave we played,
My brother John and I.

"And when the ground was white with snow,
And I could run and slide,
My brother John was forced to go,
60 And he lies by her side."

"How many are you then," said I,
If they two are in Heaven?"
The little Maiden did reply,
"O Master! we are seven."

65 "But they are dead; those two are dead!
Their spirits are in heaven!"
'Twas throwing words away; for still
The little Maid would have her will,
And said, "Nay, we are seven!"
    —1798

Lines Written in Early Spring

I heard a thousand blended notes,
  While in a grove I sat reclined,
In that sweet mood when pleasant thoughts
Bring sad thoughts to the mind.

5 To her fair works did nature link
The human soul that through me ran;
And much it griev'd my heart to think
What man has made of man.

Through primrose-tufts, in that sweet bower,
10 The periwinkle trail'd its wreathes;
And 'tis my faith that every flower
Enjoys the air it breathes.

The birds around me hopp'd and play'd:
Their thoughts I cannot measure,
15 But the least motion which they made,
It seem'd a thrill of pleasure.

The budding twigs spread out their fan,
To catch the breezy air;
And I must think, do all I can,
20 That there was pleasure there.

If I these thoughts may not prevent,
If such be of my creed the plan,
Have I not reason to lament
What man has made of man?
    —1798

The Thorn[1]

1

There is a thorn;° it looks so old,   *thorn bush*
  In truth you'd find it hard to say,
How it could ever have been young,
It looks so old and grey.
5 Not higher than a two-years' child,
It stands erect this aged thorn;
No leaves it has, no thorny points;
It is a mass of knotted joints,
A wretched thing forlorn.
10 It stands erect, and like a stone
With lichens it is overgrown.

2

Like rock or stone, it is o'ergrown
With lichens to the very top,
And hung with heavy tufts of moss,
15 A melancholy crop:
Up from the earth these mosses creep,
And this poor thorn they clasp it round

---

[1] [Wordsworth's note]   Arose from my observing, on the ridge of Quantock Hill, on a stormy day a thorn which I had often passed in calm and bright weather without noticing it. I said to myself, "Cannot I by some invention do as much to make this Thorn permanently an impressive object as the storm has made it to my eyes at this moment?"

So close, you'd say that they were bent
With plain and manifest intent,
20 To drag it to the ground;
And all had joined in one endeavour
To bury this poor thorn for ever.

3

High on a mountain's highest ridge,
Where oft the stormy winter gale
25 Cuts like a scythe, while through the clouds
It sweeps from vale to vale;
Not five yards from the mountain-path,
This thorn you on your left espy;
And to the left, three yards beyond,
30 You see a little muddy pond
Of water, never dry;
I've measured it from side to side:
'Tis three feet long, and two feet wide.

4

And close beside this aged thorn,
35 There is a fresh and lovely sight,
A beauteous heap, a hill of moss,
Just half a foot in height.
All lovely colours there you see,
All colours that were ever seen,
40 And mossy network too is there,
As if by hand of lady fair
The work had woven been,
And cups,° the darlings of the eye,   *blossoms*
So deep is their vermilion° dye.   *red*

5

45 Ah me! what lovely tints are there!
Of olive-green and scarlet bright,
In spikes, in branches, and in stars,
Green, red, and pearly white.
This heap of earth o'ergrown with moss,
50 Which close beside the thorn you see,
So fresh in all its beauteous dyes,
Is like an infant's grave in size
As like as like can be:
But never, never any where,
55 An infant's grave was half so fair.

6

Now would you see this aged thorn,
This pond and beauteous hill of moss,
You must take care and choose your time
The mountain when to cross.
60 For oft there sits, between the heap
That's like an infant's grave in size,
And that same pond of which I spoke,
A woman in a scarlet cloak,
And to herself she cries,
65 "Oh misery! oh misery!
"Oh woe is me! oh misery!"

7

At all times of the day and night
This wretched woman thither goes,
And she is known to every star,
70 And every wind that blows;
And there beside the thorn she sits
When the blue day-light's in the skies,
And when the whirlwind's on the hill,
Or frosty air is keen and still,
75 And to herself she cries,
"Oh misery! oh misery!
Oh woe is me! oh misery!"

8

"Now wherefore thus, by day and night,
In rain, in tempest, and in snow,
80 Thus to the dreary mountain-top
Does this poor woman go?
And why sits she beside the thorn
When the blue day-light's in the sky,
Or when the whirlwind's on the hill,
85 Or frosty air is keen and still,
And wherefore does she cry?
Oh wherefore? wherefore? tell me why
Does she repeat that doleful cry?"

9

I cannot tell; I wish I could;
90 For the true reason no one knows,
But if you'd gladly view the spot,
The spot to which she goes;
The heap that's like an infant's grave,

95   The pond—and thorn, so old and grey;
      Pass by her door—'tis seldom shut—
      And if you see her in her hut,
      Then to the spot away!
      I never heard of such as dare
      Approach the spot when she is there.

                    10

100   "But wherefore to the mountain-top
      Can this unhappy woman go,
      Whatever star is in the skies,
      Whatever wind may blow?"
      Nay rack your brain—'tis all in vain,
105   I'll tell you every thing I know;
      But to the thorn, and to the pond
      Which is a little step beyond,
      I wish that you would go:
      Perhaps when you are at the place
110   You something of her tale may trace.

                    11

      I'll give you the best help I can:
      Before you up the mountain go,
      Up to the dreary mountain-top,
      I'll tell you all I know.
115   'Tis now some two and twenty years,
      Since she (her name is Martha Ray)
      Gave with a maiden's true good will
      Her company to Stephen Hill;
      And she was blithe and gay,
120   And she was happy, happy still
      Whene'er she thought of Stephen Hill.

                    12

      And they had fix'd the wedding-day,
      The morning that must wed them both;
      But Stephen to another maid
125   Had sworn another oath;
      And with this other maid to church
      Unthinking Stephen went—
      Poor Martha! on that woeful day
      A cruel, cruel fire, they say,
130   Into her bones was sent:

      It dried her body like a cinder,
      And almost turn'd her brain to tinder.[1]

                    13

      They say, full six months after this,
      While yet the summer leaves were green,
135   She to the mountain-top would go,
      And there was often seen.
      'Tis said, a child was in her womb,
      As now to any eye was plain;
      She was with child, and she was mad,
140   Yet often she was sober sad
      From her exceeding pain.
      Oh me! ten thousand times I'd rather
      That he had died, that cruel father!

                    14

      Sad case for such a brain to hold
145   Communion with a stirring child!
      Sad case, as you may think, for one
      Who had a brain so wild!
      Last Christmas when we talked of this,
      Old Farmer Simpson did maintain,
150   That in her womb the infant wrought
      About its mother's heart, and brought
      Her senses back again:
      And when at last her time drew near,
      Her looks were calm, her senses clear.

                    15

155   No more I know, I wish I did,
      And I would tell it all to you;
      For what became of this poor child
      There's none that ever knew:
      And if a child was born or no,
160   There's no one that could ever tell;
      And if 'twas born alive or dead,
      There's no one knows, as I have said,
      But some remember well,
      That Martha Ray about this time
165   Would up the mountain often climb.

---

[1]   *tinder*   Dry, flammable substance that will take fire from a spark.

16

And all that winter, when at night
The wind blew from the mountain-peak,
'Twas worth your while, though in the dark,
The church-yard path to seek:
170 For many a time and oft were heard
Cries coming from the mountain-head,
Some plainly living voices were,
And others, I've heard many swear,
Were voices of the dead:
175 I cannot think, whate'er they say,
They had to do with Martha Ray.

17

But that she goes to this old thorn,
The thorn which I've described to you,
And there sits in a scarlet cloak,
180 I will be sworn is true.
For one day with my telescope,
To view the ocean wide and bright,
When to this country first I came,
Ere I had heard of Martha's name,
185 I climbed the mountain's height:
A storm came on, and I could see
No object higher than my knee.

18

'Twas mist and rain, and storm and rain,
No screen, no fence could I discover,
190 And then the wind! in faith, it was
A wind full ten times over.
I looked around, I thought I saw
A jutting crag, and off I ran,
Head-foremost, through the driving rain,
195 The shelter of the crag to gain,
And, as I am a man,
Instead of jutting crag, I found
A woman seated on the ground.

19

I did not speak—I saw her face,
200 Her face it was enough for me;
I turned about and heard her cry,
"O misery! O misery!"
And there she sits, until the moon

Through half the clear blue sky will go,
205 And when the little breezes make
The waters of the pond to shake,
As all the country know,
She shudders and you hear her cry,
"Oh misery! oh misery!"

20

210 "But what's the thorn? and what's the pond?
And what's the hill of moss to her?
And what's the creeping breeze that comes
The little pond to stir?"
I cannot tell; but some will say
215 She hanged her baby on the tree,
Some say she drowned it in the pond,
Which is a little step beyond,
But all and each agree,
The little babe was buried there,
220 Beneath that hill of moss so fair.

21

I've heard the scarlet moss is red
With drops of that poor infant's blood;
But kill a new-born infant thus!
I do not think she could.
225 Some say, if to the pond you go,
And fix on it a steady view,
The shadow of a babe you trace,
A baby and a baby's face,
And that it looks at you;
230 Whene'er you look on it, 'tis plain
The baby looks at you again.

22

And some had sworn an oath that she
Should be to public justice brought;
And for the little infant's bones
235 With spades they would have sought.
But then the beauteous hill of moss
Before their eyes began to stir;
And for full fifty yards around,
The grass it shook upon the ground;
240 But all do still aver
The little babe is buried there,
Beneath that hill of moss so fair.

23

I cannot tell how this may be,
But plain it is, the thorn is bound
245 With heavy tufts of moss, that strive
To drag it to the ground.
And this I know, full many a time,
When she was on the mountain high,
By day, and in the silent night,
250 When all the stars shone clear and bright,
That I have heard her cry,
"Oh misery! oh misery!
"Oh woe is me! oh misery!"
—1798

Expostulation and Reply

"Why William, on that old grey stone,
    Thus for the length of half a day,
Why William, sit you thus alone,
And dream your time away?

5   "Where are your books? that light bequeath'd
To beings else forlorn and blind!
Up! Up! and drink the spirit breath'd
From dead men to their kind.

"You look round on your mother earth,
10   As if she for no purpose bore you;
As if you were her first-born birth,
And none had lived before you!"

One morning thus, by Esthwaite lake,[1]
When life was sweet I knew not why,
15   To me my good friend Matthew spake,
And thus I made reply.

"The eye it cannot choose but see,
We cannot bid the ear be still;
Our bodies feel, where'er they be,
20   Against, or with our will.

"Nor less I deem that there are powers,
Which of themselves our minds impress,
That we can feed this mind of ours,
In a wise passiveness.

25   "Think you, mid all this mighty sum
Of things for ever speaking,
That nothing of itself will come,
But we must still be seeking?

"—Then ask not wherefore, here, alone,
30   Conversing as I may,
I sit upon this old grey stone,
And dream my time away."
—1798

The Tables Turned
An Evening Scene on the Same Subject

Up! up! my friend, and clear your looks,
    Why all this toil and trouble?
Up! up! my friend, and quit your books,
Or surely you'll grow double.[2]

5   The sun above the mountain's head,
A freshening lustre mellow,
Through all the long green fields has spread,
His first sweet evening yellow.

Books! 'tis a dull and endless strife,
10   Come, hear the woodland linnet,
How sweet his music; on my life
There's more of wisdom in it.

And hark! how blithe the throstle° sings!   *thrush*
And he is no mean preacher;
15   Come forth into the light of things,
Let Nature be your teacher.

She has a world of ready wealth,
Our minds and hearts to bless—

---

1 *Esthwaite lake* Located at Hawkshead (in England's Lake District), where Wordsworth attended grammar school.

2 *double* Doubled over.

Spontaneous wisdom breathed by health,
20 Truth breathed by cheerfulness.

One impulse from a vernal wood
May teach you more of man;
Of moral evil and of good,
Than all the sages can.

25 Sweet is the lore which nature brings;
Our meddling intellect
Mishapes the beauteous forms of things
—We murder to dissect.

Enough of science and of art;
30 Close up these barren leaves;
Come forth, and bring with you a heart
That watches and receives.
—1798

Among the woods and copses lose themselves,
Nor, with their green and simple hue, disturb
15 The wild green landscape. Once again I see
These hedge-rows, hardly hedge-rows, little lines
Of sportive wood run wild; these pastoral farms
Green to the very door; and wreaths of smoke
Sent up, in silence, from among the trees,
20 With some uncertain notice, as might seem,
Of vagrant dwellers in the houseless woods,
Or of some hermit's cave, where by his fire
The hermit sits alone.

                    Though absent long,
25 These forms of beauty have not been to me,
As is a landscape to a blind man's eye:
But oft, in lonely rooms, and 'mid the din
Of towns and cities, I have owed to them,
In hours of weariness, sensations sweet,
30 Felt in the blood, and felt along the heart,
And passing even into my purer mind
With tranquil restoration—feelings too
Of unremembered pleasure; such, perhaps,
As may have had no trivial influence
35 On that best portion of a good man's life;
His little, nameless, unremembered acts
Of kindness and of love. Nor less, I trust,
To them I may have owed another gift,
Of aspect more sublime; that blessed mood,
40 In which the burthen of the mystery,
In which the heavy and the weary weight
Of all this unintelligible world
Is lighten'd—that serene and blessed mood,
In which the affections gently lead us on,
45 Until, the breath of this corporeal frame,
And even the motion of our human blood
Almost suspended, we are laid asleep
In body, and become a living soul:
While with an eye made quiet by the power
50 Of harmony, and the deep power of joy,
We see into the life of things.

                    If this
Be but a vain belief, yet, oh! how oft,
In darkness, and amid the many shapes
55 Of joyless day-light; when the fretful stir

Lines Written a Few Miles above Tintern Abbey

*On Revisiting the Banks of the Wye during a Tour,
July 13, 1798*[1]

Five years have passed; five summers, with the length
Of five long winters! and again I hear
These waters, rolling from their mountain-springs
With a sweet inland murmur.[2] Once again
5 Do I behold these steep and lofty cliffs,
Which on a wild secluded scene impress
Thoughts of more deep seclusion; and connect
The landscape with the quiet of the sky.
The day is come when I again repose
10 Here, under this dark sycamore, and view
These plots of cottage-ground, these orchard-tufts,
Which, at this season, with their unripe fruits,

[1] [Wordsworth's note] No poem of mine was composed under circumstances more pleasant for me to remember than this. I began it upon leaving Tintern, after crossing the Wye, and concluded it just as I was entering Bristol in the evening, after a ramble of 4 or 5 days, with my sister. Not a line of it was altered, and not any part of it was written down till I reached Bristol.

[2] [Wordsworth's note] The river is not affected by the tides a few miles above Tintern.

Unprofitable, and the fever of the world,
Have hung upon the beatings of my heart,
How oft, in spirit, have I turned to thee
O sylvan Wye! Thou wanderer through the woods,
60 How often has my spirit turned to thee!

And now, with gleams of half-extinguish'd thought,
With many recognitions dim and faint,
And somewhat of a sad perplexity,
The picture of the mind revives again:
65 While here I stand, not only with the sense
Of present pleasure, but with pleasing thoughts
That in this moment there is life and food
For future years. And so I dare to hope
Though changed, no doubt, from what I was, when first
70 I came among these hills; when like a roe°   *deer*
I bounded o'er the mountains, by the sides
Of the deep rivers, and the lonely streams,
Wherever nature led; more like a man
Flying from something that he dreads, than one
75 Who sought the thing he loved. For nature then
(The coarser pleasures of my boyish days,
And their glad animal movements all gone by)
To me was all in all. I cannot paint
What then I was. The sounding cataract
80 Haunted me like a passion: the tall rock,
The mountain, and the deep and gloomy wood,
Their colours and their forms, were then to me
An appetite: a feeling and a love,
That had no need of a remoter charm,
85 By thought supplied, or any interest
Unborrowed from the eye. That time is past,
And all its aching joys are now no more,
And all its dizzy raptures. Not for this
Faint[1] I, nor mourn nor murmur: other gifts
90 Have followed, for such loss, I would believe,
Abundant recompence. For I have learned
To look on nature, not as in the hour
Of thoughtless youth, but hearing oftentimes
The still, sad music of humanity,
95 Not harsh nor grating, though of ample power
To chasten and subdue. And I have felt
A presence that disturbs me with the joy
Of elevated thoughts; a sense sublime

Of something far more deeply interfused,
100 Whose dwelling is the light of setting suns,
And the round ocean, and the living air,
And the blue sky, and in the mind of man,
A motion and a spirit, that impels
All thinking things, all objects of all thought,
105 And rolls through all things. Therefore am I still
A lover of the meadows and the woods,
And mountains; and of all that we behold
From this green earth; of all the mighty world
Of eye and ear, both what they half create,
110 And what perceive; well pleased to recognize
In nature and the language of the sense,
The anchor of my purest thoughts, the nurse,
The guide, the guardian of my heart, and soul
Of all my moral being.

115   Nor, perchance,
If I were not thus taught, should I the more
Suffer my genial° spirits to decay: *creative*
For thou art with me, here, upon the banks
Of this fair river; thou, my dearest Friend,[2]
120 My dear, dear Friend, and in thy voice I catch
The language of my former heart, and read
My former pleasures in the shooting lights
Of thy wild eyes. Oh! yet a little while
May I behold in thee what I was once,
125 My dear, dear Sister! And this prayer I make,
Knowing that Nature never did betray
The heart that loved her; 'tis her privilege,
Through all the years of this our life, to lead
From joy to joy: for she can so inform
130 The mind that is within us, so impress
With quietness and beauty, and so feed
With lofty thoughts, that neither evil tongues,
Rash judgments, nor the sneers of selfish men,
Nor greetings where no kindness is, nor all
135 The dreary intercourse of daily life,
Shall e'er prevail against us, or disturb
Our cheerful faith that all which we behold
Is full of blessings. Therefore let the moon
Shine on thee in thy solitary walk;
140 And let the misty mountain winds be free

---

[1] *Faint* Lose heart; grow weak.

[2] *my dearest Friend* I.e., Dorothy Wordsworth, Wordsworth's sister.

To blow against thee: and in after years,
When these wild ecstasies shall be matured
Into a sober pleasure, when thy mind
Shall be a mansion for all lovely forms,
145   Thy memory be as a dwelling-place
For all sweet sounds and harmonies; Oh! then,
If solitude, or fear, or pain, or grief,
Should be thy portion, with what healing thoughts
Of tender joy wilt thou remember me,
150   And these my exhortations! Nor, perchance,
If I should be, where I no more can hear
Thy voice, nor catch from thy wild eyes these gleams
Of past existence, wilt thou then forget
That on the banks of this delightful stream
155   We stood together; and that I, so long
A worshipper of Nature, hither came,
Unwearied in that service: rather say
With warmer love, oh! with far deeper zeal
Of holier love. Nor wilt thou then forget,
160   That after many wanderings, many years
Of absence, these steep woods and lofty cliffs,
And this green pastoral landscape, were to me
More dear, both for themselves, and for thy sake.
—1798

Composed upon Westminster Bridge
Sept. 3, 1803[3]

Earth has not any thing to show more fair:
Dull would he be of soul who could pass by
A sight so touching in its majesty:
This City now doth like a garment wear
5   This beauty of the morning; silent, bare,
Ships, towers, domes, theatres, and temples lie
Open unto the fields, and to the sky;
All bright and glittering in the smokeless air.
Never did sun more beautifully steep
10 In his first splendor valley, rock, or hill;
Ne'er saw I, never felt, a calm so deep!

---

[3] *Composed ... 1803* Wordsworth misremembered the date of composition, which was actually (according to Dorothy Wordsworth's *Grasmere Journals*) July 1802, when Wordsworth set out for a brief trip to France, where his former lover Annette Vallon lived with their daughter, Caroline.

The river glideth at his own sweet will:
Dear God! the very houses seem asleep;
And all that mighty heart is lying still!
—1807

[*The world is too much with us*]

The world is too much with us; late and soon,
Getting and spending, we lay waste our powers:
Little we see in nature that is ours;
We have given our hearts away, a sordid boon!
5   The Sea that bares her bosom to the moon;
The Winds that will be howling at all hours
And are up-gathered now like sleeping flowers;
For this, for every thing, we are out of tune;
It moves us not. Great God! I'd rather be
10   A Pagan suckled in a creed outworn;
So might I, standing on this pleasant lea,
Have glimpses that would make me less forlorn;
Have sight of Proteus coming from the sea;
Or hear old Triton blow his wreathed horn.[1]
—1807

[*It is a beauteous Evening*]

It is a beauteous Evening, calm and free;
The holy time is quiet as a Nun
Breathless with adoration; the broad sun
Is sinking down in its tranquillity;
5   The gentleness of heaven is on the Sea:
Listen! the mighty Being is awake
And doth with his eternal motion make
A sound like thunder—everlastingly.
Dear Child! dear Girl![2] that walkest with me here,
10   If thou appear'st untouch'd by solemn thought,
Thy nature is not therefore less divine:
Thou liest in Abraham's bosom[3] all the year;

---

[1]   *Proteus*   Shape-changing sea god; *Triton*   Sea god with the head
and torso of a man and the tail of a fish. He was usually depicted
blowing on a conch shell.

[2]   *Dear ... Girl*   Wordsworth's daughter Caroline.

[3]   *Abraham's bosom*   The resting place for souls bound for heaven.
See Luke 16.22: "And it came to pass, that the beggar died, and was
carried by the angels into Abraham's bosom."

And worshipp'st at the Temple's inner shrine,
God being with thee when we know it not.
—1807

London
1802[4]

Milton! thou should'st be living at this hour:
England hath need of thee: she is a fen
Of stagnant waters: altar, sword, and pen,
Fireside, the heroic wealth of hall and bower,
5   Have forfeited their ancient English dower
Of inward happiness. We are selfish men;
Oh! raise us up, return to us again;
And give us manners, virtue, freedom, power.
Thy soul was like a Star and dwelt apart:
10   Thou hadst a voice whose sound was like the sea;
Pure as the naked heavens, majestic, free,
So didst thou travel on life's common way,
In cheerful godliness; and yet thy heart
The lowliest duties on itself did lay.
—1807

The Solitary Reaper[5]

Behold her, single in the field,
Yon solitary Highland Lass!
Reaping and singing by herself;
Stop here, or gently pass!
5   Alone she cuts, and binds the grain,
And sings a melancholy strain;
O listen! for the Vale profound
Is overflowing with the sound.

---

[4]   *London, 1802*   Written immediately after Wordsworth's return
from France, when he was struck by the differences between his
native country and France after the Revolution. Milton died in
1674.

[5]   *The Solitary Reaper*   Suggested by the following passage in
Thomas Wilkinson's *Tours to the British Mountains* (1824): "Passed
a female who was reaping alone: she sung in Erse [a Gaelic language]
as she bended over her sickle; the sweetest human voice I ever heard:
her strains were tenderly melancholy, and felt delicious, long after
they were heard no more."

[*My heart leaps up*]

My heart leaps up when I behold
   A Rainbow in the sky:
So was it when my life began;
So is it now I am a Man;
So be it when I shall grow old,
      Or let me die!
The Child is Father of the Man;
And I could wish my days to be
Bound each to each by natural piety.
—1804

In Context

"I wandered lonely as a Cloud":
Stages in the Life of a Poem

The earliest version of this poem was composed in 1804 and first published in 1807. It was evidently inspired by an entry in Dorothy Wordsworth's journal from two years earlier, describing a scene at Glencoyne Bay, Ullswater, seen by Dorothy and William on their way back to Grasmere after a long ramble. Appearing below are the scene as described by Dorothy in the journal; William's first version of the poem; a facsimile copy of the page in the copy of *Poems in Two Volumes* in which William began to compose an additional stanza to the poem; a transcription of his handwritten jottings; and William's revised version, with the added stanza and some other changes (which was not published until 1815).

from Dorothy Wordsworth, *Grasmere Journal* (Thursday, 15 April 1802)

When we were in the woods beyond Gowbarrow park we saw a few daffodils close to the water side. We fancied that the lake had floated the seeds ashore and that the little colony had so sprung up. But as we went along there were more and yet more and at last under the boughs of the trees, we saw that there was a long belt of them along the shore, about the breadth of a country turnpike road. I never saw daffodils so beautiful they grew among the mossy stones about and about them, some rested their heads upon these stones as on a pillow for weariness and the rest tossed and reeled and danced and seemed as if they verily laughed with the wind that blew upon them over the lake, they looked so gay ever glancing ever changing. This wind blew directly over the lake to them. There was here and there a little knot and a few stragglers a few yards higher up but they were so few as not to disturb the simplicity and unity and life of that one busy highway.

[*I wandered lonely as a Cloud*]

I wandered lonely as a Cloud
That floats on high o'er Vales and Hills,
When all at once I saw a crowd
A host of dancing Daffodils;
5   Along the Lake, beneath the trees,
Ten thousand dancing in the breeze.

The waves beside them danced, but they
Outdid the sparkling waves in glee—
A Poet could not but be gay
10 In such a laughing company:
I gazed—and gaz'd—but little thought
What wealth the show to me had brought:

For oft when on my couch I lie
In vacant or in pensive mood,
15 They flash upon that inward eye
Which is the bliss of solitude,
And then my heart with pleasure fills,
And dances with the Daffodils.
    —1807

I wandered lonely as a cloud[1]

                    1
A host of golden Daffodi ls
Beside
~~*Along*~~ *the Lake beneath the trees*
                              vernal
All dancing ~~*dancing*~~ *in the breeze*
  Continuous
                    ⌠ *ed*
~~*Close crowd*~~ ⌡ ~~*ing. [?like]*~~
~~*As numerous*~~ ‸ *as the stars that shine*
  and twinkle
                    on⌠
At midnight, in⌡ *the milky way*
                    ⌠ *a*
They stretch'd ⌡ *in* *never ending line*
Along the margin of a bay
Ten thousand saw I at a glance
Tossing their heads in spritely dance

[*I wandered lonely as a Cloud*]

I wandered lonely as a cloud
   That floats on high o'er vales and hills,
When all at once I saw a crowd,
A host, of golden daffodils;
5   Beside the lake, beneath the trees,
Fluttering and dancing in the breeze.

Continuous as the stars that shine
And twinkle on the milky way,
They stretched in never-ending line
10   Along the margin of a bay:
Ten thousand saw I at a glance,
Tossing their heads in sprightly dance.

The waves beside them danced, but they
Outdid the sparkling waves in glee:
15   A poet could not but be gay,
In such a jocund company;
I gazed—and gazed—but little thought
What wealth the show to me had brought:

For oft, when on my couch I lie
20   In vacant or in pensive mood,
They flash upon that inward eye

Which is the bliss of solitude;
And then my heart with pleasure fills,
And dances with the daffodils.
—1815

---
[1] *I wandered ... cloud* Transcription of Wordsworth's manuscript
(see previous page for facsimile).

Percy Bysshe Shelley
1792 – 1822

Even more than Blake's, Percy Bysshe Shelley's progressive social and political ideas have been an inspiration to many readers, from nineteenth-century socialists like Marx and Engels to radical thinkers of the 1960s. Although he was born into wealth and privilege, Shelley opposed the powerful, from those who teased and harassed him in school at Eton to the Tory government and press whom he believed were responsible for the oppression of the working classes. He collaborated on *The Necessity of Atheism* (1811), a pamphlet destined to alienate not only his father, but also the bishops and authorities at Oxford, to whom Shelley sent the piece. Antagonistic to kings, priests, judges, the conservative press and aristocracy, he was called "Mad Shelley" at Oxford. He earned this sobriquet not only for his radicalism but also for his intense interest in science. These intellectual passions underwrite a body of remarkable visionary poetry characterized by an elegance and complexity that is at once very wonderful and very difficult.

Shelley was born in 1792 at Field Place in Sussex, the first of the six children of Elizabeth and Timothy Shelley, a Member of Parliament who became a baronet on the death of his father, Sir Bysshe Shelley. Percy grew up in the affluence befitting his role as heir to the estate and title of his father and grandfather. He spent his early years running free on the estate and entertaining his siblings, so he was unprepared for the rules of the boys' academy he attended, or the bullying he would suffer there. Shelley later attended Eton College, and there the teasing continued, further developing his allegiance to outcasts and the disenfranchised, and nurturing his rebellious spirit. He was still a student at Eton when he published *Zastrozzi* (1810), a Gothic romance novel. He continued to publish during his short stint at Oxford University, from which he and Thomas Jefferson Hogg, his friend and the co-author of *The Necessity of Atheism*, were expelled for writing the pamphlet.

In 1813 Shelley published his first important work: *Queen Mab*, a poetic dream-vision that vilified conventional morality and institutional religion in a utopian picture of humanity returned to a condition of innocence. Shelley's greatest utopian fantasy, *Prometheus Unbound* (1820), would essentially reprise the same picture, imagining a world grown young again as human beings learn to undo the curse of their acquired historical fears and hatreds and replace it with a program based on love, which he called "the great secret" of all morality.

Shelley's personal involvements with love, fueled by his ideals, were also fraught with that inherited curse. In 1811 Shelley married Harriet Westbrook, and the couple had a daughter born to them in 1813. But before long he would fall in love with another young woman, Mary Godwin, the daughter of the radical thinkers William Godwin and Mary Wollstonecraft.

In 1814 Shelley left Harriet and traveled to the continent with Mary and her half sister Clair Clairmont for a six-week tour. When they returned to England Shelley proposed that Harriet should live with Mary and himself as free lovers. When Harriet refused, Shelley, Mary, and Clair again traveled to Europe, where the three met Lord Byron in Switzerland in June. In the meantime, Harriet gave birth to Shelley's second child, a son, in late 1814, and at the end of 1816 she committed suicide. Mary and Percy were then married.

The summer of 1816 is one of the most famous in the history of English letters. Out of it came a series of stunning literary works: Mary's great novel *Frankenstein*; Byron's third canto of *Childe Harold* as well as various apocalyptic works, especially *Manfred*; and a series of key lyric poems by Shelley including "Mont Blanc" and the "Hymn to Intellectual Beauty." Later (1818) Shelley would write "Julian and Maddalo: A Conversation," a brilliant verse dialogue representing the conversations that he and Byron had been having since they met in 1816.

Upon this return to England from Switzerland, his life bristling with personal and political scandals, Shelley was denied custody of his two children from his first marriage. In 1818 the Shelleys moved to the Continent with their baby girl Clara in the hope of joining Byron in Italy and avoiding the judgment of English society. Unfortunately, Clara died in September, and William, born in 1816, died the following year. The only child to survive would be Percy Florence, born in 1819.

Shelley wrote his lyric masterpiece *Prometheus Unbound* that same year, to show how social life might and ought to be, and he wrote the political tragedy *The Cenci* (1819), to show the way it actually was. The distance between the two works is dialectical, as Shelley later attempted to explain in his important prose work, the *Defence of Poetry* (1821). During this prolific period Shelley also responded to the Peterloo Massacre—in which eleven workers were killed at what was meant to be a peaceful rally in Manchester—by writing "The Mask of Anarchy," "Song: To the Men of England," "A Philosophical View of Reform," and "Ode to the West Wind," a revolutionary lyric that recapitulates, in miniature, the argument and structure of *Prometheus Unbound*. Shelley hoped his verse would undermine the retrograde political institutions of his time and seed the future with a promise of rejuvenation. Enjoying scant fame or immediate influence, he nevertheless concluded his *Defence of Poetry* with the now-famous pronouncement that poets are "the unacknowledged legislators of the world."

In 1822 Shelley—who could not swim—went sailing on the Bay of Spezia in Italy with his friend Edward Williams. They were caught in a sudden squall and drowned. When Shelley's body washed up on the beach a few days later, a copy of Keats's poems was found in his pocket. A funeral pyre was hastily built and his corpse cremated—except for his heart, which was snatched from the pyre by his friend Edward Trelawney.

In a letter to some of his conservative English friends Byron famously declared: "You are all brutally mistaken about Shelley who was without exception—the *best* and least selfish man I ever knew." His ashes were placed near the recently buried Keats in the Protestant Cemetery in Rome. His inconsumable heart remained in Mary Shelley's possession, wrapped in the pages of *Adonais*, Shelley's elegy for Keats, until her death. It is buried with her in her tomb at St. Peter's Churchyard in Bournemouth.

⌘ ⌘ ⌘

To Wordsworth[1]

Poet of Nature, thou hast wept to know
That things depart which never may return:
Childhood and youth, friendship and love's first glow,
Have fled like sweet dreams, leaving thee to mourn.
These common woes I feel. One loss is mine
Which thou too feel'st, yet I alone deplore.
Thou wert as a lone star, whose light did shine
On some frail bark in winter's midnight roar:
Thou hast like to a rock-built refuge stood
Above the blind and battling multitude:
In honoured poverty thy voice did weave
Songs consecrate to truth and liberty—
Deserting these, thou leavest me to grieve,
Thus having been, that thou shouldst cease to be.
—1816

[1] *To Wordsworth*   As a young man, Wordsworth identified himself as a political radical, but as his career progressed he gradually became more conservative. His 1814 poem *The Excursion* showed a marked change in his political and religious thinking, and was received with disappointment by many of his early admirers, such as Shelley.

Mont Blanc
Lines Written in the Vale of Chamouni [3]

1

The everlasting universe of things
Flows through the mind, and rolls its rapid waves,
Now dark—now glittering—now reflecting gloom—
Now lending splendour, where from secret springs
5   The source of human thought its tribute brings
Of waters—with a sound but half its own,
Such as a feeble brook will oft assume
In the wild woods, among the mountains lone,
Where waterfalls around it leap for ever,
10 Where woods and winds contend, and a vast river
Over its rocks ceaselessly bursts and raves.

2

Thus thou, Ravine of Arve—dark, deep Ravine—
Thou many-coloured, many-voicèd vale,
Over whose pines, and crags, and caverns sail
15 Fast cloud shadows and sunbeams: awful°   *awe-inspiring*
    scene,
Where Power in likeness of the Arve comes down
From the ice gulfs that gird his secret throne,
Bursting through these dark mountains like the flame
Of lightning through the tempest—thou dost lie,
20 Thy giant brood of pines around thee clinging,
Children of elder time, in whose devotion
The chainless winds still come and ever came
To drink their odours, and their mighty swinging
To hear—an old and solemn harmony;
25 Thine earthly rainbows stretched across the sweep
Of the etherial waterfall, whose veil
Robes some unsculptured[4] image; the strange sleep
Which when the voices of the desert fail

Mutability

We are as clouds that veil the midnight moon;
How restlessly they speed, and gleam, and
    quiver,
Streaking the darkness radiantly! Yet soon
Night closes round, and they are lost for ever:

5   Or like forgotten lyres,[2] whose dissonant strings
Give various response to each varying blast,
To whose frail frame no second motion brings
One mood or modulation like the last.

We rest—A dream has power to poison sleep;
10 We rise—One wandering thought pollutes the day;
We feel, conceive or reason, laugh or weep;
Embrace fond woe, or cast our cares away:

It is the same! For, be it joy or sorrow,
The path of its departure still is free:
15 Man's yesterday may ne'er be like his morrow;
Nought may endure but Mutability.
—1816

---

[2] *lyres* Aeolian harps, stringed instruments that produce music when exposed to wind.

[3] *Mont Blanc ... Chamouni* Mont Blanc, located near France's border with Italy, is the highest peak in the Alps. Shelley conceived the idea for the poem when standing on a bridge over the Arve River in the Valley of Chamonix in southeastern France. Of the poem, Shelley wrote, "It was composed under the immediate impression of the deep and powerful feelings excited by the objects which it attempts to describe; and, as an indisciplined overflowing of the soul, rests its claim to approbation on an attempt to imitate the untameable wildness and inaccessible solemnity from which those feelings sprang."

[4] *unsculptured* I.e., not shaped by humans.

Wraps all in its own deep eternity—
30   Thy caverns echoing to the Arve's commotion,
A loud, lone sound no other sound can tame;
Thou art pervaded with that ceaseless motion,
Thou art the path of that unresting sound—
Dizzy Ravine! and when I gaze on thee
35   I seem as in a trance sublime and strange
To muse on my own separate fantasy,
My own, my human mind, which passively
Now renders and receives fast influencings,
Holding an unremitting interchange
40   With the clear universe of things around;
One legion of wild thoughts, whose wandering wings
Now float above thy darkness, and now rest
Where that or thou art no unbidden guest,
In the still cave of the witch Poesy,
45   Seeking among the shadows that pass by,
Ghosts of all things that are, some shade of thee,
Some phantom, some faint image; till the breast
From which they fled recalls them, thou art there!

3

Some say that gleams of a remoter world
50   Visit the soul in sleep—that death is slumber,
And that its shapes the busy thoughts outnumber
Of those who wake and live. I look on high;
Has some unknown omnipotence unfurled
The veil of life and death? or do I lie
55   In dream, and does the mightier world of sleep
Spread far around and inaccessibly
Its circles? For the very spirit fails,
Driven like a homeless cloud from steep to steep
That vanishes among the viewless° gales!   *invisible*
60   Far, far above, piercing the infinite sky,
Mont Blanc appears—still, snowy, and serene—
Its subject mountains their unearthly forms
Pile around it, ice and rock; broad vales between
Of frozen floods, unfathomable deeps,
65   Blue as the overhanging heaven, that spread
And wind among the accumulated steeps;
A desert peopled by the storms alone,
Save when the eagle brings some hunter's bone,
And the wolf tracks her there—how hideously
70   Its shapes are heaped around: rude, bare, and high,
Ghastly, and scarred, and riven. Is this the scene

Where the old Earthquake-daemon[1] taught her young
Ruin? Were these their toys? or did a sea
Of fire envelop once this silent snow?
75   None can reply—all seems eternal now.
The wilderness has a mysterious tongue
Which teaches awful doubt, or faith so mild,
So solemn, so serene, that man may be
But for such faith with nature reconciled;
80   Thou hast a voice, great Mountain, to repeal
Large codes of fraud and woe; not understood
By all, but which the wise, and great, and good
Interpret, or make felt, or deeply feel.

4

The fields, the lakes, the forests, and the streams,
85   Ocean, and all the living things that dwell
Within the daedal[2] earth; lightning, and rain,
Earthquake, and fiery flood, and hurricane,
The torpor of the year when feeble dreams
Visit the hidden buds, or dreamless sleep
90   Holds every future leaf and flower; the bound
With which from that detested trance they leap;
The works and ways of man, their death and birth,
And that of him and all that his may be;
All things that move and breathe with toil and sound
95   Are born and die; revolve, subside and swell.
Power dwells apart in its tranquillity
Remote, serene, and inaccessible:
And *this*, the naked countenance of earth,
On which I gaze, even these primeval mountains
100   Teach the adverting mind. The glaciers creep
Like snakes that watch their prey, from their far
         fountains,
Slow rolling on; there, many a precipice,
Frost and the Sun in scorn of mortal power
Have piled: dome, pyramid, and pinnacle,
105   A city of death, distinct with many a tower
And wall impregnable of beaming ice.
Yet not a city, but a flood of ruin
Is there, that from the boundaries of the sky
Rolls its perpetual stream; vast pines are strewing

---

[1] *daemon* In Greek mythology, supernatural being or minor deity
that controls some natural force.

[2] *daedal* Skillfully or intricately wrought. (From Daedalus of
classical myth, who built the famous labyrinth in Crete.)

110   Its destined path, or in the mangled soil
    Branchless and shattered stand; the rocks, drawn down
    From yon remotest waste, have overthrown
    The limits of the dead and living world,
    Never to be reclaimed. The dwelling-place
115   Of insects, beasts, and birds, becomes its spoil;
    Their food and their retreat for ever gone,
    So much of life and joy is lost. The race
    Of man flies far in dread; his work and dwelling
    Vanish, like smoke before the tempest's stream,
120   And their place is not known. Below, vast caves
    Shine in the rushing torrent's restless gleam,
    Which from those secret chasms in tumult welling[1]
    Meet in the vale, and one majestic River,
    The breath and blood of distant lands, for ever
125   Rolls its loud waters to the ocean waves,
    Breathes its swift vapours to the circling air.

                    5
    Mont Blanc yet gleams on high—the power is there,
    The still and solemn power of many sights
    And many sounds, and much of life and death.
130   In the calm darkness of the moonless nights,
    In the lone glare of day, the snows descend
    Upon that Mountain; none beholds them there,
    Nor when the flakes burn in the sinking sun,
    Or the star-beams dart through them. Winds contend
135   Silently there, and heap the snow with breath
    Rapid and strong, but silently! Its home
    The voiceless lightning in these solitudes
    Keeps innocently, and like vapour broods
    Over the snow. The secret strength of things
140   Which governs thought, and to the infinite dome
    Of heaven is as a law, inhabits thee!
    And what were thou, and earth, and stars, and sea,
    If to the human mind's imaginings
    Silence and solitude were vacancy?
            —1817

---

[1]   *Which from ... welling*   Cf. Coleridge's *Kubla Khan*, lines 12–24.

Hymn to Intellectual Beauty[2]

                    1

The awful shadow of some unseen Power
    Floats though unseen amongst us, visiting
        This various world with as inconstant wing
As summer winds that creep from flower to flower.
5   Like moonbeams that behind some piny mountain
            shower,
            It visits with inconstant glance
            Each human heart and countenance;
Like hues and harmonies of evening,
            Like clouds in starlight widely spread,
10   Like memory of music fled,
            Like aught that for its grace may be
Dear, and yet dearer for its mystery.

                    2
Spirit of BEAUTY, that doth consecrate
    With thine own hues all thou dost shine upon
15   Of human thought or form—where art thou gone?
Why dost thou pass away and leave our state,
This dim vast vale of tears, vacant and desolate?
            Ask why the sunlight not forever
            Weaves rainbows o'er yon mountain river,
20   Why aught should fail and fade that once is shown,
            Why fear and dream and death and birth
            Cast on the daylight of this earth
            Such gloom—why man has such a scope
For love and hate, despondency and hope?

                    3
25   No voice from some sublimer world hath ever
        To sage or poet these responses given—
        Therefore the name of God, and ghosts, and Heaven,
Remain the records of their vain endeavour,
Frail spells—whose uttered charm might not avail to
            sever,
30   From all we hear and all we see,

---

[2]   *Hymn ... Beauty*   Composed during the summer of 1816, the same summer in which Shelley wrote "Mont Blanc." The concept of "intellectual beauty" is Platonic in origin and was a popular one in contemporary writing. It denotes a beauty of the soul, or the mind and its inventions, that cannot be perceived by the senses and therefore must be grasped intuitively.

Doubt, chance, and mutability.
Thy light alone—like mist o'er mountains driven,
   Or music by the night wind sent
   Through strings of some still instrument,
35   Or moonlight on a midnight stream,
Gives grace and truth to life's unquiet dream.

4

Love, Hope, and Self-esteem, like clouds depart
   And come, for some uncertain moments lent.
   Man were° immortal, and omnipotent,   *would be*
40 Didst thou,[1] unknown and awful as thou art,
Keep with thy glorious train firm state within his heart.
   Thou messenger of sympathies
   That wax and wane in lovers' eyes—
Thou—that to human thought art nourishment,
45   Like darkness to a dying flame!
   Depart not as thy shadow came,
   Depart not—lest the grave should be,
Like life and fear, a dark reality.

5

While yet a boy I sought for ghosts, and sped
50   Through many a listening chamber, cave and ruin,
   And starlight wood, with fearful steps pursuing
Hopes of high talk with the departed dead.
I called on poisonous names with which our youth is fed,
   I was not heard—I saw them not—
55   When musing deeply on the lot
Of life, at that sweet time when winds are wooing
   All vital things that wake to bring
   News of buds and blossoming—
   Sudden, thy shadow fell on me;
60 I shrieked, and clasped my hands in ecstasy!

6

I vowed that I would dedicate my powers
   To thee and thine—have I not kept the vow?
   With beating heart and streaming eyes, even now
I call the phantoms of a thousand hours
65 Each from his voiceless grave: they have in visioned
     bowers
   Of studious zeal or love's delight
   Outwatched with me the envious night—

---

[1] *Didst thou* I.e., "if thou didst."

They know that never joy illumed my brow
   Unlinked with hope that thou wouldst free
70   This world from its dark slavery,
   That thou—O awful LOVELINESS,
Wouldst give whate'er these words cannot express.

7

The day becomes more solemn and serene
   When noon is past—there is a harmony
75   In autumn, and a lustre in its sky,
Which through the summer is not heard or seen,
As if it could not be, as if it had not been!
   Thus let thy power, which like the truth
   Of nature on my passive youth
80 Descended, to my onward life supply
   Its calm—to one who worships thee,
   And every form containing thee,
   Whom, SPIRIT fair, thy spells did bind
To fear° himself, and love all human kind.   *revere*
—1817

Ozymandias [2]

I met a traveller from an antique land
Who said: Two vast and trunkless legs of stone
Stand in the desert ... Near them, on the sand,
Half sunk, a shattered visage lies, whose frown,
5 And wrinkled lip, and sneer of cold command,
Tell that its sculptor well those passions read
Which yet survive, stamped on these lifeless things,
The hand that mocked them, and the heart that fed:
And on the pedestal these words appear:
10 "My name is Ozymandias, king of kings:
Look on my works, ye Mighty, and despair!"
Nothing beside remains. Round the decay
Of that colossal wreck, boundless and bare
The lone and level sands stretch far away.
—1818

---

[2] *Ozymandias* Greek name for King Ramses II of Egypt (1304–1237 BCE). First century BCE Greek historian Diodorus Siculus records the story of this monument (Ozymandias's tomb was in the shape of a male sphinx) and its inscription, which Diodorus says reads: "King of Kings am I, Ozymandias. If anyone would know how great I am and where I lie, let him surpass one of my exploits."

Ode to the West Wind [1]

1

O Wild West Wind, thou breath[2] of Autumn's
    being,
Thou, from whose unseen presence the leaves dead
Are driven, like ghosts from an enchanter fleeing,

Yellow, and black, and pale, and hectic° red,   *feverish*
5 Pestilence-stricken multitudes: O thou,
Who chariotest to their dark wintry bed

The winged seeds, where they lie cold and low,
Each like a corpse within its grave, until
Thine azure sister of the Spring shall blow

10 Her clarion[3] o'er the dreaming earth, and fill
(Driving sweet buds like flocks to feed in air)
With living hues and odours plain and hill:

Wild Spirit, which art moving everywhere;
Destroyer and Preserver; hear, oh, hear!

2

15 Thou on whose stream, 'mid the steep sky's commotion,
Loose clouds like earth's decaying leaves are shed,
Shook from the tangled boughs of Heaven and Ocean,

Angels° of rain and lightning: there are spread   *harbingers*
On the blue surface of thine aëry surge,
20 Like the bright hair uplifted from the head

Of some fierce Mænad,[4] even from the dim verge
Of the horizon to the zenith's height,
The locks of the approaching storm. Thou dirge

Of the dying year, to which this closing night
25 Will be the dome of a vast sepulchre,
Vaulted with all thy congregated might

Of vapours,° from whose solid atmosphere   *clouds*
Black rain, and fire, and hail will burst: oh, hear!

3

Thou who didst waken from his summer dreams
30 The blue Mediterranean, where he lay,
Lulled by the coil of his chrystàlline streams,[5]

Beside a pumice isle in Baiae's bay,[6]
And saw in sleep old palaces and towers
Quivering within the wave's intenser day,

35 All overgrown with azure moss and flowers
So sweet, the sense faints picturing them! Thou
For whose path the Atlantic's level powers

Cleave themselves into chasms, while far below
The sea-blooms and the oozy woods which wear
40 The sapless foliage of the ocean, know

Thy voice, and suddenly grow gray with fear,
And tremble and despoil themselves:[7] oh, hear!

---

[1] [Shelley's note] This poem was conceived and chiefly written in a wood that skirts the Arno, near Florence, and on a day when that tempestuous wind, whose temperature is at once mild and animating, was collecting the vapours which pour down the autumnal rains. They began, as I foresaw, at sunset with a violent tempest of hail and rain, attended by that magnificent thunder and lightning peculiar to the Cispaline regions.

[2] *breath* The Latin word for wind, *spiritus*, also means "breath" and "soul," and is the root of the word "inspiration."

[3] *clarion* High-pitched trumpet.

[4] *Mænad* Female attendant of Bacchus, the Greek god of wine.

[5] *coil … streams* Currents of the Mediterranean, the color of which are often different from the surrounding water.

[6] *pumice* Porous stone made from cooled lava; *Baiae's Bay* Bay west of Naples that contains the ruins of several imperial villas.

[7] [Shelley's note] The phenomenon alluded to at the conclusion of the third stanza is well known to naturalists. The vegetation at the bottom of the sea, of rivers, and of lakes, sympathizes with that of the land in the change of seasons, and is consequently influenced by the winds which announce it.

4

If I were a dead leaf thou mightest bear;
If I were a swift cloud to fly with thee;
45 A wave to pant beneath thy power, and share

The impulse of thy strength, only less free
Than thou, O uncontrollable! If even
I were as in my boyhood, and could be

The comrade of thy wanderings over Heaven,
50 As then, when to outstrip thy skiey speed
Scarce seemed a vision; I would ne'er have striven

As thus with thee in prayer in my sore need.
Oh! lift me as a wave, a leaf, a cloud!
I fall upon the thorns of life! I bleed!

55 A heavy weight of hours has chained and bowed
One too like thee: tameless, and swift, and proud.

5

Make me thy lyre,[1] even as the forest is:
What if my leaves are falling like its own!
The tumult of thy mighty harmonies

60 Will take from both a deep, autumnal tone,
Sweet though in sadness. Be thou, Spirit fierce,
My spirit! Be thou me, impetuous one!

Drive my dead thoughts over the universe
Like withered leaves to quicken a new birth!
65 And, by the incantation of this verse,

Scatter, as from an unextinguished hearth
Ashes and sparks, my words among mankind!
Be through my lips to unawakened Earth

The trumpet of a prophecy! O, Wind,
70 If Winter comes, can Spring be far behind?
—1820

---

1 *lyre* Aeolian harp, a stringed instrument that produces music when exposed to wind.

The Cloud

I bring fresh showers for the thirsting flowers,
    From the seas and the streams;
I bear light shade for the leaves when laid
    In their noonday dreams.
5 From my wings are shaken the dews that waken
    The sweet buds every one,
When rocked to rest on their mother's breast,
    As she dances about the sun.
I wield the flail of the lashing hail,
10   And whiten the green plains under,
And then again I dissolve it in rain,
    And laugh as I pass in thunder.

I sift the snow on the mountains below,
    And their great pines groan aghast;
15 And all the night 'tis my pillow white,
    While I sleep in the arms of the blast,
Sublime on the towers of my skiey bowers,
    Lightning my pilot sits;
In a cavern under is fettered the thunder,
20   It struggles and howls at fits;[2]
Over earth and ocean, with gentle motion,
    This pilot is guiding me,
Lured by the love of the genii that move
    In the depths of the purple sea;
25 Over the rills, and the crags, and the hills,
    Over the lakes and the plains,
Wherever he dream, under mountain or stream,
    The Spirit he loves remains;
And I all the while bask in Heaven's blue smile,
30   Whilst he is dissolving in rains.

The sanguine Sunrise, with his meteor eyes,
    And his burning plumes outspread,
Leaps on the back of my sailing rack,[3]
    When the morning star shines dead;
35 As on the jag of a mountain crag,
    Which an earthquake rocks and swings,
An eagle alit one moment may sit
    In the light of its golden wings.

---

2 *at fits* Fitfully.

3 *rack* Mass of clouds in the upper air.

And when Sunset may breathe, from the lit sea beneath,
40   Its ardours of rest and love,
And the crimson pall[1] of eve may fall
      From the depth of Heaven above,
With wings folded I rest, on mine aëry nest,
      As still as a brooding dove.

45   That orbèd maiden with white fire laden,
      Whom mortals call the Moon,
Glides glimmering o'er my fleece-like floor,
      By the midnight breezes strewn;
And wherever the beat of her unseen feet,
50   Which only the angels hear,
May have broken the woof° of my tent's   *weave*
      thin roof,
      The stars peep behind her and peer;
And I laugh to see them whirl and flee,
      Like a swarm of golden bees,
55   When I widen the rent in my wind-built tent,
      Till the calm rivers, lakes, and seas,
Like strips of the sky fallen through me on high,
      Are each paved with the moon and these.

I bind the Sun's throne with a burning zone,°   *belt*
60   And the Moon's with a girdle of pearl;
The volcanoes are dim, and the stars reel and swim,
      When the whirlwinds my banner unfurl.
From cape to cape, with a bridge-like shape,
      Over a torrent sea,
65   Sunbeam-proof, I hand like a roof—
      The mountains its columns be.
The triumphal arch through which I march
      With hurricane, fire, and snow,
When the Powers of the air are chained to my chair,
70   Is the million-coloured bow;
The sphere-fire[2] above its soft colours wove,
      While the moist Earth was laughing below.

I am the daughter of Earth and Water,
      And the nursing of the Sky;
75   I pass through the pores of the ocean and shores;
      I change, but I cannot die.
For after the rain, when with never a stain

      The pavilion of Heaven is bare,
And the winds and sunbeams with their convex gleams
80   Build up the blue dome of air,
I silently laugh at my own cenotaph,[3]
      And out of the caverns of rain,
Like a child from the womb, like a ghost from the tomb,
      I arise and unbuild it again.
—1820

To a Skylark[4]

Hail to thee, blithe Spirit!
   Bird thou never wert,
That from Heaven, or near it,
   Pourest thy full heart
5   In profuse strains of unpremeditated art.

Higher still and higher
   From the earth thou springest
Like a cloud of fire;
   The blue deep thou wingest,
10   And singing still dost soar, and soaring ever singest.

In the golden lightning
   Of the sunken sun,
O'er which clouds are bright'ning,
   Thou dost float and run;
15   Like an unbodied joy whose race is just begun.

The pale purple even
   Melts around thy flight;
Like a star of Heaven,
   In the broad daylight
20   Thou art unseen, but yet I hear thy shrill delight,

Keen as are the arrows
   Of that silver sphere,[5]
Whose intense lamp narrows

----

[1]   *pall*   Rich cloth or canopy.

[2]   *sphere-fire*   I.e., sunlight.

[3]   *cenotaph*   Empty sepulcher; monument honoring a dead person whose body lies elsewhere.

[4]   *Skylark*   Small bird that sings only when in flight, and often flies so high that it cannot be easily seen.

[5]   *silver sphere*   I.e., the morning star.

In the white dawn clear

25 Until we hardly see—we feel that it is there.

All the earth and air
    With thy voice is loud,
As, when night is bare,
    From one lonely cloud
30 The moon rains out her beams, and Heaven is
    overflowed.

What thou art we know not;
    What is most like thee?
From rainbow clouds there flow not
    Drops so bright to see
35 As from thy presence showers a rain of melody.

Like a Poet hidden
    In the light of thought,
Singing hymns unbidden,
    Till the world is wrought
40 To sympathy with hopes and fears it heeded not:

Like a high-born maiden
    In a palace-tower,
Soothing her love-laden
    Soul in secret hour
45 With music sweet as love, which overflows her bower:

Like a glow-worm golden
    In a dell of dew,
Scattering unbeholden
    Its aëreal hue
50 Among the flowers and grass, which screen it from the
    view:

Like a rose embowered
    In its own green leaves,
By warm winds deflowered,
    Till the scent it gives
55 Makes faint with too much sweet these heavy-wingèd
    thieves:

Sound of vernal° showers   *springtime*
    On the twinkling grass,
Rain-awakened flowers,

All that ever was
60 Joyous, and clear, and fresh, thy music doth surpass:

Teach us, Sprite° or Bird,   *fairy*
    What sweet thoughts are thine:
I have never heard
    Praise of love or wine
65 That panted forth a flood of rapture so divine.

Chorus Hymeneal,[1]
    Or triumphal chaunt,°   *chant*
Matched with thine would be all
    But an empty vaunt,
70 A thing wherein we feel there is some hidden want.

What objects are the fountains
    Of thy happy strain?
What fields, or waves, or mountains?
    What shapes of sky or plain?
75 What love of thine own kind? what ignorance of pain?

With thy clear keen joyance
    Languor cannot be:
Shadow of annoyance
    Never came near thee:
80 Thou lovest—but ne'er knew love's sad satiety.

Waking or asleep,
    Thou of death must deem
Things more true and deep
    Than we mortals dream,
85 Or how could thy notes flow in such a crystal stream?

We look before and after,
    And pine for what is not:
Our sincerest laughter
    With some pain is fraught;
90 Our sweetest songs are those that tell of saddest thought.

Yet if we could scorn
    Hate, and pride, and fear;
If we were things born
    Not to shed a tear,
95 I know not how thy joy we ever should come near.

----

1 *Hymeneal* Marital (Hymen is the Greek god of marriage).

Better than all measures
    Of delightful sound,
Better than all treasures
    That in books are found,
100 Thy skill to poet were, thou scorner of the ground!

Teach me half the gladness
    That thy brain must know,
Such harmonious madness
    From my lips would flow
105 The world should listen then—as I am listening now.
    —1820

———————

Mutability

1

The flower that smiles to-day
        To-morrow dies;
All that we wish to stay
        Tempts and then flies.
5   What is this world's delight?
Lightning that mocks the night,
        Brief even as bright.

2

Virtue, how frail it is!
        Friendship how rare!
10   Love, how it sells poor bliss
        For proud despair!
But we, though soon they fall,
Survive their joy, and all
        Which ours we call.

3

15   Whilst skies are blue and bright,
        Whilst flowers are gay,
Whilst eyes that change ere night
        Make glad the day;
Whilst yet the calm hours creep,
20   Dream thou—and from thy sleep
        Then wake to weep.
        —1824

Stanzas

Written in Dejection – December 1818,
near Naples

1

The sun is warm, the sky is clear,
    The waves are dancing fast and bright,
Blue isles and snowy mountains wear
    The purple noon's transparent might,
5   The breath of the moist earth is light,
Around its unexpanded buds;

Like many a voice of one delight,
The winds, the birds, the ocean floods,
The City's voice itself, is soft like Solitude's.

2

10   I see the Deep's untrampled floor
With green and purple seaweeds strown;
I see the waves upon the shore,
Like light dissolved in star-showers,[1] thrown:
I sit upon the sands alone—
15   The lightning of the noontide ocean
Is flashing round me, and a tone
Arises from its measured motion,
How sweet! did any heart now share in my emotion.

3

Alas! I have nor hope nor health,
20   Nor peace within nor calm around,
Nor that content surpassing wealth
The sage in meditation found,
And walked with inward glory crowned—
Nor fame, nor power, nor love, nor leisure.
25   Others I see whom these surround—
Smiling they live, and call life pleasure;—
To me that cup has been dealt in another measure.

4

Yet now despair itself is mild,
Even as the winds and waters are;
30   I could lie down like a tired child,
And weep away the life of care
Which I have borne and yet must bear,
Till death like sleep might steal on me,
And I might feel in the warm air
35   My cheek grow cold, and hear the sea
Breathe o'er my dying brain its last monotony.

5

Some might lament that I were cold.
As I, when this sweet day is gone,
Which my lost heart, too soon grown old,
40   Insults with this untimely moan;
They might lament—for I am one
Whom men love not—and yet regret,

Unlike this day, which, when the sun
Shall on its stainless glory set,
45   Will linger, though enjoyed, like joy in memory yet.
—1824

Sonnet [Lift Not the Painted Veil]

Lift not the painted veil which those who live
Call Life: though unreal shapes be pictured there,
And it but mimic all we would believe
With colours idly spread—behind, lurk Fear
5   And Hope, twin Destinies; who ever weave
Their shadows, o'er the chasm, sightless and drear.
I knew one who had lifted it—he sought,
For his lost heart was tender, things to love,
But found them not, alas! nor was there aught
10   The world contains, the which he could approve.
Through the unheeding many he did move,
A splendour among shadows, a bright blot
Upon this gloomy scene, a Spirit that strove
For truth, and like the Preacher[2] found it not.
—1824

To Night

1

Swiftly walk o'er the western wave,
Spirit of Night!
Out of the misty eastern cave,
Where, all the long and lone daylight,
5   Thou wovest dreams of joy and fear,
Which make thee terrible and dear,
Swift be thy flight!

2

Wrap thy form in a mantle gray,
Star-inwrought!
10   Blind with thine hair the eyes of Day;
Kiss her until she be wearied out,
Then wander o'er city, and sea, and land,

---

[1] *star-showers* Meteor showers.

[2] *Preacher* Speaker of Ecclesiastes, who says, "I have seen all the works that are done under the sun; and, behold, all is vanity and vexation of spirit" (1.14).

Touching all with thine opiate° wand—   *sleep-inducing*
    Come, long-sought!

3

15 When I arose and saw the dawn,
    I sighed for thee;
When light rode high, and the dew was gone,
And noon lay heavy on flower and tree,
And the weary Day turned to his rest,
20 Lingering like an unloved guest,
    I sighed for thee.

4

Thy brother Death came, and cried,
    Wouldst thou me?
Thy sweet child Sleep, thy filmy-eyed,
25 Murmured like a noontide bee,
Shall I nestle near thy side?
Wouldst thou me? And I replied,
    No, not thee!

5

Death will come when thou art dead,
30 Soon, too soon—
Sleep will come when thou art fled;
Of neither would I ask the boon
I ask of thee, beloved Night—
Swift be thine approaching flight,
35   Come soon, soon!
    —1824

To ——

Music, when soft voices die,
Vibrates in the memory—
Odours, when sweet violets sicken,
Live within the sense they quicken.°   *vivify*

5 Rose leaves, when the rose is dead,
Are heaped for the beloved's bed;
And so thy thoughts, when thou art gone,
Love itself shall slumber on.
    —1824

The Mask of Anarchy

On 16 August 1819, roughly 60,000 men, women, and children, led by radical orator Henry Hunt, peaceably gathered on St. Peter's Field in Manchester in support of Parliamentary reform and a repeal of the corn laws (restricting the import and export of grain). After ordering the meeting to disband, the magistrates sent out the militia to attack the crowd. Eleven people were killed and over four hundred injured. When the Home Office condoned this violent response, public outrage was widespread, and the radical journal *The Examiner* was filled with indignant reports on what became known as the "Peterloo Massacre," in mockery of the English victory in the Battle of Waterloo.

Though he was in Italy at the time, Shelley was inspired by the public outcry in *The Examiner* to write *The Mask of Anarchy*. He sent the poem to Leigh Hunt, editor of the journal, in September 1819, but Hunt thought its publication would be a risk to both Shelley's reputation and that of *The Examiner*. When Hunt did finally print the poem, in 1832, it was with the subtitle and the specific references to Jon Scott, Earl of Eldon and Lord Chancellor (who was responsible for depriving Shelley of access to his children with Harriet, his first wife) and Home Secretary Sidmouth removed. He gave the title as *The Masque of Anarchy*, which Shelley had called the poem in a letter to him, thus making explicit the reference to the literary genre of the masque, a courtly drama.

The Mask of Anarchy
Written on the Occasion of the Massacre at Manchester

I

As I lay asleep in Italy
There came a voice from over the Sea,
And with great power it forth led me
To walk in the visions of Poesy.

2

5 I met Murder on the way—
He had a mask like Castlereagh[1]—
Very smooth he looked, yet grim;
Seven bloodhounds[2] followed him:

3

All were fat; and well they might
10 Be in admirable plight,
For one by one, and two by two,
He tossed them human hearts to chew
Which from his wide cloak he drew.

4

Next came Fraud, and he had on,
15 Like Eldon, an ermined gown;[3]
His big tears, for he wept well,
Turned to mill-stones as they fell.[4]

5

And the little children, who
Round his feet played to and fro,
20 Thinking every tear a gem,
Had their brains knocked out by them.

6

Clothed with the Bible, as with light,
And the shadows of the night,
Like Sidmouth, next, Hypocrisy
25 On a crocodile rode by.[5]

7

And many more Destructions played
In this ghastly masquerade,
All disguised, even to the eyes,
Like Bishops, lawyers, peers, or spies.

8

30 Last came Anarchy: he rode
On a white horse, splashed with blood;
He was pale even to the lips,
Like Death in the Apocalypse.[6]

9

And he wore a kingly crown;
35 And in his grasp a sceptre shone;
On his brow this mark I saw—
"I AM GOD, AND KING, AND LAW!"

10

With a pace stately and fast,
Over English land he passed,
40 Trampling to a mire of blood
The adoring multitude.

11

And a mighty troop around,
With their trampling shook the ground,
Waving each a bloody sword,
45 For the service of their Lord.

12

And with glorious triumph, they
Rode through England proud and gay,
Drunk as with intoxication
Of the wine of desolation.

13

50 O'er fields and towns, from sea to sea,
Passed the Pageant swift and free,
Tearing up, and trampling down;
Till they came to London town.

[1] *Castlereagh* Robert Stuart Castlereagh, Foreign Secretary (1812–22), who was very unpopular with radicals such as Shelley. In 1815 he was responsible for Britain's joining with seven other European nations to postpone the final abolition of the slave trade.

[2] *bloodhounds* Faction of Parliament that supported war.

[3] *ermined gown* Traditional robe of office for the Lord Chancellor.

[4] *big tears ... fell* Lord Chancellor John Scott, Earl of Eldon (1751–1838), frequently shed tears during his public appearances.

[5] *Clothed with ... light* Home Secretary Henry Addington, 1st Viscount Sidmouth (1757–1844), invested in the construction of several churches for the poor, but did nothing to improve their living conditions; *crocodile* Animal often used to symbolize hypocrisy because it was fabled to shed tears as it devoured its victims.

[6] *he rode ... Apocalypse* See Revelation 6, in which John the Divine has a vision of the four horsemen of the Apocalypse. Of the fourth horse he says, "and behold a pale horse: and his name that sat on him was Death, and Hell followed him" (6.8).

14

And each dweller, panic-stricken,
55 Felt his heart with terror sicken
Hearing the tempestuous cry
Of the triumph of Anarchy.

15

For with pomp to meet him came,
Clothed in arms like blood and flame,
60 The hired murderers, who did sing
Thou art God, and Law, and King.

16

"We have waited, weak and lone
For thy coming, Mighty One!
Our purses are empty, our swords are cold,
65 Give us glory, and blood, and gold."

17

Lawyers and priests, a motley crowd,
To the earth their pale brows bowed;
Like a bad prayer not over loud,
Whispering—"Thou art Law and God."

18

70 Then all cried with one accord,
"Thou art King, and God, and Lord;
Anarchy, to thee we bow,
Be thy name made holy now!"

19

And Anarchy, the Skeleton,
75 Bowed and grinned to every one,
As well as if his education
Had cost ten millions to the nation.

20

For he knew the Palaces
Of our Kings were rightly his;
80 His the sceptre, crown, and globe,[1]
And the gold-inwoven robe.

21

So he sent his slaves before
To seize upon the Bank and Tower,[2]
And was proceeding with intent
85 To meet his pensioned Parliament

22

When one fled past, a maniac maid,
And her name was Hope, she said:
But she looked more like Despair,
And she cried out in the air:

23

90 "My father Time is weak and gray
With waiting for a better day;
See how idiot-like he stands,
Fumbling with his palsied hands!

24

"He has had child after child,
95 And the dust of death is piled
Over every one but me—
Misery, oh, Misery!"

25

Then she lay down in the street,
Right before the horses' feet,
100 Expecting, with a patient eye,
Murder, Fraud, and Anarchy.

26

When between her and her foes
A mist, a light, an image rose,
Small at first, and weak, and frail
105 Like the vapour of a vale:

27

Till as clouds grow on the blast,
Like tower-crowned giants striding fast,
And glare with lightnings as they fly
And speak in thunder to the sky,

---

[1] *globe* Golden ball that, like the scepter, is an emblem of sovereignty.

[2] *Bank* Bank of England, the national treasury; *Tower* Tower of London, where the crown jewels are kept.

28

110 It grew—a Shape arrayed in mail°   *chain mail*
Brighter than the viper's scale,
And upborne on wings whose grain°   *texture*
Was as the light of sunny rain.

29

On its helm, seen far away,
115 A planet, like the Morning's,[1] lay;
And those plumes its light rained through
Like a shower of crimson dew.

30

With step as soft as wind it passed
O'er the heads of men—so fast
120 That they knew the presence there
And looked—but all was empty air.

31

As flowers beneath May's footstep waken,
As stars from Night's loose hair are shaken,
As waves arise when loud winds call,
125 Thoughts sprung where'er that step did fall.

32

And the prostrate multitude
Looked—and ankle-deep in blood,
Hope, that maiden most serene,
Was walking with a quiet mien:°   *countenance*

33

130 And Anarchy, the ghastly birth,
Lay dead earth upon the earth;
The Horse of Death tameless as wind
Fled, and with his hoofs did grind
To dust the murderers thronged behind.

34

135 A rushing light of clouds and splendour,
A sense awakening and yet tender
Was heard and felt—and at its close
These words of joy and fear arose

35

As if their own indignant Earth
140 Which gave the sons of England birth
Had felt their blood upon her brow,
And shuddering with a mother's throe

36

Had turnèd every drop of blood
By which her face had been bedewed
145 To an accent unwithstood—
As if her heart had cried aloud:

37

"Men of England, heirs of Glory,
Heroes of unwritten story,
Nurslings of one mighty Mother,
150 Hopes of her, and one another,

38

"Rise like Lions after slumber
In unvanquishable number,
Shake your chains to earth like dew
Which in sleep had fallen on you—
155 Ye are many, they are few.

39

"What is Freedom? Ye can tell
That which slavery is, too well—
For its very name has grown
To an echo of your own.

40

160 "'Tis to work and have such pay
As just keeps life from day to day
In your limbs, as in a cell
For the tyrants' use to dwell,

41

"So that ye for them are made
165 Loom, and plough, and sword, and spade,
With or without your own will bent
To their defence and nourishment.

---

[1] *Morning* Venus, as the morning star.

42

"'Tis to see your children weak
With their mothers pine° and peak,°   *suffer / waste away*
170   When the winter winds are bleak—
They are dying whilst I speak.

43

"'Tis to hunger for such diet
As the rich man in his riot
Casts to the fat dogs that lie
175   Surfeiting beneath his eye;

44

"'Tis to let the Ghost of Gold[1]
Take from Toil a thousandfold
More than e'er its substance could
In the tyrannies of old.

45

180   "Paper coin—that forgery
Of the title-deeds, which ye
Hold to something of the worth
Of the inheritance of Earth.

46

"'Tis to be a slave in soul
185   And to hold no strong control
Over your own wills, but be
All that others make of ye.

47

"And at length when ye complain
With a murmur weak and vain
190   'Tis to see the Tyrant's crew
Ride over your wives and you—
Blood is on the grass like dew.

48

"Then it is to feel revenge
Fiercely thirsting to exchange
195   Blood for blood—and wrong for wrong—
Do not thus when ye are strong.

49

"Birds find rest, in narrow nest
When weary of their wingèd quest;
Beasts find fare, in woody lair
200   When storm and snow are in the air.

50

"Asses, swine, have litter spread
And with fitting food are fed;
All things have a home but one—
Thou, Oh, Englishman, hast none![2]

51

205   "This is Slavery—savage men,
Or wild beasts within a den,
Would endure not as ye do—
But such ills they never knew.

52

"What art thou Freedom? O! could slaves
210   Answer from their living graves
This demand—tyrants would flee
Like a dream's dim imagery:

53

"Thou art not, as impostors say,
A shadow soon to pass away,
215   A superstition, and a name
Echoing from the cave of Fame.°   *rumor*

54

"For the labourer thou art bread,
And a comely table spread
From his daily labour come
220   In a neat and happy home.

55

"Thou art clothes, and fire, and food
For the trampled multitude—
No—in countries that are free
Such starvation cannot be
225   As in England now we see.

---

[1] *Ghost of Gold* Paper money. At the time paper money was regarded as unreliable currency, and was not backed by any gold reserves. Paper money was often used to pay laborers' wages.

[2] *Asses ... none* See Matthew 8.20, in which Jesus says, "The foxes have holes, and the birds of the air have nests; but the Son of man hath not where to lay his head."

56

"To the rich thou art a check,
When his foot is on the neck
Of his victim, thou dost make
That he treads upon a snake.

57

230 "Thou art Justice—ne'er for gold
May thy righteous laws be sold
As laws are in England—thou
Shield'st alike the high and low.

58

"Thou art Wisdom—Freemen never
235 Dream that God will damn for ever
All who think those things untrue
Of which Priests make such ado.

59

"Thou art Peace—never by thee
Would blood and treasure wasted be
240 As tyrants wasted them, when all
Leagued to quench thy flame in Gaul.[1]

60

"What if English toil and blood
Was poured forth, even as a flood?
It availed, Oh, Liberty,
245 To dim, but not extinguish thee.

61

"Thou art Love—the rich have kissed
Thy feet, and like him following Christ,
Give their substance to the free
And through the rough world follow thee,[2]

62

250 "Or turn their wealth to arms, and make
War for thy belovèd sake

On wealth, and war, and fraud—whence they
Drew the power which is their prey.

63

"Science, Poetry, and Thought
255 Are thy lamps; they make the lot
Of the dwellers in a cot°   *cottage*
So serene, they curse it not.

64

"Spirit, Patience, Gentleness,
All that can adorn and bless
260 Art thou—let deeds, not words, express
Thine exceeding loveliness.

65

"Let a great Assembly be
Of the fearless and the free
On some spot of English ground
265 Where the plains stretch wide around.

66

"Let the blue sky overhead,
The green earth on which ye tread,
All that must eternal be
Witness the solemnity.

67

270 "From the corners uttermost
Of the bounds of English coast;
From every hut, village, and town
Where those who live and suffer moan
For others' misery or their own,

68

275 "From the workhouse[3] and the prison
Where pale as corpses newly risen,
Women, children, young and old
Groan for pain, and weep for cold—

---

1 *Gaul* France.

2 *like him ... thee* See Matthew 19.21, in which Jesus counsels a rich man to "go and sell that thou hast, and give to the poor, and thou shalt have treasure in heaven: and come and follow me."

3 *workhouse* Institution established to provide work, shelter, and food for the parish poor; appalling conditions were the norm at most workhouses.

69

"From the haunts of daily life
280   Where is waged the daily strife
With common wants and common cares
Which sows the human heart with tares°—   *weeds*

70

"Lastly from the palaces
Where the murmur of distress
285   Echoes, like the distant sound
Of a wind alive around

71

"Those prison halls of wealth and fashion,
Where some few feel such compassion
For those who groan, and toil, and wail
290   As must make their brethren pale—

72

"Ye who suffer woes untold,
Or° to feel, or to behold   *either*
Your lost country bought and sold
With a price of blood and gold—

73

295   "Let a vast assembly be,
And with great solemnity
Declare with measured words that ye
Are, as God has made ye, free—

74

"Be your strong and simple words
300   Keen to wound as sharpened swords,
And wide as targes° let them be,   *shields*
With their shade to cover ye.

75

"Let the tyrants pour around
With a quick and startling sound,
305   Like the loosening of a sea,
Troops of armed emblazonry.

76

"Let the charged artillery drive
Till the dead air seems alive

With the clash of clanging wheels,
310   And the tramp of horses' heels.

77

"Let the fixed bayonet
Gleam with sharp desire to wet
Its bright point in English blood
Looking keen as one for food.

78

315   "Let the horsemen's scimitars[1]
Wheel and flash, like sphereless stars
Thirsting to eclipse their burning
In a sea of death and mourning.

79

"Stand ye calm and resolute,
320   Like a forest close and mute,
With folded arms and looks which are
Weapons of unvanquished war,

80

"And let Panic, who outspeeds
The career of armèd steeds
325   Pass, a disregarded shade
Through your phalanx undismayed.

81

"Let the laws of your own land,
Good or ill, between ye stand
Hand to hand, and foot to foot,
330   Arbiters of the dispute,

82

"The old laws of England—they
Whose reverend heads with age are gray,
Children of a wiser day;
And whose solemn voice must be
335   Thine own echo—Liberty!

83

"On those who first should violate
Such sacred heralds in their state

---

[1] *scimitars* Short curved swords.

Rest the blood that must ensue,
And it will not rest on you.

84

340 "And if then the tyrants dare
Let them ride among you there,
Slash, and stab, and maim, and hew—
What they like, that let them do.

85

"With folded arms and steady eyes,
345 And little fear, and less surprise,
Look upon them as they slay
'Till their rage has died away,

86

"Then they will return with shame
To the place from which they came,
350 And the blood thus shed will speak
In hot blushes on their cheek.

87

"Every woman in the land
Will point at them as they stand—
They will hardly dare to greet
355 Their acquaintance in the street.

88

"And the bold, true warriors
Who have hugged Danger in wars
Will turn to those who would be free,
Ashamed of such base company.

89

360 "And that slaughter to the Nation
Shall steam up like inspiration,
Eloquent, oracular;
A volcano heard afar.

90

"And these words shall then become
365 Like Oppression's thundered doom
Ringing through each heart and brain,
Heard again—again—again—

91

"Rise like Lions after slumber
In unvanquishable number—
370 Shake your chains to earth like dew
Which in sleep had fallen on you—
Ye are many, they are few."
—1832 (1819)

Song to the Men of England [1]

1

Men of England, wherefore plough
For the lords who lay ye low?
Wherefore weave with toil and care
The rich robes your tyrants wear?

2

5   Wherefore feed, and clothe, and save,
From the cradle to the grave,
Those ungrateful drones who would
Drain your sweat—nay, drink your blood?

3

Wherefore, Bees of England, forge
10 Many a weapon, chain, and scourge,
That these stingless drones may spoil
The forced produce of your toil?

4

Have ye leisure, comfort, calm,
Shelter, food, love's gentle balm?
15 Or what is it ye buy so dear
With your pain and with your fear?

5

The seed ye sow, another reaps;
The wealth ye find, another keeps;
The robes ye weave, another wears;
20 The arms ye forge, another bears.

---

[1] *Song ... England*   Composed in 1819, during a time of economic depression and social turmoil following the end of the Napoleonic Wars. In this song, which became a hymn for the British labor movement, Shelley urges the proletariat to force change in the social and economic order.

6

Sow seed—but let no tyrant reap;
Find wealth—let no impostor heap;
Weave robes—let not the idle wear;
Forge arms—in your defence to bear.

7

25 Shrink to your cellars, holes, and cells;
In halls ye deck another dwells.
Why shake the chains ye wrought? Ye see
The steel ye tempered glance on[1] ye.

8

With plough and spade, and hoe and loom,
30 Trace your grave, and build your tomb,
And weave your winding-sheet, till fair
England be your sepulchre.
—1839 (1819)

England in 1819

An old, mad, blind, despised, and dying king,[2]
Princes, the dregs of their dull race, who flow
Through public scorn—mud from a muddy spring—
Rulers who neither see, nor feel, nor know,
5 But leech-like to their fainting country cling,
Till they drop, blind in blood, without a blow—
A people starved and stabbed in the untilled field[3]—
An army, which liberticide and prey
Makes as a two-edged sword to all who wield—
10 Golden and sanguine laws[4] which tempt and slay;
Religion Christless, Godless—a book sealed;
A Senate, Time's worst statute, unrepealed,[5]

Are graves, from which a glorious Phantom[6] may
Burst, to illumine our tempestuous day.

---

[1] *glance on*   Strike obliquely.

[2] *old mad ... king*   George III, who was declared insane in 1811.
His sons were known for their corruption and their licentious
behavior.

[3] *A people ... field*   Reference to the massacre at St. Peter's Field on
16 August 1819 (the Peterloo Massacre), when the militia used
undue force to disperse a crowd of men, women, and children who
were peacefully demonstrating for political reform. Several people
were killed and hundreds more injured (see "The Mask of Anarchy").

[4] *Gold ... laws*   I.e., laws, bought with gold, that lead to bloodshed.

[5] *Time's ... unrepealed*   Laws against Catholics and Dissenters.

Samuel Taylor Coleridge
1772 – 1834

Samuel Taylor Coleridge is one of the most important figures of English Romanticism. Over the course of a few years, when in his mid-twenties, he composed poems that continue to be regarded as central to the English canon, among them "The Rime of the Ancient Mariner," "Frost at Midnight," and the fragment "Kubla Khan." He wrote few poems for the last thirty-five years of his life, as he was undermined by procrastination and an addiction to opium. Nonetheless, Coleridge's story is in the end one of success. His poetry has remained fresh and affecting for generations of readers, and his later philosophical writing earned him a place as one of the most profound thinkers of the nineteenth century.

Born in 1772, Coleridge was the youngest son of the vicar of Ottery St. Mary, the Rev. John Coleridge, and his wife, Anna Bowdon. He was a voracious reader with a mind that he described as "habituated to *the Vast.*" When his father died, his mother arranged for nine-year-old Samuel to be sent to Christ's Hospital in London, a school founded to educate the promising sons of the poor. Although he received an excellent education at Christ's, Coleridge remained ambivalent about the school long after he left, continuing to feel injured by the fact that he had been a "charity boy."

In 1791, Coleridge entered Jesus College, Cambridge, where his intellectual abilities and academic success were matched only by his facility in running up debts and his increasing despair at his financial situation. He eventually attempted to escape his financial problems by enlisting (under the name Silas Tomkyn Comberbache), but he was rescued by his brother George from both the army and financial distress. In 1794 he met Robert Southey, then an Oxford undergraduate, and the two recognized a shared interest in poetry and radical political ideas. They hatched a plan to found a communitarian settlement in Pennsylvania to be run under a system they called "Pantisocracy." Both the plan and the friendship, however, foundered over the question of what role women and servants should play (Coleridge insisted on a completely egalitarian community; Southey did not). In his early exuberance for the scheme Coleridge became engaged to Sara Fricker, the sister of Southey's fiancée, and he felt bound to honor the commitment even though his feeling for her quickly waned. They married in 1795 but after a brief period of happiness they became progressively more miserable, finally separating in 1807. The marriage produced four children.

Coleridge began a short-lived liberal periodical in 1796 called *The Watchman.* He also published his first poetic collection, *Poems on Various Subjects*, which contained the poem that would later be titled "The Eolian Harp." Almost destitute, he was saved by a yearly pension granted him by Tom and Josiah Wedgwood, sons of the famous potter. The following year he met William Wordsworth and began a troubled but lifelong friendship, the first fruit of which was the joint volume *Lyrical Ballads*, which opened with Coleridge's "The Rime of the Ancyent Marinere" (revised and retitled in 1816). Shortly afterward he accompanied Wordsworth and his sister Dorothy to Germany, where he immersed himself in German philosophy.

Returning to England in 1799, Coleridge joined Wordsworth in the Lake District. Here he met Sara Hutchinson, Wordsworth's future sister-in-law, and became infatuated with her. The relationship between the two remained platonic, but it magnified Coleridge's estrangement from his wife, and the situation was made worse by his increasing dependence on laudanum, the liquid form of opium. From 1802 onward Coleridge spent only brief periods with his family. In 1804 he set off for Malta, where he took a post in the British government. From this time forth he became progressively more conservative, eventually going so far as to deny entirely his early liberal leanings. After a year and a half he returned to England penniless.

From 1808 to 1818, Coleridge intermittently delivered lectures with topics that ranged from German philosophy to current educational controversies. The highlight was a series he gave on Shakespeare and Milton, which displayed all the brilliance of his critical skills. Although frequently sidetracked onto other topics, he also offered incisive analyses of aspects of Shakespeare's plays, from a consideration of love in *Romeo and Juliet* to an anatomization of Hamlet's paradoxical psychology. He ended the series with a masterful examination of *Paradise Lost*.

Coleridge's great talents as a poet lay in his ability to combine Gothicism with complex psychological presentation and to delineate the mind as it explored itself and its relation to the larger world. His more uncanny poems, such as "The Rime of the Ancient Mariner," are haunting both because they excite tension in the reader and because the psychological complexity of the characters and relationships brings to life what might otherwise be clichéd sensationalism. Poems such as "Frost at Midnight" mingle contemplation and description to produce a richly interrelated whole, a style which influenced not only Wordsworth (specifically in "Tintern Abbey"), but poets to the present day.

From the first Coleridge was interested in newspaper writing, in which he could comment on immediate social and cultural issues. The most important of his journalistic ventures was *The Friend* (1809–10), a weekly newspaper he largely wrote himself. In 1813 his drama, *Remorse,* was staged at the Drury Lane Theatre. Three years later he took up residence in Highgate with the family of the young doctor James Gillman. He asked to stay for a month; he remained for the rest of his life. The situation offered a stable environment, and Coleridge began publishing regularly. His Gothic ballad, "Christabel," long known to other writers through private recitation (and an influence on Walter Scott's "The Lay of the Last Minstrel" and Lord Byron's "The Siege of Corinth"), was published in a collection with "Kubla Khan" and "The Pains of Sleep" in 1816, through Byron's enthusiastic support. Soon afterward Coleridge published *Sybilline Leaves*, a collection of his previous poems (including a newly revised *Ancient Mariner* with a marginal gloss) and the long work *Biographia Literaria*.

Although at times rambling and discursive, *Biographia Literaria* is a major literary and philosophical work. Its first volume is autobiographical, detailing (among other events) Coleridge's education and his first involvement with Wordsworth. This volume also begins to delve into literary analysis as, for example, in the famous passage in Chapter 13, in which Coleridge differentiates between imagination and fancy, defining the qualities of each and declaring imagination superior. The second volume consists almost entirely of literary criticism, both formal and philosophical, much of it focusing on Wordsworth's poetry. In both volumes, Coleridge anatomizes both poetry and poetic production, considering not only formal elements but also the psychology of the creative process.

Coleridge's genius and importance were gradually acknowledged by a considerable number of his contemporaries, and the "Sage of Highgate" began to be viewed as an important thinker. This opinion was cemented by the publication of *Aids to Reflection* (1825), which stressed the role of the personal in Christian faith, and *On the Constitution of Church and State* (1830), which emphasized the importance of national culture and defined the class of intellectuals needed to protect it. This latter book in particular had a profound influence on such authors as Matthew Arnold and Thomas Carlyle.

From 1832 onward Coleridge became increasingly ill, although this did not prevent him from helping to prepare *Poetical Works* (1834), a collection of his poetry—he died shortly after its publication. *Table Talk*, a posthumously-published collection of his remarks on miscellaneous topics, appeared the following year.

Kubla Khan
Or, A Vision in a Dream. A Fragment[1]

In Xanadu did Kubla Khan
A stately pleasure-dome decree:
Where Alph, the sacred river, ran

Through caverns measureless to man
5   Down to a sunless sea.
So twice five miles of fertile ground
With walls and towers were girdled round:
And there were gardens bright with sinuous rills,°   *brooks*
Where blossomed many an incense-bearing tree;
10   And here were forests ancient as the hills,
Enfolding sunny spots of greenery.

But oh! that deep romantic chasm which slanted
Down the green hill athwart a cedarn cover!
A savage place! as holy and enchanted
15   As e'er beneath a waning moon was haunted
By woman wailing for her demon-lover!
And from this chasm, with ceaseless turmoil seething,
As if this earth in fast thick pants were breathing,
A mighty fountain momently was forced:
20   Amid whose swift half-intermitted burst
Huge fragments vaulted like rebounding hail,
Or chaffy grain beneath the thresher's flail:
And 'mid these dancing rocks at once and ever
It flung up momently the sacred river.
25   Five miles meandering with a mazy° motion   *labyrinthine*
Through wood and dale the sacred river ran,
Then reached the caverns measureless to man,
And sank in tumult to a lifeless ocean:
And 'mid this tumult Kubla heard from far
30   Ancestral voices prophesying war!
      The shadow of the dome of pleasure
         Floated midway on the waves;
      Where was heard the mingled measure
         From the fountain and the caves.
35   It was a miracle of rare device,
A sunny pleasure-dome with caves of ice!

---

[1] [Coleridge's note] The following fragment is here published at the request of a poet [Lord Byron] of great and deserved celebrity, and as far as the Author's own opinions are concerned, rather as a psychological curiosity, than on the ground of any supposed poetic merits.

In the summer of the year 1797, the Author, then in ill health, had retired to a lonely farmhouse between Porlock and Linton, on the Exmoor confines of Somerset and Devonshire. In consequence of a slight indisposition [dysentery], an anodyne [opium] had been prescribed, from the effects of which he fell asleep in his chair at the moment that he was reading the following sentence, or words of the same substance, in *Purchas's Pilgrimage* [i.e., *Purchas his Pilgrimage* (1613, 1614, 1617, 1626)]: "Here the Khan Kubla commanded a palace to be built, and a stately garden thereunto. And thus ten miles of fertile ground were inclosed with a wall." The author continued for about three hours in a profound sleep, at least of the external senses, during which time he has the most vivid confidence, that he could not have composed less than from two to three hundred lines, if that indeed can be called composition in which all the images rose up before him as things, with a parallel production of the correspondent expressions, without any sensation or consciousness of effort. On awaking he appeared to himself to have a distinct recollection of the whole, and taking his pen, ink, and paper, instantly and eagerly wrote down the lines that are here preserved. At this moment he was unfortunately called out by a person on business from Porlock, and detained by him above an hour, and on his return to his room, found to his no small surprise and mortification, that though he still retained some vague and dim recollection of the general purpose of the vision, yet, with the exception of some eight or ten scattered lines and images, all the rest had passed away like the images on the surface of a stream into which a stone has been cast, but, alas! without the after restoration of the latter!

      Then all the charm
Is broken—all that phantom-world so fair
Vanishes, and a thousand circlets spread,
And each mis-shape the other. Stay awhile,
Poor youth! who scarcely dar'st lift up thine eyes—
The stream will soon renew its smoothness, soon

The visions will return! And lo, he stays,
And soon the fragments dim of lovely forms
Come trembling back, unite, and now once more
The pool becomes a mirror.
[from Coleridge's "The Picture, or the Lover's Resolution" (1802) 69–78]

Yet from the still surviving recollections in his mind, the Author has frequently purposed to finish for himself what had been originally, as it were, given to him. Σαμερον αδιον ασω [from Theocritus's *Idyll* 1.145]: but the tomorrow is yet to come.

As a contrast to this vision, I have annexed a fragment of a very different character [Coleridge's poem "The Pains of Sleep"], describing with equal fidelity the dream of pain and disease.

> A damsel with a dulcimer
> In a vision once I saw:
> It was an Abyssinian maid,
40 And on her dulcimer she played,
> Singing of Mount Abora.
> Could I revive within me
> Her symphony and song,
> To such a deep delight 'twould win me,
45 That with music loud and long,
> I would build that dome in air,
> That sunny dome! those caves of ice!
> And all who heard should see them there,
> And all should cry, Beware! Beware!
50 His flashing eyes, his floating hair!
> Weave a circle round him thrice,
> And close your eyes with holy dread,
> For he on honey-dew hath fed,
> And drunk the milk of Paradise.
> —1816 (WRITTEN 1798)

5   "The Bridegroom's doors are opened wide,
And I am next of kin;
The guests are met, the feast is set:
May'st hear the merry din."

He holds him with his skinny hand,
10   "There was a ship," quoth he.
"Hold off! unhand me, grey-beard loon!"
Eftsoons[3] his hand dropt he.

He holds him with his glittering eye—
The Wedding-Guest stood still,
15   And listens like a three years' child:
The Mariner hath his will.

The wedding-guest is spellbound by the eye of the old sea-faring man, and constrained to hear his tale.

The Wedding-Guest sat on a stone:
He cannot choose but hear;
And thus spake on that ancient man,
20   The bright-eyed Mariner.

"The ship was cheered, the harbour cleared,
Merrily did we drop
Below the kirk,[4] below the hill,
Below the lighthouse top.

The Mariner tells how the ship sailed southward with a good wind and fair weather, till it reached the line.

25   "The Sun came up upon the left,
Out of the sea came he!
And he shone bright, and on the right
Went down into the sea.

Higher and higher every day,
30   Till over the mast at noon—"
The Wedding-Guest here beat his breast,
For he heard the loud bassoon.

The bride hath paced into the hall
Red as a rose is she;
35   Nodding their heads before her goes
The merry minstrelsy.

The wedding-guest heareth the bridal music; but the mariner continueth his tale.

The Wedding-Guest he beat his breast,
Yet he cannot choose but hear;

The Rime of the Ancient Mariner
In Seven Parts[1]

Facile credo, plures esse Naturas invisibiles quam visibiles in rerum universitate. Sed horum omnium familiam quis nobis enarrabit? et gradus et cognationes et discrimina et singulorum munera? Quid agunt? quæ loca habitant? Harum rerum notitiam semper ambivit ingenium humanum, nunquam attigit. Juvat, interea, non diffiteor, quandoque in animo, tanquam in Tabulâ, majoris et melioris mundi imaginem contemplari: ne mens assuefecta hodiernæ vitæ minutiis se contrahat nimis, & tota subsidat in pusillas cogitationes. Sed veritati interea invigilandum est, modusque servandus, ut certa ab incertis, diem a nocte, distinguamus.—T. Burnet. *Archaeol. Phil.* p. 68.[2]

PART I

It is an ancient Mariner,
And he stoppeth one of three.
"By thy long grey beard and glittering eye,
Now wherefore stopp'st thou me?

An ancient Mariner meeteth three Gallants bidden to a wedding-feast, and detaineth one.

---

1 *The Rime ... Parts* This version of the poem was published in 1817.

2 *Facile ... distinguamus* From Thomas Burnet's *Archaeologiae Philosophicae* (1692), translated by Mead and Foxton (1736): "I can easily believe, that there are more invisible than visible beings in the universe. But who will declare to us the family of all these, and acquaint us with the agreements, differences, and peculiar talents which are to be found among them? It is true, human wit has always desired a knowledge of these things, though it has never yet attained it. I will own that it is very profitable, sometimes to contemplate in the mind, as in a draught, the image of the greater and better world, lest the soul being accustomed to the trifles of this present life, should contract itself too much, and altogether rest in mean cogitations, but, in the meantime, we must take care to keep to the truth, and observe moderation, that we may distinguish certain from uncertain things, and day from night."

3 *Eftsoons* At once.

4 *kirk* Church.

And thus spake on that ancient man,
40   The bright-eyed Mariner.

"And now the STORM-BLAST came, and he   The ship drawn
Was tyrannous and strong: by a storm toward
He struck with his o'ertaking wings,   the south pole.
And chased us south along.

45   With sloping masts and dipping prow,
As who pursued with yell and blow
Still treads the shadow of his foe,
And forward bends his head,
The ship drove fast, loud roared the blast,
50   And southward aye we fled.

And now there came both mist and snow,
And it grew wondrous cold:
And ice, mast-high, came floating by,
As green as emerald.

55   And through the drifts the snowy clifts   The land of ice, and
Did send a dismal sheen: of fearful sounds,
Nor shapes of men nor beasts we ken[1]—   where no living
The ice was all between.   thing was to be seen.

The ice was here, the ice was there,
60   The ice was all around:
It cracked and growled, and roared and howled,
Like noises in a swound![2]

At length did cross an Albatross,   Till a great sea-bird,
Thorough the fog it came;   called the Albatross,
65   As if it had been a Christian soul,   came through the
We hailed it in God's name.   snow-fog, and was
received with great
joy and hospitality.

It ate the food it ne'er had eat,
And round and round it flew.
The ice did split with a thunder-fit;
70   The helmsman steered us through!

And a good south wind sprung up behind;
The Albatross did follow,

And every day, for food or play,   And lo! the Alba-
Came to the Mariner's hollo!   ross proveth a bird
of good omen, and
followeth the ship
75   In mist or cloud, on mast or shroud,   as it returned north-
It perched for vespers nine;[3]   ward, through fog
Whiles all the night, through fog-smoke white, and floating ice.
Glimmered the white Moon-shine."

"God save thee, ancient Mariner!   The ancient Mariner
80   From the fiends, that plague thee thus!—   inhospitably killed
Why look'st thou so?"—"With my cross-bow   the pious bird of
I shot the ALBATROSS.   good omen.

PART 2

The Sun now rose upon the right:
Out of the sea came he,
85   Still hid in mist, and on the left
Went down into the sea.

And the good south wind still blew behind,
But no sweet bird did follow,
Nor any day for food or play
90   Came to the mariners' hollo!

And I had done a hellish thing,   His ship mates cry
And it would work 'em woe: out against the
For all averred, I had killed the bird   ancient Mariner,
That made the breeze to blow.   for killing the bird
95   Ah wretch! said they, the bird to slay,   of good luck.
That made the breeze to blow!

Nor dim nor red, like God's own head,   But when the fog
The glorious Sun uprist: cleared off, they
Then all averred, I had killed the bird   justify the same—
100   That brought the fog and mist.   and thus make
'Twas right, said they, such birds to slay,   themselves
That bring the fog and mist.   accomplices in
the crime.

The fair breeze blew, the white foam flew,   The fair breeze
The furrow followed free;   continues;
105   We were the first that ever burst
Into that silent sea.

---

[1] *ken* Recognize.
[2] *swound* Swoon.

[3] *vespers nine* I.e., nine evenings. Vespers are evening prayer.

Down dropt the breeze, the sails dropt down,
'Twas sad as sad could be;
And we did speak only to break
110 The silence of the sea!

All in a hot and copper sky,
The bloody Sun, at noon,
Right up above the mast did stand,
No bigger than the Moon.

115 Day after day, day after day,
We stuck, nor breath nor motion;
As idle as a painted ship
Upon a painted ocean.

Water, water, every where,
120 And all the boards did shrink;
Water, water, every where,
Nor any drop to drink.

The very deep did rot: O Christ!
That ever this should be!
125 Yea, slimy things did crawl with legs
Upon the slimy sea.

About, about, in reel and rout
The death-fires[1] danced at night;
The water, like a witch's oils,
130 Burnt green, and blue and white.

And some in dreams assuréd were
Of the Spirit that plagued us so;
Nine fathom deep he had followed us
From the land of mist and snow.

135 And every tongue, through utter drought,
Was withered at the root;
We could not speak, no more than if
We had been choked with soot.

Ah! well a-day! what evil looks
140 Had I from old and young!
Instead of the cross, the Albatross
About my neck was hung.

The ship enters the Pacific Ocean and sails northward, even till it reaches the Line.

The ship hath been suddenly becalmed.

And the Albatross begins to be avenged.

A spirit has followed them; one of the invisible inhabitants of this planet, neither departed souls nor angels; concerning whom the learned Jew, Josephus, and the Platonic Constantinopolitan, Michael Psellus, may be consulted, and there is no climate or element without one or more.

The shipmates in their sore distress, would fain throw the whole guilt on the ancient Mariner: in sign whereof they hang the dead sea-bird round his neck.

---

[1] *death-fires* Possibly luminescent plankton.

PART 3

There passed a weary time. Each throat
Was parched, and glazed each eye.
145 A weary time! a weary time!
How glazed each weary eye,
When looking westward, I beheld
A something in the sky.

At first it seemed a little speck,
150 And then it seemed a mist;
It moved and moved, and took at last
A certain shape, I wist.

A speck, a mist, a shape, I wist!
And still it neared and neared:
155 And as if it dodged a water-sprite,
It plunged and tacked and veered.

With throat unslacked, with black lips baked,
We could nor laugh nor wail;
Through utter drought all dumb we stood!
160 I bit my arm, I sucked the blood,
And cried, A sail! a sail!

With throat unslacked, with black lips baked,
Agape they heard me call:
Gramercy![2] they for joy did grin,
165 And all at once their breath drew in,
As they were drinking all.

See! see! (I cried) she tacks no more!
Hither to work us weal;[3]
Without a breeze, without a tide,
170 She steadies with upright keel!

The western wave was all a-flame.
The day was well nigh done!
Almost upon the western wave
Rested the broad bright Sun;
175 When that strange shape drove suddenly
Betwixt us and the Sun.

The ancient Mariner beholdeth a sign in the element afar off.

As its nearer approach, it seemeth him to be a ship; and at a dear ransom he freeth his speech from the bonds of thirst.

A flash of joy.

And horror follows. For can it be a ship that comes onward without wind or tide?

---

[2] *Gramercy* Grant mercy, i.e., may God reward you in His mercy.

[3] *us weal* Will benefit us.

And straight the Sun was flecked with bars,
(Heaven's Mother send us grace!)
As if through a dungeon-grate he peered
180 With broad and burning face.

It seemeth him but the skeleton of a ship.

Alas! (thought I, and my heart beat loud)
How fast she nears and nears!
Are those *her* sails that glance in the Sun,
Like restless gossameres?

And its ribs are seen as bars on the face of the setting Sun. The spectre-woman and her death-mate, and no other on board the skeleton-ship.

185 Are those *her* ribs through which the Sun
Did peer, as through a grate?
And is that Woman all her crew?
Is that a DEATH? and are there two?
Is DEATH that woman's mate?

190 *Her* lips were red, *her* looks were free,
Her locks were yellow as gold:
Her skin was as white as leprosy,
The Night-mare LIFE-IN-DEATH was she,
Who thicks man's blood with cold.

Like vessel, like crew! Death and Life-in-Death have diced for the ship's crew, and she (the latter) winneth the ancient Mariner.

195 The naked hulk alongside came,
And the twain were casting dice;
"The game is done! I've won! I've won!"
Quoth she, and whistles thrice.

The Sun's rim dips; the stars rush out:
200 At one stride comes the dark;
With far-heard whisper, o'er the sea,
Off shot the spectre-bark.

No twilight within the courts of the sun.

We listened and looked sideways up!
Fear at my heart, as at a cup,
205 My life-blood seemed to sip!
The stars were dim, and thick the night,
The steersman's face by his lamp gleamed white;
From the sails the dews did drip—
Till clomb above the eastern bar
210 The hornéd Moon, with one bright star
Within the nether tip.

At the rising of the Moon,

One after one, by the star-dogged Moon
Too quick for groan or sigh,
Each turned his face with a ghastly pang,
215 And cursed me with his eye.

One after another,

Four times fifty living men,
(And I heard nor sigh nor groan)
With heavy thump, a lifeless lump,
They dropped down one by one.

His ship-mates drop down dead.

220 The souls did from their bodies fly,—
They fled to bliss or woe!
And every soul, it passed me by,
Like the whiz of my cross-bow!

But Life-in-Death begins her work on the ancient Mariner.

PART 4

"I fear thee, ancient Mariner!
225 I fear thy skinny hand!
And thou art long, and lank, and brown,
As is the ribbed sea-sand.[1]

The wedding-guest feareth that a spirit is talking to him;

I fear thee and thy glittering eye,
And thy skinny hand, so brown."—
230 Fear not, fear not, thou Wedding-Guest!
This body dropt not down.

But the ancient Mariner assureth him of his bodily life, and proceedeth to relate his horrible penance.

Alone, alone, all, all alone,
Alone on a wide wide sea!
And never a saint took pity on
235 My soul in agony.

The many men, so beautiful!
And they all dead did lie:
And a thousand thousand slimy things
Lived on; and so did I.

He despiseth the creatures of the calm,

240 I looked upon the rotting sea,
And drew my eyes away;
I looked upon the rotting deck,
And there the dead men lay.

And envieth that they should live, and so many lie dead.

I looked to heaven, and tried to pray;
245 But or ever a prayer had gusht,
A wicked whisper came, and made
My heart as dry as dust.

---

[1] [Coleridge's note] For the two last lines of this stanza, I am indebted to Mr. WORDSWORTH. It was on a delightful walk from Nether Stowey to Dulverton, with him and his sister, in the Autumn of 1797, that this Poem was planned, and in part composed.

I closed my lids, and kept them close,
And the balls like pulses beat;
250 For the sky and the sea, and the sea and the sky
Lay like a load on my weary eye,
And the dead were at my feet.

The cold sweat melted from their limbs, *But the curse*
Nor rot nor reek did they: *liveth for him*
255 The look with which they looked on me   *in the eye of*
Had never passed away.   *the dead men.*

An orphan's curse would drag to hell
A spirit from on high;
But oh! more horrible than that   *In his loneliness*
260 Is the curse in a dead man's eye!   *and fixedness, he*
Seven days, seven nights, I saw that curse, *yearneth towards*
And yet I could not die.   *the journeying Moon,*
                                         and the stars that still
                                         sojourn, yet still move
The moving Moon went up the sky,   *onwards; and every*
And no where did abide: *where the blue sky*
265 Softly she was going up,   *belongs to them, and*
And a star or two beside—   *is their appointed rest,*
                                         and their native country,
                                         and their own natural
Her beams bemocked the sultry main,   *homes, which they enter*
Like April hoar-frost spread;   *unannounced, as lords*
But where the ship's huge shadow lay,   *that are certain ex-*
270 The charmèd water burnt alway   *pected, and yet there is*
A still and awful red.   *a silent joy at their*
                                         arrival.

Beyond the shadow of the ship,   *By the light of the*
I watched the water-snakes: *Moon he beholdeth*
They moved in tracks of shining white,   *God's creatures of*
275 And when they reared, the elfish light *the great calm.*
Fell off in hoary flakes.

Within the shadow of the ship
I watched their rich attire:
Blue, glossy green, and velvet black,
280 They coiled and swam; and every track
Was a flash of golden fire.

O happy living things! no tongue   *Their beauty and*
Their beauty might declare: *their happiness.*
A spring of love gushed from my heart,   *He blesseth them in*
285 And I blessed them unaware: *his heart.*

Sure my kind saint took pity on me,
And I blessed them unaware.

The selfsame moment I could pray;   *The spell begins*
And from my neck so free   *to break.*
290 The Albatross fell off, and sank
Like lead into the sea.

PART 5

Oh sleep! it is a gentle thing,
Beloved from pole to pole!
To Mary Queen the praise be given!
295 She sent the gentle sleep from Heaven,
That slid into my soul.

The silly[1] buckets on the deck,   *By grace of the holy*
That had so long remained,   *Mother, the ancient*
I dreamt that they were filled with dew; *Mariner is refreshed*
300 And when I awoke, it rained.   *with rain.*

My lips were wet, my throat was cold,
My garments all were dank;
Sure I had drunken in my dreams,
And still my body drank.

305 I moved, and could not feel my limbs:
I was so light—almost
I thought that I had died in sleep,
And was a blessèd ghost.

And soon I heard a roaring wind: *He heareth sounds,*
310 It did not come anear;   *and seeth strange*
But with its sound it shook the sails,   *sights and*
That were so thin and sere.   *commotions in*
                                         the sky and the
                                         elements.
The upper air burst into life!
And a hundred fire-flags sheen,
315 To and fro they were hurried about!
And to and fro, and in and out,
The wan stars danced between.

And the coming wind did roar more loud,
And the sails did sigh like sedge;

[1] *silly* Simple.

320 And the rain poured down from one black cloud;
The Moon was at its edge.

The thick black cloud was cleft, and still
The Moon was at its side:
Like waters shot from some high crag,
325 The lightning fell with never a jag,
A river steep and wide.

The loud wind never reached the ship,
Yet now the ship moved on!
Beneath the lightning and the Moon
330 The dead men gave a groan.

The bodies of the ship's crew are inspirited, and the ship moves on;

They groaned, they stirred, they all uprose,
Nor spake, nor moved their eyes;
It had been strange, even in a dream,
To have seen those dead men rise.

335 The helmsman steered, the ship moved on;
Yet never a breeze up-blew;
The mariners all 'gan work the ropes,
Where they were wont to do;
They raised their limbs like lifeless tools—
340 We were a ghastly crew.

The body of my brother's son
Stood by me, knee to knee:
The body and I pulled at one rope,
But he said nought to me.

But not by the souls of the men, nor by dæmons of earth or middle air, but by a blessed troop of angelic spirits, sent down by the invocation of the guardian saint.

345 "I fear thee, ancient Mariner!"
Be calm, thou Wedding-Guest!
'Twas not those souls that fled in pain,
Which to their corses[1] came again,
But a troop of spirits blest:

350 For when it dawned—they dropped their arms,
And clustered round the mast;
Sweet sounds rose slowly through their mouths,
And from their bodies passed.

Around, around, flew each sweet sound,
355 Then darted to the Sun;

Slowly the sounds came back again,
Now mixed, now one by one.

Sometimes a-dropping from the sky
I heard the sky-lark sing;
360 Sometimes all little birds that are,
How they seemed to fill the sea and air
With their sweet jargoning!

And now 'twas like all instruments,
Now like a lonely flute;
365 And now it is an angel's song,
That makes the heavens be mute.

It ceased; yet still the sails made on
A pleasant noise till noon,
A noise like of a hidden brook
370 In the leafy month of June,
That to the sleeping woods all night
Singeth a quiet tune.

Till noon we quietly sailed on,
Yet never a breeze did breathe:
375 Slowly and smoothly went the ship,
Moved onward from beneath.

Under the keel nine fathom deep,
From the land of mist and snow,
The spirit slid: and it was he
380 That made the ship to go.
The sails at noon left off their tune,
And the ship stood still also.

The lonesome spirit from the south-pole carries on the ship as far as the line, in obedience to the angelic troop, but still requireth vengeance.

The Sun, right up above the mast,
Had fixed her to the ocean:
385 But in a minute she 'gan stir,
With a short uneasy motion—
Backwards and forwards half her length
With a short uneasy motion.

Then like a pawing horse let go,
390 She made a sudden bound:
It flung the blood into my head,
And I fell down in a swound.

---

[1] *corses* Corpses.

How long in that same fit I lay,
I have not to declare;
395 But ere my living life returned,
I heard and in my soul discerned
Two voices in the air.

"Is it he?" quoth one, "Is this the man?
By Him who died on cross,
400 With his cruel bow he laid full low
The harmless Albatross.

The spirit who bideth by himself
In the land of mist and snow,
He loved the bird that loved the man
405 Who shot him with his bow."

The other was a softer voice,
As soft as honey-dew:
Quoth he, "The man hath penance done,
And penance more will do."

PART 6

FIRST VOICE
410 "But tell me, tell me! speak again,
Thy soft response renewing—
What makes that ship drive on so fast?
What is the ocean doing?"

SECOND VOICE
"Still as a slave before his lord,
415 The ocean hath no blast;
His great bright eye most silently
Up to the Moon is cast—

If he may know which way to go;
For she guides him smooth or grim.
420 See, brother, see! how graciously
She looketh down on him."

FIRST VOICE
"But why drives on that ship so fast,
Without or wave or wind?"

The Polar Spirit's fellow-dæmons, the invisible inhabitants of the element, take part in his wrong; and two of them relate, one to the other, that penance long and heavy for the ancient Mariner hath been accorded to the Polar Spirit, who returned southward.

SECOND VOICE
"The air is cut away before,
425 And closes from behind.

Fly, brother, fly! more high, more high!
Or we shall be belated:
For slow and slow that ship will go,
When the Mariner's trance is abated."

430 I woke, and we were sailing on
As in a gentle weather:
'Twas night, calm night, the Moon was high;
The dead men stood together.

All stood together on the deck,
435 For a charnel-dungeon fitter:[1]
All fixed on me their stony eyes,
That in the Moon did glitter.

The pang, the curse, with which they died,
Had never passed away:
440 I could not draw my eyes from theirs,
Nor turn them up to pray.

And now this spell was snapt: once more
I viewed the ocean green,
And looked far forth, yet little saw
445 Of what had else been seen—

Like one, that on a lonesome road
Doth walk in fear and dread,
And having once turned round, walks on,
And turns no more his head;
450 Because he knows, a frightful fiend
Doth close behind him tread.

But soon there breathed a wind on me,
Nor sound nor motion made:
Its path was not upon the sea,
455 In ripple or in shade.

It raised my hair, it fanned my cheek
Like a meadow-gale of spring—

The Mariner hath been cast into a trance; for the angelic power causeth the vessel to drive northward, faster than human life could endure.

The supernatural motion is retarded; the Mariner awakes, and his penance begins anew.

The curse is finally expiated.

---

[1] *charnel-dungeon* Mortuary; house of death.

It mingled strangely with my fears,
Yet it felt like a welcoming.

460 Swiftly, swiftly flew the ship,
Yet she sailed softly too:
Sweetly, sweetly blew the breeze—
On me alone it blew.

Oh! dream of joy! is this indeed
465 The light-house top I see?
Is this the hill? is this the kirk?
Is this mine own countree?

And the ancient Mariner beholdeth his native country.

We drifted o'er the harbour-bar,
And I with sobs did pray—
470 O let me be awake, my God!
Or let me sleep alway.

The harbour-bay was clear as glass,
So smoothly was it strewn!
And on the bay the moonlight lay,
475 And the shadow of the Moon.

The rock shone bright, the kirk no less,
That stands above the rock:
The moonlight steeped in silentness
The steady weathercock.

480 And the bay was white with silent light,
Till rising from the same,
Full many shapes, that shadows were,
In crimson colours came.

The angelic spirits leave the dead bodies,

A little distance from the prow
485 Those crimson shadows were:
I turned my eyes upon the deck—
Oh, Christ! what saw I there!

And appear in their own forms of light.

Each corse lay flat, lifeless and flat,
And, by the holy rood!
490 A man all light, a seraph-man,[1]
On every corse there stood.

---

[1] *rood* Cross; *seraph-man* Angel.

This seraph-band, each waved his hand:
It was a heavenly sight!
They stood as signals to the land,
495 Each one a lovely light;

This seraph-band, each waved his hand,
No voice did they impart—
No voice; but oh! the silence sank
Like music on my heart.

500 But soon I heard the dash of oars,
I heard the Pilot's cheer;
My head was turned perforce away
And I saw a boat appear.

The Pilot and the Pilot's boy,
505 I heard them coming fast:
Dear Lord in Heaven! it was a joy
The dead men could not blast.

I saw a third—I heard his voice:
It is the Hermit good!
510 He singeth loud his godly hymns
That he makes in the wood.
He'll shrieve[2] my soul, he'll wash away
The Albatross's blood.

PART 7

This Hermit good lives in that wood
515 Which slopes down to the sea.
How loudly his sweet voice he rears!
He loves to talk with marineres
That come from a far countree.

The Hermit of the Wood.

He kneels at morn, and noon, and eve—
520 He hath a cushion plump:
It is the moss that wholly hides
The rotted old oak-stump.

The skiff-boat neared: I heard them talk,
"Why, this is strange, I trow![3]
525 Where are those light so many and fair,
That signal made but now?"

---

[2] *shrieve* Give absolution to.

[3] *trow* Believe.

"Strange, by my faith!" the Hermit said—
"And they answered not our cheer!
The planks look warped! and see those sails,
530 How thin they are and sere!
I never saw aught like to them,
Unless perchance it were

Brown skeletons of leaves that lag
My forest-brook along;
535 When the ivy-tod[1] is heavy with snow,
And the owlet whoops to the wolf below,
That eats the she-wolf's young."

"Dear Lord! it hath a fiendish look—
(The Pilot made reply)
540 I am a-feared"—"Push on, push on!"
Said the Hermit cheerily.

The boat came closer to the ship,
But I nor spake nor stirred;
The boat came close beneath the ship,
545 And straight a sound was heard.

Under the water it rumbled on,
Still louder and more dread:
It reached the ship, it split the bay;
The ship went down like lead.

550 Stunned by that loud and dreadful sound,
Which sky and ocean smote,
Like one that hath been seven days drowned
My body lay afloat;
But swift as dreams, myself I found
555 Within the Pilot's boat.

Upon the whirl, where sank the ship,
The boat spun round and round;
And all was still, save that the hill
Was telling of the sound.

560 I moved my lips—the Pilot shrieked
And fell down in a fit;
The holy Hermit raised his eyes,
And prayed where he did sit.

Approacheth the ship with wonder.

The ship suddenly sinketh.

The ancient Mariner is saved in the Pilot's boat.

I took the oars: the Pilot's boy,
565 Who now doth crazy go,
Laughed loud and long, and all the while
His eyes went to and fro.
"Ha! ha!" quoth he, "full plain I see,
The Devil knows how to row."

570 And now, all in my own countree,
I stood on the firm land!
The Hermit stepped forth from the boat,
And scarcely he could stand.

"O shrieve me, shrieve me, holy man!"
575 The Hermit crossed his brow.
"Say quick," quoth he, "I bid thee say—
What manner of man art thou?"

Forthwith this frame of mine was wrenched
With a woful agony,
580 Which forced me to begin my tale;
And then it left me free.

Since then, at an uncertain hour,
That agony returns;
And till my ghastly tale is told,
585 This heart within me burns.

I pass, like night, from land to land;
I have strange power of speech;
That moment that his face I see,
I know the man that must hear me:
590 To him my tale I teach.

What loud uproar bursts from that door!
The wedding-guests are there:
But in the garden-bower the bride
And bride-maids singing are:
595 And hark the little vesper bell,
Which biddeth me to prayer!

O Wedding-Guest! this soul hath been
Alone on a wide wide sea:
So lonely 'twas, that God Himself
600 Scarce seeméd there to be.

The ancient Mariner earnestly entreateth the Hermit to shrieve him; and the penance of life falls on him.

And ever and anon throughout his future life an agony constraineth him to travel from land to land.

---
[1] *ivy-tod* Bush.

O sweeter than the marriage-feast,
'Tis sweeter far to me,
To walk together to the kirk
With a goodly company!—

605　To walk together to the kirk,
And all together pray,
While each to his great Father bends,
Old men, and babes, and loving friends
And youth and maidens gay!

610　Farewell, farewell! but this I tell
To thee, thou Wedding-Guest!
He prayeth well, who loveth well
Both man and bird and beast.

And to teach by his own example, love and reverence to all things that God made and loveth.

He prayeth best, who loveth best
615　All things both great and small;
For the dear God who loveth us,
He made and loveth all."

The Mariner, whose eye is bright,
Whose beard with age is hoar,[1]
620　Is gone: and now the Wedding-Guest
Turned from the bridegroom's door.

He went like one that hath been stunned,
And is of sense forlorn:
A sadder and a wiser man,
625　He rose the morrow morn.
—1817

━━━━━━━━━━

IN CONTEXT

The Origin of "The Rime of the Ancient Mariner"

from Samuel Taylor Coleridge, *Biographia Literaria*, Chapter 14 (1817)

Almost twenty years after the first publication of "The Rime of the Ancient Mariner," Coleridge gave the following account of the poem's origin and composition.

During the first year that Mr. Wordsworth and I were neighbours, our conversations turned frequently on the two cardinal points of poetry, the power of exciting the sympathy of the reader by a faithful adherence to the truth of nature, and the power of giving the interest of novelty by the modifying colours of imagination. The sudden charm, which accidents of light and shade, which moonlight or sunset diffused over a known and familiar landscape, appeared to represent the practicability of combining both. These are the poetry of nature. The thought suggested itself (to which of us I do not recollect) that a series of poems might be composed of two sorts. In the one, the incidents and agents were to be, in part at least supernatural; and the excellence aimed at was to consist in the interesting of the affections by the dramatic truth of such emotions, as would naturally accompany such situations, supposing them real. And real in *this* sense they have been to every human being who, from whatever source of delusion, has at any time believed himself under supernatural agency. For the second class, subjects were to be chosen from ordinary life; the characters and incidents were to be such, as will be found in every village and its vicinity where there is a meditative and feeling mind to seek after them, or to notice them, when they present themselves. In this idea originated the plan of the *Lyrical Ballads*; in which it was agreed, that my endeavours should be directed to persons and characters supernatural, or at least romantic; yet so as to transfer from our inward nature a human interest and a semblance of truth sufficient to procure for these shadows of

---

[1] *hoar* White, as with frost (hoarfrost).

imagination that willing suspension of disbelief for the moment, which constitutes poetic faith. Mr. Wordsworth, on the other hand, was to propose to himself as his object, to give the charm of novelty to things of every day, and to excite a feeling analogous to the supernatural, by awakening the mind's attention from the lethargy of custom, and directing it to the loveliness and the wonders of the world before us; an inexhaustible treasure, but for which, in consequence of the film of familiarity and selfish solicitude we have eyes, yet see not, and hearts that neither feel or understand. With this view I wrote "The Ancient Mariner," and was preparing among other poems, "The Dark Ladie," and the "Christabel" in which I should have more nearly realized my ideal than I had done in my first attempt.

from A Letter from the Rev. Alexander Dyce to Hartley Coleridge (1852)

In this letter to Samuel Taylor Coleridge's eldest son, Hartley, the Reverend Alexander Dyce quotes Wordsworth as saying the following about the inception of "The Rime of the Ancient Mariner":

"The Ancient Mariner" was founded on a strange dream, which a friend of Coleridge had, who fancied he saw a skeleton ship, with figures in it. We had both determined to write some poetry for a monthly magazine, the profits of which were to defer the expenses of a little excursion we were to make together. "The Ancient Mariner" was intended for this periodical, but was too long. I had very little share in the composition of it, for I soon found the style of Coleridge and myself would not assimilate. Beside the lines (in the fourth part) "And thou art long, and lank, and brown, /As in the ribbed sea-sand—" I wrote the stanza (in the first part) "He holds him with his glittering eye— / The Wedding-Guest stood still, / And listens like a three-years child: / The Mariner hath his will" and four or five lines more in different parts of the poem, which I could not now point out. The idea of shooting an albatross was mine; for I had been reading *Shelvocke's Voyages*, which probably Coleridge never saw. I also suggested the reanimation of the dead bodies, to work the ship.

GEORGE GORDON, LORD BYRON
1788 – 1824

George Gordon, Lord Byron, was one of the most influential literary figures of the nineteenth century. His works—the long poems *Childe Harold's Pilgrimage* and *Don Juan* among them —were tremendous popular successes, and the Byronic Hero has become a cultural icon. Byron himself, handsome and charming, sexually unconventional, politically iconoclastic, has been alternately celebrated and reviled from his own time to the present.

Byron's beginnings were inauspicious. He was born in near-poverty on 22 January 1788, lame in one leg (probably the result of a form of cerebral palsy). His father, Captain John ("Mad Jack") Byron, a notorious spendthrift and rake, had married Byron's mother, the Scottish heiress Catherine Gordon, for her money. This he quickly squandered, afterward fleeing to France. Byron and his mother moved to Aberdeen. Here Byron lived out his first ten years, the object of his mother's capricious mixture of love and sudden overwhelming rages, deeply conscious of his lameness, and steeped in Calvinism. Here, too, at ten years old, he was regularly molested by his nursemaid.

In 1798 Byron's great-uncle, the fifth Lord Byron, died childless, and Byron inherited the title. He and his mother moved to the family's ancestral, debt-encumbered home, Newstead Abbey, in Nottinghamshire. Byron was sent to school, first to an academy in Dulwich, then to Harrow in 1801. Around 1801 he also met for the first time his half-sister Augusta, the product of an earlier marriage of his father's. In 1805 Byron entered Trinity College, Cambridge University, where he made the most lasting friendships of his life. He also contracted huge debts to which he would only add in the future.

Byron took a degree from Cambridge in 1807. In the same year, he published his first poetry collection, *Hours of Idleness*. The book was excoriated in the press as pretentious and derivative; Byron responded in 1809 with the verse satire *English Bards and Scotch Reviewers*, in which he attacked the most notable of his critics and many of the leading poets of the day. In that same year, Byron came of age and took possession of Newstead Abbey, where he held riotous parties; as a result of carousing and redecorating, his mountain of debt grew larger. In March he made his first appearance in the House of Lords, and in July, after having incurred more debt to finance himself, he set off on a trip through Europe and the Near East, areas largely closed to the English as a result of the Napoleonic Wars. This journey began an intense attachment to Greece that would color the rest of Byron's life and writing and allowed him to fulfill the homosexual desires that he had been unable to explore in England (where sodomy was a capital crime). During this time he also began *Childe Harold's Pilgrimage,* the work that would make him a celebrity.

Featuring a journey almost identical to that which Byron himself had just completed, undertaken by a mysteriously gloomy hero, *Childe Harold's Pilgrimage*, Cantos I&II, launched both the figure of the "Byronic Hero" and the association between that figure and Byron that the poet would alternately embrace and seek to evade for the remainder of his life. The poem cunningly managed to weave elements from familiar genres such as travel writing, gothic novels, and sentimental literature with experiments in mood and tone. It enthralled its readers. Byron wrote in Spenserian stanzas, but as the poem progressed he began to bend this stiff form so that it became his own. (Harold's discoveries and the narrator's own growing observational and meditative abilities find their mirror in the rhythms of the verse.) With its panoramic focus, high-flown tone, and alluringly aloof protagonist, *Childe Harold's Pilgrimage* marked an important moment in English and European literature.

Now a celebrity, Byron played that role with gusto. He became a darling of Whig society and indulged in a series of affairs, most scandalously with Lady Caroline Lamb. In addition, some time in 1813 Byron began a sexual relationship with his half-sister Augusta. This was to prove his undoing, but it was nonetheless the deepest and most lasting attachment of his life. He also continued writing, producing a collection of hugely popular works ranging from the short lyrics of *Hebrew Melodies* to the "Eastern Tales" produced in 1813 and 1814. In this series of long narrative poems, set in the Near East, he fleshed out the anti-heroic figure he had sketched in *Childe Harold's Pilgrimage*. The protagonists of the "Tales" stood aloof from those who surround them, tortured by a mysterious but deeply-felt guilt. Brave, glamorous, and in each case devoted utterly to one woman (who herself was an idealized romantic heroine), they were nonetheless fated to be outcasts. Described most fully in the first of the "Eastern Tales," "The Giaour," the hero reached his final refinement in the last, "Lara." The public embraced this figure, and a literary type entered into the canon with a vengeance: the writing of the next hundred years would be crowded with Byronic Heroes.

In January of 1815, Byron married Annabella Millbanke, a sheltered heiress. The marriage was based on a short courtship and false hopes, and the two participants were utterly unsuited. Byron was psychologically abusive to his wife, whose piety and conventionality were a constant irritant to him. At the end of 1815, a few weeks after the birth of their daughter, Ada Augusta, Annabella left him. A public scandal, aided by unauthorized publication of Byron's poems and his wife's revelations about his incest with Augusta Leigh, followed. Now a social outcast, Byron departed for Europe, never to return. He continued to communicate with his friends in England through a voluminous and revealingly frank series of letters that detailed his sexual adventures, his political and literary beliefs, and his continued involvement with affairs in England. Even if he had written no poetry, the letters would qualify Byron for a place as one of England's foremost authors: urbane, broad-ranging, dazzling, and hilarious, they make for riveting and delightful reading.

Landing in Belgium in April of 1816, Byron made his way through scenes—including a visit to Waterloo—which he would describe in the final two cantos of *Childe Harold*. At Geneva he met Mary and Percy Shelley. They had travelled to Switzerland accompanied by Mary's stepsister Claire Clairmont, who had had a brief sexual relationship with Byron in England. The two poets formed an intimate and intellectually rich friendship, and the four lived in close proximity during the summer. Byron resumed his involvement with Claire; she bore him a daughter, Allegra, in January of 1817.

When the Shelleys departed for England in August, Byron journeyed to Venice, where he lived for the next three years. Here he flung himself into a period of promiscuity (he estimated that he had sex with over two hundred women during this time), but continued to work as well, producing his verse drama *Manfred*, the fourth canto of *Childe Harold*, and the humorous *Beppo*, written in *ottava rima*. This colloquial Italian form was fiendishly ill-adapted to English, but Byron made it his own, also using it to produce his masterpiece, *Don Juan*, which he began in July of 1818.

Don Juan is the creation of an author who has found his *métier*. It is the longest satirical poem in English, a rollicking tale of a young hero who bears the same name as the seducer but resembles him in no other way. Juan, passive and sweet-natured, is seduced by women ranging from a family friend to Catherine the Great. His adventures take him on a journey from Spain to London by way of Greece and Russia. Byron was thus able to mock not only current social mores but also his own previous poems, Don Juan standing as a kind of anti-Byronic Hero. He took as his model for the poem a slight satire written in 1817 by John Hookham Frere in *ottava rima*, but *Don Juan* is also descended from Swift's *Gulliver's Travels*, and Sterne's *Tristram Shandy*. As with the latter, the focus of Byron's poem is not so much what is narrated as its narrator, a garrulous, easily distracted gentleman who at times bears a remarkable resemblance to the author. Byron's publisher, friends, and the critical establishment condemned *Don Juan* for its immorality, but he himself relished it, asserting that he had written it only "to giggle and make giggle"—a comment typically Byronic in its attempt to deny responsibility by invoking comedy. For all its author's disclaimers, *Don Juan* is no mere comic throwaway. It is a text of great cultural and political scope and a work of questing philosophy, arguably the best of its age.

In April of 1819 Byron met Countess Teresa Guiccioli, a young Italian woman married to a much older man. Almost immediately they began a socially-sanctioned affair that would last, with reasonable fidelity, until the end of Byron's life. Through her family, Byron was drawn into nationalist schemes to free Italy from the Austrians. When the family was exiled to Pisa in 1821 as a result of this plotting, Byron followed. The Shelleys were now based in Pisa, and Byron became one of their group. Soon, however, this "Pisan circle" fell apart, first because of Shelley's anger over Byron's callous treatment of Allegra (she had joined him in Venice in 1819, only for him first to neglect her and then send her to be brought up in a convent, where she died, unvisited by him, in 1822), then because of Byron's decision to follow the Gambas to Genoa, and finally because of Shelley's own death in July 1822.

Despite these upheavals, Byron wrote at a furious pace. Between 1819 and 1823 he produced numerous works, including a series of closet dramas (including *Sardanapalus*, *The Two Foscari*, and *Cain*), and his biting satire of England under George III, *The Vision of Judgment*. He also continued *Don Juan*, finishing sixteen cantos by the end of 1823.

In 1824 Byron organized an expedition to assist the Greeks in their fight for independence from the Turks. Settled in the marsh town of Missolonghi, he financed and trained soldiers. Exhausted and worn down, he contracted a fever and died on 19 April, aged thirty-six, his death hastened by copious bloodletting performed by his incompetent doctors.

⌘⌘⌘

⌘⌘⌘

Sun of the Sleepless

Sun of the sleepless! melancholy star!
Whose tearful beam glows tremulously far,
That show'st the darkness thou canst not dispel,
How like art thou to joy remembered well!
5   So gleams the past, the light of other days,
Which shines, but warms not with its powerless rays;
A night-beam Sorrow watcheth to behold,
Distinct, but distant—clear—but, oh how cold!
—1814

She walks in beauty

1

She walks in beauty, like the night
Of cloudless climes and starry skies;
And all that's best of dark and bright
    Meet in her aspect and her eyes:
5   Thus mellow'd to that tender light
    Which heaven to gaudy day denies.

2

One shade the more, one ray the less,
    Had half impair'd the nameless grace
Which waves in every raven tress,
10   Or softly lightens o'er her face;

Where thoughts serenely sweet express
    How pure, how dear their dwelling place.

3

And on that cheek, and o'er that brow,
    So soft, so calm, yet eloquent,
15 The smiles that win, the tints that glow,
    But tell of days in goodness spent,
A mind at peace with all below,
    A heart whose love is innocent!
—1815 [WRITTEN 1814]

When we two parted [1]

1

When we two parted
    In silence and tears,
Half broken-hearted
    To sever for years,
5 Pale grew thy cheek and cold,
    Colder thy kiss;
Truly that hour foretold
    Sorrow to this.

2

The dew of the morning
10   Sunk chill on my brow—
It felt like the warning
    Of what I feel now.
Thy vows are all broken,
    And light is thy fame;
15 I hear thy name spoken,
    And share in its shame.

3

They name thee before me,

A knell to mine ear;
A shudder comes o'er me—
20   Why wert thou so dear?
They know not I knew thee,
    Who knew thee too well:—
Long, long shall I rue thee,
    Too deeply to tell.

4

25 In secret we met—
    In silence I grieve,
That thy heart could forget,
    Thy spirit deceive.
If I should meet thee
30   After long years,
How should I greet thee!—
    With silence and tears.
—1816

Stanzas for Music [2]

1

There's not a joy the world can give like that it
    takes away,
When the glow of early thought declines in feeling's
    dull decay;
'Tis not on youth's smooth cheek the blush alone,
    which fades so fast,
But the tender bloom of heart is gone, ere youth
    itself be past.

2

5 Then the few whose spirits float above the wreck
    of happiness,
Are driven o'er the shoals of guilt or ocean of excess:
The magnet of their course is gone, or only points
    in vain
The shore to which their shiver'd sail shall never
    stretch again.

---

[1] *When we two parted* This poem has a complex history, at least partially because Byron deliberately misdated the date of its composition as 1816, in order to hide its true subject. In fact, the lines were written in 1815, and their subject is Lady Frances Wedderburn Webster, the wife of a friend of Byron's; Byron had heard gossip about her affair with the Duke of Wellington. Byron himself had had a brief "platonic" affair with Lady Webster in 1813: a heated and exciting chase, kept secret from her husband and ending without consummation.

[2] *Stanzas for Music* Byron wrote this poem in 1815 to commemorate the death of one of the friends of his youth, the Duke of Dorset. He referred to it in an 1816 letter as "the truest, though the most melancholy, I ever wrote."

3

Then the mortal coldness of the soul like death
    itself comes down;
10 It cannot feel for others' woes, it dare not dream
    its own;
That heavy chill has frozen o'er the fountain of
    our tears,
And tho' the eye may sparkle still, 'tis where the
    ice appears.

4

Tho' wit may flash from fluent lips, and mirth
    distract the breast,
Through midnight hours that yield no more their
    former hope of rest;
15 'Tis but as ivy-leaves around the ruin'd turret wreath,
All green and wildly fresh without but worn and
    grey beneath.

5

Oh could I feel as 1 have felt,—or be what I have been,
Or weep as I could once have wept, o'er many a
    vanished scene:
As springs in deserts found seem sweet, all
    brackish though they be,
20 So midst the wither'd waste of life, those tears
    would flow to me.
    —1816

Darkness[1]

I had a dream, which was not all a dream.
  The bright sun was extinguish'd, and the stars
Did wander darkling in the eternal space,
Rayless, and pathless, and the icy earth

---

[1] *Darkness* The dust thrown into the atmosphere in 1815 by Mount Tamboro, an Indonesian volcano, made the summer of 1816 the coldest and wettest on record. Influenced by the weather, and perhaps by recent warnings by an Italian astronomer that sunspots might lead to the extinction of the sun, Byron produced this prescient poem, which he labeled "a Fragment." The "last man" theme was a source of fascination for the Romantics, but Byron's poem is distinctive for its absence of a last man, its unrelentingly bleak vision, and its representation of a typically Byronic faithful dog.

5 Swung blind and blackening in the moonless air;[2]
Morn came, and went—and came, and brought no day,
And men forgot their passions in the dread
Of this their desolation; and all hearts
Were chill'd into a selfish prayer for light:
10 And they did live by watchfires—and the thrones,
The palaces of crowned kings—the huts,
The habitations of all things which dwell,
Were burnt for beacons; cities were consumed,
And men were gathered round their blazing homes
15 To look once more into each other's face;
Happy were those who dwelt within the eye
Of the volcanos, and their mountain-torch:
A fearful hope was all the world contain'd;
Forests were set on fire—but hour by hour
20 They fell and faded—and the crackling trunks
Extinguish'd with a crash—and all was black.
The brows of men by the despairing light
Wore an unearthly aspect, as by fits
The flashes fell upon them; some lay down
25 And hid their eyes and wept; and some did rest
Their chins upon their clenched hands, and smiled;
And others hurried to and fro, and fed
Their funeral piles with fuel, and looked up
With mad disquietude on the dull sky,
30 The pall of a past world; and then again
With curses cast them down upon the dust,
And gnash'd their teeth and howl'd: the wild
    birds shriek'd,
And, terrified, did flutter on the ground,
And flap their useless wings; the wildest brutes
35 Came tame and tremulous; and vipers crawl'd
And twined themselves among the multitude,
Hissing, but stingless—they were slain for food:
And War, which for a moment was no more,
Did glut himself again;—a meal was bought
40 With blood, and each sate sullenly apart
Gorging himself in gloom: no love was left;
All earth was but one thought—and that was death,
Immediate and inglorious; and the pang
Of famine fed upon all entrails—men
45 Died, and their bones were tombless as their flesh;
The meagre by the meagre were devoured,

---

[2] *icy earth ... moonless air* Cf. Ezekiel 32.7–8; Joel 2.31; Revelation 6.12.

Even dogs assail'd their masters, all save one,
And he was faithful to a corse,[1] and kept
The birds and beasts and famish'd men at bay,
50 Till hunger clung them, or the dropping dead
Lured their lank jaws; himself sought out no food,
But with a piteous and perpetual moan
And a quick desolate cry, licking the hand
Which answered not with a caress—he died.
55 The crowd was famish'd by degrees; but two
Of an enormous city did survive,
And they were enemies; they met beside
The dying embers of an altar-place
Where had been heap'd a mass of holy things
60 For an unholy usage; they raked up,
And shivering scraped with their cold skeleton hands
The feeble ashes, and their feeble breath
Blew for a little life, and made a flame
Which was a mockery; then they lifted up
65 Their eyes as it grew lighter, and beheld
Each other's aspects—saw, and shriek'd, and died—
Even of their mutual hideousness they died,
Unknowing who he was upon whose brow
Famine had written Fiend. The world was void,
70 The populous and the powerful was a lump,
Seasonless, herbless, treeless, manless, lifeless—
A lump of death—a chaos of hard clay.
The rivers, lakes, and ocean all stood still,
And nothing stirred within their silent depths;
75 Ships sailorless lay rotting on the sea,
And their masts fell down piecemeal; as they dropp'd
They slept on the abyss without a surge—
The waves were dead; the tides were in their grave,
The moon their mistress had expired before;
80 The winds were withered in the stagnant air,
And the clouds perish'd; Darkness had no need
Of aid from them—She was the universe.
—1816

Prometheus [2]

Titan! to whose immortal eyes
The sufferings of mortality,
   Seen in their sad reality,
Were not as things that gods despise;
5 What was thy pity's recompense?
A silent suffering, and intense;
The rock, the vulture, and the chain,
All that the proud can feel of pain,
The agony they do not show,
10 The suffocating sense of woe,
   Which speaks but in its loneliness,
And then is jealous lest the sky
Should have a listener, nor will sigh
   Until its voice is echoless.

2

15 Titan! to thee the strife was given
   Between the suffering and the will,
   Which torture where they cannot kill;
And the inexorable Heaven,
And the deaf tyranny of Fate,
20 The ruling principle of Hate,
Which for its pleasure doth create
The things it may annihilate,
Refused thee even the boon to die:
The wretched gift eternity
25 Was thine—and thou hast borne it well.
All that the Thunderer[3] wrung from thee
Was but the menace which flung back
On him the torments of thy rack;
The fate thou didst so well foresee
30 But would not to appease him tell;
And in thy Silence was his Sentence,
And in his Soul a vain repentance,
And evil dread so ill dissembled
That in his hand the lightnings trembled.

---

2 *Prometheus* The Titan Prometheus stole fire from heaven and gave it to humanity. To punish him, Jupiter, King of the gods, had him chained to a rock in the Caucasus, where a vulture (in some versions, an eagle) tore at his liver. Each night Prometheus's liver grew afresh, to be torn out the next day.

3 *Thunderer* Jupiter.

1 *corse* Corpse.

3

35 Thy Godlike crime was to be kind,
    To render with thy precepts less
      The sum of human wretchedness,
And strengthen Man with his own mind;
But baffled as thou wert from high,
40 Still in thy patient energy,
In the endurance, and repulse
    Of thine impenetrable Spirit,
Which Earth and Heaven could not convulse,
    A mighty lesson we inherit:
45 Thou art a symbol and a sign
    To Mortals of their fate and force;
Like thee, Man is in part divine,
    A troubled stream from a pure source;
And Man in portions can foresee
50 His own funereal destiny;
His wretchedness, and his resistance,
And his sad unallied existence:
To which his Spirit may oppose
Itself—an equal to all woes,
55   And a firm will, and a deep sense,
Which even in torture can descry
    Its own concentered recompense,
Triumphant where it dares defy,
And making Death a Victory.
    —1816

So, we'll go no more a roving[1]

1

So, we'll go no more a roving
    So late into the night,

Though the heart be still as loving,
    And the moon be still as bright.

2

5 For the sword outwears its sheath,
    And the soul wears out the breast,
And the heart must pause to breathe,
    And love itself have rest.

3

Though the night was made for loving,
10   And the day returns too soon,
Yet we'll go no more a roving
    By the light of the moon.
    —1817

When a man hath no freedom to fight for at home[2]

When a man hath no freedom to fight for at home,
    Let him combat for that of his neighbors;
Let him think of the glories of Greece and of Rome,
    And get knock'd on the head for his labours.

5 To do good to mankind is the chivalrous plan,
    And is always as nobly requited;
Then battle for freedom wherever you can,
    And, if not shot or hang'd, you'll get knighted.
    —1820

---

[1] *When ... home*   Originally written as part of a letter from Byron to his friend Thomas Moore, 28 February 1817. Just before these lines Byron writes, "The Carnival ... knocked me up a little. But it is over—and it is now Lent, with all its abstinence and sacred music. The mumming closed with a masked ball ... and, though I did not dissipate much upon the whole, yet I find 'the sword wearing out the scabbard', though I have but just turned the corner of twenty-nine."

[2] *When a man ... home*   Byron first sent these lines in a letter to his friend Thomas Moore on 5 November 1820. They are based on Byron's activities with the Italian freedom-fighters, the Carbonari, and their abortive attempt to stage an uprising.

January 22nd 1842.
Missolonghi
On this day I complete my thirty sixth year[1]

1

'Tis time this heart should be unmoved
　　Since others it hath ceased to move,
Yet though I cannot be beloved
　　Still let me love.

2

5　My days are in the yellow leaf[2]
　　The flowers and fruits of love are gone—
The worm—the canker, and the grief
　　Are mine alone.

3

The fire that on my bosom preys
10　Is lone as some Volcanic Isle,
No torch is kindled at its blaze
　　A funeral pile!

4

The hope, the fear, the jealous care
　　The exalted portion of the pain
15 And power of Love I cannot share
　　But wear the chain.

5

But 'tis not *thus*—and 'tis not *here*
　　Such thoughts should shake my soul, nor *now*

(continued)

Where Glory decks the hero's bier
20　　Or binds his brow.

6

The Sword—the Banner—and the Field
　　Glory and Greece around us see!
The Spartan borne upon his shield[3]
　　Was not more free!

7

25 Awake! (not Greece—She *is* awake!)
　　Awake my spirit—think through *whom*
Thy life-blood tracks its parent lake
　　And then strike home!

8

Tread those reviving passions down
30　Unworthy Manhood;—unto thee
Indifferent should the smile or frown
　　Of Beauty be.

9

If thou regret'st thy youth, why *live?*
　　The land of honourable Death
35 Is here—up to the Field! and give
　　Away thy Breath.

10

Seek out—less often sought than found,
　　A Soldier's Grave—for thee the best,
Then look around and choose thy ground
40　　And take thy Rest.
—1824

Epistle to Augusta[4]

1

My Sister—my sweet Sister—if a name
　　Dearer and purer were—it should be thine.
Mountains and seas divide us—but I claim

[1] *On this ... year* This poem was until recently most commonly known by its subtitle, but the date and place are the correct title. Byron wrote it on his 36th birthday, in Greece. A companion who was with him at the time says, "January 22.—Lord Byron came from his bedroom into the apartment ... where some friends were assembled, and said, with a smile, 'You were complaining, the other day, that I never write any poetry now:—this is my birthday, and I have just finished something which, I think, is better than what I usually write.'" The poem is informed by Byron's relationship with two people, his young Greek companion of the time, Loukas Chalandritsanos, and a Turkish girl, Hataje, whom he had taken into his care. Byron's feelings for Chalandritsanos are commonly understood to be the stronger influence of the two.

[2] *My days ... leaf* See *Macbeth* 5.3.21–22.

[3] [Byron's note] The slain were borne on their shields—witness the Spartan mother's speech to her son, delivered with his buckler—"Either *with* this or *on* this."

[4] *Augusta* Byron's sister, Augusta Leigh (1783–1857).

No tears, but tenderness to answer mine:
5   Go where I will, to me thou art the same—
        A loved regret which I would not resign—
There yet are two things in my destiny
A world to roam through—and a home with thee.

                    2

The first were nothing—had I still the last
10   It were the haven of my happiness—
But other claims and other ties thou hast—
        And mine is not the wish to make them less.
A strange doom is thy father's son's and past
        Recalling—as it lies beyond redress—
15   Reversed for him our grandsire's fate of yore
He had no rest at sea—nor I on shore.[1]

                    3

If my inheritance of storms hath been
        In other elements—and on the rocks
Of perils overlooked or unforeseen
20   I have sustained my share of worldly shocks
The fault was mine—nor do I seek to screen
        My errors with defensive paradox—
I have been cunning in mine overthrow
The careful pilot of my proper woe.

                    4

25   Mine were my faults—and mine be their reward—
        My whole life was a contest—since the day
That gave me being gave me that which marred
        The gift—a fate, or will that walked astray—
And I at times have found the struggle hard
30   And thought of shaking off my bonds of clay—
But now I fain would for a time survive
If but to see what next can well arrive.

                    5

Kingdoms and empires in my little day
        I have outlived, and yet I am not old—
35   And when I look on this, the petty spray
        Of my own years of trouble, which have rolled
Like a wild bay of breakers, melts away:—

Something—I know not what—does still uphold
A spirit of slight patience;—not in vain,
40   Even for its own sake—do we purchase pain.

                    6

Perhaps—the workings of defiance stir
        Within me, or perhaps a cold despair—
Brought on when ills habitually recur,—
        Perhaps a kinder clime—or purer air—
45   For even to this may change of soul refer—
        And with light armour we may learn to bear—
Have taught me a strange quiet which was not
        The chief companion of a calmer lot.

                    7

I feel almost at times as I have felt
50   In happy childhood—trees, and flowers, and brooks
Which do remember me of where I dwelt
        Ere my young mind was sacrificed to books—
Come as of yore upon me—and can melt
        My heart with recognition of their looks—
55   And even at moments I could think I see
Some living thing to love—but none like thee.

                    8

Here are the Alpine landscapes—which create
        A fund for contemplation;—to admire
Is a brief feeling of a trivial date—
60   But something worthier do such scenes inspire:
Here to be lonely is not desolate—
        For much I view which I could most desire—
And, above all a Lake I can behold—
Lovelier—not dearer than our own of old.

                    9

65   Oh that thou wert but with me!—but I grow
        The fool of my own wishes—and forget
The solitude which I have vaunted so
        Has lost its praise in this but one regret—
There may be others which I less may show—
70   I am not of the plaintive mood—and yet
I feel an ebb in my philosophy
And the tide rising in my altered eye.

----

[1] *He had no ... on shore* Byron and Augusta's grandfather, Admiral
John Byron, was renowned for never making a sea voyage without
encountering a storm. He was known as "Foulweather Jack."

10

I did remind thee of our own dear lake
    By the old Hall which may be mine no more—
75 Leman's is fair—but think not I forsake
    The sweet remembrance of a dearer shore—
Sad havoc Time must with my memory make
    Ere that or thou can fade these eyes before—
Though like all things which I have loved—they are
80 Resigned for ever—or divided far.

11

The world is all before me—I but ask
    Of Nature that with which she will comply—
It is but in her Summer's sun to bask—
    To mingle with the quiet of her sky—
85 To see her gentle face without a mask
    And never gaze on it with apathy—
She was my early friend—and now shall be
My Sister—till I look again on thee.

12

I can reduce all feelings but this one,
90   And that I would not—for at length I see
Such scenes as those wherein my life begun
    The earliest—were the only paths for me.
Had I but sooner learnt the crowd to shun
    I had been better than I now can be
95 The passions which have torn me would have slept—
I had not suffered—and *thou* hadst not wept.

13

With false Ambition what had I to do?
    Little with love, and least of all with fame!
And yet they came unsought and with me grew,
100   And made me all which they can make—a Name.
Yet this was not the end I did pursue—

Surely I once beheld a nobler aim.
But all is over—I am one the more
    To baffled millions which have gone before.

14

105 And for the future—this world's future may
    From me demand but little from my care;
I have outlived myself by many a day,
    Having survived so many things that were—
My years have been no slumber—but the prey
110   Of ceaseless vigils;—for I had the share
Of life which might have filled a century
Before its fourth in time had passed me by.

15

And for the remnants which may be to come
    I am content—and for the past I feel
115 Not thankless—for within the crowded sum
    Of struggles—happiness at times would steal
And for the present—I would not benumb
    My feelings farther—nor shall I conceal
That with all this I still can look around
120 And worship Nature with a thought profound.

16

For thee—my own sweet Sister—in thy heart
    I know myself secure—as thou in mine
We were and are—I am—even as thou art—
    Beings who ne'er each other can resign
125 It is the same together or apart
    From Life's commencement to its slow decline—
We are entwined—let death come slow or fast
The tie which bound the first endures the last.
    —1830

JOHN KEATS
1795 – 1821

John Keats has come to epitomize the popular conception of the Romantic poet as a passionate dreamer whose intense, sensuous poetry celebrates the world of the imagination over that of everyday life. Keats published only 54 poems in his short lifetime, but his work ranges across a number of poetic genres, including sonnets, odes, romances, and epics. In each of these genres his poetry seeks beauty and truth that will transcend the world of suffering, always questioning its own process of interpretation.

The eldest of four children, John Keats was born in London on 31 October 1795. He lost both his parents by the time he was fourteen—his father in a riding accident and his mother of tuberculosis (then commonly known as consumption). After his mother's death, Keats came under the care of two guardians. He continued to attend Enfield School, a liberal institution where he first became acquainted with Leigh Hunt's radical paper *The Examiner*, and where his interest in poetry grew, particularly after reading the poetry of Edmund Spenser. Keats's friend Charles Brown said it was *The Faerie Queene* that awakened Keats's talent for expressing the "acute sense of beauty" he possessed.

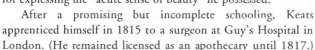

After a promising but incomplete schooling, Keats apprenticed himself in 1815 to a surgeon at Guy's Hospital in London. (He remained licensed as an apothecary until 1817.) Having befriended some of the most prolific artists and critics of his day, among them radical publisher Leigh Hunt, essayist Charles Lamb, painter Benjamin Haydon, and poets John Hamilton Reynolds and Percy Shelley (later to eulogize Keats in *Adonais*), Keats was spurred to further develop his own creative abilities. In 1816, after spending a night reading a translation of Homer with his school friend Cowden Clarke, Keats wrote "On First Looking Into Chapman's Homer" (1816), a sonnet that presents a poet reflecting on poetic tradition and discovering his talent, as an explorer surveys "with a wild surmise" another ocean of possibility.

Shortly thereafter, Keats composed "Sleep and Poetry" (1817), a poetic manifesto of sorts in which he proclaims his devotion to a new type of poetry, one in the style of Wordsworth, devoted to nature and the human heart. By aligning himself with Wordsworth's naturalism, Keats ensured the condemnation of critics; nevertheless, that same year he chose to give up surgery and devote himself entirely to poetry. This decision was most likely sealed by Leigh Hunt's first "Young Poets" article (*Examiner*, December 1816), in which he identified Keats, Shelley, and Reynolds as the leaders of a new generation of poets.

Keats's first volume, *Poems* (1817), received little critical attention. The following year he published the long and ambitious romance *Endymion* (1818), about a shepherd-prince who pursues his elusive feminine ideal. The book was sharply criticized in a famous review published in the *Quarterly Review*, where Keats and his friend Hunt were ridiculed as representing "the Cockney school of poetry." Keats endured further criticism when he read "Hymn to Pan" from *Endymion* to the contemporary poet he most admired, Wordsworth; the elder poet ungenerously dismissed it as "a very pretty piece of paganism."

His hopes undimmed, Keats continued to pursue his poetic ideals. In a series of now-famous letters to Benjamin Bailey, he explored his aesthetic ideas and sought to define the purpose of literature for modern life. Keats's letters to his friends and family are justly acclaimed for their intuitions about life, suffering, and poetry. To Keats we owe the concepts of "negative capability," the "chameleon poet," and "the vale of Soul-making." He particularly admired what he saw as Shakespeare's chameleon-like ability to escape from his personality and enter fully into the being of his characters.

During this time, Keats fell in love with the lively and flirtatious Fanny Brawne, who became a kind of muse. Though they became engaged, Keats wanted to gain financial security before marrying. He had begun as well to be haunted by fears of his own early death. (Throat ulcers that had appeared during a walking tour in poor weather the previous summer had become chronic.) It was in this set of tumultuous emotional circumstances that Keats began one of the most extraordinary periods of creativity in the history of English literature. Between January and September of 1819 he composed all seven of his "great Odes"—"Ode to Psyche," "Ode to a Nightingale," "Ode on a Grecian Urn," "Ode on Indolence," "Ode on Melancholy," and "To Autumn"—as well as "The Eve of St. Agnes," "La Belle Dame sans Merci," "Lamia," and a number of sonnets. "The Eve of St. Agnes" remains Keats's best-known narrative poem. Suffused with amorous feeling and lush imagery, "The Eve of St. Agnes" recounts a romantic story with affinities to the story of Romeo and Juliet. Generations of readers have been seduced by the sensuous immediacy of this poetry.

Keats's largest poetic project was *Hyperion*, a blank-verse epic on Jupiter's dethroning of Saturn and Apollo's overthrow of Hyperion. An intense study of cultural loss, the poem is a self-consciously Miltonic exercise that Keats kept returning to but never completed. He began the poem in the autumn of 1818, but put the manuscript aside in April of the following year. (This first fragmentary version of the poem was published as "Hyperion: A Fragment" in the 1820 volume of his verse.)

In the summer he resumed work on the project, this time casting the story within the frame of a poet's dream vision, but he stopped for a second time in September. (This second version, also fragmentary, was finally published in 1856 as "The Fall of Hyperion.")

As Keats's extraordinary poetic outpouring of 1819 was coming to a close, he began to suspect himself inadequate to the task of undertaking a Miltonic epic. As he wrote to a friend John Reynolds on 21 September 1819:

> I have given up Hyperion … Miltonic verse cannot be written but in an artful or rather artist's humour. I wish to give myself up to other sensations. English ought to be kept up.

Keats wrote little after September of 1819, but he published his third volume of poetry, *Lamia, Isabella, The Eve of St. Agnes, and Other Poems*, in 1820—defiantly advertising himself on the cover as "the author of *Endymion*." Critics were gradually acquiring a taste for Keats's work, but by this time Keats was very ill, having contracted tuberculosis. His lungs weakened and his throat still ulcerating, Keats in August of 1820 declined an invitation to join Shelley and his circle in Pisa, and instead went to Rome, where he died in the house at the base of the Spanish Steps that is now the Keats-Shelley Memorial House. Keats was buried in the Protestant Cemetery in Rome.

In the generations since his death many have wondered what Keats would have accomplished had he lived. Such thoughts, however, focus on the tragedy of the poet's death, rather than on the sustained richness of his achievement. Before his death, Keats asked that his epitaph be "Here lies one whose name was writ in water." (Though his friends complied, they added above, "This Grave contains all that was Mortal of a YOUNG ENGLISH POET, Who on his Death Bed in the Bitterness of his Heart at the Malicious Power of his Enemies, Desired these Words to be incised on his Tomb Stone.") On visiting his gravesite in 1877, Oscar Wilde supplied another epitaph: "A Priest of Beauty slain before his time." But the last sentences of Keats's last letter to Charles Brown are perhaps more evocative: "I can scarcely bid you good bye even in a letter. I always made an awkward bow."

⌘ ⌘ ⌘

⌘⌘⌘

On First Looking into Chapman's Homer[1]

Much have I travell'd in the realms of gold,
  And many goodly states and kingdoms seen;
    Round many western islands have I been
Which bards in fealty to Apollo[2] hold.
Oft of one wide expanse had I been told
    That deep-brow'd Homer ruled as his demesne;
    Yet never did I breathe its pure serene,
Till I heard Chapman speak out loud and bold:
Then felt I like some watcher of the skies
    When a new planet swims into his ken;[3]
Or like stout Cortez[4] when with eagle eyes
    He star'd at the Pacific—and all his men
Look'd at each other with a wild surmise—
    Silent, upon a peak in Darien.
          —1816

On the Grasshopper and Cricket

The poetry of earth is never dead:
  When all the birds are faint with the hot sun,
  And hide in cooling trees, a voice will run
From hedge to hedge about the new-mown mead;
That is the Grasshopper's—he takes the lead
    In summer luxury—he has never done
    With his delights; for when tired out with fun

He rests at ease beneath some pleasant weed.
The poetry of earth is ceasing never:
    On a lone winter evening, when the frost
    Has wrought a silence, from the stove there shrills
The Cricket's song, in warmth increasing ever,
    And seems to one in drowsiness half lost,
    The Grasshopper's among some grassy hills.
          —1817

Sleep and Poetry

As I lay in my bed slepe full unmete°   *unallotted*
Was unto me, but why that I ne might
Rest I ne wist,° for there n'as° erthly   *knew / was no*
    wight°   *creature*
[As I suppose] had more of hertis ese°   *heart's ease*
Than I, for I n'ad° sicknesse nor disese.[5]   *had not*
                    CHAUCER

What is more gentle than a wind in summer?
  What is more soothing than the pretty hummer
That stays one moment in an open flower,
And buzzes cheerily from bower to bower?
What is more tranquil than a musk-rose
    blowing°   *blossoming*
In a green island, far from all men's knowing?
More healthful than the leafiness of dales?
More secret than a nest of nightingales?
More serene than Cordelia's[6] countenance?
More full of visions than a high romance?
What, but thee Sleep? Soft closer of our eyes!
Low murmurer of tender lullabies!
Light hoverer around our happy pillows!
Wreather of poppy buds, and weeping willows!

---

[1] *On ... Homer* Written in October 1816, on the morning after Keats and his friend and mentor Charles Cowden Clarke had stayed up all night reading the 1614 translation of Homer by George Chapman (1559–1634).

[2] *Apollo* Greek god of poetry.

[3] *a new ... ken* William Herschel had discovered Uranus in 1781.

[4] *Cortez* The first European to see the Pacific (from the Isthmus of Darien in Panama) was not actually Hernán Cortez (1485–1547), the conqueror of Mexico, but Vasco Nuñez de Balboa in 1513 (1475–1519).

[5] *As ... disese* From *The Floure and the Leafe* 17–21, which was then thought to have been written by Chaucer.

[6] *Cordelia* Daughter of King Lear in Shakespeare's *King Lear*.

15   Silent entangler of a beauty's tresses!
     Most happy listener! when the morning blesses
     Thee for enlivening all the cheerful eyes
     That glance so brightly at the new sun-rise.

     But what is higher beyond thought than thee?
20   Fresher than berries of a mountain tree?
     More strange, more beautiful, more smooth, more
        regal,
     Than wings of swans, than doves, than dim-seen eagle?
     What is it? And to what shall I compare it?
     It has a glory, and naught else can share it:
25   The thought thereof is awful, sweet, and holy,
     Chasing away all worldliness and folly;
     Coming sometimes like fearful claps of thunder,
     Or the low rumblings earth's regions under;
     And sometimes like a gentle whispering
30   Of all the secrets of some wond'rous thing
     That breathes about us in the vacant air;
     So that we look around with prying stare,
     Perhaps to see shapes of light, aërial limning,[1]
     And catch soft floatings from a faint-heard hymning;
35   To see the laurel wreath,[2] on high suspended,
     That is to crown our name when life is ended.
     Sometimes it gives a glory to the voice,
     And from the heart up-springs, "Rejoice! rejoice!"
     Sounds which will reach the Framer of all things,
40   And die away in ardent mutterings.

     No one who once the glorious sun has seen,
     And all the clouds, and felt his bosom clean
     For his great Maker's presence, but must know
     What 'tis I mean, and feel his being glow:
45   Therefore no insult will I give his spirit,
     By telling what he sees from native merit.

     O Poesy! For thee I hold my pen
     That am not yet a glorious denizen
     Of thy wide heaven—Should I rather kneel
50   Upon some mountain-top until I feel

     A glowing splendour round about me hung,
     And echo back the voice of thine own tongue?
     O Poesy! For thee I grasp my pen
     That am not yet a glorious denizen
55   Of thy wide heaven; yet, to my ardent prayer,
     Yield from thy sanctuary some clear air,
     Smoothed for intoxication by the breath
     Of flowering bays, that I may die a death
     Of luxury, and my young spirit follow
60   The morning sun-beams to the great Apollo[3]
     Like a fresh sacrifice; or, if I can bear
     The o'erwhelming sweets, 'twill bring to me the fair
     Visions of all places: a bowery nook
     Will be elysium[4]—an eternal book
65   Whence I may copy many a lovely saying
     About the leaves, and flowers—about the playing
     Of nymphs in woods, and fountains; and the shade
     Keeping a silence round a sleeping maid;
     And many a verse from so strange influence
70   That we must ever wonder how, and whence
     It came. Also imaginings will hover
     Round my fire-side, and haply there discover
     Vistas of solemn beauty, where I'd wander
     In happy silence, like the clear Meander[5]
75   Through its lone vales; and where I found a spot
     Of awfuller shade, or an enchanted grot,°   *grotto*
     Or a green hill o'erspread with chequered dress
     Of flowers, and fearful from its loveliness,
     Write on my tablets all that was permitted,
80   All that was for our human senses fitted.
     Then the events of this wide world I'd seize
     Like a strong giant, and my spirit tease
     Till at its shoulders it should proudly see
     Wings to find out an immortality.

85   Stop and consider! Life is but a day;
     A fragile dew-drop on its perilous way
     From a tree's summit; a poor Indian's sleep
     While his boat hastens to the monstrous steep

---

[1] *limning* Painting.

[2] *laurel wreath* Wreaths made of leaves of the bay laurel were traditionally bestowed upon those who distinguished themselves in poetry.

[3] *Apollo* Greek god of poetry.

[4] *elysium* State of perfect happiness. From the Elysium of Greek mythology, the place where the blessed reside after death.

[5] *Meander* Winding river in Asia Minor.

Of Montmorenci.¹ Why so sad a moan?
90 Life is the rose's hope while yet unblown;
The reading of an ever-changing tale;
The light uplifting of a maiden's veil;
A pigeon tumbling in clear summer air;
A laughing school-boy, without grief or care,
95 Riding the springy branches of an elm.

O for ten years, that I may overwhelm
Myself in poesy; so I may do the deed
That my own soul has to itself decreed.
Then will I pass the countries that I see
100 In long perspective, and continually
Taste their pure fountains. First the realm I'll pass
Of Flora, and old Pan:² sleep in the grass,
Feed upon apples red, and strawberries,
And choose each pleasure that my fancy sees;
105 Catch the white-handed nymphs in shady places,
To woo sweet kisses from averted faces,
Play with their fingers, touch their shoulders white
Into a pretty shrinking with a bite
As hard as lips can make it: till agreed,
110 A lovely tale of human life we'll read
And one will teach a tame dove how it best
May fan the cool air gently o'er my rest;
Another, bending o'er her nimble tread,
Will set a green robe floating round her head,
115 And still will dance with ever varied ease,
Smiling upon the flowers and the trees:
Another will entice me on, and on
Through almond blossoms and rich cinnamon;
Till in the bosom of a leafy world
120 We rest in silence, like two gems upcurl'd
In the recesses of a pearly shell.

And can I ever bid these joys farewell?
Yes, I must pass them for a nobler life,
Where I may find the agonies, the strife
125 Of human hearts: for lo! I see afar,

O'er sailing the blue cragginess, a car°   chariot
And steeds with streamy manes—the charioteer
Looks out upon the winds with glorious fear:
And now the numerous tramplings quiver lightly
130 Along a huge cloud's ridge; and now with sprightly
Wheel downward come they into fresher skies,
Tipt round with silver from the sun's bright eyes.
Still downward with capacious whirl they glide,
And now I see them on the green-hill's side
135 In breezy rest among the nodding stalks.
The charioteer with wond'rous gesture talks
To the trees and mountains; and there soon appear
Shapes of delight, of mystery, and fear,
Passing along before a dusky space
140 Made by some mighty oaks: as they would chase
Some ever-fleeting music on they sweep.
Lo! how they murmur, laugh, and smile, and weep:
Some with upholden hand and mouth severe;
Some with their faces muffled to the ear
145 Between their arms; some, clear in youthful bloom,
Go glad and smilingly athwart the gloom;
Some looking back, and some with upward gaze;
Yes, thousands in a thousand different ways
Flit onward—now a lovely wreath of girls
150 Dancing their sleek hair into tangled curls;
And now broad wings. Most awfully intent
The driver of those steeds is forward bent,
And seems to listen: O that I might know
All that he writes with such a hurrying glow.

155 The visions all are fled—the car is fled
Into the light of heaven, and in their stead
A sense of real things comes doubly strong,
And, like a muddy stream, would bear along
My soul to nothingness: but I will strive
160 Against all doubtings, and will keep alive
The thought of that same chariot, and the strange
Journey it went.

Is there so small a range
In the present strength of manhood, that the high
165 Imagination cannot freely fly
As she was wont of old? prepare her steeds,
Paw up against the light, and do strange deeds
Upon the clouds? Has she not shown us all?

---

¹ *Montmorenci* Montmorency Falls near Québec City, Canada.

² *Flora ... Pan* In Greek mythology, the goddess of flowers and the shepherd god of nature, respectively. The realm of Flora and Pan is that of pastoral poesy, which, according to Virgil, should be the genre with which the aspiring poet begins, eventually working his way up to the epic.

From the clear space of ether, to the small
170 Breath of new buds unfolding? From the meaning
Of Jove's[1] large eyebrow, to the tender greening
Of April meadows? Here her altar shone,
E'en in this isle; and who could paragon
The fervid choir that lifted up a noise
175 Of harmony, to where it aye will poise
Its mighty self of convoluting sound,
Huge as a planet, and like that roll round,
Eternally around a dizzy void?
Ay, in those days the Muses[2] were nigh cloy'd
180 With honours; nor had any other care
Than to sing out and sooth their wavy hair.

Could all this be forgotten? Yes, a schism
Nurtured by foppery and barbarism,
Made great Apollo blush for this his land.
185 Men were thought wise who could not understand
His glories: with a puling infant's force
They sway'd about upon a rocking horse,
And thought it Pegasus.[3] Ah dismal soul'd!
The winds of heaven blew, the ocean roll'd
190 Its gathering waves—ye felt it not. The blue
Bared its eternal bosom, and the dew
Of summer nights collected still to make
The morning precious: beauty was awake!
Why were ye not awake? But ye were dead
195 To things ye knew not of—were closely wed
To musty laws lined out with wretched rule
And compass vile: so that ye taught a school
Of dolts to smooth, inlay, and clip, and fit,
Till, like the certain wands of Jacob's wit,[4]
200 Their verses tallied. Easy was the task:
A thousand handicraftsmen wore the mask
Of Poesy. Ill-fated, impious race!

That blasphemed the bright Lyrist[5] to his face,
And did not know it—no, they went about,
205 Holding a poor, decrepit standard out
Mark'd with most flimsy mottos, and in large
The name of one Boileau![6]

                    O ye whose charge
It is to hover round our pleasant hills!
210 Whose congregated majesty so fills
My boundly[7] reverence, that I cannot trace
Your hallowed names, in this unholy place,
So near those common folk; did not their shames
Affright you? Did our old lamenting Thames°   river
215 Delight you? Did ye never cluster round
Delicious Avon,° with a mournful sound,   river
And weep? Or did ye wholly bid adieu
To regions where no more the laurel grew?
Or did ye stay to give a welcoming
220 To some lone spirits[8] who could proudly sing
Their youth away, and die? 'Twas even so:
But let me think away those times of woe:
Now 'tis a fairer season; ye have breathed
Rich benedictions o'er us; ye have wreathed
225 Fresh garlands: for sweet music has been heard
In many places—some has been upstirr'd
From out its crystal dwelling in a lake,
By a swan's ebon bill;[9] from a thick brake,°   thicket
Nested and quiet in a valley mild,
230 Bubbles a pipe;[10] fine sounds are floating wild
About the earth: happy are ye and glad.

---

[1] *Jove* Roman king of the gods.

[2] *Muses* In Greek mythology, nine daughters of Zeus and Mnemosyne, each of whom presided over and provided inspiration for an aspect of learning or the arts.

[3] *Pegasus* Great winged horse of Greek mythology. This line is a reference to William Hazlitt's essay "On Milton's Versification" (1815), in which he says, on the use of the heroic couplet by eighteenth-century poets, "Dr. Johnson and Pope would have turned [Milton's] vaulting Pegasus into a rocking-horse."

[4] *Jacob's wit* See Genesis 30.27–43, in which Jacob increases his wealth at the expense of Laban.

[5] *the bright Lyrist* I.e., Apollo.

[6] *Boileau* French literary critic Nicolas Boileau Despréaux (1636–1711), whose *L'Art Poétique* (1674), a verse treatise on literary aesthetics, was extremely influential among English poets.

[7] *boundly* Term coined by Keats, meaning either "boundless" or "bounden."

[8] *some lone spirits* Reference to poets Thomas Chatterton (1752–70), Henry White (1785–1806), and others, who died young, without receiving the critical attention their work deserved.

[9] *swan's ebon bill* Reference to William Wordsworth (1770–1850), who, along with Coleridge and Southey, was known as a "Lake Poet."

[10] *from a ... pipe* Reference to poet Leigh Hunt (1784–1859).

These things are doubtless: yet in truth we've had
Strange thunders from the potency of song;
Mingled indeed with what is sweet and strong,
235 From majesty: but in clear truth the themes
Are ugly clubs, the poets Polyphemes[1]
Disturbing the grand sea. A drainless shower
Of light is poesy; 'tis the supreme of power;
'Tis might half slumb'ring on its own right arm.
240 The very archings of her eye-lids charm
A thousand willing agents to obey,
And still she governs with the mildest sway:
But strength alone though of the Muses born
Is like a fallen angel: trees uptorn,
245 Darkness, and worms, and shrouds, and sepulchres
Delight it; for it feeds upon the burrs,
And thorns of life; forgetting the great end
Of poesy, that it should be a friend
To sooth the cares, and lift the thoughts of man.

250   Yet I rejoice: a myrtle fairer than
E'er grew in Paphos,[2] from the bitter weeds
Lifts its sweet head into the air, and feeds
A silent space with ever sprouting green.
All tenderest birds there find a pleasant screen,
255 Creep through the shade with jaunty fluttering,
Nibble the little cupped flowers and sing.
Then let us clear away the choking thorns
From round its gentle stem; let the young fawns,
Yeaned° in after times, when we are flown,   *brought forth*
260 Find a fresh sward° beneath it, overgrown   *turf*
With simple flowers: let there nothing be
More boisterous than a lover's bended knee;
Nought more ungentle than the placid look
Of one who leans upon a closed book;
265 Nought more untranquil than the grassy slopes
Between two hills. All hail delightful hopes!
As she was wont, th'imagination
Into most lovely labyrinths will be gone,
And they shall be accounted poet kings
270 Who simply tell the most heart-easing things.
O may these joys be ripe before I die.

Will not some say that I presumptuously
Have spoken? that from hastening disgrace
'Twere better far to hide my foolish face?
275 That whining boyhood should with reverence bow
Ere the dread thunderbolt could reach? How!
If I do hide myself, it sure shall be
In the very fane, the light of Poesy:
If I do fall, at least I will be laid
280 Beneath the silence of a poplar shade;
And over me the grass shall be smooth shaven;
And there shall be a kind memorial graven.
But off Despondence! miserable bane!
They should not know thee, who athirst to gain
285 A noble end, are thirsty every hour.
What though I am not wealthy in the dower
Of spanning wisdom; though I do not know
The shiftings of the mighty winds that blow
Hither and thither all the changing thoughts
290 Of man: though no great minist'ring reason sorts
Out the dark mysteries of human souls
To clear conceiving: yet there ever rolls
A vast idea before me, and I glean
Therefrom my liberty; thence too I've seen
295 The end and aim of Poesy. 'Tis clear
As any thing most true; as that the year
Is made of the four seasons—manifest
As a large cross, some old cathedral's crest,
Lifted to the white clouds. Therefore should I
300 Be but the essence of deformity,
A coward, did my very eyelids wink
At speaking out what I have dared to think.
Ah! rather let me like a madman run
Over some precipice; let the hot sun
305 Melt my Dedalian wings,[3] and drive me down
Convuls'd and headlong! Stay! an inward frown
Of conscience bids me be more calm awhile.
An ocean dim, sprinkled with many an isle,
Spreads awfully before me. How much toil!
310 How many days! what desperate turmoil!
Ere I can have explored its widenesses.

---

[1] *Polyphemes* One-eyed, club-wielding giant in Homer's *Odyssey*.

[2] *Paphos* City in Cyprus that is the site of a famous temple to Venus, goddess of love and beauty. Myrtle (line 248) is also associated with Venus.

[3] *Dedalian wings* According to Greek mythology, the sculptor Daedalus built wings of wax and feathers so that he and his son Icarus could escape from the island of Crete, where they were imprisoned. Icarus flew too close to the sun, and his wings melted, causing him to fall into the sea.

Ah, what a task! upon my bended knees,
I could unsay those—no, impossible!
Impossible!

315   For sweet relief I'll dwell
On humbler thoughts, and let this strange assay
Begun in gentleness die so away.
E'en now all tumult from my bosom fades:
I turn full hearted to the friendly aids
320 That smooth the path of honour; brotherhood,
And friendliness the nurse of mutual good.
The hearty grasp that sends a pleasant sonnet
Into the brain ere one can think upon it;
The silence when some rhymes are coming out;
325 And when they're come, the very pleasant rout:
The message certain to be done to-morrow.
'Tis perhaps as well that it should be to borrow
Some precious book from out its snug retreat,
To cluster round it when we next shall meet.
330 Scarce can I scribble on; for lovely airs
Are fluttering round the room like doves in pairs;
Many delights of that glad day recalling,
When first my senses caught their tender falling.
And with these airs come forms of elegance
335 Stooping their shoulders o'er a horse's prance,
Careless, and grand—fingers soft and round
Parting luxuriant curls—and the swift bound
Of Bacchus from his chariot, when his eye
Made Ariadne's cheek look blushingly.[1]
340 Thus I remember all the pleasant flow
Of words at opening a portfolio.

Things such as these are ever harbingers
To trains of peaceful images: the stirs
Of a swan's neck unseen among the rushes:
345 A linnet starting all about the bushes:
A butterfly, with golden wings broad parted,
Nestling a rose, convuls'd as though it smarted
With over pleasure—many, many more,
Might I indulge at large in all my store

350 Of luxuries: yet I must not forget
Sleep, quiet with his poppy coronet:[2]
For what there may be worthy in these rhymes
I partly owe to him: and thus, the chimes
Of friendly voices had just given place
355 To as sweet a silence, when I 'gan retrace
The pleasant day, upon a couch at ease.
It was a poet's house who keeps the keys
Of pleasure's temple.[3] Round about were hung
The glorious features of the bards who sung
360 In other ages—cold and sacred busts
Smiled at each other. Happy he who trusts
To clear Futurity his darling fame!
Then there were fauns and satyrs taking aim
At swelling apples with a frisky leap
365 And reaching fingers, 'mid a luscious heap
Of vine leaves. Then there rose to view a fane°   *temple*
Of liny° marble, and thereto a train   *veined*
Of nymphs approaching fairly o'er the sward:
One, loveliest, holding her white hand toward
370 The dazzling sun-rise: two sisters sweet
Bending their graceful figures till they meet
Over the trippings of a little child:
And some are hearing, eagerly, the wild
Thrilling liquidity of dewy piping.
375 See, in another picture, nymphs are wiping
Cherishingly Diana's[4] timorous limbs;
A fold of lawny mantle dabbling swims
At the bath's edge, and keeps a gentle motion
With the subsiding crystal: as when ocean
380 Heaves calmly its broad swelling smoothness o'er
Its rocky marge, and balances once more
The patient weeds; that now unshent°   *unharmed*
     by foam
Feel all about their undulating home.

Sappho's[5] meek head was there half smiling down
385 At nothing; just as though the earnest frown

---

[1] *Of Bacchus ... blushingly* Adriane, daughter of King Minos of Crete, was abandoned by her lover, Theseus, on the island of Naxos. Bacchus, god of wine, found her there, consoled her, and married her (Ovid, *Metamorphses* 8.172–82). Keats would also have been familiar with the painting *Bacchus and Ariadne* (1523) by Venetian painter Titian (1490–1576).

[2] *poppy coronet* The seed capsules of some species of poppy contain opium, and therefore were associated with sleep.

[3] *It was ... temple* Poet Leigh Hunt kept a bed for Keats in his study. Hunt's cottage was filled with busts and pictures, on which the following descriptions are probably based.

[4] *Diana* Roman goddess of chastity, childbirth, and the hunt.

[5] *Sappho* Greek lyric poet of the sixth century BCE.

Of over thinking had that moment gone
From off her brow, and left her all alone.

Great Alfred's[1] too, with anxious, pitying eyes,
As if he always listened to the sighs
390 Of the goaded world; and Kosciusko's[2] worn
By horrid suffrance—mightily forlorn.

Petrarch, outstepping from the shady green,
Starts at the sight of Laura;[3] nor can wean
His eyes from her sweet face. Most happy they!
395 For over them was seen a free display
Of out-spread wings, and from between them shone
The face of Poesy: from off her throne
She overlook'd things that I scarce could tell.
The very sense of where I was might well
400 Keep Sleep aloof: but more than that there came
Thought after thought to nourish up the flame
Within my breast; so that the morning light
Surprised me even from a sleepless night;
And up I rose refresh'd, and glad, and gay,
405 Resolving to begin that very day
These lines; and howsoever they be done,
I leave them as a father does his son.
—1817

On Seeing the Elgin Marbles[4]

My spirit is too weak; mortality
Weighs heavily on me like unwilling sleep,
And each imagined pinnacle and steep
Of godlike hardship, tells me I must die
5 Like a sick Eagle looking at the sky.

Yet 'tis a gentle luxury to weep,
That I have not the cloudy winds to keep
Fresh for the opening of the morning's eye.
Such dim-conceived glories of the brain
10 Bring round the heart an indescribable feud;
So do these wonders a most dizzy pain,
That mingles Grecian grandeur with the rude
Wasting of old Time—with a billowy main,°   sea
A sun, a shadow of a magnitude.
—1817

On Sitting Down to Read
King Lear Once Again

O golden tongued Romance, with serene lute!
Fair plumed Syren![5] Queen of far-away!
Leave melodizing on this wintry day,
Shut up thine olden pages, and be mute:
5 Adieu! for once again the fierce dispute
Betwixt damnation and impassion'd clay
Must I burn through; once more humbly assay
The bitter-sweet of this Shakespearian fruit.
Chief Poet! and ye clouds of Albion,[6]
10 Begetters of our deep eternal theme,
When through the old oak forest I am gone,
Let me not wander in a barren dream,
But when I am consumed in the fire,
Give me new Phœnix[7] wings to fly at my desire.
—1838

When I Have Fears that I May Cease to Be

When I have fears that I may cease to be
Before my pen has glean'd my teeming brain,
Before high piled books, in charact'ry,[8]
Hold like rich garners the full-ripen'd grain;

[1] *Great Alfred* Alfred the Great, King of Wessex from 871 to 899.

[2] *Kosciusko* Polish patriot Tadeusz Kosciusko (1746–1817), who led his countrymen in an uprising against Russia, and also fought for the United States Army in the American struggle for independence.

[3] *Petrarch ... Laura* Italian poet Petrarch (1304–74) wrote odes and sonnets in celebration of his beloved, Laura.

[4] *Elgin Marbles* In 1806 Lord Elgin brought friezes and other sculptures that had decorated the exterior of the Parthenon, in Athens, to England. In 1816 the government purchased them for display in the British Museum, where they remain today. See the "In Context" section on this topic.

[5] *Syren* Monster of classical mythology who is half woman, half serpent, and whose enchanted singing lures sailors to their deaths.

[6] *Albion* England.

[7] *Phoenix* Mythical Egyptian bird that is consumed by fire, and then reborn, once every 500 years.

[8] *charact'ry* Symbols or characters.

5   When I behold, upon the night's starr'd face,
      Huge cloudy symbols of a high romance,
   And think that I may never live to trace
      Their shadows, with the magic hand of chance;
   And when I feel, fair creature of an hour!
10   That I shall never look upon thee more,
   Never have relish in the fairy power
      Of unreflecting love—then on the shore
   Of the wide world I stand alone, and think
   Till love and fame to nothingness do sink.
   —1848 (WRITTEN 1818)

Epistle to John Hamilton Reynolds[1]

Dear Reynolds! as last night I lay in bed,
   There came before my eyes that wonted thread
Of shapes, and shadows, and remembrances,
That every other minute vex and please:
5   Things all disjointed come from north and south—
Two witch's eyes above a cherub's mouth,
Voltaire with casque and shield and habergeon,[2]
And Alexander[3] with his night-cap on;
Old Socrates[4] a-tying his cravat,
10   And Hazlitt playing with Miss Edgeworth's cat;[5]
And Junius Brutus, pretty well so so,[6]
Making the best of's way towards Soho.[7]

   Few are there who escape these visitings—
Perhaps one or two whose lives have patent wings,
15   And through whose curtains peeps no hellish nose,
No wild-boar tushes,° and no mermaid's toes;   *tusks*

But flowers bursting out with lusty pride,
And young Æolian harps[8] personified;
Some, Titian[9] colours touch'd into real life—
20   The sacrifice goes on; the pontiff knife
Gleams in the sun, the milk-white heifer lows,
The pipes go shrilly, the libation flows:
A white sail shows above the green-head cliff,
Moves round the point, and throws her anchor stiff;
25   The mariners join hymn with those on land.

   You know the Enchanted Castle[10]—it doth stand
Upon a rock, on the border of a lake,
Nested in trees, which all do seem to shake
From some old magic like Urganda's sword.[11]
30   O Phoebus![12] that I had thy sacred word
To show this Castle, in fair dreaming wise,
Unto my friend, while sick and ill he lies!

   You know it well enough, where it doth seem
A mossy place, a Merlin's Hall,[13] a dream;
35   You know the clear lake, and the little isles,
The mountains blue, and cold near neighbour rills,
All which elsewhere are but half animate;
There do they look alive to love and hate,
To smiles and frowns; they seem a lifted mound
40   Above some giant, pulsing underground.

   Part of the building was a chosen see,°   *dwelling-place*
Built by a banish'd Santon° of Chaldee;   *holy man*
The other part, two thousand years from him,
Was built by Cuthbert de Saint Aldebrim;[14]
45   Then there's a little wing, far from the sun,

---

[1] *John Hamilton Reynolds* Poet and lawyer (1794–1852) who was a close friend of Keats. Reynolds was ill at the time, and Keats sent him this verse letter to cheer him.

[2] *Voltaire* French philosopher François-Marie Arouet de Voltaire (1694–1778); *casque* Helmet; *habergeon* Sleeveless jacket of chain mail.

[3] *Alexander* Poet Alexander Pope (1688–1744).

[4] *Socrates* Greek philosopher of the fifth century BCE.

[5] *Hazlitt* Painter and writer William Hazlitt (1778–1830); *Miss Edgeworth* Novelist Maria Edgeworth (1767–1849).

[6] *Junius Brutus* Actor Junius Brutus Booth (1796–1852); *so so* Tipsy.

[7] *Soho* Area in London, then rather disreputable.

[8] *Æolian harps* Harps that produce sound when exposed to the wind or open air. From Æolus, the Greek god of the winds.

[9] *Titian* I.e, rich; in the style of Titian, a Venetian Renaissance painter whose work was characterized by bold colors. The following lines most likely describe *Sacrifice to Apollo*, by French painter Claude Lorraine (1600–82).

[10] *the Enchanted Castle* Painting by Claude Lorraine.

[11] *Urganda's sword* Enchantress figure in *Amadis of Gaul*, a fifteenth-century romance.

[12] *Phoebus* Apollo, Greek god of poetry and of the sun.

[13] *Merlin's Hall* I.e., a hall built by magicians such as the sorcerer Merlin, from Arthurian legend.

[14] *Cuthbert ... Aldebrim* Character invented by Keats.

Built by a Lapland witch[1] turn'd maudlin nun;
And many other juts of aged stone
Founded with many a mason-devil's groan.

The doors all look as if they oped themselves,
50   The windows as if latched by fays° and elves,   *fairies*
And from them comes a silver flash of light,
As from the westward of a summer's night;
Or like a beauteous woman's large blue eyes
Gone mad through olden songs and poesies.

55   See! what is coming from the distance dim!
A golden galley all in silken trim!
Three rows of oars are lightening, moment whiles,
Into the verd'rous bosoms of those isles;
Towards the shade, under the Castle wall,
60   It comes in silence—now 'tis hidden all.
The clarion sounds, and from a postern-gate
An echo of sweet music doth create
A fear in the poor herdsman, who doth bring
His beasts to trouble the enchanted spring—
65   He tells of the sweet music, and the spot,
To all his friends, and they believe him not.

O that our dreamings all, of sleep or wake,
Would all their colours from the sunset take:
From something of material sublime,
70   Rather than shadow our own soul's daytime
In the dark void of night. For in the world
We jostle—but my flag is not unfurl'd
On the admiral-staff—and to philosophise
I dare not yet! Oh, never will the prize,
75   High reason, and the lore of good and ill,
Be my award! Things cannot to the will
Be settled, but they tease us out of thought;
Or is it that imagination brought
Beyond its proper bound, yet still confin'd,
80   Lost in a sort of Purgatory blind,
Cannot refer to any standard law
Of either earth or heaven? It is a flaw
In happiness, to see beyond our bourn—
It forces us in summer skies to mourn,
85   It spoils the singing of the nightingale.

---

[1]   *Lapland witch*   Lapland was supposed to be the dwelling-place of
witches.

Dear Reynolds! I have a mysterious tale,
And cannot speak it: the first page I read
Upon a lampit° rock of green sea-weed   *limpet*
Among the breakers; 'twas a quiet eve,
90   The rocks were silent, the wide sea did weave
An untumultuous fringe of silver foam
Along the flat brown sand; I was at home
And should have been most happy—but I saw
Too far into the sea, where every maw°   *throat, gullet*
95   The greater on the less feeds evermore.
But I saw too distinct into the core
Of an eternal fierce destruction,
And so from happiness I far was gone.
Still am I sick of it, and tho', to-day,
100   I've gather'd young spring-leaves, and flowers gay
Of periwinkle and wild strawberry,
Still do I that most fierce destruction see—
The shark at savage prey, the hawk at pounce,
The gentle robin, like a pard° or ounce,°   *leopard / lynx*
105   Ravening a worm—Away, ye horrid moods!
Moods of one's mind! You know I hate them well.
You know I'd sooner be a clapping bell
To some Kamschatkan[2] missionary church,
Than with these horrid moods be left i'the lurch.
110   Do you get health—and Tom the same—I'll dance,
And from detested moods in new romance[3]
Take refuge—Of bad lines a centaine[4] dose
Is sure enough—and so "here follows prose."[5]
—1848

To Homer[6]

Standing aloof in giant ignorance,
S   Of thee I hear and of the Cyclades,[7]
As one who sits ashore and longs perchance

---

[2]   *Kamschatkan*   From the Kamchatka Peninsula in Siberia.

[3]   *new romance*   Probably Keats's *Isabella* (1820), a romance based
on a tale from Italian poet Giovanni Boccaccio's *Decameron* (written
1348–53).

[4]   *centaine*   Company of one hundred.

[5]   *here follows prose*   See Shakespeare's *Twelfth Night* 2.5.154.

[6]   *Homer*   Early Greek poet, believed to be the author of *The Iliad*
and *Odyssey*.

[7]   *Cyclades*   Group of islands in the Aegean Sea, off the southeast
coast of Greece.

To visit dolphin-coral in deep seas.
5   So thou wast blind!¹—but then the veil was rent;
         For Jove² uncurtain'd Heaven to let thee live,
And Neptune³ made for thee a spumy⁴ tent,
         And Pan⁵ made sing for thee his forest-hive;
Aye, on the shores of darkness there is light,
10   And precipices show untrodden green;
There is a budding morrow in midnight;
         There is a triple sight in blindness keen;
Such seeing hast thou, as it once befell
To Dian, Queen of Earth, and Heaven, and Hell.⁶
—1848 (WRITTEN C.1818)

The Eve of St. Agnes⁷

1

St. Agnes' Eve—Ah, bitter chill it was!
    The owl, for all his feathers, was a-cold;
The hare limp'd trembling through the frozen grass,
And silent was the flock in woolly fold:
5   Numb were the Beadsman's⁸ fingers, while he told
His rosary, and while his frosted breath,
Like pious incense from a censer⁹ old,
Seem'd taking flight for heaven, without a death,

---

¹ *thou wast blind*   Homer was said to have been blind.

² *Jove*   Roman King of the gods.

³ *Neptune*   Roman god of the sea.

⁴ *spumy*   Covered in sea foam.

⁵ *Pan*   Greek shepherd god of nature who was half goat and half man. After the nymph Syrinx turned herself into a bed of reeds in order to escape him, Pan created an instrument (the panpipe) out of the reeds.

⁶ *To Dian … Hell*   Diana was sometimes envisioned as a three-figured goddess, presiding over the moon, childbirth, and the hunt, and hell.

⁷ *St. Agnes*   Fourth-century Christian martyr, executed at the age of thirteen, who is the patron saint of virgins. It was tradition that young women could obtain a vision of their future husbands if they performed the proper rituals on 20 January, the night before St. Agnes's Feast Day.

⁸ *Beadsman*   Pensioner paid to say prayers for the souls of his benefactors. He "tells," or counts, the beads of his rosary, saying a prayer at each bead.

⁹ *censer*   Incense burner.

Past the sweet Virgin's¹⁰ picture, while his prayer he
    saith.

2

10   His prayer he saith, this patient, holy man;
Then takes his lamp, and riseth from his knees,
And back returneth, meagre, barefoot, wan,
Along the chapel aisle by slow degrees:
The sculptur'd dead, on each side, seem to freeze,
15   Emprison'd in black, purgatorial rails:
Knights, ladies, praying in dumb orat'ries,°   *chapels*
He passeth by; and his weak spirit fails
To think how they may ache in icy hoods and mails.

3

Northward he turneth through a little door,
20   And scarce three steps, ere Music's golden tongue
Flatter'd to tears this aged man and poor;
But no—already had his deathbell rung:
The joys of all his life were said and sung:
His was harsh penance on St. Agnes' Eve:
25   Another way he went, and soon among
Rough ashes sat he for his soul's reprieve,
And all night kept awake, for sinners' sake to grieve.

4

That ancient Beadsman heard the prelude soft;
And so it chanc'd, for many a door was wide,
30   From hurry to and fro. Soon, up aloft,
The silver, snarling trumpets 'gan to chide:
The level chambers, ready with their pride,
Were glowing to receive a thousand guests:
The carved angels, ever eager-eyed,
35   Star'd, where upon their heads the cornice rests,
With hair blown back, and wings put cross-wise on
    their breasts.

5

At length burst in the argent¹¹ revelry,
With plume, tiara, and all rich array,
Numerous as shadows haunting fairily
40   The brain, new stuff'd, in youth, with triumphs gay
Of old romance. These let us wish away,

---

¹⁰ *Virgin*   I.e., Mary, virgin mother of Christ.

¹¹ *argent*   Adorned with silver.

And turn, sole-thoughted, to one Lady there,
Whose heart had brooded, all that wintry day,
On love, and wing'd St. Agnes' saintly care,
45   As she had heard old dames full many times declare.

6

They told her how, upon St. Agnes' Eve,
Young virgins might have visions of delight,
And soft adorings from their loves receive
Upon the honey'd middle of the night,
50   If ceremonies due they did aright;°   *arranged properly*
As, supperless to bed they must retire,
And couch supine their beauties, lily white;
Nor look behind, nor sideways, but require
Of Heaven with upward eyes for all that they desire.

7

55   Full of this whim was thoughtful Madeline:
The music, yearning like a God in pain,
She scarcely heard: her maiden eyes divine,
Fix'd on the floor, saw many a sweeping train
Pass by—she heeded not at all: in vain
60   Came many a tiptoe, amorous cavalier,
And back retir'd; not cool'd by high disdain,
But she saw not: her heart was otherwhere:
She sigh'd for Agnes' dreams, the sweetest of the year.

8

She danc'd along with vague, regardless eyes,
65   Anxious her lips, her breathing quick and short:
The hallow'd hour was near at hand: she sighs
Amid the timbrels,° and the throng'd resort   *tambourines*
Of whisperers in anger, or in sport;
'Mid looks of love, defiance, hate, and scorn,
70   Hoodwink'd° with faery fancy; all   *blindfolded*
    amort,°   *dead*
Save to St. Agnes and her lambs unshorn,[1]
And all the bliss to be before to-morrow morn.

9

So, purposing each moment to retire,
She linger'd still. Meantime, across the moors,
75   Had come young Porphyro, with heart on fire

For Madeline. Beside the portal doors,
Buttress'd from moonlight, stands he, and implores
All saints to give him sight of Madeline,
But for one moment in the tedious hours,
80   That he might gaze and worship all unseen;
Perchance speak, kneel, touch, kiss—in sooth such
    things have been.

10

He ventures in: let no buzz'd whisper tell:
All eyes be muffled, or a hundred swords
Will storm his heart, Love's fev'rous citadel:
85   For him, those chambers held barbarian hordes,
Hyena foemen, and hot-blooded lords,
Whose very dogs would execrations howl
Against his lineage: not one breast affords
Him any mercy, in that mansion foul,
90   Save one old beldame,[2] weak in body and in soul.

11

Ah, happy chance! the aged creature came,
Shuffling along with ivory-headed wand,°   *staff*
To where he stood, hid from the torch's flame,
Behind a broad hall-pillar, far beyond
95   The sound of merriment and chorus bland:°   *soft*
He startled her; but soon she knew his face,
And grasp'd his fingers in her palsied hand,
Saying, "Mercy, Porphyro! hie thee from this place;
They are all here to-night, the whole blood-thirsty race!"

12

100   "Get hence! get hence! there's dwarfish Hildebrand;
He had a fever late, and in the fit
He cursed thee and thine, both house and land:
Then there's that old Lord Maurice, not a whit
More tame for his gray hairs—Alas me! flit!
105   Flit like a ghost away."—"Ah, Gossip[3] dear,
We're safe enough; here in this arm-chair sit,
And tell me how"—"Good Saints! not here, not here;
Follow me, child, or else these stones will be thy bier."

13

He follow'd through a lowly arched way,
110   Brushing the cobwebs with his lofty plume,

---

[1] *St. Agnes ... unshorn* The Latin for lamb is *agnus*; thus the
traditional association of St. Agnes with lambs, which also carry
connotations of whiteness and purity.

[2] *beldame* Grandmother, old woman, or elderly nurse.

[3] *Gossip* Good friend; godmother.

And as she mutter'd "Well-a—well-a-day!"
He found him in a little moonlight room,
Pale, lattic'd, chill, and silent as a tomb.
"Now tell me where is Madeline," said he,
115   "O tell me, Angela, by the holy loom
Which none but secret sisterhood may see,
When they St. Agnes' wool are weaving piously."

14

"St. Agnes! Ah! it is St. Agnes' Eve—
Yet men will murder upon holy days:
120   Thou must hold water in a witch's sieve,
And be liege-lord of all the Elves and Fays,°   *fairies*
To venture so: it fills me with amaze
To see thee, Porphyro!—St. Agnes' Eve!
God's help! my lady fair the conjuror plays
125   This very night: good angels her deceive!
But let me laugh awhile, I've mickle° time to grieve.   *much*

15

Feebly she laugheth in the languid moon,
While Porphyro upon her face doth look,
Like puzzled urchin on an aged crone
130   Who keepeth clos'd a wond'rous riddle-book,
As spectacled she sits in chimney nook.
But soon his eyes grew brilliant, when she told
His lady's purpose; and he scarce could brook°   *prevent*
Tears, at the thought of those enchantments cold
135   And Madeline asleep in lap of legends old.

16

Sudden a thought came like a full-blown rose,
Flushing his brow, and in his pained heart
Made purple riot: then doth he propose
A stratagem, that makes the beldame start:
140   "A cruel man and impious thou art:
Sweet lady, let her pray, and sleep, and dream
Alone with her good angels, far apart
From wicked men like thee. Go, go!—I deem
Thou canst not surely be the same that thou didst seem."

17

145   "I will not harm her, by all saints I swear,"
Quoth Porphyro: "O may I ne'er find grace
When my weak voice shall whisper its last prayer,
If one of her soft ringlets I displace,

Or look with ruffian passion in her face:
150   Good Angela, believe me by these tears;
Or I will, even in a moment's space,
Awake, with horrid shout, my foemen's ears,
And beard° them, though they be more fang'd than
    wolves and bears."   *oppose*

18

"Ah! why wilt thou affright a feeble soul?
155   A poor, weak, palsy-stricken, churchyard thing,
Whose passing-bell may ere the midnight toll;
Whose prayers for thee, each morn and evening,
Were never miss'd."—Thus plaining,°   *complaining*
    doth she bring
A gentler speech from burning Porphyro;
160   So woeful, and of such deep sorrowing,
That Angela gives promise she will do
Whatever he shall wish, betide her weal or woe.

19

Which was, to lead him, in close secrecy,
Even to Madeline's chamber, and there hide
165   Him in a closet, of such privacy
That he might see her beauty unespied,
And win perhaps that night a peerless bride,
While legion'd fairies pac'd the coverlet,
And pale enchantment held her sleepy-eyed.
170   Never on such a night have lovers met,
Since Merlin paid his Demon all the monstrous debt.[1]

20

"It shall be as thou wishest," said the Dame:
"All cates° and dainties shall be stored there   *delicacies*
Quickly on this feast-night: by the tambour frame[2]
175   Her own lute thou wilt see: no time to spare,
For I am slow and feeble, and scarce dare
On such a catering trust my dizzy head.
Wait here, my child, with patience; kneel in prayer
The while: Ah! thou must needs the lady wed,
180   Or may I never leave my grave among the dead."

---

[1] *Since ... debt* Probably a reference to the episode in Arthurian legend in which the enchanter Merlin falls in love with the enchantress Vivien, or Nimue, who turns one of his spells against him and imprisons him in a cave.

[2] *tambour frame* Circular frame for embroidery.

21

So saying, she hobbled off with busy fear.
The lover's endless minutes slowly pass'd:
The dame return'd, and whisper'd in his ear
To follow her; with aged eyes aghast
185   From fright of dim espial. Safe at last,
Through many a dusky gallery, they gain
The maiden's chamber, silken, hush'd, and chaste;
Where Porphyro took covert, pleas'd amain.°   *completely*
His poor guide hurried back with agues°   *fever*
   in her brain.

22

190   Her falt'ring hand upon the balustrade,
Old Angela was feeling for the stair,
When Madeline, St. Agnes' charmed maid,
Rose, like a mission'd spirit, unaware:
With silver taper's light, and pious care,
195   She turn'd, and down the aged gossip led
To a safe level matting. Now prepare,
Young Porphyro, for gazing on that bed;
She comes, she comes again, like ring-dove
   fray'd° and fled.   *frightened*

23

Out went the taper° as she hurried in;   *candle*
200   Its little smoke, in pallid moonshine, died:
She clos'd the door, she panted, all akin
To spirits of the air, and visions wide:
No uttered syllable, or, woe betide!
But to her heart, her heart was voluble,
205   Paining with eloquence her balmy side;
As though a tongueless nightingale should swell
Her throat in vain, and die, heart-stifled, in her dell.

24

A casement high and triple-arch'd there was,
All garlanded with carven imag'ries
210   Of fruits, and flowers, and bunches of knot-grass,
And diamonded with panes of quaint device,
Innumerable of stains and splendid dyes,
As are the tiger-moth's deep-damask'd wings;
And in the midst, 'mong thousand heraldries,[1]
215   And twilight saints, and dim emblazonings,

---

[1]   *heraldries*   Emblems of rank and genealogy.

A shielded scutcheon blush'd with blood of queens
   and kings.[2]

25

Full on this casement shone the wintry moon,
And threw warm gules[3] on Madeline's fair breast,
As down she knelt for heaven's grace and boon;°   *blessing*
220   Rose-bloom fell on her hands, together prest,
And on her silver cross soft amethyst,
And on her hair a glory, like a saint:
She seem'd a splendid angel, newly drest,
Save wings, for heaven—Porphyro grew faint:
225   She knelt, so pure a thing, so free from mortal taint.

26

Anon his heart revives: her vespers° done,   *evening prayers*
Of all its wreathed pearls her hair she frees;
Unclasps her warmed jewels one by one;
Loosens her fragrant boddice; by degrees
230   Her rich attire creeps rustling to her knees:
Half-hidden, like a mermaid in sea-weed,
Pensive awhile she dreams awake, and sees,
In fancy, fair St. Agnes in her bed,
But dares not look behind, or all the charm is fled.

27

235   Soon, trembling in her soft and chilly nest,
In sort of wakeful swoon, perplex'd[4] she lay,
Until the poppied° warmth of sleep oppress'd   *narcotic*
Her soothed limbs, and soul fatigued away;
Flown, like a thought, until the morrow-day;
240   Blissfully haven'd both from joy and pain;
Clasp'd like a missal[5] where swart Paynims[6] pray;
Blinded alike from sunshine and from rain,
As though a rose should shut, and be a bud again.

28

Stol'n to this paradise, and so entranced,
245   Porphyro gazed upon her empty dress,
And listen'd to her breathing, if it chanced

---

[2]   *scutcheon* I.e., escutcheon: shield; *blushed ... kings* I.e.,
indicates she is of royal blood.

[3]   *gules*   Red bars (a heraldic device).

[4]   *perplexed*   I.e., between sleep and waking.

[5]   *missal*   Christian mass- or prayer-book.

[6]   *swart Paynims*   Dark-skinned pagans.

To wake into a slumberous tenderness;
Which when he heard, that minute did he bless,
And breath'd himself: then from the closet crept,
250   Noiseless as fear in a wide wilderness,
And over the hush'd carpet, silent, stept,
And 'tween the curtains peep'd, where, lo!—how fast
   she slept.

29

Then by the bed-side, where the faded moon
Made a dim, silver twilight, soft he set
255   A table, and, half anguish'd, threw thereon
A cloth of woven crimson, gold, and jet—
O for some drowsy Morphean amulet![1]
The boisterous, midnight, festive clarion,°   *trumpet*
The kettle-drum, and far-heard clarinet,
260   Affray his ears, though but in dying tone—
The hall door shuts again, and all the noise is gone.

30

And still she slept an azure-lidded sleep,
In blanched linen, smooth, and lavender'd,
While he from forth the closet brought a heap
265   Of candied apple, quince, and plum, and gourd;°   *melon*
With jellies soother[2] than the creamy curd,
And lucent° syrops, tinct° with cinnamon;   *clear / imbued*
Manna[3] and dates, in argosy[4] transferr'd
From Fez;[5] and spiced dainties, every one,
270   From silken Samarkand[6] to cedar'd Lebanon.

31

These delicates he heap'd with glowing hand
On golden dishes and in baskets bright
Of wreathed silver: sumptuous they stand
In the retired quiet of the night,
275   Filling the chilly room with perfume light.
"And now, my love, my seraph° fair, awake!   *angel*

---

[1] *Morphean amulet* Sleep-inducing medicine or charm. (Morpheus is the god of dreams.)

[2] *soother* A word of Keats's own invention, meaning more soothing, softer.

[3] *Manna* Dried, sweet gum taken from various plants.

[4] *argosy* Merchant vessels.

[5] *Fez* City in Morocco.

[6] *Samarkand* City in Uzbekistan.

Thou art my heaven, and I thine eremite:°   *hermit*
Open thine eyes, for meek St. Agnes' sake,
Or I shall drowse beside thee, so my soul doth ache."

32

280   Thus whispering, his warm, unnerved arm
Sank in her pillow. Shaded was her dream
By the dusk curtains—'twas a midnight charm
Impossible to melt as iced stream:
The lustrous salvers° in the moonlight gleam;   *trays*
285   Broad golden fringe upon the carpet lies:
It seem'd he never, never could redeem
From such a stedfast spell his lady's eyes;
So mus'd awhile, entoil'd in woofed° phantasies.   *woven*

33

Awakening up, he took her hollow lute—
290   Tumultuous—and, in chords that tenderest be,
He play'd an ancient ditty, long since mute,
In Provence call'd, "La belle dame sans mercy":[7]
Close to her ear touching the melody—
Wherewith disturb'd, she utter'd a soft moan:
295   He ceased—she panted quick—and suddenly
Her blue affrayed eyes wide open shone:
Upon his knees he sank, pale as smooth-sculptured
   stone.

34

Her eyes were open, but she still beheld,
Now wide awake, the vision of her sleep:
300   There was a painful change, that nigh expell'd
The blisses of her dream so pure and deep,
At which fair Madeline began to weep,
And moan forth witless words with many a sigh;
While still her gaze on Porphyro would keep;
305   Who knelt, with joined hands and piteous eye,
Fearing to move or speak, she look'd so dreamingly.

35

"Ah, Porphyro!" said she, "but even now
Thy voice was at sweet tremble in mine ear,
Made tuneable with every sweetest vow;
310   And those sad eyes were spiritual and clear:

---

[7] *La belle … mercy* French: "The beautiful woman without pity." Title of a long poem by medieval poet Alain Chartier (c. 1385–1433); Keats had not yet written his own poem with this title.

How chang'd thou art! how pallid, chill, and drear!
Give me that voice again, my Porphyro,
Those looks immortal, those complainings° *lamentings*
    dear!
Oh leave me not in this eternal woe,
315 For if thou diest, my Love, I know not where to go."

36

Beyond a mortal man impassion'd far
At these voluptuous accents, he arose,
Ethereal, flush'd, and like a throbbing star
Seen mid the sapphire heaven's deep repose;
320 Into her dream he melted, as the rose
Blendeth its odour with the violet—
Solution sweet: meantime the frost-wind blows
Like Love's alarum° pattering the sharp sleet   *warning bell*
Against the window-panes; St. Agnes' moon hath set.

37

325 'Tis dark: quick pattereth the flaw-blown° sleet:*gust-driven*
"This is no dream, my bride, my Madeline!"
'Tis dark: the iced gusts still rave and beat:
"No dream, alas! alas! and woe is mine!
Porphyro will leave me here to fade and pine.
330 Cruel! what traitor could thee hither bring?
I curse not, for my heart is lost in thine,
Though thou forsakest a deceived thing—
A dove forlorn and lost with sick unpruned wing."

38

"My Madeline! sweet dreamer! lovely bride!
335 Say, may I be for aye° thy vassal blest?   *ever*
Thy beauty's shield, heart-shap'd and
    vermeil° dyed?   *vermilion (red)*
Ah, silver shrine, here will I take my rest
After so many hours of toil and quest,
A famish'd pilgrim, saved by miracle.
340 Though I have found, I will not rob thy nest
Saving of thy sweet self; if thou think'st well
To trust, fair Madeline, to no rude infidel.

39

"Hark! 'tis an elfin-storm from faery land,
Of haggard° seeming, but a boon indeed: *wild*
345 Arise—arise! the morning is at hand;
The bloated wassaillers° will never heed—   *drinkers*

Let us away, my love, with happy speed;
There are no ears to hear, or eyes to see—
Drown'd all in Rhenish and the sleepy mead:[1]
350 Awake! arise! my love, and fearless be,
For o'er the southern moors I have a home for thee."

40

She hurried at his words, beset with fears,
For there were sleeping dragons all around,
At glaring watch, perhaps, with ready spears—
355 Down the wide stairs a darkling[2] way they found.
In all the house was heard no human sound.
A chain-droop'd lamp was flickering by each door;
The arras,° rich with horseman, hawk, and   *tapestries*
    hound,
Flutter'd in the besieging wind's uproar;
360 And the long carpets rose along the gusty floor.

41

They glide, like phantoms, into the wide hall;
Like phantoms, to the iron porch, they glide;
Where lay the Porter, in uneasy sprawl,
With a huge empty flaggon by his side:
365 The wakeful bloodhound rose, and shook his hide,
But his sagacious eye an inmate owns:
By one, and one, the bolts full easy slide—
The chains lie silent on the footworn stones—
The key turns, and the door upon its hinges groans.

42

370 And they are gone: ay, ages long ago
These lovers fled away into the storm.
That night the Baron dreamt of many a woe,
And all his warrior-guests, with shade and form
Of witch, and demon, and large coffin-worm,
375 Were long be-nightmar'd. Angela the old
Died palsy-twitch'd, with meagre face deform;
The Beadsman, after thousand aves[3] told,
For aye unsought for slept among his ashes cold.
    —1820

---

1 *Rhenish* Wine from the Rhine region; *mead* Alcoholic beverage
made from fermented honey and water.

2 *darkling* Obscure, gloomy.

3 *aves* Latin: abbreviation for *Ave Marias*, or Hail Marys, prayers
to the Virgin Mary.

Bright Star

Bright star, would I were steadfast as thou art—
Not in lone splendour hung aloft the night
And watching, with eternal lids apart,
   Like nature's patient, sleepless Eremite,°   *hermit*
5 The moving waters at their priestlike task
   Of pure ablution[1] round earth's human shores,
Or gazing on the new soft fallen mask
   Of snow upon the mountains and the moors—
No—yet still steadfast, still unchangeable,
10   Pillow'd upon my fair love's ripening breast,
To feel for ever its soft fall and swell,
   Awake for ever in a sweet unrest,
Still, still to hear her tender-taken breath,
And so live ever—or else swoon to death.
—1838 (WRITTEN 1819)

La Belle Dame sans Merci[2]

O what can ail thee, knight-at-arms,
   Alone and palely loitering?
The sedge[3] has wither'd from the lake,
   And no birds sing.

5 O what can ail thee, knight-at-arms,
   So haggard, and so woe-begone?
The squirrel's granary is full,
   And the harvest's done.

I see a lily[4] on thy brow,
10   With anguish moist and fever dew
And on thy cheeks a fading rose
   Fast withereth too.

I met a lady in the meads,°   *meadows*
   Full beautiful—a faery's child,

15 Her hair was long, her foot was light,
   And her eyes were wild.

I made a garland for her head,
   And bracelets too, and fragrant zone;°   *belt*
She look'd at me as she did love,
20   And made sweet moan.

I set her on my pacing steed,
   And nothing else saw all day long,
For sidelong would she bend and sing
   A faery's song.

25 She found me roots of relish sweet,
   And honey wild, and manna dew,[5]
And sure in language strange she said
   "I love thee true."

She took me to her elfin grot,°   *grotto*
30   And there she wept and sigh'd full sore,
And there I shut her wild wild eyes
   With kisses four.

And there she lulled me asleep,
   And there I dream'd—Ah! woe betide!
35 The latest° dream I ever dream'd   *last*
   On the cold hill side.

I saw pale kings and princes too,
   Pale warriors, death-pale were they all;
They cried, "La belle dame sans merci
40   Hath thee in thrall!"°   *captivity*

I saw their starved lips in the gloam,°   *twilight*
   With horrid warning gaped wide,
And I awoke, and found me here,
   On the cold hill's side.

45 And this is why I sojourn here,
   Alone and palely loitering,
Though the sedge is wither'd from the lake,
   And no birds sing.
—1848 (WRITTEN 1819)

---

[1] *ablution* Religious ritual washing of the body.

[2] *La Belle Dame sans Merci* French: the beautiful lady without pity. This original version of the poem, found in a journal letter to George and Georgiana Keats, was first published in 1848. Keats's revised version was published in 1820.

[3] *sedge* Rush-like grass.

[4] *lily* Flower traditionally symbolic of death.

[5] *manna dew* See Exodus 16, in which God provides the Israelites with a food that falls from heaven, called manna.

La Belle Dame sans Mercy[1]

Ah, what can ail thee, wretched wight,°   *being*
    Alone and palely loitering;
The sedge[2] is wither'd from the lake,
    And no birds sing.

5   Ah, what can ail thee, wretched wight,
    So haggard and so woe-begone?
The squirrel's granary is full,
    And the harvest's done.

I see a lily[3] on thy brow,
10   With anguish moist and fever dew;
And on thy cheek a fading rose
    Fast withereth too.

I met a lady in the meads°   *meadows*
    Full beautiful, a fairy's child;
15   Her hair was long, her foot was light,
    And her eyes were wild.

I set her on my pacing steed,
    And nothing else saw all day long;
For sideways would she lean, and sing
20   A fairy's song.

I made a garland for her head,
    And bracelets too, and fragrant zone:°   *belt*
She look'd at me as she did love,
    And made sweet moan.

25   She found me roots of relish sweet,
    And honey wild, and manna[4] dew;
And sure in language strange she said,
    "I love thee true."

She took me to her elfin grot,°   *grotto*
30   And there she gaz'd and sighed deep.

And there I shut her wild sad eyes—
    So kiss'd to sleep.

And there we slumber'd on the moss,
    And there I dream'd, ah woe betide,
35   The latest dream I ever dream'd
    On the cold hill side.

I saw pale kings, and princes too,
    Pale warriors, death-pale were they all;
Who cry'd—"La belle dame sans mercy
40   Hath thee in thrall!"°   *captivity*

I saw their starv'd lips in the gloom
    With horrid warning gaped wide,
And I awoke, and found me here
    On the cold hill side.

45   And this is why I sojourn here
    Alone and palely loitering,
Though the sedge is wither'd from the lake,
    And no birds sing.
—1820 (WRITTEN 1819)

Incipit altera Sonneta[5]

I have been endeavouring to discover a better sonnet stanza than we have. The legitimate[6] does not suit the language over-well from the pouncing rhymes—the other kind appears too elegaiac—and the couplet at the end of it has seldom a pleasing effect—I do not pretend to have succeeded—it will explain itself—

If by dull rhymes our English must be chain'd
  And, like Andromeda,[7] the Sonnet sweet
Fetter'd in spite of pained loveliness;
Let us find out, if we must be constrain'd
5 Sandals more interwoven & complete

---

[1] *La Belle ... Mercy* French: the beautiful lady without pity. Keats's revised version was published in 1820.

[2] *sedge* Rush-like grass.

[3] *lily* Flower traditionally symbolic of death.

[4] *manna* See Exodus 16, in which God provides the Israelites with a food that falls from heaven, called manna.

[5] *Incipit altera Sonneta* Latin: another sonnet begins.

[6] *The legitimate* I.e., the Petrarchan sonnet. The "other kind" to which Keats refers is the Shakespearean sonnet.

[7] *Andromeda* In Greek myth, Andromeda is tied to a rock to be devoured by a sea serpent after her mother boasts that she is more beautiful than the sea nymphs. Perseus, on his winged horse Pegasus (a symbol of poetic inspiration), rescues her.

To fit the naked foot of Poesy;
Let us inspect the Lyre,[1] & weigh the stress
Of every chord & see what may be gain'd
By ear industrious & attention meet;°   *fitting*
10   Misers of sound & syllable, no less
Than Midas of his coinage,[2] let us be
Jealous of dead leaves in the bay wreath Crown;[3]
So if we may not let the Muse[4] be free,
She will be bound with Garlands of her own.
—1836 (WRITTEN 1819)

---

[1] *Lyre* Stringed instrument.

[2] *Midas … coinage* In Ovid's *Metamorphoses*, King Midas of
Phrygia gets his wish that everything he touches will turn to gold.

[3] *bay wreath Crown* Wreaths made of leaves of the bay laurel were
traditionally bestowed upon those who distinguished themselves in
poetry.

[4] *Muse* One of nine daughters of Zeus and Mnemosyne, each of
whom presided over and provided inspiration for an aspect of
learning or the arts.

15 They lay calm-breathing on the bedded grass;
      Their arms embraced, and their pinions° too; *wings*
      Their lips touch'd not, but had not bade adieu,
As if disjoined by soft-handed slumber,
And ready still past kisses to outnumber
20   At tender eye-dawn of aurorean[8] love:
      The winged boy° I knew;   *Cupid*
   But who wast thou, O happy, happy dove?
      His Psyche true!

O latest born and liveliest vision far
25   Of all Olympus'[9] faded hierarchy!
Fairer than Phœbe's[10] sapphire-region'd star,
   Or Vesper,[11] amorous glow-worm of the sky;
Fairer than these, though temple thou hast none,
      Nor altar heap'd with flowers;
30 Nor virgin-choir to make delicious moan
      Upon the midnight hours;
No voice, no lute, no pipe, no incense sweet
   From chain-swung censer° teeming;   *incense burner*
No shrine, no grove, no oracle, no heat
35   Of pale-mouth'd prophet dreaming.

O brightest! Though too late for antique vows,
   Too, too late for the fond believing
      lyre,°   *stringed instrument*
When holy were the haunted forest boughs,
   Holy the air, the water, and the fire;
40 Yet even in these days so far retir'd
   From happy pieties, thy lucent fans,°   *wings*
   Fluttering among the faint Olympians,
I see, and sing, by my own eyes inspired.
So let me be thy choir, and make a moan
45   Upon the midnight hours;
Thy voice, thy lute, thy pipe, thy incense sweet
   From swinged censer teeming;
Thy shrine, thy grove, thy oracle, thy heat
      Of pale-mouth'd prophet dreaming.

50 Yes, I will be thy priest, and build a fane°   *temple*
   In some untrodden region of my mind,

Ode to Psyche[5]

O Goddess! hear these tuneless numbers, wrung
   By sweet enforcement and remembrance dear,
And pardon that thy secrets should be sung
   Even into thine own soft-conched[6] ear:
5 Surely I dreamt to-day, or did I see
   The winged Psyche with awaken'd eyes?
I wander'd in a forest thoughtlessly,
   And, on the sudden, fainting with surprise,
Saw two fair creatures, couched side by side
10   In deepest grass, beneath the whisp'ring roof
   Of leaves and trembled blossoms, where there ran
      A brooklet, scarce espied:

'Mid hush'd, cool-rooted flowers, fragrant-eyed,
   Blue, silver-white, and budded Tyrian,[7]

[5] *Psyche* In classical mythology, a young woman who was beloved by Cupid, winged god of love and son of Venus. After winning over Venus, who was jealous of Psyche's beauty, Psyche was granted immortality by Jupiter. In Greek myth she is often a personification of the soul: her name in Greek means soul or mind as well as butterfly.

[6] *soft-conched* Shaped like a conch shell, but soft.

[7] *Tyrian* Purple. From the Phoenician city of Tyre, where purple or crimson dyes were made in ancient times.

[8] *aurorean* I.e., dawning. Aurora was the goddess of the dawn.

[9] *Olympus* Mount Olympus, home of the gods.

[10] *Phoebe* Diana, goddess of the moon.

[11] *Vesper* Venus, the evening star.

Where branched thoughts, new grown with pleasant
      pain,
      Instead of pines shall murmur in the wind:
Far, far around shall those dark-cluster'd trees
55   Fledge the wild-ridged mountains steep by steep;
And there by zephyrs,° streams, and birds,   *breezes*
      and bees,
      The moss-lain Dryads° shall be lull'd   *wood nymphs*
      to sleep;
And in the midst of quietness
A rosy sanctuary will I dress
60 With the wreath'd trellis of a working brain,
      With buds, and bells, and stars without a name,
With all the gardener Fancy e'er could feign,
      Who breeding flowers, will never breed the same:
And there shall be for thee all soft delight
65   That shadowy thought can win,
A bright torch, and a casement ope°   *window opened*
      at night,
To let the warm Love in!
—1820

Ode to a Nightingale[1]

1

My heart aches, and a drowsy numbness pains
My sense, as though of hemlock° I had   *poison*
      drunk,
Or emptied some dull opiate to the drains
One minute past, and Lethe-wards[2] had sunk:
5 'Tis not through envy of thy happy lot,
      But being too happy in thine happiness—

That thou, light-winged Dryad°   *wood-nymph*
      of the trees,
      In some melodious plot
Of beechen green, and shadows numberless,
10   Singest of summer in full-throated ease.

2

O, for a draught of vintage! that hath been
      Cool'd a long age in the deep-delved earth,
Tasting of Flora[3] and the country green,
      Dance, and Provençal song,[4] and sunburnt mirth!
15 O for a beaker full of the warm South,
      Full of the true, the blushful Hippocrene,[5]
      With beaded bubbles winking at the brim,
            And purple-stained mouth;
      That I might drink, and leave the world unseen,
20   And with thee fade away into the forest dim:

3

Fade far away, dissolve, and quite forget
      What thou among the leaves hast never known,
The weariness, the fever, and the fret
      Here, where men sit and hear each other groan;
25 Where palsy shakes a few, sad, last gray hairs,
      Where youth grows pale, and spectre-thin, and dies;
      Where but to think is to be full of sorrow
            And leaden-eyed despairs,
      Where Beauty cannot keep her lustrous eyes,
30   Or new Love pine at them beyond to-morrow.

4

Away! away! for I will fly to thee,
      Not charioted by Bacchus and his pards,[6]
But on the viewless wings of Poesy,
      Though the dull brain perplexes and retards:
35 Already with thee! tender is the night,
      And haply° the Queen-Moon is on her throne,   *maybe*
            Cluster'd around by all her starry Fays;°   *fairies*

[1] *Ode to a Nightingale* Written about 1 May 1819. Twenty years later, Keats's friend and housemate Charles Armitage Brown remembered the composition of the poem: "In the spring of 1819 a nightingale had built her nest near my house. Keats felt a tranquil and continual joy in her song; and one morning he took his chair from the breakfast-table to the grass-plot under a plum-tree, where he sat for two or three hours. When he came into the house, I perceived he had some scraps of paper in his hand, and these he was quietly thrusting behind the books. On enquiry, I found those scraps, four or five in number, contained his poetic feeling on the song of our nightingale."

[2] *Lethe-wards* Towards Lethe, the river of forgetfulness which, in classical mythology, the dead must cross to reach Hades, the underworld.

[3] *Flora* Roman goddess of flowers.

[4] *Provençal song* The region of Provence, in southern France, was known in the Middle Ages for its poet-singers, or troubadours.

[5] *Hippocrene* Fountain of the Muses (nine sister goddesses who presided over aspects of learning and the arts) located on the sacred Mount Helicon. Its waters were said to provide poetic inspiration.

[6] *Bacchus ... pards* Bacchus, the god of wine, rides a chariot drawn by pards, or leopards.

But here there is no light,
  Save what from heaven is with the breezes blown
40   Through verdurous glooms and winding mossy ways.

5

I cannot see what flowers are at my feet,
  Nor what soft incense hangs upon the boughs,
But, in embalmed° darkness, guess each sweet   *fragrant*
  Wherewith the seasonable month endows
45 The grass, the thicket, and the fruit-tree wild;
  White hawthorn, and the pastoral eglantine;
    Fast fading violets cover'd up in leaves;
      And mid-May's eldest child,
  The coming musk-rose, full of dewy wine,
50   The murmurous haunt of flies on summer eves.

6

Darkling[1] I listen; and, for many a time
  I have been half in love with easeful Death,
Call'd him soft names in many a mused rhyme,
  To take into the air my quiet breath;
55 Now more than ever seems it rich to die,
  To cease upon the midnight with no pain,
    While thou art pouring forth thy soul abroad
      In such an ecstasy!
  Still wouldst thou sing, and I have ears in vain—
60   To thy high requiem[2] become a sod.

7

Thou wast not born for death, immortal Bird!
  No hungry generations tread thee down;
The voice I hear this passing night was heard
  In ancient days by emperor and clown:°   *rustic*
65 Perhaps the self-same song that found a path
  Through the sad heart of Ruth, when, sick for home,
    She stood in tears amid the alien corn;[3]
      The same that oft-times hath
  Charm'd magic casements, opening on the foam
70   Of perilous seas, in faery lands forlorn.

8

Forlorn! the very word is like a bell
  To toll me back from thee to my sole self!
Adieu! the fancy cannot cheat so well
  As she is fam'd to do, deceiving elf.
75 Adieu! adieu! thy plaintive anthem fades
  Past the near meadows, over the still stream,
    Up the hill-side; and now 'tis buried deep
      In the next valley-glades:
  Was it a vision, or a waking dream?
80   Fled is that music—Do I wake or sleep?
—1819

Ode on a Grecian Urn

1

Thou still unravish'd bride of quietness,
  Thou foster-child of silence and slow time,
Sylvan° historian, who canst thus express   *woodland*
  A flowery tale more sweetly than our rhyme:
5 What leaf-fring'd legend haunts about thy shape
  Of deities or mortals, or of both,
    In Tempe or the dales of Arcady?[4]
  What men or gods are these? What maidens loth?
What mad pursuit? What struggle to escape?
10   What pipes and timbrels?° What   *tambourines*
    wild ecstasy?

2

Heard melodies are sweet, but those unheard
  Are sweeter; therefore, ye soft pipes, play on;
Not to the sensual° ear, but, more endear'd,   *physical*
  Pipe to the spirit ditties of no tone:
15 Fair youth, beneath the trees, thou canst not leave
  Thy song, nor ever can those trees be bare;
    Bold Lover, never, never canst thou kiss,
Though winning near the goal—yet, do not grieve;
  She cannot fade, though thou hast not thy bliss,
20   For ever wilt thou love, and she be fair!

---

[1] *Darkling* In the dark.
[2] *requiem* Mass sung for the dead.
[3] *Ruth ... corn* Widow in the Book of Ruth (1-4) who leaves Moab for Judah with her mother-in-law Naomi because of famine.

---

[4] *Tempe* Valley in ancient Greece renowned for its beauty; *Arcady* Ideal region of rural life, named for a mountainous district in Greece.

3

Ah, happy, happy boughs! that cannot shed
    Your leaves, nor ever bid the Spring adieu;
And, happy melodist, unwearied,
    For ever piping songs for ever new;
25 More happy love! more happy, happy love!
    For ever warm and still to be enjoy'd,
        For ever panting, and for ever young;
All breathing human passion far above,
    That leaves a heart high-sorrowful and cloy'd,
30   A burning forehead, and a parching tongue.

4

Who are these coming to the sacrifice?
    To what green altar, O mysterious priest,
Lead'st thou that heifer lowing at the skies,
    And all her silken flanks with garlands drest?
35 What little town by river or sea shore,
    Or mountain-built with peaceful citadel,
        Is emptied of this folk, this pious morn?
And, little town, thy streets for evermore
    Will silent be; and not a soul to tell
40   Why thou art desolate, can e'er return.

5

O Attic[1] shape! Fair attitude! with brede°   *interwoven design*
    Of marble men and maidens overwrought,°   *overlaid*
With forest branches and the trodden weed;
    Thou, silent form, dost tease us out of thought
45 As doth eternity: Cold Pastoral!
    When old age shall this generation waste,
        Thou shalt remain, in midst of other woe
Than ours, a friend to man, to whom thou say'st,
    "Beauty is truth, truth beauty,"—that is all
50   Ye know on earth, and all ye need to know.[2]
—1820

---

1 *Attic* I.e., Greek. Attica was an ancient region of Greece that had Athens as its capital.

2 *Beauty is ... know* The quotation marks in line 49 are present in Keats's 1820 volume of poems, but are absent in transcripts of the poem made by Keats's friends and in the version of the poem published in *Annals of the Fine Arts* in 1820. As a result, their presence has engendered much critical debate. It is unclear whether Keats meant the last line and a half to be spoken by the poet, or whether the entire final two lines are the imagined declaration of the urn.

Ode on Melancholy[3]

1

No, No, go not to Lethe,[4] neither twist
Wolf's-bane,[5] tight-rooted, for its poisonous
    wine;
Nor suffer thy pale forehead to be kiss'd
By nightshade, ruby grape of Proserpine;[6]
5 Make not your rosary of yew-berries,[7]
    Nor let the beetle, nor the death-moth[8] be
        Your mournful Psyche,[9] nor the downy owl
A partner in your sorrow's mysteries;[10]

---

3 *Ode on Melancholy* In the original manuscript version, the poem opened with the following stanza:
Though you should build a bark of dead men's bones,
    And rear a phantom gibbet for a mast,
Stitch creeds together for a sail, with groans
    To fill it out, bloodstained and aghast;
Although your rudder be a Dragon's tail,
    Long sever'd, yet still hard with agony,
Your cordage large uprootings from the skull
Of bald Medusa; certes you would fail
    To find Melancholy, whether she
        Dreameth in any isle of Lethe dull.
(Medusa was one of the Gorgons, three monstrous, winged sisters who had snakes for hair.)

4 *Lethe* River in Hades, the classical underworld, whose waters produce forgetfulness.

5 *Wolf's-bane* Poisonous plant native to Europe.

6 *nightshade* Plants with poisonous berries; *Proserpine* Daughter of Demeter who was abducted by Pluto, god of the underworld, and made queen of Hades. Her mother, goddess of the harvest, mourned for her daughter and so caused an eternal winter until Pluto was prevailed upon to allow Proserpine to return to her mother six months of every year.

7 *yew-berries* Poisonous berries of the yew tree, which is commonly planted in graveyards and is therefore often regarded as symbolic of death or sadness.

8 *beetle* The scarab, a large black beetle that Egyptians placed in their tombs as a symbol of resurrection; *death-moth* Death's-head moth, whose wings carry a mark resembling a human skull.

9 *Psyche* In classical mythology, a young woman who was beloved by Cupid, winged god of love and son of Venus. After winning over Venus, who was jealous of Psyche's beauty, Psyche was granted immortality by Jupiter. In Greek myth she is often a personification of the soul. Her name in Greek means butterfly as well as soul. Psyche was often represented as a butterfly flying out of a dying person's mouth.

10 *mysteries* I.e., secret rites or ceremonies.

For shade to shade will come too drowsily,
10   And drown the wakeful anguish of the soul.

2

But when the melancholy fit shall fall
      Sudden from heaven like a weeping cloud,
That fosters the droop-headed flowers all,
      And hides the green hill in an April shroud;
15 Then glut thy sorrow on a morning rose,
      Or on the rainbow of the salt sand-wave,
            Or on the wealth of globed peonies;
Or if thy mistress some rich anger shows,
      Emprison her soft hand, and let her rave,
20   And feed deep, deep upon her peerless eyes.

3

She dwells with Beauty—Beauty that must die;
      And Joy, whose hand is ever at his lips
Bidding adieu; and aching Pleasure nigh,
      Turning to poison while the bee-mouth sips:
25 Ay, in the very temple of Delight
      Veil'd Melancholy has her sovran° shrine,   *sovereign*
            Though seen of none save him whose
                  strenuous tongue
Can burst Joy's grape against his palate fine;°   *refined*
      His soul shall taste the sadness of her might,
30   And be among her cloudy trophies hung.
—1820

Ode on Indolence[1]

"They toil not, neither do they spin."[2]

1

One morn before me were three figures seen,
      With bowed necks, and joined hands, side-faced;
And one behind the other stepp'd serene,
      In placid sandals, and in white robes graced;
5 They pass'd, like figures on a marble urn,

When shifted round to see the other side;
      They came again; as when the urn once more
Is shifted round, the first seen shades return;
      And they were strange to me, as may betide
10   With vases, to one deep in Phidian lore.[3]

2

How is it, shadows, that I knew ye not?
      How came ye muffled in so hush a masque?°   *play*
Was it a silent deep-disguised plot
      To steal away, and leave without a task
15 My idle days? Ripe was the drowsy hour;
      The blissful cloud of summer-indolence
            Benumb'd my eyes; my pulse grew less and less;
Pain had no sting, and pleasure's wreath no flower:
      O, why did ye not melt, and leave my sense
20   Unhaunted quite of all but—nothingness?

3

A third time pass'd they by, and, passing, turn'd
      Each one the face a moment whiles to me;
Then faded, and to follow them I burn'd
      And ached for wings because I knew the three;
25 The first was a fair Maid, and Love her name;
      The second was Ambition, pale of cheek,
            And ever watchful with fatigued eye;
The last, whom I love more, the more of blame
      Is heap'd upon her, maiden most unmeek,
30   I knew to be my demon Poesy.

4

They faded, and, forsooth! I wanted wings:
      O folly! What is Love! and where is it?
And for that poor Ambition! It springs
      From a man's little heart's short fever-fit;
35 For Poesy! No—she has not a joy—
      At least for me—so sweet as drowsy noons,
            And evenings steep'd in honeyed indolence;
O, for an age so shelter'd from annoy,°   *harm*
      That I may never know how change the moons,
40   Or hear the voice of busy common sense!

---

[1] *Ode on Indolence*   See the 1919 letter to George and Georgiana Keats, reprinted below, in which Keats describes the bout of indolence that is thought to have inspired this poem.

[2] *They toil … spin*   From Matthew 6.28–89: "Consider the lilies of the field, how they grow; they toil not, neither do they spin: And yet I say unto you, That even Solomon in all his glory was not arrayed like one of these."

[3] *Phidian lore*   Lore concerning Phidias, the fifth-century Athenian sculptor of what were later named the Elgin Marbles, the marble sculptures that decorated the outside of the Parthenon and were brought to England by Lord Elgin.

5

A third time came they by—alas! wherefore?
  My sleep had been embroider'd with dim dreams;
My soul had been a lawn besprinkled o'er
  With flowers, and stirring shades, and baffled beams:
45 The morn was clouded, but no shower fell,
  Tho' in her lids hung the sweet tears of May;
    The open casement press'd a new-leav'd vine,
Let in the budding warmth and
    throstle's° lay;°   *thrush's / song*
  O shadows! 'twas a time to bid farewell!
50   Upon your skirts had fallen no tears of mine.

6

So, ye three ghosts, adieu! Ye cannot raise
  My head cool-bedded in the flowery grass;
For I would not be dieted with praise,
  A pet-lamb in a sentimental farce!
55 Fade softly from my eyes, and be once more
  In masque-like figures on the dreamy urn;
    Farewell! I yet have visions for the night,
And for the day faint visions there is store;
  Vanish, ye phantoms! from my idle spright,°   *spirit*
60   Into the clouds, and never more return!
  —1848 (WRITTEN 1819)

15   Thy hair soft-lifted by the winnowing wind;
  Or on a half-reap'd furrow sound asleep,
    Drows'd with the fume of poppies, while thy hook[1]
      Spares the next swath and all its twined flowers:
  And sometimes like a gleaner[2] thou dost keep
20   Steady thy laden head across a brook;
      Or by a cider-press, with patient look,
        Thou watchest the last oozings hours by hours.

3

Where are the songs of Spring? Ay, where are they?
  Think not of them, thou hast thy music too—
25 While barred clouds bloom the soft-dying day,
  And touch the stubble-plains with rosy hue;
Then in a wailful choir the small gnats mourn
  Among the river sallows,° borne aloft   *willows*
    Or sinking as the light wind lives or dies;
30 And full-grown lambs loud bleat from hilly bourn;° *realm*
  Hedge-crickets sing; and now with treble soft
  The red-breast whistles from a
    garden-croft;°   *enclosed garden*
      And gathering swallows twitter in the skies.
  —1820

To Autumn

1

S eason of mists and mellow fruitfulness,
   Close bosom-friend of the maturing sun;
Conspiring with him how to load and bless
  With fruit the vines that round the thatch-eves run;
5 To bend with apples the moss'd cottage-trees,
  And fill all fruit with ripeness to the core;
    To swell the gourd, and plump the hazel shells
With a sweet kernel; to set budding more,
  And still more, later flowers for the bees,
10 Until they think warm days will never cease,
    For Summer has o'er-brimm'd their clammy cells.

2

Who hath not seen thee oft amid thy store?
  Sometimes whoever seeks abroad may find
Thee sitting careless on a granary floor,

OSCAR WILDE
1854 – 1900

For his epigrammatic genius, his challenges to bourgeois sensibilities, and his dazzling essays, dramas, and other writings, Oscar Wilde has been both reverenced and reviled for more than a century. Notorious for his flamboyance and wit before he had ever published a word, Wilde established himself in the literary world with his sole novel, *The Picture of Dorian Gray*, and even more with such sparkling social comedies as *An Ideal Husband* and *The Importance of Being Earnest*. He was a vocal advocate of aestheticism; Wilde saw in art the possibility for a life beyond the day-to-day monotony of ordinary existence. The "aesthetic movement," he writes, "produced certain colours, subtle in their loveliness and fascinating in their almost mystical tone. They were, and are, our reaction against the crude primaries of a doubtless more respectable but certainly less cultivated age."

Wilde began his life as Oscar Fingal O'Flahertie Wills Wilde. His parents, themselves no strangers to controversy, were Lady Jane Francesca Elgee and Dr. (later Sir) William Wilde. Both were accomplished writers. William, an ear and eye surgeon, wrote a book on medical and literary institutions in Austria and another about his voyage to North Africa and the Middle East. He achieved fame for his work on the Irish Census, for which he conducted a groundbreaking demographic study of the Great Famine, earning a knighthood in 1864. His reputation was somewhat tainted, however, by his womanizing; he fathered three children out of wedlock. Lady Wilde was also a prominent figure. Born Jane Frances Agnes Elgee, she adopted the more Italian-sounding "Francesca" to reinforce the family's claim that they were descended from Dante Alighieri (truth never stood in the way of a good Wilde family story). Lady Wilde took yet another name, "Speranza," when she published poems in *The Nation*, a weekly Dublin newspaper published by an anti-British revolutionary group called the Young Irelanders.

Wilde grew up in the colorful environment of his mother's famous salon, where she hosted leading Dublin artists and writers. Once when Wilde returned from college, he invited a friend to Lady Wilde's weekly "conversazione," saying: "I want to introduce you to my mother. We have founded a society for the suppression of virtue." Wilde was a brilliant student at Trinity College, graduating in 1874 with the Berkeley Gold Medal for Classics and receiving a scholarship to study at Oxford. Before long, he was celebrated at Oxford's Magdalen College for his wit, decadence, and ostentatious appearance. He was most influenced in his academic years by two rivals at Oxford, John Ruskin and Walter Pater. From Ruskin, perhaps the most influential art critic of the century, Wilde took counsel on what the older scholar believed to be the spiritual, ethical, and moral nature of art. From Pater, who was already infamous following the publication of his *Studies in the History of the Renaissance* (1873), Wilde picked up elements of aestheticism he would eventually transform into his own theories of art. Wilde would later describe Pater's *Renaissance* as "the holy writ of beauty."

After winning the Newdigate prize for poetry and graduating with first class honors, Wilde moved to London and began his career as a divisive public figure. He was known, for example, for a formal jacket, called his "cello coat," that he wore to the opening of the Grosvenor Gallery in 1877, and for being more generally a poster-boy of the emerging aesthetic movement. By the time he published a book of poems in 1881, he had already become the butt of many caricatures in *Punch* magazine; he had taken to modeling his look on the character of Bunthorne in Gilbert and Sullivan's satirical comic opera *Patience*. For the next few years Wilde delivered lectures in the United States and Great Britain about the aesthetic movement, for which he had ambitious plans: "I want to make this artistic movement the basis for a new civilization." In Boston he voiced some of the ideas about art and life for which he would best be known: "The supreme object of life is to live. Few people live. It is true life only to realize one's own perfection, to make one's every dream a reality. Even this is possible."

In 1884 Wilde married Constance Lloyd, with whom he would have two sons, Cyril and Vyvyan. From 1887 to 1889 he edited *Woman's World*, a popular magazine. Through the late 1880s, Wilde wrote reviews of many of his most famous contemporaries, including the painter James Whistler and the poets D.G. Rossetti, William Morris, Algernon Swinburne, and others. He was also at work on the volume that would ultimately constitute the most thorough account of his aesthetic philosophy, *Intentions* (1891), which included the essays "The Decay of Lying" and "The Critic as Artist." The essays argue for the paramount importance of art in human life: "[Art's] are ... the great archetypes of which things that have existence are but unfinished copies." Rather than artists copying from the world about them, writes Wilde, we as individuals interpret the world *through art*, through the "archetypes" presented to us by works of art. Hence "[T]here may have been fogs for centuries in London," but "no one saw them .... till Art had invented them." The early 1890s also saw the publication of Wilde's novel, *The Picture of Dorian Gray*, which both puts forward Wilde's aesthetic beliefs and suggests some of the dangers of a life given over to aesthetic consumption.

Wilde was clearly at his very best in the early 1890s. In addition to *Intentions, Dorian Gray*, and poems such as "Helas," Wilde penned a string of brilliant social comedies, including *Lady Windermere's Fan* (1892), *A Woman of No Importance* (1893), and *An Ideal Husband* (1895). His final comedy was his masterpiece of farce, *The Importance of Being Earnest*; it first played in 1895 to wildly enthusiastic crowds at the St. James Theatre in London. Success came to an end only through Wilde's ill-fated affair with a young aristocrat, Lord Alfred Douglas ("Bosie"). Douglas's father, the mentally-unstable Marquis of Queensbury, was infuriated by the relationship, and in 1895 he publicly accused Wilde of sodomy. Convinced he had to defend his own and Douglas's honor, Wilde sued the Marquis for libel. After Wilde failed in his suit against Queensbury, the government used evidence from the trial to launch a criminal investigation against Wilde because homosexuality was a criminal offence. Wilde was found guilty of "gross indecency" and sentenced to two years of imprisonment with hard labor.   Prison left Wilde financially and emotionally broken. The horrid conditions of late-Victorian prison life—including a poor diet, enforced silence, and physically-taxing labor—were especially difficult to handle. From prison Wilde wrote a moving autobiographical letter to Bosie, later entitled *De Profundis*, that accuses the younger man of heartless and selfish behavior. (Bosie had treated Wilde poorly all along, and he abandoned Wilde during his imprisonment.) Even from his cell, however, Wilde wrote of seeing "new developments in Art and Life." Upon his release he composed "The Ballad of Reading Gaol " (1898), a heartfelt indictment of the prison system and capital punishment, as well as a meditation on the universal characteristics of human nature.

Wilde's last years were spent in Italy and France. He seems never to have recovered fully from his prison experience, and by late in 1900 he was quite ill. He died and was buried in Paris before the year ended; the immediate cause of his death has never been conclusively established. In 1995 a window in the Poets' Corner of Westminster Abbey was dedicated in his honor.

⌘ ⌘ ⌘

The Importance of Being Earnest
A Trivial Comedy for Serious People

THE PERSONS IN THE PLAY

John Worthing, J.P.[3]
Algernon Moncrieff
Rev. Canon Chasuble, D.D.[4]
Merriman, *Butler*
Lane, *Manservant*
Lady Bracknell
Hon.[5] Gwendolen Fairfax
Cecily Cardew
Miss Prism, *Governess*

THE SCENES IN THE PLAY

ACT 1.   Algernon Moncrieff's Flat in Half-Moon Street,[6] W.
ACT 2. The Garden at the Manor House, Woolton.[7]
ACT 3. Drawing-Room at the Manor House, Woolton.

TIME: The Present.

---

[3] *J.P.*   Justice of the Peace.

[4] *D.D.*   Doctor of Divinity.

[5] *Hon.*   I.e., The Honorable. The honorific in this case designates the daughter of a peer below the rank of Earl.

[6] *Half-Moon Street*   Street located in a fashionable area of London.

[7] *Woolton*   A fictional location.

ACT 1

SCENE

(*Morning-room in Algernon's flat in Half-Moon Street. The room is luxuriously and artistically furnished. The sound of a piano is heard in the adjoining room.*)

(*Lane is arranging afternoon tea on the table, and after the music has ceased, Algernon enters.*)

ALGERNON.   Did you hear what I was playing, Lane?

LANE.   I didn't think it polite to listen, sir.

ALGERNON.   I'm sorry for that, for your sake. I don't play accurately—any one can play accurately—but I
5   play with wonderful expression. As far as the piano is concerned, sentiment is my forte. I keep science for Life.

LANE.   Yes, sir.

ALGERNON.   And, speaking of the science of Life, have you got the cucumber sandwiches[1] cut for Lady
10   Bracknell?

LANE.   Yes, sir. (*Hands them on a salver.[2]*)

ALGERNON.   (*Inspects them, takes two, and sits down on the sofa.*) Oh! ... by the way, Lane, I see from your book that on Thursday night, when Lord Shoreman and Mr.
15   Worthing were dining with me, eight bottles of champagne are entered as having been consumed.

LANE.   Yes, sir; eight bottles and a pint.

ALGERNON.   Why is it that at a bachelor's establishment the servants invariably drink the champagne? I ask
20   merely for information.

LANE.   I attribute it to the superior quality of the wine, sir. I have often observed that in married households the champagne is rarely of a first-rate brand.

ALGERNON.   Good heavens! Is marriage so demoralising
25   as that?

LANE.   I believe it is a very pleasant state, sir. I have had very little experience of it myself up to the present. I have only been married once. That was in consequence of a misunderstanding between myself and a young
30   person.

---

[1]   *cucumber sandwiches*   Small sandwiches of cucumber on thinly-sliced bread, a staple of afternoon tea in polite English society.

[2]   *salver*   Serving tray, typically silver.

ALGERNON.   (*Languidly.*) I don't know that I am much interested in your family life, Lane.

LANE.   No, sir; it is not a very interesting subject. I never think of it myself.

35   ALGERNON. Very natural, I am sure. That will do, Lane, thank you.

LANE.   Thank you, sir. (*Lane goes out.*)

ALGERNON.   Lane's views on marriage seem somewhat lax. Really, if the lower orders don't set us a good
40   example, what on earth is the use of them? They seem, as a class, to have absolutely no sense of moral responsibility.

(*Enter Lane.*)

LANE.   Mr. Ernest Worthing.

(*Enter Jack. Lane goes out.*)

ALGERNON. How are you, my dear Ernest? What brings
45   you up to town?

JACK.   Oh, pleasure, pleasure! What else should bring one anywhere? Eating as usual, I see, Algy!

ALGERNON.   (*Stiffly.*) I believe it is customary in good society to take some slight refreshment at five o'clock.
50   Where have you been since last Thursday?

JACK.   (*Sitting down on the sofa.*) In the country.

ALGERNON.   What on earth do you do there?

JACK.   (*Pulling off his gloves.*) When one is in town[3] one amuses oneself. When one is in the country one amuses
55   other people. It is excessively boring.

ALGERNON.   And who are the people you amuse?

JACK.   (*Airily.*) Oh, neighbours, neighbours.

ALGERNON.   Got nice neighbours in your part of Shropshire?

60   JACK.   Perfectly horrid! Never speak to one of them.

ALGERNON.   How immensely you must amuse them! (*Goes over and takes sandwich.*) By the way, Shropshire is your county, is it not?

JACK.   Eh? Shropshire? Yes, of course. Hallo! Why all
65   these cups? Why cucumber sandwiches? Why such reckless extravagance in one so young? Who is coming to tea?

---

[3]   *in town*   In London.

ALGERNON.   Oh! merely Aunt Augusta and Gwendolen.

JACK.   How perfectly delightful!

70 ALGERNON.   Yes, that is all very well; but I am afraid Aunt Augusta won't quite approve of your being here.

JACK.   May I ask why?

ALGERNON.   My dear fellow, the way you flirt with Gwendolen is perfectly disgraceful. It is almost as bad as

75 the way Gwendolen flirts with you.

JACK.   I am in love with Gwendolen. I have come up to town expressly to propose to her.

ALGERNON.   I thought you had come up for pleasure? … I call that business.

80 JACK.   How utterly unromantic you are!

ALGERNON.   I really don't see anything romantic in proposing. It is very romantic to be in love. But there is nothing romantic about a definite proposal. Why, one may be accepted. One usually is, I believe. Then the

85 excitement is all over. The very essence of romance is uncertainty. If ever I get married, I'll certainly try to forget the fact.

JACK.   I have no doubt about that, dear Algy. The Divorce Court was specially invented for people whose

90 memories are so curiously constituted.

ALGERNON.   Oh! there is no use speculating on that subject. Divorces are made in Heaven—(*Jack puts out his hand to take a sandwich. Algernon at once interferes.*) Please don't touch the cucumber sandwiches. They are

95 ordered specially for Aunt Augusta. (*Takes one and eats it.*)

JACK.   Well, you have been eating them all the time.

ALGERNON.   That is quite a different matter. She is my aunt. (*Takes plate from below.*) Have some bread and

100 butter. The bread and butter is for Gwendolen. Gwendolen is devoted to bread and butter.

JACK.   (*Advancing to table and helping himself.*) And very good bread and butter it is too.

ALGERNON. Well, my dear fellow, you need not eat as if

105 you were going to eat it all. You behave as if you were married to her already. You are not married to her already, and I don't think you ever will be.

JACK. Why on earth do you say that?

ALGERNON. Well, in the first place girls never marry the

110 men they flirt with. Girls don't think it right.

JACK. Oh, that is nonsense!

ALGERNON. It isn't. It is a great truth. It accounts for the extraordinary number of bachelors that one sees all over the place. In the second place, I don't give my consent.

115 JACK.   Your consent!

ALGERNON.   My dear fellow, Gwendolen is my first cousin. And before I allow you to marry her, you will have to clear up the whole question of Cecily. (*Rings bell.*)

120 JACK.   Cecily! What on earth do you mean? What do you mean, Algy, by Cecily! I don't know any one of the name of Cecily.

(*Enter Lane.*)

ALGERNON.   Bring me that cigarette case Mr. Worthing left in the smoking-room the last time he dined here.

125 LANE.   Yes, sir.

(*Lane goes out.*)

JACK.   Do you mean to say you have had my cigarette case all this time? I wish to goodness you had let me know. I have been writing frantic letters to Scotland Yard about it. I was very nearly offering a large reward.

130 ALGERNON.   Well, I wish you would offer one. I happen to be more than usually hard up.

JACK.   There is no good offering a large reward now that the thing is found.

(*Enter Lane with the cigarette case on a salver. Algernon takes it at once. Lane goes out.*)

ALGERNON.   I think that is rather mean of you, Ernest,

135 I must say. (*Opens case and examines it.*) However, it makes no matter, for, now that I look at the inscription inside, I find that the thing isn't yours after all.

JACK.   Of course it's mine. (*Moving to him.*) You have seen me with it a hundred times, and you have no right

140 whatsoever to read what is written inside. It is a very ungentlemanly thing to read a private cigarette case.

ALGERNON.   Oh! it is absurd to have a hard and fast rule about what one should read and what one shouldn't. More than half of modern culture depends on what one

145 shouldn't read.

JACK. I am quite aware of the fact, and I don't propose to discuss modern culture. It isn't the sort of thing one should talk of in private. I simply want my cigarette case back.

150 ALGERNON. Yes; but this isn't your cigarette case. This cigarette case is a present from some one of the name of Cecily, and you said you didn't know any one of that name.

JACK. Well, if you want to know, Cecily happens to be
155 my aunt.

ALGERNON. Your aunt!

JACK. Yes. Charming old lady she is, too. Lives at Tunbridge Wells. Just give it back to me, Algy.

ALGERNON. (*Retreating to back of sofa.*) But why does
160 she call herself little Cecily if she is your aunt and lives at Tunbridge Wells? (*Reading.*) "From little Cecily with her fondest love."

JACK. (*Moving to sofa and kneeling upon it.*) My dear fellow, what on earth is there in that? Some aunts are
165 tall, some aunts are not tall. That is a matter that surely an aunt may be allowed to decide for herself. You seem to think that every aunt should be exactly like your aunt! That is absurd! For Heaven's sake give me back my cigarette case. (*Follows Algernon round the room.*)

170 ALGERNON. Yes. But why does your aunt call you her uncle? "From little Cecily, with her fondest love to her dear Uncle Jack." There is no objection, I admit, to an aunt being a small aunt, but why an aunt, no matter what her size may be, should call her own nephew her
175 uncle, I can't quite make out. Besides, your name isn't Jack at all; it is Ernest.

JACK. It isn't Ernest; it's Jack.

ALGERNON. You have always told me it was Ernest. I have introduced you to every one as Ernest. You answer
180 to the name of Ernest. You look as if your name was Ernest. You are the most earnest-looking person I ever saw in my life. It is perfectly absurd your saying that your name isn't Ernest. It's on your cards. Here is one of them. (*Taking it from case.*) "Mr. Ernest Worthing, B.
185 4, The Albany." I'll keep this as a proof that your name is Ernest if ever you attempt to deny it to me, or to Gwendolen, or to any one else. (*Puts the card in his pocket.*)

JACK. Well, my name is Ernest in town and Jack in the
190 country, and the cigarette case was given to me in the country.

ALGERNON. Yes, but that does not account for the fact that your small Aunt Cecily, who lives at Tunbridge Wells, calls you her dear uncle. Come, old boy, you had
195 much better have the thing out at once.

JACK. My dear Algy, you talk exactly as if you were a dentist. It is very vulgar to talk like a dentist when one isn't a dentist. It produces a false impression.

ALGERNON. Well, that is exactly what dentists always
200 do. Now, go on! Tell me the whole thing. I may mention that I have always suspected you of being a confirmed and secret Bunburyist; and I am quite sure of it now.

JACK. Bunburyist? What on earth do you mean by a
205 Bunburyist?

ALGERNON. I'll reveal to you the meaning of that incomparable expression as soon as you are kind enough to inform me why you are Ernest in town and Jack in the country.

210 JACK. Well, produce my cigarette case first.

ALGERNON. Here it is. (*Hands cigarette case.*) Now produce your explanation, and pray make it improbable. (*Sits on sofa.*)

JACK. My dear fellow, there is nothing improbable about
215 my explanation at all. In fact it's perfectly ordinary. Old Mr. Thomas Cardew, who adopted me when I was a little boy, made me in his will guardian to his granddaughter, Miss Cecily Cardew. Cecily, who addresses me as her uncle from motives of respect that you could
220 not possibly appreciate, lives at my place in the country under the charge of her admirable governess, Miss Prism.

ALGERNON. Where in that place in the country, by the way?

225 JACK. That is nothing to you, dear boy. You are not going to be invited … I may tell you candidly that the place is not in Shropshire.

ALGERNON. I suspected that, my dear fellow! I have Bunburyed all over Shropshire on two separate occa-
230 sions. Now, go on. Why are you Ernest in town and Jack in the country?

JACK. My dear Algy, I don't know whether you will be able to understand my real motives. You are hardly serious enough. When one is placed in the position of guardian, one has to adopt a very high moral tone on all subjects. It's one's duty to do so. And as a high moral tone can hardly be said to conduce very much to either one's health or one's happiness, in order to get up to town I have always pretended to have a younger brother of the name of Ernest, who lives in the Albany, and gets into the most dreadful scrapes. That, my dear Algy, is the whole truth pure and simple.

ALGERNON.   The truth is rarely pure and never simple. Modern life would be very tedious if it were either, and modern literature a complete impossibility!

JACK.   That wouldn't be at all a bad thing.

ALGERNON.   Literary criticism is not your forte, my dear fellow. Don't try it. You should leave that to people who haven't been at a University. They do it so well in the daily papers. What you really are is a Bunburyist. I was quite right in saying you were a Bunburyist. You are one of the most advanced Bunburyists I know.

JACK.   What on earth do you mean?

ALGERNON.   You have invented a very useful younger brother called Ernest, in order that you may be able to come up to town as often as you like. I have invented an invaluable permanent invalid called Bunbury, in order that I may be able to go down into the country whenever I choose. Bunbury is perfectly invaluable. If it wasn't for Bunbury's extraordinary bad health, for instance, I wouldn't be able to dine with you at Willis's to-night, for I have been really engaged to Aunt Augusta for more than a week.

JACK.   I haven't asked you to dine with me anywhere to-night.

ALGERNON.   I know. You are absurdly careless about sending out invitations. It is very foolish of you. Nothing annoys people so much as not receiving invitations.

JACK.   You had much better dine with your Aunt Augusta.

ALGERNON.   I haven't the smallest intention of doing anything of the kind. To begin with, I dined there on Monday, and once a week is quite enough to dine with one's own relations. In the second place, whenever I do dine there I am always treated as a member of the family, and sent down[1] with either no woman at all, or two. In the third place, I know perfectly well whom she will place me next to, to-night. She will place me next Mary Farquhar, who always flirts with her own husband across the dinner-table. That is not very pleasant. Indeed, it is not even decent … and that sort of thing is enormously on the increase. The amount of women in London who flirt with their own husbands is perfectly scandalous. It looks so bad. It is simply washing one's clean linen in public. Besides, now that I know you to be a confirmed Bunburyist I naturally want to talk to you about Bunburying. I want to tell you the rules.

JACK.   I'm not a Bunburyist at all. If Gwendolen accepts me, I am going to kill my brother, indeed I think I'll kill him in any case. Cecily is a little too much interested in him. It is rather a bore. So I am going to get rid of Ernest. And I strongly advise you to do the same with Mr. … with your invalid friend who has the absurd name.

ALGERNON.   Nothing will induce me to part with Bunbury, and if you ever get married, which seems to me extremely problematic, you will be very glad to know Bunbury. A man who marries without knowing Bunbury has a very tedious time of it.

JACK.   That is nonsense. If I marry a charming girl like Gwendolen, and she is the only girl I ever saw in my life that I would marry, I certainly won't want to know Bunbury.

ALGERNON.   Then your wife will. You don't seem to realise, that in married life three is company and two is none.

JACK.   (*Sententiously.*) That, my dear young friend, is the theory that the corrupt French Drama has been propounding for the last fifty years.

ALGERNON.   Yes; and that the happy English home has proved in half the time.

JACK.   For heaven's sake, don't try to be cynical. It's perfectly easy to be cynical.

ALGERNON.   My dear fellow, it isn't easy to be anything nowadays. There's such a lot of beastly competition about. (*The sound of an electric bell is heard.*) Ah! that must be Aunt Augusta. Only relatives, or creditors, ever ring in that Wagnerian[2] manner. Now, if I get her out

---

[1]   *sent down* I.e., sent from the drawing-room (typically upstairs) down to the dining-room (typically on a lower floor).

[2]   *Wagnerian* Suggesting the music of German composer Richard Wagner (1813–83), known for dramatic, stirring compositions such as *Tannhäuser, Lohergrin,* and *Der Ring des Nibelungen.*

of the way for ten minutes, so that you can have an opportunity for proposing to Gwendolen, may I dine with you to-night at Willis's?

JACK.   I suppose so, if you want to.

ALGERNON.   Yes, but you must be serious about it. I hate people who are not serious about meals. It is so shallow of them.

(*Enter Lane.*)

Lady Bracknell and Miss Fairfax.

(*Algernon goes forward to meet them. Enter Lady Bracknell and Gwendolen.*)

LADY BRACKNELL.   Good afternoon, dear Algernon, I hope you are behaving very well.

ALGERNON.   I'm feeling very well, Aunt Augusta.

LADY BRACKNELL.   That's not quite the same thing. In fact the two things rarely go together. (*Sees Jack and bows to him with icy coldness.*)

ALGERNON.   (*To Gwendolen.*) Dear me, you are smart!

GWENDOLEN.   I am always smart! Am I not, Mr. Worthing?

JACK.   You're quite perfect, Miss Fairfax.

GWENDOLEN.   Oh! I hope I am not that. It would leave no room for developments, and I intend to develop in many directions.

(*Gwendolen and Jack sit down together in the corner.*)

LADY BRACKNELL.   I'm sorry if we are a little late, Algernon, but I was obliged to call on dear Lady Harbury. I hadn't been there since her poor husband's death. I never saw a woman so altered; she looks quite twenty years younger. And now I'll have a cup of tea, and one of those nice cucumber sandwiches you promised me.

ALGERNON.   Certainly, Aunt Augusta. (*Goes over to tea-table.*)

LADY BRACKNELL.   Won't you come and sit here, Gwendolen?

GWENDOLEN.   Thanks, mamma, I'm quite comfortable where I am.

ALGERNON.   (*Picking up empty plate in horror.*) Good heavens! Lane! Why are there no cucumber sandwiches? I ordered them specially.

LANE.   (*Gravely.*) There were no cucumbers in the market this morning, sir. I went down twice.

ALGERNON.   No cucumbers!

LANE.   No, sir. Not even for ready money.

ALGERNON.   That will do, Lane, thank you.

LANE.   Thank you, sir. (*Goes out.*)

ALGERNON.   I am greatly distressed, Aunt Augusta, about there being no cucumbers, not even for ready money.

LADY BRACKNELL.   It really makes no matter, Algernon. I had some crumpets with Lady Harbury, who seems to me to be living entirely for pleasure now.

ALGERNON.   I hear her hair has turned quite gold from grief.

LADY BRACKNELL.   It certainly has changed its colour. From what cause I, of course, cannot say. (*Algernon crosses and hands tea.*) Thank you. I've quite a treat for you to-night, Algernon. I am going to send you down with Mary Farquhar. She is such a nice woman, and so attentive to her husband. It's delightful to watch them.

ALGERNON.   I am afraid, Aunt Augusta, I shall have to give up the pleasure of dining with you to-night after all.

LADY BRACKNELL.   (*Frowning.*) I hope not, Algernon. It would put my table completely out. Your uncle would have to dine upstairs. Fortunately he is accustomed to that.

ALGERNON.   It is a great bore, and, I need hardly say, a terrible disappointment to me, but the fact is I have just had a telegram to say that my poor friend Bunbury is very ill again. (*Exchanges glances with Jack.*) They seem to think I should be with him.

LADY BRACKNELL.   It is very strange. This Mr. Bunbury seems to suffer from curiously bad health.

ALGERNON.   Yes; poor Bunbury is a dreadful invalid.

LADY BRACKNELL.   Well, I must say, Algernon, that I think it is high time that Mr. Bunbury made up his mind whether he was going to live or to die. This shilly-shallying with the question is absurd. Nor do I in any way approve of the modern sympathy with invalids. I consider it morbid. Illness of any kind is hardly a thing to be encouraged in others. Health is the primary duty of life. I am always telling that to your poor uncle, but

he never seems to take much notice ... as far as any
improvement in his ailment goes. I should be much
obliged if you would ask Mr. Bunbury, from me, to be
kind enough not to have a relapse on Saturday, for I rely
on you to arrange my music for me. It is my last recep-
tion, and one wants something that will encourage
conversation, particularly at the end of the season when
every one has practically said whatever they had to say,
which, in most cases, was probably not much.

ALGERNON. I'll speak to Bunbury, Aunt Augusta, if he
is still conscious, and I think I can promise you he'll be
all right by Saturday. Of course the music is a great
difficulty. You see, if one plays good music, people don't
listen, and if one plays bad music people don't talk. But
I'll run over the programme I've drawn out, if you will
kindly come into the next room for a moment.

LADY BRACKNELL. Thank you, Algernon. It is very
thoughtful of you. (*Rising, and following Algernon.*) I'm
sure the programme will be delightful, after a few
expurgations. French songs I cannot possibly allow.
People always seem to think that they are improper, and
either look shocked, which is vulgar, or laugh, which is
worse. But German sounds a thoroughly respectable
language, and indeed, I believe is so. Gwendolen, you
will accompany me.

GWENDOLEN. Certainly, mamma.

(*Lady Bracknell and Algernon go into the music-room,
Gwendolen remains behind.*)

JACK. Charming day it has been, Miss Fairfax.

GWENDOLEN. Pray don't talk to me about the weather,
Mr. Worthing. Whenever people talk to me about the
weather, I always feel quite certain that they mean
something else. And that makes me so nervous.

JACK. I do mean something else.

GWENDOLEN. I thought so. In fact, I am never wrong.

JACK. And I would like to be allowed to take advantage
of Lady Bracknell's temporary absence ...

GWENDOLEN. I would certainly advise you to do so.
Mamma has a way of coming back suddenly into a
room that I have often had to speak to her about.

JACK. (*Nervously.*) Miss Fairfax, ever since I met you I
have admired you more than any girl ... I have ever met
since ... I met you.

GWENDOLEN. Yes, I am quite well aware of the fact.
And I often wish that in public, at any rate, you had
been more demonstrative. For me you have always had
an irresistible fascination. Even before I met you I was
far from indifferent to you. (*Jack looks at her in amaze-
ment.*) We live, as I hope you know, Mr. Worthing, in
an age of ideals. The fact is constantly mentioned in the
more expensive monthly magazines, and has reached the
provincial[1] pulpits, I am told; and my ideal has always
been to love some one of the name of Ernest. There is
something in that name that inspires absolute confi-
dence. The moment Algernon first mentioned to me
that he had a friend called Ernest, I knew I was destined
to love you.

JACK. You really love me, Gwendolen?

GWENDOLEN. Passionately!

JACK. Darling! You don't know how happy you've made
me.

GWENDOLEN. My own Ernest!

JACK. But you don't really mean to say that you couldn't
love me if my name wasn't Ernest?

GWENDOLEN. But your name is Ernest.

JACK. Yes, I know it is. But supposing it was something
else? Do you mean to say you couldn't love me then?

GWENDOLEN. (*Glibly.*) Ah! that is clearly a metaphysical
speculation, and like most metaphysical speculations has
very little reference at all to the actual facts of real life, as
we know them.

JACK. Personally, darling, to speak quite candidly, I
don't much care about the name of Ernest ... I don't
think the name suits me at all.

GWENDOLEN. It suits you perfectly. It is a divine name.
It has a music of its own. It produces vibrations.

JACK. Well, really, Gwendolen, I must say that I think
there are lots of other much nicer names. I think Jack,
for instance, a charming name.

GWENDOLEN. Jack? ... No, there is very little music in
the name Jack, if any at all, indeed. It does not thrill. It
produces absolutely no vibrations ... I have known
several Jacks, and they all, without exception, were more
than usually plain. Besides, Jack is a notorious domestic-
ity for John! And I pity any woman who is married to a

---

[1] *provincial* "Province" does not indicate a formal British jurisdic-
tion; "the provinces" is a colloquial term for all areas of the country
that are some distance from London.

man called John. She would probably never be allowed to know the entrancing pleasure of a single moment's solitude. The only really safe name is Ernest.

485 JACK. Gwendolen, I must get christened at once—I mean we must get married at once. There is no time to be lost.

GWENDOLEN. Married, Mr. Worthing?

JACK. (*Astounded.*) Well … surely. You know that I love
490 you, and you led me to believe, Miss Fairfax, that you were not absolutely indifferent to me.

GWENDOLEN. I adore you. But you haven't proposed to me yet. Nothing has been said at all about marriage. The subject has not even been touched on.

495 JACK. Well … may I propose to you now?

GWENDOLEN. I think it would be an admirable opportunity. And to spare you any possible disappointment, Mr. Worthing, I think it only fair to tell you quite frankly before-hand that I am fully determined to accept
500 you.

JACK. Gwendolen!

GWENDOLEN. Yes, Mr. Worthing, what have you got to say to me?

JACK. You know what I have got to say to you.

505 GWENDOLEN. Yes, but you don't say it.

JACK. Gwendolen, will you marry me? (*Goes on his knees.*)

GWENDOLEN. Of course I will, darling. How long you have been about it! I am afraid you have had very little
510 experience in how to propose.

JACK. My own one, I have never loved any one in the world but you.

GWENDOLEN. Yes, but men often propose for practice. I know my brother Gerald does. All my girl-friends tell
515 me so. What wonderfully blue eyes you have, Ernest! They are quite, quite, blue. I hope you will always look at me just like that, especially when there are other people present. (*Enter Lady Bracknell.*)

LADY BRACKNELL. Mr. Worthing! Rise, sir, from this
520 semi-recumbent posture. It is most indecorous.

GWENDOLEN. Mamma! (*He tries to rise; she restrains him.*) I must beg you to retire. This is no place for you. Besides, Mr. Worthing has not quite finished yet.

LADY BRACKNELL. Finished what, may I ask?

525 GWENDOLEN. I am engaged to Mr. Worthing, mamma.

(*They rise together.*)

LADY BRACKNELL. Pardon me, you are not engaged to any one. When you do become engaged to some one, I, or your father, should his health permit him, will inform you of the fact. An engagement should come on a young
530 girl as a surprise, pleasant or unpleasant, as the case may be. It is hardly a matter that she could be allowed to arrange for herself … And now I have a few questions to put to you, Mr. Worthing. While I am making these inquiries, you, Gwendolen, will wait for me below in
535 the carriage.

GWENDOLEN. (*Reproachfully.*) Mamma!

LADY BRACKNELL. In the carriage, Gwendolen!

(*Gwendolen goes to the door. She and Jack blow kisses to each other behind Lady Bracknell's back. Lady Bracknell looks vaguely about as if she could not understand what the noise was. Finally turns round.*)

Gwendolen, the carriage!

GWENDOLEN. Yes, mamma. (*Goes out, looking back at
540 Jack.*)

LADY BRACKNELL. (*Sitting down.*) You can take a seat, Mr. Worthing. (*Looks in her pocket for note-book and pencil.*)

JACK. Thank you, Lady Bracknell, I prefer standing.

545 LADY BRACKNELL. (*Pencil and note-book in hand.*) I feel bound to tell you that you are not down on my list of eligible young men, although I have the same list as the dear Duchess of Bolton has. We work together, in fact. However, I am quite ready to enter your name, should
550 your answers be what a really affectionate mother requires. Do you smoke?

JACK. Well, yes, I must admit I smoke.

LADY BRACKNELL. I am glad to hear it. A man should always have an occupation of some kind. There are far
555 too many idle men in London as it is. How old are you?

JACK. Twenty-nine.

LADY BRACKNELL. A very good age to be married at. I have always been of opinion that a man who desires to get married should know either everything or nothing.
560 Which do you know?

JACK. (*After some hesitation.*) I know nothing, Lady Bracknell.

LADY BRACKNELL. I am pleased to hear it. I do not approve of anything that tampers with natural igno-
565 rance. Ignorance is like a delicate exotic fruit; touch it and the bloom is gone. The whole theory of modern education is radically unsound. Fortunately in England, at any rate, education produces no effect whatsoever. If it did, it would prove a serious danger to the upper
570 classes, and probably lead to acts of violence in Grosvenor Square.[1] What is your income?

JACK. Between seven and eight thousand a year.

LADY BRACKNELL. (*Makes a note in her book.*) In land, or in investments?

575 JACK. In investments, chiefly.

LADY BRACKNELL. That is satisfactory. What between the duties[2] expected of one during one's lifetime, and the duties exacted from one after one's death, land has ceased to be either a profit or a pleasure. It gives one
580 position, and prevents one from keeping it up. That's all that can be said about land.

JACK. I have a country house with some land, of course, attached to it, about fifteen hundred acres, I believe; but I don't depend on that for my real income. In fact, as far
585 as I can make out, the poachers are the only people who make anything out of it.

LADY BRACKNELL. A country house! How many bedrooms? Well, that point can be cleared up afterwards. You have a town house, I hope? A girl with a simple,
590 unspoiled nature, like Gwendolen, could hardly be expected to reside in the country.

JACK. Well, I own a house in Belgrave Square, but it is let by the year to Lady Bloxham. Of course, I can get it back whenever I like, at six months' notice.

595 LADY BRACKNELL. Lady Bloxham? I don't know her.

JACK. Oh, she goes about very little. She is a lady considerably advanced in years.

LADY BRACKNELL. Ah, nowadays that is no guarantee of respectability of character. What number in Belgrave
600 Square?

JACK. 149.

LADY BRACKNELL. (*Shaking her head.*) The unfashionable side. I thought there was something. However, that could easily be altered.

605 JACK. Do you mean the fashion, or the side?

LADY BRACKNELL. (*Sternly.*) Both, if necessary, I presume. What are your politics?

JACK. Well, I am afraid I really have none. I am a Liberal Unionist.[3]

610 LADY BRACKNELL. Oh, they count as Tories. They dine with us. Or come in the evening, at any rate. Now to minor matters. Are your parents living?

JACK. I have lost both my parents.

LADY BRACKNELL. To lose one parent, Mr. Worthing,
615 may be regarded as a misfortune; to lose both looks like carelessness. Who was your father? He was evidently a man of some wealth. Was he born in what the Radical papers call the purple of commerce,[4] or did he rise from the ranks of the aristocracy?

620 JACK. I am afraid I really don't know. The fact is, Lady Bracknell, I said I had lost my parents. It would be nearer the truth to say that my parents seem to have lost me … I don't actually know who I am by birth. I was … well, I was found.

625 LADY BRACKNELL. Found!

JACK. The late Mr. Thomas Cardew, an old gentleman of a very charitable and kindly disposition, found me, and gave me the name of Worthing, because he happened to have a first-class ticket for Worthing in his
630 pocket at the time. Worthing is a place in Sussex. It is a seaside resort.

LADY BRACKNELL. Where did the charitable gentleman who had a first-class ticket for this seaside resort find you?

635 JACK. (*Gravely.*) In a hand-bag.

LADY BRACKNELL. A hand-bag?

JACK. (*Very seriously.*) Yes, Lady Bracknell. I was in a hand-bag—a somewhat large, black leather hand-bag, with handles to it—an ordinary hand-bag in fact.

640 LADY BRACKNELL. In what locality did this Mr. James, or Thomas, Cardew come across this ordinary hand-bag?

JACK. In the cloak-room at Victoria Station. It was given

---

1 *Grosvenor Square* Located in a fashionable part of central London.

2 *duties* Taxes.

3 *Liberal Unionist* The Liberal Unionists, who in 1886 had broken away from the Liberal party in reaction to Prime Minister William Gladstone's support for Irish Home Rule, occupied the political center between the two large parties, the Liberals and the Conservatives.

4 *Was he born … the purple of commerce* I.e., was he born into a wealthy merchant or trading family. (The color purple is traditionally associated with royalty.)

to him in mistake for his own.

LADY BRACKNELL.   The cloak-room at Victoria Station?

645 JACK.   Yes. The Brighton line.

LADY BRACKNELL.   The line is immaterial. Mr. Worthing, I confess I feel somewhat bewildered by what you have just told me. To be born, or at any rate bred, in a hand-bag, whether it had handles or not, seems to me to

650 display a contempt for the ordinary decencies of family life that reminds one of the worst excesses of the French Revolution. And I presume you know what that unfortunate movement led to? As for the particular locality in which the hand-bag was found, a cloak-room at a

655 railway station might serve to conceal a social indiscretion— has probably, indeed, been used for that purpose before now—but it could hardly be regarded as an assured basis for a recognised position in good society.

JACK.   May I ask you then what you would advise me to

660 do? I need hardly say I would do anything in the world to ensure Gwendolen's happiness.

LADY BRACKNELL.   I would strongly advise you, Mr. Worthing, to try and acquire some relations as soon as possible, and to make a definite effort to produce at any

665 rate one parent, of either sex, before the season¹ is quite over.

JACK.   Well, I don't see how I could possibly manage to do that. I can produce the hand-bag at any moment. It is in my dressing-room at home. I really think that

670 should satisfy you, Lady Bracknell.

LADY BRACKNELL.   Me, sir! What has it to do with me? You can hardly imagine that I and Lord Bracknell would dream of allowing our only daughter—a girl brought up with the utmost care—to marry into a

675 cloak-room, and form an alliance with a parcel? Good morning, Mr. Worthing!

(*Lady Bracknell sweeps out in majestic indignation.*)

JACK.   Good morning! (*Algernon, from the other room, strikes up the Wedding March. Jack looks perfectly furious,*

680 *and goes to the door.*) For goodness' sake don't play that ghastly tune, Algy. How idiotic you are!

---

¹ *the season*   The London social season, which ran while Parliament was sitting. Many wealthy families spent the rest of the year at their country homes.

(*The music stops and Algernon enters cheerily.*)

ALGERNON.   Didn't it go off all right, old boy? You don't mean to say Gwendolen refused you? I know it is a way she has. She is always refusing people. I think it is

685 most ill-natured of her.

JACK.   Oh, Gwendolen is as right as a trivet.² As far as she is concerned, we are engaged. Her mother is perfectly unbearable. Never met such a Gorgon³ ... I don't really know what a Gorgon is like, but I am quite sure that

690 Lady Bracknell is one. In any case, she is a monster, without being a myth, which is rather unfair ... I beg your pardon, Algy, I suppose I shouldn't talk about your own aunt in that way before you.

ALGERNON.   My dear boy, I love hearing my relations

695 abused. It is the only thing that makes me put up with them at all. Relations are simply a tedious pack of people, who haven't got the remotest knowledge of how to live, nor the smallest instinct about when to die.

JACK.   Oh, that is nonsense!

700 ALGERNON.   It isn't!

JACK.   Well, I won't argue about the matter. You always want to argue about things.

ALGERNON.   That is exactly what things were originally made for.

705 JACK.   Upon my word, if I thought that, I'd shoot myself ... (*A pause.*) You don't think there is any chance of Gwendolen becoming like her mother in about a hundred and fifty years, do you, Algy?

ALGERNON.   All women become like their mothers. That

710 is their tragedy. No man does. That's his.

JACK.   Is that clever?

ALGERNON.   It is perfectly phrased! and quite as true as any observation in civilized life should be.

JACK.   I am sick to death of cleverness. Everybody is

715 clever nowadays. You can't go anywhere without meeting clever people. The thing has become an absolute public nuisance. I wish to goodness we had a few fools left.

ALGERNON.   We have.

---

² *as right as a trivet*   Proverbial expression indicating stability (a trivet is a three-footed stand or support).

³ *Gorgon*   In Greek mythology the three Gorgons are sisters who have repulsive features (including snakes growing out of their heads instead of hair); anyone who looks at them turns into stone.

JACK. I should extremely like to meet them. What do they talk about?

ALGERNON.   The fools? Oh! about the clever people, of course.

JACK. What fools!

ALGERNON. By the way, did you tell Gwendolen the truth about your being Ernest in town, and Jack in the country?

JACK. (*In a very patronising manner.*) My dear fellow, the truth isn't quite the sort of thing one tells to a nice, sweet, refined girl. What extraordinary ideas you have about the way to behave to a woman!

ALGERNON. The only way to behave to a woman is to make love to her, if she is pretty, and to some one else, if she is plain.

JACK. Oh, that is nonsense.

ALGERNON. What about your brother? What about the profligate Ernest?

JACK. Oh, before the end of the week I shall have got rid of him. I'll say he died in Paris of apoplexy.[1] Lots of people die of apoplexy, quite suddenly, don't they?

ALGERNON. Yes, but it's hereditary, my dear fellow. It's a sort of thing that runs in families. You had much better say a severe chill.

JACK. You are sure a severe chill isn't hereditary, or anything of that kind?

ALGERNON. Of course it isn't!

JACK. Very well, then. My poor brother Ernest is carried off suddenly, in Paris, by a severe chill. That gets rid of him.

ALGERNON. But I thought you said that … Miss Cardew was a little too much interested in your poor brother Ernest? Won't she feel his loss a good deal?

JACK. Oh, that is all right. Cecily is not a silly romantic girl, I am glad to say. She has got a capital appetite, goes on long walks, and pays no attention at all to her lessons.

ALGERNON. I would rather like to see Cecily.

JACK. I will take very good care you never do. She is excessively pretty, and she is only just eighteen.

ALGERNON. Have you told Gwendolen yet that you have an excessively pretty ward who is only just eighteen?

JACK. Oh! one doesn't blurt these things out to people. Cecily and Gwendolen are perfectly certain to be extremely great friends. I'll bet you anything you like that half an hour after they have met, they will be calling each other sister.

ALGERNON. Women only do that when they have called each other a lot of other things first. Now, my dear boy, if we want to get a good table at Willis's, we really must go and dress. Do you know it is nearly seven?

JACK. (*Irritably.*) Oh! It always is nearly seven.

ALGERNON. Well, I'm hungry.

JACK. I never knew you when you weren't …

ALGERNON. What shall we do after dinner? Go to a theatre?

JACK. Oh no! I loathe listening.

ALGERNON. Well, let us go to the Club?

JACK. Oh, no! I hate talking.

ALGERNON. Well, we might trot round to the Empire[2] at ten?

JACK. Oh, no! I can't bear looking at things. It is so silly.

ALGERNON. Well, what shall we do?

JACK. Nothing!

ALGERNON. It is awfully hard work doing nothing. However, I don't mind hard work where there is no definite object of any kind.

(*Enter Lane.*)

LANE. Miss Fairfax.

(*Enter Gwendolen. Lane goes out.*)

ALGERNON. Gwendolen, upon my word!

GWENDOLEN. Algy, kindly turn your back. I have something very particular to say to Mr. Worthing.

ALGERNON. Really, Gwendolen, I don't think I can allow this at all.

GWENDOLEN. Algy, you always adopt a strictly immoral attitude towards life. You are not quite old enough to do that. (*Algernon retires to the fireplace.*)

JACK. My own darling!

GWENDOLEN. Ernest, we may never be married. From the expression on mamma's face I fear we never shall. Few parents nowadays pay any regard to what their children say to them. The old-fashioned respect for the young is fast dying out. Whatever influence I ever had

---

[1] *apoplexy* Stroke.

[2] *the Empire* Theater that often featured risqué variety shows.

over mamma, I lost at the age of three. But although she may prevent us from becoming man and wife, and I may marry some one else, and marry often, nothing that she can possibly do can alter my eternal devotion to you.

JACK.   Dear Gwendolen!

GWENDOLEN.   The story of your romantic origin, as related to me by mamma, with unpleasing comments, has naturally stirred the deeper fibres of my nature. Your Christian name has an irresistible fascination. The simplicity of your character makes you exquisitely incomprehensible to me. Your town address at the Albany[1] I have. What is your address in the country?

JACK.   The Manor House, Woolton, Hertfordshire.

(Algernon, who has been carefully listening, smiles to himself, and writes the address on his shirt-cuff. Then picks up the Railway Guide.)

GWENDOLEN.   There is a good postal service, I suppose? It may be necessary to do something desperate. That of course will require serious consideration. I will communicate with you daily.

JACK.   My own one!

GWENDOLEN.   How long do you remain in town?

JACK.   Till Monday.

GWENDOLEN.   Good! Algy, you may turn round now.

ALGERNON.   Thanks, I've turned round already.

GWENDOLEN.   You may also ring the bell.

JACK.   You will let me see you to your carriage, my own darling?

GWENDOLEN.   Certainly.

JACK.   *(To Lane, who now enters.)* I will see Miss Fairfax out.

LANE.   Yes, sir. *(Jack and Gwendolen go off.)*

(Lane presents several letters on a salver to Algernon. It is to be surmised that they are bills, as Algernon, after looking at the envelopes, tears them up.)

ALGERNON.   A glass of sherry, Lane.

LANE.   Yes, sir.

ALGERNON.   To-morrow, Lane, I'm going Bunburying.

LANE.   Yes, sir.

ALGERNON.   I shall probably not be back till Monday.

You can put up my dress clothes, my smoking jacket, and all the Bunbury suits …

LANE.   Yes, sir. *(Handing sherry.)*

ALGERNON.   I hope to-morrow will be a fine day, Lane.

LANE.   It never is, sir.

ALGERNON.   Lane, you're a perfect pessimist.

LANE.   I do my best to give satisfaction, sir.

(Enter Jack. Lane goes off.)

JACK.   There's a sensible, intellectual girl! the only girl I ever cared for in my life. *(Algernon is laughing immoderately.)* What on earth are you so amused at?

ALGERNON.   Oh, I'm a little anxious about poor Bunbury, that is all.

JACK.   If you don't take care, your friend Bunbury will get you into a serious scrape some day.

ALGERNON.   I love scrapes. They are the only things that are never serious.

JACK.   Oh, that's nonsense, Algy. You never talk anything but nonsense.

ALGERNON.   Nobody ever does.

(Jack looks indignantly at him, and leaves the room. Algernon lights a cigarette, reads his shirt-cuff, and smiles.)

ACT DROP

ACT 2

SCENE

(Garden at the Manor House. A flight of grey stone steps leads up to the house. The garden, an old-fashioned one, full of roses. Time of year, July. Basket chairs, and a table covered with books, are set under a large yew-tree. Miss Prism discovered seated at the table. Cecily is at the back watering flowers.)

MISS PRISM.   *(Calling.)* Cecily, Cecily! Surely such a utilitarian occupation as the watering of flowers is rather Moulton's duty than yours? Especially at a moment when intellectual pleasures await you. Your German grammar is on the table. Pray open it at page fifteen. We will repeat yesterday's lesson.

---

[1] *the Albany*   Fashionable men's club in London.

CECILY. (*Coming over very slowly.*) But I don't like German. It isn't at all a becoming language. I know perfectly well that I look quite plain after my German lesson.

MISS PRISM. Child, you know how anxious your guardian is that you should improve yourself in every way. He laid particular stress on your German, as he was leaving for town yesterday. Indeed, he always lays stress on your German when he is leaving for town.

CECILY. Dear Uncle Jack is so very serious! Sometimes he is so serious that I think he cannot be quite well.

MISS PRISM. (*Drawing herself up.*) Your guardian enjoys the best of health, and his gravity of demeanour is especially to be commended in one so comparatively young as he is. I know no one who has a higher sense of duty and responsibility.

CECILY. I suppose that is why he often looks a little bored when we three are together.

MISS PRISM. Cecily! I am surprised at you. Mr. Worthing has many troubles in his life. Idle merriment and triviality would be out of place in his conversation. You must remember his constant anxiety about that unfortunate young man his brother.

CECILY. I wish Uncle Jack would allow that unfortunate young man, his brother, to come down here sometimes. We might have a good influence over him, Miss Prism. I am sure you certainly would. You know German, and geology, and things of that kind influence a man very much. (*Cecily begins to write in her diary.*)

MISS PRISM. (*Shaking her head.*) I do not think that even I could produce any effect on a character that according to his own brother's admission is irretrievably weak and vacillating. Indeed I am not sure that I would desire to reclaim him. I am not in favour of this modern mania for turning bad people into good people at a moment's notice. As a man sows so let him reap.[1] You must put away your diary, Cecily. I really don't see why you should keep a diary at all.

CECILY. I keep a diary in order to enter the wonderful secrets of my life. If I didn't write them down, I should probably forget all about them.

MISS PRISM. Memory, my dear Cecily, is the diary that we all carry about with us.

CECILY. Yes, but it usually chronicles the things that have never happened, and couldn't possibly have happened. I believe that Memory is responsible for nearly all the three-volume novels that Mudie sends us.[2]

MISS PRISM. Do not speak slightingly of the three-volume novel, Cecily. I wrote one myself in earlier days.

CECILY. Did you really, Miss Prism? How wonderfully clever you are! I hope it did not end happily? I don't like novels that end happily. They depress me so much.

MISS PRISM. The good ended happily, and the bad unhappily. That is what Fiction means.

CECILY. I suppose so. But it seems very unfair. And was your novel ever published?

MISS PRISM. Alas! no. The manuscript unfortunately was abandoned. (*Cecily starts.*) I use the word in the sense of lost or mislaid. To your work, child, these speculations are profitless.

CECILY. (*Smiling.*) But I see dear Dr. Chasuble coming up through the garden.

MISS PRISM. (*Rising and advancing.*) Dr. Chasuble! This is indeed a pleasure.

(*Enter Canon Chasuble.*)

CHASUBLE. And how are we this morning? Miss Prism, you are, I trust, well?

CECILY. Miss Prism has just been complaining of a slight headache. I think it would do her so much good to have a short stroll with you in the Park, Dr. Chasuble.

MISS PRISM. Cecily, I have not mentioned anything about a headache.

CECILY. No, dear Miss Prism, I know that, but I felt instinctively that you had a headache. Indeed I was thinking about that, and not about my German lesson, when the Rector came in.

CHASUBLE. I hope, Cecily, you are not inattentive.

CECILY. Oh, I am afraid I am.

CHASUBLE. That is strange. Were I fortunate enough to be Miss Prism's pupil, I would hang upon her lips. (*Miss Prism glares.*) I spoke metaphorically.—My metaphor was drawn from bees. Ahem! Mr. Worthing, I suppose, has not returned from town yet?

---

[1] *As a man sows so let him reap* Galatians 6.7: "whatsoever a man soweth, that shall he also reap."

[2] *nearly all ... Mudie sends us* Commercial lending libraries of the time, such as Mudie's, specialized in lending novels that were published in three volumes.

MISS PRISM. We do not expect him till Monday after-
90 noon.

CHASUBLE. Ah yes, he usually likes to spend his Sunday in London. He is not one of those whose sole aim is enjoyment, as, by all accounts, that unfortunate young man his brother seems to be. But I must not disturb
95 Egeria and her pupil any longer.

MISS PRISM. Egeria? My name is Lætitia, Doctor.

CHASUBLE. (*Bowing.*) A classical allusion merely, drawn from the Pagan authors.[1] I shall see you both no doubt at Evensong?[2]

100 MISS PRISM. I think, dear Doctor, I will have a stroll with you. I find I have a headache after all, and a walk might do it good.

CHASUBLE. With pleasure, Miss Prism, with pleasure. We might go as far as the schools and back.

105 MISS PRISM. That would be delightful. Cecily, you will read your Political Economy in my absence. The chapter on the Fall of the Rupee you may omit. It is somewhat too sensational. Even these metallic problems have their melodramatic side.[3]

(*Goes down the garden with Dr. Chasuble.*)

110 CECILY. (*Picks up books and throws them back on table.*) Horrid Political Economy! Horrid Geography! Horrid, horrid German!

(*Enter Merriman with a card on a salver.*)

MERRIMAN. Mr. Ernest Worthing has just driven over from the station. He has brought his luggage with him.

115 CECILY. (*Takes the card and reads it.*) "Mr. Ernest Worthing, B. 4, The Albany, W." Uncle Jack's brother! Did you tell him Mr. Worthing was in town?

MERRIMAN. Yes, Miss. He seemed very much disap-pointed. I mentioned that you and Miss Prism were in

---

[1] *A classical allusion … Pagan authors* In Roman mythology, the nymph Egeria taught Numa, the second King of Rome, the lessons of wisdom and law which he then used to found the institutions of Rome.

[2] *Evensong* The evening service in the Anglican church (and various other Christian denominations).

[3] *The chapter … melodramatic side* The rupee (India's currency) declined dramatically in the early 1890s as a result of a variety of disasters, including an outbreak of plague.

---

120 the garden. He said he was anxious to speak to you privately for a moment.

CECILY. Ask Mr. Ernest Worthing to come here. I suppose you had better talk to the housekeeper about a room for him.

125 MERRIMAN. Yes, Miss.

(*Merriman goes off.*)

CECILY. I have never met any really wicked person before. I feel rather frightened. I am so afraid he will look just like every one else. (*Enter Algernon, very gay and debonair.*) He does!

130 ALGERNON. (*Raising his hat.*) You are my little cousin Cecily, I'm sure.

CECILY. You are under some strange mistake. I am not little. In fact, I believe I am more than usually tall for my age. (*Algernon is rather taken aback.*) But I am your
135 cousin Cecily. You, I see from your card, are Uncle Jack's brother, my cousin Ernest, my wicked cousin Ernest.

ALGERNON. Oh! I am not really wicked at all, cousin Cecily. You mustn't think that I am wicked.

140 CECILY. If you are not, then you have certainly been deceiving us all in a very inexcusable manner. I hope you have not been leading a double life, pretending to be wicked and being really good all the time. That would be hypocrisy.

145 ALGERNON. (*Looks at her in amazement.*) Oh! Of course I have been rather reckless.

CECILY. I am glad to hear it.

ALGERNON. In fact, now you mention the subject, I have been very bad in my own small way.

150 CECILY. I don't think you should be so proud of that, though I am sure it must have been very pleasant.

ALGERNON. It is much pleasanter being here with you.

CECILY. I can't understand how you are here at all. Uncle Jack won't be back till Monday afternoon.

155 ALGERNON. That is a great disappointment. I am obliged to go up by the first train on Monday morning. I have a business appointment that I am anxious … to miss!

CECILY. Couldn't you miss it anywhere but in London?

160 ALGERNON. No: the appointment is in London.

CECILY.   Well, I know, of course, how important it is not to keep a business engagement, if one wants to retain any sense of the beauty of life, but still I think you had better wait till Uncle Jack arrives. I know he wants to
165   speak to you about your emigrating.

ALGERNON.   About my what?

CECILY.   Your emigrating. He has gone up to buy your outfit.

ALGERNON.   I certainly wouldn't let Jack buy my outfit.
170   He has no taste in neckties at all.

CECILY.   I don't think you will require neckties. Uncle Jack is sending you to Australia.[1]

ALGERNON.   Australia! I'd sooner die.

CECILY.   Well, he said at dinner on Wednesday night,
175   that you would have to choose between this world, the next world, and Australia.

ALGERNON.   Oh, well! The accounts I have received of Australia and the next world are not particularly encouraging. This world is good enough for me, cousin Cecily.

180   CECILY.   Yes, but are you good enough for it?

ALGERNON.   I'm afraid I'm not that. That is why I want you to reform me. You might make that your mission, if you don't mind, cousin Cecily.

CECILY.   I'm afraid I've no time, this afternoon.

185   ALGERNON.   Well, would you mind my reforming myself this afternoon?

CECILY.   It is rather Quixotic of you. But I think you should try.

ALGERNON.   I will. I feel better already.

190   CECILY.   You are looking a little worse.

ALGERNON.   That is because I am hungry.

CECILY.   How thoughtless of me. I should have remembered that when one is going to lead an entirely new life, one requires regular and wholesome meals. Won't you
195   come in?

ALGERNON.   Thank you. Might I have a buttonhole[2] first? I never have any appetite unless I have a buttonhole first.

CECILY.   A Maréchal Niel?[3]   (*Picks up scissors.*)

200   ALGERNON.   No, I'd sooner have a pink rose.

CECILY.   Why?   (*Cuts a flower.*)

ALGERNON.   Because you are like a pink rose, Cousin Cecily.

CECILY.   I don't think it can be right for you to talk to
205   me like that. Miss Prism never says such things to me.

ALGERNON.   Then Miss Prism is a short-sighted old lady. (*Cecily puts the rose in his buttonhole.*) You are the prettiest girl I ever saw.

CECILY.   Miss Prism says that all good looks are a snare.

210   ALGERNON.   They are a snare that every sensible man would like to be caught in.

CECILY.   Oh, I don't think I would care to catch a sensible man. I shouldn't know what to talk to him about.

(*They pass into the house. Miss Prism and Dr. Chasuble return.*)

215   MISS PRISM.   You are too much alone, dear Dr. Chasuble. You should get married. A misanthrope I can understand—a womanthrope,[4] never!

CHASUBLE.   (*With a scholar's shudder.*) Believe me, I do not deserve so neologistic a phrase. The precept as well
220   as the practice of the Primitive Church[5] was distinctly against matrimony.

MISS PRISM.   (*Sententiously.*) That is obviously the reason why the Primitive Church has not lasted up to the present day. And you do not seem to realize, dear
225   Doctor, that by persistently remaining single, a man converts himself into a permanent public temptation. Men should be more careful; this very celibacy leads weaker vessels astray.

CHASUBLE.   But is a man not equally attractive when
230   married?

MISS PRISM.   No married man is ever attractive except to his wife.

CHASUBLE.   And often, I've been told, not even to her.

MISS PRISM.   That depends on the intellectual sympa-
235   thies of the woman. Maturity can always be depended on. Ripeness can be trusted. Young women are green. (*Dr. Chasuble starts.*) I spoke horticulturally. My metaphor was drawn from fruits. But where is Cecily?

---

[1]   *Australia*   A former penal colony, at the time still considered to be largely composed of wilderness.

[2]   *buttonhole*   Boutonniere, flower for one's lapel.

[3]   *Maréchal Niel*   Variety of yellow rose.

[4]   *misanthrope … womanthrope*   The correct word for someone who hates women is a "misogynist"; a "misanthrope" is someone who hates all humanity.

[5]   *Primitive Church*   Early Christian church.

CHASUBLE.   Perhaps she followed us to the schools.

(*Enter Jack slowly from the back of the garden. He is dressed in the deepest mourning, with crepe hatband and black gloves.*)

240 MISS PRISM.   Mr. Worthing!

CHASUBLE.   Mr. Worthing?

MISS PRISM.   This is indeed a surprise. We did not look for you till Monday afternoon.

JACK.   (*Shakes Miss Prism's hand in a tragic manner.*) I
245 have returned sooner than I expected. Dr. Chasuble, I hope you are well?

CHASUBLE.   Dear Mr. Worthing, I trust this garb of woe does not betoken some terrible calamity?

JACK.   My brother.

250 MISS PRISM.   More shameful debts and extravagance?

CHASUBLE.   Still leading his life of pleasure?

JACK.   (*Shaking his head.*) Dead!

CHASUBLE.   Your brother Ernest dead?

JACK.   Quite dead.

255 MISS PRISM.   What a lesson for him! I trust he will profit by it.

CHASUBLE.   Mr. Worthing, I offer you my sincere condolence. You have at least the consolation of knowing that you were always the most generous and forgiv-
260 ing of brothers.

JACK.   Poor Ernest! He had many faults, but it is a sad, sad blow.

CHASUBLE.   Very sad indeed. Were you with him at the end?

265 JACK.   No. He died abroad; in Paris, in fact. I had a telegram last night from the manager of the Grand Hotel.

CHASUBLE.   Was the cause of death mentioned?

JACK.   A severe chill, it seems.

270 MISS PRISM.   As a man sows, so shall he reap.

CHASUBLE.   (*Raising his hand.*) Charity, dear Miss Prism, charity! None of us are perfect. I myself am peculiarly susceptible to draughts. Will the interment take place here?

275 JACK.   No. He seems to have expressed a desire to be buried in Paris.

CHASUBLE.   In Paris! (*Shakes his head.*) I fear that hardly points to any very serious state of mind at the last. You

would no doubt wish me to make some slight allusion
280 to this tragic domestic affliction next Sunday. (*Jack presses his hand convulsively.*) My sermon on the meaning of the manna in the wilderness[1] can be adapted to almost any occasion, joyful, or, as in the present case, distressing. (*All sigh.*) I have preached it at harvest
285 celebrations, christenings, confirmations,[2] on days of humiliation and festal days. The last time I delivered it was in the Cathedral, as a charity sermon on behalf of the Society for the Prevention of Discontent among the Upper Orders. The Bishop, who was present, was much
290 struck by some of the analogies I drew.

JACK.   Ah! that reminds me, you mentioned christenings I think, Dr. Chasuble? I suppose you know how to christen all right? (*Dr. Chasuble looks astounded.*) I mean, of course, you are continually christening, aren't you?

295 MISS PRISM.   It is, I regret to say, one of the Rector's most constant duties in this parish. I have often spoken to the poorer classes on the subject. But they don't seem to know what thrift is.

CHASUBLE.   But is there any particular infant in whom
300 you are interested, Mr. Worthing? Your brother was, I believe, unmarried, was he not?

JACK.   Oh yes.

MISS PRISM.   (*Bitterly.*) People who live entirely for pleasure usually are.

305 JACK.   But it is not for any child, dear Doctor. I am very fond of children. No! the fact is, I would like to be christened myself, this afternoon, if you have nothing better to do.

CHASUBLE.   But surely, Mr. Worthing, you have been
310 christened already?

JACK.   I don't remember anything about it.

CHASUBLE.   But have you any grave doubts on the subject?

JACK.   I certainly intend to have. Of course I don't know
315 if the thing would bother you in any way, or if you think I am a little too old now.

CHASUBLE.   Not at all. The sprinkling, and, indeed, the

---

1 *manna in the wilderness*   See Exodus 16.

2 *christenings, confirmations*   Whereas a christening formally admits a person to the Christian church through baptism (usually as an infant), in many Christian denominations a person's standing as a full member of the church must be confirmed at a later ceremony (typically as a young adult).

immersion of adults is a perfectly canonical practice.

JACK.   Immersion!

320 CHASUBLE.   You need have no apprehensions. Sprinkling is all that is necessary, or indeed I think advisable. Our weather is so changeable. At what hour would you wish the ceremony performed?

JACK.   Oh, I might trot round about five if that would

325 suit you.

CHASUBLE. Perfectly, perfectly! In fact I have two similar ceremonies to perform at that time. A case of twins that occurred recently in one of the outlying cottages on your own estate. Poor Jenkins the carter,[1] a

330 most hard-working man.

JACK.   Oh! I don't see much fun in being christened along with other babies. It would be childish. Would half-past five do?

CHASUBLE. Admirably! Admirably! (*Takes out watch.*)

335 And now, dear Mr. Worthing, I will not intrude any longer into a house of sorrow. I would merely beg you not to be too much bowed down by grief. What seem to us bitter trials are often blessings in disguise.

MISS PRISM.   This seems to me a blessing of an extremely

340 obvious kind.

(*Enter Cecily from the house.*)

CECILY.   Uncle Jack! Oh, I am pleased to see you back. But what horrid clothes you have got on! Do go and change them.

345 MISS PRISM.   Cecily!

CHASUBLE.   My child! my child!

(*Cecily goes towards Jack; he kisses her brow in a melancholy manner.*)

CECILY.   What is the matter, Uncle Jack? Do look happy! You look as if you had toothache, and I have got such a surprise for you. Who do you think is in the dining-

350 room? Your brother!

JACK.   Who?

CECILY.   Your brother Ernest. He arrived about half an hour ago.

JACK.   What nonsense! I haven't got a brother.

355 CECILY.   Oh, don't say that. However badly he may have

---

[1] *carter* Cart driver.

behaved to you in the past he is still your brother. You couldn't be so heartless as to disown him. I'll tell him to come out. And you will shake hands with him, won't you, Uncle Jack? (*Runs back into the house.*)

360 CHASUBLE.   These are very joyful tidings.

MISS PRISM.   After we had all been resigned to his loss, his sudden return seems to me peculiarly distressing.

JACK.   My brother is in the dining-room? I don't know what it all means. I think it is perfectly absurd.

(*Enter Algernon and Cecily hand in hand. They come slowly up to Jack.*)

365 JACK.   Good heavens! (*Motions Algernon away.*)

ALGERNON.   Brother John, I have come down from town to tell you that I am very sorry for all the trouble I have given you, and that I intend to lead a better life in the future. (*Jack glares at him and does not take his*

370 *hand.*)

CECILY.   Uncle Jack, you are not going to refuse your own brother's hand?

JACK.   Nothing will induce me to take his hand. I think his coming down here disgraceful. He knows perfectly

375 well why.

CECILY.   Uncle Jack, do be nice. There is some good in every one. Ernest has just been telling me about his poor invalid friend Mr. Bunbury whom he goes to visit so often. And surely there must be much good in one who

380 is kind to an invalid, and leaves the pleasures of London to sit by a bed of pain.

JACK.   Oh! he has been talking about Bunbury, has he?

CECILY.   Yes, he has told me all about poor Mr. Bunbury, and his terrible state of health.

385 JACK.   Bunbury! Well, I won't have him talk to you about Bunbury or about anything else. It is enough to drive one perfectly frantic.

ALGERNON.   Of course I admit that the faults were all on my side. But I must say that I think that Brother John's

390 coldness to me is peculiarly painful. I expected a more enthusiastic welcome, especially considering it is the first time I have come here.

CECILY.   Uncle Jack, if you don't shake hands with Ernest I will never forgive you.

395 JACK.   Never forgive me?

CECILY.   Never, never, never!

JACK. Well, this is the last time I shall ever do it. (*Shakes hands with Algernon and glares.*)

CHASUBLE. It's pleasant, is it not, to see so perfect a
400 reconciliation? I think we might leave the two brothers together.

MISS PRISM. Cecily, you will come with us.

CECILY. Certainly, Miss Prism. My little task of reconciliation is over.

405 CHASUBLE. You have done a beautiful action to-day, dear child.

MISS PRISM. We must not be premature in our judgments.

CECILY. I feel very happy.

(*They all go off except Jack and Algernon.*)

410 JACK. You young scoundrel, Algy, you must get out of this place as soon as possible. I don't allow any Bunburying here.

(*Enter Merriman.*)

MERRIMAN. I have put Mr. Ernest's things in the room next to yours, sir. I suppose that is all right?

415 JACK. What?

MERRIMAN. Mr. Ernest's luggage, sir. I have unpacked it and put it in the room next to your own.

JACK. His luggage?

MERRIMAN. Yes, sir. Three portmanteaus, a dressing-
420 case, two hat-boxes, and a large luncheon-basket.

ALGERNON. I am afraid I can't stay more than a week this time.

JACK. Merriman, order the dog-cart[1] at once. Mr. Ernest has been suddenly called back to town.

425 MERRIMAN. Yes, sir. (*Goes back into the house.*)

ALGERNON. What a fearful liar you are, Jack. I have not been called back to town at all.

JACK. Yes, you have.

ALGERNON. I haven't heard any one call me.

430 JACK. Your duty as a gentleman calls you back.

ALGERNON. My duty as a gentleman has never interfered with my pleasures in the smallest degree.

---

[1] *dog-cart* Small horse-drawn carriage in which the occupants would sit back-to-back; a box for conveying hunting dogs was also typically part of the contraption.

JACK. I can quite understand that.

ALGERNON. Well, Cecily is a darling.

435 JACK. You are not to talk of Miss Cardew like that. I don't like it.

ALGERNON. Well, I don't like your clothes. You look perfectly ridiculous in them. Why on earth don't you go up and change? It is perfectly childish to be in deep
440 mourning for a man who is actually staying for a whole week with you in your house as a guest. I call it grotesque.

JACK. You are certainly not staying with me for a whole week as a guest or anything else. You have got to leave
445 ... by the four-five train.

ALGERNON. I certainly won't leave you so long as you are in mourning. It would be most unfriendly. If I were in mourning you would stay with me, I suppose. I should think it very unkind if you didn't.

450 JACK. Well, will you go if I change my clothes?

ALGERNON. Yes, if you are not too long. I never saw anybody take so long to dress, and with such little result.

JACK. Well, at any rate, that is better than being always over-dressed as you are.

455 ALGERNON. If I am occasionally a little over-dressed, I make up for it by being always immensely over-educated.

JACK. Your vanity is ridiculous, your conduct an outrage, and your presence in my garden utterly absurd.
460 However, you have got to catch the four-five, and I hope you will have a pleasant journey back to town. This Bunburying, as you call it, has not been a great success for you. (*Goes into the house.*)

ALGERNON. I think it has been a great success. I'm in
465 love with Cecily, and that is everything.

(*Enter Cecily at the back of the garden. She picks up the can and begins to water the flowers.*)

But I must see her before I go, and make arrangements for another Bunbury. Ah, there she is.

CECILY. Oh, I merely came back to water the roses. I thought you were with Uncle Jack.

470 ALGERNON. He's gone to order the dog-cart for me.

CECILY. Oh, is he going to take you for a nice drive?

ALGERNON. He's going to send me away.

CECILY. Then have we got to part?

ALGERNON. I am afraid so. It's a very painful parting.

475 CECILY. It is always painful to part from people whom one has known for a very brief space of time. The absence of old friends one can endure with equanimity. But even a momentary separation from anyone to whom one has just been introduced is almost unbear-

480 able.

ALGERNON. Thank you.

(*Enter Merriman.*)

MERRIMAN. The dog-cart is at the door, sir.

(*Algernon looks appealingly at Cecily.*)

CECILY. It can wait, Merriman for … five minutes.

MERRIMAN. Yes, Miss.

(*Exit Merriman.*)

ALGERNON. I hope, Cecily, I shall not offend you if I

485 state quite frankly and openly that you seem to me to be in every way the visible personification of absolute perfection.

CECILY. I think your frankness does you great credit, Ernest. If you will allow me, I will copy your remarks

490 into my diary. (*Goes over to table and begins writing in diary.*)

ALGERNON. Do you really keep a diary? I'd give anything to look at it. May I?

CECILY. Oh no. (*Puts her hand over it.*) You see, it is

495 simply a very young girl's record of her own thoughts and impressions, and consequently meant for publication. When it appears in volume form I hope you will order a copy. But pray, Ernest, don't stop. I delight in taking down from dictation. I have reached "absolute

500 perfection." You can go on. I am quite ready for more.

ALGERNON. (*Somewhat taken aback.*) Ahem! Ahem!

CECILY. Oh, don't cough, Ernest. When one is dictating one should speak fluently and not cough. Besides, I don't know how to spell a cough. (*Writes as Algernon*

505 *speaks.*)

ALGERNON. (*Speaking very rapidly.*) Cecily, ever since I first looked upon your wonderful and incomparable beauty, I have dared to love you wildly, passionately,

devotedly, hopelessly.

510 CECILY. I don't think that you should tell me that you love me wildly, passionately, devotedly, hopelessly. Hopelessly doesn't seem to make much sense, does it?

ALGERNON. Cecily!

(*Enter Merriman.*)

MERRIMAN. The dog-cart is waiting, sir.

515 ALGERNON. Tell it to come round next week, at the same hour.

MERRIMAN. (*Looks at Cecily, who makes no sign.*) Yes, sir.

(*Merriman retires.*)

CECILY. Uncle Jack would be very much annoyed if he knew you were staying on till next week, at the same

520 hour.

ALGERNON. Oh, I don't care about Jack. I don't care for anybody in the whole world but you. I love you, Cecily. You will marry me, won't you?

CECILY. You silly boy! Of course. Why, we have been

525 engaged for the last three months.

ALGERNON. For the last three months?

CECILY. Yes, it will be exactly three months on Thursday.

ALGERNON. But how did we become engaged?

530 CECILY. Well, ever since dear Uncle Jack first confessed to us that he had a younger brother who was very wicked and bad, you of course have formed the chief topic of conversation between myself and Miss Prism. And of course a man who is much talked about is always

535 very attractive. One feels there must be something in him, after all. I daresay it was foolish of me, but I fell in love with you, Ernest.

ALGERNON. Darling! And when was the engagement actually settled?

540 CECILY. On the 14th of February last. Worn out by your entire ignorance of my existence, I determined to end the matter one way or the other, and after a long struggle with myself I accepted you under this dear old tree here. The next day I bought this little ring in your

545 name, and this is the little bangle with the true lover's knot I promised you always to wear.

ALGERNON. Did I give you this? It's very pretty, isn't it?

CECILY. Yes, you've wonderfully good taste, Ernest. It's the excuse I've always given for your leading such a bad life. And this is the box in which I keep all your dear letters. (*Kneels at table, opens box, and produces letters tied up with blue ribbon.*)

ALGERNON. My letters! But, my own sweet Cecily, I have never written you any letters.

CECILY. You need hardly remind me of that, Ernest. I remember only too well that I was forced to write your letters for you. I wrote always three times a week, and sometimes oftener.

ALGERNON. Oh, do let me read them, Cecily?

CECILY. Oh, I couldn't possibly. They would make you far too conceited. (*Replaces box.*) The three you wrote me after I had broken off the engagement are so beautiful, and so badly spelled, that even now I can hardly read them without crying a little.

ALGERNON. But was our engagement ever broken off?

CECILY. Of course it was. On the 22nd of last March. You can see the entry if you like. (*Shows diary.*) "To-day I broke off my engagement with Ernest. I feel it is better to do so. The weather still continues charming."

ALGERNON. But why on earth did you break it off? What had I done? I had done nothing at all. Cecily, I am very much hurt indeed to hear you broke it off. Particularly when the weather was so charming.

CECILY. It would hardly have been a really serious engagement if it hadn't been broken off at least once. But I forgave you before the week was out.

ALGERNON. (*Crossing to her, and kneeling.*) What a perfect angel you are, Cecily.

CECILY. You dear romantic boy. (*He kisses her, she puts her fingers through his hair.*) I hope your hair curls naturally, does it?

ALGERNON. Yes, darling, with a little help from others.

CECILY. I am so glad.

ALGERNON. You'll never break off our engagement again, Cecily?

CECILY. I don't think I could break it off now that I have actually met you. Besides, of course, there is the question of your name.

ALGERNON. Yes, of course. (*Nervously.*)

CECILY. You must not laugh at me, darling, but it had always been a girlish dream of mine to love some one whose name was Ernest. (*Algernon rises, Cecily also.*) There is something in that name that seems to inspire absolute confidence. I pity any poor married woman whose husband is not called Ernest.

ALGERNON. But, my dear child, do you mean to say you could not love me if I had some other name?

CECILY. But what name?

ALGERNON. Oh, any name you like—Algernon—for instance ...

CECILY. But I don't like the name of Algernon.

ALGERNON. Well, my own dear, sweet, loving little darling, I really can't see why you should object to the name of Algernon. It is not at all a bad name. In fact, it is rather an aristocratic name. Half of the chaps who get into the Bankruptcy Court are called Algernon. But seriously, Cecily ... (*Moving to her*) ... if my name was Algy, couldn't you love me?

CECILY. (*Rising.*) I might respect you, Ernest, I might admire your character, but I fear that I should not be able to give you my undivided attention.

ALGERNON. Ahem! Cecily! (*Picking up hat.*) Your Rector here is, I suppose, thoroughly experienced in the practice of all the rites and ceremonials of the Church?

CECILY. Oh, yes. Dr. Chasuble is a most learned man. He has never written a single book, so you can imagine how much he knows.

ALGERNON. I must see him at once on a most important christening—I mean on most important business.

CECILY. Oh!

ALGERNON. I shan't be away more than half an hour.

CECILY. Considering that we have been engaged since February the 14th, and that I only met you to-day for the first time, I think it is rather hard that you should leave me for so long a period as half an hour. Couldn't you make it twenty minutes?

ALGERNON. I'll be back in no time.

(*Kisses her and rushes down the garden.*)

CECILY. What an impetuous boy he is! I like his hair so much. I must enter his proposal in my diary.

(*Enter Merriman.*)

MERRIMAN. A Miss Fairfax has just called to see Mr. Worthing. On very important business, Miss Fairfax states.

CECILY.   Isn't Mr. Worthing in his library?

MERRIMAN.   Mr. Worthing went over in the direction of
635   the Rectory some time ago.

CECILY.   Pray ask the lady to come out here; Mr. Worth-
ing is sure to be back soon. And you can bring tea.

MERRIMAN.   Yes, Miss. (*Goes out.*)

CECILY.   Miss Fairfax! I suppose one of the many good
640   elderly women who are associated with Uncle Jack in
some of his philanthropic work in London. I don't quite
like women who are interested in philanthropic work. I
think it is so forward of them.

(*Enter Merriman.*)

MERRIMAN.   Miss Fairfax.

(*Enter Gwendolen. Exit Merriman.*)

645   CECILY.   (*Advancing to meet her.*) Pray let me introduce
myself to you. My name is Cecily Cardew.

GWENDOLEN.   Cecily Cardew? (*Moving to her and
shaking hands.*) What a very sweet name! Something tells
me that we are going to be great friends. I like you
650   already more than I can say. My first impressions of
people are never wrong.

CECILY.   How nice of you to like me so much after we
have known each other such a comparatively short time.
Pray sit down.

655   GWENDOLEN.   (*Still standing up.*) I may call you Cecily,
may I not?

CECILY.   With pleasure!

GWENDOLEN.   And you will always call me Gwendolen,
won't you?

660   CECILY.   If you wish.

GWENDOLEN.   Then that is all quite settled, is it not?

CECILY.   I hope so. (*A pause. They both sit down together.*)

GWENDOLEN.   Perhaps this might be a favourable
opportunity for my mentioning who I am. My father is
665   Lord Bracknell. You have never heard of Papa, I sup-
pose?

CECILY.   I don't think so.

GWENDOLEN.   Outside the family circle, Papa, I am glad
to say, is entirely unknown. I think that is quite as it
670   should be. The home seems to me to be the proper

sphere for the man. And certainly once a man begins to
neglect his domestic duties he becomes painfully effemi-
nate, does he not? And I don't like that. It makes men
so very attractive. Cecily, Mamma, whose views on
675   education are remarkably strict, has brought me up to be
extremely short-sighted; it is part of her system; so do
you mind my looking at you through my glasses?

CECILY.   Oh! not at all, Gwendolen. I am very fond of
being looked at.

680   GWENDOLEN.   (*After examining Cecily carefully through
a lorgnette.*) You are here on a short visit, I suppose.

CECILY.   Oh no! I live here.

GWENDOLEN.   (*Severely.*) Really? Your mother, no
doubt, or some female relative of advanced years, resides
685   here also?

CECILY.   Oh no! I have no mother, nor, in fact, any
relations.

GWENDOLEN.   Indeed?

CECILY.   My dear guardian, with the assistance of Miss
690   Prism, has the arduous task of looking after me.

GWENDOLEN.   Your guardian?

CECILY.   Yes, I am Mr. Worthing's ward.

GWENDOLEN.   Oh! It is strange he never mentioned to
me that he had a ward. How secretive of him! He grows
695   more interesting hourly. I am not sure, however, that
the news inspires me with feelings of unmixed delight.
(*Rising and going to her.*) I am very fond of you, Cecily;
I have liked you ever since I met you! But I am bound
to state that now that I know that you are Mr. Worth-
700   ing's ward, I cannot help expressing a wish you were—
well, just a little older than you seem to be—and not
quite so very alluring in appearance. In fact, if I may
speak candidly—

CECILY.   Pray do! I think that whenever one has anything
705   unpleasant to say, one should always be quite candid.

GWENDOLEN.   Well, to speak with perfect candour,
Cecily, I wish that you were fully forty-two, and more
than usually plain for your age. Ernest has a strong
upright nature. He is the very soul of truth and honour.
710   Disloyalty would be as impossible to him as deception.
But even men of the noblest possible moral character are
extremely susceptible to the influence of the physical
charms of others. Modern, no less than Ancient History,
supplies us with many most painful examples of what I
715   refer to. If it were not so, indeed, History would be

quite unreadable.

CECILY. I beg your pardon, Gwendolen, did you say Ernest?

GWENDOLEN. Yes.

720 CECILY. Oh, but it is not Mr. Ernest Worthing who is my guardian. It is his brother—his elder brother.

GWENDOLEN. (*Sitting down again.*) Ernest never mentioned to me that he had a brother.

CECILY. I am sorry to say they have not been on good
725 terms for a long time.

GWENDOLEN. Ah! that accounts for it. And now that I think of it I have never heard any man mention his brother. The subject seems distasteful to most men. Cecily, you have lifted a load from my mind. I was
730 growing almost anxious. It would have been terrible if any cloud had come across a friendship like ours, would it not? Of course you are quite, quite sure that it is not Mr. Ernest Worthing who is your guardian?

CECILY. Quite sure. (*A pause.*) In fact, I am going to be
735 his.

GWENDOLEN. (*Inquiringly.*) I beg your pardon?

CECILY. (*Rather shy and confidingly.*) Dearest Gwendolen, there is no reason why I should make a secret of it to you. Our little county newspaper is sure to chronicle
740 the fact next week. Mr. Ernest Worthing and I are engaged to be married.

GWENDOLEN. (*Quite politely, rising.*) My darling Cecily, I think there must be some slight error. Mr. Ernest Worthing is engaged to me. The announcement will
745 appear in the *Morning Post* on Saturday at the latest.

CECILY. (*Very politely, rising.*) I am afraid you must be under some misconception. Ernest proposed to me exactly ten minutes ago. (*Shows diary.*)

GWENDOLEN. (*Examines diary through her lorgnette
750 carefully.*) It is certainly very curious, for he asked me to be his wife yesterday afternoon at 5.30. If you would care to verify the incident, pray do so. (*Produces diary of her own.*) I never travel without my diary. One should always have something sensational to read in the train.
755 I am so sorry, dear Cecily, if it is any disappointment to you, but I am afraid I have the prior claim.

CECILY. It would distress me more than I can tell you, dear Gwendolen, if it caused you any mental or physical anguish, but I feel bound to point out that since Ernest
760 proposed to you he clearly has changed his mind.

GWENDOLEN. (*Meditatively.*) If the poor fellow has been entrapped into any foolish promise I shall consider it my duty to rescue him at once, and with a firm hand.

CECILY. (*Thoughtfully and sadly.*) Whatever unfortunate
765 entanglement my dear boy may have got into, I will never reproach him with it after we are married.

GWENDOLEN. Do you allude to me, Miss Cardew, as an entanglement? You are presumptuous. On an occasion of this kind it becomes more than a moral duty to speak
770 one's mind. It becomes a pleasure.

CECILY. Do you suggest, Miss Fairfax, that I entrapped Ernest into an engagement? How dare you? This is no time for wearing the shallow mask of manners. When I see a spade I call it a spade.

775 GWENDOLEN. (*Satirically.*) I am glad to say that I have never seen a spade. It is obvious that our social spheres have been widely different.

(*Enter Merriman, followed by the footman. He carries a salver, table cloth, and plate stand. Cecily is about to retort. The presence of the servants exercises a restraining influence, under which both girls chafe.*)

MERRIMAN. Shall I lay tea here as usual, Miss?

CECILY. (*Sternly, in a calm voice.*) Yes, as usual.

(*Merriman begins to clear table and lay cloth. A long pause. Cecily and Gwendolen glare at each other.*)

780 GWENDOLEN. Are there many interesting walks in the vicinity, Miss Cardew?

CECILY. Oh! yes! a great many. From the top of one of the hills quite close one can see five counties.

GWENDOLEN. Five counties! I don't think I should like
785 that; I hate crowds.

CECILY. (*Sweetly.*) I suppose that is why you live in town?

(*Gwendolen bites her lip, and beats her foot nervously with her parasol.*)

GWENDOLEN. (*Looking round.*) Quite a well-kept garden this is, Miss Cardew.

790 CECILY. So glad you like it, Miss Fairfax.

GWENDOLEN. I had no idea there were any flowers in

the country.

CECILY.   Oh, flowers are as common here, Miss Fairfax, as people are in London.

795 GWENDOLEN.   Personally I cannot understand how anybody manages to exist in the country, if anybody who is anybody does. The country always bores me to death.

CECILY.   Ah! This is what the newspapers call agricultural
800 depression,[1] is it not? I believe the aristocracy are suffering very much from it just at present. It is almost an epidemic amongst them, I have been told. May I offer you some tea, Miss Fairfax?

GWENDOLEN.   (*With elaborate politeness.*) Thank you.
805 (*Aside.*) Detestable girl! But I require tea!

CECILY.   (*Sweetly.*) Sugar?

GWENDOLEN.   (*Superciliously.*) No, thank you. Sugar is not fashionable any more. (*Cecily looks angrily at her, takes up the tongs and puts four lumps of sugar into the*
810 *cup.*)

CECILY.   (*Severely.*) Cake or bread and butter?

GWENDOLEN.   (*In a bored manner.*) Bread and butter, please. Cake is rarely seen at the best houses nowadays.

CECILY.   (*Cuts a very large slice of cake, and puts it on the*
815 *tray.*) Hand that to Miss Fairfax.

(*Merriman does so, and goes out with footman. Gwendolen drinks the tea and makes a grimace. Puts down cup at once, reaches out her hand to the bread and butter, looks at it, and finds it is cake. Rises in indignation.*)

GWENDOLEN.   You have filled my tea with lumps of sugar, and though I asked most distinctly for bread and butter, you have given me cake. I am known for the gentleness of my disposition, and the extraordinary
820 sweetness of my nature, but I warn you, Miss Cardew, you may go too far.

CECILY.   (*Rising.*) To save my poor, innocent, trusting boy from the machinations of any other girl there are no lengths to which I would not go.

825 GWENDOLEN.   From the moment I saw you I distrusted you. I felt that you were false and deceitful. I am never deceived in such matters. My first impressions of people

---

[1] *agricultural depression*   The British economy in general was in depression from 1873 until the mid-1890s; the agricultural sector was depressed from 1875 until the mid-1890s.

are invariably right.

CECILY.   It seems to me, Miss Fairfax, that I am trespass-
830 ing on your valuable time. No doubt you have many other calls of a similar character to make in the neighbourhood.

(*Enter Jack.*)

GWENDOLEN.   (*Catching sight of him.*) Ernest! My own Ernest!

835 JACK.   Gwendolen! Darling! (*Offers to kiss her.*)

GWENDOLEN.   (*Draws back.*) A moment! May I ask if you are engaged to be married to this young lady? (*Points to Cecily.*)

JACK.   (*Laughing.*) To dear little Cecily! Of course not!
840 What could have put such an idea into your pretty little head?

GWENDOLEN.   Thank you. You may! (*Offers her cheek.*)

CECILY.   (*Very sweetly.*) I knew there must be some misunderstanding, Miss Fairfax. The gentleman whose
845 arm is at present round your waist is my guardian, Mr. John Worthing.

GWENDOLEN.   I beg your pardon?

CECILY.   This is Uncle Jack.

GWENDOLEN.   (*Receding.*) Jack! Oh!

(*Enter Algernon.*)

850 CECILY.   Here is Ernest.

ALGERNON.   (*Goes straight over to Cecily without noticing any one else.*) My own love! (*Offers to kiss her.*)

CECILY.   (*Drawing back.*) A moment, Ernest! May I ask you—are you engaged to be married to this young lady?

855 ALGERNON.   (*Looking round.*) To what young lady? Good heavens! Gwendolen!

CECILY.   Yes! to good heavens, Gwendolen, I mean to Gwendolen.

ALGERNON.   (*Laughing.*) Of course not! What could
860 have put such an idea into your pretty little head?

CECILY.   Thank you. (*Presenting her cheek to be kissed.*) You may.

(*Algernon kisses her.*)

GWENDOLEN.   I felt there was some slight error, Miss

Cardew. The gentleman who is now embracing you is my cousin, Mr. Algernon Moncrieff.

CECILY. (*Breaking away from Algernon.*) Algernon Moncrieff! Oh!

(*The two girls move towards each other and put their arms round each other's waists as if for protection.*)

CECILY. Are you called Algernon?

ALGERNON. I cannot deny it.

CECILY. Oh!

GWENDOLEN. Is your name really John?

JACK. (*Standing rather proudly.*) I could deny it if I liked. I could deny anything if I liked. But my name certainly is John. It has been John for years.

CECILY. (*To Gwendolen.*) A gross deception has been practised on both of us.

GWENDOLEN. My poor wounded Cecily!

CECILY. My sweet wronged Gwendolen!

GWENDOLEN. (*Slowly and seriously.*) You will call me sister, will you not? (*They embrace. Jack and Algernon groan and walk up and down.*)

CECILY. (*Rather brightly.*) There is just one question I would like to be allowed to ask my guardian.

GWENDOLEN. An admirable idea! Mr. Worthing, there is just one question I would like to be permitted to put to you. Where is your brother Ernest? We are both engaged to be married to your brother Ernest, so it is a matter of some importance to us to know where your brother Ernest is at present.

JACK. (*Slowly and hesitatingly.*) Gwendolen—Cecily—it is very painful for me to be forced to speak the truth. It is the first time in my life that I have ever been reduced to such a painful position, and I am really quite inexperienced in doing anything of the kind. However, I will tell you quite frankly that I have no brother Ernest. I have no brother at all. I never had a brother in my life, and I certainly have not the smallest intention of ever having one in the future.

CECILY. (*Surprised.*) No brother at all?

JACK. (*Cheerily.*) None!

GWENDOLEN. (*Severely.*) Had you never a brother of any kind?

JACK. (*Pleasantly.*) Never. Not even of an kind.

GWENDOLEN. I am afraid it is quite clear, Cecily, that neither of us is engaged to be married to any one.

CECILY. It is not a very pleasant position for a young girl suddenly to find herself in. Is it?

GWENDOLEN. Let us go into the house. They will hardly venture to come after us there.

CECILY. No, men are so cowardly, aren't they?

(*They retire into the house with scornful looks.*)

JACK. This ghastly state of things is what you call Bunburying, I suppose?

ALGERNON. Yes, and a perfectly wonderful Bunbury it is. The most wonderful Bunbury I have ever had in my life.

JACK. Well, you've no right whatsoever to Bunbury here.

ALGERNON. That is absurd. One has a right to Bunbury anywhere one chooses. Every serious Bunburyist knows that.

JACK. Serious Bunburyist! Good heavens!

ALGERNON. Well, one must be serious about something, if one wants to have any amusement in life. I happen to be serious about Bunburying. What on earth you are serious about I haven't got the remotest idea. About everything, I should fancy. You have such an absolutely trivial nature.

JACK. Well, the only small satisfaction I have in the whole of this wretched business is that your friend Bunbury is quite exploded. You won't be able to run down to the country quite so often as you used to do, dear Algy. And a very good thing too.

ALGERNON. Your brother is a little off colour, isn't he, dear Jack? You won't be able to disappear to London quite so frequently as your wicked custom was. And not a bad thing either.

JACK. As for your conduct towards Miss Cardew, I must say that your taking in a sweet, simple, innocent girl like that is quite inexcusable. To say nothing of the fact that she is my ward.

ALGERNON. I can see no possible defence at all for your deceiving a brilliant, clever, thoroughly experienced young lady like Miss Fairfax. To say nothing of the fact that she is my cousin.

JACK. I wanted to be engaged to Gwendolen, that is all. I love her.

ALGERNON. Well, I simply wanted to be engaged to

Cecily. I adore her.

JACK. There is certainly no chance of your marrying Miss Cardew.

950 ALGERNON. I don't think there is much likelihood, Jack, of you and Miss Fairfax being united.

JACK. Well, that is no business of yours.

ALGERNON. If it was my business, I wouldn't talk about it. (*Begins to eat muffins.*) It is very vulgar to talk about 955 one's business. Only people like stock-brokers do that, and then merely at dinner parties.

JACK. How can you sit there, calmly eating muffins when we are in this horrible trouble, I can't make out. You seem to me to be perfectly heartless.

960 ALGERNON. Well, I can't eat muffins in an agitated manner. The butter would probably get on my cuffs. One should always eat muffins quite calmly. It is the only way to eat them.

JACK. I say it's perfectly heartless your eating muffins at 965 all, under the circumstances.

ALGERNON. When I am in trouble, eating is the only thing that consoles me. Indeed, when I am in really great trouble, as any one who knows me intimately will tell you, I refuse everything except food and drink. At 970 the present moment I am eating muffins because I am unhappy. Besides, I am particularly fond of muffins. (*Rising.*)

JACK. (*Rising.*) Well, that is no reason why you should eat them all in that greedy way. (*Takes muffins from* 975 *Algernon.*)

ALGERNON. (*Offering tea-cake.*) I wish you would have tea-cake instead. I don't like tea-cake.

JACK. Good heavens! I suppose a man may eat his own muffins in his own garden.

980 ALGERNON. But you have just said it was perfectly heartless to eat muffins.

JACK. I said it was perfectly heartless of you, under the circumstances. That is a very different thing.

ALGERNON. That may be. But the muffins are the same.

(*He seizes the muffin-dish from Jack.*)

985 JACK. Algy, I wish to goodness you would go.

ALGERNON. You can't possibly ask me to go without having some dinner. It's absurd. I never go without my dinner. No one ever does, except vegetarians and people like that. Besides I have just made arrangements with 990 Dr. Chasuble to be christened at a quarter to six under the name of Ernest.

JACK. My dear fellow, the sooner you give up that nonsense the better. I made arrangements this morning with Dr. Chasuble to be christened myself at 5:30, 995 and I naturally will take the name of Ernest. Gwendolen would wish it. We can't both be christened Ernest. It's absurd. Besides, I have a perfect right to be christened if I like. There is no evidence at all that I have ever been christened by anybody. I should think it 1000 extremely probable I never was, and so does Dr. Chasuble. It is entirely different in your case. You have been christened already.

ALGERNON. Yes, but I have not been christened for years.

1005 JACK. Yes, but you have been christened. That is the important thing.

ALGERNON. Quite so. So I know my constitution can stand it. If you are not quite sure about your ever having been christened, I must say I think it rather 1010 dangerous your venturing on it now. It might make you very unwell. You can hardly have forgotten that some one very closely connected with you was very nearly carried off this week in Paris by a severe chill.

JACK. Yes, but you said yourself that a severe chill was 1015 not hereditary.

ALGERNON. It usen't to be, I know—but I daresay it is now. Science is always making wonderful improvements in things.

JACK. (*Picking up the muffin-dish.*) Oh, that is non- 1020 sense; you are always talking nonsense.

ALGERNON. Jack, you are at the muffins again! I wish you wouldn't. There are only two left. (*Takes them.*) I told you I was particularly fond of muffins.

JACK. But I hate tea-cake.

1025 ALGERNON. Why on earth then do you allow tea-cake to be served up for your guests? What ideas you have of hospitality!

JACK. Algernon! I have already told you to go. I don't want you here. Why don't you go!

1030 ALGERNON. I haven't quite finished my tea yet! and there is still one muffin left. (*Jack groans, and sinks into a chair. Algernon still continues eating.*)

ACT DROP

ACT 3

SCENE

(*Morning-room at the Manor House. Gwendolen and Cecily are at the window, looking out into the garden.*)

GWENDOLEN. The fact that they did not follow us at once into the house, as any one else would have done, seems to me to show that they have some sense of shame left.

5 CECILY. They have been eating muffins. That looks like repentance.

GWENDOLEN. (*After a pause.*) They don't seem to notice us at all. Couldn't you cough?

CECILY. But I haven't got a cough.

10 GWENDOLEN. They're looking at us. What effrontery!

CECILY. They're approaching. That's very forward of them.

GWENDOLEN. Let us preserve a dignified silence.

CECILY. Certainly. It's the only thing to do now.

(*Enter Jack followed by Algernon. They whistle some dreadful popular air from a British Opera.*)

15 GWENDOLEN. This dignified silence seems to produce an unpleasant effect.

CECILY. A most distasteful one.

GWENDOLEN. But we will not be the first to speak.

CECILY. Certainly not.

20 GWENDOLEN. Mr. Worthing, I have something very particular to ask you. Much depends on your reply.

CECILY. Gwendolen, your common sense is invaluable. Mr. Moncrieff, kindly answer me the following question. Why did you pretend to be my guardian's brother?

25 ALGERNON. In order that I might have an opportunity of meeting you.

CECILY. (*To Gwendolen.*) That certainly seems a satisfactory explanation, does it not?

GWENDOLEN. Yes, dear, if you can believe him.

30 CECILY. I don't. But that does not affect the wonderful beauty of his answer.

GWENDOLEN. True. In matters of grave importance, style, not sincerity is the vital thing. Mr. Worthing, what explanation can you offer to me for pretending to

35 have a brother? Was it in order that you might have an opportunity of coming up to town to see me as often as possible?

JACK. Can you doubt it, Miss Fairfax?

GWENDOLEN. I have the gravest doubts upon the

40 subject. But I intend to crush them. This is not the moment for German scepticism.[1] (*Moving to Cecily.*) Their explanations appear to be quite satisfactory, especially Mr. Worthing's. That seems to me to have the stamp of truth upon it.

45 CECILY. I am more than content with what Mr. Moncrieff said. His voice alone inspires one with absolute credulity.

GWENDOLEN. Then you think we should forgive them?

CECILY. Yes. I mean no.

50 GWENDOLEN. True! I had forgotten. There are principles at stake that one cannot surrender. Which of us should tell them? The task is not a pleasant one.

CECILY. Could we not both speak at the same time?

GWENDOLEN. An excellent idea! I nearly always speak at

55 the same time as other people. Will you take the time from me?

CECILY. Certainly.

(*Gwendolen beats time with uplifted finger.*)

GWENDOLEN and CECILY (*Speaking together.*) Your Christian names are still an insuperable barrier. That is

60 all!

JACK and ALGERNON (*Speaking together.*) Our Christian names! Is that all? But we are going to be christened this afternoon.

GWENDOLEN. (*To Jack.*) For my sake you are prepared

65 to do this terrible thing?

JACK. I am.

CECILY. (*To Algernon.*) To please me you are ready to face this fearful ordeal?

ALGERNON. I am!

70 GWENDOLEN. How absurd to talk of the equality of the sexes! Where questions of self-sacrifice are concerned, men are infinitely beyond us.

JACK. We are. (*Clasps hands with Algernon.*)

---

[1] *German scepticism* According to the school of philosophy deriving from Immanuel Kant, we do not always perceive the true state of things-in-themselves.

CECILY. They have moments of physical courage of
75 which we women know absolutely nothing.
GWENDOLEN. (*To Jack.*) Darling!
ALGERNON. (*To Cecily.*) Darling! (*They fall into each other's arms.*)

(*Enter Merriman. When he enters he coughs loudly, seeing the situation.*)

MERRIMAN. Ahem! Ahem! Lady Bracknell!
80 JACK. Good heavens!

(*Enter Lady Bracknell. The couples separate in alarm. Exit Merriman.*)

LADY BRACKNELL. Gwendolen! What does this mean?
GWENDOLEN. Merely that I am engaged to be married to Mr. Worthing, Mamma.
LADY BRACKNELL. Come here. Sit down. Sit down
85 immediately. Hesitation of any kind is a sign of mental decay in the young, of physical weakness in the old. (*Turns to Jack.*) Apprised, sir, of my daughter's sudden flight by her trusty maid, whose confidence I purchased by means of a small coin, I followed her at once by a
90 luggage train. Her unhappy father is, I am glad to say, under the impression that she is attending a more than usually lengthy lecture by the University Extension Scheme on the Influence of a permanent income on Thought. I do not propose to undeceive him. Indeed I
95 have never undeceived him on any question. I would consider it wrong. But of course, you will clearly understand that all communication between yourself and my daughter must cease immediately from this moment. On this point, as indeed on all points, I am firm.
100 JACK. I am engaged to be married to Gwendolen, Lady Bracknell!
LADY BRACKNELL. You are nothing of the kind, sir. And now, as regards Algernon!… Algernon!
ALGERNON. Yes, Aunt Augusta.
105 LADY BRACKNELL. May I ask if it is in this house that your invalid friend Mr. Bunbury resides?
ALGERNON. (*Stammering.*) Oh! No! Bunbury doesn't live here. Bunbury is somewhere else at present. In fact, Bunbury is dead.
110 LADY BRACKNELL. Dead! When did Mr. Bunbury die?

His death must have been extremely sudden.
ALGERNON. (*Airily.*) Oh! I killed Bunbury this afternoon. I mean poor Bunbury died this afternoon.
LADY BRACKNELL. What did he die of?
115 ALGERNON. Bunbury? Oh, he was quite exploded.
LADY BRACKNELL. Exploded! Was he the victim of a revolutionary outrage? I was not aware that Mr. Bunbury was interested in social legislation. If so, he is well punished for his morbidity.
120 ALGERNON. My dear Aunt Augusta, I mean he was found out! The doctors found out that Bunbury could not live, that is what I mean—so Bunbury died.
LADY BRACKNELL. He seems to have had great confidence in the opinion of his physicians. I am glad,
125 however, that he made up his mind at the last to some definite course of action, and acted under proper medical advice. And now that we have finally got rid of this Mr. Bunbury, may I ask, Mr. Worthing, who is that young person whose hand my nephew Algernon is now
130 holding in what seems to me a peculiarly unnecessary manner?
JACK. That lady is Miss Cecily Cardew, my ward.

(*Lady Bracknell bows coldly to Cecily.*)

ALGERNON. I am engaged to be married to Cecily, Aunt Augusta.
135 LADY BRACKNELL. I beg your pardon?
CECILY. Mr. Moncrieff and I are engaged to be married, Lady Bracknell.
LADY BRACKNELL. (*With a shiver, crossing to the sofa and sitting down.*) I do not know whether there is anything
140 peculiarly exciting in the air of this particular part of Hertfordshire, but the number of engagements that go on seems to me considerably above the proper average that statistics have laid down for our guidance. I think some preliminary inquiry on my part would not be out
145 of place. Mr. Worthing, is Miss Cardew at all connected with any of the larger railway stations in London? I merely desire information. Until yesterday I had no idea that there were any families or persons whose origin was a Terminus.

(*Jack looks perfectly furious, but restrains himself.*)

150 JACK. (*In a clear, cold voice.*) Miss Cardew is the grand-daughter of the late Mr. Thomas Cardew of 149 Belgrave Square, S.W.; Gervase Park, Dorking, Surrey; and the Sporran, Fifeshire, N.B.

LADY BRACKNELL. That sounds not unsatisfactory.
155 Three addresses always inspire confidence, even in tradesmen. But what proof have I of their authenticity?

JACK. I have carefully preserved the Court Guides[1] of the period. They are open to your inspection, Lady Bracknell.

160 LADY BRACKNELL. (*Grimly.*) I have known strange errors in that publication.

JACK. Miss Cardew's family solicitors are Messrs. Markby, Markby, and Markby.

LADY BRACKNELL. Markby, Markby, and Markby? A
165 firm of the very highest position in their profession. Indeed I am told that one of the Mr. Markbys is occasionally to be seen at dinner parties. So far I am satisfied.

JACK. (*Very irritably.*) How extremely kind of you, Lady Bracknell! I have also in my possession, you will be
170 pleased to hear, certificates of Miss Cardew's birth, baptism, whooping cough, registration, vaccination, confirmation, and the measles; both the German and the English variety.

LADY BRACKNELL. Ah! A life crowded with incident, I
175 see; though perhaps somewhat too exciting for a young girl. I am not myself in favour of premature experiences. (*Rises, looks at her watch.*) Gwendolen! the time approaches for our departure. We have not a moment to lose. As a matter of form, Mr. Worthing, I had better
180 ask you if Miss Cardew has any little fortune?

JACK. Oh! about a hundred and thirty thousand pounds in the Funds. That is all. Goodbye, Lady Bracknell. So pleased to have seen you.

LADY BRACKNELL. (*Sitting down again.*) A moment, Mr.
185 Worthing. A hundred and thirty thousand pounds! And in the Funds! Miss Cardew seems to me a most attractive young lady, now that I look at her. Few girls of the present day have any really solid qualities, any of the qualities that last, and improve with time. We live, I
190 regret to say, in an age of surfaces. (*To Cecily.*) Come over here, dear. (*Cecily goes across.*) Pretty child! your

---

[1] *Court Guides* Directory of names and addresses of those members of the nobility, gentry, and society who have been presented at court.

dress is sadly simple, and your hair seems almost as Nature might have left it. But we can soon alter all that. A thoroughly experienced French maid produces a really
195 marvellous result in a very brief space of time. I remember recommending one to young Lady Lancing, and after three months her own husband did not know her.

JACK. And after six months nobody knew her.

LADY BRACKNELL. (*Glares at Jack for a few moments.*
200 *Then bends, with a practised smile, to Cecily.*) Kindly turn round, sweet child. (*Cecily turns completely round.*) No, the side view is what I want. (*Cecily presents her profile.*) Yes, quite as I expected. There are distinct social possibilities in your profile. The two weak points in our age
205 are its want of principle and its want of profile. The chin a little higher, dear. Style largely depends on the way the chin is worn. They are worn very high, just at present. Algernon!

ALGERNON. Yes, Aunt Augusta!

210 LADY BRACKNELL. There are distinct social possibilities in Miss Cardew's profile.

ALGERNON. Cecily is the sweetest, dearest, prettiest girl in the whole world. And I don't care twopence about social possibilities.

215 LADY BRACKNELL. Never speak disrespectfully of Society, Algernon. Only people who can't get into it do that. (*To Cecily.*) Dear child, of course you know that Algernon has nothing but his debts to depend upon. But I do not approve of mercenary marriages. When I
220 married Lord Bracknell I had no fortune of any kind. But I never dreamed for a moment of allowing that to stand in my way. Well, I suppose I must give my consent.

ALGERNON. Thank you, Aunt Augusta.

225 LADY BRACKNELL. Cecily, you may kiss me!

CECILY. (*Kisses her.*) Thank you, Lady Bracknell.

LADY BRACKNELL. You may also address me as Aunt Augusta for the future.

CECILY. Thank you, Aunt Augusta.

230 LADY BRACKNELL. The marriage, I think, had better take place quite soon.

ALGERNON. Thank you, Aunt Augusta.

CECILY. Thank you, Aunt Augusta.

LADY BRACKNELL. To speak frankly, I am not in favour
235 of long engagements. They give people the opportunity of finding out each other's character before marriage,

which I think is never advisable.

JACK. I beg your pardon for interrupting you, Lady Bracknell, but this engagement is quite out of the question. I am Miss Cardew's guardian, and she cannot marry without my consent until she comes of age. That consent I absolutely decline to give.

LADY BRACKNELL. Upon what grounds may I ask? Algernon is an extremely, I may almost say an ostentatiously, eligible young man. He has nothing, but he looks everything. What more can one desire?

JACK. It pains me very much to have to speak frankly to you, Lady Bracknell, about your nephew, but the fact is that I do not approve at all of his moral character. I suspect him of being untruthful.

(Algernon and Cecily look at him in indignant amazement.)

LADY BRACKNELL. Untruthful! My nephew Algernon? Impossible! He is an Oxonian.[1]

JACK. I fear there can be no possible doubt about the matter. This afternoon during my temporary absence in London on an important question of romance, he obtained admission to my house by means of the false pretence of being my brother. Under an assumed name he drank, I've just been informed by my butler, an entire pint bottle of my Perrier-Jouet, Brut, '89; wine I was specially reserving for myself. Continuing his disgraceful deception, he succeeded in the course of the afternoon in alienating the affections of my only ward. He subsequently stayed to tea, and devoured every single muffin. And what makes his conduct all the more heartless is, that he was perfectly well aware from the first that I have no brother, that I never had a brother, and that I don't intend to have a brother, not even of any kind. I distinctly told him so myself yesterday afternoon.

LADY BRACKNELL. Ahem! Mr. Worthing, after careful consideration I have decided entirely to overlook my nephew's conduct to you.

JACK. That is very generous of you, Lady Bracknell. My own decision, however, is unalterable. I decline to give my consent.

LADY BRACKNELL. *(To Cecily.)* Come here, sweet child.

---

[1] *Oxonian*   One who has attended Oxford University.

(Cecily goes over.) How old are you, dear?

CECILY. Well, I am really only eighteen, but I always admit to twenty when I go to evening parties.

LADY BRACKNELL. You are perfectly right in making some slight alteration. Indeed, no woman should ever be quite accurate about her age. It looks so calculating … *(In a meditative manner.)* Eighteen, but admitting to twenty at evening parties. Well, it will not be very long before you are of age and free from the restraints of tutelage. So I don't think your guardian's consent is, after all, a matter of any importance.

JACK. Pray excuse me, Lady Bracknell, for interrupting you again, but it is only fair to tell you that according to the terms of her grandfather's will Miss Cardew does not come legally of age till she is thirty-five.

LADY BRACKNELL. That does not seem to me to be a grave objection. Thirty-five is a very attractive age. London society is full of women of the very highest birth who have, of their own free choice, remained thirty-five for years. Lady Dumbleton is an instance in point. To my own knowledge she has been thirty-five ever since she arrived at the age of forty, which was many years ago now. I see no reason why our dear Cecily should not be even still more attractive at the age you mention than she is at present. There will be a large accumulation of property.

CECILY. Algy, could you wait for me till I was thirty-five?

ALGERNON. Of course I could, Cecily. You know I could.

CECILY. Yes, I felt it instinctively, but I couldn't wait all that time. I hate waiting even five minutes for anybody. It always makes me rather cross. I am not punctual myself, I know, but I do like punctuality in others, and waiting, even to be married, is quite out of the question.

ALGERNON. Then what is to be done, Cecily?

CECILY. I don't know, Mr. Moncrieff.

LADY BRACKNELL. My dear Mr. Worthing, as Miss Cardew states positively that she cannot wait till she is thirty-five—a remark which I am bound to say seems to me to show a somewhat impatient nature— I would beg of you to reconsider your decision.

JACK. But my dear Lady Bracknell, the matter is entirely in your own hands. The moment you consent to my marriage with Gwendolen, I will most gladly allow your nephew to form an alliance with my ward.

LADY BRACKNELL.   (*Rising and drawing herself up.*) You must be quite aware that what you propose is out of the

325   question.

JACK.   Then a passionate celibacy is all that any of us can look forward to.

LADY BRACKNELL.   That is not the destiny I propose for Gwendolen. Algernon, of course, can choose for him-

330   self. (*Pulls out her watch.*) Come, dear, (*Gwendolen rises*) we have already missed five, if not six, trains. To miss any more might expose us to comment on the platform.

(*Enter Dr. Chasuble.*)

CHASUBLE.   Everything is quite ready for the christen-ings.

335   LADY BRACKNELL.   The christenings, sir! Is not that somewhat premature?

CHASUBLE.   (*Looking rather puzzled, and pointing to Jack and Algernon.*) Both these gentlemen have expressed a desire for immediate baptism.

340   LADY BRACKNELL.   At their age? The idea is grotesque and irreligious! Algernon, I forbid you to be baptized. I will not hear of such excesses. Lord Bracknell would be highly displeased if he learned that that was the way in which you wasted your time and money.

345   CHASUBLE.   Am I to understand then that there are to be no christenings at all this afternoon?

JACK.   I don't think that, as things are now, it would be of much practical value to either of us, Dr. Chasuble.

CHASUBLE.   I am grieved to hear such sentiments from

350   you, Mr. Worthing. They savour of the heretical views of the Anabaptists,[1] views that I have completely refuted in four of my unpublished sermons. However, as your present mood seems to be one peculiarly secular, I will return to the church at once. Indeed, I

355   have just been informed by the pew-opener[2] that for the last hour and a half, Miss Prism has been waiting for me in the vestry.

---

[1]   *heretical views ... Anabaptists*   Although Anabaptists, members of a Protestant sect that rejects Anglican doctrine, believe in baptism, they reject the Anglican custom of baptizing infants. Dr. Chasuble is suggesting that Jack is heretical in denying the value of baptism in the Anglican church.

[2]   *pew-opener*   One assigned to open the doors of pews for privileged churchgoers.

LADY BRACKNELL.   (*Starting.*) Miss Prism! Did I hear you mention a Miss Prism?

360   CHASUBLE.   Yes, Lady Bracknell. I am on my way to join her.

LADY BRACKNELL.   Pray allow me to detain you for a moment. This matter may prove to be one of vital importance to Lord Bracknell and myself. Is this Miss

365   Prism a female of repellent aspect, remotely connected with education?

CHASUBLE.   (*Somewhat indignantly.*) She is the most cultivated of ladies, and the very picture of respectabil-ity.

370   LADY BRACKNELL.   It is obviously the same person. May I ask what position she holds in your household?

CHASUBLE.   (*Severely.*) I am a celibate, madam.

JACK.   (*Interposing.*) Miss Prism, Lady Bracknell, has been for the last three years Miss Cardew's esteemed

375   governess and valued companion.

LADY BRACKNELL.   In spite of what I hear of her, I must see her at once. Let her be sent for.

CHASUBLE.   (*Looking off.*) She approaches; she is nigh.

(*Enter Miss Prism hurriedly.*)

MISS PRISM.   I was told you expected me in the vestry,

380   dear Canon. I have been waiting for you there for an hour and three-quarters.

(*Catches sight of Lady Bracknell, who has fixed her with a stony glare. Miss Prism grows pale and quails. She looks anxiously round as if desirous to escape.*)

LADY BRACKNELL.   (*In a severe, judicial voice.*) Prism! (*Miss Prism bows her head in shame.*) Come here, Prism! (*Miss Prism approaches in a humble manner.*) Prism!

385   Where is that baby? (*General consternation. The Canon starts back in horror. Algernon and Jack pretend to be anxious to shield Cecily and Gwendolen from hearing the details of a terrible public scandal.*) Twenty-eight years ago, Prism, you left Lord Bracknell's house, Number

390   104, Upper Grosvenor Street, in charge of a perambula-tor that contained a baby of the male sex. You never returned. A few weeks later, through the elaborate investigations of the Metropolitan police, the perambu-lator was discovered at midnight, standing by itself in a

remote corner of Bayswater. It contained the manuscript of a three-volume novel of more than usually revolting sentimentality. (*Miss Prism starts in involuntary indignation.*) But the baby was not there! (*Every one looks at Miss Prism.*) Prism! Where is that baby? (*A pause.*)

MISS PRISM.   Lady Bracknell, I admit with shame that I do not know. I only wish I did. The plain facts of the case are these. On the morning of the day you mention, a day that is for ever branded on my memory, I prepared as usual to take the baby out in its perambulator. I had also with me a somewhat old, but capacious hand-bag in which I had intended to place the manuscript of a work of fiction that I had written during my few unoccupied hours. In a moment of mental abstraction, for which I never can forgive myself, I deposited the manuscript in the bassinette, and placed the baby in the hand-bag.

JACK.   (*Who has been listening attentively.*) But where did you deposit the hand-bag?

MISS PRISM.   Do not ask me, Mr. Worthing.

JACK.   Miss Prism, this is a matter of no small importance to me. I insist on knowing where you deposited the hand-bag that contained that infant.

MISS PRISM.   I left it in the cloak-room of one of the larger railway stations in London.

JACK.   What railway station?

MISS PRISM.   (*Quite crushed.*) Victoria. The Brighton line. (*Sinks into a chair.*)

JACK.   I must retire to my room for a moment. Gwendolen, wait here for me.

GWENDOLEN.   If you are not too long, I will wait here for you all my life.

(*Exit Jack in great excitement.*)

CHASUBLE.   What do you think this means, Lady Bracknell?

LADY BRACKNELL.   I dare not even suspect, Dr. Chasuble. I need hardly tell you that in families of high position strange coincidences are not supposed to occur. They are hardly considered the thing.

(*Noises heard overhead as if some one was throwing trunks about. Every one looks up.*)

CECILY.   Uncle Jack seems strangely agitated.

CHASUBLE.   Your guardian has a very emotional nature.

LADY BRACKNELL.   This noise is extremely unpleasant.

It sounds as if he was having an argument. I dislike arguments of any kind. They are always vulgar, and often convincing.

CHASUBLE.   (*Looking up.*) It has stopped now. (*The noise is redoubled.*)

LADY BRACKNELL.   I wish he would arrive at some conclusion.

GWENDOLEN.   This suspense is terrible. I hope it will last.

(*Enter Jack with a hand-bag of black leather in his hand.*)

JACK.   (*Rushing over to Miss Prism.*) Is this the handbag, Miss Prism? Examine it carefully before you speak. The happiness of more than one life depends on your answer.

MISS PRISM.   (*Calmly.*) It seems to be mine. Yes, here is the injury it received through the upsetting of a Gower Street omnibus[1] in younger and happier days. Here is the stain on the lining caused by the explosion of a temperance beverage,[2] an incident that occurred at Leamington. And here, on the lock, are my initials. I had forgotten that in an extravagant mood I had had them placed there. The bag is undoubtedly mine. I am delighted to have it so unexpectedly restored to me. It has been a great inconvenience being without it all these years.

JACK.   (*In a pathetic voice.*) Miss Prism, more is restored to you than this hand-bag. I was the baby you placed in it.

MISS PRISM.   (*Amazed.*) You?

JACK.   (*Embracing her.*) Yes ... mother!

MISS PRISM.   (*Recoiling in indignant astonishment.*) Mr. Worthing! I am unmarried!

JACK.   Unmarried! I do not deny that is a serious blow. But after all, who has the right to cast a stone against one who has suffered? Cannot repentance wipe out an act of folly? Why should there be one law for men, and another for women? Mother, I forgive you. (*Tries to embrace her again.*)

MISS PRISM.   (*Still more indignant.*) Mr. Worthing, there

---

[1]   *Gower Street omnibus*   Public horse-drawn bus on a route in central London.

[2]   *temperance beverage*   Non-alcoholic drink. (The temperance movement aimed to prohibit all alcoholic beverages.)

is some error. (*Pointing to Lady Bracknell.*) There is the lady who can tell you who you really are.

475 JACK. (*After a pause.*) Lady Bracknell, I hate to seem inquisitive, but would you kindly inform me who I am?

LADY BRACKNELL.   I am afraid that the news I have to give you will not altogether please you. You are the son of my poor sister, Mrs. Moncrieff, and consequently 480 Algernon's elder brother.

JACK. Algy's elder brother! Then I have a brother after all. I knew I had a brother! I always said I had a brother! Cecily,—how could you have ever doubted that I had a brother? (*Seizes hold of Algernon.*) Dr. Chasuble, my 485 unfortunate brother. Miss Prism, my unfortunate brother. Gwendolen, my unfortunate brother. Algy, you young scoundrel, you will have to treat me with more respect in the future. You have never behaved to me like a brother in all your life.

490 ALGERNON.   Well, not till to-day, old boy, I admit. I did my best, however, though I was out of practice. (*Shakes hands.*)

GWENDOLEN. (*To Jack.*) My own! But what own are you? What is your Christian name, now that you have 495 become some one else?

JACK.   Good heavens! ... I had quite forgotten that point. Your decision on the subject of my name is irrevocable, I suppose?

GWENDOLEN.   I never change, except in my affections.

500 CECILY.   What a noble nature you have, Gwendolen!

JACK.   Then the question had better be cleared up at once. Aunt Augusta, a moment. At the time when Miss Prism left me in the hand-bag, had I been christened already?

505 LADY BRACKNELL.   Every luxury that money could buy, including christening, had been lavished on you by your fond and doting parents.

JACK.   Then I was christened! That is settled. Now, what name was I given? Let me know the worst.

510 LADY BRACKNELL.   Being the eldest son you were naturally christened after your father.

JACK. (*Irritably.*) Yes, but what was my father's Christian name?

LADY BRACKNELL. (*Meditatively.*) I cannot at the present 515 moment recall what the General's Christian name was. But I have no doubt he had one. He was eccentric, I admit. But only in later years. And that was the result of

the Indian climate, and marriage, and indigestion, and other things of that kind.

520 JACK.   Algy! Can't you recollect what our father's Christian name was?

ALGERNON.   My dear boy, we were never even on speaking terms. He died before I was a year old.

JACK.   His name would appear in the Army Lists[1] of the 525 period, I suppose, Aunt Augusta?

LADY BRACKNELL.   The General was essentially a man of peace, except in his domestic life. But I have no doubt his name would appear in any military directory.

JACK.   The Army Lists of the last forty years are here. 530 These delightful records should have been my constant study. (*Rushes to bookcase and tears the books out.*) M. Generals ... Mallam, Maxbohm, Magley, what ghastly names they have—Markby, Migsby, Mobbs, Moncrieff! Lieutenant 1840, Captain, Lieutenant-Colonel, Colo- 535 nel, General 1869, Christian names, Ernest John. (*Puts book very quietly down and speaks quite calmly.*) I always told you, Gwendolen, my name was Ernest, didn't I? Well, it is Ernest after all. I mean it naturally is Ernest.

LADY BRACKNELL.   Yes, I remember now that the 540 General was called Ernest, I knew I had some particular reason for disliking the name.

GWENDOLEN.   Ernest! My own Ernest! I felt from the first that you could have no other name!

JACK.   Gwendolen, it is a terrible thing for a man to find 545 out suddenly that all his life he has been speaking nothing but the truth. Can you forgive me?

GWENDOLEN.   I can. For I feel that you are sure to change.

JACK.   My own one!

550 CHASUBLE. (*To Miss Prism.*) Laetitia! (*Embraces her.*)

MISS PRISM. (*Enthusiastically.*) Frederick! At last!

ALGERNON.   Cecily! (*Embraces her.*)   At last!

JACK.   Gwendolen! (*Embraces her.*)   At last!

LADY BRACKNELL.   My nephew, you seem to be display- 555 ing signs of triviality.

JACK.   On the contrary, Aunt Augusta, I've now realized for the first time in my life the vital Importance of Being Earnest.

TABLEAU

—1895

---

[1] *Army Lists*   Directories of officers.

ALFRED, LORD TENNYSON
1809 – 1892

In 1850, the novelist and critic Charles Kingsley praised Tennyson's dramatic monologue, "Locksley Hall," as the poem that "has had most influence on the minds of the young men of our day." Throughout his long career, Tennyson's poems continued to resonate with Victorian audiences. The self-reflective grief of *In Memoriam* (1850) touched a chord of genuine sympathy in nineteenth-century readers, including Queen Victoria herself, much as Tennyson's re-telling of Arthurian legend in *Idylls of the King* (1859–85) echoed the nationalistic zeal of the later Victorian period. Britain's Poet Laureate from 1850 to his death in 1892, Tennyson was the quintessential poet of his age.

He was born in 1809 in Somersby, Lincolnshire, to a privileged family, and his poetic gifts became apparent early on. At age eight, Tennyson was composing pages of blank verse in the style of James Thomson; by ten or eleven he had graduated to studying the work of Alexander Pope, imitating hundreds of lines of Pope's translation of Homer's *Iliad*. At twelve, Tennyson set to work on his first epic, a six-thousand-line experiment that mimicked Walter Scott's octosyllabic extravaganzas of war and romance. "I wrote as much as seventy lines at one time," he later recalled, "and used to go shouting them about the fields in the dark." By age fourteen, with an Elizabethan-style drama entitled *The Devil and the Lady*, Tennyson's work was approaching the sonorous agility and understated pathos for which it would be known. His first publication, *Poems by Two Brothers* (1827), a collaborative effort by Tennyson and his two older brothers, Frederick and Charles, was completed just prior to Tennyson's entrance to Trinity College, Cambridge.

Tennyson distinguished himself at Cambridge, establishing his reputation as both a deep thinker and a poet. In June of 1829, he won the Chancellor's Gold Medal with a blank-verse poem, *Timbuctoo*. Some time in that year, Tennyson met Arthur Henry Hallam, who was to become the poet's closest friend and companion. It was also in 1829 that Tennyson joined the Cambridge Apostles, an undergraduate debating society of which Hallam and many of Tennyson's other Cambridge friends were a part. 1830 saw the publication of Tennyson's first important volume, *Poems, Chiefly Lyrical*, which Hallam reviewed for the *Englishman's Magazine* in an essay entitled "On Some of the Characteristics of Modern Poetry and on the Lyrical Poems of Alfred Tennyson." Hallam describes Tennyson as a poet of "sensation," one of a school of poets, including Shelley and Keats, whose "fine organs tremble into emotion at colors, and sounds, and movements" and who translate this physiological sensitivity into their verses. It was precisely such sensitivity that Christopher North (the pseudonym of John Wilson) later attacked in his 1832 *Blackwood's* review of the volume. Subsequently many critics have charted Tennyson's gradual movement away from a poetics of sensation and toward a more restrained poetic style.

The early 1830s were a difficult time for the young poet. Following the death of his father in 1831, Tennyson left Cambridge without taking his degree. Soon afterward, his brother Edward lost his sanity, succumbing to what was known as the "black blood" of the Tennyson family. Finally, and perhaps most devastatingly, Arthur Hallam died suddenly in 1833 of a hemorrhage to his brain. Having published one volume, *Poems*, in 1832, Tennyson would remain silent as a poet for the next ten years, refusing to publish his many works in progress until the *Poems* of 1842, the volume that brought him his reputation as both a remarkable poet and a great voice of his age. During the "ten years' silence," however, Tennyson composed much of what many consider his masterwork, *In Memoriam* (1850), in addition to the innovative dramatic monologues of the 1842 volume, including "Ulysses," "Locksley Hall," and "St. Simeon Stylites."

In 1847, Tennyson published *The Princess*, a poetic medley that explored, through a wildly improbable narrative, the relations between the sexes and the viability of education for women. Interspersed throughout the work are many of Tennyson's best-known lyrics: "Sweet and Low," "The Splendour Falls," and "Tears, Idle Tears," among others. In 1850, Tennyson ascended to the Laureateship and married Emily Sellwood, to whom he had been engaged for fourteen years. That same year, Tennyson also published *In Memoriam*, the elegy on which he had been at work since Arthur Hallam's death. The first of many of Tennyson's books to sell in large numbers, *In Memoriam* went into three editions in its first year alone. Amid a rising swell of scientific discovery and industrial transformation, the poem captured the mood of the era, alternating between faith in science and faith in religion, and reflecting the hopes, doubts, and beliefs of the Victorians.

Tennyson's life changed notably as a result of both his marriage and his suddenly public role as Poet Laureate. The Tennysons had two sons within the next four years, the elder of whom was named Hallam after Tennyson's deceased friend. (After his father's death, Hallam Tennyson wrote a biography entitled *Alfred Lord Tennyson: A Memoir*, and he penned a second volume in 1911, *Tennyson and His Friends*. Alfred Tennyson's grandson Charles also wrote a biography in 1949.)

Many critics have argued that Tennyson's style changed after his appointment as Poet Laureate. Certainly it is true that he assumed a different voice in the occasional poems composed in his role as Poet Laureate, most notably the "Ode on the Death of the Duke of Wellington" (1852); likewise "The Charge of the Light Brigade" (1854) projects an explicit political stance largely absent in his earlier works. But Tennyson continued to evolve as a poet, publishing an experimental "monodrama," *Maud*, in 1855 and the first four segments of his epic, *Idylls of the King*, in 1859. *Maud* was in many ways Tennyson's most controversial publication. Critics complained of the poem's irregular rhythms and of the "screed of bombast" that seemed to some like "the rasping of a blacksmith's file." *Idylls of the King*, on the other hand, was largely—though not universally—hailed as a *magnum opus*. Tennyson had contemplated writing an epic from his childhood; the finished *Idylls* reflects the poet's mature thoughts about Victorian life, politics, and culture through the world of Camelot and King Arthur.

Tennyson's later publications include the plays *Queen Mary* (1875), *The Falcon* (1879), and *The Promise of May* (1882), all of which were produced on the Victorian stage, and numerous volumes of poetry, including *Enoch Arden* (1864), *Tiresias, and Other Poems* (1885), *Locksley Hall Sixty Years After* (1886), and *Demeter and Other Poems* (1889). In 1883, Tennyson accepted a baronetcy from the Queen and took a seat in the House of Lords. He died in 1892 at his second home, Aldworth, and is buried beside Robert Browning in the Poets' Corner of Westminster Abbey.

⌘⌘⌘

Julia Margaret Cameron, *Mariana*, 1875.

Mariana

Mariana in the moated grange
(Measure for Measure)[1]

With blackest moss the flower-plots
    Were thickly crusted, one and all:
The rusted nails fell from the knots
    That held the pear to the gable-wall.[2]
5 The broken sheds looked sad and strange:
    Unlifted was the clinking latch;
    Weeded and worn the ancient thatch
Upon the lonely moated grange.
      She only said, "My life is dreary,

10   He cometh not," she said;
      She said, "I am aweary, aweary,
      I would that I were dead!"

Her tears fell with the dews at even;°   *evening*
    Her tears fell ere° the dews were dried;   *before*
15 She could not look on the sweet heaven,
    Either at morn or eventide.
After the flitting of the bats,
    When thickest dark did trance° the sky,   *entrance*
    She drew her casement-curtain by,
20 And glanced athwart the glooming flats.[3]
      She only said, "The night is dreary,
      He cometh not," she said;
      She said, "I am aweary, aweary,
      I would that I were dead!"

25 Upon the middle of the night,
    Waking she heard the night-fowl crow:
The cock sung out an hour ere light:
    From the dark fen° the oxen's low   *lowlands*
Came to her: without hope of change,
30   In sleep she seemed to walk forlorn,
    Till cold winds woke the gray-eyed morn
About the lonely moated grange.
      She only said, "The day is dreary,
      He cometh not," she said;
35   She said, "I am aweary, aweary,
      I would that I were dead!"

About a stone-cast from the wall
    A sluice with blackened waters slept,
And o'er it many, round and small,
40   The clustered marish-mosses[4] crept.
Hard by a poplar shook alway,
    All silver-green with gnarlèd bark:
    For leagues no other tree did mark
The level waste, the rounding gray.
45   She only said, "My life is dreary,
      He cometh not," she said;
      She said, "I am aweary, aweary,
      I would that I were dead!"

---

[1] *Mariana ... Measure* Tennyson's epigraph is adapted from the words of the Duke in Shakespeare's *Measure for Measure*, 3.1.277: "There, at the moated grange, lies this dejected Mariana." Earlier in the scene, the Duke has recounted how Mariana, having lost her dowry (and her brother) in a shipwreck, has been deserted by her betrothed; *moated grange* Cottage or small farmhouse surrounded by a moat, or water-filled ditch.

[2] *The rusted ... gable-wall* The pear has been espaliered, or trained to grow against a wall on a lattice or framework of stakes.

[3] *flats* Flatlands or lowlands.

[4] [Tennyson's note] *Marish-mosses*, the little marsh-moss lumps that float on the surface of the water.

And ever when the moon was low,
50   And the shrill winds were up and away,
In the white curtain, to and fro,
      She saw the gusty shadow sway.
But when the moon was very low,
      And wild winds bound within their cell,[1]
55   The shadow of the poplar fell
Upon her bed, across her brow.
            She only said, "The night is dreary,
                  He cometh not," she said;
            She said, "I am aweary, aweary,
60   I would that I were dead!"

All day within the dreamy house,
      The doors upon their hinges creaked;
The blue fly° sung in the pane; the mouse   *bluebottle*
      Behind the mouldering wainscot shrieked,
65 Or from the crevice peered about.
      Old faces glimmered through the doors,
      Old footsteps trod the upper floors,
Old voices called her from without.
            She only said, "My life is dreary,
70   He cometh not," she said;
            She said, "I am aweary, aweary,
                  I would that I were dead!"

The sparrow's chirrup on the roof,
      The slow clock ticking, and the sound
75 Which to the wooing wind aloof
      The poplar made, did all confound
Her sense; but most she loathed the hour
      When the thick-moted[2] sunbeam lay
      Athwart the chambers, and the day
80 Was sloping toward his western bower.
            Then, said she, "I am very dreary,
                  He will not come," she said;
            She wept, "I am aweary, aweary,
                  Oh God, that I were dead!"
—1830

---

[1] *wild ... cell* A reference to Virgil's *Aeneid*, 1.52, in which Aeolus, god of winds, keeps the winds imprisoned in a cavern.

[2] *thick-moted* I.e., thick with motes of dust.

The Palace of Art

I built my soul a lordly pleasure-house,
      Wherein at ease for aye° to dwell.   *ever*
I said, "O Soul, make merry and carouse,
      Dear soul, for all is well."

5 A huge crag-platform, smooth as burnished brass
      I chose. The rangèd ramparts bright
From level meadow-bases of deep grass
      Suddenly scaled the light.

Thereon I built it firm. Of ledge or shelf
10   The rock rose clear, or winding stair.
My soul would live alone unto herself
      In her high palace there.

And "while the world runs round and round," I said,
      "Reign thou apart, a quiet king,
15 Still as, while Saturn whirls, his steadfast shade
      Sleeps on his luminous ring."

To which my soul made answer readily:
      "Trust me, in bliss I shall abide
In this great mansion, that is built for me,
20   So royal-rich and wide."

Four courts I made, East, West and South and North,
      In each a squared lawn, wherefrom
The golden gorge of dragons spouted forth
      A flood of fountain-foam.

25 And round the cool green courts there ran a row
      Of cloisters, branched like mighty woods,
Echoing all night to that sonorous flow
      Of spouted fountain-floods.

And round the roofs a gilded gallery
30   That lent broad verge° to distant lands,   *view*
Far as the wild swan wings, to where the sky
      Dipped down to sea and sands.

From those four jets four currents in one swell
    Across the mountain streamed below
35 In misty folds, that floating as they fell
    Lit up a torrent-bow.[1]

And high on every peak a statue seemed
    To hang on tiptoe, tossing up
A cloud of incense of all odour steamed
40   From out a golden cup.

So that she thought, "And who shall gaze upon
    My palace with unblinded eyes,
While this great bow will waver in the sun,
    And that sweet incense rise?"

45 For that sweet incense rose and never failed,
    And, while day sank or mounted higher,
The light aerial gallery, golden-railed,
    Burnt like a fringe of fire.

Likewise the deep-set windows, stained and traced,
50   Would seem slow-flaming crimson fires
From shadowed grots° of arches interlaced,   *grottoes*
    And tipped with frost-like spires.

Full of long-sounding corridors it was,
    That over-vaulted grateful° gloom,   *pleasing*
55 Through which the livelong day my soul did pass,
    Well-pleased, from room to room.

Full of great rooms and small the palace stood,
    All various, each a perfect whole
From living Nature, fit for every mood
60   And change of my still soul.

For some were hung with arras° green and blue,   *tapestries*
    Showing a gaudy summer-morn,
Where with puffed cheek the belted hunter blew
    His wreathèd bugle-horn.

65 One seemed all dark and red—a tract of sand,
    And someone pacing there alone,
Who paced forever in a glimmering land,
    Lit with a low large moon.

---

[1] *torrent-bow* Rainbow formed in the spray of a torrent.

One showed an iron coast and angry waves.
70   You seemed to hear them climb and fall
And roar rock-thwarted under bellowing caves,
    Beneath the windy wall.

And one, a full-fed river winding slow
    By herds upon an endless plain,
75 The ragged rims of thunder brooding low,
    With shadow-streaks of rain.

And one, the reapers at their sultry toil.
    In front they bound the sheaves. Behind
Were realms of upland, prodigal in oil,
80   And hoary to the wind.[2]

And one a foreground black with stones and slags,
    Beyond, a line of heights, and higher
All barred with long white cloud the scornful crags,
    And highest, snow and fire.

85 And one, an English home—gray twilight poured
    On dewy pastures, dewy trees,
Softer than sleep—all things in order stored,
    A haunt of ancient Peace.

Nor these alone, but every landscape fair,
90   As fit for every mood of mind,
Or gay, or grave, or sweet, or stern, was there
    Not less than truth designed.

Or the maid-mother by a crucifix,
    In tracts of pasture sunny-warm,
95 Beneath branch-work of costly sardonyx[3]
    Sat smiling, babe in arm.

Or in a clear-walled city on the sea,
    Near gilded organ-pipes, her hair
Wound with white roses, slept St. Cecily;[4]
100   An angel looked at her.

---

[2] *hoary ... wind* The white underside of the olive leaves are exposed by the wind.

[3] *sardonyx* Onyx striped with sard, a yellow or orange quartz.

[4] *St. Cecily* St. Cecilia, patron saint of music.

Or thronging all one porch of Paradise
    A group of Houris[1] bowed to see
The dying Islamite, with hands and eyes
    That said, We wait for thee.

105   Or mythic Uther's deeply-wounded son[2]
    In some fair space of sloping greens
Lay, dozing in the vale of Avalon,
    And watched by weeping queens.

Or hollowing one hand against his ear,
110   To list° a foot-fall, ere he saw   *hear*
The wood-nymph, stayed the Ausonian king[3] to hear
    Of wisdom and of law.

Or over hills with peaky tops engrailed,°   *serrated*
    And many a tract of palm and rice.
115   The throne of Indian Cama[4] slowly sailed
    A summer fanned with spice.

Or sweet Europa's[5] mantle blew unclasped,
    From off her shoulder backward borne:
From one hand drooped a crocus: one hand grasped
120   The mild bull's golden horn.

Or else flushed Ganymede,[6] his rosy thigh
    Half-buried in the Eagle's down,
Sole as a flying star shot through the sky
    Above the pillared town.

125 Nor these alone: but every legend fair
    Which the supreme Caucasian mind
Carved out of Nature for itself, was there,
    Not less than life, designed.

Then in the towers I placed great bells that swung,
130   Moved of themselves, with silver sound;
And with choice paintings of wise men I hung
    The royal dais round.

For there was Milton like a seraph° strong,   *angel*
    Beside him Shakespeare bland and mild;
135 And there the world-worn Dante grasped his song,
    And somewhat grimly smiled.

And there the Ionian father[7] of the rest;
    A million wrinkles carved his skin;
A hundred winters snowed upon his breast,
140   From cheek and throat and chin.

Above, the fair hall-ceiling stately-set
    Many an arch high up did lift,
And angels rising and descending met
    With interchange of gift.

145 Below was all mosaic choicely planned
    With cycles of the human tale
Of this wide world, the times of every land
    So wrought, they will not fail.

The people here, a beast of burden slow,
150   Toiled onward, pricked with goads and stings;
Here played, a tiger, rolling to and fro
    The heads and crowns of kings;

Here rose, an athlete, strong to break or bind
    All force in bonds that might endure,
155 And here once more like some sick man declined,
    And trusted any cure.

But over these she trod: and those great bells
    Began to chime. She took her throne:
She sat betwixt the shining Oriels,°   *windows*
160   To sing her songs alone.

---

[1] *Houris* Nymphs of Muslim paradise.

[2] *Uther's … son* King Arthur, son of Uther Pendragon, badly wounded in his last battle and carried to the mystic island of Avalon to heal.

[3] *Ausonian king* Numa, the legendary second king of Rome, who was said to have received the laws of the kingdom from the nymph Egeria; *Ausonia* was an ancient name for Italy often used by poets.

[4] [Tennyson's note] The Hindu God of young love, son of Brahma.

[5] *Europa* In Greek legend, the beautiful daughter of the king of Phoenicia. Zeus fell in love with her and assumed the shape of a bull in order to carry her off.

[6] *Ganymede* In Greek legend, a beautiful youth who was carried up to heaven at the command of Zeus, who made him cup-bearer to the gods.

[7] *Ionian father* Homer.

And through the topmost Oriels' coloured flame
    Two godlike faces gazed below;
Plato the wise, and large-browed Verulam,[1]
    The first of those who know.

165 And all those names, that in their motion were
    Full-welling fountainheads of change,
Betwixt the slender shafts were blazoned fair
    In diverse raiment° strange: *clothing*

Through which the lights, rose, amber, emerald, blue,
170   Flushed in her temples and her eyes,
And from her lips, as morn from Memnon, drew
    Rivers of melodies.[2]

No nightingale delighteth to prolong
    Her low preamble all alone,
175 More than my soul to hear her echoed song
    Throb through the ribbèd stone;

Singing and murmuring in her feastful mirth,
    Joying to feel herself alive,
Lord over Nature, Lord of the visible earth,
180   Lord of the senses five;

Communing with herself: "All these are mine,
    And let the world have peace or wars,
'Tis one to me." She—when young night divine
    Crowned dying day with stars,

185 Making sweet close of his delicious toils—
    Lit light in wreaths and anadems,°   *garlands*
And pure quintessences of precious oils
    In hollowed moons of gems,

To mimic heaven; and clapped her hands and cried,
190   "I marvel if my still° delight   *constant*
In this great house so royal-rich, and wide,
    Be flattered to the height.

"O all things fair to sate my various eyes!
    O shapes and hues that please me well!
195 O silent faces of the Great and Wise,
    My Gods, with whom I dwell!

"O God-like isolation which art mine,
    I can but count thee perfect gain,
What time I watch the darkening droves of swine
200   That range on yonder plain.

"In filthy sloughs they roll a prurient skin,
    They graze and wallow, breed and sleep;
And oft some brainless devil enters in,
    And drives them to the deep."[3]

205 Then of the moral instinct would she prate
    And of the rising from the dead,
As hers by right of full-accomplished Fate;
    And at the last she said:

"I take possession of man's mind and deed.
210   I care not what the sects may brawl.
I sit as God holding no form of creed,
    But contemplating all."

Full oft the riddle of the painful earth
    Flashed through her as she sat alone,
215 Yet not the less held she her solemn mirth,
    And intellectual throne.

And so she throve and prospered: so three years
    She prospered: on the fourth she fell,
Like Herod, when the shout was in his ears,
220   Struck through with pangs of hell.[4]

Lest she should fail and perish utterly,
    God, before whom ever lie bare
The abysmal deeps of Personality,
    Plagued her with sore despair.

---

[1] *Oriels' ... Verulam* Recessed windows decorated with colored stained glass in images of Plato and Francis Bacon, one of whose titles was Baron Verulam.

[2] *morn ... melodies* The statue of the legendary Ethiopian king Memnon at Thebes was said by the ancient Greeks to produce beautiful music when touched by the rays of the dawning sun.

[3] *oft ... deep* A reference to Matthew 8.28–32, in which Jesus casts devils out of two men and into a herd of swine, whereupon the herd stampedes off a cliff into the sea.

[4] *Herod ... hell* A reference to Acts 12.21–23, in which King Herod is struck dead as a crowd of his subjects shout that he is a god and not a man.

"Yet pull not down my palace towers, that are
    So lightly, beautifully built:
295 Perchance I may return with others there
      When I have purged my guilt."
—1832 (REVISED 1842)

The Lady of Shalott [1]

PART 1

On either side the river lie
  Long fields of barley and of rye,
That clothe the wold° and meet the sky;   *plain*
And through the field the road runs by
5   To many-towered Camelot;
And up and down the people go,
Gazing where the lilies blow
Round an island there below,
    The island of Shalott.

10 Willows whiten,[2] aspens quiver,
Little breezes dusk° and shiver   *darken*
Through the wave that runs for ever
By the island in the river
    Flowing down to Camelot.
15 Four gray walls, and four gray towers,
Overlook a space of flowers,
And the silent isle imbowers°   *encloses*
    The Lady of Shalott.

By the margin, willow-veiled,
20 Slide the heavy barges trailed
By slow horses; and unhailed
The shallop[3] flitteth silken-sailed
    Skimming down to Camelot:
But who hath seen her wave her hand?

Or at the casement seen her stand?
Or is she known in all the land,
    The Lady of Shalott?

Only reapers, reaping early
In among the bearded barley,
30 Hear a song that echoes cheerly
From the river winding clearly,
    Down to towered Camelot:
And by the moon the reaper weary,
Piling sheaves in uplands airy,
35 Listening, whispers "'Tis the fairy
    Lady of Shalott."

PART 2

There she weaves by night and day
A magic web with colours gay.
She has heard a whisper say,
40 A curse is on her if she stay
    To look down to Camelot.
She knows not what the curse may be,
And so she weaveth steadily,
And little other care hath she,
45   The Lady of Shalott.

And moving through a mirror clear
That hangs before her all the year,
Shadows of the world appear.
There she sees the highway near
50   Winding down to Camelot:
There the river eddy whirls,
And there the surly village-churls,
And the red cloaks of market girls,
    Pass onward from Shalott.

55 Sometimes a troop of damsels glad,
An abbot on an ambling pad,°   *horse*
Sometimes a curly shepherd-lad,
Or long-haired page in crimson clad,
    Goes by to towered Camelot;
60 And sometimes through the mirror blue
The knights come riding two and two:
She hath no loyal knight and true,
    The Lady of Shalott.

---

[1] *The Lady of Shalott* Elaine of the Arthurian romances, who dies of love for Lancelot; she is called "the lily maid of Astolat" in Malory's *Morte Darthur*. Tennyson first encountered the story, however, in a medieval Italian romance called "La Donna di Scalotta" and changed the name to Shalott for a softer sound.

[2] *Willows whiten* I.e., the wind exposes the white undersides of the leaves.

[3] *shallop* Light open boat for use in shallow water.

225 When she would think, where'er she turned her sight
  The airy hand confusion wrought,
Wrote, "Mene, mene,"[1] and divided quite
  The kingdom of her thought.

Deep dread and loathing of her solitude
230   Fell on her, from which mood was born
Scorn of herself; again, from out that mood
  Laughter at her self-scorn.

"What! is not this my place of strength," she said,
  "My spacious mansion built for me,
235 Whereof the strong foundation-stones were laid
  Since my first memory?"

But in dark corners of her palace stood
  Uncertain shapes; and unawares
On white-eyed phantasms weeping tears of blood,
240   And horrible nightmares,

And hollow shades enclosing hearts of flame,
  And, with dim fretted foreheads all,
On corpses three-months-old at noon she came,
  That stood against the wall.

245 A spot of dull stagnation, without light
  Or power of movement, seemed my soul,
'Mid onward-sloping motions infinite
  Making for one sure goal.

A still salt pool, locked in with bars of sand,
250   Left on the shore; that hears all night
The plunging seas draw backward from the land
  Their moon-led waters white.

A star that with the choral starry dance
  Joined not, but stood, and standing saw
255 The hollow orb of moving Circumstance
  Rolled round by one fixed law.

Back on herself her serpent pride had curled.
  "No voice," she shrieked in that lone hall,
"No voice breaks through the stillness of this world:
260   One deep, deep silence all!"

She, mouldering with the dull earth's mouldering sod,
  Inwrapt tenfold in slothful shame,
Lay there exilèd from eternal God,
  Lost to her place and name;

265 And death and life she hated equally,
  And nothing saw, for her despair,
But dreadful time, dreadful eternity,
  No comfort anywhere;

Remaining utterly confused with fears,
270   And ever worse with growing time,
And ever unrelieved by dismal tears,
  And all alone in crime:

Shut up as in a crumbling tomb, girt round
  With blackness as a solid wall,
275 Far off she seemed to hear the dully° sound   *faint*
  Of human footsteps fall.

As in strange lands a traveller walking slow,
  In doubt and great perplexity,
A little before moon-rise hears the low
280   Moan of an unknown sea;

And knows not if it be thunder, or a sound
  Of rocks thrown down, or one deep cry
Of great wild beasts; then thinketh, "I have found
  A new land, but I die."

285 She howled aloud, "I am on fire within.
  There comes no murmur of reply.
What is it that will take away my sin,
  And save me lest I die?"

So when four years were wholly finished,
290   She threw her royal robes away.
"Make me a cottage in the vale," she said,
  "Where I may mourn and pray.

---

1 *"Mene, mene"* The first of the words, seen by the Babylonian king Belshazzar, that are mysteriously written on the wall by a disembodied hand in Daniel 5.25–26. Daniel's interpretation of the words for the frightened king concludes with the phrase "Thy kingdom is divided."

But in her web she still delights
65 To weave the mirror's magic sights,
For often through the silent nights
A funeral, with plumes and lights
    And music, went to Camelot:
Or when the moon was overhead,
70 Came two young lovers lately wed;
"I am half sick of shadows," said
    The Lady of Shalott.

PART 3

A bow-shot from her bower-eaves,
He rode between the barley-sheaves,
75 The sun came dazzling through the leaves,
And flamed upon the brazen greaves[1]
    Of bold Sir Lancelot.
A red-cross knight for ever kneeled
    To a lady in his shield,
80 That sparkled on the yellow field,
    Beside remote Shalott.

The gemmy° bridle glittered free,   *brilliant*
Like to some branch of stars we see
Hung in the golden Galaxy.
85 The bridle bells rang merrily
    As he rode down to Camelot:
And from his blazoned baldric° slung   *shoulder-strap*
A mighty silver bugle hung,
And as he rode his armour rung,
90   Beside remote Shalott.

All in the blue unclouded weather
Thick-jewelled shone the saddle-leather,
The helmet and the helmet-feather
Burned like one burning flame together,
95   As he rode down to Camelot.
As often through the purple night,
Below the starry clusters bright,
Some bearded meteor, trailing light,
    Moves over still Shalott.

100 His broad clear brow in sunlight glowed;
On burnished hooves his war-horse trode;
From underneath his helmet flowed
His coal-black curls as on he rode,
    As he rode down to Camelot.
105 From the bank and from the river
He flashed into the crystal mirror,
"Tirra lirra," by the river
    Sang Sir Lancelot.

She left the web, she left the loom,
110 She made three paces through the room,
She saw the water-lily bloom,
She saw the helmet and the plume,
    She looked down to Camelot.
Out flew the web and floated wide;
115 The mirror cracked from side to side;
"The curse is come upon me," cried
    The Lady of Shalott.

PART 4

In the stormy east-wind straining,
The pale yellow woods were waning,
120 The broad stream in his banks complaining,
Heavily the low sky raining
    Over towered Camelot;
Down she came and found a boat
Beneath a willow left afloat,
125 And round about the prow she wrote
    The Lady of Shalott.

And down the river's dim expanse
Like some bold seer in a trance,
Seeing all his own mischance—
130 With a glassy countenance
    Did she look to Camelot.
And at the closing of the day
She loosed the chain, and down she lay;
The broad stream bore her far away,
135   The Lady of Shalott.

---

[1] *greaves* Armor worn below the knee.

Lying, robed in snowy white
That loosely flew to left and right—
The leaves upon her falling light—
Through the noises of the night
140   She floated down to Camelot:
And as the boat-head wound along
The willowy hills and fields among,
They heard her singing her last song,
      The Lady of Shalott.

145   Heard a carol, mournful, holy,
Chanted loudly, chanted lowly,
Till her blood was frozen slowly,
And her eyes were darkened wholly,
      Turned to towered Camelot.
150   For ere she reached upon the tide
The first house by the water-side,
Singing in her song she died,
      The Lady of Shalott.

Under tower and balcony,
155   By garden-wall and gallery,
A gleaming shape she floated by,
Dead-pale between the houses high,
      Silent into Camelot.
Out upon the wharfs they came,
160   Knight and burgher, lord and dame,
And round the prow they read her name,
      The Lady of Shalott.

Who is this? and what is here?
And in the lighted palace near
165   Died the sound of royal cheer;
And they crossed themselves for fear,
      All the knights at Camelot:
But Lancelot mused a little space;
He said, "She has a lovely face;
170   God in his mercy lend her grace,
      The Lady of Shalott."
      —1832 (REVISED 1842)

The Lotos-Eaters[1]

"Courage!" he said, and pointed toward the land,
   "This mounting wave will roll us shoreward
      soon."
In the afternoon they came unto a land
In which it seemed always afternoon.
5   All round the coast the languid air did swoon,
Breathing like one that hath a weary dream.
Full-faced above the valley stood the moon;
And like a downward smoke, the slender stream
Along the cliff to fall and pause and fall did seem.

10   A land of streams! some, like a downward smoke,
Slow-dropping veils of thinnest lawn,[2] did go;
And some through wavering lights and shadows broke,
Rolling a slumbrous sheet of foam below.
They saw the gleaming river seaward flow
15   From the inner land: far off, three mountain-tops,
Three silent pinnacles of agèd snow,
Stood sunset-flushed: and, dewed with showery drops,
Up-clomb the shadowy pine above the woven
      copse.°   *thicket*

The charmèd sunset lingered low adown
20   In the red West: through mountain clefts the dale
Was seen far inland, and the yellow down
Bordered with palm, and many a winding vale
And meadow, set with slender galingale;[3]
A land where all things always seemed the same!
25   And round about the keel with faces pale,
Dark faces pale against that rosy flame,
The mild-eyed melancholy Lotos-eaters came.

Branches they bore of that enchanted stem,
Laden with flower and fruit, whereof they gave
30   To each, but whoso did receive of them,

---

[1] *Lotos-Eaters* In Greek mythology, the Lotus Eaters (or Loto-phagi) were a race of people who inhabited an island near north Africa. They existed in peaceful apathy because of the narcotic effects of the lotus plants they ate. When Odysseus landed on the island, some of his men ate the lotus plants and wanted to stay on the island, rather than return home to their families. The incident is documented in Homer's *Odyssey* 9.2.

[2] *lawn* Fine fabric.

[3] *galingale* Species of sedge.

And taste, to him the gushing of the wave
Far far away did seem to mourn and rave
On alien shores; and if his fellow spake,
His voice was thin, as voices from the grave;
35   And deep-asleep he seemed, yet all awake,
And music in his ears his beating heart did make.

They sat them down upon the yellow sand,
Between the sun and moon upon the shore;
And sweet it was to dream of Fatherland,
40   Of child, and wife, and slave; but evermore
Most weary seemed the sea, weary the oar,
Weary the wandering fields of barren foam.
Then some one said, "We will return no more";
And all at once they sang, "Our island home
45   Is far beyond the wave; we will no longer roam."

CHORIC SONG[1]

I

There is sweet music here that softer falls
Than petals from blown roses on the grass,
Or night-dews on still waters between walls
Of shadowy granite, in a gleaming pass;
50   Music that gentlier on the spirit lies,
Than tired eyelids upon tired eyes;
Music that brings sweet sleep down from the blissful
    skies.
Here are cool mosses deep,
And through the moss the ivies creep,
55   And in the stream the long-leaved flowers weep,
And from the craggy ledge the poppy hangs in sleep.

2

Why are we weighed upon with heaviness,
And utterly consumed with sharp distress,
While all things else have rest from weariness?
60   All things have rest: why should we toil alone,
We only toil, who are the first of things,
And make perpetual moan,
Still from one sorrow to another thrown:
Nor ever fold our wings,
65   And cease from wanderings,
Nor steep our brows in slumber's holy balm;
Nor harken what the inner spirit sings,

"There is no joy but calm!"
Why should we only toil, the roof and crown of things?

3

70   Lo! in the middle of the wood,
The folded leaf is wooed from out the bud
With winds upon the branch, and there
Grows green and broad, and takes no care,
Sun-steeped at noon, and in the moon
75   Nightly dew-fed; and turning yellow
Falls, and floats adown the air.
Lo! sweetened with the summer light,
The full-juiced apple, waxing over-mellow,
Drops in a silent autumn night.
80   All its allotted length of days,
The flower ripens in its place,
Ripens and fades, and falls, and hath no toil,
Fast-rooted in the fruitful soil.

4

Hateful is the dark-blue sky,
85   Vaulted o'er the dark-blue sea.
Death is the end of life; ah, why
Should life all labour be?
Let us alone. Time driveth onward fast,
And in a little while our lips are dumb.
90   Let us alone. What is it that will last?
All things are taken from us, and become
Portions and parcels of the dreadful Past.
Let us alone. What pleasure can we have
To war with evil? Is there any peace
95   In ever climbing up the climbing wave?
All things have rest, and ripen toward the grave
In silence; ripen, fall and cease:
Give us long rest or death, dark death, or dreamful ease.

5

How sweet it were, hearing the downward stream,
100   With half-shut eyes ever to seem
Falling asleep in a half-dream!
To dream and dream, like yonder amber light,
Which will not leave the myrrh-bush on the height;
To hear each other's whispered speech;
105   Eating the Lotos day by day,
To watch the crisping ripples on the beach,

---
[1] *Choric Song*   As performed by the Chorus in an ancient Greek play.

And tender curving lines of creamy spray;
To lend our hearts and spirits wholly
To the influence of mild-minded melancholy;
110 To muse and brood and live again in memory,
With those old faces of our infancy
Heaped over with a mound of grass,
Two handfuls of white dust,[1] shut in an urn of brass!

6

Dear is the memory of our wedded lives,
115 And dear the last embraces of our wives
And their warm tears: but all hath suffered change:
For surely now our household hearths are cold:
Our sons inherit us: our looks are strange:
And we should come like ghosts to trouble joy.
120 Or else the island princes over-bold
Have eat our substance, and the minstrel sings
Before them of the ten years' war in Troy,
And our great deeds, as half-forgotten things.
Is there confusion in the little isle?
125 Let what is broken so remain.
The Gods are hard to reconcile:
'Tis hard to settle order once again.
There *is* confusion worse than death,
Trouble on trouble, pain on pain,
130 Long labour unto agèd breath,
Sore task to hearts worn out by many wars
And eyes grown dim with gazing on the pilot-stars.

7

But, propped on beds of amaranth[2] and moly,[3]
How sweet (while warm airs lull us, blowing lowly)
135 With half-dropped eyelid still,
Beneath a heaven dark and holy,
To watch the long bright river drawing slowly
His waters from the purple hill—
To hear the dewy echoes calling
140 From cave to cave through the thick-twinèd vine—
To watch the emerald-coloured water falling
Through many a woven acanthus[4]-wreath divine!

---

[1] *white dust* I.e., cremated remains.

[2] *amaranth* Mythical flowers that never wilted.

[3] *moly* Herb with magical protective powers.

[4] *acanthus* Plant native to Mediterranean shores. The Greeks and Romans esteemed the plant for the elegance of its leaves.

Only to hear and see the far-off sparkling brine,
Only to hear were sweet, stretched out beneath the pine.

8

145 The Lotos blooms below the barren peak:
The Lotos blows by every winding creek:
All day the wind breathes low with mellower tone:
Through every hollow cave and alley lone
Round and round the spicy downs the yellow
     Lotos-dust is blown.
150 We have had enough of action, and of motion we,
Rolled to starboard, rolled to larboard,° when   *port*
     the surge was seething free,
Where the wallowing monster spouted his foam-
     fountains in the sea.
Let us swear an oath, and keep it with an equal mind,
In the hollow Lotos-land to live and lie reclined
155 On the hills like Gods together, careless of mankind.
For they lie beside their nectar, and the bolts are
     hurled
Far below them in the valleys, and the clouds are
     lightly curled
Round their golden houses, girdled with the gleaming
     world:
Where they smile in secret, looking over wasted lands,
160 Blight and famine, plague and earthquake, roaring
     deeps and fiery sands,
Clanging fights, and flaming towns, and sinking
     ships, and praying hands.
But they smile, they find a music centred in a doleful
     song
Steaming up, a lamentation and an ancient tale of
     wrong,
Like a tale of little meaning though the words are strong;
165 Chanted from an ill-used race of men that cleave the
     soil,
Sow the seed, and reap the harvest with enduring toil,
Storing yearly little dues of wheat, and wine and oil;
Till they perish and they suffer—some, 'tis whispered
     —down in hell
Suffer endless anguish, others in Elysian[5] valleys
     dwell,

---

[5] *Elysian* Heavenly. According to the ancient Greeks, Elysium was the dwelling place of the blessed after death.

170　Resting weary limbs at last on beds of asphodel.[1]
　　Surely, surely, slumber is more sweet than toil, the shore
　　Than labour in the deep mid-ocean, wind and wave
　　　　and oar;
　　Oh rest ye, brother mariners, we will not wander more.
　　　　—1832 (REVISED 1842)

Ulysses[2]

　　It little profits that an idle king,
　　By this still hearth, among these barren crags,
　　Matched with an agèd wife, I mete and dole
　　Unequal laws unto a savage race,
5　　That hoard, and sleep, and feed, and know not me.

　　I cannot rest from travel: I will drink
　　Life to the lees:° all times I have enjoyed   *dregs*
　　Greatly, have suffered greatly, both with those
　　That loved me, and alone; on shore, and when
10　　Thro' scudding drifts the rainy Hyades[3]
　　Vexed the dim sea: I am become a name;
　　For always roaming with a hungry heart
　　Much have I seen and known; cities of men
　　And manners, climates, councils, governments,
15　　Myself not least, but honoured of them all;
　　And drunk delight of battle with my peers,
　　Far on the ringing plains of windy Troy.
　　I am a part of all that I have met;
　　Yet all experience is an arch wherethrough
20　　Gleams that untravelled world, whose margin°   *horizon*
　　　　fades
　　For ever and for ever when I move.
　　How dull it is to pause, to make an end,
　　To rust unburnished, not to shine in use!
　　As though to breathe were life. Life piled on life
25　　Were all too little, and of one to me
　　Little remains: but every hour is saved
　　From that eternal silence, something more,

　　A bringer of new things; and vile it were
　　For some three suns to store and hoard myself,
30　　And this gray spirit yearning in desire
　　To follow knowledge like a sinking star,
　　Beyond the utmost bound of human thought.

　　　　This is my son, mine own Telemachus,
　　To whom I leave the sceptre and the isle—
35　　Well-loved of me, discerning to fulfil
　　This labour, by slow prudence to make mild
　　A rugged people, and through soft degrees
　　Subdue them to the useful and the good.
　　Most blameless is he, centred in the sphere
40　　Of common duties, decent not to fail
　　In offices of tenderness, and pay
　　Meet adoration to my household gods,
　　When I am gone. He works his work, I mine.

　　　　There lies the port; the vessel puffs her sail:
45　　There gloom the dark broad seas. My mariners,
　　Souls that have toiled, and wrought, and thought
　　　　with me—
　　That ever with a frolic welcome took
　　The thunder and the sunshine, and opposed
　　Free hearts, free foreheads—you and I are old;
50　　Old age hath yet his honour and his toil;
　　Death closes all: but something ere the end,
　　Some work of noble note, may yet be done,
　　Not unbecoming men that strove with Gods.

　　The lights begin to twinkle from the rocks:
55　　The long day wanes: the slow moon climbs: the deep
　　Moans round with many voices. Come, my friends,
　　'Tis not too late to seek a newer world.
　　Push off, and sitting well in order smite
　　The sounding furrows; for my purpose holds
60　　To sail beyond the sunset, and the baths
　　Of all the western stars, until I die.
　　It may be that the gulfs will wash us down:
　　It may be we shall touch the Happy Isles,[4]
　　And see the great Achilles,[5] whom we knew.

---

[1]　*asphodel*　Plant said to cover the Elysian fields.

[2]　*Ulysses*　Latin name for Odysseus, the protagonist of Homer's *Odyssey*. Here, long after the adventures recounted in that book, the aged, yet restless, Ulysses prepares to embark on one last voyage of discovery.

[3]　*Hyades*　Group of stars near the constellation Taurus and associated with rainstorms.

[4]　*Happy Isles*　Elysium, or Isles of the Blessed, where heroes enjoyed the afterlife.

[5]　*Achilles*　Hero from Greek mythology, also the central character of Homer's *Iliad*.

65 Though much is taken, much abides; and though
    We are not now that strength which in old days
    Moved earth and heaven; that which we are, we are;
    One equal temper of heroic hearts,
    Made weak by time and fate, but strong in will
70 To strive, to seek, to find, and not to yield.
                —1842 (WRITTEN 1833)

The Epic [Morte d'Arthur]

At Francis Allen's on the Christmas-eve,—
    The game of forfeits done—the girls all kissed
Beneath the sacred bush[1] and past away—
The parson Holmes, the poet Everard Hall,
5   The host, and I sat round the wassail-bowl,[2]
Then half-way ebbed: and there we held a talk,
How all the old honour had from Christmas gone,
Or gone, or dwindled down to some odd games
In some odd nooks like this; till I, tired out
10 With cutting eights[3] that day upon the pond,
Where, three times slipping from the outer edge,
I bumped the ice into three several stars,
Fell in a doze; and half-awake I heard
The parson taking wide and wider sweeps,
15 Now harping on the church-commissioners,
Now hawking at Geology and schism;
Until I woke, and found him settled down
Upon the general decay of faith
Right through the world, "at home was little left,
20 And none abroad: there was no anchor, none,
To hold by." Francis, laughing, clapped his hand
On Everard's shoulder, with "I hold by him."
"And I," quoth Everard, "by the wassail-bowl."
"Why yes," I said, "we knew your gift that way
25 At college: but another which you had,
I mean of verse (for so we held it then),
What came of that?" "You know," said Frank, "he
        burnt
His epic, his King Arthur, some twelve books"—
And then to me demanding why? "Oh, sir,
30 He thought that nothing new was said, or else

---

[1] *sacred bush* Mistletoe.

[2] *wassail-bowl* Punch bowl containing spiced ale.

[3] *cutting eights* Skating figure-eights.

Something so said 'twas nothing—that a truth
Looks freshest in the fashion of the day:
God knows: he has a mint of reasons: ask.
It pleased *me* well enough." "Nay, nay," said Hall,
35 "Why take the style of those heroic times?
For nature brings not back the Mastodon,
Nor we those times; and why should any man
Remodel models? these twelve books of mine
Were faint Homeric echoes, nothing-worth,
40 Mere chaff and draff,[4] much better burnt." "But I,"
Said Francis, "picked the eleventh from this hearth
And have it: keep a thing, its use will come.
I hoard it as a sugar-plum for Holmes."
He laughed, and I, though sleepy, like a horse
45 That hears the corn-bin open, pricked my ears;
For I remembered Everard's college fame
When we were freshmen: then at my request
He brought it; and the poet little urged,
But with some prelude of disparagement,
50 Read, mouthing out his hollow oes and aes,
Deep-chested music, and to this result.

Morte d'Arthur[5]

So all day long the noise of battle rolled
    Among the mountains by the winter sea;
Until King Arthur's table, man by man,
Had fallen in Lyonnesse[6] about their Lord,
5   King Arthur: then, because his wound was deep,
The bold Sir Bedivere uplifted him,
Sir Bedivere, the last of all his knights,
And bore him to a chapel nigh the field,
A broken chancel[7] with a broken cross,
10 That stood on a dark strait of barren land.
On one side lay the ocean, and on one
Lay a great water, and the moon was full.

    Then spake King Arthur to Sir Bedivere:
"The sequel of today unsolders all

---

[4] *chaff and draff* Here, refuse, material of little worth.

[5] *Morte d'Arthur* French: the death of [King] Arthur.

[6] [Tennyson's note] The country of legend that lay between Cornwall and the Scilly Islands.

[7] *chancel* Area around the altar.

15 The goodliest fellowship of famous knights
Whereof this world holds record. Such a sleep
They sleep—the men I loved. I think that we
Shall never more, at any future time,
Delight our souls with talk of knightly deeds,
20 Walking about the gardens and the halls
Of Camelot, as in the days that were.
I perish by this people which I made,—
Though Merlin sware that I should come again
To rule once more—but let what will be, be,
25 I am so deeply smitten through the helm
That without help I cannot last till morn.
Thou therefore take my brand° Excalibur,   *sword*
Which was my pride: for thou rememberest how
In those old days, one summer noon, an arm
30 Rose up from out the bosom of the lake,
Clothed in white samite,° mystic, wonderful,   *silk*
Holding the sword—and how I rowed across
And took it, and have worn it, like a king:
And, wheresoever I am sung or told
35 In aftertime, this also shall be known:
But now delay not: take Excalibur,
And fling him far into the middle mere:[1]
Watch what thou seest, and lightly bring me word."

To him replied the bold Sir Bedivere:
40 "It is not meet,° Sir King, to leave thee thus,   *appropriate*
Aidless, alone, and smitten through the helm.
A little thing may harm a wounded man.
Yet I thy hest° will all perform at full,   *command*
Watch what I see, and lightly bring thee word."

45 So saying, from the ruined shrine he stepped
And in the moon athwart the place of tombs,
Where lay the mighty bones of ancient men,
Old knights, and over them the sea-wind sang
Shrill, chill, with flakes of foam. He, stepping down
50 By zig-zag paths, and juts of pointed rock,
Came on the shining levels of the lake.

There drew he forth the brand Excalibur,
And o'er him, drawing it, the winter moon,
Brightening the skirts of a long cloud, ran forth
55 And sparkled keen with frost against the hilt:

For all the haft° twinkled with diamond sparks,   *handle*
Myriads of topaz-lights, and jacinth[2]-work
Of subtlest jewellery. He gazed so long
That both his eyes were dazzled, as he stood,
60 This way and that dividing the swift mind,
In act to throw: but at the last it seemed
Better to leave Excalibur concealed
There in the many-knotted waterflags,°   *iris*
That whistled stiff and dry about the marge.°   *shore*
65 So strode he back slow to the wounded King.

Then spake King Arthur to Sir Bedivere:
"Hast thou performed my mission which I gave?
What is it thou hast seen? or what hast heard?"

And answer made the bold Sir Bedivere:
70 "I heard the ripple washing in the reeds,
And the wild water lapping on the crag."

To whom replied King Arthur, faint and pale:
"Thou hast betrayed thy nature and thy name,
Not rendering true answer, as beseemed
75 Thy fealty,° nor like a noble knight: *sworn allegiance*
For surer sign had followed, either hand,
Or voice, or else a motion of the mere.
This is a shameful thing for men to lie.
Yet now, I charge thee, quickly go again
80 As thou art lief° and dear, and do the thing   *beloved*
I bad[3] thee, watch, and lightly bring me word."

Then went Sir Bedivere the second time
Across the ridge, and paced beside the mere,
Counting the dewy pebbles, fix'd in thought;
85 But when he saw the wonder of the hilt,
How curiously and strangely chased,° he smote   *engraved*
His palms together, and he cried aloud,

"And if indeed I cast the brand away,
Surely a precious thing, one worthy note,
90 Should thus be lost for ever from the earth,
Which might have pleased the eyes of many men.
What good should follow this, if this were done?
What harm, undone? deep harm to disobey,

[1] *middle mere* Middle of the lake.

[2] *jacinth* Reddish-orange gem.

[3] *bad* I.e., bade, commanded.

Seeing obedience is the bond of rule.
95 Were it well to obey then, if a king demand
An act unprofitable, against himself?
The King is sick, and knows not what he does.
What record, or what relic of my lord
Should be to aftertime, but empty breath
100 And rumours of a doubt? but were this kept,
Stored in some treasure-house of mighty kings,
Some one might show it at a joust of arms,
Saying, "King Arthur's sword, Excalibur,
Wrought by the lonely maiden of the Lake.
105 Nine years she wrought it, sitting in the deeps
Upon the hidden bases of the hills."
So might some old man speak in the aftertime
To all the people, winning reverence.
But now much honour and much fame were lost."

110 So spake he, clouded with his own conceit,
And hid Excalibur the second time,
And so strode back slow to the wounded King.

Then spoke King Arthur, breathing heavily:
"What is it thou hast seen? or what hast heard?"
115 And answer made the bold Sir Bedivere:
"I heard the water lapping on the crag,
And the long ripple washing in the reeds."

To whom replied King Arthur, much in wrath:
"Ah, miserable and unkind, untrue,
120 Unknightly, traitor-hearted! Woe is me!
Authority forgets a dying king,
Laid widowed of the power in his eye
That bowed the will. I see thee what thou art,
For thou, the latest-left of all my knights,
125 In whom should meet the offices of all,
Thou wouldst betray me for the precious hilt;
Either from lust of gold, or like a girl
Valuing the giddy pleasure of the eyes.
Yet, for a man may fail in duty twice,
130 And the third time may prosper, get thee hence:
But, if thou spare to fling Excalibur,
I will arise and slay thee with my hands."

Then quickly rose Sir Bedivere, and ran,
And, leaping down the ridges lightly, plunged
135 Among the bulrush-beds, and clutched the sword,
And strongly wheeled and threw it. The great brand
Made lightnings in the splendour of the moon,
And flashing round and round, and whirled in an arch,
Shot like a streamer of the northern morn,
140 Seen where the moving isles of winter shock
By night, with noises of the northern sea.
So flashed and fell the brand Excalibur:
But ere he dipped the surface, rose an arm
Clothed in white samite, mystic, wonderful,
145 And caught him by the hilt, and brandished him
Three times, and drew him under in the mere.
And lightly went the other to the King.

Then spoke King Arthur, drawing thicker breath:
"Now see I by thine eyes that this is done.
150 Speak out: what is it thou hast heard, or seen?"

And answer made the bold Sir Bedivere:
"Sir King, I closed mine eyelids, lest the gems
Should blind my purpose, for I never saw,
Nor shall see, here or elsewhere, till I die,
155 Not though I live three lives of mortal men,
So great a miracle as yonder hilt.
Then with both hands I flung him, wheeling him;
But when I looked again, behold an arm,
Clothed in white samite, mystic, wonderful,
160 That caught him by the hilt, and brandished him
Three times, and drew him under in the mere."

And answer made King Arthur, breathing hard:
"My end draws nigh; 'tis time that I were gone.
Make broad thy shoulders to receive my weight,
165 And bear me to the margin; yet I fear
My wound hath taken cold, and I shall die."

So saying, from the pavement he half rose,
Slowly, with pain, reclining on his arm,
And looking wistfully with wide blue eyes
170 As in a picture. Him Sir Bedivere
Remorsefully regarded through his tears,
And would have spoken, but he found not words,
Then took with care, and kneeling on one knee,
O'er both his shoulders drew the languid hands,
175 And rising bore him through the place of tombs.

But, as he walked, King Arthur panted hard,
Like one that feels a nightmare on his bed
When all the house is mute. So sighed the King,
Muttering and murmuring at his ear, "Quick, quick!
180   I fear it is too late, and I shall die."
But the other swiftly strode from ridge to ridge,
Clothed with his breath, and looking, as he walked,
Larger than human on the frozen hills.
He heard the deep behind him, and a cry
185   Before. His own thought drove him, like a goad.
Dry clashed his harness in the icy caves
And barren chasms, and all to left and right
The bare black cliff clanged round him, as he based
His feet on juts of slippery crag that rang
190   Sharp-smitten with the dint of armèd heels—
And on a sudden, lo! the level lake,
And the long glories of the winter moon.
      Then saw they how there hove a dusky barge,
Dark as a funeral scarf from stem to stern,
195   Beneath them; and descending they were ware°   *aware*
That all the decks were dense with stately forms
Black-stoled, black-hooded, like a dream—by these
Three Queens with crowns of gold—and from them rose
A cry that shivered to the tingling stars,
200   And, as it were one voice, an agony
Of lamentation, like a wind, that shrills
All night in a waste land, where no one comes,
Or hath come, since the making of the world.

      Then murmured Arthur, "Place me in the barge,"
205   And to the barge they came. There those three Queens
Put forth their hands, and took the King, and wept.
But she, that rose the tallest of them all
And fairest, laid his head upon her lap,
And loosed the shattered casque,° and chafed   *helmet*
         his hands,
210   And called him by his name, complaining loud,
And dropping bitter tears against his brow
Striped with dark blood: for all his face was white
And colourless, and like the withered moon
Smote by the fresh beam of the springing east;
215   And all his greaves and cuisses[1] dashed with drops
Of onset; and the light and lustrous curls—

That made his forehead like a rising sun
High from the dais-throne—were parched with dust;
Or, clotted into points and hanging loose,
220   Mix'd with the knightly growth that fringed his lips.
So like a shattered column lay the King;
Not like that Arthur who, with lance in rest,
From spur to plume a star of tournament,
Shot through the lists[2] at Camelot, and charged
225   Before the eyes of ladies and of kings.

      Then loudly cried the bold Sir Bedivere,
"Ah! my Lord Arthur, whither shall I go?
Where shall I hide my forehead and my eyes?
For now I see the true old times are dead,
230   When every morning brought a noble chance,
And every chance brought out a noble knight.
Such times have been not since the light that led
The holy Elders with the gift of myrrh.
But now the whole Round Table is dissolved
235   Which was an image of the mighty world;
And I, the last, go forth companionless,
And the days darken round me, and the years,
Among new men, strange faces, other minds."

      And slowly answered Arthur from the barge:
240   "The old order changeth, yielding place to new,
And God fulfils Himself in many ways,
Lest one good custom should corrupt the world.
Comfort thyself: what comfort is in me?
I have lived my life, and that which I have done
245   May He within Himself make pure! but thou,
If thou shouldst never see my face again,
Pray for my soul. More things are wrought by prayer
Than this world dreams of. Wherefore, let thy voice
Rise like a fountain for me night and day.
250   For what are men better than sheep or goats
That nourish a blind life within the brain,
If, knowing God, they lift not hands of prayer
Both for themselves and those who call them friend?
For so the whole round earth is every way
255   Bound by gold chains about the feet of God.
But now farewell. I am going a long way
With these thou seest—if indeed I go—
(For all my mind is clouded with a doubt)

---

[1] *greaves and cuisses* Armor for shins and thighs.

[2] *lists* Arenas in which jousting and tilting tournaments were held.

To the island-valley of Avilion;°   *i.e., Avalon*
260　Where falls not hail, or rain, or any snow,
Nor ever wind blows loudly; but it lies
Deep-meadowed, happy, fair with orchard-lawns
And bowery hollows crown'd with summer sea,
Where I will heal me of my grievous wound."

265　　So said he, and the barge with oar and sail
Moved from the brink, like some full-breasted swan
That, fluting a wild carol ere her death,[1]
Ruffles her pure cold plume, and takes the flood
With swarthy webs.[2] Long stood Sir Bedivere
270　Revolving many memories, till the hull
Looked one black dot against the verge of dawn,
And on the mere the wailing died away.
　　—1842 (WRITTEN 1833–34)

[*Break, break, break*]

Break, break, break,
　On thy cold gray stones, O Sea!
And I would that my tongue could utter
　　The thoughts that arise in me.

5　O well for the fisherman's boy,
　　That he shouts with his sister at play!
O well for the sailor lad,
　　That he sings in his boat on the bay!

And the stately ships go on
10　　To their haven under the hill;
But O for the touch of a vanished hand,
　　And the sound of a voice that is still![3]

Break, break, break,
　　At the foot of thy crags, O Sea!
15　But the tender grace of a day that is dead
　　Will never come back to me.
　　—1842 (WRITTEN 1834?)

---

[1] *swan ... death* Swans were said to sing only once, at their deaths.

[2] *webs* I.e., webbed feet.

[3] *But ... still* Probably a reference to Tennyson's closest friend, Arthur Hallam, who had died in 1833.

ROBERT BROWNING
1812 – 1889

"The spirit of passionate and imaginative poetry is not dead among us," wrote an exultant R.H. Horne in 1844, while reviewing the poems of the young Robert Browning. But Browning, for all his passion and imagination, was not a popular poet for much of his lifetime. Indeed, until the 1860s, Browning was better known as the husband of Elizabeth Barrett. His own poetry, in the eyes of many of his contemporaries, was far too obscure, littered as it was with recondite historical and literary references and with dubious subject matter—husbands murdering their wives, artists frolicking with prostitutes. Fame did come, however, and scholars now credit Browning for having realized new

possibilities in the dramatic monologue, a form of poetry that, like a monologue in a dramatic production, showcases the speech of a character to an implied or imaginary audience. The poems are, in Browning's own words, "so many utterances of so many imaginary persons, not mine." As Browning's dramatic monologues unfold, their speakers reveal levels of psychological complexity that have inspired generations of poets, from the Pre-Raphaelites who were coming of age in the 1840s to Modernists such as Ezra Pound and T.S. Eliot.

Browning was the eldest of two children born in an upper middle-class suburb of London to a scholarly father and a devout, Protestant mother, Sarah Anna Wiedemann. An opponent of slavery, Robert Browning Sr. rejected employment on his family's plantation in St. Kitts in favor of less lucrative but more morally-acceptable work as a clerk for the Bank of England. Both parents helped to shape Browning's religious, social, and intellectual tastes and values, with Browning Sr. in particular feeding his son's voracious appetite for knowledge. The young Browning composed his first poem at the age of six. He attended Peckham School between the ages of ten and twelve and later some classes at University College in London. But the great majority of his schooling took place at home with tutors, and he spent many hours studying the books in his family's voluminous library. Despite his relative lack of formal schooling, then, Browning had an exceptionally bookish education—which may help to explain the intellectual cast of Browning's poetic vision.

Browning first arrived on the literary scene with the publication in 1833 of *Pauline: A Fragment of a Confession*, a long poem in the style of Shelley's *Alastor* (1816), which John Stuart Mill credited with "considerable poetic powers" that yet revealed "a more intense and morbid self-consciousness than I ever knew in any sane human being." The volume, published with family funds, apparently sold not even a single copy. It was followed in 1835 by *Paracelsus*, which, though similarly obscure, at least made Browning known to a few important critics and ultimately brought him into contact with Carlyle, Dickens, and Wordsworth, among others. With *Sordello* (1840), Browning secured his reputation for writing poetry of bewildering difficulty. Browning claimed that his "stress [in *Sordello*] lay on the incidents in the development of a soul: little else is worth study," and yet few could make sense of such incidents as Browning had chosen to portray them.

In 1842 Browning published a volume of shorter poems, *Dramatic Lyrics*, which marked an important break from his earlier productions. Included were many of the poems on which his reputation came to be based: "My Last Duchess," "Soliloquy of the Spanish Cloister," "Johannes Agricola in Meditation," and "Porphyria's Lover," the last two of which had been published in the

Monthly Repository of 1836 under the heading "Madhouse Cells." With *Dramatic Romances and Lyrics* (1845) and *Men and Women* (1855), Browning confirmed his literary reputation as the foremost innovator of the dramatic monologue; he remained, however, little known among contemporary Victorians. *Men and Women* contained now-canonical poems such as "Fra Lippo Lippi" and "Andrea del Sarto." "Here," wrote George Eliot in the *Westminster Review*, the reader will find "no conventionality, no melodious commonplace, but freshness, originality, sometimes eccentricity of expression; no didactic laying-out of a subject, but dramatic indication, which requires the reader to trace by his own mental activity the underground stream of thought that jets out in elliptical and pithy verse." Eliot's commentary draws attention not only to Browning's unconventional subject matter and dramatic presentation, but also to the range of his accomplishment in poetic form, his lack of "melodious commonplace." Victorian critics noted with varying degrees of wonder and consternation the degree to which Browning experimented with rhythm and meter, an experimentation that in the early twentieth century earned him the nickname "Old Hippety-Hop o' the accents" from Ezra Pound.

In January of 1845 Browning began what became a celebrated correspondence with the already-famous poet Elizabeth Barrett. Even before meeting her personally (an event that took place after four months of writing), Browning praised Barrett's 1844 volume *Poems* with the words, "I do, as I say, love these books with all my heart—and I love you too." Barrett fell in love with Browning after meeting him, and in 1846, despite her semi-invalid state and her father's command never to marry, the two eloped in London and moved to Italy, where they remained for the rest of her life. Their only child, Robert Wiedemann Barrett Browning (nicknamed "Pen"), was born in 1849 in their Florence home, Casa Guidi.

Browning returned to London and society life after his wife's death in 1861. 1864 brought the publication of *Dramatis Personae*, the first of his volumes to be popular among British readers. This was followed in 1868–69 by his twelve-part epic "murder-poem" (as Browning called it), *The Ring and the Book*. Browning conceived the idea of writing this epic in 1860, when in a Florence market he chanced upon a book of documents concerning a 1698 murder trial. He organized the story so that each book in the epic gives voice to a different participant in the event: the murderer, various onlookers, the victim, and even the Pope. In juxtaposing these varying testimonies, Browning suggests the impossibility of ever finding a coherent or truthful narrative and the importance of recognizing the relativity of points of view—something enacted in his dramatic monologues. These "filthy rags of speech," says the Pope, are "tatters all too contaminate for use."

The 1879–80 volumes of *Dramatic Idyls* brought the poet even greater fame, both in England and internationally; the public in the United States flocked to buy his books, and wearing brown articles of clothing in his honor became fashionable. In 1889, on the day his final volume of poems, *Asolando*, was published, Robert Browning died at his son's home in Venice. He is buried next to Alfred, Lord Tennyson, in the Poets' Corner of Westminster Abbey.

⌘ ⌘ ⌘

Porphyria's Lover

The rain set early in tonight,
   The sullen wind was soon awake,
It tore the elm tops down for spite,
   And did its worst to vex the lake:

5   I listened with heart fit to break.
When glided in Porphyria; straight
   She shut the cold out and the storm,
And kneeled and made the cheerless grate
   Blaze up, and all the cottage warm;
10   Which done, she rose, and from her form

Withdrew the dripping cloak and shawl,
    And laid her soiled gloves by, untied
Her hat and let the damp hair fall,
    And, last, she sat down by my side
15   And called me. When no voice replied,
She put my arm about her waist,
    And made her smooth white shoulder bare,
And all her yellow hair displaced,
    And, stooping, made my cheek lie there,
20   And spread, o'er all, her yellow hair,
Murmuring how she loved me—she
    Too weak, for all her heart's endeavour,
To set its struggling passion free
    From pride, and vainer ties dissever,
25   And give herself to me forever.
But passion sometimes would prevail,
    Nor could tonight's gay feast restrain
A sudden thought of one so pale
    For love of her, and all in vain:
30   So, she was come through wind and rain.
Be sure I looked up at her eyes
    Happy and proud; at last I knew
Porphyria worshipped me; surprise
    Made my heart swell, and still it grew
35   While I debated what to do.
That moment she was mine, mine, fair,
    Perfectly pure and good: I found
A thing to do, and all her hair
    In one long yellow string I wound
40   Three times her little throat around,
And strangled her. No pain felt she;
    I am quite sure she felt no pain.
As a shut bud that holds a bee,
    I warily oped her lids: again
45   Laughed the blue eyes without a stain.
And I untightened next the tress
    About her neck; her cheek once more
Blushed bright beneath my burning kiss:
    I propped her head up as before,
50   Only, this time my shoulder bore
Her head, which droops upon it still:
    The smiling rosy little head,
So glad it has its utmost will,
    That all it scorned at once is fled,
55   And I, its love, am gained instead!

Porphyria's love: she guessed not how
    Her darling one wish would be heard.
And thus we sit together now,
    And all night long we have not stirred,
60   And yet God has not said a word!
—1836

My Last Duchess[7]

Ferrara

That's my last Duchess painted on the wall,
Looking as if she were alive. I call
That piece a wonder, now: Frà° Pandolf's hands   *Brother*

---

[7] *My Last Duchess* According to Louis S. Friedland, Browning likely modeled the speaker of this poem on Alfonso II (1533–1598), Duke of Ferrara. His first wife, a member of the wealthy Medici family, was only fourteen years old when they married. Only three days after the wedding, Alfonso left his wife for two years, and she died of suspicious causes a year after he returned. Four years later the duke negotiated with a servant to marry the daughter of the Count of Tyrol.

Worked busily a day, and there she stands.
5 Will't please you sit and look at her? I said
"Frà Pandolf" by design, for never read
Strangers like you that pictured countenance,
The depth and passion of its earnest glance,
But to myself they turned (since none puts by
10 The curtain I have drawn for you, but I)
And seemed as they would ask me, if they durst,
How such a glance came there; so, not the first
Are you to turn and ask thus. Sir, 'twas not
Her husband's presence only, called that spot
15 Of joy into the Duchess' cheek: perhaps
Frà Pandolf chanced to say "Her mantle laps
Over my lady's wrist too much," or "Paint
Must never hope to reproduce the faint
Half-flush that dies along her throat": such stuff
20 Was courtesy, she thought, and cause enough
For calling up that spot of joy. She had
A heart—how shall I say?—too soon made glad,
Too easily impressed; she liked whate'er
She looked on, and her looks went everywhere.
25 Sir, 'twas all one! My favour° at her breast,   *gift*
The dropping of the daylight in the West,
The bough of cherries some officious fool
Broke in the orchard for her, the white mule
She rode with round the terrace—all and each
30 Would draw from her alike the approving speech,
Or blush, at least. She thanked men—good! but
      thanked
Somehow—I know not how—as if she ranked
My gift of a nine-hundred-years-old name
With anybody's gift. Who'd stoop to blame
35 This sort of trifling? Even had you skill
In speech—(which I have not)—to make your will
Quite clear to such an one, and say, "Just this
Or that in you disgusts me; here you miss,
Or there exceed the mark"—and if she let
40 Herself be lessoned so, nor plainly set
Her wits to yours, forsooth, and made excuse,
—E'en then would be some stooping; and I choose
Never to stoop. Oh sir, she smiled, no doubt,
Whene'er I passed her; but who passed without

45 Much the same smile? This grew; I gave commands;
Then all smiles stopped together. There she stands
As if alive. Will't please you rise? We'll meet
The company below, then. I repeat,
The Count your master's known munificence
50 Is ample warrant that no just pretence
Of mine for dowry will be disallowed;
Though his fair daughter's self, as I avowed
At starting, is my object. Nay, we'll go
Together down, sir. Notice Neptune,[1] though,
55 Taming a seahorse, thought a rarity,
Which Claus of Innsbruck cast in bronze for me!
                                         —1842

---

[1] *Neptune* Roman god of the sea, who rides in a chariot pulled by seahorses.

ELIZABETH BARRETT BROWNING
1806 – 1861

Once considered for the position of poet laureate of England, Elizabeth Barrett Browning was a highly renowned poet in her day, admired by contemporaries such as Wordsworth and Dickinson, critics, and the general public alike. Her poetry fell out of fashion in the first half of the twentieth century, but Barrett Browning began to be lauded once again in the past generation, particularly for her long narrative poem *Aurora Leigh*. Best known among the general public for the romantic vision of her *Sonnets from the Portuguese* ("How do I love thee? Let me count the ways" from "Sonnet XLII" is one of the most famous lines in English literature), Barrett Browning also addressed significant moral and political issues in her work.

Elizabeth Barrett was the eldest of twelve children born to a wealthy plantation-owning family in Durham, England. Just prior to her birth her parents, Edward Barrett Moulton-Barrett and Mary Graham Clarke Moulton-Barrett, moved from their slave plantation in Jamaica to raise a family in England. The young Barrett grew up in the sheltered environment of a country manor called Hope End, learning languages and studying the classics, at a time when a young woman's education was typically restricted to the domestic sphere. An exceptional and intellectually voracious student, Barrett learned Latin, Greek, and French from her brothers' tutors and studied philosophical, historical, and religious works on her own. She had read Milton's *Paradise Lost* by the time she was 10 years old and, encouraged by her parents, anonymously published her first poem, an epic entitled *The Battle of Marathon*, a few years later. In 1826, she published *An Essay on Mind and Other Poems*. In 1833 she published her translation from the Greek of Aeschylus's *Prometheus Unbound*; she also included some of her own poems in the volume.

Due to the abolition of slavery, the Barretts' fortune began to wane, and in 1832 they were required to sell Hope End, eventually moving to Wimpole Street in London. Her father was overly protective of his children, however, and Barrett fell into semi-seclusion within the family home; her seclusion was compounded by illnesses that had begun to plague her when she was about 12 years old. Critics speculate as to the name of those illnesses, but there is evidence to suggest that Barrett may have suffered from tuberculosis and possibly from a spinal injury. Her maladies were no doubt exacerbated by the opiates prescribed by doctors and the depression that followed the accidental death of her beloved brother Edward, who had accompanied her while she recuperated in the south of England. This tragedy, and Barrett's subsequent feelings of anguish and guilt, inspired some of her best-known poems, including the elegiac sonnet "Grief."

Much has been written about Barrett's middle years, but the image of the bed-ridden recluse remains somewhat at odds with the prolific reader and writer who wrote poetry, essays, reviews, and criticism for magazines and journals and published *The Seraphim and Other Poems* in 1838. The two-volume collection of her *Poems* published in 1844 contains some of her most politically-charged poetry, including "The Cry of the Children," which condemned the employment of children in factories. During these years, Barrett kept up an active correspondence with many writers, critics, and artists and accepted occasional visitors in the confines of her family home. It was in this way that she met Robert Browning, who called upon her after the 1844 collection appeared. He visited her after first writing to express his admiration for work that had already made Barrett famous in England and was rapidly gaining recognition in the United States.

The subsequent exchange of 574 letters between Barrett and Browning, six years her junior, and their eventual elopement have received much attention, with some suggesting that Barrett Browning's best work was inspired by this passionate relationship. It is worth noting here that she had already begun to write love poetry, having translated Petrarch's sonnets and written her own before she met Browning. There is no doubt, however, that the force of their relationship inspired some of her most enduring work, notably her famous *Sonnets from the Portuguese*, written during her courtship with Browning and published in 1850. "My little Portuguese," an allusion to her dark skin, was Browning's pet name for his wife.

Her 1846 marriage to Browning and their ensuing life together in Italy were a boon to Barrett Browning's health and her work. Her beloved father, however, who had forbidden his children to marry, refused to speak to or see his daughter again, going so far as to return her letters unopened. In 1849 the Brownings' only child, Robert Wiedemann Barrett Browning (nicknamed "Pen"), was born in Casa Guidi, just outside Florence.

Not long after the publication of *Sonnets*, Barrett Browning published *Casa Guidi Windows*, which promoted the cause of *Risorgimento*, the Italian struggle for unification and independence from foreign domination (the subject also of many of the later *Poems before Congress*). In 1850, she published the abolition poem "The Runaway Slave at Pilgrim's Point," one of the great dramatic monologues and political-protest poems written in English in the nineteenth century. Barrett Browning's comment on Harriet Beecher Stowe's *Uncle Tom's Cabin* summarizes her consistent response to critics who questioned her choice of subjects: "… is it possible you think a woman has no business with questions like the question of slavery? Then she had better use a pen no more. She had better subside into slavery and concubinage herself, I think, as in the times of old, shut herself up with the Penelopes in the 'women's apartment,' and take no rank among thinkers and speakers." The 1856 work *Aurora Leigh* further cemented Barrett Browning's immense popularity, even though its subject matter was deemed scandalous by many at the time. Coventry Patmore, Victorian author of *The Angel in the House*, a book of poems lauding feminine domestic virtues, was among those who attacked Barrett Browning's candor and audacity in *Aurora Leigh*. An ambitious, epic poem, *Aurora Leigh* is narrated in nine books of blank verse and is the zenith of Barrett Browning's life work, encompassing her convictions on desire, power, art, love, romance, race, class structures, and the subjugation of women. The independent and progressive heroine of the books is named in part after Barrett Browning's idol, French writer Georges Sand (née Aurore Dupin), known for her liberal, feminist views and her penchant for wearing men's clothing. Like Sand, and also like Barrett Browning herself, Aurora Leigh is a writer, one who questions her identity as both artist and woman and struggles to achieve independence from subjugation by staid societal mores and manners and yet still preserve the ability to attain love and companionship.

Elizabeth Barrett Browning predeceased her husband by 28 years when she passed away in his arms in 1861; she is buried in the Protestant cemetery in Florence.

⌘⌘⌘

from *Sonnets from the Portuguese*

1

I thought once how Theocritus[1] had sung
Of the sweet years, the dear and wished-for years,
Who each one in a gracious hand appears
To bear a gift for mortals, old or young:
5 And, as I mused it in his antique tongue,[2]
I saw, in gradual vision through my tears,
The sweet, sad years, the melancholy years,
Those of my own life, who by turns had flung
A shadow across me. Straightway I was 'ware,
10 So weeping, how a mystic Shape did move
Behind me, and drew me backward by the hair;
And a voice said in mastery, while I strove—
"Guess now who holds thee?"—"Death," I said. But,
    there,
The silver answer rang—"Not Death, but Love."

7

The face of all the world is changed, I think,
Since first I heard the footsteps of thy soul
Move still, oh, still, beside me, as they stole
Betwixt me and the dreadful outer brink
5 Of obvious death, where I, who thought to sink,
Was caught up into love, and taught the whole
Of life in a new rhythm. The cup of dole
God gave for baptism, I am fain to drink,
And praise its sweetness, Sweet, with thee anear.
10 The names of country, heaven, are changed away
For where thou art or shalt be, there or here;
And this … this lute and song … loved yesterday,
(The singing angels know) are only dear
Because thy name moves right in what they say.

13

And wilt thou have me fasten into speech
The love I bear thee, finding words enough,
And hold the torch out, while the winds are rough,
Between our faces, to cast light on each?—
5 I drop it at thy feet. I cannot teach

My hand to hold my spirit so far off
From myself—me—that I should bring thee proof
In words, of love hid in me out of reach.
Nay, let the silence of my womanhood
10 Commend my woman-love to thy belief—
Seeing that I stand unwon, however wooed,
And rend the garment of my life, in brief,
By a most dauntless, voiceless fortitude,
Lest one touch of this heart convey its grief.

21

Say over again, and yet once over again,
That thou dost love me. Though the word repeated
Should seem "a cuckoo-song," as thou dost treat it,
Remember, never to the hill or plain,
5 Valley and wood, without her cuckoo-strain
Comes the fresh Spring in all her green completed.
Belovèd, I, amid the darkness greeted
By a doubtful spirit-voice, in that doubt's pain
Cry, "Speak once more—thou lovest!" Who can fear
10 Too many stars, though each in heaven shall roll,
Too many flowers, though each shall crown the year?
Say thou dost love me, love me, love me—toll
The silver iterance![3]—only minding, Dear,
To love me also in silence with thy soul.

22

When our two souls stand up erect and strong,
Face to face, silent, drawing nigh and nigher,
Until the lengthening wings break into fire
At either curvèd point—what bitter wrong
5 Can the earth do to us, that we should not long
Be here contented? Think. In mounting higher,
The angels would press on us and aspire
To drop some golden orb of perfect song
Into our deep, dear silence. Let us stay
10 Rather on earth, Belovèd—where the unfit
Contrarious moods of men recoil away
And isolate pure spirits, and permit
A place to stand and love in for a day,
With darkness and the death hour rounding it.

---

[1] *Theocritus* Greek poet of the third century BCE who created the genre of the pastoral (characterized by idyllic country life and love between shepherds and shepherdesses).

[2] *antique tongue* Greek language.

---

[3] *iterance* Repetition.

24

Let the world's sharpness, like a clasping knife,
    Shut in upon itself and do no harm
In this close hand of Love, now soft and warm,
And let us hear no sound of human strife
5   After the click of the shutting. Life to life—
I lean upon thee, Dear, without alarm,
And feel as safe as guarded by a charm
Against the stab of worldlings, who if rife
Are weak to injure. Very whitely still
10 The lilies of our lives may reassure
Their blossoms from their roots, accessible
Alone to heavenly dews that drop not fewer,
Growing straight, out of man's reach, on the hill.
God only, who made us rich, can make us poor.

26

I lived with visions for my company
    Instead of men and women, years ago,
And found them gentle mates, nor thought to know
A sweeter music than they played to me.
5   But soon their trailing purple was not free
Of this world's dust, their lutes did silent grow,
And I myself grew faint and blind below
Their vanishing eyes. Then *thou* didst come—to be,
Belovèd, what they seemed. Their shining fronts,
10 Their songs, their splendours (better, yet the same,
As river water hallowed into fonts),
Met in thee, and from out thee overcame
My soul with satisfaction of all wants:
Because God's gifts put man's best dreams to shame.

28

My letters! all dead paper, mute and white!
    And yet they seem alive and quivering
Against my tremulous hands which loose the string
And let them drop down on my knee tonight.
5   This said—he wished to have me in his sight
Once, as a friend: this fixed a day in spring
To come and touch my hand … a simple thing,
Yet I wept for it!—this, … the paper's light …
Said, *Dear, I love thee;* and I sank and quailed
10 As if God's future thundered on my past.
This said, *I am thine*—and so its ink has paled
With lying at my heart that beat too fast.

And this … O Love, thy words have ill availed
If, what this said, I dared repeat at last!

43

How do I love thee? Let me count the ways.
    I love thee to the depth and breadth and height
My soul can reach, when feeling out of sight
For the ends of Being and ideal Grace.
5   I love thee to the level of every day's
Most quiet need, by sun and candle-light.
I love thee freely, as men strive for Right;
I love thee purely, as they turn from Praise.
I love thee with the passion put to use
10 In my old griefs, and with my childhood's faith.
I love thee with a love I seemed to lose
With my lost saints—I love thee with the breath,
Smiles, tears, of all my life!—and, if God choose,
I shall but love thee better after death.
—1845–47

Elizabeth Barrett Browning
From _Sonnets from the Portuguese_

Sonnet 32

THE FIRST time that the sun rose on thine oath
To love me, I looked forward to the moon
To slacken all those bonds which seemed too soon
And quickly tied to make a lasting troth.
Quick-loving hearts, I thought, may quickly loathe;
And, looking on myself, I seemed not one
For such man's love;—more like an out-of-tune
Worn viol, a good singer would be wroth
To spoil his song with, and which, snatched in haste,
Is laid down at the first ill-sounding note.
I did not wrong myself so, but I placed
A wrong on _thee._ For perfect strains may float
'Neath master-hands, from instruments defaced,—
And great souls, at one stroke, may do and dote.

MATTHEW ARNOLD
1822 – 1888

Nicknamed "the Emperor" by his friends and family, Matthew Arnold was an ardent and, in the view of some Victorians, arrogant critic of modernity. Arnold embodied both the idealist expectations and the apocalyptic anxieties of the approaching *fin-de-siécle* in his poetry and prose. In the face of an increasingly materialistic mass culture, dominated by the vacuity of what he called "the average man" or "Philistine" of the democratized middle classes, Arnold sought to revive culture in the image of liberal humanism. Only an education in the ostensibly timeless and universal works of masters like Marcus Aurelius, Tolstoy, Homer and Wordsworth, Arnold believed, could cure the *malaise* of modern life.

"For the creation of a masterwork of literature, two powers must concur," Arnold wrote in 1865, "The power of the man and the power of the moment, and the man is not enough without the moment." Arnold believed that modern industrial life and the materialism it had made possible were radically indisposed towards artistic genius and indeed had created a climate of psychological and moral enervation that poetry was powerless to heal. The *Zeitgeist* (one of his terms for the powerful work of modern popular culture) was profoundly "unpoetical," and was best anatomized through prose. His own career shows symptoms of the fragmentation he analyzed. Arnold incisively broke with the often melancholic poetry of his early years in order to pursue prose criticism, for him the best possible literary work, he believed, in an era that he saw as spiritually bankrupt. Modern society was in no condition to produce great poets; the best that modern life could muster, according to Arnold, were powerful critics—*if* they stayed away from the politics of the passing moment.

The River Thames ran past the village of Laleham where Matthew Arnold was born in 1822. Arnold was the eldest son of Mary Penrose Arnold and Dr. Thomas Arnold. His father, a clergyman and headmaster of Rugby School, was celebrated for reforming the school's curriculum to foreground Christian values, classical languages, and competitive games. Ironically, Arnold, who in later life would come to resemble his father by valuing above all else great humanist texts and a classical education, was lazy, laconic and flippant as a student. Upon meeting the young dilettante, Charlotte Brontë wrote that "his manner displeases, from its seeming foppery." Yet, in spite of a flamboyant indifference to academia and a studied attempt to dissociate himself from all that his father represented, he amazed family and friends by winning a scholarship to Oxford's Balliol College in 1840, the prodigious Newdigate Prize for poetry in 1843, and a Fellowship at Oriel College in 1845.

Wordsworth, a friend of the family, was one of the most tangible influences on Arnold's poetry. When Wordsworth died, Arnold wondered sadly, "Who will teach us how to feel?" He frequently fled from classes to wander the countryside around the Lake District or to hike in the Alps, landscapes memorialized by Wordsworth and Coleridge. Many critics claim that Arnold was most accomplished as a poet of nature. The "simple joy the country yields," rendered in poems like "Thyrsis," reveals a surprising affinity with the quiet style of Thomas Gray; his "Resignation" speaks to Wordsworth's "Tintern Abbey." Arnold's personal manner, reminiscent of his idols Lord Byron and Goethe, did not cancel out a heartfelt relation to nature, whose unadorned expression modelled the "high seriousness" he admired in Sophocles and Aeschylus.

In 1847, Arnold obtained employment in London as a private secretary to the liberal politician Lord Lansdowne, a period during which he produced most of his poetry. 1849 saw the publication of *The Strayed Reveller, and Other Poems*, by "A," followed by *Empedocles on Etna, and Other Poems* (1852). The controversial preface to *Poems* (1853) provoked heated debate. Here Arnold focused on the ponderous force of the "unpoetical" nineteenth century writ large over his earlier work and damned the "dialogue of the mind with itself" that his *Empedocles on Etna* exhibited. Great poetry, Arnold claimed, must be distinguished from verse produced by a restless intellect fragmented by attempts to address the problems of contemporary life. Poetry should create works of beauty and unity that rise above the historical moment to "inspirit and rejoice" readers.

Letters to his best friend and fellow poet Arthur Hugh Clough, who did address the intellectual issues of the current moment, provide valuable insight into the demanding standards Arnold set for poetry. "I am glad you like the *Gypsy Scholar*," he wrote, "—but what does it *do* for you? Homer *animates*—Shakespeare *animates*— in its poor way I think *Sohrab and Rustum animates*—the *Gypsy Scholar* at best awakens a pleasing melancholy." Considered an often biting critic of the work of his contemporaries, including Clough, Arnold's harshest criticisms were first addressed to his own work. His poem "Dover Beach," probably written in 1851, but published in 1867, is one of English literature's profound expressions of modernity's disaffection with itself. Yet perceiving that his own poetry seemed passively ensnared in the "continual state of mental distress" that he took to task in the preface to *Poems*, he largely ceased writing poetry from the mid-1850s onward. After *New Poems* (1867), Arnold would refashion himself as a prose writer. According to Lionel Trilling, Arnold "perceived in himself the poetic power, but knew that his genius was not of the greatest, that the poetic force was not irresistible in him," not enough, at any rate, to act as a transformative agent in an age of disillusionment.

In 1851, Arnold married Frances Lucy Wightman and to support his family accepted a position as a public school inspector. Initially thinking the job would suffice "for the next three or four years," Arnold continued to be employed in the public service for thirty-five years. In contrast to writers like Tennyson or Carlyle, Arnold had to work for a living, writing only in his spare time. He believed that his inspections of schools in Britain and across Europe gave him first-hand experience to support his conviction that educating the public in a classical humanist tradition was key to "civilizing the next generation of the lower classes."

Arnold was elected Professor of Poetry at Oxford University in 1857, where he delivered public lectures for the following ten years. Though a proponent of an exacting standard of classical scholarship, Arnold was the first to lecture in English rather than Latin, altering an elitist institutional practice that acted as a barrier to the kind of education that the nineteenth century urgently needed, in his opinion. Arnold turned many of his lectures into essays and books, including *On Translating Homer* (1861) and *Friendship's Garland* (1871).

Though by his own standards of greatness Arnold could not *transform* society as a poet, as a critic he was determined to *reform* it. In his famous essay "The Function of Criticism at the Present Time," published in *Essays in Criticism* (1865), Arnold helped raise the value of criticism from its status as a "baneful and injurious employment" to a creative activity in its own right. Deftly juxtaposing snatches from tabloids alongside texts of high culture, Arnold's critical methodology foreshadowed the kind of work pursued in cultural studies today. While few have unanimously agreed with Arnold's pronouncements on literature and society, he has influenced almost every significant English-speaking critic since his time, including T.S. Eliot, F.R. Leavis, Lionel Trilling, and Raymond Williams.

In *Culture and Anarchy* (1869), arguably his most important work of social criticism, Arnold proposed that antagonistic factions of British society could learn to overcome their differences through an education in "disinterested" and universal human values. The differences allowed expression in democratic societies would disintegrate into anarchic disorder, thought Arnold, unless tethered to the "higher" ideals of the humanist tradition. His witty veneer and Apollonian appeal to transcendent virtues of "sweetness and light" sometimes enamored, and sometimes exasperated, a public whose prominent figures he often singled out by name for critical interrogation. Leslie Stephen, Virginia Woolf's father, remarked drily: "I often wished ... that I too had a little sweetness and light that I might be able to say such nasty things of my enemies."

During the 1870s, Arnold published a series of attacks on orthodox religion: *St. Paul and Protestantism* (1870), *Literature and Dogma* (1873) and *God and the Bible* (1875). Even in a period that witnessed the challenges to traditional religious belief posed by Darwin's theories, the work of geologists, and the "higher criticism" of the Bible that came from Germany and elsewhere, Arnold's religious critiques scandalized many Victorians. He recommended that Victorians exchange their faith in a religion founded on the assumption of the truth of the Bible for faith in a transcendent, secular humanism. When he returned to literary criticism in "The Study of Poetry" (1880), he claimed, as Thomas Carlyle had before him in the 1830s, that "most of what now passes for religion and philosophy will be replaced by poetry."

Like Dickens and Thackeray before him, Arnold embarked on a lecture tour of the United States, in 1883. Tired and burdened by debts, Arnold saw the trip as a money-making venture that would also allow him to visit a daughter who had married an American. He was loved in Washington but received with mixed success in other cities. He compiled his lectures in *Discourses in America* (1885), which contains his discussion of Emerson as well as the essay "Literature and Science." Here Arnold responds to Thomas Huxley's claim in "Science and Culture" (1881) that "for the purpose of attaining real culture, an exclusively scientific education is at least as effectual as an exclusively literary education." Especially in America, Arnold argued, where the democratic impulse to glorify "the average man" was particularly enthusiastic, education must safeguard the guiding ideals of the Western tradition, "the best that is known and thought."

Arnold died suddenly of a heart attack in 1888, leaving behind him a remarkable body of cultural criticism and a few poems familiar to all readers of English poetry. His statement about Oxford and modernity in *Culture and Anarchy* may well be taken as fitting epitaph: "We in Oxford ... have not failed to seize one truth,—the truth that beauty and sweetness are essential characters of a complete human perfection. ... We have not won our political battles, we have not carried our main points, we have not stopped our adversaries' advance, we have not marched victoriously with the modern world; but we have told silently upon the mind of the century, we have prepared currents of feeling which sap our adversaries' position when it seems gained, we have kept up our communications with the future."

Dover Beach

The sea is calm tonight.
The tide is full, the moon lies fair
Upon the straits—on the French coast the light
Gleams and is gone; the cliffs of England stand,
5   Glimmering and vast, out in the tranquil bay.
Come to the window, sweet is the night-air!

Only, from the long line of spray
Where the sea meets the moon-blanched land,
Listen! you hear the grating roar
Of pebbles which the waves draw back, and fling,   10
At their return, up the high strand,°   *shore*
Begin, and cease, and then again begin,
With tremulous cadence slow, and bring
The eternal note of sadness in.

Sophocles long ago   15
Heard it on the Aegaean, and it brought
Into his mind the turbid ebb and flow
Of human misery;[1] we
Find also in the sound a thought,
Hearing it by this distant northern sea.   20

The Sea of Faith
Was once, too, at the full, and round earth's shore
Lay like the folds of a bright girdle furled.
But now I only hear
Its melancholy, long, withdrawing roar,   25
Retreating, to the breath
Of the night-wind, down the vast edges drear
And naked shingles[2] of the world.

Ah, love, let us be true
To one another! for the world, which seems   30
To lie before us like a land of dreams,
So various, so beautiful, so new,
Hath really neither joy, nor love, nor light,
Nor certitude, nor peace, nor help for pain;
And we are here as on a darkling plain   35
Swept with confused alarms of struggle and flight,
Where ignorant armies clash by night.[3]   —1867

---

1 *Sophocles ... misery* See Sophocles's *Antigone* 583–91: "Blest are those whose days have
not tasted of evil. For when a house has once been shaken by the gods, no form of ruin is
lacking, but it spreads over the bulk of the race, just as, when the surge is driven over the
darkness of the deep by the fierce breath of Thracian sea-winds, it rolls up the black sand
from the depths, and the wind-beaten headlands that front the blows of the storm give
out a mournful roar"; *Aegaean* Arm of the Mediterranean Sea near Greece.

2 *shingles* Water-worn pebbles.

3 *ignorant ... by night* Reference to Thucydides's *History of the Peloponnesian War*, in which
the invading Athenians became confused as night fell on the battle at Epipolae. Combat-
ants could not tell friend from foe in the moonlight.

Christina Rossetti
1830 – 1894

To the late-Victorian critic Edmund Gosse, Christina Rossetti was "one of the most perfect poets of the age." Of her works, Rossetti's fellow-poet Algernon Charles Swinburne claimed that "nothing more glorious in poetry has ever been written." Rossetti may have been less popular than contemporaries such as Alfred Tennyson and Elizabeth Barrett Browning, but her melding of

sensuous imagery and stringent form earned her the admiration and devotion of many nineteenth-century readers. Her lyricism elicited praise for being, as one critic wrote in 1862, "remarkably fresh and free," as well as "true and most genuine." The ease of Rossetti's lyric voice remains apparent in works as diverse as the sensual *Goblin Market* and the subtle religious hymns she penned throughout her career.

She was born in London in 1830, the youngest of four children. Her father, Gabriel Rossetti, was a scholar and an Italian exile, and her mother, Frances Polidori, was the English-Italian daughter of another Italian exile. Italian revolutionaries-in-exile frequented the Rossetti home, creating a provocative and unconventional environment for the Rossetti children. Other influences included their mother's devotion to Christianity and visits to their maternal grandfather's rural home. "If any one thing schooled me in the direction of poetry," Rossetti was later to write, "it was perhaps the delightful idle liberty to prowl all alone about my grandfather's cottage-grounds some thirty miles from London."

Rossetti's grandfather Polidori printed her first volume of poems, *Verses: Dedicated to Her Mother*, in 1847. Though immature in light of the works that would follow, the poems of the sixteen-year-old Rossetti already exhibited many of the qualities for which her work would later be known: directness of expression and simplicity of narrative colored with vivid and often sensuous detail. In 1850 several of her poems were published in *The Germ*, the journal of the Pre-Raphaelite Brotherhood founded in part by her two brothers, Dante Gabriel and William Michael. Although she was not formally a member of the Brotherhood, Rossetti's aesthetic sense—and especially her attention to color and detail—link her to the movement. Other Pre-Raphaelite values were also central to Rossetti's poetic vision, including a devotion to the faithful representation of nature and, at the same time, a penchant for symbolic representation.

The 1850s were a difficult time for Rossetti. Early in the decade she rejected, most likely on religious grounds, a suitor to whom she had been engaged for two years, the Pre-Raphaelite painter James Collinson. Collinson had converted to Anglicanism to please Rossetti, but he ultimately returned to his original faith, Catholicism. (In 1866 Rossetti appears to have rejected a second suitor, Charles Bagot Cayley, perhaps because he was an agnostic.) In 1854 Rossetti volunteered to join Florence Nightingale's nursing efforts in the Crimean War, but she was rejected for being too young. She volunteered instead at the Highgate Penitentiary for "fallen women." Throughout this period, she lived with her mother, sister, and brother William in the family home.

Rossetti first gained attention in the literary world with her 1862 publication of *Goblin Market and Other Poems*. Before publication of the volume, the eminent critic John Ruskin had declared the poems irregular in both their rhyme schemes and meters. Ruskin advised Rossetti to "exercise herself in the severest commonplace of metre until she [could] write as the public like." Rossetti nevertheless went ahead with publication, and the vast majority of her Victorian critics praised the volume for what one reviewer called its "very decided character and originality, both in theme and treatment." "Here," notes the *Eclectic Review*, "is a volume of really true poetry." "Goblin Market" remains among her most discussed works. Few readers have believed William Michael Rossetti's insistence that his sister "did not mean anything profound" by "Goblin Market," but many have found the precise nature of its deep suggestiveness elusive.

More volumes followed, among the most important of which were *The Prince's Progress and Other Poems* (1866), *Sing-Song* (1872), *A Pageant and Other Poems* (1881), and *Verses* (1893). In *Sing-Song* Rossetti proved herself a talented writer of children's verses. With "Monna Innominata," the "sonnet of sonnets" published in *A Pageant and Other Poems*, Rossetti offered her own bold contribution to the sonnet-sequence tradition. In the prose preface to "Monna Innominata," Rossetti notes that women such as Dante's Beatrice and Petrarch's Laura were denied the opportunity to speak for themselves. If either had spoken in her own voice, Rossetti writes, "the portrait left us might have appeared more tender, if less dignified, than any drawn even by a devoted friend." According to Rossetti, even the *Sonnets from the Portuguese* of the "Great Poetess" Elizabeth Barrett Browning do not offer us a voice "drawn from feeling": her circumstances, that is, her happy love-story, precluded her from giving her speaker such a voice. Rossetti's sonnets, in contrast, speak of unfulfilled yearning and painful loss, bringing to the sonnet form the voice of a woman's suffering such as Rossetti believed had never before been written. Critics have often read the poem in biographical terms, following from William Michael Rossetti's suggestion that the "introductory prose-note ... is a blind ... interposed to draw off attention from the writer in her proper person." But such readings, however tempting, limit interpretation of the poems and fail to account for the deep complexities of Rossetti's work.

In 1871, Rossetti was stricken with exophthalmic bronchocele, or Graves's disease, a disease causing protrusion of the eyeballs, which led her to retreat even further into an already quiet life. Rossetti continued to live with and care for her mother and two aunts. She lived to see editions of her collected poems published in 1875 and then again in 1890, and in 1892 she was among those mentioned as a possible successor to Tennyson as England's Poet Laureate. She died in 1894 from cancer, having undergone surgery for breast cancer in 1892.

⌘ ⌘ ⌘

Illustration by Laurence Housman from the 1893
Macmillan edition.

A Triad

Three sang of love together: one with lips
    Crimson, with cheeks and bosom in a glow,
Flushed to the yellow hair and finger tips;
    And one there sang who soft and smooth as snow

5 Bloomed like a tinted hyacinth at a show;
And one was blue with famine after love,
    Who like a harpstring snapped rang harsh and low
The burden of what those were singing of.
One shamed herself in love; one temperately
10   Grew gross in soulless love, a sluggish wife;
One famished died for love. Thus two of three
    Took death for love and won him after strife;
One droned in sweetness like a fattened bee:
    All on the threshold, yet all short of life.
—1862

Remember

Remember me when I am gone away,
    Gone far away into the silent land;
    When you can no more hold me by the hand,
Nor I half turn to go yet turning stay.
5 Remember me when no more day by day
    You tell me of our future that you planned:
    Only remember me; you understand
It will be late then to counsel or to pray.
Yet if you should forget me for a while
10   And afterwards remember, do not grieve:
    For if the darkness and corruption leave
A vestige of the thoughts that once I had,
Better by far you should forget and smile
    Than that you should remember and be sad.
—1862

A Birthday

My heart is like a singing bird
    Whose nest is in a watered shoot;
My heart is like an apple tree
    Whose boughs are bent with thickset fruit;
5 My heart is like a rainbow shell
    That paddles in a halcyon° sea;   calm
My heart is gladder than all these
    Because my love is come to me.

Raise me a dais of silk and down;
10   Hang it with vair° and purple dyes;   squirrel fur

Carve it in doves and pomegranates,
  And peacocks with a hundred eyes;
Work it in gold and silver grapes,
  In leaves, and silver fleurs-de-lys;
15 Because the birthday of my life
  Is come, my love is come to me.
    —1861

After Death

The curtains were half drawn, the floor was swept
  And strewn with rushes, rosemary and may
  Lay thick upon the bed on which I lay,
Where thro' the lattice ivy-shadows crept.
5 He leaned above me, thinking that I slept
  And could not hear him; but I heard him say:
  "Poor child, poor child": and as he turned away
Came a deep silence, and I knew he wept.
He did not touch the shroud, or raise the fold
10   That hid my face, or take my hand in his,
    Or ruffle the smooth pillows for my head:
    He did not love me living; but once dead
  He pitied me; and very sweet it is
To know he still is warm tho' I am cold.
    —1862

An Apple-Gathering

I plucked pink blossoms from mine apple tree
  And wore them all that evening in my hair:
Then in due season when I went to see
  I found no apples there.

5 With dangling basket all along the grass
  As I had come I went the selfsame track:
My neighbours mocked me while they saw me pass
  So empty-handed back.

Lilian and Lilias smiled in trudging by,
10   Their heaped-up basket teazed me like a jeer;
Sweet-voiced they sang beneath the sunset sky,
  Their mother's home was near.

Plump Gertrude passed me with her basket full,
  A stronger hand than hers helped it along;
15 A voice talked with her thro' the shadows cool
  More sweet to me than song.

Ah Willie, Willie, was my love less worth
  Than apples with their green leaves piled above?
I counted rosiest apples on the earth
20   Of far less worth than love.

So once it was with me you stooped to talk
  Laughing and listening in this very lane;
To think that by this way we used to walk
  We shall not walk again!

25 I let my neighbours pass me, ones and twos
  And groups; the latest said the night grew chill,
And hastened: but I loitered, while the dews
  Fell fast I loitered still.
    —1862

Echo

Come to me in the silence of the night;
  Come in the speaking silence of a dream;
Come with soft rounded cheeks and eyes as bright
  As sunlight on a stream;
    Come back in tears,
O memory, hope, love of finished years.

O dream how sweet, too sweet, too bitter sweet,
  Whose wakening should have been in Paradise,
Where souls brimfull of love abide and meet;
10   Where thirsting longing eyes
    Watch the slow door
That opening, letting in, lets out no more.

Yet come to me in dreams, that I may live
  My very life again tho' cold in death:
15 Come back to me in dreams, that I may give
  Pulse for pulse, breath for breath:
    Speak low, lean low,
As long ago, my love, how long ago.
    —1862

Winter: My Secret

I tell my secret? No indeed, not I:
  Perhaps some day, who knows?
But not today; it froze, and blows, and snows,
  And you're too curious: fie!
5 You want to hear it? well:
Only, my secret's mine, and I won't tell.

Or, after all, perhaps there's none:
Suppose there is no secret after all,
  But only just my fun.
10 Today's a nipping day, a biting day;
  In which one wants a shawl,
A veil, a cloak, and other wraps:
I cannot ope to every one who taps,
And let the draughts come whistling thro' my hall;
15 Come bounding and surrounding me,
  Come buffeting, astounding me,
Nipping and clipping thro' my wraps and all.
I wear my mask for warmth: who ever shows
  His nose to Russian snows
20 To be pecked at by every wind that blows?
You would not peck? I thank you for good will,
Believe, but leave that truth untested still.

Spring's an expansive time: yet I don't trust
  March with its peck of dust,
25 Nor April with its rainbow-crowned brief showers,
  Nor even May, whose flowers
One frost may wither thro' the sunless hours.

Perhaps some languid summer day,
  When drowsy birds sing less and less,
30 And golden fruit is ripening to excess,
If there's not too much sun nor too much cloud,
And the warm wind is neither still nor loud,
Perhaps my secret I may say,
  Or you may guess.
—1862

"No, Thank You, John"

I never said I loved you, John:
  Why will you teaze me day by day,
And wax a weariness to think upon
  With always "do" and "pray"?

5 You know I never loved you, John;
  No fault of mine made me your toast:[1]
Why will you haunt me with a face as wan
  As shows an hour-old ghost?

I dare say Meg or Moll would take
10 Pity upon you, if you'd ask:
And pray don't remain single for my sake
  Who can't perform that task.

I have no heart?—Perhaps I have not;
  But then you're mad to take offence
15 That I don't give you what I have not got:
  Use your own common sense.

Let bygones be bygones:
  Don't call me false, who owed not to be true:
I'd rather answer "No" to fifty Johns
20 Than answer "Yes" to you.

Let's mar our pleasant days no more,
  Songbirds of passage, days of youth:
Catch at today, forget the days before:
  I'll wink at your untruth.

25 Let us strike hands as hearty friends;
  No more, no less; and friendship's good:
Only don't keep in view ulterior ends,
  And points not understood

In open treaty. Rise above
30 Quibbles and shuffling off and on:
Here's friendship for you if you like; but love,—
  No, thank you, John.
—1862

---

[1] *your toast* I.e., the woman to whom John would raise a glass when toasting his lady.

A Pause of Thought

I looked for that which is not, nor can be,
    And hope deferred made my heart sick in truth:
But years must pass before a hope of youth
    Is resigned utterly.

5   I watched and waited with a steadfast will:
    And though the object seemed to flee away
    That I so longed for, ever day by day
    I watched and waited still.

Sometimes I said, "This thing shall be no more;
10   My expectation wearies and shall cease;
    I will resign it now and be at peace:"
    Yet never gave it o'er.

Sometimes I said, "It is an empty name
    I long for; to a name why should I give
15   The peace of all the days I have to live?"—
    Yet gave it all the same.

Alas, thou foolish one! alike unfit
    For healthy joy and salutary pain:
    Thou knowest the chase useless, and again
20   Turnest to follow it.
—1848

Song

She sat and sang alway
    By the green margin of a stream,
Watching the fishes leap and play
    Beneath the glad sunbeam.

5   I sat and wept alway
    Beneath the moon's most shadowy beam,
Watching the blossoms of the May
    Weep leaves into the stream.

I wept for memory;
10   She sang for hope that is so fair:
My tears were swallowed by the sea;
    Her songs died on the air.
—1862

Song

When I am dead, my dearest,
    Sing no sad songs for me;
Plant thou no roses at my head,
    Nor shady cypress tree.
5   Be the green grass above me
    With showers and dewdrops wet;
And if thou wilt, remember,
    And if thou wilt, forget.

I shall not see the shadows,
10   I shall not feel the rain;
I shall not hear the nightingale
    Sing on as if in pain.
And dreaming through the twilight
    That doth not rise nor set,
15   Haply° I may remember,   *by chance*
    And haply may forget.
—1862

Dead Before Death

Ah! changed and cold, how changed and very cold!
    With stiffened smiling lips and cold calm eyes:
    Changed, yet the same; much knowing, little wise;
This was the promise of the days of old!
5   Grown hard and stubborn in the ancient mould,
    Grown rigid in the sham of lifelong lies:
    We hoped for better things as years would rise,
But it is over as a tale once told.
All fallen the blossom that no fruitage bore,
10   All lost the present and the future time,
All lost, all lost, the lapse that went before:
So lost till death shut-to the opened door,
    So lost from chime to everlasting chime,
So cold and lost for ever evermore.
—1862

Monna Innominata [1]
A Sonnet of Sonnets

Beatrice, immortalized by "*altissimo poeta … cotanto amante*";[2] Laura, celebrated by a great though an inferior bard[3]—have alike paid the exceptional penalty of exceptional honour, and have come down to us resplendent with charms, but (at least, to my apprehension) scant of attractiveness.

These heroines of worldwide fame were preceded by a bevy of unnamed ladies "*donne innominate*" sung by a school of less conspicuous poets; and in that land and that period which gave simultaneous birth to Catholics, to Albigenses, and to Troubadours,[4] one can imagine many a lady as sharing her lover's poetic aptitude, while the barrier between them might be one held sacred by both, yet not such as to render mutual love incompatible with mutual honour.

Had such a lady spoken for herself, the portrait left us might have appeared more tender, if less dignified, than any drawn even by a devoted friend. Or had the Great Poetess[5] of our own day and nation only been unhappy instead of happy, her circumstances would have invited her to bequeath to us, in lieu of the "Portuguese Sonnets," an inimitable "*donna innominata*" drawn not from fancy but from feeling, and worthy to occupy a niche beside Beatrice and Laura.

I

"Lo dì che han detto a' dolci amici addio."—DANTE
"Amor, con quanto sforzo oggi mi vinci!"—PETRARCA [6]

Come back to me, who wait and watch for you:—
　Or come not yet, for it is over then,
　　And long it is before you come again,
So far between my pleasures are and few.

5 While, when you come not, what I do I do
　Thinking "Now when he comes," my sweetest "when":
　For one man is my world of all the men
This wide world holds; O love, my world is you.
Howbeit, to meet you grows almost a pang
10 　Because the pang of parting comes so soon;
　　My hope hangs waning, waxing, like a moon
　　　Between the heavenly days on which we meet:
Ah me, but where are now the songs I sang
　When life was sweet because you called them sweet?

2

"Era già l'ora che volge il desio."—DANTE
"Ricorro al tempo ch' io vi vidi prima."—PETRARCA [7]

I wish I could remember that first day,
　First hour, first moment of your meeting me,
　If bright or dim the season, it might be
Summer or winter for aught I can say;
5 So unrecorded did it slip away,
　So blind was I to see and to foresee,
　So dull to mark the budding of my tree
That would not blossom yet for many a May.
If only I could recollect it, such
10 　A day of days! I let it come and go
　　As traceless as a thaw of bygone snow;
It seemed to mean so little, meant so much;
If only now I could recall that touch,
　First touch of hand in hand—Did one but know!

3

"O ombre vane, fuor che ne l'aspetto!"—DANTE
"Immaginata guida la conduce."—PETRARCA [8]

I dream of you to wake: would that I might
　Dream of you and not wake but slumber on;
　Nor find with dreams the dear companion gone,
As summer ended summer birds take flight.
5 In happy dreams I hold you full in sight,
　I blush again who waking look so wan;

---

[1] *Monna Innominata* Italian: unnamed lady.

[2] *altissimo poeta … cotanto amante* Italian: loftiest poet … equally great lover (Italian). Rossetti refers to Italian poet Dante Alighieri (1265–1321), whose muse was Beatrice.

[3] *great … bard* Italian poet Francesco Petrarca (1304–74) wrote many love songs to Laura.

[4] *Albigenses* Albigensians were members of a religious sect of the twelfth and thirteenth centuries; *Troubadours* Wandering lyric poets of the eleventh to thirteenth centuries.

[5] *Great Poetess* Elizabeth Barrett Browning.

[6] *Dante* From *Purgatorio* 8.3: "Who in the morn have bid sweet friends farewell"; *Petrarca* From *Canzone* 85.12: "Love, with what forces you conquer me now!"

[7] *Dante* From *Purgatorio* 8.1: "Now was the hour that wakens fond desire"; *Petrarca* From Sonnet 20.3: "I remember when I saw you for the first time."

[8] *Dante* From *Purgatorio* 2.79: "Oh vain shadows, except in outward aspect"; *Petrarca* From *Canzone* 277.9: "An imagined guide leads her."

Brighter than sunniest day that ever shone,
In happy dreams your smile makes day of night.
Thus only in a dream we are at one,
10   Thus only in a dream we give and take
        The faith that maketh rich who take or give;
    If thus to sleep is sweeter than to wake,
        To die were surely sweeter than to live,
Tho' there be nothing new beneath the sun.

4

"Poca favilla gran fiamma seconda."—DANTE
"Ogni altra cosa, ogni pensier va fore,
E sol ivi con voi rimansi amore."—PETRARCA[1]

I loved you first: but afterwards your love,
    Outsoaring mine, sang such a loftier song
As drowned the friendly cooings of my dove.
    Which owes the other most? My love was long,
5   And yours one moment seemed to wax more strong;
I loved and guessed at you, you construed me
And loved me for what might or might not be—
    Nay, weights and measures do us both a wrong.
For verily love knows not "mine" or "thine";
10   With separate "I" and "thou" free love has done,
        For one is both and both are one in love:
Rich love knows nought of "thine that is not mine";
    Both have the strength and both the length
        thereof,
    Both of us, of the love which makes us one.

5

"Amor che a nullo amato amar perdona."—DANTE
"Amor m'addusse in sì gioiosa spene."—PETRARCA[2]

O my heart's heart, and you who are to me
    More than myself myself, God be with you,
    Keep you in strong obedience leal° and true   *loyal*
To Him whose noble service setteth free;
5 Give you all good we see or can foresee,
    Make your joys many and your sorrows few,

Bless you in what you bear and what you do,
Yea, perfect you as He would have you be.
So much for you; but what for me, dear friend?
10   To love you without stint and all I can
Today, tomorrow, world without an end;
    To love you much and yet to love you more,
    As Jordan at his flood sweeps either shore;
Since woman is the helpmeet made for man.

6

"Or puoi la quantitate
Comprender de l'amor che a te mi scalda."—DANTE
"Non vo'che da tal nodo amor mi sciolglia."—PETRARCA[3]

Trust me, I have not earned your dear rebuke,
    I love, as you would have me, God the most;
    Would lose not Him, but you, must one be lost,
Nor with Lot's wife cast back a faithless look,[4]
5 Unready to forego what I forsook;
    This say I, having counted up the cost,
    This, tho' I be the feeblest of God's host,
The sorriest sheep Christ shepherds with His crook.
Yet while I love my God the most, I deem
10   That I can never love you overmuch;
        I love Him more, so let me love you too;
    Yea, as I apprehend it, love is such
I cannot love you if I love not Him,
    I cannot love Him if I love not you.

7

"Qui primavera sempre ed ogni frutto."—DANTE
"Ragionando con meco ed io con lui."—PETRARCA[5]

"Love me, for I love you"—and answer me,
    "Love me, for I love you": so shall we stand
    As happy equals in the flowering land
Of love, that knows not a dividing sea.
5 Love builds the house on rock and not on sand,
    Love laughs what while the winds rave desperately;

---

[1] *Dante* From *Paradiso* 1.34: "From a small spark a great flame rises"; *Petrarca* From *Canzone* 72.44–45: "All other hopes, all other thoughts are gone, and love with you remains there alone."

[2] *Dante* From *Inferno* 5.103: "Love, that denial takes from none beloved"; *Petrarca* From Sonnet 56.11: "Love urged me in this gladness to believe."

[3] *Dante* From *Purgatorio* 21.133–34: "Now has thou proved the force and ardor of the love I bear thee"; *Petrarca* From Canzone 59.17: "I do not wish love to release me from this knot."

[4] *Lot's wife ... look* See Genesis 19.26: "[Lot's] wife looked back from behind him, and she became a pillar of salt."

[5] *Dante* From *Purgatorio* 28.143: "Perpetual spring and every fruit"; *Petrarca* From Canzone 35.14: "Speaking with me and I with him."

And who hath found love's citadel unmanned?
    And who hath held in bonds love's liberty?—
My heart's a coward tho' my words are brave—
    We meet so seldom, yet we surely part
10   So often; there's a problem for your art!
Still I find comfort in his Book, who saith,
Tho' jealousy be cruel as the grave,
    And death be strong, yet love is strong as death.[1]

8

    "Come dicesse a Dio, D'altro non calme." —DANTE
    "Spero trovar pietà non che perdono."—PETRARCA[2]

"I, if I perish, perish"—Esther spake:[3]
    And bride of life or death she made her fair
    In all the lustre of her perfumed hair
And smiles that kindle longing but to slake.
5 She put on pomp of loveliness, to take
    Her husband through his eyes at unaware;
    She spread abroad her beauty for a snare,
Harmless as doves and subtle as a snake.
She trapped him with one mesh of silken hair,
10   She vanquished him by wisdom of her wit,
      And built her people's house that it should
        stand:—
      If I might take my life so in my hand,
And for my love to Love put up my prayer,
    And for love's sake by Love be granted it!

9

    "O dignitosa coscienza e netta!"—DANTE
    "Spirto più acceso di virtuti ardenti."—PETRARCA[4]

Thinking of you, and all that was, and all
    That might have been and now can never be,
    I feel your honoured excellence, and see
Myself unworthy of the happier call:
5 For woe is me who walk so apt to fall,
    So apt to shrink afraid, so apt to flee,
    Apt to lie down and die (ah woe is me!)
Faithless and hopeless turning to the wall.
And yet not hopeless quite nor faithless quite,
10 Because not loveless; love may toil all night,
    But take at morning; wrestle till the break
     ·Of day, but then wield power with God and
        man:—
      So take I heart of grace as best I can,
    Ready to spend and be spent for your sake.

10

    "Con miglior corso e con migliore stella."—DANTE
    "La vita fugge e non s'arresta un' ora."—PETRARCA[5]

Time flies, hope flags, life plies a wearied wing;
    Death following hard on life gains ground apace;
    Faith runs with each and rears an eager face,
Outruns the rest, makes light of everything,
5 Spurns earth, and still finds breath to pray and sing;
    While love ahead of all uplifts his praise,
    Still asks for grace and still gives thanks for grace,
Content with all day brings and night will bring.
Life wanes; and when love folds his wings above
10   Tired hope, and less we feel his conscious pulse,
      Let us go fall asleep, dear friend, in peace:
      A little while, and age and sorrow cease;
    A little while, and life reborn annuls
Loss and decay and death, and all is love.

---

[1] *his Book ... death* See The Song of Solomon 6: "Set me as a seal upon your heart, as a seal upon your arm; for love is strong as death, passion fierce as the grave."

[2] *Dante* From *Purgatorio* 8.12: "As if telling God, 'I care for nothing else'"; *Petrarca* From *Canzone* 1.8: "I hope to find pity, not just forgiveness."

[3] *I ... spake* From Esther 4.16, in which Queen Esther says to Mordecai, before donning beautiful robes and appealing to her husband to cease his mission to kill her people, the Jews: "Go, gather together all the Jews ... and neither eat nor drink three days, night or day: I also and my maidens will fast likewise; and so will I go in unto the king, which is not according to the law: and if I perish, I perish."

[4] *Dante* From *Purgatorio* 3.8: "Oh conscience clear and upright!"; *Petrarca* From *Canzone* 283.3: "Spirit dazzling with blazing virtues."

[5] *Dante* From *Paradiso* 1.40: "In best course and in happiest constellation"; *Petrarca* From *Canzone* 272.1: "Life flies and doesn't stay for an hour."

11

"Vien dietro a me e lascia dir le genti."—DANTE
"Contando i casi della vita nostra."—PETRARCA[1]

Many in aftertimes will say of you
   "He loved her"—while of me what will they say?
   Not that I loved you more than just in play,
For fashion's sake as idle women do.
5 Even let them prate; who know not what we knew
   Of love and parting in exceeding pain,
   Of parting hopeless here to meet again,
Hopeless on earth, and heaven is out of view.
But by my heart of love laid bare to you,
10 My love that you can make not void nor vain,
Love that foregoes you but to claim anew
   Beyond this passage of the gate of death,
   I charge you at the Judgment make it plain
     My love of you was life and not a breath.

12

"Amor, che ne la mente mi ragiona."—DANTE
"Amor vien nel bel viso di costei."—PETRARCA[2]

If there be any one can take my place
   And make you happy whom I grieve to grieve,
   Think not that I can grudge it, but believe
I do commend you to that nobler grace,
5 That readier wit than mine, that sweeter face;
   Yea, since your riches make me rich, conceive
   I too am crowned, while bridal crowns I weave,
And thread the bridal dance with jocund° pace.   *merry*
For if I did not love you, it might be
10 That I should grudge you some one dear delight;
   But since the heart is yours that was mine own,
   Your pleasure is my pleasure, right my right,
Your honourable freedom makes me free,
     And you companioned I am not alone.

13

"E drizzeremo glí occhi al Primo Amore."—DANTE
"Ma trovo peso non de le mie braccia."—PETRARCA[3]

If I could trust mine own self with your fate,
   Shall I not rather trust it in God's hand?
   Without Whose Will one lily doth not stand,
Nor sparrow fall at His appointed date;
5 Who numbereth the innumerable sand,
Who weighs the wind and water with a weight,
To Whom the world is neither small nor great,
   Whose knowledge foreknew every plan we planned.
Searching my heart for all that touches you,
10 I find there only love and love's goodwill
Helpless to help and impotent to do,
   Of understanding dull, of sight most dim;
   And therefore I commend you back to Him
     Whose love your love's capacity can fill.

14

"E la Sua Volontade è nostra pace."—DANTE
"Sol con questi pensier, con altre chiome."—PETRARCA[4]

Youth gone, and beauty gone if ever there
   Dwelt beauty in so poor a face as this;
   Youth gone and beauty, what remains of bliss?
I will not bind fresh roses in my hair,
5 To shame a cheek at best but little fair,—
   Leave youth his roses, who can bear a thorn,—
I will not seek for blossoms anywhere,
   Except such common flowers as blow with corn.[5]
Youth gone and beauty gone, what doth remain?
10 The longing of a heart pent up forlorn,
   A silent heart whose silence loves and longs;
   The silence of a heart which sang its songs
   While youth and beauty made a summer morn,
Silence of love that cannot sing again.
—1881

---

[1] *Dante* From *Purgatorio* 5.13: "Come after me, and leave behind the people's babblings"; *Petrarca* From *Canzone* 285.12: "Telling of the changes in our lives."

[2] *Dante* From *Purgatorio* 2.112: "Love that discourses in my thoughts"; *Petrarca* From *Canzone* 13.2: "Love appears in the beautiful face of this lady."

[3] *Dante* From *Paradiso* 32.142: "And our eyes will turn unto the first Love"; *Petrarca* From Sonnet 20.5: "The burden I find too great a weight for my arms."

[4] *Dante* From *Paradiso* 3.85: "And in his will is our tranquility"; *Petrarca* From *Canzone* 30.32: "Alone with these thoughts, with time-altered locks of hair."

[5] *corn* Grain.

Cobwebs

It is a land with neither night nor day,
Nor heat nor cold, nor any wind, nor rain,
   Nor hills nor valleys; but one even plain
Stretches thro' long unbroken miles away:
5   While thro' the sluggish air a twilight grey
   Broodeth; no moons or seasons wax and wane,
   No ebb and flow are there along the main,
No bud-time no leaf-falling there for aye,°   any
No ripple on the sea, no shifting sand,
10   No beat of wings to stir the stagnant space,
No pulse of life thro' all the loveless land:
And loveless sea; no trace of days before,
   No guarded home, no toil-won resting place
No future hope no fear for evermore.
—1896 (WRITTEN 1855)

In an Artist's Studio

One face[1] looks out from all his canvasses,
   One selfsame figure sits or walks or leans:
   We found her hidden just behind those screens,
That mirror gave back all her loveliness.
5   A queen in opal or in ruby dress,
   A nameless girl in freshest summer-greens,
   A saint, an angel;—every canvass means
The same one meaning, neither more nor less.
He feeds upon her face by day and night,
10   And she with true kind eyes looks back on him,
Fair as the moon and joyful as the light:
   Not wan with waiting, nor with sorrow dim;
Not as she is, but was when hope shone bright;
   Not as she is, but as she fills his dream.
—1896

Dante Gabriel Rossetti's *Beata Beatrix* (1864–70).

Promises like Pie-Crust [2]

Promise me no promises,
   So will I not promise you;
Keep we both our liberties,
   Never false and never true:
5 Let us hold the die uncast,
   Free to come as free to go;
For I cannot know your past,
   And of mine what can you know?

[1] *One face* I.e., Elizabeth (Lizzie) Siddal's. Siddal (1829–62) was
D.G. Rossetti's model for *Beata Beatrix* and many other paintings;
the two eventually married. She was a poet and artist in her own
right.

[2] *Promises like Pie-Crust* See Jonathan Swift's comment: "Promises
and pie-crust are made to be broken."

You, so warm, may once have been
    Warmer towards another one;
I, so cold, may once have seen
    Sunlight, once have felt the sun:
Who shall show us if it was
    Thus indeed in time of old?
Fades the image from the glass
    And the fortune is not told.

If you promised, you might grieve
    For lost liberty again;
If I promised, I believe
    I should fret to break the chain:
Let us be the friends we were,
    Nothing more but nothing less;
Many thrive on frugal fare
    Who would perish of excess.
—1896 (WRITTEN 1861)

In Progress

Ten years ago it seemed impossible
    That she should ever grow so calm as this,
    With self-remembrance in her warmest kiss
And dim dried eyes like an exhausted well.
Slow-speaking when she has some fact to tell,
    Silent with long-unbroken silences,
    Centred in self yet not unpleased to please,

Gravely monotonous like a passing bell.
Mindful of drudging daily common things,
    Patient at pastime, patient at her work,
Wearied perhaps but strenuous certainly.
Sometimes I fancy we may one day see
    Her head shoot forth seven stars from where they
        lurk
And her eyes lightnings and her shoulders wings.
—1896

Sleeping at Last

Sleeping at last, the trouble & tumult over,
    Sleeping at last, the struggle & horror past,
Cold & white out of sight of friend & of lover
Sleeping at last.

No more a tired heart downcast or overcast,
No more pangs that wring or shifting fears that hover,
Sleeping at last in a dreamless sleep locked fast.

Fast asleep. Singing birds in their leafy cover
Cannot wake her, nor shake her gusty blast.
Under the purple thyme & the purple clover
Sleeping at last.
—1896

WILLIAM BUTLER YEATS
1865 – 1939

In *On Poetry and Poets* (1957), fellow poet and contemporary T.S. Eliot wrote of William Butler Yeats: "Born into a world in which the doctrine of "Art for Art's Sake" was generally accepted, and living on into one in which art has been asked to be instrumental to social purposes, he held firmly to the right view which is between these, though not in any way a compromise between them, and showed that an artist, by serving his art with entire integrity, is at the same time rendering the greatest service he can to his own nation and to the whole world." In truth, few poets of the twentieth century have contributed as much to the cultural, political, and social framework of their own country, and to English literature in general. An analysis of Yeats's poetry, however, is impossible without understanding the deeply personal and biographical nature of his writing, and Yeats's own endeavor to shape his entire canon of work into a unified body of art.

William Butler Yeats was born in the Dublin suburb of Sandymount on 13 June 1865. His father, John Butler Yeats, had given up law to take up portrait painting, a decision that, though artistically and intellectually stimulating, led to many years of uprooted existence and strained finances for his family. When William was two, the family moved to London, yet much of his childhood was spent moving between schooling in London and retreats to the family home of his mother, Susan Pollexfen, in County Sligo, Ireland. In County Sligo, Yeats would find inspiration in the beauty of the countryside, the local folklore, and Irish tradition. That would remains apparent throughout his lifetime, as evidenced in early poems such as "The Lake Isle of Innisfree" and in later works such as "Under Ben Bulben." In 1880, the family returned permanently to Ireland and settled in Howth, close to Dublin. In 1883, having completed high school, Yeats decided to be an artist and enrolled in the Metropolitan School of Art, but he soon left to pursue his true passion, poetry. His first published poems appeared in the *Dublin University Review* in 1885. Yeats also capitalized on his burgeoning literary talent and interest in Irish folklore by editing two anthologies, *Poems and Ballads of Young Ireland* (1888) and *Fairy and Folk Tales of the Irish Peasantry* (1888). From an early age, Yeats is said to have followed an inner voice that commanded him to "hammer his thoughts into unity."

Also at an early age, influenced by his father's religious skepticism, Yeats developed a strong interest in occultism, folklore, and theosophism, a system of philosophical thought based on the direct and immediate experience of the divine. In 1885 he joined with friends to form the Dublin Hermetic Society, a group devoted to discussion of occult sciences and pseudo-sciences of the day. This group was predominantly influenced by a more famous mystical society, The Theosophical Society, founded in New York by Madame Helena Blavatsky. In 1887, Yeats met with Madame Blavatsky and later joined the Esoteric section of the London chapter of the Theosophical Society. In 1890, Yeats left the Society to join the Hermetic Order of the Golden Dawn, an occult society that drew upon astrology, tarot, kabbala, and Eastern mysticism for its teachings. Throughout his life and career, Yeats would turn to mythology and the occult as tools for developing his own vision of history and imagination.

In his poetry, this vision is evident in an elaborate system of images and symbols that Yeats would continually investigate and refine.

In 1889 Yeats's first collection, *The Wanderings of Oisin and Other Poems*, was published. The collection was well received, but the attention of one reader in particular would be responsible for what Yeats would term "the troubling of my life." The beautiful actress and Irish nationalist Maud Gonne was introduced to Yeats by a mutual friend, John O'Leary, shortly after the collection was published. The meeting marked a fateful moment in the life of Yeats, as Gonne would become his obsession for the next quarter-century, and his poetry would resonate with his love and despair for her in poems such as "Adam's Curse" (1904), "No Second Troy" (1910), and "A Prayer for My Daughter" (1921). Despite remaining intimate with Yeats for many years, Maud Gonne persistently refused to marry him, and added to his turmoil with her marriage to an Irish soldier, John MacBride, in 1903. Yet in spite of the heartache Yeats endured through his relationship with Gonne, she helped inspire him in two new cultural endeavors: the establishment of an Irish national theatre and the development of a public voice for the Irish nationalist movement for independence.

For several years after the publication of *The Wanderings of Oisin and Other Poems*, Yeats continued to gain literary prominence with further collections of poetry and studies of Irish folklore and fairy tales. In 1896 Yeats met Lady Augusta Gregory, a fellow writer and promoter of Irish literature, who invited him to stay in her country house at Coole Park. Through her influence, Yeats became involved in the founding of the Irish National Theatre in 1899. In writing for the theater, Yeats found a new voice for his interest in mythology, mysticism, Irish nationalism, and Maud Gonne. In 1902, Gonne played the title role in Yeats's nationalist play *Cathleen Ni Houlihan*. In 1904, the Irish National Theatre's permanent home, The Abbey Theatre, opened with Yeats's play *On Baile's Strand*. As the Abbey's director and dramatist, Yeats helped develop it into one of the world's leading theaters and, perhaps more importantly to him, into the center of the Irish literary renaissance.

In 1908, eight volumes of Yeats's *Collected Works* were published. Although Yeats was most interested in the Abbey Theatre during this period, this publication by no means heralded the slowdown of his poetic career. On the contrary, as he was becoming a figure of national importance, Yeats began to develop a more public voice in his poetry. Abandoning the more lyrical and self-conscious mode of his earlier poems, Yeats began to trace the growing political upheaval of the period. The publication of *The Green Helmet and Other Poems* in 1910 marks Yeats's transition into the second phase of his poetic career. Where his early poems often offered romantic melancholy and idyllic meditations on pagan themes, the poetry of this second phase became more direct in its analysis of the events and attitudes of the period. As Yeats became embittered by the small-minded nationalism of The Abbey's middle-class audiences, and as he watched with horror the growing violence in the struggle for Irish independence, poems such as "Easter 1916," "Meditations In Time of Civil War," and "Nineteen Hundred and Nineteen" began to reflect his distrust of popular judgement and concern for the future of his country.

At the same time, Yeats continued to develop his complex system of symbolism and esoteric theories regarding the movement of history and human intellect. In 1917, having exhausted his proposals to Maud Gonne and suffered another humiliating refusal by Gonne's daughter Iseult, Yeats married Georgie Hyde-Lees, whom he had met in 1911. On their honeymoon, Hyde-Lees delighted Yeats with her gift for automatic writing (believed by Yeats to be dictated by spirits), and for several years her writings inspired Yeats to refine his symbolic system, as described in his book *A Vision* (1925). Although Yeats's poetry is by no means unintelligible without an understanding of *A Vision*, many of his poems refer directly to the patterns and imagery examined within its pages. According to Yeats, the progress of art and thought is directly interwoven through the spirals, or gyres, of human history, represented in *A Vision* by two interpenetrating cones that make up antithetical cycles of 2000 years. These ideas became increasingly evident in his poetic works, particularly later poems such as "Byzantium" and "Sailing to Byzantium."

In 1922 Yeats was elected Senator of the Irish Free State; a year later, he was awarded the Nobel Prize for Literature, becoming the first Irish writer to receive the award. Yeats continued to produce major poetry well into his later years. As his health began to decline, his poetry took on a defiant tone, reflecting an awareness of his own mortality. Poems of this period, such as "Lapis Lazuli," "The Circus Animals' Desertion," and "Under Ben Bulben," rage against old age while reflecting on his life and body of work. Poems published in *The Tower* (1928), *The Winding Stair* (1933), and *Last Poems* (1939) are thought by many critics to be among his finest.

Following a long period of heart trouble, Yeats died on 28 January 1939, and was buried in Roquebrune, France, where he had been spending the winter. In 1948, his remains were reinterred, as he had wished, in Drumcliff, County Sligo. Also according to his wishes, his epitaph is taken from "Under Ben Bulben": "Cast a cold eye / On life, on death. / Horseman, pass by!"

When You Are Old[3]

When you are old and gray and full of sleep,
    And nodding by the fire, take down this book,
And slowly read, and dream of the soft look
Your eyes had once, and of their shadows deep;

5   How many loved your moments of glad grace,
And loved your beauty with love false or true,
But one man loved the pilgrim soul in you,
And loved the sorrows of your changing face;

And bending down beside the glowing bars,
10 Murmur, a little sadly, how Love fled
And paced upon the mountains overhead
And hid his face amid a crowd of stars.
                —1892

---

[3] *When You Are Old*   Based on one of Pierre de Ronsard's (1524–85) *Sonnets pour Hélène*, "*Quand vous serez bien vieille, au soir, à la chandelle*," which translates to: "When you very old, sitting by the candlelight at night."

I saw, before I had well finished,
All suddenly mount
And scatter wheeling in great broken rings
Upon their clamorous wings.

I have looked upon those brilliant creatures,
And now my heart is sore.
All's changed since I, hearing at twilight,
The first time on this shore,
The bell-beat of their wings above my head,
Trod with a lighter tread.

Unwearied still, lover by lover,
They paddle in the cold
Companionable streams or climb the air;
Their hearts have not grown old;
Passion or conquest, wander where they will,
Attend upon them still.

But now they drift on the still water,
Mysterious, beautiful;
Among what rushes will they build,
By what lake's edge or pool
Delight men's eyes, when I awake some day
To find they have flown away?
　—1917

The Wild Swans at Coole [4]

The trees are in their autumn beauty,
　The woodland paths are dry,
Under the October twilight the water
Mirrors a still sky;
Upon the brimming water among the stones
Are nine-and-fifty swans.

The nineteenth autumn [5] has come upon me
Since I first made my count;

[4] *Coole*   Coole Park, County Galway estate of Lady Gregory, friend and patron of Yeats.

[5] *nineteenth autumn*   Yeats first visited Coole Park in 1897, nineteen years before he wrote this poem.

The Second Coming [1]

Turning and turning in the widening gyre[2]
The falcon cannot hear the falconer;
Things fall apart; the centre cannot hold;
Mere anarchy is loosed upon the world,
5 The blood-dimmed tide is loosed, and everywhere
The ceremony of innocence is drowned;
The best lack all conviction, while the worst
Are full of passionate intensity.

Surely some revelation is at hand;
10 Surely the Second Coming is at hand.
The Second Coming! Hardly are those words out
When a vast image out of *Spiritus Mundi*[3]
Troubles my sight: somewhere in sands of the desert
A shape with lion body and the head of a man,[4]
15 A gaze blank and pitiless as the sun,
Is moving its slow thighs, while all about it
Reel shadows of the indignant desert birds.
The darkness drops again; but now I know
That twenty centuries of stony sleep
20 Were vexed to nightmare by a rocking cradle,[5]
And what rough beast, its hour come round at last,
Slouches towards Bethlehem to be born?

—1920

---

[1] *The Second Coming* The return of Christ, as predicted in the New Testament. See Revelation 1.7: "Behold, he cometh with clouds; and every eye shall see him."

[2] *gyre* Spiral formed from concentric circles.

[3] *Spiritus Mundi* Universal spirit that houses the images of civilization's past memories and provides divine inspiration for the poet; the human race is a connected whole in the *spiritus mundi*.

[4] *shape ... man* The Egyptian Sphinx.

[5] *rocking cradle* Cradle of the Christ Child.

Ephemera[1]

"Your eyes that once were never weary of mine
Are bowed in sorrow under
         pendulous° lids,   *heavy-hanging*
Because our love is waning."
         And then she:
5   "Although our love is waning, let us stand
By the lone border of the lake once more,
Together in that hour of gentleness
When the poor tired child, Passion, falls asleep:
How far away the stars seem, and how far
10 Is our first kiss, and ah, how old my heart!"

Pensive they paced along the faded leaves,
While slowly he whose hand held hers replied:
"Passion has often worn our wandering hearts."

The woods were round them, and the yellow leaves
15 Fell like faint meteors in the gloom, and once
A rabbit old and lame limped down the path;
Autumn was over him: and now they stood
On the lone border of the lake once more:
Turning, he saw that she had thrust dead leaves
20 Gathered in silence, dewy as her eyes,
In bosom and hair.
         "Ah, do not mourn," he said,
"That we are tired, for other loves await us:
Hate on and love through unrepining[2] hours;
25 Before us lies eternity; our souls
Are love, and a continual farewell."
         —1887 (REVISED 1895)

The Lake Isle of Innisfree[3]

I will arise and go now, and go to Innisfree,
And a small cabin build there, of clay and wattles[4]
   made;
Nine bean-rows will I have there, a hive for the honey
   bee,
And live alone in the bee-loud glade.

5   And I shall have some peace there, for peace comes
      dropping slow,
Dropping from the veils of the morning to where the
   cricket sings;
There midnight's all a glimmer, and noon a purple glow,
And evening full of the linnet's° wings.   *small songbird's*

I will arise and go now, for always night and day
10 I hear lake water lapping with low sounds by the shore;
While I stand on the roadway, or on the pavements grey,
I hear it in the deep heart's core.
—1890

Into the Twilight[5]

Out-worn heart, in a time out-worn,
Come clear of the nets of wrong and right;
Laugh heart again in the grey twilight,
Sigh, heart, again in the dew of the morn.

5   Your mother Eire° is always young,   *Ireland*
Dew ever shining and twilight gray;
Though hope fall from you and love decay,
Burning in fires of a slanderous tongue.

---

[1] *Ephemera*   Short-lived things, or things that are enjoyed only briefly.

[2] *unrepining*   Contented, without brooding.

[3] *Lake Isle of Innisfree*   A small island in Lough Gill, County Sligo; Innisfree (*Inis Fraoigh* in Gaelic) means "Heather Island."

[4] *wattles*   Poles and reeds interwoven to create a thatched wall or roof.

[5] *Into the Twilight*   Originally published under the title "The Celtic Twilight."

Come, heart, where hill is heaped upon hill:
10 For there the mystical brotherhood
Of sun and moon and hollow and wood
And river and stream work out their will;

And God stands winding° His lonely horn,   *blowing*
And time and the world are ever in flight;
15 And love is less kind than the gray twilight,
And hope is less dear than the dew of the morn.
—1893

The Secret Rose[1]

Far-off, most secret, and inviolate Rose,
Enfold me in my hour of hours; where those
Who sought thee in the Holy Sepulchre,[2]
Or in the wine vat, dwell beyond the stir
5   And tumult of defeated dreams; and deep
Among pale eyelids, heavy with the sleep
Men have named beauty. Thy great leaves enfold
The ancient beards, the helms of ruby and gold
Of the crowned Magi;[3] and the king whose eyes
10 Saw the Pierced Hands and Rood° of elder rise   *Cross*
In druid vapour and make the torches dim;
Till vain frenzy awoke and he died;[4] and him

Who met Fand walking among flaming dew
By a grey shore where the wind never blew,
15 And lost the world and Emer for a kiss;[5]
And him who drove the gods out of their liss,[6]
And till a hundred morns had flowered red,
Feasted, and wept the barrows° of his dead;   *grave mounds*
And the proud dreaming king who flung the crown
20 And sorrow away, and calling bard and clown
Dwelt among wine-stained wanderers in deep woods:[7]
And him who sold tillage,° and house,   *farmland*
    and goods,
And sought through lands and islands numberless years,
Until he found with laughter and with tears,
25 A woman, of so shining loveliness
That men threshed corn at midnight by a tress,°   *lock of hair*
A little stolen tress.[8] I, too, await
The hour of thy great wind of love and hate.
When shall the stars be blown about the sky,
30 Like the sparks blown out of a smithy,°   *blacksmith's forge*
    and die?
Surely thine hour has come, thy great wind blows,
Far-off, most secret, and inviolate Rose?
—1896

---

[1] *The Secret Rose*   First published under the title "O'Sullivan Rua to the Secret Rose."

[2] *Holy Sepulchre*   Cave in which Jesus Christ's body was placed before his resurrection.

[3] *Magi*   Three wise men who came from the East to bring gifts to the baby Jesus.

[4] *the king … he died*   King Conchobar, who was said to have the same birth date and death date as Jesus Christ. Conchobar had an object embedded in his head, an injury from a past battle; when he was told of Christ's execution, he grew so angry that the object burst out of his skull and he died. Here, Yeats imagines Conchobar witnessing the crucifixion in a vision brought by Druids, priests of Celtic religion. Yeats identifies this and the poem's other references to Irish myth and folktale in an extensive note accompanying some editions of the poem.

[5] *and him … a kiss*   In Irish myth, the great hero Cúchulainn became a lover to the goddess Fand and accompanied her to the otherworld, leaving his wife Emer.

[6] *And him … their liss*   Caoilte, a hero of Irish legend. Seized by rage after almost all of his friends were killed in a battle, he drove the nearby gods out of their home; *liss* Circular fort common in iron-age Ireland.

[7] *And the proud … deep woods*   Legendary Irish king Fergus. According to Yeats, he fell so deeply in love with a woman that he was motivated to give up his throne to her son Conchobar, and he spent the rest of his days feasting and hunting in the forest.

[8] *And him who sold … stolen tress*   Reference to an Irish folktale in which a working man, while traveling on the road in the dark, discovers a box containing a brightly glowing lock of hair. He uses it as a lamp to work at night until the king learns of the hair and sends him to find the woman to whom it belongs.

He Remembers Forgotten Beauty[1]

When my arms wrap you round I press
   My heart upon the loveliness
That has long faded from the world;
The jewelled crowns that kings have hurled
5   In shadowy pools, when armies fled;
The love-tales wrought with silken thread
By dreaming ladies upon cloth
That has made fat the murderous moth;
The roses that of old time were
10   Woven by ladies in their hair,
The dew-cold lilies ladies bore
Through many a sacred corridor
Where such gray clouds of incense rose
That only the gods' eyes did not close:
15   For that pale breast and lingering hand
Come from a more dream-heavy land,
A more dream-heavy hour than this;
And when you sigh from kiss to kiss
I hear white Beauty sighing, too,
20   For hours when all must fade like dew
But flame on flame, deep under deep,
Throne over throne, where in half sleep
Their swords upon their iron knees
Brood her high lonely mysteries.
—1896

The Travail of Passion[2]

When the flaming lute-thronged angelic door is wide;
   When an immortal passion breathes in mortal
      clay;
Our hearts endure the scourge,° the plaited[3]   *whip*
   thorns, the way
Crowded with bitter faces, the wounds in palm and side,
5   The hyssop-heavy sponge,[4] the flowers by Kidron stream;[5]
We will bend down and loosen our hair over you,
That it may drop faint perfume, and be heavy with dew,
Lilies of death-pale hope, roses of passionate dream.
—1899

---

[1] *He Remembers … Beauty* Originally published under the title "O'Sullivan Rua to Mary Lavell" (1896) and then, with small revisions, as "Michael Robartes Remembers Forgotten Beauty" (1899) before being reprinted under the present title (1906).

[2] *Travail* Toil, struggle; *Passion* Throughout this poem are allusions to the Passion of Christ, the sufferings of Jesus surrounding his crucifixion. Among other tortures, Christ was whipped, forced to wear a crown of thorns, made to carry his cross through a jeering crowd, nailed to the cross by his hands, and speared in the side.

[3] *plaited* Braided (i.e., into a crown).

[4] *hyssop-heavy sponge* In John 19.29 Christ, dying on the cross, is given a drink of vinegar on a sponge attached to a stick from a hyssop plant.

[5] *Kidron stream* Small river that passes through the garden of Gethsemane, where Jesus spent the night in prayer before his arrest.

T.S. Eliot
1888–1965

No twentieth-century writer did more to shape the direction of modern poetry and criticism than T.S. Eliot. In poems such as "The Love Song of J. Alfred Prufrock" (1915) and *The Waste Land* (1922), Eliot founded a radical new poetical idiom to express the alienation and the "chaotic, irregular, fragmentary" experience of the modern mind, which he considered disconnected from any meaningful sense of tradition. Eliot's many essays and reviews, notably "Tradition and the Individual Talent" (1919) and "The Metaphysical Poets" (1921), were scarcely less influential. Such writings not only provided a theoretical foundation for New Criticism, one of the most prominent critical schools of the early to mid-twentieth century; they also introduced new terms and concepts—"objective correlative," "the dissociation of sensibility," the ideal development of the poet as a "continual extinction of personality"—that have enriched the study of modern literature, not least by illuminating Eliot's own complex poetics.

Eliot's poetry is challenging, but in his reckoning it could hardly be otherwise, for he believed that "poets in our civilization, as it exists at present, must be *difficult*. Our civilization comprehends great variety and complexity, and this variety and complexity, playing upon a refined sensibility, must produce various and complex results." Among the most striking of these results is the absence—particularly in his early poetry—of fluid transitions: images are precise but often jarring and incongruous, arrestingly juxtaposed to suggest broader patterns of meaning. At once colloquial and erudite, fragmentary and unified, much of Eliot's poetry relies on ironies, tensions, and paradoxes. These qualities are ideally suited to the rigorous methodology of close reading championed by the New Critics, who focused not on the mind of the poet or the external conditions of the text's creation but on the details of the text itself.

Eliot's thought and technique evolved over his career, particularly following his conversion to Anglo-Catholicism, when—as in "Journey of the Magi" (1927) and *Four Quartets* (1943)—he began to explore more religious themes. Although his poetic output was relatively modest, his body of work occupies the very centre of literary modernism. As Northrop Frye remarked, "a thorough knowledge of Eliot is compulsory for anyone interested in contemporary literature. Whether he is liked or disliked is of no importance, but he must be read."

The Love Song of J. Alfred Prufrock[1]

S'io credesse che mia risposta fosse
A persona che mai tornasse al mondo,
Questa fiamma staria senza piu scosse.
Ma perciocche giammai di questo fondo
Non torno viva alcun, s'i'odo il vero,   5
Senza tema d'infamia ti rispondo.[2]

Let us go then, you and I,
When the evening is spread out against the sky
Like a patient etherized upon a table;
Let us go, through certain half-deserted streets,   10
The muttering retreats
Of restless nights in one-night cheap hotels
And sawdust restaurants with oyster-shells:
Streets that follow like a tedious argument
Of insidious intent   15
To lead you to an overwhelming question …
Oh, do not ask, "What is it?"
Let us go and make our visit.

In the room the women come and go
Talking of Michelangelo.   20

The yellow fog that rubs its back upon the window-panes,
The yellow smoke that rubs its muzzle on the window-panes
Licked its tongue into the corners of the evening,
Lingered upon the pools that stand in drains,
Let fall upon its back the soot that falls from chimneys, 25
Slipped by the terrace, made a sudden leap,
And seeing that it was a soft October night,
Curled once about the house, and fell asleep.

And indeed there will be time
For the yellow smoke that slides along the street,   30

---

1   *J. Alfred Prufrock* The name is likely taken from the The Prufrock-Littau Company, a
    furniture dealer located in St. Louis, Eliot's birthplace.
2   *S'io credesse … ti rispondo* Italian: "If I thought that my reply were given to anyone who
    might return to the world, this flame would stand forever still; but since never from this
    deep place has anyone ever returned alive, if what I hear is true, without fear of infamy
    I answer thee," Dante's *Inferno* 27.61–66; Guido da Montefeltro's speech as he burns in
    Hell.

Rubbing its back upon the window panes;
There will be time, there will be time[1]
To prepare a face to meet the faces that you meet
There will be time to murder and create,
35 And time for all the works and days[2] of hands
That lift and drop a question on your plate;
Time for you and time for me,
And time yet for a hundred indecisions,
And for a hundred visions and revisions,
40 Before the taking of a toast and tea.

In the room the women come and go
Talking of Michelangelo.

And indeed there will be time
To wonder, "Do I dare?" and, "Do I dare?"
45 Time to turn back and descend the stair,
With a bald spot in the middle of my hair—
(They will say: "How his hair is growing thin!")
My morning coat,[3] my collar mounting firmly to the chin,
My necktie rich and modest, but asserted by a simple pin—
50 (They will say: "But how his arms and legs are thin!")
Do I dare
Disturb the universe?
In a minute there is time
For decisions and revisions which a minute will reverse.

55 For I have known them all already, known them all—
Have known the evenings, mornings, afternoons,
I have measured out my life with coffee spoons;
I know the voices dying with a dying fall[4]
Beneath the music from a farther room.
60   So how should I presume?

And I have known the eyes already, known them all—
The eyes that fix you in a formulated phrase,

---

1   *there will be time* See Ecclesiastes 3.1–8. "To everything there is a season, and a time to every purpose under heaven: A time to be born, and a time to die; a time to plant, and a time to pluck up that which is planted; a time to kill, and a time to heal...."

2   *works and days* Title of a poem by eighth-century BCE Greek poet Hesiod.

3   *morning coat* Formal coat with tails.

4   *with a dying fall* In Shakespeare's *Twelfth Night* 1.1.1–15 Duke Orsino commands, "That strain again, it had a dying fall."

And when I am formulated, sprawling on a pin,
When I am pinned and wriggling on the wall,
Then how should I begin   65
To spit out all the butt-ends of my days and ways?
        And how should I presume?

And I have known the arms already, known them all—
Arms that are braceleted and white and bare
(But in the lamplight, downed with light brown hair!)   70
Is it perfume from a dress
That makes me so digress?
Arms that lie along a table, or wrap about a shawl.
        And should I then presume?
        And how should I begin?   75

                *   *   *

Shall I say, I have gone at dusk through narrow streets
And watched the smoke that rises from the pipes
Of lonely men in shirt-sleeves, leaning out of windows? …[1]

I should have been a pair of ragged claws
Scuttling across the floors of silent seas.[2]   80

                *   *   *

And the afternoon, the evening, sleeps so peacefully!
Smoothed by long fingers,
Asleep … tired … or it malingers,
Stretched on the floor, here beside you and me.
Should I, after tea and cakes and ices,   85
Have the strength to force the moment to its crisis?
But though I have wept and fasted, wept and prayed,
Though I have seen my head (grown slightly bald) brought in
        upon a platter,[3]
I am no prophet[4]—and here's no great matter;

---

1   … The ellipsis here makes note of a 38 line insertion written by Eliot, entitled *Pru-
     frock's Pervigilium*. The subtitle and 33 of the lines were later removed.
2   *I should … seas* See Shakespeare's *Hamlet* 2.2, in which Hamlet tells Polonius, "for you
     yourself, sir, should be old as I am, if like a crab you could go backwards."
3   *brought in upon a platter* Reference to Matthew 14.1–12, in which the prophet John
     the Baptist is beheaded at the command of Herod, and his head presented to Salomé
     upon a platter.
4   *I am no prophet* See Amos 7.14. When commanded by King Amiziah not to proph-
     esize, the Judean Amos answered; "I was no prophet, neither was I a prophet's son; but
     I was a herdsman, and a farmer of sycamore fruit."

90 I have seen the moment of my greatness flicker,
And I have seen the eternal Footman hold my coat, and snicker,
And in short, I was afraid.

And would it have been worth it, after all,
After the cups, the marmalade, the tea,
95 Among the porcelain, among some talk of you and me,
Would it have been worth while,
To have bitten off the matter with a smile,
To have squeezed the universe into a ball[1]
To roll it toward some overwhelming question,
100 To say: "I am Lazarus,[2] come from the dead,
Come back to tell you all, I shall tell you all"—
If one, settling a pillow by her head,
    Should say: "That is not what I meant at all;
    That is not it, at all."

105 And would it have been worth it, after all,
Would it have been worth while,
After the sunsets and the dooryards and the sprinkled streets,[3]
After the novels, after the teacups, after the skirts that trail along
    the floor—
And this, and so much more?—
110 It is impossible to say just what I mean!
But as if a magic lantern[4] threw the nerves in patterns on a screen:
Would it have been worth while
If one, settling a pillow or throwing off a shawl,
And turning toward the window, should say:
115   "That is not it at all,
    That is not what I meant, at all."

      *   *   *

No! I am not Prince Hamlet, nor was meant to be;
Am an attendant lord, one that will do
To swell a progress,[5] start a scene or two,
120 Advise the prince; no doubt, an easy tool,

---

1   *squeezed ... ball* See Andrew Marvell's "To His Coy Mistress," 41–42: "Let us roll our strength and all / Our sweetness up into one ball."
2   *Lazarus* Raised from the dead by Jesus in John 11.1–44.
3   *sprinkled streets* Streets sprayed with water to keep dust down.
4   *magic lantern* In Victorian times, a device used to project images painted on glass onto a blank screen or wall.
5   *progress* Journey made by royalty through the country.

Deferential, glad to be of use,
Politic, cautious, and meticulous;
Full of high sentence,[1] but a bit obtuse;
At times, indeed, almost ridiculous—
Almost, at times, the Fool.   125

I grow old ... I grow old ...
I shall wear the bottoms of my trousers rolled.

Shall I part my hair behind? Do I dare to eat a peach?
I shall wear white flannel trousers, and walk upon the beach.
I have heard the mermaids singing,[2] each to each.   130

I do not think that they will sing to me.

I have seen them riding seaward on the waves
Combing the white hair of the waves blown back
When the wind blows the water white and black.

We have lingered in the chambers of the sea   135
By sea-girls wreathed with seaweed red and brown
Till human voices wake us, and we drown.

—1915, 1917

---

1   *high sentence* Serious, elevated sentiments or opinions.
2   *I have ... singing* See John Donne's "Song": "Teach me to hear the mermaids singing."

ELIOT, POUND, AND THE VORTEX OF MODERNISM

CONTEXTS

According to Virginia Woolf's oft-quoted formulation (from a 1924 essay excerpted in this section), "on or about December 1910 human character changed." Woolf saw that date as marking the moment at which writers began smashing literary conventions in an effort to represent the complexity of human experience through "the spasmodic, the obscure, the fragmentary." At the same moment, painting and sculpture were breaking visual reality into fragments to express the reality of fragmented experience—or indeed to express the reality of what increasingly seemed a fragmented world. Such is now a conventional account of the birth of Modernism.

There was, of course, a mock-precision in Woolf's dating, but many others have linked the birth of Modernism to developments that occurred at *about* this time: in painting, the development of Cubism by Pablo Picasso and Georges Braque; in music, the development of strikingly discordant styles such as that of Schoenberg's *The Rite of Spring*; in poetry, the development of Imagism and its offshoots by Ezra Pound, H.D. and, a few years later, T.S. Eliot; in fiction, the development by Dorothy Richardson, James Joyce, Virginia Woolf, and others, of "stream of consciousness" techniques of narration; and, in the world of art as well as of ideas, the development of Futurism by F.T. Marinetti and others. Arguably, though, the birth of Modernism can be traced to developments that occurred in France considerably earlier—developments such as Arthur Rimbaud's wholesale rejection in 1871 of the conventions of Western poetry. In the 1880s and 90s the Symbolist aesthetic of poets Jules Laforgue and Stephane Mallarmé foreshadowed the coming of Modernism even more directly than had that of Rimbaud. In the 1891 interview excerpted below, Mallarmé asserted that "when a society is without stability, without unity, it cannot create a stable and definitive art," and suggested that we must not try to elude the intellectual work that is entailed in coming to terms with the appropriate obscurity of poetry. A generation later, T.S. Eliot declared (in his essay "The Metaphysical Poets") that "poets in our civilization must be *difficult*. Our civilization comprehends great variety and complexity, and this variety and complexity ... must produce various and complex results. The poet must become ... more allusive, more indirect, in order to force, to dislocate if necessary, language into his meaning."

The vortex of Modernism includes within it a wide variety of narrower "isms"—including not only post-Impressionism, Symbolism, Imagism, and Futurism, but also Vorticism, Absurdism, Dadaism, and a number of others. All shun the linear, the decorative, and the sentimental. All tend towards the presentation of reality fractured into its component pieces—and conversely, towards a rejection of all traditions within which reality is represented through the construction of convention-ally unified wholes. Often, however, it was suggested that the fractured forms might represent the world as humans *perceive* it more realistically than other, seemingly more "realistic" forms of representation. Such was the case with stream of consciousness narration in fiction, for example, and also with Cubism; Picasso is famously reported to have said of his Cubist work, "I paint objects as I think them, not as I see them."

In the revolutionary ferment of the late eighteenth and early nineteenth centuries, there was a close correlation between literary or artistic positions and political ones; those who held radical political views tended also to hold radical aesthetic ones. In the revolutionary ferment of Modernism a century later, however, the lines of association between the aesthetic and the political are much more tangled; certainly it would be difficult to argue that Modernism was particularly friendly towards the political left. While Woolf and most of the Bloomsbury circle held progressive political views, Pound and many of the Futurists gravitated towards fascism, Eliot towards conservative High Anglicanism. Modernism's strong desire to recognize the force of often anarchic psychological impulse eventually found its most venomous expression in the racism and anti-Semitism of Pound ("Let us be done with Jews … / Let us spit on those who fawn on the Jews for their money"). Nor was Modernism on the whole friendly towards feminism—or, more generally, towards women. H.D., Richardson, and Woolf must be numbered among the major figures of Modernism—and in the long run, their writing on issues relating to gender has counted more than the less progressive pronouncements of some other Modernist figures. But in their own time, the virulent misogyny of such figures as Marinetti and Pound (and the much milder variety of Eliot) had a wide-ranging impact, on literature as in other contexts. The "modern woman" that had been so central to the cultural world at the turn of the century was of little interest to the major male figures of Modernism. (Paradoxically, though, the climate that Modernism helped to create may not, finally, have been hostile to women or to progressive causes, if only because Modernism promoted the belief that nothing is stable—and thus implicitly that change can occur in surprising directions, and with surprising speed.)

A particular focus in this section is placed on the reception of the Modernist poetry of T.S. Eliot, which was as influential upon later twentieth-century generations as it was controversial when first published.

⌘⌘⌘

JAMES JOYCE
1882 – 1941

Irish novelist James Joyce's prose style and subject matter were so innovative and influential that fellow writer T.S. Eliot was prompted to declare that Joyce had helped to make "the modern world possible for art" by discovering "a way of controlling, or ordering, of giving a shape and a significance to the panorama of futility and anarchy which is contemporary history." Joyce's works as a whole redefined realism as they sought to access reality as perceived by the mind—whether awake or dreaming. Although throughout his life Joyce battled publishers, critics, and readers who objected to his frank treatment of the more "vulgar" aspects of his characters' thoughts and actions, Joyce became a literary figure of the first magnitude during his lifetime, and has remained so since.

James Augustus Aloysius Joyce was born in the middle-class Dublin suburb of Rathgar and was the first surviving son in a family of twelve siblings. Through his father's fecklessness, Joyce's family situation would eventually devolve into poverty. John Joyce's increasing dependence on alcohol created strains both on the family's finances and on its morale. On the other hand, Joyce's mother, Mary Jane Joyce, exposed the young Joyce to the arts and to religion, as she was both accomplished in music and devout in her Catholicism. The former he would embrace with as much fervor as he rejected the latter.

At the age of 6, Joyce started his studies under the tutorship of the Jesuits. During the course of his schooling, however, he became increasingly cynical about the Church. His intellectual and spiritual rebelliousness grew so that by the time he entered university he had begun to believe that religion, family, and nation were all traps of conventionality that the true artist must avoid.

While at University College, Joyce attempted to write poetry and enjoyed writing articles parodying various literary styles. A penchant for experimentation with form stayed with him, from the economy of voice exhibited in *Dubliners*, to the variety of narrative expressions created for *A Portrait of the Artist as a Young Man* and *Ulysses*, to the radical linguistic experimentation of *Finnegan's Wake*. In political matters, he rejected the single-minded nationalism of his peers and wrote outspoken articles that were published privately after the school advisory board barred publication in the school newspaper. Meanwhile, he was very successful in his chosen field of study—modern languages.

Joyce originally moved to Paris in 1902 to study medicine, but it was not until about 1904 that he took up his artistic mission in earnest and decided to leave Ireland. Apart from some brief periods, Joyce remained an exile from the country about which he would spend his life writing. For Joyce, exile was a prerequisite for artistic objectivity and freedom; he believed that his self-imposed exile allowed him to see the truth of Ireland and Irishness with clarity, precision, and detachment.

In June 1904, Joyce was invited by the paper *The Irish Homestead* to submit a short story. In the end he wrote a series of fifteen stories that were published in 1914 under the title *Dubliners*. Along the way Joyce had a series of arguments with publishers that would also dog and delay the publication of *A Portrait of the Artist as a Young Man,* as editors objected to what they saw as the inappropriate subject matter and language of his work. In 1909, he wrote to London publisher Grant Richards, with whom he was in negotiations for *Dubliners,* "I seriously believe that you will retard the course of civilization in Ireland by preventing the Irish people from having one good look at themselves in my nicely polished looking-glass." Richards, however, was in no financial position to advance the course of Irish civilization, and the book was rejected, not to be published until 1914.

Joyce described *Dubliners* as "a chapter of the moral history of my country." The book is divided—according to a letter Joyce wrote to his publisher—into four sections, representing childhood, adolescence, maturity, and public life. The fifteenth story, "The Dead," was not part of Joyce's original manuscript. This story, the longest in the collection, became the showpiece of the book upon its publication. Thematically, each of the stories in *Dubliners* deals with the lives of ordinary people, many of whom suffer from a sort of emotional paralysis—as a result of internal or external forces or moral decay—that makes them unable to move forward.

Many of these stories have as their focus a moment of self-recognition on the part of a character, a moment Joyce referred to as an "epiphany." The triggers to an epiphany are often accidental, "little errors and gestures—mere straws in the wind," as Joyce described them in a letter to his brother Stanislaus. The sharp focus allowed by a sudden flash of clarity is fleeting but allows characters a moment in which to see above their particular circumstances.

1904 was also the year Joyce met the woman who would be his lifelong partner. As legend has it, it was on 16 June, or "Bloomsday" (the day on which the events in *Ulysses* take place), that James Joyce first went out walking with Nora Barnacle, a chambermaid from Galway. Uninterested in literature, but with a fresh charm and wit and, like Joyce, an interest in music, she followed Joyce to the city of Pola, in the Austro-Hungarian Empire, four months after their meeting. They lived there a short time, without the sanction of marriage, and later moved to Trieste, Italy, where Joyce continued to write and eked out a meager living teaching English. The couple produced two children, Lucia and Georgio, and ultimately married, in 1931.

During their time in Trieste, in the fall of 1907, Joyce started editing, cutting, and reshaping the almost 1,000 pages of *Stephen Hero,* a novel he had begun in 1904. The result would be *A Portrait of the Artist as a Young Man,* on which Joyce continued to work intermittently for the next nine years. The novel-in-progress began to be published serially in *The Egoist* in 1914. It was not published as a volume until 1916, by the New York publisher B.W. Huebsch. It had been rejected by every London publisher to whom Joyce had sent it, despite the support of some major literary figures of the day, including W.B. Yeats, H.G. Wells, and Ezra Pound.

The hero of *Portrait,* Stephen Dedalus, bears a striking similarity to Joyce himself. The novel details the artistic growth of a writer, from childhood to the age of twenty, and outlines Joyce's artistic mission in life: to "record ... with extreme care" epiphanic moments of sublime self-awareness; it also extends Joyce's experiments with style. The voice of the implied narrator changes and develops in correspondence with the development of the central character.

Ulysses details a day in Dublin life. Events in the novel follow the comings and goings of Stephen Dedalus, continuing the artistic journey on which Joyce set him in *A Portrait of the Artist as a Young Man,* and Leo Bloom, the Jewish-Irish Everyman who is the hero of the novel. *Ulysses* takes as its model Homer's *Odyssey*; an everyday journey through the neighborhoods of Dublin becomes highly symbolic as Leo Bloom follows a path that parallels that of Homer's hero. Meanwhile, Stephen Dedalus plays the role of Homer's Telemachus; Joyce imagines him an artist and visionary cut off from society. Joyce believed that Odysseus was perhaps the most well-rounded character in Western literature, embodying the best and the worst in human behavior: he was both brave and cowardly, a liar and an intellectual. Joyce's endeavors to portray these traits in his hero make Leo Bloom one of the most warmly compelling characters in all of twentieth-century literature.

In form, each chapter is an ironic rewriting of a chapter from Homer's *Odyssey,* and is written in a broadly different literary style from the one that precedes it. The novel adopts a stream-of-consciousness approach that makes little or no distinction between what is happening externally and what takes place in a character's mind. Perspectives move fluidly from internal to external dialogue, from character to character, and from event to event, with little to indicate the change. The novel's central themes are those that recur in Joyce's work: the inner life of Dublin in all its beauty and hollowness, and the outsider status of Leo Bloom (because of his Jewishness) and Stephen Dedalus (because of his artistic mission). This shared experience of Leo and Stephen, and Stephen's figurative search for an absent father, link the two thematically throughout the story.

Ulysses began to be published serially in the *Little Review* beginning in 1918, but in 1920 publication ceased in the face of obscenity charges. Not until 1922 was *Ulysses* published, and even then it was printed in Paris, not Britain. An American edition was published in 1934, after a landmark court case decided the book was not pornography. The weary judge at the time acquiesced to the view that the book was a work of art, even if many readers would not understand it. A British edition of *Ulysses* finally appeared in 1937.

It was not until about 1920 that the Joyce family began to attain a modest level of financial security, largely the result of the support and patronage of a number of people who had as much faith in Joyce's genius as he himself did. The family moved from Trieste to Zurich in 1914, then to Paris in 1920, then back to Zurich in 1940, where Joyce died of a perforated ulcer, just after seeing the publication of his final—and perhaps least understood—novel, *Finnegan's Wake* (1939). In stylistic terms, the novel goes beyond the playful, self-conscious mode of *Ulysses* and enters a far more obscure territory. The title refers to a common folk song in which a laborer, Finnegan, falls and hits his head. His friends assume he is dead and hold a wake for him; he finally awakens after having whiskey spilled on him. *Finnegan's Wake* is ostensibly the dream of Finnegan's successor, a Dublin Everyman with the initials H.C.E. (which stand for a variety of names, including Humphrey Chimpden Earwicker and Here Comes Everybody), and also features H.C.E.'s wife, A.L.P. (Anna Livia Plurabelle, Amnis Limina Permanent) and their twin sons, Shem and Shaun. Everything that occurs, and all the characters present, belong at least partially to the realm of dream. The novel's form relies on the cyclical view of history set out by Italian philosopher Giambattista Vico (detailed in Samuel Beckett's essay "Dante … Bruno. Vico … Joyce," included here). The narrative is largely composed of multi-leveled puns that are fraught with symbolic meaning. Joyce used elements of English and seven other languages to create the texture of the novel, reinventing not just the form of the novel but the structure of language itself in order to escape the stifling traditions in which he felt conventional language was steeped.

During his lifetime Joyce promised his writing would "keep the professors busy," and in this he has succeeded, and continues to succeed, to an extent that even he might not have expected. For many years scholars were occupied with historical, cultural, and anthropological research into the background of Joyce's Dublin. While this research continues, developments in critical theory (such as postcolonialism) have also opened up many new ways to interpret Joyce's texts. During his lifetime much of his work was, as one of Joyce's friends said, "outside of literature"; "literature" has since shifted to accommodate Joyce.

⌘⌘⌘

Araby[1]

North Richmond Street, being blind,[2] was a quiet street except at the hour when the Christian Brothers' School set the boys free. An uninhabited house of two storeys stood at the blind end, detached from its neighbours in a square ground. The other houses of the street, conscious of decent lives within them, gazed at one another with brown imperturbable faces.

The former tenant of our house, a priest, had died in the back drawing-room. Air, musty from having been long enclosed, hung in all the rooms, and

---

1   *Araby* Charity bazaar held in Dublin in 1894; it was advertised as a "grand, Oriental fête."
2   *being blind* I.e., being a dead-end street.

the waste room behind the kitchen was littered with old useless papers. Among these I found a few paper-covered books, the pages of which were curled and damp: *The Abbot*, by Walter Scott, *The Devout Communicant* and *The Memoirs of Vidocq*.[1] I liked the last best because its leaves were yellow. The wild garden behind the house contained a central apple-tree and a few straggling bushes under one of which I found the late tenant's rusty bicycle-pump. He had been a very charitable priest; in his will he had left all his money to institutions and the furniture of his house to his sister.

When the short days of winter came dusk fell before we had well eaten our dinners. When we met in the street the houses had grown sombre. The space of sky above us was the colour of ever-changing violet and towards it the lamps of the street lifted their feeble lanterns. The cold air stung us and we played till our bodies glowed. Our shouts echoed in the silent street. The career of our play brought us through the dark muddy lanes behind the houses where we ran the gantlet of the rough tribes from the cottages, to the back doors of the dark dripping gardens where odours arose from the ash-pits, to the dark odorous stables where a coachman smoothed and combed the horse or shook music from the buckled harness. When we returned to the street light from the kitchen windows had filled the areas.[2] If my uncle was seen turning the corner we hid in the shadow until we had seen him safely housed. Or if Mangan's sister came out on the doorstep to call her brother in to his tea we watched her from our shadow peer up and down the street. We waited to see whether she would remain or go in and, if she remained, we left our shadow and walked up to Mangan's steps resignedly. She was waiting for us, her figure defined by the light from the half-opened door. Her brother always teased her before he obeyed and I stood by the railings looking at her. Her dress swung as she moved her body and the soft rope of her hair tossed from side to side.

Every morning I lay on the floor in the front parlour watching her door. The blind was pulled down to within an inch of the sash so that I could not be seen. When she came out on the doorstep my heart leaped. I ran to the hall, seized my books and followed her. I kept her brown figure always in my eye and, when we came near the point at which our ways diverged, I quickened my pace and passed her. This happened morning after morning. I had never spoken to her, except for a few casual words, and yet her name was like a summons to all my foolish blood.

---

1   *The Abbot* 1820 historical novel by Sir Walter Scott about Mary, Queen of Scots; *The Devout Communicant* Title common to several nineteenth-century religious tracts; *The Memoirs of Vidocq* Autobiography of François Vidocq, a nineteenth-century Parisian criminal turned police detective.

2   *areas* Spaces between the railings and the fronts of houses, below street level.

Her image accompanied me even in places the most hostile to romance. On Saturday evenings when my aunt went marketing I had to go to carry some of the parcels. We walked through the flaring streets, jostled by drunken men and bargaining women, amid the curses of labourers, the shrill litanies of shop-boys who stood on guard by the barrels of pigs' cheeks, the nasal chanting of street-singers, who sang a *come-all-you* about O'Donovan Rossa,[1] or a ballad about the troubles in our native land. These noises converged in a single sensation of life for me: I imagined that I bore my chalice safely through a throng of foes. Her name sprang to my lips at moments in strange prayers and praises which I myself did not understand. My eyes were often full of tears (I could not tell why) and at times a flood from my heart seemed to pour itself out into my bosom. I thought little of the future. I did not know whether I would ever speak to her or not or, if I spoke to her, how I could tell her of my confused adoration. But my body was like a harp and her words and gestures were like fingers running upon the wires.

One evening I went into the back drawing-room in which the priest had died. It was a dark rainy evening and there was no sound in the house. Through one of the broken panes I heard the rain impinge upon the earth, the fine incessant needles of water playing in the sodden beds. Some distant lamp or lighted window gleamed below me. I was thankful that I could see so little. All my senses seemed to desire to veil themselves and, feeling that I was about to slip from them, I pressed the palms of my hands together until they trembled, murmuring: *O love! O love!* many times.

At last she spoke to me. When she addressed the first words to me I was so confused that I did not know what to answer. She asked me was I going to *Araby*. I forget whether I answered yes or no. It would be a splendid bazaar, she said; she would love to go.

—And why can't you? I asked.

While she spoke she turned a silver bracelet round and round her wrist. She could not go, she said, because there would be a retreat that week in her convent.[2] Her brother and two other boys were fighting for their caps and I was alone at the railings. She held one of the spikes, bowing her head towards me. The light from the lamp opposite our door caught the white curve of her neck, lit up her hair that rested there and, falling, lit up the hand upon the railing. It fell over one side of her dress and caught the white border of a petticoat, just visible as she stood at ease.

—It's well for you, she said.

---

1   *come-all-you* Ballad, so called because many ballads started with this phrase; *O'Donovan Rossa* Jeremiah O'Donovan Rossa (1831–1915), an activist for Irish independence.
2   *convent* I.e., convent school.

—If I go, I said, I will bring you something.

What innumerable follies laid waste my waking and sleeping thoughts after that evening! I wished to annihilate the tedious intervening days. I chafed against the work of school. At night in my bedroom and by day in the classroom her image came between me and the page I strove to read. The syllables of the word *Araby* were called to me through the silence in which my soul luxuriated and cast an Eastern enchantment over me. I asked for leave to go to the bazaar on Saturday night. My aunt was surprised and hoped it was not some Freemason[1] affair. I answered few questions in class. I watched my master's face pass from amiability to sternness; he hoped I was not beginning to idle. I could not call my wandering thoughts together. I had hardly any patience with the serious work of life which, now that it stood between me and my desire, seemed to me child's play, ugly monotonous child's play.

On Saturday morning I reminded my uncle that I wished to go to the bazaar in the evening. He was fussing at the hallstand, looking for the hatbrush, and answered me curtly:

—Yes, boy, I know.

As he was in the hall I could not go into the front parlour and lie at the window. I left the house in bad humour and walked slowly towards the school. The air was pitilessly raw and already my heart misgave me.

When I came home to dinner my uncle had not yet been home. Still it was early. I sat staring at the clock for some time and, when its ticking began to irritate me, I left the room. I mounted the staircase and gained the upper part of the house. The high cold empty gloomy rooms liberated me and I went from room to room singing. From the front window I saw my companions playing below in the street. Their cries reached me weakened and indistinct and, leaning my forehead against the cool glass, I looked over at the dark house where she lived. I may have stood there for an hour, seeing nothing but the brown-clad figure cast by my imagination, touched discreetly by the lamplight at the curved neck, at the hand upon the railings and at the border below the dress.

When I came downstairs again I found Mrs. Mercer sitting at the fire. She was an old garrulous woman, a pawnbroker's widow, who collected used stamps for some pious purpose. I had to endure the gossip of the tea-table. The meal was prolonged beyond an hour and still my uncle did not come. Mrs. Mercer stood up to go: she was sorry she couldn't wait any longer, but it was after eight o'clock and she did not like to be out late, as the night air was bad for her. When she had gone I began to walk up and down the room, clenching my fists. My aunt said:

---

1   *Freemason* In reference to the Freemasons, a secret society believed by many in Ireland to be anti-Catholic.

—I'm afraid you may put off your bazaar for this night of Our Lord.

At nine o'clock I heard my uncle's latchkey in the halldoor. I heard him talking to himself and heard the hallstand rocking when it had received the weight of his overcoat. I could interpret these signs. When he was midway through his dinner I asked him to give me the money to go to the bazaar. He had forgotten.

—The people are in bed and after their first sleep now, he said.

I did not smile. My aunt said to him energetically:

—Can't you give him the money and let him go? You've kept him late enough as it is.

My uncle said he was very sorry he had forgotten. He said he believed in the old saying: *All work and no play makes Jack a dull boy.* He asked where I was going and, when I had told him a second time he asked me did I know *The Arab's Farewell to his Steed.*[1] When I left the kitchen he was about to recite the opening lines of the piece to my aunt.

I held a florin tightly in my hand as I strode down Buckingham Street towards the station. The sight of the streets thronged with buyers and glaring with gas recalled to me the purpose of my journey. I took my seat in a third-class carriage of a deserted train. After an intolerable delay the train moved out of the station slowly. It crept onward among ruinous houses and over the twinkling river. At Westland Row Station a crowd of people pressed to the carriage doors; but the porters moved them back, saying that it was a special train for the bazaar. I remained alone in the bare carriage. In a few minutes the train drew up beside an improvised wooden platform. I passed out on to the road and saw by the lighted dial of a clock that it was ten minutes to ten. In front of me was a large building which displayed the magical name.

I could not find any sixpenny entrance and, fearing that the bazaar would be closed, I passed in quickly through a turnstile, handing a shilling to a weary-looking man. I found myself in a big hall girdled at half its height by a gallery. Nearly all the stalls were closed and the greater part of the hall was in darkness. I recognized a silence like that which pervades a church after a service. I walked into the centre of the bazaar timidly. A few people were gathered about the stalls which were still open. Before a curtain, over which the words *Café Chantant* were written in coloured lamps, two men were counting money on a salver.[2] I listened to the fall of the coins.

Remembering with difficulty why I had come I went over to one of the stalls and examined porcelain vases and flowered tea-sets. At the door of the

1   *The Arab's ... his Steed* Popular Romantic poem by Caroline Norton (1808–77).
2   *Café Chantant* Café that provides musical entertainment; *salver* Tray.

stall a young lady was talking and laughing with two young gentlemen. I remarked their English accents and listened vaguely to their conversation.

—O, I never said such a thing!

—O, but you did!

—O, but I didn't!

—Didn't she say that?

—Yes. I heard her.

—O, there's a ... fib!

Observing me the young lady came over and asked me did I wish to buy anything. The tone of her voice was not encouraging; she seemed to have spoken to me out of a sense of duty. I looked humbly at the great jars that stood like eastern guards at either side of the dark entrance to the stall and murmured:

—No, thank you.

The young lady changed the position of one of the vases and went back to the two young men. They began to talk of the same subject. Once or twice the young lady glanced at me over her shoulder.

I lingered before her stall, though I knew my stay was useless, to make my interest in her wares seem the more real. Then I turned away slowly and walked down the middle of the bazaar. I allowed the two pennies to fall against the sixpence in my pocket. I heard a voice call from one end of the gallery that the light was out. The upper part of the hall was now completely dark.

Gazing up into the darkness I saw myself as a creature driven and derided by vanity; and my eyes burned with anguish and anger.

—1914

Virginia Woolf
1882 – 1941

A towering figure in the history of twentieth-century feminist thought, Virginia Woolf also occupies a central place in the development of the twentieth-century novel. Woolf, along with contemporaries such as James Joyce and Dorothy Richardson, rejected the traditional conventions of fiction, which included narrative coherence, omniscient narration, and emphasis on external settings and events. Instead, she explored the everyday, internal lives of her characters in a style—often called stream-of-consciousness—that mimics the flow of her characters' thoughts. In her fiction and essays alike, she examined the ways in which social roles and values are constructed and the effects these have on the lives and interactions of individuals.

Virginia Woolf was born Adeline Virginia Stephen, the third child of an illustrious, upper-middle-class London family. Her father, Leslie Stephen, a philosopher and literary critic, was primarily known as editor of the *Dictionary of National Biography* and President of the London Library. Her mother, born Julia Jackson, had been married into the Duckworth publishing family, and then married Stephen some time after the death of her first husband. Deeply connected to Victorian literary circles, the Stephen family included among its friends Henry James, Matthew Arnold, and George Eliot. From childhood, Woolf was drawn to a literary career, and her father in particular encouraged her, as she says, "to read what one liked because one liked it, never to pretend to admire what one did not. ... To write in the fewest possible words, as clearly as possible, exactly what one meant."

Surrounded by her father's impressive library, Woolf immersed herself in the study of languages and literary classics. While her brothers Thoby and Adrian went to public schools and eventually to university at Cambridge, Woolf and her sister Vanessa were educated at home by their father and private tutors. The lack of formal education for women would become a pervasive issue in Woolf's novels and later essays such as *A Room of One's Own* (1929) and *Three Guineas* (1938). A frequent exploration into the emotional effects of death in her later writing would also stem from Woolf's youthful experience. In 1895, her mother died of influenza; a few months later, at the age of thirteen, Woolf suffered a mental breakdown, symptoms of which included hearing voices, avoiding food, and experiencing extreme anxiety. Her mother's death was followed by that of her beloved half-sister and maternal substitute, Stella Duckworth, in childbirth, and then by that of her father, from cancer, in 1904. A second breakdown resulted. These breakdowns were harbingers of Woolf's lifelong struggle with manic and depressive episodes, which were generally brought about by stress—such as the emotional and mental anxiety that accompanied the completion of a book.

Despite Woolf's emotional turmoil in the year following her father's death, the event freed her from her family's inhibiting influence and facilitated her emergence amongst London's intelligentsia. With an unsigned review, she received her first publication in *The Guardian*, and against her extended family's attempts to introduce her into polite society, Woolf and several of her siblings moved to the Bloomsbury area of London. There they began associating with her brother Thoby's Cambridge friends, and what began as a social gathering of casual friends for drinks and conversation eventually came to be known as the Bloomsbury Group, a cultural circle bound together by an intense interest in current literary, philosophical, artistic, sexual, and political issues. Its members included novelist E.M. Forster, biographer and essayist Lytton Strachey, painter Duncan Grant, art critics Roger Fry and Clive Bell (the future husband of Woolf's sister Vanessa), economist John Maynard Keynes, and political theorist Leonard Woolf. Although Thoby Stephen died of typhoid in 1906, the group continued to meet throughout Woolf's lifetime. It attracted a certain amount of controversy as a result of the new ideas (particularly concerning sexuality) and frank artistic expression it fostered, and also because of the class snobbery it was perceived to exhibit (to the extent that the word *Bloomsbury* later became widely used to connote an insular and patronizing aestheticism).

In 1912, Virginia Stephen married Leonard Woolf, who throughout her life provided her with the time, encouragement, and emotional support necessary for her to continue writing as she alternated between periods of stability and intense productivity and episodes of immobilizing emotional collapse. In 1915, *The Voyage Out*, Woolf's first major novel, was published, introducing her readers for the first time to the character of Clarissa Dalloway, whom Woolf would make central to her later novel *Mrs. Dalloway* (1925). *The Voyage Out* and its successor, *Night and Day* (1919), are Woolf's most conventional works.

In 1917, Woolf and her husband Leonard bought a hand press and established Hogarth Press at their London home, intending to publish their own works and those of their friends. The Hogarth Press soon became a highly successful enterprise, publishing the early works of authors such as E.M. Forster, Katherine Mansfield, and T.S. Eliot, as well as English translations of the works of Sigmund Freud.

Woolf's 1922 novel, *Jacob's Room*, based on the life and death of Woolf's brother Thoby, represented a stylistic breakthrough for her. In this novel, she tried an entirely different approach, ignoring much of the framework of external events and descriptions present in her earlier work. In this novel, she said, there was "no scaffolding; scarcely a brick to be seen; all crepuscular." By 1925, Woolf had completed *Mrs. Dalloway*, the culmination of many years' experimentation with narrative technique. Originally titled *The House*, *Mrs. Dalloway* takes place in a twenty-four hour period in London, and explores the subjectivities of characters who never meet, but whose observations, experiences, and memories reveal a curious kinship between them. Describing her new method of characterization, Woolf said, "I dig out beautiful caves behind my characters.... The idea is that the caves shall connect and each come to daylight at the present moment."

In Woolf's next novel, *To the Lighthouse* (1927), Woolf further developed her stream-of-consciousness style, relying heavily on imagery and rich symbolism to convey meaning. Divided into three distinct parts that take place against the backdrop of ordinary domestic events, the novel experiments with the passage of time through the consciousness of its various characters. By alternating between various viewpoints, Woolf demonstrates how rare, tenuous, and fleeting the moments of real connection between people are.

In 1929, Woolf's best-known work of non-fiction was published. Originally constructed as lecture notes for talks to be given at Newnham and Girton Colleges at Cambridge, the work was expanded and published as *A Room of One's Own*. The essay, which has become a foundational text of literary feminism, explores the traditional barriers and prejudices faced by women writers. At the core of Woolf's argument is her conclusion that a woman must have financial independence and privacy (a room of her own) if she is to write fiction successfully. In presenting the concept of the androgynous mind, Woolf also provides insight into her own literary process. As defined by Woolf, the successful author of whatever sex must possess the ability to draw creative forces from all facets of his or her emotional and intellectual being—regardless of whether these facets are traditionally classified as "masculine" or "feminine." To do so, the author must move beyond any awareness of his or her own gender role as dictated by social customs; as Woolf says, "It is fatal for anyone who writes to think of their sex." In her novel of the previous year, *Orlando*, Woolf had celebrated what she saw as the androgynous creative mind of her friend Vita Sackville-West. Subtitled *A Biography*, *Orlando* plays overtly with the form of genre as Woolf follows her main character—who is able to change sex as the times and his or her desires demanded—across several hundred years of British history.

For the next twelve years, Woolf continued to pursue more radical experiments with form while developing her ideas about writing, genre, and gender roles in numerous essays (most of which are collected in two volumes of her *Common Readers*). Woolf's next novel, *The Waves* (1931), is a poem-novel written "to a rhythm and not to a plot" that focuses on the mutability of life. In 1938, Woolf extended the feminist critique of male privilege begun in *A Room of One's Own* with *Three Guineas*, which implicitly links the values of patriarchal society with those of fascism. Less popular at the time than its predecessor, *Three Guineas*, and the pacifism is advocates, have found a more receptive audience in the later twentieth and early twenty-first centuries.

Just as *The Waves* sought to combine poetry and the novel, Woolf described her 1937 work, *The Years*, as an "essay-novel," and her final novel, *Between the Acts* (1941), is something of a drama-novel, focusing on the audience reception of an amateur pageant that takes place as the threat of war is imminent. Woolf herself, discouraged by the progress of World War II and its implications for herself and her Jewish husband, and dreading the critical reception this work would receive, faced another emotional breakdown. Before she could complete the revisions of *Between the Acts*, she began to feel mental illness engulf her. She composed a note to her husband explaining that she felt that this time she would not recover, filled her pockets with stones, and drowned herself in the River Ouse near her home.

Throughout her lifetime, Woolf was offered numerous honors, all of which she refused because of her avowed contempt for patriarchal society. After declining an honorary degree from Manchester University, she wrote in her diary, "It is an utterly corrupt society ..., and I will take nothing that it can give me." She did not want to be condescended to or used as a "token woman." Nevertheless, the honors continued to be offered, and, after her death, the loss of her unique vision and style were greatly mourned. She has since been hailed as a pioneer of the modernist novel, a central early figure in the development of feminist theory, and a central figure in the twentieth-century world of letters. Her personal diaries and letters, published posthumously in several volumes, provide unique insight into her aims as an artist and her intellectual development in a remarkable literary and artistic milieu.

The Mark on the Wall

Perhaps it was the middle of January in the present year that I first looked up and saw the mark on the wall. In order to fix a date it is necessary to remember what one saw. So now I think of the fire; the steady film of yellow light upon the page of my book; the three chrysanthemums in the round glass bowl on the mantelpiece. Yes, it must have been the winter time, and we had just finished our tea, for I remember that I was smoking a cigarette when I looked up and saw the mark on the wall for the first time. I looked up through the smoke of my cigarette and my eye lodged for a moment upon the burning coals, and that old fancy of the crimson flag flapping from the castle tower came into my mind, and I thought of the cavalcade of red knights riding up the side of the black rock. Rather to my relief the sight of the mark interrupted the fancy, for it is an old fancy, an automatic fancy, made as a child perhaps. The mark was a small round mark, black upon the white wall, about six or seven inches above the mantelpiece.

How readily our thoughts swarm upon a new object, lifting it a little way, as ants carry a blade of straw so feverishly, and then leave it.... If that mark was made by a nail, it can't have been for a picture, it must have been for a miniature—the miniature of a lady with white powdered curls, powder-dusted cheeks, and lips like red carnations. A fraud of course, for the people who had this house before us would have chosen pictures in that way—an old picture for an old room. That is the sort of people they were—very interesting people, and I think of them so often, in such queer places, because one will never see them again, never know what happened next. They wanted to leave this house because they wanted to change their style of furniture, so he said, and he was in process of saying that in his opinion art should have ideas behind it when we were torn asunder, as one is torn from the old lady about to pour out tea and the young man about to hit the tennis ball in the back garden of the suburban villa as one rushes past in the train.

But as for that mark, I'm not sure about it; I don't believe it was made by a nail after all; it's too big, too round, for that. I might get up, but if I got up and looked at it, ten to one I shouldn't be able to say for certain; because once a thing's done, no one ever knows how it happened. Oh! dear me, the mystery of life! The inaccuracy of thought! The ignorance of humanity! To show how very little control of our possessions we have—what an accidental affair this living is after all our civilization—let me just count over a few of the things lost in our lifetime, beginning, for that seems always the most mysterious of losses—what cat would gnaw, what rat would nibble—three pale blue canisters of book-binding tools? Then there were the bird cages, the iron hoops, the steel skates, the Queen Anne coal-scuttle, the bagatelle board,[1] the hand organ—all gone, and jewels too. Opals and emeralds, they lie about the roots of turnips. What a scraping paring affair it is to be sure! The wonder is that I've any clothes on my back, that I sit surrounded by solid furniture at this moment. Why, if one wants to compare life to anything, one must liken it to being blown through the Tube[2] at fifty miles an hour—landing at the other end without a single hairpin in one's hair! Shot out at the feet of God entirely naked! Tumbling head over heels in the asphodel[3] meadows like brown paper parcels pitched down a shoot in the post office! With one's hair flying back like the tail of a racehorse. Yes, that seems to express the rapidity of life, the perpetual waste and repair; all so casual, all so haphazard.…

But after life. The slow pulling down of thick green stalks so that the cup of the flower, as it turns over, deluges one with purple and red light. Why, after all, should one not be born there as one is born here, helpless, speechless, unable to focus one's eyesight, groping at the roots of the grass, at the toes of the Giants? As for saying which are trees, and which are men and women, or whether there are such things, that one won't be in a condition to do for fifty years or so. There will be nothing but spaces of light and dark, intersected by thick stalks, and rather higher up perhaps, rose-shaped blots of an indistinct colour—dim pinks and blues—which will, as time goes on, become more definite, become—I don't know what.…

And yet the mark on the wall is not a hole at all. It may even be caused by some round black substance, such as a small rose leaf, left over from the summer, and I, not being a very vigilant housekeeper—look at the dust on the mantelpiece, for example, the dust which, so they say, buried Troy three times over, only fragments of pots utterly refusing annihilation, as one can believe.

The tree outside the window taps very gently on the pane … I want to think quietly, calmly, spaciously, never to be interrupted, never to have to rise from my chair, to slip easily from one thing to another, without any sense of hostility, or obstacle. I want to sink deeper and deeper, away from the surface, with its hard separate facts. To steady myself, let me catch hold of the first idea that passes … Shakespeare … Well, he will do as well as another. A man who sat himself solidly in an arm-chair, and looked into the fire, so—A shower of ideas fell perpetually from some very high Heaven down through his mind. He leant his forehead on his hand, and people, looking in through the open door—for this scene is supposed to take place on a summer's evening—But how dull this is, this historical fiction! It

---

[1] *bagatelle board* Playing surface for a game similar to billiards.

[2] *Tube* Nickname for the London Underground, the system of subway lines that underlies the city of London.

[3] *asphodel* Genus of liliaceous flowers; said to cover the Elysian fields, the paradise where (according to Greek mythology) the blessed would reside after death.

doesn't interest me at all. I wish I could hit upon a pleasant track of thought, a track indirectly reflecting credit upon myself, for those are the pleasantest thoughts, and very frequent even in the minds of modest mouse-coloured people, who believe genuinely that they dislike to hear their own praises. They are not thoughts directly praising oneself; that is the beauty of them; they are thoughts like this:

"And then I came into the room. They were discussing botany. I said how I'd seen a flower growing on a dust heap on the site of an old house in Kingsway. The seed, I said, must have been sown in the reign of Charles the First. What flowers grew in the reign of Charles the First?" I asked—(but I don't remember the answer). Tall flowers with purple tassels to them perhaps. And so it goes on. All the time I'm dressing up the figure of myself in my own mind, lovingly, stealthily, not openly adoring it, for if I did that, I should catch myself out, and stretch my hand at once for a book in self-protection. Indeed, it is curious how instinctively one protects the image of oneself from idolatry or any other handling that could make it ridiculous, or too unlike the original to be believed in any longer. Or is it not so very curious after all? It is a matter of great importance. Suppose the looking-glass smashes, the image disappears, and the romantic figure with the green of forest depths all about it is there no longer, but only that shell of a person which is seen by other people—what an airless, shallow, bald, prominent world it becomes! A world not to be lived in. As we face each other in omnibuses and underground railways we are looking into the mirror; that accounts for the vagueness, the gleam of glassiness, in our eyes. And the novelists in future will realise more and more the importance of these reflections, for of course there is not one reflection but an almost infinite number; those are the depths they will explore, those the phantoms they will pursue, leaving the description of reality more and more out of their stories, taking a knowledge of it for granted, as the Greeks did and Shakespeare perhaps—but these generalisations are very worthless. The military sound of the word is enough. It recalls leading articles, cabinet ministers—a whole class of things indeed which as a child one thought the thing itself, the standard thing, the real thing, from which one could not depart save at the risk of nameless damnation.

Generalisations bring back somehow Sunday in London, Sunday afternoon walks, Sunday luncheons, and also ways of speaking of the dead, clothes, and habits—like the habit of sitting all together in one room until a certain hour, although nobody liked it. There was a rule for everything. The rule for tablecloths at that particular period was that they should be made of tapestry with little yellow compartments marked upon them, such as you may see in photographs of the carpets in the corridors of the royal palaces. Tablecloths of a different kind were not real tablecloths. How shocking, and yet how wonderful it was to discover that these real things, Sunday luncheons, Sunday walks, country houses, and tablecloths were not entirely real, were indeed half phantoms, and the damnation which visited the disbeliever in them was only a sense of illegitimate freedom. What now takes the place of those things I wonder, those real standard things? Men perhaps, should you be a woman; the masculine point of view which governs our lives, which sets the standard, which establishes Whitaker's Table of Precedency,[1] which has become, I suppose, since the war half a phantom to many men and women, which soon, one may hope, will be laughed into the dustbin where the phantoms go, the mahogany sideboards and the Landseer prints,[2] Gods and Devils, Hell and so forth, leaving us all with an intoxicating sense of illegitimate freedom—if freedom exists. …

In certain lights that mark on the wall seems actually to project from the wall. Nor is it entirely circular. I cannot be sure, but it seems to cast a perceptible shadow, suggesting that if I ran my finger down that strip of the wall it would, at a certain point, mount and descend a small tumulus, a smooth tumulus like those barrows on the South Downs[3] which are, they say, either tombs or camps. Of the two I should prefer them to be tombs, desiring melancholy like most English people, and finding it natural at the end of a walk to think of the bones stretched beneath the turf … There must be

---

[1] *Table of Precedency* Table in *Whitaker's Almanac* that illustrates the hierarchy of the various ranks of the British social order.

[2] *Landseer prints* Edwin Henry Landseer (1802–73) produced paintings and engravings of animals.

[3] *South Downs* Range of chalk hills in southeastern England; *barrows* Mounds of earth or stone.

some book about it. Some antiquary[1] must have dug up those bones and given them a name ... What sort of a man is an antiquary, I wonder? Retired Colonels for the most part, I daresay, leading parties of aged labourers to the top here, examining clods of earth and stone, and getting into correspondence with the neighbouring clergy, which, being opened at breakfast time, gives them a feeling of importance, and the comparison of arrowheads necessitates cross-country journeys to the country towns, an agreeable necessity both to them and to their elderly wives, who wish to make plum jam or to clean out the study, and have every reason for keeping that great question of the camp or the tomb in perpetual suspension, while the Colonel himself feels agreeably philosophic in accumulating evidence on both sides of the question. It is true that he does finally incline to believe in the camp; and, being opposed, indites a pamphlet which he is about to read at the quarterly meeting of the local society when a stroke lays him low, and his last conscious thoughts are not of wife or child, but of the camp and that arrowhead there, which is now in the case at the local museum, together with the foot of a Chinese murderess, a handful of Elizabethan nails, a great many Tudor clay pipes, a piece of Roman pottery, and the wine-glass that Nelson drank out of—proving I really don't know what.

No, no, nothing is proved, nothing is known. And if I were to get up at this very moment and ascertain that the mark on the wall is really—what shall I say?—the head of a gigantic old nail, driven in two hundred years ago, which has now, owing to the patient attrition of many generations of housemaids, revealed its head above the coat of paint, and is taking its first view of modern life in the sight of a white-walled fire-lit room, what should I gain? Knowledge? Matter for further speculation? I can think sitting still as well as standing up. And what is knowledge? What are our learned men save the descendants of witches and hermits who crouched in caves and in woods brewing herbs, interrogating shrew-mice and writing down the language of the stars? And the less we honour them as our superstitions dwindle and our respect for beauty and health of mind increases ... Yes, one could imagine a very pleasant world. A quiet spacious world, with the

flowers so red and blue in the open fields. A world without professors or specialists or house-keepers with the profiles of policemen, a world which one could slice with one's thought as a fish slices the water with his fin, grazing the stems of the water-lilies, hanging suspended over nests of white sea eggs.... How peaceful it is down here, rooted in the centre of the world and gazing up through the grey waters, with their sudden gleams of light, and their reflections—if it were not for Whitaker's Almanack—if it were not for the Table of Precedency!

I must jump up and see for myself what that mark on the wall really is—a nail, a rose-leaf, a crack in the wood?

Here is Nature once more at her old game of self-preservation. This train of thought, she perceives, is threatening mere waste of energy, even some collision with reality, for who will ever be able to lift a finger against Whitaker's Table of Precedency? The Archbishop of Canterbury is followed by the Lord High Chancellor; the Lord High Chancellor is followed by the Archbishop of York. Everybody follows somebody, such is the philosophy of Whitaker; and the great thing is to know who follows whom. Whitaker knows, and let that, so Nature counsels, comfort you, instead of enraging you; and if you can't be comforted, if you must shatter this hour of peace, think of the mark on the wall.

I understand Nature's game—her prompting to take action as a way of ending any thought that threatens to excite or to pain. Hence, I suppose, comes our slight contempt for men of action—men, we assume, who don't think. Still, there's no harm in putting a full stop to one's disagreeable thoughts by looking at a mark on the wall.

Indeed, now that I have fixed my eyes upon it, I feel that I have grasped a plank in the sea; I feel a satisfying sense of reality which at once turns the two Archbishops and the Lord High Chancellor to the shadows of shades. Here is something definite, something real. Thus, waking from a midnight dream of horror, one hastily turns on the light and lies quiescent, worshipping the chest of drawers, worshipping solidity, worshipping reality, worshipping the impersonal world which is proof of some existence other than ours. That is what one wants to be sure of. ... Wood is a pleasant thing to think about. It comes from a tree; and trees grow, and we don't know how they grow. For years and years they grow, without paying any attention to us, in meadows, in forests, and by the side of rivers—all things one likes to think about. The cows swish their tails beneath them on hot afternoons; they paint rivers so green that when a moorhen dives one expects to see its feathers all green when it comes up again. I like to think of the fish balanced against the stream like flags blown out; and of water-beetles slowly raising domes of mud upon the bed of the river. I like to think of the tree itself: first the close dry sensation of being wood; then the grinding of the storm; then the slow, delicious ooze of sap. I like to think of it, too, on winter's nights standing in the empty field with all leaves close-furled, nothing tender exposed to the iron bullets of the moon, a naked mast upon an earth that goes tumbling, tumbling all night long. The song of birds must sound very loud and strange in June; and how cold the feet of insects must feel upon it, as they make laborious progresses up the creases of the bark, or sun themselves upon the thin green awning of the leaves, and look straight in front of them with diamond-cut red eyes.... One by one the fibres snap beneath the immense cold pressure of the earth, then the last storm comes and, falling, the highest branches drive deep into the ground again. Even so, life isn't done with; there are a million patient, watchful lives still for a tree, all over the world, in bedrooms, in ships, on the pavement, lining rooms, where men and women sit after tea, smoking cigarettes. It is full of peaceful thoughts, happy thoughts, this tree. I should like to take each one separately—but something is getting in the way.... Where was I? What has it all been about? A tree? A river? The Downs? Whitaker's Almanack? The fields of asphodel? I can't remember a thing. Everything's moving, falling, slipping, vanishing.... There is a vast upheaval of matter. Someone is standing over me and saying—

"I'm going out to buy a newspaper."

"Yes?"

"Though it's no good buying newspapers.... Nothing ever happens. Curse this war; God damn this war! ... All the same, I don't see why we should have a snail on our wall."

Ah, the mark on the wall! It was a snail.

—1921

Blue & Green

GREEN

The pointed fingers of glass hang downwards. The light slides down the glass, and drops a pool of green. All day long the ten fingers of the lustre drop green upon the marble. The feathers of parakeets—their harsh cries—sharp blades of palm trees—green, too; green needles glittering in the sun. But the hard glass drips on to the marble; the pools hover above the desert sand; the camels lurch through them; the pools settle on the marble; rushes edge them; weeds clog them; here and there a white blossom; the frog flops over; at night the stars are set there unbroken. Evening comes, and the shadow sweeps the green over the mantelpiece; the ruffled surface of ocean. No ships come; the aimless waves sway beneath the empty sky. It's night; the needles drip blots of blue. The green's out.

BLUE

The snub-nosed monster rises to the surface and spouts through his blunt nostrils two columns of water, which, fiery-white in the centre, spray off into a fringe of blue beads. Strokes of blue line the black tarpaulin of his hide. Slushing the water through mouth and nostrils he sinks, heavy with water, and the blue closes over him dowsing the polished pebbles of his eyes. Thrown upon the beach he lies, blunt, obtuse, shedding dry blue scales. Their metallic blue stains the rusty iron on the beach. Blue are the ribs of the wrecked rowing boat. A wave rolls beneath the blue bells. But the cathedral's different, cold, incense laden, faint blue with the veils of madonnas.

—1921

Kew Gardens

From the oval-shaped flower-bed there rose perhaps a hundred stalks spreading into heart-shaped or tongue-shaped leaves half way up and unfurling at the tip red or blue or yellow petals marked with spots of colour raised upon the surface; and from the red, blue or yellow gloom of the throat emerged a straight bar, rough with gold dust and slightly clubbed at the end. The petals were voluminous enough to be stirred by the summer breeze, and when they moved, the red, blue, and yellow lights passed one over the other, staining an inch of the brown earth beneath with a spot of the most intricate colour. The light fell either upon the smooth grey back of a pebble, or the shell of a snail with its brown circular veins, or, falling into a raindrop, it expanded with such intensity of red, blue, and yellow the thin walls of water that one expected them to burst and disappear. Instead, the drop was left in a second silver grey once more, and the light now settled upon the flesh of a leaf, revealing the branching thread of fibre beneath the surface, and again it moved on and spread its illumination in the vast green spaces beneath the dome of the heart-shaped and tongue-shaped leaves. Then the breeze stirred rather more briskly overhead and the colour was flashed into the air above, into the eyes of the men and women who walk in Kew Gardens in July.

The figures of these men and women straggled past the flower-bed with a curiously irregular movement not unlike that of the white and blue butterflies who crossed the turf in zig-zag flights from bed to bed. The man was about six inches in front of the woman, strolling carelessly, while she bore on with greater purpose, only turning her head now and then to see that the children were not too far behind. The man kept this distance in front of the woman purposely, though perhaps unconsciously, for he wanted to go on with his thoughts.

"Fifteen years ago I came here with Lily," he thought. "We sat somewhere over there by a lake, and I begged her to marry me all through the hot afternoon. How the dragon-fly kept circling round us: how clearly I see the dragon-fly and her shoe with the square silver buckle at the toe. All the time I spoke I saw her shoe and when it moved impatiently I knew without looking up what she was going to say: the whole of her seemed to be in her shoe. And my love, my desire, were in the dragon-fly; for some reason I thought that if it settled there, on that leaf, the broad one with the red flower in the middle of it, if the dragonfly settled on the leaf she would say 'Yes' at once. But the dragon-fly went round and round: it never settled anywhere—of course not, happily not, or I shouldn't be walking here with Eleanor and the children —Tell me, Eleanor, d'you ever think

of the past?"

"Why do you ask, Simon?"

"Because I've been thinking of the past. I've been thinking of Lily, the woman I might have married … Well, why are you silent? Do you mind my thinking of the past?"

"Why should I mind, Simon? Doesn't one always think of the past, in a garden with men and women lying under the trees? Aren't they one's past, all that remains of it, those men and women, those ghosts lying under the trees … one's happiness, one's reality?"

"For me, a square silver shoe-buckle and a dragon-fly—"

"For me, a kiss. Imagine six little girls sitting before their easels twenty years ago, down by the side of a lake, painting the water-lilies, the first red water-lilies I'd ever seen. And suddenly a kiss, there on the back of my neck. And my hand shook all the afternoon so that I couldn't paint. I took out my watch and marked the hour when I would allow myself to think of the kiss for five minutes only—it was so precious—the kiss of an old grey-haired woman with a wart on her nose, the mother of all my kisses all my life. Come Caroline, come Hubert."

They walked on past the flower-bed, now walking four abreast, and soon diminished in size among the trees and looked half transparent as the sunlight and shade swam over their backs in large trembling irregular patches.

In the oval flower-bed the snail, whose shell had been stained red, blue and yellow for the space of two minutes or so, now appeared to be moving very slightly in its shell, and next began to labour over the crumbs of loose earth which broke away and rolled down as it passed over them. It appeared to have a definite goal in front of it, differing in this respect from the singular high-stepping angular green insect who attempted to cross in front of it, and waited for a second with its antennae trembling as if in deliberation, and then stepped off as rapidly and strangely in the opposite direction. Brown cliffs with deep green lakes in the hollows, flat blade-like trees that waved from root to tip, round boulders of grey stone, vast crumpled surfaces of a thin crackling texture—all these objects lay across the snail's progress between one stalk and another to his goal. Before he had decided whether to circumvent the arched tent of a dead leaf or to breast it there came past the bed the feet of other human beings.

This time they were both men. The younger of the two wore an expression of perhaps unnatural calm; he raised his eyes and fixed them very steadily in front of him while his companion spoke, and directly his companion had done speaking he looked on the ground again and sometimes opened his lips only after a long pause and sometimes did not open them at all. The elder man had a curiously uneven and shaky method of walking, jerking his hand forward and throwing up his head abruptly, rather in the manner of an impatient carriage horse tired of waiting outside a house; but in the man these gestures were irresolute and pointless. He talked almost incessantly; he smiled to himself and again began to talk, as if the smile had been an answer. He was talking about spirits—the spirits of the dead, who, according to him, were even now telling him all sorts of odd things about their experiences in Heaven.

"Heaven was known to the ancients as Thessaly, William, and now, with this war, the spirit matter is rolling between the hills like thunder." He paused, seemed to listen, smiled, jerked his head and continued:—

"You have a small electric battery and a piece of rubber to insulate the wire—isolate?—insulate?—well, we'll skip the details, no good going into details that wouldn't be understood—and in short the little machine stands in any convenient position by the head of the bed, we will say, on a neat mahogany stand. All arrangements being properly fixed by workmen under my direction, the widow applies her ear and summons the spirit by sign as agreed. Women! Widows! Women in black—"

Here he seemed to have caught sight of a woman's dress in the distance, which in the shade looked a purple black. He took off his hat, placed his hand upon his heart, and hurried towards her muttering and gesticulating feverishly. But William caught him by the sleeve and touched a flower with the tip of his walking-stick in order to divert the old man's attention. After looking at it for a moment in some confusion the old man bent his ear to it and seemed to answer a voice speaking from it, for he began talking about the forests of Uruguay which he had visited hundreds of years ago in company with

the most beautiful young woman in Europe. He could be heard murmuring about forests of Uruguay blanketed with the wax petals of tropical roses, nightingales, sea beaches, mermaids and women drowned at sea, as he suffered himself to be moved on by William, upon whose face the look of stoical patience grew slowly deeper and deeper.

Following his steps so closely as to be slightly puzzled by his gestures came two elderly women of the lower middle class, one stout and ponderous, the other rosy-cheeked and nimble. Like most people of their station[1] they were frankly fascinated by any signs of eccentricity betokening a disordered brain, especially in the well-to-do; but they were too far off to be certain whether the gestures were merely eccentric or genuinely mad. After they had scrutinised the old man's back in silence for a moment and given each other a queer, sly look, they went on energetically piecing together their very complicated dialogue:

"Nell, Bert, Lot, Cess, Phil, Pa, he says, I says, she says, I says, I says, I says—"

"My Bert, Sis, Bill, Grandad, the old man, sugar,
    Sugar, flour, kippers, greens
    Sugar, sugar, sugar."

The ponderous woman looked through the pattern of falling words at the flowers standing cool, firm and upright in the earth, with a curious expression. She saw them as a sleeper waking from a heavy sleep sees a brass candlestick reflecting the light in an unfamiliar way, and closes his eyes and opens them, and seeing the brass candlestick again, finally starts broad awake and stares at the candlestick with all his powers. So the heavy woman came to a standstill opposite the oval-shaped flower-bed, and ceased even to pretend to listen to what the other woman was saying. She stood there letting the words fall over her, swaying the top part of her body slowly backwards and forwards, looking at the flowers. Then she suggested that they should find a seat and have their tea.

The snail had now considered every possible method of reaching his goal without going round the dead leaf or climbing over it. Let alone the effort needed for climbing a leaf, he was doubtful whether the thin texture which vibrated with such an alarming crackle

[1] *their station* I.e., their position in English society.

when touched even by the tip of his horns would bear his weight; and this determined him finally to creep beneath it, for there was a point where the leaf curved high enough from the ground to admit him. He had just inserted his head in the opening and was taking stock of the high brown roof and was getting used to the cool brown light when two other people came past outside on the turf. This time they were both young, a young man and a young woman. They were both in the prime of youth, or even in that season which precedes the prime of youth, the season before the smooth pink folds of the flower have burst their gummy case, when the wings of the butterfly, though fully grown, are motionless in the sun.

"Lucky it isn't Friday," he observed.

"Why? D'you believe in luck?"

"They make you pay sixpence on Friday."

"What's sixpence anyway? Isn't it worth sixpence?"

"What's 'it'—what do you mean by 'it'?"

"O anything—I mean—you know what I mean."

Long pauses came between each of these remarks: they were uttered in toneless and monotonous voices. The couple stood still on the edge of the flower-bed, and together pressed the end of her parasol deep down into the soft earth. The action and the fact that his hand rested on the top of hers expressed their feelings in a strange way, as these short insignificant words also expressed something, words with short wings for their heavy body of meaning, inadequate to carry them far and thus alighting awkwardly upon the very common objects that surrounded them and were to their inexperienced touch so massive: but who knows (so they thought as they pressed the parasol into the earth) what precipices aren't concealed in them, or what slopes of ice don't shine in the sun on the other side? Who knows? Who has ever seen this before? Even when she wondered what sort of tea they gave you at Kew, he felt that something loomed up behind her words, and stood vast and solid behind them; and the mist very slowly rose and uncovered—O Heavens,—what were those shapes?—little white tables, and waitresses who looked first at her and then at him; and there was a bill that he would pay with a real two shilling piece, and it was real, all real, he assured himself, fingering the coin in his pocket, real to everyone except to him and to her; even

to him it began to seem real; and then—but it was too exciting to stand and think any longer, and he pulled the parasol out of the earth with a jerk and was impatient to find the place where one had tea with other people, like other people.

"Come along, Trissie; it's time we had our tea."

"Wherever does one have one's tea?" she asked with the oddest thrill of excitement in her voice, looking vaguely round and letting herself be drawn on down the grass path, trailing her parasol, turning her head this way and that way, forgetting her tea, wishing to go down there and then down there, remembering orchids and cranes among wild flowers, a Chinese pagoda and a crimson-crested bird; but he bore her on.

Thus one couple after another with much the same irregular and aimless movement passed the flower-bed and were enveloped in layer after layer of green-blue vapour, in which at first their bodies had substance and a dash of colour, but later both substance and colour dissolved in the green-blue atmosphere. How hot it was! So hot that even the thrush chose to hop, like a mechanical bird, in the shadow of the flowers, with long pauses between one movement and the next; instead of rambling vaguely the white butterflies danced one above another, making with their white shifting flakes the outline of a shattered marble column above the tallest flowers; the glass roofs of the palm house shone as if a whole market full of shiny green umbrellas had opened in the sun; and in the drone of the aeroplane the voice of the summer sky murmured its fierce soul. Yellow and black, pink and snow white, shapes of all these colours, men, women, and children, were spotted for a second upon the horizon, and then, seeing the breadth of yellow that lay upon the grass, they wavered and sought shade beneath the trees, dissolving like drops of water in the yellow and green atmosphere, staining it faintly with red and blue. It seemed as if all gross and heavy bodies had sunk down in the heat motionless and lay huddled upon the ground, but their voices went wavering from them as if they were flames lolling from the thick waxen bodies of candles. Voices, yes, voices, wordless voices, breaking the silence suddenly with such depth of contentment, such passion of desire, or, in the voices of children, such freshness of surprise; breaking the silence? But there was no silence; all the time the motor omnibuses were turning their wheels and changing their gear; like a vast nest of Chinese boxes all of wrought steel turning ceaselessly one within another the city murmured; on the top of which the voices cried aloud and the petals of myriads of flowers flashed their colours into the air.

—1921

INDEX